United Nations University S

CW00733063

Volume 17

The United Nations University Series on Regionalism, launched by UNU-CRIS and Springer, offers a platform for innovative work on (supra-national) regionalism from a global and inter-disciplinary perspective. It includes the *World Reports* on *Regional Integration*, published in collaboration with other UN agencies, but it is also open for theoretical, methodological and empirical contributions from academics and policy-makers worldwide.

Book proposals will be reviewed by an International Editorial Board.

The series editors are particularly interested in book proposals dealing with:

– comparative regionalism;
– comparative work on regional organizations;
– inter-regionalism;
– the role of regions in a multi-level governance context;
– the interactions between the UN and the regions;
– the regional dimensions of the reform processes of multilateral institutions;
– the dynamics of cross-border micro-regions and their interactions with supra-national regions;
– methodological issues in regionalism studies.

Accepted book proposals can receive editorial support from UNU-CRIS for the preparation of manuscripts.

Please send book proposals to: pdelombaerde@cris.unu.edu and lvanlangenhove@cris.unu.edu.

More information about this series at http://www.springer.com/series/7716

Madeleine O. Hosli • Joren Selleslaghs
Editors

The Changing Global Order

Challenges and Prospects

 Springer

Editors
Madeleine O. Hosli
Institute of Security and Global Affairs
Leiden University
The Hague, The Netherlands

Joren Selleslaghs
Faculty of Governance and Global Affairs
Leiden University
The Hague, The Netherlands

ISSN 2214-9848   ISSN 2214-9856   (electronic)
United Nations University Series on Regionalism
ISBN 978-3-030-21605-4   ISBN 978-3-030-21603-0   (eBook)
https://doi.org/10.1007/978-3-030-21603-0

This Springer imprint is published by the registered company Springer Nature Switzerland AG.
The registered company address is: Gewerbestrasse 11, 6330 Cham, Switzerland

Preface

This edited volume explicitly targets the following questions: How are international relations (IR) changing? How can global peace and stability be maintained? In so doing, the volume addresses important contemporary issues of international affairs, conflict, peace and security by bringing together a range of prominent experts from different, but related, academic disciplines to share their perspectives on the topic at hand. The volume also addresses additional related aspects of IR, such as knowledge based on international law, the operation of international and regional organisations and emerging players in today's changing global order. The multidisciplinary approach provides the essential knowledge for students and scholars of IR and international studies, in general, to analyse current events and problems from a wide range of perspectives. This volume also presents its readers with a solid theoretical foundation to examine and better understand global political events. As such, the book aims to provide insights into several important themes and theories of international relations and an understanding of how the global order is gradually changing and how regional and international organisations contribute to the maintenance of international peace and security in today's multipolar world.

The first part provides a state-of-the-art overview of theories of international relations. To this end, Chap. 1, written by D. de Buck and M.O. Hosli, introduces the reader to the key concepts and general academic discipline of IR. It addresses, in detail, the traditional or mainstream IR theories, namely, realism, liberalism and constructivism. The mainstream theories aim to explain how the world is in reality rather than how it ideally should be. The origins of IR theory aimed to answer questions related to the conditions of peace and warfare as follows: Why and when do nations go to war? What are the underlying motives of warfare? When are peaceful relations most likely? These questions were particularly prominent in the twentieth century following the devastating global impacts of two world wars. Although still central to the discipline today, the causes of peace and warfare are not the only subjects addressed. IR scholars are equally interested in the emergence and role of international organisations. They investigate the impact institutions have on existing power structures and whether they constrain the behaviour of the most powerful players. Other questions focus on how and when states cooperate and the factors that contribute to hostile or peaceful relations. Regardless of the topic investigated, the crucial tools in understanding global problems, order and relations are theoretical frameworks. Therefore, this chapter pays close attention to the integral elements pertaining to theoretical frameworks in IR. It provides students with a sound theoretical base to further comprehend and analyse current events, conflicts and changing global orders. The first section of the chapter reveals what the mainstream theories of international relations are and how they vary from alternative approaches in the field. The second section analyses the three above-mentioned theories by identifying their key components and contrasts how the theories diverge from one another. The chapter concludes with a brief comparison of the three theories with regard to how they explain, and what factors they attribute, to changes in the global order. At the end of the chapter, the reader is left well equipped with a solid understanding of the theoretical world of IR.

In Chap. 2, I. Baruah and J. Selleslaghs provide an overview of alternative postpositivist theories of IR and the need for a global IR scholarship. It addresses various key elements, including the notion of positivism as well as that of postpositivism. There is often a misunderstanding in the scientific tradition that somehow positivism and postpositivism are contradictory to one another, and there is a perpetual war between the two perspectives. According to some scholars, IR is a justifiably divided discipline which is currently split between a positivist mainstream camp on the one hand and a postpositivist camp on the other hand. Consequently, in the recent past, there occurred a theoretical upheaval as positivism, the foundational epistemology of the mainstream schools of IR thinking (realism and liberalism), was criticised by other emerging theories. These include post-modernism, normative theory, feminism, critical theory, constructivism and green theory. It is also noteworthy that the only key unifying element amidst the latter theories is their mutual critique towards core positivist assumptions. This chapter addresses the key elements of each camp, the shift towards postpositivist approaches, and maintains that IR can benefit from both positivism and postpositivism. Ultimately, the (need for a) move towards a global IR scholarship is discussed by providing a critical overview of the most important scholars' positions on this (including B. Buzan, A. Achaya, Z. Capan, V. Morozov and Y. Qin).

In part two, attention turns to the rise of 'New Powers' in the changing global order. It starts with a chapter on Power Politics by R. De Wijk who claims that the notion of power is central to the politics among nations in the twenty-first century. Essentially, this chapter presents a historical narrative of the exercise of power politics, by states great and small alike. It highlights the fundamentals of power in politics, how states exercise it and on what grounds. Power is essentially the ability to get others to do what one wants. This can be done either in a positive way through encouragement (incentives) or in a negative way through force (coercion). This study also describes states' instruments for exercising power in foreign policy, i.e. economic sanctions, and the use of military power. It has been established that the power of modern states is dependent upon the three factors or variables: wealth, innovation and conventional military capabilities. In addition to an evaluation of how great powers exercise state power, the chapter also examines how highly developed medium-sized industrialised democracies, such as the Netherlands, the Scandinavian countries and Canada exercise power. Furthermore, it highlights the shift of global power towards Asia and away from the Western world. The discussion about the relative decline in American power and the emergence of a multipolar world is an important one. The conclusion is that due to the rising powers and the development of multiple centres of power, international relations is becoming not only less 'Western' but also more complex. The chapter answers questions such as the following: Does a state need a large economy to influence world politics? Is a powerful military necessary to be a key player on the global stage? What impact do powerful players have on the world order? The chapter additionally illustrates how emerging powers often have to compete with existing, mainly Western, powers over economic and geopolitical interests and the consequences this has on patterns of international cooperation.

In Chap. 4, J. Shi and Z. Langjia shed further light on the rise of China, as China's ascent is undoubtedly one of the prominent topics in IR today. However, the nature of China's rise has been controversial. This chapter explores China's rise mainly from its strategic view of the global order, the strategic intention at both regional and global levels, focusing on major powers (like the United States, Russia, India, Japan) and its narrative of peaceful rising. It examines in detail the Chinese global order and world view. The chapter also describes Confucianism and Chinese practice and further examines it from IR theory and Chinese actions in IR in the contemporary era. It also investigates whether the Chinese narrative of its peaceful rise to power reflects the behaviour and actions taken by the state on the global stage. This chapter highlights China's Asia-Pacific strategic intentions and also that of the East Asian region. From the 1990s, China had the intention of transforming its economic power into political and military power. It focused on economic development and neglected political participation in international issues, but now it is becoming increasingly assertive. The authors argue that China advocates a multipolar world order and combats unipolar or bipolar hegemonism, which is very much conducive to its rise and strategic interests. Additionally, they discuss the relations between China and the United States in detail. Evidently, the global order is changing, or shifting, as great changes are taking place in Asia and China's strategic focus is on the Asia-Pacific and neighbouring regions. This chapter concludes by stating that while China's economic growth has bestowed on it a greater confidence and an opportunity to engage in international affairs, its levels of international responsibility, political participation and global leadership still do not reflect its economic status. This prevents China from achieving full international legitimacy and becoming a regional (or global) hegemon.

In Chap. 5, A. Gerrits discusses, in detail, the Russian Federation's foreign and political interactions within the changing global context. He focuses on two related aspects of Russia's foreign policies: multipolarity and multilateralism. This chapter also discusses the concept of revisionism and its relevance vis-a-vis Russia. It addresses interesting questions such as the following: Is Russia a revisionist power? If so, what does Russia aim to revise? What does it want to keep constant? The author also outlines the role of the President in Russian politics and gives a detailed account of Putin's political activities, domestic, rule and foreign relations. Gerrits argues that Russia is as much a re-emerging or 'recovering' power, as it is an emerging one. In addition, Russia is a great power not only by virtue of its size, nuclear arsenal and energy resources, but also because it is the successor state to the superpower Soviet Union. Furthermore, Russia inherited its most prestigious symbol of great power status, its permanent seat in the UN Security Council, from its predecessor. The focus is on Eurasianism, which has deeply penetrated official discourse in Russia and serves as an ideological driver for strengthening Russian influence in the Eurasian region (the former Soviet space) and for policy initiatives as the Eurasian Union, a fundamental component of Putin's foreign policy strategy. Gerrits argues that multipolarity is Russia's answer to the post-Cold War global dominance of the United States and its tendency towards unilateralism, which Russia considers as a danger to global peace and as a threat to its national security. If Russia can be considered as an emerging power at all, it is not for its economy but for its political potential. And it is also for political reasons that the Russian leadership values its affiliation with the BRICS group, which provides Russia with a platform to present its ideas and ambitions about global reform. This chapter also discusses Russia's relations and foreign policy vis-a-vis the United States and the EU. The partnership with China in various international and regional institutions is also described. Russia aspires to create a strong, dynamic regional order under its own leadership, as a building block towards the global multipolar order it envisions.

In Chap. 6, C. van de Wetering proposes some innovative ideas for understanding India's 'rise' on the global stage. Contemporary political narratives seek to portray India as an emerging power in the international system. This is firstly because the Indian economy is one of the fastest-growing ones in the world. New Delhi's military power is also significant, as India boasts one of the largest armies globally, and is one of the biggest markets for imported weapons and defence-related equipment. Furthermore, the BRICs grouping is gaining renewed attention owing to the economic growth potential of its members. This chapter addresses the question as to how India came to be understood as an emerging power during the last two decades. The representation of India's emergence assumes that India is experiencing large economic growth, is expanding its military and is taking on a larger role in the world. These assumptions are based on realist theory which argues that India's rapid economic growth will help it to become a great power on the grounds that 'wealth and military power go hand in hand'. Drawing on the theories in the first chapter, Chap. 6 makes use of a social constructivist approach. First, it goes through some recent political and economic developments in India. It asks whether these 'facts' can be viewed in different ways. It then asks how one interpretation can gain more prominence. This shows that the discussion of India's emergence is part of a larger debate on the rising Asia and declining United States. What is less well articulated in common discourse is that India's economy could also be portrayed as not very strong, that it is still confronted with poverty and other social deficiencies and that it also experienced large economic growth in the past. The chapter also illustrates the internal dynamics of India's shortfalls, such as illiteracy, corruption, lack of adequate infrastructure, etc.

To end the part, F. Lala elaborates Africa's position in the changing global order by analysing African agency and its role played in multilateral negotiations. The post-Cold War era of multipolarity and shifts in global governance have opened doors for emerging powers, and Africa is one of them. The rise of nations from the global South, especially China, opened new avenues for the African continent and increased its role in global politics. The author starts by looking at African agency in international relations discourse, with a focus on the birth and rise of the African Union (AU) as the continent's prime intergovernmental institution. It illustrates how the AU has come to be a voice for Africa and its ability to exercise agency internationally in such cases as UN system reform, the African Common Position on Climate Change, the AU-EU partnership and the Doha Development Agenda. It also looks at the rise of South Africa as the regional hegemon and continental giant. The author concludes by claiming that African agency is an incontrovertible fact and its significance is increasing gradually.

Whereas part two of the book critically analyses the role of nations and nation-states in contemporary international relations, part three focuses on regional organisations in global affairs. The part begins with a chapter on 'The Rise of Regions: Introduction to Regional Integration and Organisations' by J. Selleslaghs and L. Van Langenhove. Regionalism has gained considerable strategic clout in the twenty-first century, not only as a form of economic, political and social organisation but also as a field of study. The debate on the rise of regionalism shows we need to adopt a clear understanding of what we mean by regionalism and how we measure it. More than 40 years ago, Joseph Nye complained that 'integration theorists have talked past each other' using different concepts and measurements. His criticism still holds today – there is a Babylonian variety of definitions and analytical frameworks, and only a few scholars of regionalism have engaged in a systemic comparison of different forms around the globe. In some ways, research on old regionalism was more comparative than many studies of new regionalism. Yet, it is only with the turn of the millennium that solid comparative studies have been undertaken in this particular subfield of international relations/international political economy. There are many 'roads to regionalism', and not all of them lead to new forms of regionalism. Regions outside Europe leave much to be explored with regard to why states build, develop, join and leave regional organisations and standard international relations theories are still yet to develop ways of explaining the (final) outcome/outlook of regionalisms' different manifestations. These issues are central to this chapter, which is organised in three parts. Part I, The field of regionalism, regional cooperation and regional integration in international relations, focuses on the theoretical understanding of 'the rise of regions' and the importance of regional integration systems for the changing global order. In contrast, Part II, Classification of regionalism and regional organisations, adopts a more practical approach by providing clear categories and indicators of regionalism worldwide. Finally, Part III, Studying regionalism and regional integration through standard IR lenses and related research challenges, provides valuable insights and understandings on researching regionalist tendencies in a changing global order.

Written by the editors, Chap. 9 looks at the European Union (EU): its integration process, institutions and external relations in a globalised and regionalised world. In the early phases of the European integration process, the European Community was more concerned with its internal development and functioning than with its place and role in the international community. Neither the European Commission nor the European Community was very relevant in international politics, as international relations and representation were very much dominated by the different member states. The limited external relations were largely restricted to former European colonies and almost exclusively oriented around trade and development relations. But assessing the EU's external relations and the EU's clout in international politics today, things have (drastically) changed. The EU now has its own High Representative of the Union for Foreign Affairs and Security Policy and its own diplomatic services, the 'European External Action Service' (EEAS). It has established a worldwide network of 141 delegations/representations, signed numerous cooperation and association agreements with different countries and cooperates closely with various regions globally. Today, the EU is seen by many as a (especially economic) global power, and its voice is increasingly heard at the international level. An important aspect of the EU's external relations is its so-called 'interregional' interactions with other regional entities around the world. Before providing a more detailed account of this way of conducting external relations, this chapter provides an overview of the scholarly research on interregionalism and its relation to international relations (theory). Sections 3 and 4 of the chapter then provide a thorough analysis of the main rationale behind EU-driven interregionalism, its current form and outreach, as well as its strategic place within today's EU foreign policy, particularly as contained in the 2016 Global Strategy.

G. Scott-Smith carefully analyses the Shanghai Cooperation Organisation (SCO) in Chap. 10. The SCO is an intergovernmental organisation founded in Shanghai on 15 June 2001 by six countries, China, Russia, Kazakhstan, Kyrgyzstan, Tajikistan and Uzbekistan, which was established to ensure the security of the Central Asian region in the post-Soviet era. Initially, the SCO was interpreted by many studies as being little more than an extension of Russian foreign policy interests, but more recently, it is clear that the initiative has shifted to Beijing. In 2015, its membership was expanded for the first time with the addition of India and Pakistan, and this was formalised at the 2016 Summit. Including the two new members will means the SCO represents 45 percent of the world's population and 19 percent of the world's GDP. As Russia and China further develop their cooperation, the SCO is now 'increasingly viewed by governments across the world as an organisation reflecting the political and economic ascendancy of the Eurasian region'. This chapter outlines the origins and purposes of the SCO and its position in relation to other post-Soviet regional entities that have been formed since 1991 under the heading of the Commonwealth of Independent States (CIS), such as the Collective Security Treaty Organisation (CSTO, 1992) and the Eurasian Economic Union (EAEU, 2015). The questions it poses are as follows: To what extent are these formations moving beyond simply being expressions of great power interests, and are they instead beginning to represent an interconnected, multilayered regional governance structure that could have consequences in a global context?

Moving further east, Chap. 11, written by F. Queen and Y. H. Sheng, analyses the role of the ASEAN as a Conflict Manager. Intrastate conflict has become the most common conflict trend in the world since the middle of the twentieth century. As the series of conflicts in Southeast Asia account for nearly half of all intrastate conflicts in the Asian region, the question of how they have been resolved arises. Responding to this, mediation has been considered as the most efficient means to bring the conflicting parties to a mutually acceptable agreement. This chapter analyses what factors explain the dynamics of ASEAN's involvement in intrastate conflicts as a Mediator. Through analysing three different cases – the Cambodia conflict, the Aceh conflict and the East Timor conflict – this chapter suggests that the relevant factors have a variety of levels of influence towards the dynamic of ASEAN mediation.

In Chap. 12, J. Selleslaghs, J. Briceño Ruiz and P. de Lombaerde look at the complex phenomenon that is regionalism in Latin America. This chapter argues that following the various waves of regionalisation efforts, Latin-American regionalism today is multilayered, multifaceted and eclectic. It is characterised by a large set of different arrangements, both formal and informal in nature and structure, in which various regimes and regional institutions coexist. It is the result of a large variety of different drivers and influential factors, both endogenous and exogenous, that resulted in what has been labelled 'the alphabet soup of Latin American regionalism'. Regionalism as a political project has been present in Latin American politics since its early days after independence. However, rather than going through a process of enlargement, deepening and/or 'spillover' effects as happened in Western Europe, no single regional organisation has come to dominate Latin American (or South American) regionalism, and its pervasiveness and cast have changed over time. As new organisations were created, old ones were reconstructed and reframed, leading in turn to the different waves or stages of regional cooperation and to the superposition of various layers. This chapter provides a critical account of the different phases, drivers and limitations of Latin American regional integration efforts, as well as a structural overview of today's most well-known regional (integration) organisations. Section 1 first reflects on the definition of the 'Latin American region' and argues that due to a variation in possible geopolitical and geoeconomic interpretations of the 'region', different visions – and consequently outcomes – of regional integration efforts have been generated. Section 2 gives an overview of the various waves of Latin American regional integration efforts. In Section 3, a selection of today's most well-known Latin American regional organisations or cooperation schemes are presented to empirically show how multi-faced and multilayered the Latin American regional architecture really is. Finally, the end of the chapter offers some reflections as to how the authors believe Latin American regionalism will likely evolve in the (near) future, and it provides suggestions for further readings.

The last chapter of the part on regional organisations in global affairs, Chap. 13 written by I. Baruah, analyses regional integration in South Asia, utilising the regional organisation SAARC as a case study. South Asia is often considered the least integrated region in the world. As the name of the regional organisation itself suggests, the institution was established with the purpose of 'regional cooperation'. At the beginning of this volume, it is stated that regional cooperation is characterised by cooperation between states within a region on specific policy areas of mutual concern. Furthermore, that cooperation is a step towards regional integration, which is the end result (Chap. 8). In this chapter, the regional scenarios in Europe, North America, South America and Southeast Asia are compared to that of South Asia. Such a comparison allows to derive crucial insights for South Asia and other regions globally. Baruah posits that regional power rivalry in South Asia (or any other region) severely impedes integration or even cooperation in the said region. Most notably, he presents a critical outlook on regionalism and regional integration. Outright hostility or the lack of cooperation and trust between key regional players severely impedes processes of regional integration. Furthermore, the effects of key player rivalry can also be seen in Latin America. For example, the bilateral relations between Brazil and Argentina led to the creation of additional overlapping institutions. It is argued regional integration can be utilised as a tool for conflict management. Moreover, the crucial elements to the above assumption are the partnerships between regional powers. It is difficult to imagine the EU project without the mutual cooperation between the continental powers of France and Germany after centuries of warfare. Contrastingly, in South Asia, the lack of cooperation between India and Pakistan has impeded regional integration.

Part four deals with the changing nature of international (global) organisations and 'global governance 2.0'. In Chap. 14, A. Kasper commences by addressing the conceptual challenges related to the term 'global governance'. This is important due to the lack of clarity in the IR discipline regarding global governance as a concept, which in turn has led to its methodological and analytical misuse. This chapter also touches upon the different but intimately related concepts of globalisation and global governance. Furthermore, it also focuses on other (related) key conceptualisations, which are useful while investigating global governance, for example, the concept of state sovereignty. Next, it mentions briefly the institutions linked to global governance, such as the UN, ICC, World Bank, etc. Moreover, the concept applies not only amidst states but also non-state actors; groups based on religion, health and gender; NGOs; IGOs; MNCs; private entities; etc. This chapter also highlights the 'economic aspect' or 'business side' of global governance. Additionally, this chapter systematically compares authoritarian and democratic systems and highlights their advantages and disadvantages in light of globalisation and global governance. Finally, it outlines the 'implications' of globalisation on democratic systems of governance. The objective of this chapter is not only to provide information about global governance in and of itself. Rather, it aims to present the foundational concepts of, and approaches to, global governance so that students and non-specialists may gain a strong grasp of the basics. It also outlines key IR theoretical approaches to global governance. Furthermore, for purposes of objectivity, the chapter also outlines the adverse effects of, and critical views on, global governance. For example, the very notion of global governance strips citizens and local forms of governance of their authority, transferring it to a distant global body with very little connection to local issues. Like all other chapters, this one also provides a very useful list of academic readings, for those interested in developing an advanced understanding of global governance, and its increasing relevance to IR in today's changing global order.

In Chap. 15, M.O. Hosli and T. Dörfler look at the United Nations Security Council (UNSC): its history, composition and reform proposals in an ever-changing world order. This chapter begins by presenting a brief sketch of the historical underpinnings which led to the foundation of the United Nations Organisation in 1945. The authors discuss the structure of the UNSC and address key contemporary debates concerning the UN, such as 'reform proposals' for the UNSC. The chapter succinctly discusses previous proposals and counterproposals. When the UN was founded, permanent seats were created in the Security Council for those member states that were deemed to have the available power and resources to secure and enforce world peace. However, in today's changing global order, other powers are rising, while certain members of the current UNSC no longer have as much power and authority as compared to 1945. Therefore, since the creation of the UN, there has been a growing debate as to who should be the UNSC members. The discussions on possible reform of this institution became even more intense after the end of the Cold War and the superpower blockade. UNSC reform is relevant because the ability of the Council to maintain international peace and security is a vital global concern. Nevertheless, the authors acknowledge that reform of the UNSC – and any amendment to the UN Charter – is a truly global enterprise that necessitates political support on all continents. The chapter demonstrates that instead of formal reform, it is also possible to focus on a reform of the UNSC's working methods. Generally, it seems that emerging powers have not disengaged from the UNSC as an institution but rather developed adaptation strategies to overcome the 'structural constraints' of the UNSC setup. By engaging in informal interstate discussions in cases where the UNSC is blocked, states can still be proactive and then subsequently engage with the UNSC in providing ex post legitimacy. This chapter also sheds a light on specific dynamics pertaining to the UN, such as the involvement of the UN member states in coercive diplomacy, military measures and economic sanctions. For instance, it discusses the contribution of troops for UN peacekeeping missions from different UN member states. Additionally, the chapter discusses the UN's involvement in different conflicts around the globe and its contribution in maintaining global peace and security. Lastly, the chapter briefly addresses the functions and role of international law and legal enforcement vis-à-vis the UN.

In Chap. 16, R. A. Tosbotn and E. Cusumano address the area of transnational security governance by analysing the role of NATO in a changing world. A changing global order entails a rearrangement of relations, and not necessarily just of those among nation-states but also those between states and other types of actors, such as multilateral and international organisations, non-state actors and a plethora of other global players. Even the large interstate security organisation, the North Atlantic Treaty Organisation (NATO), was not immune to this process. Intrinsic to the changes, NATO is being forced to pose questions about its identity, its origin and, most importantly, its future with regard to the former two. Originally, following the mass destruction and human suffering of World War II, the alliance's creation served three purposes: (1) deterring Soviet expansionism, (2) forbidding the revival of nationalist militarism in Europe and (3) encouraging European integration. However, the collapse of the Soviet Union not only stripped NATO of one of its original raison d'êtres but also spawned a less defined world in which the strongest actors in the international fora are not always nation-states. This has led some to ask the following question: What is the role of NATO today? To answer this guiding question, the chapter is structured as follows: (1) it firstly scrutinises NATO's history, paying particular attention to its role within coercive diplomatic strategies; subsequently, (2) it builds on the previous chapters to outline the aspects of the changing global order relevant to NATO's imperatives; and lastly, (3) it examines and details the way forward to valorise its existence. It particularly focuses on the organisation's potential role in countering its traditional nemesis's revivalism, in Eastern Europe and in the Mediterranean. It makes the case for the positive role NATO should play in the Mediterranean, after years of negligent and misguided/misconducted military operations.

Finally, J. Kantorowicz meticulously describes the role of international economic organisations, such as the G20, in addressing the challenges – and opportunities – related to globalisation. In Chap. 17, J. Kantorowicz describes how both the inception and the upgrade of the Group of 20 (hereinafter G20) were marked by crisis events. A series of financial crises in developing countries and emerging economies in the late 1990s demonstrated that the G7 was an outdated mode of governance as it was unable to effectively respond to these challenges to the global economy. G7 Finance Ministers and Central Bank Governors suggested to broaden the dialogue on crucial economic issues, and thus, the G20 was formed. Currently, the role of the G20 seems to have evolved from an abrupt global response to the global financial crisis to a forum for international cooperation in multiple policy areas, in other words from a 'crisis committee' to a 'steering committee'. Although initially preoccupied with financial regulation reforms and balanced economic growth, the G20 has experienced a noticeable expansion of its objectives to issues such as corruption, climate change, aid and development. Against this background, this chapter describes the institutional design and effectiveness of the G20 with the goal being to position the G20 as an essential part of the changing global order. It will provide a detailed account of the institutions' main strengths and weaknesses, as well as threats and opportunities as one of the world's most important diplomatic mechanisms for international economic governance.

Part five of the edited volume deals with a topic area which is increasingly dominating both the policy and the academic agenda at the time of writing: conflict, conflict resolution and international security. The part begins with a chapter on the enforcement of international law written by E. Kantorowicz-Reznichenko. At the national level, the state has a monopoly over law enforcement. The procedure of law making and enforcement is clear. Legislators (or courts) enact laws and specify the expected consequences of failure to comply; police or other official authorities monitor compliance; prosecutors and courts impose punishment on violators who were apprehended; and finally, authorities such as the prison service, probation service and fine collection agencies execute the sanctions. Conversely, there is no world governor, and the creation of international laws depends on the consent of states for which those laws are binding. As states continue to enjoy sovereignty and possess exclusive decision-making power within their territories, the following question arises: Can international law be enforced? International norms emerge over time, and once they enjoy wide acceptance, they become part of a customary law and sometimes are even entrenched in multilateral agreements (treaties and conventions). In a globalised world, there is an increasing need for a larger number of laws to govern the intercourse of states and other organs. However, the existence of rules does not guarantee a change of behaviour or compliance. To affect behaviour, rules need to be enforceable. The global world today faces many security challenges, including armed international and national conflicts, civil wars and international terrorism. In the twenty-first century, there are three major players in the enforcement of international law that are recognised by most states in the world: the United Nations, the International Court of Justice and the International Criminal Court. Despite their prominence in the changing global order, all three institutions have weaknesses. For instance, the special decision-making structure of the UN Security Council, i.e. the veto power of the five permanent members, has prevented it from adequately addressing all relevant international conflicts. The purpose of this chapter is to introduce the reader to the concept of international law and the three major players in its enforcement. In addition, the chapter will try to explain the existence of international law from the perspective of IR theories.

Following on from this general introduction on the legal possibilities of establishing international security and peace, Chap. 19, written by J. Speiser, focuses on the international norm dynamics of the Responsibility to Protect (R2P). R2P is an UN principle that was enshrined in the 2005 World Summit Outcome Document. It essentially asserts that each individual state has the responsibility to protect its population from genocide, war crimes, ethnic cleansing and crimes against humanity. When a national government is either unwilling or unable to put an end to the ongoing and persistent mass atrocities, the international community has the responsibility to use appropriate diplomatic, humanitarian and other peaceful means to protect civilian populations. Additionally, the international community, via the UN Security Council, should also be prepared to take collective action, in accordance with the Charter, if peaceful means prove inadequate and national authorities manifestly fail to protect their populations from mass atrocities. The adoption of the R2P principle is the result of a succession of debates that took place in the wake of several humanitarian catastrophes in the 1990s, such as in Somalia, Rwanda, Bosnia-Herzegovina and Kosovo. This chapter engages with the main theoretical considerations of R2P and provides the reader with all the details attached to this norm, its emergence and its applicability. Furthermore, this chapter assesses R2P's stages of normative progress through the constructivist theoretical framework of the norm 'life cycle'. This framework comprehensively integrates intersubjective features to distinguish three stages of norm evolution in international relations: norm emergence, norm cascade and internalisation. The research questions addressed in this chapter include the following: What is the current stage reached by

R2P on Finnemore and Sikkink's scale of international norm dynamics? Why has it reached this particular stage? Debates over the norm of R2P are centred around the dual understandings of responsibility vs. sovereignty. This chapter outlines the reasons behind the emergence of the R2P norm. Libya and the contestation of R2P among the permanent members of the Security Council are discussed in detail. This event constituted the first time that the use of force had been authorised by invoking R2P. The official positions of the five permanent members of the Security Council, concerning R2P from 2009 until 2015, are examined in detail, as it is ultimately these states which have the final say on the use of force.

Chapter 20, written by P. Meerts, looks at of the most integral method of conflict resolution and the practice of IR: negotiation. It examines international negotiations from the perspective of procedure and process, party and people, perception and power and preference and product. The chapter studies, in detail, the fundamental aspects of international negotiation, such as context, timing, etc. Furthermore, it addresses the definition of negotiation from a variety of perspectives, depending on the elements, such as outcome, communication, process, behaviour and so on. This study limits itself to interstate negotiation, asking questions about negotiation's nature and utility and relating it on its fringes to warfare and adjudication. Additionally, the strategy of cooperation (integrative negotiation), as compared to a competing approach (distributive negotiation), is also discussed. It is argued that a lasting peace is dependent on institutionalising the process of cooperation. The European Union is a typical example of such an institutionalised process. The four developments which led to the strengthening of negotiation in Europe are also outlined in this chapter. The notion of power in negotiations is classified into three components: power that is marginal and originates from the negotiator (power of conduct), power of the state being represented (structural power) and power that belongs to the state regarding the issues being negotiated (comparative power). This chapter addresses integral elements of the negotiation process, such as mutual hurting stalemate (MHS), mutual enticing opportunity (MEO) and mutual beneficial stalemate (MBS); the notion of trust, power and personal qualities of the diplomat; etc. Furthermore, a negotiation process means going through various phases: preparation and diagnosis, information, searching for formulations, bargaining and drafting of details. Finally, the current context and future trajectory of diplomacy is outlined, as is the nature of the work of the contemporary diplomat, as compared to previous epochs of diplomacy. With the dichotomies of globalisation and polarisation occurring together, it is argued that national and international negotiation methods are needed more than ever. This chapter provides insightful lessons for negotiators and anyone interested in negotiation and diplomacy.

To conclude this volume, S. Vukovic describes the role of international mediation in restoring (international) security in Chap. 21. International mediation represents the most cost-effective and thus the most commonly used form of conflict management. It represents an assisted form of negotiations, where one or more external actors help the disputants in finding a solution to their conflict that, on their own, they are either unable or unwilling to reach. In respect to other types of third-party-led conflict management activities, its appeal is derived from an expectation that the process will be conducted in a voluntary, *ad hoc*, noncoercive and legally nonbinding manner. In an international system deprived of an overarching authority and effective enforcement mechanisms, this flexible and non-assertive approach provides an enticing structure for international actors motivated to preserve the autonomy of decision-making. International mediation is conducted in situations that are regularly characterised by a complete breakdown of communication between the conflicting parties, coupled with high levels of mutual suspicion and mistrust. In such circumstances, success is contingent upon mediators' ability to move the parties away from their confrontational attitudes towards a mutually acceptable agreement. In other words, the role of a mediator is to increase the appeal of a negotiated agreement while decreasing the appeal of unilateral solutions that parties might be inclined to pursue through belligerent and destructive activities. As this chapter aims to show, despite its previously announced definitional characteristics, international mediation represents a power dynamic, through which the third parties shape an outcome that they are interested in endorsing. This inherent prejudice that mediators bring to the process represents the core reason why mediators are accepted in the first place: their biases provide the clarity and direction needed in a highly anarchical international system. The purpose of this chapter is to elaborate on the inevitability and utility of mediation bias (both towards a specific actor and a particular outcome), the essence of the power or leverage that mediators are required to use in order to shape an outcome and the elusive nature of success in international mediation as it is marked by at least three distinct degrees of success: bringing the parties to the table, making them sign an agreement and ensuring it sticks.

Based on – and extending – contents of the MOOC *The Changing Global Order*, this volume presents an overview of the various aspects of international relations in the changing global context. It demonstrates how regional organisations and international institutions can crucially contribute to the maintenance of peace and stability but also to the challenges they face in this endeavour.

We thank all the authors for their contributions to this book. In addition to this, the volume would not have come about without invaluable research assistance. We gratefully acknowledge the contributions of Denise de Buck, Rory Johnson, Fridon Lala, Ewout Ramon, Indraneel Baruah and Konstantinos Adamidis.

We hope our readers will learn about the various aspects of the changing global order and understand both the complexities and opportunities arising from current developments in international affairs.

Zuid-Holland, The Netherlands   Madeleine O. Hosli
                                                                 Joren Selleslaghs

Contents

Editors and Contributors

About the Editors

Madeleine O. Hosli is full Professor of International Relations and a Jean Monnet Chair *ad personam* at Leiden University. She is also the Director of the two-year advanced MSc in International Relations and Diplomacy. She is Author of *The Euro: A Concise Introduction to European Monetary Integration* (2005) and a Coeditor of *Decision-Making in the European Union Before and After the Lisbon Treaty* (2015). Her work has appeared in journals such as *International Organization, International Studies Quarterly, Journal of European Public Policy, European Journal of Political Research, Journal of Common Market Studies, Review of International Organizations, Governance, Political Studies* and *Journal of International Relations and Development.*

Joren Selleslaghs is the Belgian Consul for Peru, Bolivia, and Ecuador since October 2018. He entered the Belgian Ministry of Foreign Affairs as a Diplomat in October 2017 and has worked at the Brussels headquarters (Brexit, Benelux, Consular Affairs) and the Belgian Embassy in Luxemburg as diplomatic Counselor.

He graduated *cum laude* from the College of Europe (MA EU International Relations and Diplomacy Studies) and magna cum laude at the Institute for European Studies of the Université Libre de Bruxelles (MSc European Studies). He previously worked as a Lecturer and Researcher on the EU and International Relations at Leiden University, and as an Associate Research Fellow at the United Nations University Institute of Comparative Regional Integration Studies, UNU-CRIS (Belgium). He also worked as an EU Innovation Consultant at PNO Consultants (the Netherlands), at The Hague Centre for Strategic Studies, the cabinet of a Belgian Member of the European Parliament, and the External Relations department of the Belgian Permanent Representation to the European Union. Until October 2017, Joren Selleslaghs was also an external evaluator/expert for the European Commission and member of the Board of Directors of the Europe-Central America Chamber of Commerce. He was the Belgian Youth Ambassador toward the

UN in 2011–2012 and also active as a development worker for UNICEF in Tanzania and Central America (2007–2008 and 2012).

About the Contributors

Indraneel Baruah is a recent graduate from Leiden University, where he attained his MSc in International Relations and Diplomacy. He wrote a master's thesis (cum laude) on Regional Integration in South Asia: An investigation of the Kashmir conflict and prospects for international mediation. Prior to this, he received his Bachelor of Arts (BA) degree in Political Science (Honours) from Hindu College, University of Delhi. He is currently an EU Research and Innovation Consultant at PNO Consultants. He has consulted a range of organisations including Shell, BNP Paribas, DISA, Scania, CNH Industrial Europe and various institutions of higher education within Europe. He has also been a Research Assistant at the Faculty of Governance and Global Affairs, Leiden University. Currently, he is on a 1-year sabbatical from PNO, conducting research in his home state of Assam, India. The research is focused on the migration crisis between India and Bangladesh, which is centred in India's North-Eastern Province of Assam. In addition, he works part-time as a Research Consultant at ActionAid.

Denise de Buck currently works as Head of the Donor Management Department for the International Humanitarian Mine Clearance Organization the HALO Trust in Afghanistan. Previously, she completed a traineeship at the European External Action Service (EEAS) in Brussels, dealing with conflict prevention, security sector reform and post-conflict peacebuilding and stabilisation. She holds an MSc (*cum laude*) in International Relations and Diplomacy from Leiden University.

Eugenio Cusumano is an Assistant Professor in International Relations at Leiden University. His research concentrates on the role of non-state actors in military operations and humanitarian crises both on land and at sea. He has published for leading academic outlets like Stanford University Press, *Journal of Strategic Studies*, *Cooperation and Conflict* and *Armed Forces & Society*.

Philippe de Lombaerde is currently Associate Professor of International Economics at NEOMA Business School (Reims, Rouen, Paris). Previously, he was Associate Director at the United Nations University Institute on Comparative Regional Integration Studies (UNU-CRIS) in Bruges and Associate Professor of International Economics at the National University of Colombia.

Rob De Wijk is the Founder of The Hague Centre for Strategic Studies (HCSS) and Professor of International Relations and Security at the Institute of Security and Global Affairs, Leiden University. He studied Contemporary History and International Relations at Groningen University and wrote his PhD dissertation on

NATO's 'Flexibility in Response' strategy at the Political Science Department of Leiden University. He started his career in 1977 as a Freelance Journalist and later became Head of the Defence Concepts Department of the Dutch Ministry of Defence, Head of the Security Studies unit at the Clingendael Institute and Professor of International Relations at the Royal Netherlands Military Academy.

Thomas Dörfler holds a PhD in Political Science from the University of Bamberg, Germany, and a master's degree from Leiden University, the Netherlands. He has been a Japan Society for the Promotion of Science (JSPS)-UNU Postdoctoral Research Fellow with the UNU Centre for Policy Research, a Visiting Scholar at John Jay College of Criminal Justice (City University of New York) and a Consultant for the Security Council Affairs Division of the UN Secretariat. Most recently, he held a postdoctoral position at the Technical University Munich (Germany) (TUM) School of Governance and currently holds a research fellow position at the University of Potsdam (Germany). He has published in academic journals including *Regulation & Governance*; *Global Governance: A Review of Multilateralism and International Organizations*; *Journal of International Relations and Development*; *Terrorism and Political Violence;* and *Journal of Economic Policy Reform*, as well as several chapters in edited volumes and policy-relevant articles. For his work on UN sanctions, he has received the 2018 Hans-Löwel Prize and the 2017 Award of the UN Association of Germany.

André Gerrits is Professor of International Studies and Global Politics and Chair of the MA International Relations (European Union Studies/International Studies) and the BA International Studies, based in The Hague. Previously, he held the Chair in Russian History and Politics at Leiden University and the Jean Monnet Chair in European Studies at the University of Amsterdam. He was also a Senior Research Fellow at the Netherlands Institute of International Studies Clingendael.

Rory Johnson currently works within the Office of the Director at the United Nations Institute on Comparative Regional Integration Studies (UNU-CRIS) in Brugge, Belgium. He is a graduate of Leiden University, where he attained an MA in International Studies (cum laude). He is also pursuing an MSc in Environmental Studies at Bangor University in the UK. His specific interests are in environmental governance and security and development issues in Africa.

Jaroslaw Kantorowicz is an Assistant Professor at the Institute of Security and Global Affairs, Faculty of Governance and Global Affairs, Leiden University. He graduated (summa cum laude) from the European Doctorate in Law and Economics (Hamburg University). His research interests are focused on global economic governance, political economy, intergovernmental fiscal relations and empirical legal studies. In the past few years, he has been collaborating on various projects with the European Commission, the European Parliament and the Organisation for Economic Cooperation and Development.

Elena Kantorowicz-Reznichenko is a Researcher and a Lecturer at Rotterdam Institute of Law and Economics, Erasmus School of Law, Erasmus University Rotterdam. Her main areas of expertise are public law and economics, international criminal law and behavioural and experimental law and economics. In addition, she is the Academic Coordinator of the European Doctorate in Law and Economics (EDLE). She holds multiple academic degrees from different internationally recognised universities in the fields of law, psychology and law and economics. Prior to her academic career, she worked as a Criminal Prosecutor in the District Attorney's Office in Israel. She published in a variety of prestigious international journals, such as *Journal of International Criminal Justice* (forthcoming 2017), *Washington University Law Review* (forthcoming 2018), *International Review of Law and Economics*.

Amy E. P. Kasper is a PhD student at the University of St. Gallen in Switzerland. She has earlier been a Researcher at the Institute of Security and Global Affairs at Leiden University. She is a recent graduate (*cum laude*) of Leiden University's MSc in International Relations and Diplomacy. She wrote her MSc thesis on patterns of compliance within international human rights law, tying these patterns to the presence/absence of domestic acceptance of international norms. Her background has been shaped by her time working on the terrorism and counterterrorism team at Leiden's Institute of Security and Global Affairs, as a Programme Officer at the World Affairs Council in Seattle, managing professional exchange programmes for the US Department of State, and as a Teacher of English as a second language in multiple countries.Recently, she worked as a Tutor/Lecturer for Leiden University's minor in Global Affairs.

Fridon Lala is a Graduate Student in Public Administration at the School of Public Policy, Central European University, in Budapest. He is specialising in governance, focusing on governance beyond the nation-state, and related changes to the structure of the global political economy. He has conducted an internship at the United Nations University Institute on Comparative Regional Integration Studies (UNU-CRIS) in Bruges, Belgium.

Zeren Langjia is a Doctoral Researcher of the Centre for European Studies of Sichuan University, China, and Department of Political Science of Ghent University, Belgium. His research focuses on the Normative Power Europe and the EU's external policy.

Paul Meerts is Senior Associate with the Netherlands Institute of International Relations 'Clingendael' at The Hague, Netherlands, and an International/Diplomatic Negotiation Analyst. He holds a PhD in International Public Law from Leiden University (2014). He is a Member of the Steering Committees of the network Processes of International Negotiation (PIN) and Founder of the Program on International Negotiation Training (POINT), as well as Advisor to the journal *International Negotiation*.

Fathania Queen Genisa is currently working in the Governor's Delivery Unit of Special Capital Region of Jakarta as a Member of the staff. She studied at Leiden University, where she obtained her MSc degree in International Relations and Diplomacy degree and took her Bachelor's degree at the Universiti Utara Malaysia. She had working experience at the Grotius Centre for International Legal Studies in which she worked on issues related to non-state actors in global governance. Before that, she worked at the Indonesian Teaching Movement (Jakarta, Indonesia) and the Institute of Diplomacy and Foreign Relations (IDFR) in Malaysia.

Ewout Ramon was formerly a Research Assistant to the Director at the UNU-CRIS. He acted as UNU-CRIS' focal point in the UNU network for communications, ICT and project management and coordinated the UNU-CRIS internship programme. Prior to joining UNU-CRIS, he obtained a bachelor's degree in International Politics from the University of Ghent and a master's degree in European Studies: Transnational and Global Perspectives from the University of Leuven before starting at UNU-CRIS as a Communication Intern in April 2013. As an Exchange Student, he also spent one year studying international relations at Istanbul Bilgi University in Turkey. He currently works as a Project Coordinator in the International Affairs Department at Voka, the Flanders' Chamber of Commerce and Industry, West Flanders.

José Briceño Ruiz holds a PhD in Political Science from the Institut d'Études Politiques d'Aix-en-Provence, France. He is Professor and Researcher at the Faculty of Economics and Administration and the Centro de Pensamiento Global (CEPEG) at the Universidad Cooperativa de Colombia. He was Professor at the Faculty of Social and Economic Sciences of the University of the Andes, Venezuela, between 2003 and 2017. He is a Specialist on Regional Integration and International Political Economy. He has written and edited books on regional integration, the most recent of them being *Brazil and Latin America: Between the Separation and Integration Paths* (Lanham, Maryland: Lexington Books, 2017) in collaboration with Andrés Rivarola Puntigliano and *Post-Hegemonic Regionalism in the Americas: Toward a Pacific-Atlantic Divide?* (London: Routledge, 2017) in collaboration with Isidro Morales (Tec de Monterrey).

Giles Scott-Smith holds the Roosevelt Chair in New Diplomatic History at Leiden University and is the Academic Director of the Roosevelt Institute for American Studies in Middelburg, the Netherlands. From 2013 to 2016, he was Chair of the Transatlantic Studies Association. In 2017, as one of the Organisers of the New Diplomatic History Network (http://www.newdiplomatichistory.com), he was one of the Founding Editors of *Diplomatica: A Journal of Diplomacy and Society* published with Brill.

Ying-Hsien Sheng was born in Taiwan in 1982. She studied political science at Tunghai University, where she received her doctor's degree in 2012. She proceeded to serve in some local universities, such as the National Chung Hsing University,

Central Taiwan University of Science and Technology, Providence University and Tunghai University, as Adjunct Assistant Professor for years. Her articles have been included in the *Journal of National Development Studies, International and Public Affairs, Journal of Law and Public Governance, Review of Global Politics, Tamkang International and Area Studies Semiannual, Chang Gung Journal of Humanities* and *Social Sciences,* among others. She has passed the Level One Civil Service Senior Exam and worked for the government since February 2018.

Jian Shi is Jean Monnet Professor in European Society and Director of the Jean Monnet Centre of Excellence at the School of International Studies, Sichuan University, Chengdu, China, where he lectures in European Studies. He has a PhD from Lehigh University, PA, USA. His research focuses on European civilisation and EU-China relations, particularly on the bilateral cooperation in higher education.

Jérémie Speiser is an Assistant Administrator at the Council of Europe in Strasbourg and follows up on the work of the Steering Committee for Human Rights (CDDH) regarding the system of the European Convention on Human Rights. His academic interests focus on international mechanisms for the protection of civilians in situations of conflict and/or humanitarian distress. Prior to that, he was an Intern at the Organisation for the Prohibition of Chemical Weapons (OPCW) and the International Criminal Court (ICC). He holds a Master of Science degree in International Relations and Diplomacy from Leiden University and a Bachelor of Arts in War Studies from King's College London.

Mario Telò is an Italian Political Scientist and Researcher who focuses on European studies, political theory and international relations. He has been a Researcher and Professor in many European, Asian and American universities. Since 1995, he has been a 'Jean Monnet Chair' and, since 2006, a Member of the Royal Academies for Science and the Arts of Belgium.

Roger A. Tosbotn is a Temporary Project Officer at the Financial Mechanism Office of the EEA and Norway Grants in Brussels, having completed a 12-month traineeship in the same organisation. He obtained his master's degree diploma from Leiden University in 2016, specialising in international security, international organisations and global politics. His master's thesis, NATO and Cyber Security: Critical Junctures as Catalysts for Change, was an in-depth quantitative and qualitative content analysis of the prominence and conceptualisation of the 'cyber' concept over time. He has also worked on the 510.global Red Cross Netherlands initiative where he, among other things, helped develop a Data Responsibility Policy. Additionally, he has assisted Dr. Eugenio Cusumano in a research project on hybrid threats commissioned by the NATO CIMIC Centre of Excellence. This project was published by Palgrave Macmillan.

Carina van de Wetering is a Lecturer at the Leiden University Department of Political Science, the Netherlands. She received her PhD in Politics at the University of Bristol, UK, in 2014. She is the Author of *Changing US Foreign Policy Towards India: US-India Relations Since the Cold War* (2016).

Luk Van Langenhove is a Research Professor and former Academic Director at the Institute for European Studies (IES) of the Vrije Universiteit Brussel (VUB). He previously held the position of Director at the United Nations University Institute on Comparative Regional Integration Studies (UNU-CRIS) in Bruges and Representative of the Rector at the UNESCO in Paris. Moreover, he was Deputy Secretary-General of the Belgian Federal Ministry of Science Policy, Deputy Chief of Cabinet of the Belgian Federal Minister of Science Policy and Researcher and Lecturer at the VUB.

Siniŝa Vuković is Senior Lecturer in Conflict Management and Global Policy and Associate Director of the Conflict Management Programme at Johns Hopkins University's School of Advanced International Studies (SAIS). He is also Assistant Professor at the Institute of Security and Global Affairs, Leiden University, and a Visiting Professor at the Amsterdam University College. He received his PhD (*cum laude*) in International Relations and Conflict Resolution at Leiden University, an MA (*cum laude*) in International Relations and Diplomacy from Leiden University and the Netherlands Institute of International Relations 'Clingendael' and a BA (*laurea*) in Political Science from the University of Rome 'La Sapienza'.

Part I
Theories of International Relations to Understand the Changing Global Order

Chapter 1
Traditional Theories of International Relations

Denise de Buck and Madeleine O. Hosli

1.1 Introduction

The study of international relations in its early origins aimed to answer questions related to the conditions of peace and warfare. Why and when do nations go to war? What are the underlying motives of warfare? And when are peaceful relations most likely? These questions were particularly prominent in the twentieth century after having experienced two world wars with devastating impacts globally. Although such questions remain central to the discipline today, the causes of peace and warfare are not the only subjects addressed. International relations scholars are equally interested in understanding why international organizations emerged and what role they play on the global stage. They investigate the impact institutions have on existing power structures and whether they constrain the behavior of the most powerful players. Other questions focus on how and when states cooperate and the factors that contribute to hostile or peaceful relations. Regardless of the topic investigated, a crucial tool in understanding global problems, order and relations are theoretical frameworks.

International relations theories generate assumptions to explain and predict state behavior and interests. The theories attempt to rationalize why states act the way they do in particular situations. This chapter introduces you to the theories of international relations and illustrates in what way mainstream approaches interpret how global affairs change, what the role of states is in the international system, whether international institutions matter and whether international cooperation between states is both possible and sustainable. Although the chapter content may be a bit

D. de Buck
Faculty of Governance and Global Affairs, Leiden University, The Hague, The Netherlands
e-mail: denise_debuck@hotmail.nl

M. O. Hosli (✉)
Institute of Security and Global Affairs, Leiden University, The Hague, The Netherlands
e-mail: m.o.hosli@fgga.leidenuniv.nl

© Springer Nature Switzerland AG 2020
M. O. Hosli, J. Selleslaghs (eds.), *The Changing Global Order*, United Nations University Series on Regionalism 17,
https://doi.org/10.1007/978-3-030-21603-0_1

difficult to comprehend at times, the theoretical assumptions are useful for you to understand, because they provide you with a solid basis for the various chapters on diverse topics throughout the book. The theories will help you grasp subjects like the role of China and Russia in today's global structure, the role of regional organizations such as the European Union in global politics and the contribution of diverse institutions, including the United Nations Security Council and the North Atlantic Treaty Organization, to the maintenance of international peace and security. This chapter will thus provide you with a sound theoretical base to further comprehend and analyze current events, conflicts and the changing global order.

The chapter introduces you to three mainstream approaches to international relations, namely realism, liberalism and constructivism. The underlying assumptions of the theories are addressed, including how each theory interprets the interaction and behavior of states on the global stage, what factors explain conflict and cooperation, and the role that regional and international organizations play. The first section of the chapter reveals what mainstream theories of international relations are and how they vary from alternative approaches in the field. The second section analyzes the three abovementioned theories by identifying their key components and contrasts how the theories diverge from one another. The chapter concludes with a brief comparison of the three theories in regards to how they explain and what factors they attribute to changes in the global order.

1.2   Mainstream Theories of International Relations

Mainstream theories, also known as rationalist approaches to international relations, in contrast to post-modern theories aim to explain how the world is in reality rather than how it ideally should be. Mainstream theories attempt to take an empirical or scientific approach to international relations, as opposed to the normative or philosophical approach used by post-modern theories. The scholars of mainstream theories implement the scientific method to the field of international relations by (1) observing and describing state behavior and interaction, (2) explaining why states act the way they do or why an event occurred, (3) identifying and analyzing causal mechanisms between a set of phenomen a, and (4) using the theoretical assumptions to make predictions of state behavior and current events (Acharya 2008: 2). Consequently, mainstream theories have a positivist epistemology in which they investigate and explain objective data and so-called 'brute facts'. In comparison, post-modern or reflectivist theories of international relations have a post-positivist epistemology with the underlying goal of international relations being to understand rather than explain. Mainstream approaches regularly condemn and delegitimize reflectivist theories "precisely because reflectivist approaches do not share the commitment to the form of foundational positivism found in rationalist approaches, they are increasingly criticized for not being social science and, thereby, not counting as reliable knowledge about the world" (Smith 2000: 385). Chapter 2 of this book will discuss the post-modern, reflectivist approaches to international relations in further detail.

Traditionally, realism and liberalism have been characterized as the two main, competing approaches in the field of international relations – an assumption that still faces little discussion today. However, the popularity and acceptance of constructivism has increased immensely since its introduction to the international relations discipline in the 1980s. "Fifteen years ago, constructivism was only beginning to be firmly established as a mainstream research approach in international relations and a challenger to other approaches, mainly rationalism. Today, constructivism has become firmly established in mainstream IR theory, both in North America and around the world" (Adler 2013: 112). Particularly the end of the Cold War set the stage for new debates. This is especially the case as both liberalism and realism failed to predict the collapse of the Soviet Union, the end of the rivalry between the superpowers, and "simply had difficulty explaining the end of the Cold War, or systemic change more generally" (Wendt 1999: 4). This sparked a search for alternative theories and explanations in the field of international relations. In sum, realism, liberalism and constructivism are classified as the three major theories in the discipline and consist of the most frequently applied theories by academics in the field of international relations.

Nevertheless, it is also important to acknowledge that while liberalism and realism have always been categorized as mainstream theories, this is not the case for constructivism. Even today, the labelling of constructivism as a mainstream theory remains controversial, mainly because it does not share its ontology with the other two approaches. While realism and liberalism have a state-centric, materialistic ontology, this is not true for constructivism. Instead, constructivism has a social and ideational ontology. The theory does, however, share a positivist or empirical epistemology with realism and liberalism, thereby taking a so-called 'middle way' (Adler 2013: 112). As a result of this, on a spectrum ranging from empirical mainstream approaches on the left end and reflectivist or post-modern theories on the right end, constructivism is often placed in the middle and labeled a 'metatheory'.

Although the classification of constructivism as a mainstream theory remains debated, the rapid development of the approach and the large-scale use of constructivism in mainstream research has resulted in the theory being progressively accepted as mainstream. As such, this chapter has also branched constructivism under the mainstream heading. The differences between the core assumptions of the theories will become more apparent when discussed in the following sections. The first mainstream international relations theory addressed is realism and the later extension of the theory, neorealism.

1.3   (Neo-) Realism: Power, Rationality and Anarchy

Realism is one of the oldest, and most well-known theories in international relations and centers its explanation on the notions of power. The realist school is often thought of holding a pessimistic view of the world, as the theory attributes conflict and warfare to the egoistic behavior of states and power politics. It is important to mention and keep in mind throughout the section that despite their negative view of cooperation, realists are often concerned with the maintenance of global peace and stability. Realist scholars do not describe the world as conflictual because they felt that this is how it should be. But instead they try to describe, and understand state behavior, exactly in an attempt to prevent violence and war. The realist approach will help you understand what drives state behavior, why states may feel insecure in the system, and with this how situations can be prevented when states go to war with each other.

In traditional realist thinking, individuals or groups of individuals are seen as rational actors that aim to maximize their power to increase their chances of survival. Individuals feel threatened when others are stronger than they are themselves, because this poses a security challenge. Without a central authority to govern over and regulate the actions of individuals or groups, the state of nature in Hobbesian terms is "a war of all against all". In other words, without an absolute sovereign to enforce rules and punish deviance, the powerful players can dominate and take what they want from the weaker ones (Forde 1992: 376). As such, it is crucial to accumulate as much power as possible to ensure self-preservation. To guarantee order and stability, a central governing authority is necessary to dictate over the self-interested nature and behavior of humans. The realist approach to international relations transfers these thoughts to the global level to explain state behavior and world politics.

In classical realism, particularly based on the teachings of the prominent realist thinker Hans Morgenthau, conflict and international politics is driven by human nature. Humans are self-interested, insecure, aggressive and power hungry beings. As stated by Waltz (1959: 35), "struggles for power arise because men are born seekers of power [...] One who accepts [this] idea will define national interests in terms of power". It is this flawed human nature that persuades nations and their leaders to strive for power maximization on the global stage, often at the expense of other states. In the words of Hans Morgenthau, as stated in his renowned book 'Politics Among Nations' published in 1948, "political leaders think and act in term of interests defined as power". Hence, interests revolving around building up power are prioritized over ethics and human wellbeing. Despite the focus on human nature, states are defined as the unit of analysis and the main actors in world politics. States crave power, because unlike in domestic politics, there is no overarching international authority to govern over states, resulting in the need to fend for themselves.

The realist theory of international relations is based on three core assumptions. As aforementioned, the first assumption characterizes states as the core players in international relations, and thus also the units of analysis. Consequently, realism is a state-centric approach. The second assumption argues that all states seek to survive and aim to increase their power, as this enhances their security in comparison to other states on the global stage (Jervis 1985: 60). The third assumption claims that states are rational actors and strategically calculate and weigh the costs and benefits of a move carefully prior to acting in order to predict potential outcomes. Hans Morgenthau (1948: 5) alleges that to study the foreign policy and interests of states, we must "ask ourselves what the rational alternatives are from which a states-man can choose [...] and which of these rational alternatives this particular statesman, acting under these circumstances, is likely to choose". Accordingly, states select the rational action with the predicted best optimal outcome. Based on this logic, predominance of power for one side tends to deter conflict, as weaker states will not attack stronger ones because they know they likely will lose.

Power, according to Hans Morgenthau (1948: 13), "may comprise anything that establishes and maintains the control of man over man". Modern interpretations of realism define power in materialistic terms, consisting predominantly of economic resources and military might, with the latter being most important. Economic resources are imperative for states to fuel their military capabilities and enhance their abilities to both defend from attacks and carry out attacks themselves, thereby playing a security-enhancing role (Mearsheimer 2010: 78). States are constantly investing and expanding their security forces to prevent other states from becoming more powerful than they are themselves. Additionally, states also tend to be con-cerned with what is called **relative gains**, in which they constantly compare their power accumulations or gains to other players (Waltz 1959: 198). To put it more simply, they are not so much concerned with the amount they have obtained in **absolute** terms, but how much they have gained in comparison to other states.

In the modern version of realism, also called **neorealism** or **structural realism**, human nature is no longer characterized as the driving force for conflict. Instead, it is the structure of the international system and the interaction between states – the units of analysis – that fuels conflict and determines state behavior. The structure encourages or discourages states to take certain actions based on their ability to survive (Waltz 1988: 618). States are additionally perceived as "black boxes", of which the domestic differences between countries such as regime type, economic system, and institutions are irrelevant to their behavior in the international system. In other words, in neorealism no distinctions are made between states except on dif-ferences in geography, military strength and power, since regardless of domestic organization, all states are interested in optimizing their chances of survival and thus behave comparably.

Neorealism is based on five core assumptions. The first assumption, and as shared with classical realism, is that the international system is **anarchic**. This does not mean that the system is subjugated to chaos, disorder and conflict, but instead that there is "no government over governments" (Claude 1971: 14). Mearsheimer states anarchy "is an ordering principle, which says that the system comprises inde-pendent political units (states) that have no central authority above them" (Mearsheimer 1994: 10). The second assumption is that all states possess at least some offensive military capabilities, providing the ability to cause harm to one another. The third assumption argues that the intentions of other states are always uncertain, therefore, a state can never be confident whether another will use military forces against it or not, particularly because intentions are also subject to change. The assumption of mutual mistrust makes cooperation immensely difficult. The fourth assumption entails that all states seek to survive and maintain their sovereignty. The fifth and final assumption postulates that all states are rational actors, and in order to survive, must strategically calculate their actions (Mearsheimer 1994: 10). Thus, **rational** calculations about their own position in the system determine states' interests and their strategies. States additionally define their interest in terms of power and position. Political leaders respond to the incentives and the constraints that the system provides, and to the distribution of capabilities within it. So variations in state behavior are due to discrepancies in the characteristics of the international system.

However, as the world operates on imperfect information, actions are frequently miscalculated. Mearsheimer (1994: 11) argues that states are suspicious and afraid of each other due to a lack of certainty about one another's intentions, leading to mutual mistrust. Consequently, cooperation is difficult to achieve and sustain, instigating self-interested behavior since states instead compete to maximize their relative gains. Peaceful relations are maintained by alliances and **balances of power.** When faced with a common enemy or threat, states may form coalitions or alliances with other actors to increase their strength as an attempt to balance the power of other entities in the system (Waltz 1967). For instance, when state X is becoming too powerful, states Y and Z will perceive this as threatening and fear their survival is in jeopardy. As such, states Y and Z may form an alliance and combine their power and resources to balance that of state X. The alliances are thus built upon common strategic and security interests. Although the members of the coalition work together and pool resources to deter or attack a rival, no stable trusting relationship is built between them. The entities refrain from fighting each other simply because it will weaken their common front against the enemy if they do. Instead, as soon as the threat is defeated, the partnership dissolves (Waltz 1993: 75). It is also important to mention that the formation of an alliance may also spark the establishment of a counter-alliance. In the global system such balances of power will form on a regular basis.

States, or coalitions of states, may also face a **security dilemma**. Jervis (1978: 170) asserts a security dilemma occurs when "one state's gain in security often inadvertently threatens others". Although states might prefer to disarm, the fear that a rival will get stronger than they are themselves if they stop building up their military capabilities prevents them from doing so. Since there is no supranational authority controlling the system, states often feel forced to continue the armaments process. A prominent example of a security dilemma is that of the Cold War, where the United States and the Soviet Union formed the two countering poles of the bipolar international system. They balanced each other's power, but equally feared that if they discontinued building up nuclear arms, the other side would have an advantage. Therefore, both actors continued strengthening military resources, resulting in the escalation of tensions. The example also illustrates that the security dilemma often results in an arms race between great powers.

In neorealist thinking, within the structure of the international system, changes in the distribution of capabilities based on power can vary over time and cause changes in the relations between states. In contrast to classical realism, neorealism sees the structure of the international system as largely determining state behavior. Although realists disagree about the most stable distribution of power, they agree that the polarity impacts state behavior (Powell 1996: 240). The international system can be **bipolar**, meaning that it is dominated by two great powers or opposing blocs as was the case during the Cold War. The international system may at times also be dominated by a **multipolar** world, in which there are several great powers with comparable capabilities. Both structures are argued to have distinct advantages and disadvantages on state interaction. For instance, in a bipolar world, the two entities tend to have equal amounts of power and may refrain from attacking each other due to the possibility of **mutually assured destruction**. Yet, with only two great powers, tensions increase since the attention of both actors will almost solely be focused on each other, as was the case during the Cold War. Contrarily, in a multipolar world, great powers can form alliances to confront an aggressive state with overwhelming amounts of power, but this also increases the likelihood of miscalculation and outbreaks of war between the actors (Mearsheimer 2010: 85). For instance, both world wars occurred during a multipolar global order.

The international system can also be dominated by a single power, resulting in a **unipolar** world. A state with significantly more power than any other actor and that holds geopolitical and sometimes also cultural dominance is called a **hegemon**. Although states may fear the rise of a hegemon and may try to form coalitions or balance against a potential hegemon, a unipolar world is believed by some to be relatively stable since security struggles are less likely and war between great powers is less probable. However, it is important to keep in mind that states and hegemons may also lose power in a global system, allowing for challenging powers to rise, often resulting in a period of conflict and instability. Currently, the rise of major powers, such as China, challenges the existing global power balance and may upset the order if the United States feels threatened. The stable rule of a hegemon and chaos of power transition when new powers rise is referred to as the **hegemonic stability theory.** In the words of Robert Keohane (1980: 132), hegemonic stability theory "holds that hegemonic structures of power, dominated by a single country, are most conducive to the development of strong international regimes whose rules are relatively precise and well obeyed [...] the decline of hegemonic structures of power can be expected to presage a decline in the strength and corresponding international economic regimes."

Since realism argues that cooperation between states is unlikely to happen, the existence of international institutions facilitating multilateral collaboration appears to refute the assumptions of the theory. This raises the question, how does realism account for the formation of international and regional organizations? Realists argue that the establishment of international institutions is unlikely to occur, because it not only requires collaboration but also constrains state behavior and actions. According to the article "The False Promise of International Institutions" by Mearsheimer (1994), states are only willing to create international rules and institutions if they are consistent with their interests. Thus, international institutions, if they are created, are likely to be established by the most powerful players on the international arena and will largely reflect the preferences and power of the most influential states in the system. The institutions are unlikely to be able to act independently of the interests of these powers. Mearsheimer asserts that organizations like the United Nations (UN) are created by the most powerful states as a way to reassert their power over less powerful actors and change the international system according to their preferences. For instance, the most powerful states including the US ensured that the UN would not be able to restrict their behavior through establishing a veto power within the UN Security Council. As such, the permanent five members of the UNSC are able to exercise their power and self-interests over other states, while simultaneously not being constrained by the institution themselves.

Similarly, regional integration is seen by neorealists as an attempt to balance the power of a major state or coalitions of states within the international system. For example, cooperation among the states of the European Union is initially determined by realism as unlikely to happen. But European integration, from this theoretical perspective, makes more sense if it is seen as an attempt to increase Europe's power and standing in the global system. The formation of regional integration schemes around the world, including those focused predominantly on economic integration, are characterized as deliberate attempts of its member states to increase their collective power and influence on the global level. Organizations such as the North Atlantic Treaty Organization (NATO), an organization that we will address in more detail later in this book, is another example of alliance formation in the global system (Waltz 1993: 75). Finally, the rise of new powers will likely lead to the establishment of new international institutions and regional integration schemes.

Since the global political system is assumed to be anarchical, it largely constitutes what is called a **self-help** system. Key neorealist scholars disagree on the best methods for states to help themselves on the global stage. According to some neorealist thinkers, including Kenneth Waltz, states mainly act to ensure their survival. States should attempt to accumulate enough power to defend themselves or what Waltz calls (1979: 40) "an appropriate amount of power", but should refrain from pursuing hegemony. This is because if too much power is obtained, other states will likely balance against it. This approach is called **defensive realism**. In contrast, other neorealist thinkers, including John Mearsheimer, have argued that states and mainly great powers, should aim to maximize their power and attempt to dominate the international system. It is argued that although obtaining too much power may encourage a balance of power to occur, balancing efforts are often unsuccessful and the pursuance of hegemony may pay off. This approach is called **offensive realism** (Mearsheimer 2010: 78). Thus, within the realist paradigm, several variations in the school of thought exist.

To sum up, realism is one of the oldest theories of international relations. It has been extended to account for the dynamics of the international system in what is called neorealism. Neorealists assume that the world is anarchical and conflictual in nature. States aim to continuously increase their power due to fears that others might become more powerful than they are themselves and with this, their security could be threatened. But we have to keep in mind that realism and neorealism are not prescriptions as to how individuals and states should behave. They simply aim to understand what drives behavior, and with this on the international level, how patterns could be established that prevent states from going to war with each other. In the next section, we will look at another approach to international relations that is very different from realism, namely liberalism and its later extension, neoliberalism.

1.4   (Neo-) Liberalism

In comparison to realism, liberalism has an abundantly more optimistic view of the world, despite sharing several core assumptions with the previously discussed theory. Like realism, liberalism believes that states are the main actors in the international arena and must operate under the conditions of an anarchic world system. However, contrary to realism, the theory argues that cooperation is not only likely, but feasible and sustainable. Moreover, liberalism opens the "black box" of states in order to take factors such as the role of domestic institutions, regime type and economic system into account when analyzing the behavior of states (Oneal and Russett 1999: 4). These key differences are addressed in further detail when discussing neoliberalism. But first let us review the foundations of the liberalist approach to international relations.

Liberalism is a paradigm composed of several strands of theories. In its political versions, summarizing from various different trends of this major theoretical stream, it focuses on aspects and values such as individual liberty, political freedom, and equality. In what is sometimes called **republican liberalism**, for example, democracies are believed to be more peaceful than non-democracies. The so-called **Democratic Peace Theory** assumes that two democracies will never go to war with one another. According to Immanuel Kant, the father of republican liberalism, democracies will not fight each other, because they hold common norms and values. Leaders in democratic states recognize that other democracies operate on common principles and will turn to peaceful conflict resolution strategies when tensions arise (Doyle 1983). In comparison, authoritarian regimes or dictatorships are expected to threaten other states, take advantage of weaker entities, and use force in the face of conflict. Additionally, unlike in autocracies, leaders in democratic societies are elected and held responsible by the people. Thus, if the public does not agree with the war, the conflict is taking too long, is too costly, or if the country loses the confrontation, democratic leaders risk being removed from office. In result, if two democracies have a conflict, both leaders are constrained by their people and instead will attempt to find alternative, peaceful solutions to maintain their position in power (Russett 2010: 103).

Aspects of liberalism can also be found extensively, for example, in the principles of neo-classical economics where the unit of analysis or focus tends to be the firm or the individual. The economic approach to the theory emphasizes free market conditions and trade for peaceful relations between states. In neo-classical economics, there is a sense that the economy should be as free as possible from political interference. Based on the theory of Adam Smith, markets should operate and be fully functional on their own, causing an **'invisible hand'** to generate favorable economic conditions and generally lead to welfare gains for all. There are only a few areas were collective action would fail and where government interference would be needed, namely in the case of 'market failures' (Wyatt-Walter 1996). Additionally, in the economic version of liberalism, a special emphasis is placed on so-called **comparative advantage**. This means that every state should focus on the production of certain goods or services that it actually can produce best and cheapest. If all states do this and exchange, the global economy will be beneficial to all and states will converge to comparable levels of economic performance (Gilpin 2011: 198). In fact, Burchill (2005: 63) argues free trade is a "a more peaceful means of achieving national wealth because, according to the theory of comparative advantage, each economy would be materially better off than if it had been pursuing nationalism and self-sufficiency (**autarky**)".

Economic liberalism was largely a response to approaches that emphasized the importance of government interference in markets, such as mercantilism. In the framework of what is at times called **commercial liberalism**, economic independence is believed to allow for the development of peaceful relations between states. If states regularly engage in commercial relations with one another, channels of dialogue are often opened whereby information regarding the needs, interests and preferences of the actors are exchanged. Such communication can move beyond the realm of economics and can generate trust, empathy and shared identities between the trading partners (Russett 2010: 103). Moreover, states are less likely to go to war with countries that they hold economic ties to, as violence will dissolve the mutual beneficial economic activities between the states. According to Russett (2010: 103), "the larger the contribution of trade between two countries to their national economies, the stronger the political base that has an interest in preserving peaceful relations between them". Likewise, Burchill (2005: 63) contends, "free trade would expand the range of contacts and levels of understanding between the peoples of the world and encourage international friendship and understanding". Thus, commercial liberalism argues that economic relations between states can facilitate cooperation. Although economic liberalism has been extremely influential in most parts of the world over the last decades, more concerns have been voiced about the effects of economic liberalism in recent years, especially in the aftermath of the global financial crisis.

In international relations theory, the liberal strands of thought have been adapted and incorporated under one approach labeled as **neoliberalism** or also known as **neoliberal institutionalism**. As formerly mentioned, this tradition shares some of the core principles with realism and neorealism, including the assumptions that states are the most important actors in world politics and that they behave rationally. Additionally, neoliberalists concur with realists that the anarchic system creates conditions of uncertainty, mistrust and fear between states, thereby making cooperation difficult. Nonetheless, there also some key differences between the theories on other significant aspects.

Important authors who developed the neoliberalist school of thought are Robert Keohane and Joseph Nye, who in 1989, published a world famous book, 'Power and Interdependence'. According to Keohane and Nye, in addition to states, there are several other actors on the global stage that influence world politics. Trans-national linkages, and the various patterns of interdependence between states crucially influence the ways in which states behave and conduct their foreign policy. In neoliberalism, like in neorealism, the global system is believed to be anarchic, but states are not seen as the unit of analysis acting as cohesive entities and instead as being constituted by a range of different actors. Domestic politics and international institutions shape the priorities of governments and co-determine their behavior. In addition to this, actors can cooperate across state borders. Multinational corporations and transnational interest groups, for example, are seen as playing an imperative role in shaping the incentives for states to act. International institutions and what is called '**regimes**' – essentially sets of rules, norms and principles that govern behavior in giving issues areas – are seen to affect state behavior. In fact, Stephen Krasner (1982: 186) defined international regimes as being "implicit or explicit principles, norms, rules and decision-making procedures around which actors' expectations converge in a given area of international relations".

In neoliberalism, international institutions are assigned a significantly more important role than they are in realism. For instance, in the article by Robert Keohane and Helen Milner titled 'The Promise of Institutionalist Theory' (1995), these well-known scholars assert that institutions affect the ways in which states define their self-interest. Instead of emphasizing relative gains, the interaction via institutions over time can influence states to prioritize collective or **absolute gains** over relative gains. This is because institutions provide platforms where states can share information and their interests and devious behavior can be punished. As such, cooperation between states is then possible, partially because of the existence of institutions and regimes, and the effect of **reciprocity**. When states cheat or fail to cooperate, other states may no longer wish to collaborate with the cheating state, resulting in a damaged reputation and the inability to profit from the absolute gains facilitated by cooperation. Moreover, although states may be tempted to break the rules of cooperation, and display non-cooperative behavior, institutions can exercise important functions that allow for cooperation. For instance, institutions can monitor the behavior of actors, provide information, allow for repeated interaction and for the reduction of transaction costs. They can sanction actors if they display non-cooperative behavior and with this, they create the foundations for long-term stable patterns of cooperative interaction. Through institutions and reciprocity, states learn that cooperation can be a better strategy and more beneficial than conflict. Additionally, liberalism argues that states do not view international relations as a **zero-sum game**, in which a gain for another is a loss for oneself. Rather, "states feel secure enough to maximize their own gains regardless of what accrues to others" (Burchill 2005: 63). In sum, cooperation and sustainable peace are possible according to the neoliberalist perspective.

Another key difference between realism and liberalism is how power is defined and the role it plays in international relations. While liberalism agrees that power is the ability to get others to do what you want, to maintain control over others, and the main sources largely consist of material factors—including the size of the population, territory, economy, amount of natural resources and the size of the military (Nye 1990: 154)—according to a prominent neoliberalist thinker, Joseph Nye, there is also another crucial component of power, namely what he calls '**soft power**'. Nye claims soft or co-optive power is "when one country gets other countries to *want* what it wants […] in contrast with the hard or command power of *ordering* others to do what it wants" (Nye 1990: 166). When a state is deemed legitimate by other actors, they are less likely to resist its interests and actions on the global stage. Additionally, if others find the culture and ideology of the state attractive, they may want to follow its lead and implement similar policies, adhere to common norms, and become more like the attractive state. As such, in neoliberalism, power does not only include the resources an actor has, but also the influence and ability of an actor to change the behavior of others on the global stage.

As liberalism argues that international institutions facilitate cooperative interaction between states, reducing the effects of anarchy on state behavior, the question arises: is cooperation feasible between states also without the assistance of international institutions? Neoliberalists assert that although international institutions play a key role in facilitating cooperation, peaceful relations are possible without the inference and assistance of institutions. For instance, if states hold common norms as seen by the Democratic Peace Theory or by engaging in sustainable, commercial relations. Nonetheless, institutions clearly can help create systems and frameworks that increase prospects for states to engage in cooperative behavior also for longer time spans.

In essence, the work of neoliberal institutionalists can be seen as a reaction to realism and neorealism: a school of thought they believe that is too pessimistic in terms of explaining the behavior of states and notably, their assumptions regarding the likelihood that cooperation between states can occur. However, there is middle ground between the two theories. Robert Keohane describes himself more as what he calls a '**rational institutionalist**', because he also believes that some of the realist assumptions are actually relevant and very useful. He criticized neorealism but sees this more as an attempt to adapt to theory, rather to reject it entirely. According to neoliberalism, international institutions will not simply be reflections of the interests of the most powerful actors in the global system. Clearly, the preferences of such actors will matter. But they, like smaller or medium-sized countries, are constrained in their behavior by their embedding into networks of international or regional institutions, or regimes. International institutions are believed to be able to crucially influence the behavior of states in the global system. Interdependence between states, according to this school of thought, does not create dependence, and with this a fear of gaining less than others in relative terms, but it adds to the prospects for stability and peace over time (Keohane and Martin 1995). In fact, we could see a project like European integration in the light of this theory.

In the aftermath of World War II, former enemies such as Germany and France, integrated some of the most important sectors of the economy at the time, coal and steel. This economic inter-dependence created the foundations for a long-lasting pattern of stability and peace in what today is the European Union. Moreover, the European integration process has led to the establishment of institutions that have further stimulated the integration process and they do not simply reflect the preferences and power of its most important member states (see Chap. 9 for more information on the European Union and regional integration).

To conclude, liberalism has a rich tradition in terms of both its political and its economic features. Political liberalism emphasizes values such as individual liberty, political rights, equality, human freedom, and democracy. Economic strains of liberalism focus on the importance of markets, the benefits of trade and the need to keep markets as free as possible from government interference. Neoliberalism or neoliberal institutionalism emphasizes the role of a range of different actors on the domestic and the international level, including transnational actors, in terms of constraining and shaping the behavior of states and most importantly, in this theoretical school of thought, international institutions do matter. In the next section, we will investigate a third major theory, which differs in terms of quite a few aspects from realism and liberalism: constructivism.

1.5 Constructivism

In essence, constructivism in international relations theory is based on many different approaches, but can broadly be seen as a reaction to both neorealism and neoliberalism. In fact, constructivism has largely developed as a response to the domination of the rationalist theories in the international relations paradigm, criticizes some of the core assumptions of these trends of theorizing and offers alternative explanations of state interests and behavior in world politics beyond the conditions of anarchy and rationality.

Constructivism, like other major theories of international relations, has many different authors and sub-schools. What is common to most of these approaches is that social reality is not assumed to just be given, but instead **constructed**. Knowledge does not exist independently of interpretation and the use of language; we give what we see a meaning. Most objects of international relations are not material in nature but rather **social facts** that exist because we have constructed them and assigned a meaning to them (Fierke 2010: 182). For instance, monetary bills would be nothing more than a piece of paper if we detached the shared social meaning attributed. How we and others interpret the world around us depends on how the social reality is constructed. It is not so much material interests and power that matter, but rather ideas, norms, identities, and processes of learning that shape our interests and actions (Hopf 1998: 177). Moreover, constructivism argues that power is not merely composed of material factors such as military and economic resources, but also incorporates **ideational** factors that are grounded in shared intersubjective or collective norms and values. These intersubjective norms construct the identities and interests of actors, which are mutually dependent on each other as interests transform when identities do (Finnemore and Sikkink 2001: 393). As such, constructivism distinguishes itself from neoliberalism and neorealism by emphasizing ideational factors as more important than material ones to explain state behavior.

The behavior of states is influenced by how they perceive each other rather than the structure of the international system determining how states act. According to Wendt (1992: 404) via repeated interaction, socialization and mirroring each other's practices, states form perceptions of their own and each other's identities. Through their identities, states determine their interests regarding a particular situation. Hence, the behavior of states is not determined by structural constraints such as anarchy, but rather through collective meaning and interests assigned to a situation that was established by interaction. Wendt (1992: 397) argues that states act towards objects and other states based on the meanings that they have assigned to those objects or other states. In other words, a rivaling state is not an enemy simply because it holds a specific amount of power, but because it is perceived as an enemy due to prior conflictual encounters or tense interaction. Another state with a similar or higher level of economic or military power can equally be perceived as a friend or an ally and with this, not be seen as a security threat. Thus, the level of threat that a state poses to another state is not something that can solely be measured by its military weight or its economic power.

In comparison to realism and liberalism, constructivism assigns an even more important role to institutions. For constructivists, institutions may not only offer formal rules of interaction, but they also shape actor behavior: actors will learn in the setting of formal or informal institutions and get socialized by them. Institutions both create and spread norms forming **standards of appropriate behavior** and socializes states according to these norms (Wendt 1992: 405). For instance, institutions such as international organizations can assist in a newly emerging norm to become widely recognized by the international community. Through promoting the norm and institutionalizing it in organizational platforms and international rules, the norm will become legitimized and states will feel pressured to conform to avoid harming their reputation, as the norm defines appropriate behavior. By acting in accordance with the norm, eventually it will be internalized in the identity of the actor and a taken-for-granted status will be achieved, where deviance from the norm is perceived as severely undesirable or inappropriate (Finnemore and Sikkink 1998). For example, the value of human rights or democracy may be learned and be determined as valuable via mutual interaction over time. Once a human rights norm is fully internalized, the violation of the human right is highly discouraged. Thus, institutions can help with the gradual acquisitions and development of norms and values, which in turn shape behavior. In this edited volume, Chap. 19 by Jérémie Speiser addresses the spreading and institutionalization of norms in further detail when applying the constructivist norm cycle to the 'Responsibility-to-Protect' concept.

Shared norms and values therefore play an imperative role in the constructivist approach. It is the spread of norms and values, changing identities, and patterns of socialization that will mainly affect actor behavior, including interactions between states. Images and perceptions of each other matter, such as whether actors perceive others as belonging to 'self', or to the 'other' (Wendt 1992: 397). For instance, when former US president George W. Bush stated, "you are either with us or you are with the enemy" in the aftermath of the 9/11 terrorist attacks, he constructed identities that belong either to the self or the other: you either believe in American values of freedom and democracy, or you will be perceived as the enemy. The example illustrates that constructivism does not necessarily see actors as utility maximizing or rational. Instead, ideational factors are generally understood as being more important than material interests.

In 1992 Alexander Wendt wrote an influential article, in which he presented some of the most important elements of what now is called **social constructivism**. His article was titled "Anarchy is What States Make of It: The Social Construction of Power Politics". In essence, he criticized some of the core assumptions of neo-realism, but also of neoliberalism. A main message of his article is that states do not (only) act on the basis of the constraints and opportunities that the global system offers, but rather the ways in which they perceive each other and their actions. Wendt (1992: 397), for instance, rejects the realist notion that structural aspects of anarchy and distribution of power will automatically lead to self-help. This is because anarchy and distribution of power do not reveal a priori how a state or object will be labeled, thus failing to account for states being viewed as friends or rivals. Social reality, in this sense, is constructed, and with this also the patterns of interaction between states in international relations.

For constructivism, cooperation between states may be possible, but the focus of analysis is different compared to other theories of international relations. For example, when analyzing an entity such as the European Union, a constructivist is more interested in aspects such as how this regional organization is affected by, and supports, values and norms such as democracy, the rule of law, and human rights than how material features shape the behavior of this organization. Similarly, identities matter, such as the question to which extent citizens of the European Union, for example, will feel they are French, German, Polish, rather than citizens of the European Union. The European Union in turn will affect these identities and citizens will perceive the regional organization based on this identity. For instance, British nationals in recent years have become increasingly skeptical of EU policies, such as the single currency in the Eurozone in the aftermath of the financial crisis and the Schengen Treaty that relaxed EU borders, particularly when facing one of the largest migrant crises in history. As a result, constructivists would argue that the British identity as opposed to a European identity has strengthened, resulting in a rise in Euroscepticism and nationalism in the country. As identity influences the interests and behavior of actors, the nationalist identity in the country persuaded British nationals to vote for EU departure, thereby accounting for Brexit.

The example of Brexit illustrates how constructivism differs from other major strands of international relations theorizing by its emphasis on how states perceive each other, by the importance of identities, and of images such as self and the other, by whether states see each other as friends or as enemies, and finally by a focus on socialization and learning. In constructivism, institutions matter, but as formal or informal rules that affect actor behavior. For most constructivists, it is not so much material forces that are assumed to influence the behavior of actors, but rather ideational ones. In another example, constructivists argue that the Cold War was largely caused by the clashing identities and interests of the US and USSR. The repeated, tense interaction between the superpowers frequently reaffirmed their perceptions of each other as enemies. The end of the rivalry alternatively is argued to be largely the result of changes in the identity of the Soviet Union. Robert Snyder (2005) claims that the end of the decades-long rivalry should be explained in terms of agency, and of ideas, and the so-called pro-western 'new thinking' of Mikhail Gorbachev. The argument is made that the Cold War ended not because of strategic or military reasons, but because of a change in identity, and a change in thinking within the Soviet Union itself, which in turn altered the interests and the behavior of the USSR. The example illustrates the importance of normative values and identity to the constructivist approach.

To sum up, constructivism is now one of the major strands of theories in international relations. It does not consist of one single school of thought. But most constructivists in international relations believe that social reality is constructed by mutual interaction and that material interests are not as important as non-material ones, including norms, ideas and identities. The theory criticizes the rational and anarchic approach of liberalism and realism and attempts to offer an alternative way of looking at the world. As you will see in Chap. 2, several of the post-modern theories share assumptions with constructivism or use constructivist logic.

1.6 Conclusion: International Relations Theories and the Changing Global Order

This chapter introduced you to the three major theories of international relations and outlined the core assumptions of each approach. Theories of international relations break down the complexity of foreign affairs and state behavior to explainable and applicable assumptions. Each of the discussed approaches strives to understand why states behave the way they do and how the world is in reality. There are significant variations in how the three mainstream theories explain the same phenomena on the global stage: they stress diverse actors as the key players, assign various degrees of importance to international institutions, and disagree on whether cooperation is feasible and how stable relations can be maintained.

Realism and liberalism both use a materialistic ontology, categorize states as the main actors and assert that the international system is anarchic. Nevertheless, liberalism holds a more positive view of the world in comparison to realism by arguing that states can cooperate, prioritize absolute gains, and an important role is assigned to international organizations. Likewise, constructivists also believe international institutions are key to spreading norms and values, constructing favorable intersubjective understandings of one another, and thereby foster cooperation. However, unlike the previous two approaches, constructivism attributes the relations between states to social or ideational factors consisting of norms, values and identities as opposed to materialistic ones. As such, each of theories takes alternative components into consideration when explaining the behavior of states on the international arena.

As the content throughout this book largely revolves around changes in the international structure, cooperation and power relations, it is crucial to have a sound theoretical understanding of what causes change. Thus, the chapter concludes by briefly targeting the question: how do international relations theories explain changes in the global order?

Starting with neorealism, academics from this strand emphasize the structure of the international system to understand the changes of global order. A change in the order originates from changes in the structure of the system, which is largely determined by the distribution of power or the polarity of the system. Fluctuations in the number of major powers, the polarity, and the relative power between the actors – most frequently caused by warfare, the decline of existing powers, and the rise of new powers – results in the transformations of the global order. Consequently, the rise of new major players like China and India will likely alter the rules of the game on the international arena.

Alternatively, liberalism takes a notably different approach to explain changes in the global order. Key to explaining transformations is the emergence of new institutions that provide platforms for cooperative behavior between states. Additionally, the more states engage with one another within institutions and the more independent they become, the less likely conflictual relations will occur. Also an increase in the number of democratic states changes the relations states have with other actors on the global stage. For instance, based on the democratic peace thesis, the more democracies that exist, the less conflict will occur between these states, resulting in a more stable global order.

Finally, constructivists argue that the world we live in and the structure of the international system is socially constructed and as famously stated by Alexander Wendt, "anarchy is what states make of it". Through collectively engaging with one another, states reinforce or discourage certain practices, behavior, and beliefs. As repeated interaction with other actors in the international system generates intersubjective understandings of one another and perceptions of the global order, for changes to occur, deviations in state behavior must also take place. Changes in the social behavior of states will alter the perception of the global order and likewise, the behavior of states. However, as long as states continue to engage in insecurity-producing practices, the global order will continue to be seen as a hostile environment dominated by power politics.

Further Readings

Keohane, R. O., & Martin, L. L. (1995). The promise of institutionalist theory. *International Security, 20*(1), 39–51.

Mearsheimer, J. J. (1994). The false promise of international institutions. *International Security, 19*(3), 5–49.

Wendt, A. (1992). Anarchy is what states make of it: The social construction of power politics. *International Organization, 46*(02), 391–425.

References

Acharya, A. (2008). *The limitations of mainstream international relations theories for understanding the politics of forced migration, 27*. Centre for International Studies, Oxford University.

Adler, E. (2013). Constructivism in international relations: Sources, contributions, an debates. *Handbook of International Relations, 2*, 112–144.

Burchill, S. (2005). Liberalism. In J. True, S. Burchill, A. Linklater, R. Devetack, J. Donnely, M. Patterson, & C. Reus-Smit (Eds.), *Theories of international relations* (3rd ed.). Basingstoke: Palgrave.

Claude, I. L. (1971). *Swords into plowshares: The problems and progress of international organization*. New York: Random House.

Doyle, M. W. (1983). Kant, liberal legacies, and foreign affairs. *Philosophy & Public Affairs, 12*, 205–235.

Finnemore, M., & Sikkink, K. (1998). International norm dynamics and political change. *International Organization, 52*(04), 887–917.

Finnemore, M., & Sikkink, K. (2001). Taking stock: The constructivist research program in international relations and comparative politics. *Annual Review of Political Science, 4*, 391–416.

Forde, S. (1992). Varieties of realism: Thucydides and Machiavelli. *The Journal of Politics, 54*(02), 372–393.

Fierke, K. M. (2010). Constructivism. In T. Dunne, M. Kurki, & S. Smith (Eds.), *International relations theories: Discipline and diversity* (2nd ed.). Oxford: Oxford University Press.

Gilpin, R. (2011). *Global political economy: Understanding the international economic order*. Princeton, Princeton University Press.

Hopf, T. (1998). The promise of constructivism in international relations theory. *International Security, 23*(1), 171–200.

Jervis, R. (1978). Cooperation under the security dilemma. *World Politics, 30*(02), 167–214.

Jervis, R. (1985). From balance to concert: A study of international security cooperation. *World Politics, 38*(01), 58–79.

Keohane, R. (1980). The theory of hegemonic stability and changes in international economic regimes, 1967–1977. In O. Holsti, R. Siverson, & A. George (Eds.), *Change in the international system* (pp. 131–162). Boulder: Westview Press.

Keohane, R. O., & Martin, L. L. (1995). The promise of institutionalist theory. *International Security, 20*(1), 39–51.

Krasner, S. (Ed.). (1982). Regimes and the limits of realism: Regimes as autonomous variables. *International Organization, 36*, 185–205.

Mearsheimer, J. J. (1994). The false promise of international institutions. *International Security, 19*(3), 5–49.

Mearsheimer, J. J. (2010). Structural realism. In T. Dunne, M. Kurki, & S. Smith (Eds.), *International relations theories: Discipline and diversity* (2nd ed.). Oxford: Oxford University Press.

Morgenthau, H. (1948). *Politics amongst nations. The struggle for power and peace*. Nova York: Alfred Kopf.

Nye, J. S. (1990). Soft power. *Foreign Policy, 80*, 153–171.

Oneal, J. R., & Russett, B. (1999). The Kantian peace: The Pacific benefits of democracy, interdependence, and international organizations, 1885–1992. *World Politics, 51*(1), 1–37.

Powell, R. (1996). Stability and the distribution of power. *World Politics, 48*(02), 239–267.

Russett, B. (2010). Liberalism. In T. Dunne, M. Kurki, & S. Smith (Eds.), *International relations theories: Discipline and diversity* (2nd ed.). Oxford: Oxford University Press.

Smith, S. (2000). The discipline of international relations: Still an American social science? *The British Journal of Politics and International Relations, 2*(3), 374–402.

Snyder, R. S. (2005). Bridging the realist/constructivist divide: The case of the counterrevolution in soviet foreign policy at the end of the cold war. *Foreign Policy Analysis, 1*(1), 55–71.

Waltz, K. N. (1959). *Man, the state, and war: A theoretical analysis*. New York, Columbia University Press.

Waltz, K. N. (1967). International structure, national force, and the balance of world power. *Journal of International Affairs, 21*(2), 215–231.

Waltz, K. N. (1979). *Theory of international relations*. Reading: Addison-Wesley.

Waltz, K. N. (1988). The origins of war in neorealist theory. *The Journal of Interdisciplinary History, 18*(4), 615–628.

Waltz, K. N. (1993). The emerging structure of international politics. *International Security, 18*(2), 44–79.

Wendt, A. (1992). Anarchy is what states make of it: The social construction of power politics. *International Organization, 46*(02), 391–425.

Wendt, A. (1999). *Social theory of international politics*. Cambridge: Cambridge University Press.

Wyatt-Walter, A. (1996). Adam Smith and the liberal tradition in international relations. *Review of International Studies, 22*(01), 5–28.

Chapter 2
Alternative Post-Positivist Theories of IR and the Quest for a Global IR Scholarship

Indraneel Baruah and Joren Selleslaghs

2.1 Introduction

This chapter is a continuation of the previous one, at least in terms of the theoretical foundations of IR to enrich the understanding of the changing global order. It is interesting to note that the global system and IR theory both undergo change and interact consistently in order to adapt to developments on either side. The main area of focus will be post-positivist theories of international relations, as the previous chapters focused primarily on positivist theories such as realism and liberalism. In other words, this chapter looks at different substantive theories which share a post-positivist (or reflectivist) methodology, or philosophy of science. Before proceeding, some key issues will be addressed, such as the philosophical notion, and purposes of post-positivism, as well as that of its predecessor, positivism. There is often a misunderstanding in the scientific/academic tradition that somehow positivism and post-positivism are (or have to be) contradictory to one another, and thus there is a perpetual war between the two camps of thought. Certain scholars characterize IR as a justifiably divided discipline which is currently split between a positivist mainstream camp and a post-positivist camp (Kurki 2006: 194). Consequently, in recent theoretical narratives, there has been a degree of turmoil caused by a consortium of theories (i.e. post-positivist theories) aiming to primarily criticise the core positivist assumptions, i.e. the social world can be studied scientifically like the natural world. To reiterate, in IR theory, post-positivism broadly refers to the consortium of theories which epistemologically reject positivism, the idea that the

I. Baruah (✉) · J. Selleslaghs
Faculty of Governance and Global Affairs, Leiden University, The Hague, The Netherlands
e-mail: I.Baruah16@gmail.com; selleslaghs.joren@gmail.com

© Springer Nature Switzerland AG 2020
M. O. Hosli, J. Selleslaghs (eds.), *The Changing Global Order*, United Nations University Series on Regionalism 17,
https://doi.org/10.1007/978-3-030-21603-0_2

empiricist observation of the natural sciences can be applied to the social sciences.[1] It is useful to note the only key unifying element amidst this consortium is a mutual critique towards core positivist assumptions. Nevertheless, due to their relevance in today's changing global order, it is crucial to understand the basic elements of such theories. Therefore, this chapter highlights a few key post-positivist approaches, namely: constructivism, critical theory, postmodernism, and relational theory. These are not all post-positivist approaches, but a few of them. Some of which are not addressed in this chapter are feminism, normative theory, and green theory, among others. This chapter also sheds light on the quest for a global IR scholarship, and recent developments therein. It is important to note that there is no such thing as "a post-positivist approach, only post-positivist approaches" (Smith et al. 1996: 35). After addressing a few post-positivist approaches in the first part, the recent debate on the Global IR project will be addressed in the second part of this chapter.

There are influential thinkers and substantive insights on both camps, positivist and post-positivist, which impacts social science, and IR theory in general. For conceptual clarity, it seems useful to lay the groundwork for some key essential semantic debates and differences. For instance, positivist theories tried to organise the early social scientific theories by using similar methods to those used to study the natural sciences. In fact, from a historical perspective, positivism was an ancient literary point of dispute between philosophy and poetry,[2] before being reformulated as one amidst social science (humanities) and natural science.

Further, another recent development within the discipline of IR is the call for a 'Global IR' scholarship. Amitav Acharya postulates the discipline of IR does not reflect the voices, experiences, knowledge claims, and contributions of most societies and states on the globe, often marginalizing those outside the core countries of the West (Acharya 2014: 647–659).

Stanley Hoffman famously described the field of International Relations as an "American social science" (Hoffmann 1977). The connection of the IR discipline with the West, i.e. North America as well as Europe must be acknowledged, owing to scientific and methodological developments pertaining to the Renaissance, and Enlightenment movements, and resulting experiences and advances in statehood, and statecraft in the Modern Era before and after the Peace of Westphalia in 1648 (The Peace of Westphalia is widely accepted as the event after which sovereign nation states started to function as actors in the international system).

---

[1] Another notable element is that there occurs some conflation in philosophical ontology, and scientific ontology from this debate. This is not addressed in this chapter, as it would exceed its scope.

[2] The debate involving positivism as a quarrel between philosophy and poetry was formulated as far back as Plato. See Egan, Kieran (1997). *The Educated Mind.* University of Chicago Press. pp. 115–116. "Positivism is marked by the final recognition that science provides the only valid form of knowledge and that facts are the only possible objects of knowledge; philosophy is thus recognised as essentially no different from science […] Ethics, politics, social interactions, and all other forms of human life about which knowledge was possible would eventually be drawn into the orbit of science […] The positivists' program for mapping the inexorable and immutable laws of matter and society seemed to allow no greater role for the contribution of poets than had Plato. […] What Plato represented as the quarrel between philosophy and poetry is resuscitated in the "two cultures" quarrel of more recent times between the humanities and the sciences."

Nevertheless, in today's increasingly globalized and inter-connected world, the analogy of IR as an American, or even a Western field does not have a valid claim as it lacks salience. Although there has been a great deal of interaction between Western and non-western scholars and institutions, the universities, scholars, and publishing outlets in the West mainly dominate the narrative and set the agenda (Acharya 2014). Only a few countries and institutions outside the Western world seem to have somewhat competitive mechanisms. The non-Western world is often viewed as being of interest mainly to area specialists, and hence a place for "cameras" rather than of "thinkers". This part of the globe is often percieved as ideal for fieldwork and theory-testing, rather than to discover new ideas and approaches. It is useful to note that the political and economic circumstances of the developing world also contributed to this trajectory. Conditions such as scarcity of resources, political interventions, and the lack of freedom of expression and opportunities have also stymied the development of IR as a global discipline (Acharya 2014: 648). Nevertheless, scholars have demonstrated that the international studies community also bears responsibility for IR being too focused on the Western world (Shea 1997).

To put this in perspective, a few brief examples are in order. For instance, whilst considering the ideas that have shaped Realist theory in IR, much if not all of the literature is grounded on the ideas of Thucydides, Machiavelli, Hobbes, but not on Kautilya, or Sun-Tzu, or others from the so called developing world.[3] Investigating the Realist school of IR indicates the roots of the field as grounded on the writings and thought of Machiavelli during the Medici era in the Florentine Republic, without any substantive reference or acknowledgement of Kautilya, who predated him by centuries, and can be regarded as the first great realist (Boesche 2002). Reading Kautilya's *Arthashastra* demonstrates several ideas outlined in Machiavelli's *Prince*. The Arthashastra is an ancient Indian treatise on statecraft, diplomacy, economic policy and military strategy, originally written in Sanskrit. Composed, expanded and redacted between the second and third century BCE, it was influential until the twelfth century, when it disappeared (Olivelle 2013: 30–31). Rediscovered in 1905 by R. Shamasastry, who published it in 1909 (Allen 2012). The first English translation was published in 1915 (Boesche 2002: 8). The title "Arthashastra" is often translated to "the science of politics", but has a much broader scope. It includes texts on the nature of government, law, civil and criminal court systems, diplomacy, theories on war, nature of peace, ethics, economics, markets and trade, the methods for screening ministers, the duties and obligations of a king, as well as ancient economic and cultural details on agriculture, mineralogy, mining and metals, animal husbandry, medicine, forests and wildlife (Olivelle 2013; Trautmann 1971). Moreover, the Arthashastra explores issues of social welfare, and the collective ethics that hold a society together (Olivelle 2013: 101, 228–229, 286–287). The purpose of this example is to indicate how different the school of IR Realism would seem today, if rationality and social welfare was considered vital, as well as elements linked to schooling and health care. Similarly, there were other notable experts who have made significant contributions in their field but are often

---

[3] This distinction exceeds the domain of Realism, and is added for the purpose of substantiating a specific claim, which entails realist thinkers.

unacknowledged. For example, ninth century mathematician Muhammad ibn Musa al-Khwarizmi, also known as the "father of algebra". The word algebra itself is derived from the title of his book, Kitab al-Jabr, yet this is not mainstream knowledge. For example, 9th century mathematician Muhammad ibn Musa al-Khwarizmi, also known as the "father of algebra". The word algebra itself is derived from the title of his book, Kitab al-Jabr, yet this is not mainstream knowledge. Another example pertains to the ignorance of colonial wars, or extra-systemic conflicts, in assessing war and peace in the international system, especially in constructing the democratic peace theory.[4] Taking these wars into account would challenge established claims about the pacific nature of Western Liberal Democracies (Ravlo et al. 2003; Mann 2001; Haas 1995). The Democratic Peace theory in general (both monadic and dyadic) has also been criticised for being Eurocentric, with little relevance for explaining war and peace in the non-Western world (Barkawi and Laffey 2001; Adem 2007).

This chapter highlights the relative advantages and disadvantages of positivism and post-positivism in IR theory. This is grounded on the firm belief that IR can benefit from both positivism and post-positivism. In other words, instead of critically comparing the two lines of thought, or discussing their contradictions, or strengths and weaknesses, it seems apposite to consider the complementary strengths of both these camps of thought. Further, an argument can be made that despite all its boons and banes, positivism was influenced by the wider political and social context of the time, just like post-positivism is influenced by the contemporary social and international contexts. The structure of this chapter, which is divided into two parts is organized as follows: the first section introduced the content of this chapter, including the recent scholarly debate on the need for a "Global IR". The second section studies Positivism, its rationale, and why there has been a shift towards post-positivism. The third section outlines Post-positivism and its rationale.[5] The fourth section briefly outlines some of the main post-positivist approaches mentioned earlier. The fifth section addresses the Global IR project, and outlines a few of its key elements and developments. This section also presents the recently conceived relational theory based on Confucian Chinese *zhongyong* dialectics as an example. Notably, it was developed in response to the call for a global IR. The final section will draw conclusions and provide insights into theoretically innovative approaches.

---

[4] For example, the "Correlates of War" (COW) project, founded at the University of Michigan in 1963 coded wars since 1816 but neglected "extra-state" wars, that is, imperial and colonial wars. It was criticized for reflecting a "historical legacy of Western Imperialism and racism that simply did not regard non-Western groups as civilized or as human beings equal to whites" and thus "did not bother to record in any systematic way the fatalities sustained by non-national groupings in imperial wars of conquest or pacification". For details see Vasquez, John. (1993). *The War Puzzle.* Cambridge: Cambridge University Press. p.27. The COW database later added 129 extra-state wars, with the help of revised methodology and new historical research (COW 2006: News & Notes).

[5] Sections 2.1 and 2.2 will also include advantages and disadvantages, to maintain objectivity.

2.2   Positivism

Positivism is often known as the foundational epistemology of the mainstream schools of IR thought ([neo-] realism and liberalism as described in Chap. 1). It was devised as part of the broader Enlightenment project, in order to study social activity in an organised, scientific, and methodological manner. It was akin to a scientific experiment which only allows empirical facts, and dominated the social sciences until the rise of post-positivism (George 1989: 279). Essentially then, positivism can be understood as a philosophical theory which states positive knowledge is based on natural phenomena and their properties and relations. It was believed by (early) positivists that the social sciences can be understood via (empirical) observation through the senses, just like the natural sciences. In other words, positivism pertains to the basic idea that the empirical observation techniques of the natural sciences can be applied to the social sciences as well.

Positivism also emphasises the centrality of empirical propositions, based on the careful observation of reality through the senses. According to Nicholson, "We observe events and on the basis of these observations hope to predict the consequences of actions carried out now or in the future" (Nicholson 1996: 132). Subsequently, information which is derived from sensory experience through observation, and interpreted through reason and logic, forms the exclusive source of all authoritative knowledge. Positivism holds that valid knowledge can only be found via derived knowledge. "The kernel of positivism is the belief that scholars can make empirical generalisations about the social world, including international relations, which are verifiable" (Jackson and Sørensen 2010: 285). Positivist theories rest upon propositions that are (or are striving to be) related in a logical way: "some propositions imply other propositions" (Nicholson 1996: 129). Further, as verifiable data or positive facts received from the senses are regarded as empirical (as per the dictionary), thus positivism was increasingly based on empiricism. Positivism can also be characterised through Hume's radical empiricist conception of cause: "knowledge does not exist outside of what we can observe, and thus what we claim to know is simply the associations or 'conjunctions' made on these observations" (Kurki 2006: 192). One of the simplest and most basic characterisations of Positivism is "the adoption of methodologies of the natural sciences to explain the social world" (Smith 1996: 11).

At the time when positivism was formulated, it is useful to consider two important factors: the founder of positivism, and the wider international context at the time. The foundations for positivist thought, at least in the modern sense of the term was laid by Auguste Comte (1798–1857) in the nineteenth century. Furthermore, in order to understand positivism, it is helpful to know the basic principles driving Comte's thought in the remarkable academic contribution known as, *'The course of positive philosophy'* (or the *Course*).[6] In this volume, Comte has essentially organised the concept of a philosophy of science, arguably with good intentions in mind.

---

[6] This is recommended to anyone who is interested in the philosophical details about positivism.

It can be postulated that his classification was to systematise social sciences by organising the measurement of data and avoid the fragmentation of knowledge (Bourdeau 2015). According to Comte, just as the physical world operates according to gravity and other absolute laws, society also operates according to general laws. Therefore, Comte's Course presented in sequence a philosophy of mathematics, astronomy, physics, chemistry, biology, and sociology.

Based on the 'unity of all the sciences conception', which also includes social sciences, Positivism views the social and political world, (including the international world), as having regularities and patterns that can be explained if the correct methodology is applied (Jackson and Sørensen 2010: 284). Consequently, the social scientist is no different from any other (natural) scientist in this regard. According to positivist methodology, observation and experience are keys to constructing objective judgement of scientific theories. Furthermore, positivism asserts there can be an objective knowledge of the world, or at least "a great deal of intersubjective agreement" (Nicholson 1996: 131). From a critical point of view, this assertion seems justifiable in investigating natural sciences, but not necessarily the social world, which is in constant flux, as asserted by Alexander Wendt in the theory of Constructivism. The relational theory based on Chinese Confucian Chinese *zhongyong* dialectics, which is discussed later in this chapter also addresses the ever changing and complex social world. Therefore, positivism has been subject to criticism. From such a vantage point, it has been postulated that positivism fails to acknowledge the possibility that all theories are at some level "politically and socially contextualised" (Kurki 2009: 442). Consequently, this leads to the creation of positivist predictions which are fundamentally flawed, resulting from a failure to take into account the very context within which social facts are constructed.

From an IR perspective, more than one point explains the shift towards post-positivism. Positivism became increasingly marginalised due to wider systemic developments. First, it included only traditional political thought (mostly relating [neo] realism and liberalism), due to the social and international context at the time. It was the era of a realist global order, as it preceded two World Wars and the Cold War. Second, its founder Comte's work on the political philosophy of positivism is less known, and the wider debate got entangled in divergent academic debates. Third, the World Wars, and the Cold War gave birth to a wide range of issues, voices, and political thoughts and movements. The entire notions of institutionalism, constructivism, NGOs, IGOs, activists, and spread of ideas and opinions directly contradicted the positivist school. Fourth, the failure of positivism to appropriately address the Cold War, the rise of social constructivism, and the spread of activist movements of many hues quickly consolidated post-positivism as an influential camp in the contemporary context. Nevertheless, the useful contribution to science made by positivism cannot be ignored, as it strived for the foundation of a discipline which is aimed towards making the study of society positively scientific, akin to the natural sciences. It can be said that positivism was a step that led to the formulation of post-positivism (the next step). These two modes of thought were not concieved as inherently opposing to one another. For example, automobiles running on refined crude oil were invented first, before the advent of electric cars, which is a relatively recent development, stemming from changing needs and structural contexts. Both have their advantages and disadvantages as per changing contexts, and it is arguably unfair to seperate either development from one another and pose it distinctly.

2.3 Post-Positivism

As indicated earlier, post-positivism refers to the consortium of relatively newly formulated IR theories which emerged after the Cold War. Post-positivist methodology and process of theorising epistemologically reject positivist thought. From a practical standpoint, post-positivism (also known as anti-positivism, or reflectivism), grew in popularity within the academic IR debate during the 1980s and surged into the fore of mainstream IR thought when positivism was deemed a failure for being unable to aptly predict the end of the Cold War (Monteiro and Ruby 2009: 15–48). Post-positivism has advanced the debate pertaining to theory and method in social science. Consequently, it attempts to integrate, or include a larger variety of variables pertaining to international security concerns. Post-positivism allows the raising of questions regarding *accepted* practice, i.e. questioning paradigms, questioning perspectives, and questioning methodology, which invigorates the wider academic project. Therefore, the optimistic potential of what post-positivism signifies, and can achieve in IR is significant (Lapid 1989: 235).

It is also useful to understand the structural changes which led to the shift towards post-positivism. The two World Wars, and especially the Cold War contributed heavily to the changing social and international contexts. Therefore, it demanded theoretical adaptations, which had to be made as the descriptive and explanatory power of traditional modes of Realist (and Liberal) thought was severely limited with the rise of new thought patterns and ideas. As addressed earlier in this chapter, one of the primary positivist assumptions was that the same methodologies could be applied to both the natural and social scientific disciplines. However, such a viewpoint is outrightly, and according to the current context, justifiably rejected by IR scholars, such as Alexander Wendt (see Chap. 1) who posits social constructivism perceives social facts as socially constructed, and in constant flux. Therefore, this rejected, or rather built upon the earlier positivist assumption that unlike natural scientific facts, social scientific facts cannot be studied with the same methodologies.

Furthermore, it has been postulated that "post-positivist methodology rests on the proposition that people conceive, construct and constitute the worlds in which they live, including the international world, which is an entirely human arrangement" (Jackson and Sørensen 2010: 286). It is useful to emphasise there are several versions or models of post-positivist theoretical frameworks and methodologies. Due to the limits of this chapter, it is not possible to give a full overview of all the post-positivist theories ever formulated. Notably, only a few renowned ones will be addressed in this chapter. The most adopted and widely accepted post-positivist approach or methodology is Constructivism, which is already addressed in the previous chapter. The constructivists believe the social world cannot be measured with the same methodologies as the natural world because social knowledge is made up of ever-changing, ever-modifying facts, and therefore bears no resemblance to knowledge of the natural world (Wendt 1992). For a detailed account on constructivism, please refer to the previous chapter.

2.4   Post-Positivist Theories of IR

2.4.1   Critical Theory

Critical theory was conceived by a group of German scholars who were often known collectively as the 'Frankfurt school'. The term was coined in 1937, and refers to the works of the Frankfurt institute of social research. A few key scholars from this group are: Max Horkheimer, Theodor Adorno, Herbert Marcus (first generation), and Jürgen Habermas (second generation) for example. In IR, critical theory is often closely linked to Marxist International Political Economy (Jackson and Sørensen 2010: 181–196). As a result, critical theory is also at times regarded as neo-Marxism. Critical theory is essentially the critical analysis of positivist thought, which is in turn the main strength of post-positivism, or post-positivist approaches in general. It encourages social science to think more critically about the status quo, and the reaction against positivist epistemology. It has been postulated that Karl Marx's theory of historical materialism and critical analysis drew upon positivism, a tradition which would continue in the development of critical theory (Kołakowski 1978: 327–331). Critical theory rejects the "three basic postulates of positivism: an objective external reality, the subject object distinction, and value free social science". It therefore strikes at the epistemological core of positivism, by denying the subject-object distinction.

Whilst earlier positivist scholars like Comte and Hume seem to have believed that knowledge can be found only on what we observe, post-positivist critical theorists believe individual human ideas, norms, needs, interests, actions, and purposes heavily influence social observations. Individual in this sense can vary to one, or a group of any number of persons, anything short of a country. In the global system in which positivism thrived, states were considered to be the sole actors. In contrast, today's global system includes a wide variety of abstract social groups and organisations who have a role in global affairs, and are not states. Therefore, it can be inferred that the positivist theories are not as 'value-neutral' as claimed, and even less relevant in today's international system. In fact, it can be argued that many scholars who are criticised as positivists are actually post-positivists. It is revealing to look at Waltz's epistemologically positivist approach that "only through some sort of systems structure can international politics be understood" (Waltz 2007: 30).

Thus, a major strength of the critical theory approach, (and post-positivist approaches in general) is giving precedence to "what" or "who" theories represent. Such an approach has been able to aptly address the changing nature of the international system, and international relations between states in the post Cold War era. As per one perspective, "one of the reasons IR has failed as an intellectual project is its failure to move beyond the traditional conception of relationships between states" (Buzan and Little 2001: 19). This could be viewed as an extreme narrative of sorts, but the essential point is evident, as is its complementarity with post-positivist approaches.

The critical approach shifted the attention away from states as the sole actors in the international system, towards the implications of violence, gender, and development issues, among others. Conception of frameworks such as the Millenium Development Goals, and Sustainable Development Goals can be seen as examples in this context and subsequent developments. This post-positivist approach is deemed to be in a better position to understand this new trajectory because it is not dogmatic in an ontological sense. Importantly, the academic debate is widened, or rather advanced, and marginalised actors and groups which have previously been denied agency in the traditional IR realm (only consisting of state actors), are now empowered. "Critical theory questions the dominant world order by taking a reflective stance on the framework of this order. By doing so it also questions the origins and legitimacy of political and social institutions and the way they change over time" (Roach et al. 2014: 62). Barnett and Duvall conceive of a type of 'productive power' which refers partly to 'the discursive production of the subjects, the fixing of meanings, and the terms of action, of world politics' and this productive power is inherent in the positivist universality of assumptions based on conjunctions of the Western experience (Barnett and Duvall 2005: 56).

Furthermore, everything that is social, including IR is not immutable, i.e. they are changeable and thus historical, as history is a continuous process of change. "Since world politics are constructed rather than discovered, there is no fundamental distinction between subject (the analyst) and object (the focus of analysis)" (Barnett and Duvall 2005: 287). Robert Cox is another central figure in critical theory, his contributions to which are noteworthy. Cox affirms the connection between knowledge and interests, and distinguishes two perspectives on theory depending on its purpose, i.e. (1) problem-solving theory; and (2) critical theory (Cox 1981). According to the first, theory serves as a guide to find solutions to problems from the point of view of, and within, its own framework. In the second perspective, the presumptions of the theory itself and the process of theorising are reflected upon. To do so means to open up the possibility of choice.

According to critical theorists, knowledge is not and cannot be neutral, either morally or politically or ideologically, as all knowledge reflects the interests of the observer and is always biased because it is produced from the social perspective of the analyst. Knowledge thus discloses an inclination- conscious or unconscious-towards certain interests, values, groups, parties, classes, nations, and so on. Therefore, from a purely critical perspective, all IR theories are in a way biased too (Jackson and Sørensen 2010: 287).

Critical theorists express political opinions, advocate and promote progressive (usually socialist) ideology of emancipation believing that conservative scholars and liberal scholars are defending and simply promoting their respective political values. Critical theorists thus believe that theoretical debates are political debates, and thus knowledge is inherently political (Jackson and Sørensen 2010: 288). According to critical theorists, IR scholars cannot conduct an objective and unbiased investigation, as they themselves cannot be detached form the subject matter they are studying, as they are also a part of the social world and interactions under investigation therein. According to Jackson and Sørensen, the main problem with this outlook is the difficulty it poses in terms of academic relevance and the integrity of scholarly and scientific research. Critical theory rejects all other (positivist) approaches as overly political, which are also unable to provide an objective assessment of the social world. Further, as certain authors posit: If IR theory is political rather than scientific or scholarly, there can justifiably be no real academic debates, disagreements and controversies. But if IR theories and all other social science theories really are solely political, how can we justify them as academic subjects to begin with? By that logic, why should any theory (including critical theory) be taken as a statement of knowledge if it is really a statement of politics? (Jackson and Sørensen 2010). Critical theories are researched, applied and taught in many universities especially outside the US, due to a concern that "a myopic discipline of IR might contribute to the continued development of a civil society in the U.S. that thinks, reflects and analyses complex international events through a very narrow set of theoretical lenses" (Smith 2002).

2.4.2   Postmodernism

Akin to all other post-positivist approaches, postmodernism too entered the realm of IR around the end of the Cold War. Nonetheless, the historical roots of this theoretical approach can be traced back to a group of post-world war II French thinkers who refused existentialism and its philosophy, which was prevalent during late 1940s (and early 1960s) in France. Postmodernism is also deemed similar to critical theory, in the sense that it strives to illustrate the "conceptual prisons" of the other mainstream theorists (Vasquez 1995: 217–40).

Postmodernists reject the claim of mainstream theories such as (neo) realism and liberalism which claim to discover the objective truth about the social world in an IR context. There is a succinct definition of postmodernist view of knowledge and power. "All power requires knowledge and all knowledge relies on and reinforces existing power relations. Thus there is no such thing as 'truth', existing outside of power. To paraphrase Foucault, 'how can history have a truth if truth has a history?'[7,8] Truth is not something external to social settings, but is instead part of them. Postmodern international theorists have used this insight to examine the 'truths' of international relations to see how the concepts and knowledge- claims that dominate the discipline in fact are highly contingent on specific power relations" (Smith 1997: 181).

Further, Postmodernism can be characterised by three main themes: "First, post-modernists are hostile towards claims to universal or objective truth, as they reject the idea of an external reality independent of our perceptions and the language we use to express those perceptions, and therefore they claim to undermine the traditional distinction between theory and practice. Second, postmodernists seek to unmask putatively emancipatory grand narratives as oppressive, and believe that truth itself is a mask for power. Third, in so far as postmodernism does turn out to have a distinctive ethical position of its own, it might be summed up as 'respect for difference'" (Roach et al. 2014).

Postmodernism disputes the notions of reality, truth, and of the idea that there is or can be ever-expanding knowledge of the human world. Narratives, including metanarratives, are constructed by a theorist and are most likely contaminated by his or her perspectives and prejudices (Jackson and Sørensen 2010: 296). A metanarrative in postmodernism (and in critical theory in general) is a narrative about narratives of historical meaning, experience, and knowledge, which offers society legitimation through the anticipated completion of a (as yet unrealised) master idea (Lyotard 1992: 29). Postmodernists are also sceptical of the idea that institutions can ever be fair and just for all of humankind: men and women everywhere (Jackson and Sørensen 2010: 289). Social science is not neutral; rather, it is historical, cultural, political and therefore biased more often than not. Empirical theory is often regarded as a myth, as every theory decides for itself what counts as 'truth' or 'facts'. In other words, there is no objective reality; everything involving human beings is subjective. Further, knowledge and power are intimately related, as knowledge is not at all "immune from the workings of power" (Smith 1997: 181).

It can be deduced that essentially, postmodernists are deconstructivists who regard theories in terms of 'narratives' and 'metanarratives' which are devised by a theorist, who has his or her own distinct perspectives, values, ideas, culture, prides, and prejudices. The main target of postmodernist deconstruction in IR are the mainstream theories, for the latter's claim that only a few elements or variables of information about sovereign nation states in an anarchical international system can explain the important things needed to know about IR, in Waltz's words "through all the centuries we can contemplate" (Waltz 1993). According to Richard Ashley, a postmodernist critique of neorealism is specifically targeted towards the anarchical structure and ahistorical bias of the theory (Ashley 1986: 289).

---

[7]Foucault, M. (1997). *Ethics, Subjectivity and Truth: Essential Works of Foucault 1954–1984* (Vol. 1). Trans. C. Porter, New York: The New Press.

[8]Taylor, C. (1984). Foucault on freedom and truth. *Political Theory*, 12(2), 152–183.

The benefit of postmodernism is the crucial argument presented to established academic traditions. It is opined by postmodernists (and critical theorists in general) that mainstream scholars typically claim too much for their theories, which do not live up to their claims from a critical perspective. In other words, positivist theories for example (neo) realism, and (neo) liberalism (among others) do not provide objective knowledge or complete information of the world, as they claim.

However, there is also a negative side to postmodernist thought, which is sort of self-contradictory in nature. As per postmodernist ideology, all theories are biased and none can explain objective reality. Such a line of reasoning can be turned on its head, as Jackson and Sørensen have addressed these questions succinctly and accurately: "Why should we accept the analysis of the postmodernists if theory is always biased in some way? Why should the deconstruction be believed any more than the original construction? If every account of the social world is arbitrary and biased, then postmodernism cannot be spared: its critique can be turned upon itself" (Jackson and Sørensen 2010: 290).

According to postmodernism, there are essentially no stable platforms or certitudes upon which social speech, writing, and action can be based.

> ironically, what makes postmodernism intelligible, including the work of its proponents, is its conformity to the basic conventions of academic inquiry which are the very foundations of all knowledge, including social knowledge. Their own writing conform to the conventions of English grammar and vocabulary, and no doubt postmodernists live their own lives as we live our lives within the compass of interpersonal standards of time, space, and no on which are marked and measured calendars, clocks, miles, kilometres, etc. There are similar conventions of international law, politics, and economics (Jackson and Sørensen 2010). For example, security protocols in airports and train stations on one hand, and even corportate institutions or other non-corporate organisations on the other hand are examples, as everyone is required to follow certain conventions, although not everyone technically agreed to every specific clause therein. Such measures and standards are some of the most fundamental elements of the modern world.

Therefore, in its extreme, postmodernism can also often deteriorate into nihilism, i.e. negativism for its own sake, or criticisms made solely for the purpose of criticism. "Many (mostly younger) scholars have welcomed the participation of postmodernist inspired critiques of epistemological orthodoxies. What unites post-positivist critics (postmodernist or otherwise) is the shared frustration with the way in which 'the discipline' adjudicates what is to count as proper theory on the basis of narrow metatheoretical criteria overly indebted to the philosophy of the natural sciences" (Roach et al. 2014: 280).

2.5   The Quest for a Global IR Scholarship

Mainstream (mostly Western) IR theory pertains to the schools of thought, or theorising which generated in the American school and the English school. The American school needs no introduction, as the most popular IR theories of Realism, Liberalism, and Constructivism (and their sub-schools), and methodologies were conceived in the United States and are described at length in Chap. 1. The English school mainly pertains to norms and international society, but places international anarchy at the centre of IR Theory.[9] English scholars share affinities and made major contributions especially to constructivism and realism for which the English School is often regarded as a major contribution to Western Mainstream IR theory. Although the field is dominated by the American schools of thought, a transatlantic connection or affinity between the American mainstream and the English School is manifest, especially via the elementary (and metaphysical) concepts of individual rationality, and also of international norms. Brown defines the international society as a "norm-governed relationship whose members accept that they have at least limited responsibilities towards one another and the society as a whole" (Brown 2009: 484). Another way of looking at this would be through Adam Watson's term 'raison de système', a counterpoint to 'raison d'état', and defined as 'the idea that it pays to make the system work' (Watson 1992). Buzan posits that the English School should "make more substantial inroads into the US IR community" especially in terms of the centrality of norms, rules, and institutions to both approaches (Buzan 2001). It can be inferred that the transatlantic link persists mainly because of the shared metaphysical component: individualistic rationality.

Mainstream or Western IR theory, especially its expression in America largely dominates the disciplinary discourse.[10] Acharya and Buzan initiated a project asking the question "Why is there no non-Western IR theory?" (Acharya and Buzan 2007). More recently, Acharya has put forward the concept of a "Global IR" project, stressing the significance of the evolution of IR toward an inclusive discipline, whilst also "recognizing its multiple and diverse foundations" (Acharya 2014). The quest for a Global IR is not a distinctive theory, concept or method, but it draws from a broad canvas of human and social interactions, with their multiple and diverse origins, histories, norms, societal patterns, and distinctions, in order to challenge IR's existing boundary markers set by dominant mainstream scholarship and encourage new understandings and approaches to the study of global politics. It serves as a framework for advancing IR toward a truly inclusive and universal discipline (Acharya 2016: 4-5). This is sensible at least, as the global order has evidently transformed into a multipolar order, from a unipolar one after the end of the Cold War. Briefly, the six main elements of a Global IR approach are: (1) It is founded upon a pluralistic universalism: not "applying to all," but recognizing and respecting the diversity in us; (2) It is grounded in world history, not just Greco-Roman, European, or US history; (3) It subsumes, rather than supplants, existing IR theories and methods; (4) It integrates the study of regions, regionalisms, and area studies; (5) It eschews exceptionalism; and (6) It recognizes multiple forms of agency beyond material

---

[9] See for instance, Buzan, B. (2004). *From international to world society? English school theory and the social structure of globalisation.* Cambridge: Cambridge University Press.

[10] This holds for the past, as well as present era of IR scholarship. For facts and figures, see Wiebke Wemheuer-Vogelaar et al. (2016). The IR of the Beholder: Examining Global IR Using the 2014 TRIP Survey. *International Studies Review* 18(1): 16–32.

power, including resistance, normative action, and local constructions of global order (Acharya 2014: 647).

Furthermore, a Global IR research agenda calls scholars to discover new patterns, theories, and methods from world histories, which will enable and indeed supplement an analysis of changes in the distribution of power and ideas after 200 plus years of Western dominance. As per Amitav Acharya, the three main issues revolving around the Global IR debate include: (1) the American/Western dominance of the discipline; (2) the issue of geographic and regional specialization; and (3) the claim that it is the Western scholars who do the most of the theoretical work, whereas their non-Western counterparts supply raw data by primarily engaging in regional and area studies. The core of the debate on Global IR is the question of Western and American dominance of the discipline (Acharya 2016: 5). Acharya postulates that if IR is to overcome Western dominance, it must offer concepts and theories that are derived from other societies and cultures. In addition, "Global IR does not mean globalized IR or the formation and dominance of a singular global epistemic community" (Acharya 2016: 12). In other words, Global IR should not aim to displace but subsume, complement, or supplement existing IR theories and approaches (Acharya 2014: 649–50). For instance, certain ideas, concepts and mechanisms used to measure the current success of the Asian economic system, are often grounded on the mechanisms used to measure the Western dominated economic system in terms of trade, finance, infrastructure networks. But this does not mean Asia and America (or Europe) had very similar systems and norms from a historical vantage point. Nor, does it mean that Asia can return to its age old multi-civilisational cultures and systems to maintain and advance its current economic trajectory. Nonetheless, after a period of dominance and success of the Western, or mainly American dominated global economy, the future economy and economic success stories seem increasingly centred to be Asian. As per Parag Khanna, "in the nineteenth century, the world was Europeanized. In the twentieth century, it was Americanized. Now, in the twenty-first century, the world is being irreversibly Asianized" (Khanna 2019). This view clearly portrays an Asian centred global economy and future. Nevertheless, this does not mean that Asia's growth is seperate from the western economic and global order, but rather complementary to it. It can also be postulated that Asia is returning to the stable multipolar order that existed long before European colonialism and American dominance (Khanna 2019, 2016). Other scholars opine that Global IR could advance by positing a broader range of analytical and research questions, paying attention to the context of theories and scholars and expanding its methodological toolkit rather than privileging often parsimonious and self-contained paradigms and research cultures: in other words, methodological cross-fertilization and analytic eclecticism (Sil and Katzenstein 2010).

2.6 A Relational Theory of World Politics

Responding to the call for a Global IR, Yaqing Qin proposes a relational theory of world politics that emphasizes the primacy of social context and action, and with relationality as the metaphysical component of its theoretical hard core (Qin 2016). A solid non-Western, yet generalisable and falsifiable conception, grounded on Chinese interpretation or conception of IR, relational theory entails another stream of theorising. From a relational perspective, the IR world represents itself as a complexly related whole. Culture is a vital component of social theory construction because the metaphysical component of the theoretical hard core is primarily shaped by the background knowledge of a cultural community (Qin 2016). A relational theory conceives the IR world as one composed of ongoing relations, assumes international actors as actors-in-relations, and processes defined in terms of relations in motion as ontologically significant. It puts forward the logic of relationality, arguing that actors base their actions on relations. It uses the Chinese *zhongyong* dialectics as its epistemological nucleus for understanding relationships in an increasingly complex world. This theoretical framework allows for a different and unique perspective, reconceptualisation of key elements such as power, and makes a broader comparison of international systems for the enrichment of the Global IR project. The Global IR project has arguably raised the question about the role of culture in IR theory, because a "pluralistic universality" inevitably involves the multiple cultures that coexist across the globe.

A theory is essentially a system of ideas. By deductive reasoning, theory construction is therefore, a process of organizing ideas and thoughts into a system. Most often, a theory contains parts, of which the most important is the theoretical hard core (Lakatos 1978: 6). The hard core of a social theory, furthermore, consists of two components, one substantive and the other metaphysical. The former plays the role of perception, taking signals from the real world and presenting them to the latter, which plays the role of conception, processing signals through the ideational filter, and representing them as a meaningful construct. It is about understanding and interpretation. These two components of the theoretical hard core are complementary to and conditioned by one another. What defines a distinct social theory, however, is the metaphysical component, which is in turn shaped by the background knowledge of a cultural community. Searle's "Background" is most illustrative in this respect, for he defines it as "the set of nonintentional or preintentional capacities that enables intentional states of function, structuring consciousness, enabling human interpretation, and disposing an actor toward certain behavior" (Searle 1995: 129, 132–37). It is the background knowledge of a cultural community that nurtures and shapes the metaphysical component of a theoretical hard core.

2.6.1 Logic of Relationality

Relationality is a concept abstracted from the interrelated world, which means that a social actor bases its action on relations. In other words, the logic of relationality is that an actor tends to make decisions according to the degrees of intimacy and/or importance of relationships to specific others, with the totality of the relational circles as the background (Qin 2016). Certain scholars have argued that intimate relationship, such as friendship, is a much neglected concept and should be inserted into the reading of IR (Berenskoetter 2007: 647–76). In IR, for the self, there can be friends, rivals, and enemies, indicating the degrees of intimacy of their respective relationships to the self, and each of the categories can be further divided into sub-categories such as allies, close friends, and average friends within the category of friends. An actor tends to take different actions for different relationships. A friend is treated differently from the way a stranger is treated, and similarly, a country provides special policy toward its allies, which it would not offer to other countries (Qin 2016: 37–38). It is the social relationships that define what is rational and appropriate. "The Chinese tend to see the manipulation of human relationships as the natural and normal approach for accomplishing most things in life," for they see "society as a web of human relations and associations" (Pye 1968: 173–174; Gold et al. 2002: 11).

The relational theory of world politics rests upon the culturally oriented view that "the world is a universe of interrelatedness. It holds that actors are actors-in-relations, that relations constitute the most significant component in the social world, and that the logic of relationality provides explanation to much of socially meaningful action" (Qin 2016: 44). It offers alternative understandings of key IR concepts such as power, and international systems.

2.6.2 Relational Power

Power is one of the integral concepts in IR. A relational theory, while recognizing the importance of both hard and soft power, provides another understanding, of "relational power." It means that power comes from relations, or simply, relations are power. Western IR theory usually takes power as being possessed by the actor. For proponents of hard power, it is the material capabilities enabling an actor to take coercive actions. For soft power theorists, it is "the ability to get what you want through attraction rather than coercion or payments. It arises from the attractiveness of a country's culture, political ideals, and policies" (Nye 2004: 10). These two kinds of power are possessed by the actor and utilized to exert influence on others. Relational power is similar to both hard and soft power in that it is the ability to change the attitude, motivation, or behavior of others and thus make them conform to one's will during the process of social interaction (Hwang 1987: 947). However, it differs from those types of power because it is not a possession or acquisition of a particular actor. Rather, it is a process of constantly manipulating and managing one's relational circles to one's advantage. An actor is more powerful because it has larger relational circles, more intimate and important others in these circles, and more social prestige because of these circles. It is not the relational circles themselves but the manipulation of such circles that makes an actor more capable to influence others. It is reflected in Chinese society particularly by the term of *mianzi* (face or reputation), which itself is called "the power game" (Hwang 2004).

2.6.3   Relational International System

The relational approach sees the international system as a relational one, a system of complex relations rather than individual units or actors. An argument can be made that international systems differ not because their constituent units differ, but because they have different types of relationships among actors. Comparative studies of international systems have explored international systems which existed in history and found there have been both hierarchical and anarchical ones. For instance, Ringmar demonstrates that the Westphalian system is an anarchy, the Sino-centric system a hierarchy, and the Tokugawa system is something in between: politically anarchical and socially hierarchical (Ringmar 2012: 7). It can be deduced that the terms of anarchy and hierarchy cannot refer to the nature of the individual actor, but rather they denote relationships among the actors. Simply put, an international system is *defined by relations*.

2.7   Concluding Remarks

This chapter began by introducing positivism, and post-positivism, their similarities and differences, and the advantages and disadvantages in IR theory. It also tries to explain the 'shift' towards the post-positivist camp, from the previously well-established positivist camp. This chapter acknowledges both camps, i.e. positivists and post-positivists for their merits, and outlined their shortfalls. This is grounded on the firm belief that IR can and ought to benefit from both positivism and post-positivism.

The inception of positivism in the nineteenth century was a success, and significantly relevant for the international system of the time for two reasons: (1) it developed a philosophy of social science based on scientific method; and (2) the international system at that time gave precedence to states above any other actors. In other words, when states were the most important, or in fact the only actors comprising the international system, traditional positivist approaches (realism and liberalism) aptly addressed IR. With time, and advancements in IR theory and practice, positivism lost it stronghold, and gave way to post-positivism, which succeeded by criticising the epistemological core of the former. The main reason behind this, as this chapter has explained, is that it lacks sense to not include social and ideological variables in measuring social science. In fact they are considered as crucial to study social phenomena, as per the post-positivists. But what post-positivists are often unwilling or unable to acknowledge is the positivist initiative of developing a theoretical framework based on scientific principles, in the advancement of science and knowledge. For instance, an important question can be raised as to how far post-positivism actually departs from the very positivist perspective it critiques to begin with. According to some scholars, positivist concepts are present in the work of critical theorists (Kurki 2006: 198). Thus, it can be deduced what the post-positivists purport to reject is also evident in their own work.

Therefore, on a semantical level, it is not only that positivists are post-positivists, but also that post-positivists are positivists as well. Therefore, it is not absurd for scholars or students of IR to be positivists and post-positivists at the same time. In fact, it can be postulated that any objective analysis of the international system and IR would demand positivist as well as post-positivist ideologies and reasoning. Although this chapter acknowledges the benefits of post-positivism in critiquing the positivist mainstream in IR, it must be noted that post-positivism has its disadvantages as well. According to Biestecker, "however desirable it may be to open international relations to methodological pluralism and relativism, post-positivist scholarship does not offer us any clear criteria for choosing among the multiple and competing explanations it produces" (Biersteker 1989: 265).

It can also be argued that post-positivism may lead to intellectual incoherence in IR. In other words, it is not just a case of numerous unlinked and confusing explanations, but within the broad post-positivist camp there is no consensus. For instance, whilst critical theory and post-modernism are both characterised as post-positivist in nature, postmodernism "eschews the very goal of critical theory" and postulates critical theory itself is hegemonic, where "all conversation is power, and it is not possible to move beyond a place tainted by power" (Jackson and Sørenson 2003: 165). We therefore have an example of post-positivism criticising post-positivism, which makes it difficult to discuss the relative merits of post-modernism and critical theory.

Therefore, in accordance to George, we should be careful to avoid "intellectual anarchy" (George 1989: 270). Although this chapter gives precedence to the relative advantages of post-positivism to positivism, especially in the current global context, this is not to say that positivism is no longer important. Post-positivist scholars argue that if IR is the study of interstate, or foreign affairs and relations, it ought to also include non-state actors in addition to state actors. This is especially relevant in the globalised and deeply inter-connected international system of today. We should thus view positivism and post-positivism as complementary in strengthening the discipline of IR as a whole. This chapter seeks to give due credit to both academic developments and to describe the circumstances which lead to the advantages and disadvantages of both.

Further Readings

Jackson, R., & Sørensen, G. (2010). *Introduction to international relations: Theories and approaches*. Oxford: Oxford University Press.
Reus-Smit, C., & Snidal, D. (Eds.). (2008). *The Oxford handbook of international relations*. Oxford: Oxford University Press.
Smith, S., Booth, K., & Zalewski, M. (Eds.). (1996). *International theory: Positivism and beyond*. Cambridge: Cambridge University Press.

References

Acharya, A. (2014). Global international relations (IR) and regional worlds: A new agenda for international studies. *International Studies Quarterly, 58*(4), 647–659.
Acharya, A. (2016). Advancing global IR: Challenges, contentions, and contributions. *International Studies Review, 18*, 4–15.
Acharya, A., & Buzan, B. (2007). Why is there no Non-Western IR theory: An introduction. *International Relations of the Asia Pacific, 7*(3), 287–312.
Adem, S. (2007). *Democratic peace theory and Africa's international relations*. Paper Presented at the ISA Convention, Chicago, IL, February 28–March 3.
Allen, C. (2012). *Ashoka: The search for India's lost emperor*. London: Hachette.
Ashley, R. K. (1986). The poverty of neorealism. In R. O. Keohane (Ed.), *Neo-realism and its critics* (pp. 255–301). New York: Columbia University Press.
Barkawi, T., & Laffey, M. (2001). Introduction: The international relations of democracy, liberalism, and war. In T. Barkawi & M. Laffey (Eds.), *Democracy, liberalism, and war: Rethinking the democratic peace debate*. Boulder: Lynne Rienner.
Barnett, M., & Duvall, R. (2005). Power in international politics. *International Organization, 59*(01), 39–75.
Berenskoetter, F. (2007). Friends, there are no friends? An intimate reframing of the international. *Millennium: Journal of International Studies, 35*(3), 647–676.
Biersteker, T. J. (1989). Critical reflections on post-positivism in international relations. *International Studies Quarterly, 33*(3), 236–267.
Boesche, R. (2002). *The first great political realist: Kautilya and his Arthashastra*. Lanham: Lexington Books.
Bourdeau, M. (2015). Auguste Comte. *The Stanford Encyclopaedia of Philosophy* (Winter 2015 Edition) (E. N. Zalta (Ed.)). Access at: https://plato.stanford.edu/entries/comte/
Brown, C. (2009). *Understanding international relations* (pp. 48–52). Basingstoke: Palgrave.
Buzan, B. (2001). The English school: An underexploited resource in IR. *Review of International Studies, 27*(3), 471–488.
Buzan, B., & Little, R. (2001). Why international relations has failed as an intellectual project and what to do about it. *Millennium-Journal of International Studies, 30*(1), 19–39.
Cox, R. (1981). Social forces, states and world orders: Beyond international relations theory. *Millennium: Journal of International Studies, 10*, 126–155.
George, J. (1989). International relations and the search for thinking space: Another view of the third debate. *International Studies Quarterly, 33*(3), 269–279.
Gold, T., Guthrie, D., & Wank, D. (2002). An introduction to the study of Guanxi. In T. Gold, D. Guthrie, & D. Wank (Eds.), *Social connections in China: Institutions, culture, and the changing nature of Guanxi* (pp. 3–20). Cambridge: Cambridge University Press.
Haas, M. (1995). *When democracies fight one another, just what is the punishment for disobeying the law?* Paper presented at the 91st annual meeting of the American Political Science Association, Chicago, IL, September 1.

Hoffmann, S. (1977). An American social science: International relations. *Daedalus, 106*(3), 41–60.

Hwang, K.-G. (1987). Face and favor: The Chinese power game. *American Journal of Sociology, 92*(4), 944–974.

Hwang, K.-G (Eds.). (2004). *Mianzi: Zhongguoren de Quanli Youxi* (Face: Power game of Chinese people). Beijing: Remin University Press.

Jackson, R., & Sørenson, G. (2003). Methodological debates: Classical versus positivism approaches. In R. Jackson & G. Sørensen (Eds.), *Introduction to international relations: Theories and approaches*. Oxford University Press.

Jackson, R., & Sørensen, G. (2010). *Introduction to international relations: Theories and approaches*. Oxford: Oxford University Press.

Khanna, P. (2016). *Connectography: Mapping the future of global civilization* (First ed.). New York: Random House.

Khanna, P. (2019). *The future is Asian: Commerce, conflict, and culture in the 21st century*. New York: Simon & Schuster.

Kołakowski, L. (1978). *Main currents of Marxism* (1st ed.). Oxford: Oxford University Press.

Kurki, M. (2006). Causes of a divided discipline: Rethinking the concept of cause in international relations theory. *Review of International Studies, 32*(2), 189–216.

Lakatos, I. (1978). *The methodology of scientific research programmes: Philosophical papers* (Vol. 1 vol). London: Cambridge University Press.

Lapid, Y. (1989). The third debate: On the prospects of international theory in a post-positivist era. *International Studies Quarterly, 33*(3), 235–254.

Lyotard, J. F. (1992). *The postmodern explained: Correspondence, 1982–1985*. Minneapolis: University of Minnesota Press.

Mann, M. (2001). Democracy and ethnic war. In T. Barkawi & M. Laffey (Eds.), *Democracy, liberalism, and war: Rethinking the democratic peace debate*. Boulder: Lynne Rienner.

Monteiro, N. P., & Ruby, K. G. (2009). IR and the false promise of philosophical foundations. *International Theory, 1*(1), 15–48.

Nicholson, M. (1996). The continued significance of positivism? In S. Smith, K. Booth, & M. Zalewski (Eds.), *International theory: Positivism and beyond*. Cambridge: Cambridge University Press.

Nye, J. S. J. (2004). *Soft power: The means to success in world politics*. New York: Public Affairs.

Olivelle, P. (2013). *King, governance, and law in ancient India: Kauṭilya's Arthaśāstra*. Oxford: Oxford University Press.

Pye, L. (1968). *The spirit of Chinese politics: A psychological study of the authority crisis in political development*. Cambridge, MA: The MIT Press.

Qin, Y. (2016). A relational theory of world politics. *International Studies Review, 18*(1), 33–47.

Ravlo, H., Gleditsch, N. P., & Dorussen, H. (2003). Colonial war and the democratic peace. *Journal of Conflict Resolution, 47*(4), 520–548.

Ringmar, E. (2012). Performing international systems: Two East-Asian alternatives to the Westphalian order. *International Organization, 66*(1), 1–25.

Roach, S. C., Griffiths, M., & O'Callaghan, T. (2014). *International relations: The key concepts*. London/New York: Routledge/Taylor and Francis Group.

Searle, J. R. (1995). *The construction of social reality*. New York: The Free Press.

Shea, C. (1997). Political scientists clash over value of area studies. *Chronicle of Higher Education*, January 10. Available at http://chronicle.com/article/Political-ScientistsClash/75248/

Sil, R., & Katzenstein, P. (2010). *Beyond paradigms: Analytic eclecticism in the study of world politics*. New York: Palgrave Macmillan.

Smith, S. (1996). Positivism and beyond. In S. Smith, K. Booth, & M. Zalewski (Eds.), *International theory: Positivism and beyond*. Cambridge: Cambridge University Press.

Smith, S. (1997). New approaches to international theory. In J. Baylis & S. Smith (Eds.), *The globalisation of world politics* (pp. 165–190). Oxford: Oxford University Press.

Smith, S. (2002). The United States and the discipline of international relations: Hegemonic country, hegemonic discipline? *International Studies Review, 4*(2), 67–86.

Smith, S., Booth, K., & Zalewski, M. (1996). *Positivism and beyond* (1st ed.). Cambridge: Cambridge University Press.

Trautmann, T. R. (1971). *Kauṭilya and the Arthaśāstra: A statistical investigation of the authorship and evolution of the text.* Leiden: E.J. Brill.

Vasquez, J. (1995). The post-positivist debate. In K. Booth & S. Smith (Eds.), *International relations theory today* (pp. 217–240). Cambridge: Polity.

Waltz, K. N. (1993). The emerging structure of international politics. *International Security, 18*(2), 44–79.

Waltz, K. N. (2007). The anarchic structure of world politics. In R. Art & R. Jervis (Eds.), *International politics: Enduring concepts and contemporary issues.* Boston: Pearson Higher Ed.

Watson, A. (1992). *The evolution of international society* (p. 14). London: Routledge.

Wemheuer-Vogelaar, W., et al. (2016). The IR of the beholder: Examining global IR using the 2014 TRIP survey. *International Studies Review, 18*(1), 16–32.

Wendt, A. (1992). Anarchy is what states make of it. *International Organization, 46*(2), 391–425.

Part II
The Changing World Order: The Rise of New Powers

Chapter 3
Power Politics

Rob De Wijk

3.1 Power Politics

Power is central to the politics among nations.[1] As explained in Chap. 1 a core assumption of realism is that all states seek to survive and aim to increase their power. In this chapter power is defined as the ability to get others to do what one wants. This can be done in a positive way through encouragement (incentives), or in a negative way through force (coercion). An example of the former is the way the Greek sovereign debt crisis was dealt with. After the sovereign debt crisis the European Union pressed Greece for the structural reform of its economy. In return, Greece would gain access to the rescue funds. Recent examples of the latter are the sanctions imposed on Iran to give up its nuclear program and the sanctions imposed on Russia after the annexation of the Crimea in 2014 and Russia's support for the rebels in eastern Ukraine. In return, Russia imposed counter sanctions on the United States and the European Union.

If diplomacy is reinforced with economic sanctions and the threat or limited use of military power, then we call this 'coercive diplomacy' (De Wijk 2014). Strategy is the critical success factor for exercising power successfully. Strategy determines how political aims should be met using instruments of power. For the political aim, what is essential is not to convince one's opponent that they are wrong – after all, this would not work – but to manipulate and influence his politico-strategic choices.

States have only a few instruments for exercising power. Economic resources and the use of military might be the only instruments to exercise real power in

---

[1] This chapter is based on De Wijk, Rob (2015), Power Politics: How China and Russia Reshape the World, Amsterdam: Amsterdam University Press.

R. De Wijk (✉)
Leiden University, Leiden, The Netherlands
e-mail: robdewijk@hcss.nl

© Springer Nature Switzerland AG 2020
M. O. Hosli, J. Selleslaghs (eds.), *The Changing Global Order*, United Nations University Series on Regionalism 17,
https://doi.org/10.1007/978-3-030-21603-0_3

foreign policy. How those two instruments are used determines the effectiveness of a country's diplomacy.

Traditionally, a country's power is determined by a combination of factors: its population size, territory, economy and military apparatus. In the eighteenth and nineteenth centuries, the size of a country's land forces was the most important expression of its power. During the inter-war period, naval capabilities were the most important expression of power. During the Cold War, power was expressed by having massive armed forces and nuclear weapons, which had to deter the opponent from using its armed force.

A study by the American RAND Corporation has established that the power of modern states is dependent upon three variables: wealth, innovation and conventional military capabilities (Tellis et al. 2000). Wealth, as expressed by GDP, provides independence, can be used to put pressure on opponents and offers a good starting point for negotiations. Innovation is needed for prosperity and to achieve greater military capabilities than potential opponents. The RAND study did not identify nuclear weapons as an instrument of power. This is because nuclear weapons cannot or can hardly be used on the battlefield, as their use can lead to mutual destruction. These weapons are mainly suitable for deterrence and as an ultimate security guarantee.

Wealth, innovation and military might play a deciding role in how effectively the two instruments of foreign policy can be used. The two are interlinked and are decisive for the extent to which a country is able to get its way in international relations. The size of a country's GDP is determined by its population size, degree of urbanization, state of technological development and access to raw materials and energy. The size of a country's GDP does not tell us everything, however. At the beginning of the nineteenth century China had the largest economy in the world, but it was much too focused on domestic affairs to be a global player. In the same century, Great Britain was the global power, but it certainly did not have the largest economy. Britain gained its position due to the high income per capita of the population and its innovative ability, which found expression in the Industrial Revolution. Size does matter, then, but it does not tell us everything. Germany is a powerful country in terms of wealth, but is shows little readiness to use its power. After the end of the Second World War, Germany became a post-modern state that is reluctant to use its military power. Instead, Germany puts much emphasis on multilateralism, international law and the use of its armed forces for humanitarian purposes. However, Germany took the lead in the EU-efforts to force the structural economic reform on Greece mentioned above. Russia, by contrast, is a weak economy, and has relatively weak armed forces, but is willing to use its armed force. Russia is a classic modern state with a traditional view on security. For Russia, security equals territorial integrity and non-interference.

Tiny states such as Luxembourg have a high income per capita, but they cannot mobilize any sizeable military force. Therefore, they cannot exercise any meaningful power. Only when tiny states gain crucial positions in multilateral organisations can they punch above their weight. The appointment of the former prime minister of Luxemburg Jean-Claude Juncker as chairman of the European Commission is a case in point. The same is true of the most highly developed medium-sized industrialized democracies, such as the Netherlands, the Scandinavian countries and Canada. These countries have to focus on their persuasive power and the status quo in international relations. Power can only be exercised by these countries in coalitions and through effective multilateralism.

Regardless of their actual power, countries attempt to achieve their aims through a combination of cooperation and confrontation. Countries therefore play the cultural, normative and ideological card, as well as the military one. Soft power is important for this, and can be seen as a third instrument of power. As was explained in Chap. 1, the concept was popularized by Joseph Nye (1990). He argued that international relations is not only about forcing a change of course by exercising hard power, but also through enticement, or soft power. We should note that Nye (2011) concluded that it was not possible to have an effective foreign policy based on soft power alone. He therefore introduced the term 'smart power', a combination of hard and soft power.

Dhruva Jaishankar (2014) has added a fourth instrument, namely a country's resilience. He points out that the Soviet Union collapsed despite its overwhelming military potential. Resilience is about a state's ability to keep going, even if it is facing economic, political and social difficulties. He argues that the United States, for example, may be a young country, but it is one of the countries with the longest experience of democracy and internal stability, in contrast to China, for example, where the social contract between population and leaders hangs in a fragile balance.

Whether a country actually pursues power politics is dependent upon its power relative to other countries. By definition, superpowers and great powers have global interests that they have to defend in the interests of their own prosperity and security. These interests can be material or immaterial in nature. Material interests, for example, include access to raw materials and energy supplies. Immaterial interests are usually of an ideological nature, such as democracy and human rights.

Therefore, great powers such as the United States take a more instrumental view of international law and international institutions. If they serve their interests, then they are used; if not, then international law and intergovernmental institutions are passed over. The ambivalent attitude of the United States with respect to the UN is one example of this, as were the American-led interventions without explicit mandates in Kosovo (1999) and Iraq (2003). As will be seen, the same applies to assertive powers such as China and Russia.

Highly developed medium-sized democracies, such as Canada, Australia, the Netherlands and the Scandinavian countries, have been the most effective in determining their position in – and even developing alternatives to – the geopolitical power game of the great powers. These countries have an interest in maintaining a stable and peaceful world for their own economic development. For this reason, they advocate a well-functioning international legal order and want to use their military might largely for humanitarian reasons. This means that they believe there should be compliance with international law and that the intergovernmental institutions that reflect this legal order, such as the UN and the Organization for Security and Co-operation in Europe (OSCE), should be made more effective. Other highly developed medium-sized democracies, such as Finland, Sweden and Switzerland, attempt to preserve their neutrality in the geopolitical power game.

Another group of countries has organized itself as the Non-Aligned Movement. From 1961 onwards, on the initiative of countries such as Egypt, Yugoslavia, Indonesia and India, this group attempted to find a third way alongside capitalism and communism. The movement still exists, although the goal has since shifted to finding common standpoints, for example in the UN and other intergovernmental organizations.

Other smaller countries are by definition the object of a power struggle between the great powers and the superpowers. During the Cold War the leaders of both systems, the United States and the Soviet Union, attempted to bring other countries into their spheres of influence or to limit their opponent's sphere of influence. This led to conflicts about the demarcation of the spheres of influence, such as the Cuban missile crisis (1962) and the war in Vietnam (from the 1960s to 1973).

That is not to say that smaller countries do not pursue power politics. By cleverly picking a side, they can exercise more influence than one might expect, given their position. The best example is the Netherlands, which after the Golden Age was too small to wield decisive influence in world politics. By concluding alliances, first with the United Kingdom and later with the United States, the Netherlands managed to augment its influence. Both the Pax Britannica and the Pax Americana were masterly examples of balance-of-power politics, whereby the Netherlands was protected by great powers and was also able to use these great powers to realize part of its foreign policy agenda. This mainly concerned the promotion of immaterial issues, such as the strengthening of the international legal order and the reinforcement of intergovernmental institutions. Moreover, the Netherlands made itself into a bridge between the United States and Europe, allowing it to act as an intermediary in the realization of American policy with its European allies. Both the Pax Britannica and the Pax Americana were types of power politics, because they helped the Netherlands to form a counterweight to the large, dominant continental European powers of Germany and France. As a result, a small country such as the Netherlands could maximize the amount of latitude it had in Europe for its foreign policy. However, global power shifts, increased American isolationism and the Brexit forced The Netherlands to rethink the fundamentals of its foreign policy.

The major difference between small and great-power politics is the lack of opportunities to change things to one's advantage without taking account of other countries, institutions or international law. Allies profit from this 'shaping power'. Smaller countries have two options in the geopolitical game: to take sides or remain neutral. NATO was composed of allies that defended themselves collectively against the Soviet Union and the Warsaw Pact. It even included a country without an army: Iceland. Owing to its location between Europe and America, Iceland was of major logistical significance to NATO during a conflict with the Warsaw Pact.

3.2   The Western World Order

Only superpowers and great powers have the economic and military resources to exercise real power in the world. These countries play a decisive role in the system of international relations; in short, the world order. The current 'Western world order' was institutionalized after the Second World War and reflects the power of liberal democracies and American leadership. One important milestone was the financial-economic Bretton Woods Agreement, initiated by the United States and agreed by 44 countries in 1944. This provided for a system of fixed exchange rates whereby only the dollar could be exchanged for a fixed amount of gold at the American Federal Reserve. Whilst other currencies were indeed fixed against the dollar, they could not be exchanged for gold. The Bretton Woods system also provided for the establishment of the International Monetary Fund (IMF) and the World Bank. With this agreement, the global primacy of the American – and with it, the Western – economy became a fact. Furthermore, the victors of the Second World War also founded the United Nations (UN) and were given permanent seats on the UN Security Council. A system of global governance was thereby created that covered almost every aspect of global society, but that largely expressed Western preferences. The International Court of Justice (ICJ) in The Hague is also a Western invention. In 1942 the US Secretary of State and the Foreign Secretary of the United Kingdom kicked off the process that led to the establishment of a permanent court after the war. The way in which international law is applied by the International Criminal Tribunal for the former Yugoslavia, the Special Tribunal for Lebanon and the International Criminal Court (ICC), for example, all of which are based in The Hague, likewise reflects Western conceptions of good and evil. The same is even true of 'universal' fundamental principles, such as the Universal Declaration of Human Rights (1948). The same is even true of 'universal' fundamental principles, such as the Universal Declaration of Human Rights (1948). In contrast to Asia, Africa and South America the West has always used normative justifications to carry out interventions in distant parts of the world.

The world order, which has been shaped to a major extent by Western countries, is becoming less 'Western', however, due to the rise of countries such as China. One way to assess the changing world order is to measure the assertiveness of rising powers and of those powers taking advantage of the relative decline of the West. Studies show that the assertiveness of China and Russia are increasing (HCSS 2014a). 'Assertiveness' is a neutral concept that refers both to word and deed, rhetoric and actual dealings, diplomatic and economic or military pressure. Assertiveness is positive if a country devotes its efforts to bringing about peace or negotiating a climate accord. Assertiveness is negative when self-interest prevails and a country uses its power to impose its own will. The average level of assertiveness of both China and the Soviet Union (later Russia) has increased gradually over the last decades. In this period, China's assertiveness, both in reality and rhetorically, has become stronger than Russia's, although as far as the number of actions is concerned, it has not yet reached Russian levels.[2] A second conclusion is that actual assertiveness has increased more than rhetorical assertiveness in both countries; in effect, there have been more deeds than words. In the case of both countries, there have been more positive or neutral expressions of assertiveness than negative ones.

In relation to diplomatic assertiveness, at the UN Security Council, the two countries are proving unwilling to join the West in interventions in other countries, even if these are for purely humanitarian reasons. They have not agreed to put pressure on Iran and North Korea, which the West suspects of having nuclear weapons programmes. Economic assertiveness, in turn, can take the form of protectionism or foreign investments. Sovereign Wealth Funds and state enterprises thus play an important role in this area, but cyber-attacks can also be included in this category. Military activities include the Ukraine crisis and the seizure of the Crimea, for instance, and China's ongoing problems with the countries around the South China Sea. In the area of military assertiveness, there has been a considerable increase in Chinese power. Although the level of Russian military assertiveness remains much higher than that of China, the general trend here is less unequivocal.

A clear turnaround took place around 2008. Russia has been attempting to achieve more and more influence in the area that used to belong to the Soviet Union by putting pressure on countries such as Ukraine that are unable to pay their energy bills, and by occupying territory, as happened in South Ossetia in August 2008. In the view of the West, this marked a turning point in relations with Russia. As of 2008, China is increasingly active in the South China Sea and is safeguarding its raw materials and energy interests all over the world – including in countries that are seen by the West as rogue states. Moreover, both Russia and China sell arms to such regimes. The first signs that China was starting to behave more assertively date from 1995. In that year, China occupied the oil-rich Mischief Reef, territory that was claimed by the Philippines. Moreover, that year saw the holding of the first large-scale military manoeuvres and missile tests near Taiwan, in response to President Clinton's granting of a visa to the Taiwanese President Lee Teng-hui to visit Cornell University. China's change in policy caused problems with ASEAN countries, whilst the United States stationed two aircraft carriers near Taiwan.

Remarkably enough, little research has been done on China's preparedness to cooperate with other countries. One of the few studies is 'Regime Insecurity and International Cooperation' by M. Taylor Fravel (2005), published in International Security. Fravel states that since 1996, China has settled 17 of 23 territorial conflicts peacefully, that China has not avoided making compromises, and that it has actually obtained no more than half of the territory it had claimed. A number of the claims are non-negotiable, such as those concerning Taiwan and Tibet, and in the past, Hong Kong and Macao. Reneging on these would backfire on the regime in Beijing. In relation to the other claims, China has proved willing to compromise.

Assertiveness should always be put in context. Assertiveness and nationalism – a combination that can be seen in both Russia and China – can be dangerous. In Asia

---

[2]The dataset covers the period up to mid-2013. It does not cover recent examples of Russian assertiveness in Ukraine.

in particular, there seems to be a lack of awareness of the risks. François Godement (2013) of the European Council of Foreign Relations has called this 'nationalism without guilt'. Only Japan seems to have a historical awareness of the risks due to its wartime past, which has contributed to its pacifism today. Other Asian countries frame their rhetoric in terms of 'humiliation'. China, for example, even refers to the 'Century of Humiliation', the consequence of Western and Japanese interference. This century began with the First Opium War or the Anglo-Chinese War of 1839–1842 and ended with the founding of the People's Republic in 1949. After this, China regained true independence and became less and less susceptible to Western ideas. In addition, many Asian countries only partly share the Western vision of institutions. What is more, Western powers have refused to admit China and Russia to Western institutions or only allowed them to join at a later stage. It took Russia great effort to gain admittance in 1997 to the G7, the group of the richest industrial countries. According to the American researcher Strobe Talbot (2002), the objective was to sweeten the bitter pill of NATO expansion for Russia.

Asian countries rarely or never solve their conflicts by means of international arbitration. Problems are dealt with bilaterally, and recourse to the ICJ in The Hague, for example, is seen as an escalation of a conflict. The ICJ has only been brought in on a few occasions, such as during a dispute between Japan and South Korea over Dokdo/Takeshima. China will never permit the internationalization of the conflict with Taiwan, however, and sees Japan's recourse to the ICJ over the issue of the Senkaku/Diaoyutai islands as an act of aggression.

3.3 The End of the 'Unipolar Moment'

The increased assertiveness of China and Russia confirmed prediction by scholars that after the end of the Cold War unipolarity would be replaced by multipolarity. In 1990 Charles Krauthammer published a notorious article in Foreign Affairs entitled 'The Unipolar Moment'. He argued that now that the relatively stable bipolar world order had been consigned to history, the United States found itself in a historically unprecedented position of power and that the world had become unipolar. In this world, the United States could act unilaterally as a superpower if necessary. His claims were supported by heavyweights such as Layne (1993), Mearsheimer (2001), Schweller and Pu (2011), Kenneth Waltz (2000) and Fareed Zakaria (2008).

The unipolar moment lasted until after 11 September 2001 at any rate, and reached its apex under President George W. Bush. In line with unipolar thinking, the president took far-reaching measures that undermined multilateralism and institutionalism: the Anti-Ballistic Missile (ABM) treaty, which put limits on the American and Russian missile defence systems, had to be amended; the Kyoto climate agreements were rejected; the ban on landmines was likewise rejected; and the United States did not ratify the statutes of the ICC and the Biological Weapons Convention. However, in Krauthammer's view, the way in which the United States responded to the terrorist attacks led to the 'first crisis of unilateralism'. Neorealists such as

Kenneth Waltz also predicted that emerging powers would attempt to challenge American dominion in order to create a new balance of power.

The academic discussion continued, however. Professor of international relations William C. Wohlforth (1999) suggested that unipolarity was actually sustainable. America's power was so great that the system would remain unipolar for the foreseeable future. A unipolar system, he reasoned, is the most stable system, and provides an opportunity to shape the world in accordance with (in this case) American ideas. No single potential rival would risk entering into a conflict with the hegemon. The exception was Al-Qaeda, with the attacks on the World Trade Center in New York and the Pentagon in Washington in 2001.

Wohlforth also argued that such a superpower is able to prevent conflicts between other states. For these reasons, according to Wohlforth, it is important that the United States manages to maintain its position of power in the world. The American political scientist Nuno P. Monteiro (2011/2) has countered this last claim. According to him, the United States has been involved in a relatively large number of conflicts as a hegemonic power: Kuwait (1991), Kosovo (1999), Afghanistan (from 2001), Iraq (from 2003) and, albeit indirectly, Libya (2011). He also observes that in multipolar world orders, great powers have historically spent 18 per cent of their time as great powers waging war. In the bipolar world order, the two superpowers spent 16 per cent of their time as superpowers waging war, whilst in the era of unipolarity after the Cold War, the United States was involved in wars for 56% of the time. How could this be the case? The answer is simple: the extent to which a superpower becomes involved in war is up to the superpower itself. Monteiro argues that an important explanation for America's 'thirst for war' is that this superpower capitalized upon unipolarity in order to shape the world order in accordance with its own preferences. This is known as an offensive strategy of domination. This strategy is theoretically underpinned by the approach of offensive realism mentioned in Chap. 1. The manner in which President George W. Bush designed his foreign and defence security after 9/11 is consistent with this. An alternative would be a strategy of defensive domination, which would focus on maintenance of the status quo in terms of the global division of power, territorial integrity and alliances. This strategy is explained by the approach of defensive realism, as elaborated in Chap. 1. In principle a superpower does not want to wage war, but it can be provoked into doing so if another country undermines the status quo. It is precisely this emphasis on maintenance of the status quo that can inspire a despot elsewhere in the world to test the borders of what is acceptable. On 2 August 1990, the Iraqi leader Saddam Hussein invaded Kuwait in the belief that the United States would accept this infringement of the status quo. This proved a fatal misconception, because the American President George H.W. Bush, supported by a large part of the international community, responded with 'Operation Desert Storm' – the military intervention intended to drive the troops of the Iraqi leader Saddam Hussein out of Iraqi-occupied Kuwait and liberated the country within 6 weeks.

This example demonstrates that power and values were determining factors in the global order and thus for global peace. At least, this was the idea. Precisely for this reason, President Bush stated on the eve of Operation Desert Storm that a 'new world order' was within reach. According to the president, this would be a world guided by fundamental principles such as law and justice, and the protection of the weak against the strong. He saw a world in which the UN would be freed from the crippling deadlock that had developed during the Cold War and would finally be able to do what its founders had intended, namely, to create a world of freedom and respect for human rights (Bush 1991).

Both American presidents George Bush and his successor William Clinton assumed that a hegemonic power could bring stability to the world. This is consistent with regime theory. The American professor of international relations Stephen Krasner (1983) defines a regime as a 'set of rules, norms of behaviour around which the expectations of actors converge in a certain issue area'. A superpower can impose regimes on other countries that influence their behaviour and thus promote world peace.

In a multipolar system, a number of great powers have almost equal influence in terms of military, economic and cultural power A variation on this theme is the concept of nonpolarity, introduced by the American diplomat Richard Haass (2008). This exists when there are multiple centres of power, but none of them can dominate the others.

The increasing level of assertiveness of China and Russia seems to confirm the realist claim that a multipolar system is less stable than a unipolar or bipolar one. In a multipolar system, individual countries have greater freedom to act and to choose their allies. As a result there is an increased risk of misperceptions, because the intentions of a number of players have to be assessed. Smaller states can also potentially play a greater role in a multipolar system, certainly when this concerns states that possess 'strategic goods' such as raw materials, or that are strategically located on trade routes or between spheres of influence. If such states change alliances or shift loyalties, this produces friction and a significant likelihood of conflict. Ukraine and Egypt are examples of 'pivot states' such as these (HCSS 2014b). It is certain that during the transition from a unipolar to a multipolar system, when the new constellation of power has yet to crystallize, the chance of accidents is at its greatest.

3.4   The Changing Balance of Power

It has been clear for years that the world is changing. The same is true of the countries that are rising. In 2001 the American investment bank Goldman Sachs adopted the term 'BRIC', which was coined by the economist Jim O'Neill to refer to Brazil, Russia, India and China. From 2010, South Africa was also included in this group, and the BRIC countries became the BRICS. In 2003 the bank predicted that Brazil, Russia, India and China would be among the world's top five global economies in 2050 (Wilson and Purushothaman 2003). Due to their huge economic weight and their different political systems, these countries could change international relations fundamentally and present a great challenge to the Western world.

According to the IMF, Asia accounted for 18% of the global gross domestic product (GDP) in 2010, as compared to 8% in 2002. During the same period, the eurozone saw its share of global GDP shrink from 21 to 17%. In Global Trends 2030 of the National Intelligence Council (2012) the rise of Asia is seen as a defining development. It is argued that by 2030 the balance of power will have tipped in Asia's favour in all respects. Asia will have overtaken Europe and the United States not only in terms of GDP, but also in terms of military expenditure and technology and innovation. In 2012 the size of the American and European economies amounted to 56% of the global total; in 2030, this will have fallen to less than 50%. The World Bank observed in 2013 that due to geopolitical changes, for the first time in history there was a greater volume of South-South trade than trade between the countries belonging to the Organization for Economic Co-operation and Development (OECD). Developing countries now account for around a third of world trade. Also notable is the unmistakable trend whereby trade is shifting in the direction of the BRICS countries. Another example of the intensification of South-South relations is that of changing energy relations. Two-thirds of all oil exports from the Gulf region now go to East Asia. China, Japan, South Korea and Taiwan already receive 70% of their oil from the Gulf region (Manning 2012).

The real leader of global change, however, is China. If a country with 1.3 billion inhabitants develops, this is by definition a game-changer, as Elizabeth Economy (2010) wrote in Foreign Affairs. Its importance was also revealed by the American President's four-yearly survey of future trends, carried out by the combined intelligence services, the National Intelligence Council (NIC).

Goldman Sachs also coined the term 'Next Eleven,' or N-11. It appeared that Bangladesh, Egypt, the Philippines, Indonesia, Iran, Mexico, Nigeria, Pakistan, Turkey, Vietnam and South Korea could also develop into regional great powers. The list includes countries such as Bangladesh that have been affected by disasters and poverty in the past, but that nevertheless show enormous potential for development. This is not to say, though, that all of these countries will by definition grow rapidly and start to practise power politics.

After the financial crisis of 2008, developing countries proved not to have been hit hard by the crisis. It is notable that in Africa in particular, growth rates rose well above the world average. From 2000, Africa experienced rapid growth. The continent recovered quickly from the economic crisis and was back to enjoying a growth rate of over 5% in 2010 (United Nations 2013). This growth was mainly boosted by the extraction of raw materials, but agriculture also did well. Moreover, Africa has the fastest-growing labour market in the world. These positive developments are the result of economic cooperation with BRICS countries and a number of developing countries.

3.5 Consequences of the Power Shifts

The world order will change if the West becomes less powerful relative to other countries. And if hegemonic power is so important for global stability, then a decline in American power must lead to less stability. There is much evidence to support these hypotheses.

If power has to be shared with other upcoming countries, then American 'shaping power' – its power to induce other countries and international organizations to engage in 'desirable' behaviour – will diminish. If this power is eroded, then other countries will also gain influence over the rules of the game, and the old centre of power will start to compete with emerging powers on world-views and norms.

After centuries of world domination, Western powers find it difficult to accept that other powers try to shape the world as well. When Russia made moves to annex the Crimea at the beginning of 2014 Western leaders reacted with disbelief. 'This Putin is living in a different world', remarked the German Chancellor Angela Merkel. John Kerry, the American Secretary of State, also condemned Russia: in the twenty-first century, 'You just don't … behave in 19th-century fashion by invading another country on a completely trumped up pretext.' (Reuters 2014). What Putin did, however, was more than many imagined: it was the 'normal' power politics of great powers, or countries that see themselves as such. At the same time, a similar power struggle was taking place on the other side of the world. At the beginning of 2014, China, which lays claim to large parts of the South China Sea, was engaged in a sharp confrontation with the Philippines and Vietnam over the control of small islands.

But history teaches us that transitions of power are always accompanied by friction, and even by conflicts. In the longer term, the system of international relations itself can change radically. This process is being further strengthened by political and societal polarization in the United States and Europe, meaning that democracy has become less effective at solving far-reaching crises. This proved to be the case, for example, during the financial crisis that erupted in 2008.

All of this allows upcoming countries to question the dominance of the West and to strive for a multipolar system. The shift of economic, military and associated political power to the East has implications for the way in which the West is able to determine the rules of international relations, protect its interests and promote its values. Upcoming countries want to see international institutions adapted in ways that reflect their new positions and values. The first 'victim' of this development has been Western 'soft power', or the ability to co-opt and attract. This is based on values, but is being backed up less and less by military 'hard power', political unity and superior economic power.

Due to power shifts it will become more difficult to impose traditional Western preferences, such as a foreign policy that gives a prominent place to the promotion of humanity and democracy, because upcoming countries do not tolerate any interference by other countries in their domestic affairs.

Geopolitical conflicts are fought out between superpowers and great powers, and can be about the ordering and organization of international relations, access to supplies of energy and raw materials, control over space and the Arctic region, or spheres of influence. These kinds of developments are dangerous if they take place on geopolitical fault lines, where frictions in international relations have been manifest for centuries. A variant of this idea was popularized by Samuel Huntington. In The Clash of Civilizations and the Remaking of World Order (1996), Huntington argued that crises and conflicts occur when civilizations clash. In Europe, Western civilization is clashing with orthodoxy and the Islamic world. In the East, the East Asian, Japanese and Western civilizations are clashing. Huntington's thesis contains important observations, but it leaves many questions unanswered. In Asia, for example, Huntington would count the many countries that are clashing around the South China Sea as belonging to the same civilization; after all, East Asian civilization includes not only China, but also Korea, Singapore, Taiwan and Vietnam. If we consider the ongoing conflicts in the Middle East, it is clear that clashes are also occurring within Islamic civilization. These are local or regional crises, however, that do not have an effect on the system of international relations.

If we start from geopolitical fault lines, then we can make predictions about where future power struggles will take place. In Europe, there is a struggle for power between the European Union and NATO and Russia. The Ukraine crisis, which started with the annexation of the Crimea, clearly demonstrates this point. In Asia, there is a struggle for power between China and the countries around the South China Sea, and between China and the United States. We would not expect important upcoming countries, such as Brazil and South Africa, to develop into power-political players that become involved in these kinds of conflicts, as these countries are located in parts of the world where there are no geopolitical fault lines. Thus we should not expect all BRICS or N-11 countries to start behaving in the same way in this fragmented world, or to see discord develop everywhere. There are also areas, however, where the spheres of influence have not yet crystallized fully: in space and in the Polar Regions.

In sum, global power transitions are accompanied by friction and even by conflicts. Countries that see their position worsening will want to counter this, whereas countries that are rising will not allow their ascent to be thwarted. Moreover, there is a much greater chance of misinterpreting each other's intentions if not one, or two, but a number of countries are dominant. Misinterpretation of other states' intentions is a major cause of conflict in international relations. Leaders also tend to underestimate the effects of their actions on the leaders of other countries, to endow their convictions with the status of truth and to judge their opponents on moral and ethical grounds.

3.6 A New World Order?

The consequences of geopolitical change were not unexpected. The Ukraine crisis of 2014 saw Russian resentment and revanchism vis-à-vis the West collide with Europe's inability to safeguard what it had achieved with its soft power. The Ukraine crisis made it clear that European power had declined to the extent that the continent was no longer able to protect its interests. Most important, however, was the fact that due to the crisis in Ukraine, European fault-lines resurfaced, cooperation faltered and security and prosperity had eroded. As a result, the order that had been established with the Charter of Paris for a New Europe, signed by Russia, the United States and the European countries, appeared to come to an end. In this charter, which was solemnly signed by the heads of state and government leaders of the OSCE member states in November 1990, all European countries and North America committed themselves to an undivided Europe; to desist from using military force in territorial disputes, but to settle differences peacefully; to develop confidence-building measures and mechanisms for peaceful dispute settlement; and to respect countries' economic and political choices. With this charter the signatories bid farewell to the Cold War, and a new, undivided Europe was established. The Ukraine crisis is so fundamental in nature because almost every one of the agreements in the charter has been broken by Russia.

Subsequently, Russia rejected a resolution of the UN General Assembly titled "Territorial integrity of Ukraine". The resolution affirmed the Assembly's commitment to Ukraine's sovereignty and called on international organizations and specialized agencies not to recognize any change in the status of Crimea or the Black Sea port city of Sevastopol, and to refrain from actions or dealings that might be interpreted as such. Moreover, the Assembly called on States to "desist and refrain" from actions aimed at disrupting Ukraine's national unity and territorial integrity, including by modifying its borders through the threat or use of force. (United Nations 2014).

China rejected a ruling on the South China Sea by the Permanent Court of Arbitration in The Hague. The UN tribunal ruled in 2016 overwhelmingly against Chinese claims to huge swaths of the strategically important South China Sea. Beijing rebuffed the verdict, calling it "a piece of paper that is destined to come to naught" (Philips 2016).

Like Russia, China feels excluded from Western institutions. Just like Russia, China has therefore taken initiatives to improve its status by setting up multinational organizations. In 1996 it took the initiative to found the Shanghai Five, along with Kazakhstan, Kyrgyzstan, Russia and Tajikistan. The fall of the Soviet Union and the founding of the Shanghai Cooperation Council, which grew out of the Shanghai Five, led to a substantial improvement in relations with Russia. This meant that China could focus more of its attention on other strategic issues, such as Taiwan, the South China Sea and the East China Sea (Liao 2013). The objective of this initiative was to demarcate borders and agree confidence-building measures. After the Asian financial crisis, China helped to create the ASEAN Plus Three, along with Japan and South Korea, in order to increase financial stability in the region. In 2002 China signed a free trade agreement with ASEAN, which came into force in 2010. On the one hand, China's involvement in multilateral institutions is driven by economic growth, while on the other, it is prompted by a desire to achieve greater influence in the region. Despite this, China is ambivalent about international cooperation. As noted above, emerging powers such as China do not reject the international order, but their overriding objective is to ensure that it reflects their own preferences to a greater extent. This will help China to protect its interests more effectively.

The relative decline in the power of the West will also come at the expense of representation in international institutions, in which they currently enjoy a large voting share. Within the IMF, an 85% 'super majority' is required for major decisions. At present, the American voting share is 16.75%. If this voting share falls under 15%, the United States will lose its right of veto. It is also certain that this relative decline in power will demand more of diplomacy than has been the case until now. This is less of a major problem for the United States than it is for an increasingly fragmented Europe.

As a result of its economic successes, China's soft power has also increased. China can now present the Beijing Consensus with great conviction as a challenger to the neoliberal order of the Washington Consensus. China has been promoting the Beijing Consensus since 2004 as an alternative model of development, based on autocracy and state capitalism. In line with this, unlike the West, China does not attach any conditions relating to human rights, good governance, democracy, accountability, fighting corruption and environmental standards to its commercial dealings in other countries. In this model, Western values are replaced by Confucian values such as harmony, union, co-existence and shared prosperity (Limin 2010) Various emerging countries, even those in Europe, are attracted by this growth model. The Prime Minister of Hungary, Victor Orbán, has been more explicit than any other European leader on this point. He has argued that Hungary should no longer be a traditional constitutional state, but an autocracy based on the Chinese, Russian or Turkish model. Traditional liberal democracies, in Orbán's view, will no longer be able to generate prosperity in the new era (Mahony 2014).

Globalization has always produced winners and losers. According to Yang Jiemian, chair of the Shanghai Institute for Strategic Studies, the world contains countries that win, countries that are forced onto the defensive, countries that see their position harmed and countries that are clear losers (Godement 2010: 3). In Yang's prediction, the new world order that is being created by the shift in the geopolitical centre of gravity to Asia may hit European citizens particularly hard. Europe finds it difficult to adapt, because the debt crisis that hit Europe in 2009 was followed by a political and institutional crisis. Partly as a result of this, Europe, or rather the European Union, has not become as powerful as it could have been, and as a result, Europe is finding it increasingly hard to protect its global interests.

Nevertheless, aspects of Yang's vision should be questioned. For one thing, it is by no means inevitable that rising countries will assume a dominant place in the world. This will depend on the manner in which they manage to take their place in the complex network of international relations. Russia presents an interesting case in this regard. Russia belongs to the BRICS group, but the economic outlook for this country is less positive, even though it behaves like an emerging superpower. Moreover, it is by no means certain that the United States will become so weak that it can no longer play a meaningful role.

3.7 Conclusion

The main lines of the development of international relations are relatively predictable. The discussion about multipolarity and the question of which powers would become dominant had already begun at the beginning of the 1990s. Many authors made relatively good predictions about which way the world was heading. Detailed predictions about how, where and when each type of conflict would arise could not be made, however. We can draw a comparison here with the climate and the weather. The climate changes slowly, just like international relations. Climate change influences the weather, but it is not possible to make precise predictions over the long run. Just as with the weather, it is not easy to predict how, where and when actual incidents will occur in international relations. For this reason, humanity is repeatedly overcome by crises and events, which are indeed unpredictable, but fit very well into the changing 'climate' of international relations.

Due to the rise of countries such as China, the power of the West had already been declining from the mid-1990s in a relative, if not in an absolute, sense. As a result, these emerging powers gained more latitude in international relations, and the West, less. For President George W. Bush, who took office in 2001, the rise of China was an absolute priority for American foreign policy. This priority was pushed aside, however, by the attacks on 11 September 2001. Ironically, it was the military interventions in Afghanistan and Iraq, which were indeed direct outcomes of the September 11th attacks, which in fact contributed to the acceleration of the geopolitical changes, to the creation of new local crises and even to the relative decline of American power.

The discussion about the relative decline in American power and the emergence of a multipolar world is an important one. If the United States wanted to remain the key global player, then we would expect the Americans to hold back China's ascendancy by strengthening the liberal economic world order and the American military presence in Asia. If the United States were nevertheless to become weaker, then the Americans would try to curb China's growth with neo-mercantilist policies and by forging new alliances in Asia. Both developments would lead to geopolitical friction.

The conclusion is that due to rising powers and the development of multiple centres of power, international relations is not only becoming less 'Western', but also more complex. This means that more will be demanded of the quality of foreign and security policy, and of politicians, who have not actually engaged in the practice of power politics since the end of the Cold War.

For many Western countries, geopolitical change requires a mental and practical adjustment of their foreign and security policy, an adjustment that starts with the acknowledgment that in international relations power-political considerations are becoming more important, and moral and ethical considerations less so. Only countries that are able to deal with the new complex reality of the multipolar world will be able to benefit from it, in terms of more prosperity, stability and influence on the shaping of the new world order. This does not mean that other countries, by definition, will be left completely powerless, but they will not be players that can shape the new world order in such a way that they profit maximally from it. Time-honoured beliefs will have to be abandoned. For the countries that have dominated international relations in recent centuries, this will not be easy.

Further Readings

Bull, H. (1971) Order vs. justice in international society. *Political Studies, 19*(3), 269–283.

Gaddis, J. L. (1986. Spring). The long peace: Elements of stability in the postwar international system. *International Security, 10*(4), 99–142. MIT Press.

Gross-Stein, J. (2013). Building politics into psychology: The misperception of threat. In L. Huddy, D. O. Sears, & J. S. Levy (Eds.), *The Oxford handbook of political psychology* (2nd ed.). Oxford: Oxford University Press.

Jervis, R. (1978). Cooperation under security dilemma. *World Politics, 30*(2), 167–214. Cambridge University Press.

Jervis, R.(1988, Spring). War and misperception. *The Journal of Interdisciplinary History, 18*(4), 675–700. The origin and prevention of major wars. MIT Press.

Kissinger, H.. (1994). *Diplomacy*. Simon & Schuster.

Mearsheimer, J. (2014). America Unhinged. *The National Interest*.

References

Bush, G. (1991, January 29). *Address before a joint session of the congress on the state of the union*. http://www.presidency.ucsb.edu/ws/?pid=19253

De Wijk, R. (2014). *The art of military coercion: Why the West's military might scarcely matters*. Amsterdam: Amsterdam University Press and Chicago University Press.

De Wijk, R. (2015). *Power politics: How China and Russia reshape the world*. Amsterdam: Amsterdam University Press.

Economy, E. (2010, November–December). The game changer. *Foreign Affairs*, 142–152.

Godement, F. (2010), *Geopolitics on Chinese Terms* (European Council on Foreign Relations), September, p. 3.

Godement, F. (2013) *Divided Asia: The implications of Europe*. (European Council on Foreign Relations), November, p. 3.

Haass, R. N., (2008, May–June). *The age of nonpolarity*. Council on Foreign Relations.

HCSS (2014a). *Strategic monitor 2014, Monograph 2. The assertions of assertiveness: The Chinese and Russian cases*. The Hague: The Hague Centre for Strategic Studies.

HCSS. (2014b). *Why are pivot states so pivotal? The role of pivot states in regional and global security*. The Hague: The Hague Centre for Strategic Studies.

Jaishankar, D. (2014, June-July). Resilience and the future balance of power. *Survival, 56*(3).

Krasner, D. S. (Ed.). (1983). *International regimes*. Ithaca: Cornell University Press.

Layne, C. (1993). The unipolar illusion: Why new greats powers will rise. *International Security, 17*(4), 5–41.

Liao, K. (2013). The Pentagon and the pivot. *Survival, 55*(3), 104.

Limin, L. (2010). Global political changes and China's strategic choices. *Xiandai guoji guanxi, 4*, 1–10.

Mahony, H. (2014). Orbán wants to build 'illiberal state'. *EU Observer*, 28 July 2014. http://euob-server.com/political/125128

Manning, R. A. (2012). *US strategy in a post-Western world* (p. 118). Washington: Atlantic Council.

Mearsheimer, J. J. (2001). *The tragedy of great power politics* (p. 2001). New York: W.W. Norton & Company.

Monteiro, N. P. (2011, Winter). Unrest assured: Why unipolarity is not peaceful. *International Security, 36*(3).

National Intelligence Council. (2012, December). *Global trends 2030: Alternative worlds*, p. 16.

Nye, J. (1990). *Bound to Lead: The changing nature of American power*. New York: Basic Books.

Nye, J. (2011). *The future of power*. New York: Public Affairs.

Phillips, T. (2016). China attacks international court after South China Sea ruling. *The Guardian*, 13 July, https://www.theguardian.com/world/2016/jul/13/china-damns-international-court-after-south-china-sea-slapdown

Reuters. (2014). *Kerry condemns Russia's 'incredible act of aggression' in Ukraine*, 2 March. http://www.reuters.com/article/2014/03/02/us-ukraine-crisis-usa-kerry-idUSBREA210DG20140302

Schweller, R. L., & Pu, X. (2011). After unipolarity: China's visions of international order in an era of U.S. decline. *International Security, 36*(1), 41–72.

Talbot, S. (2002). *The Russia hand: A memoir of presidential diplomacy*. New York: Random House.

Taylor Fravel, M. (2005). Regime insecurity and international cooperation. *International Security, 30*(2), 46–83.

Tellis, A.J., Bially, J., Layne, C. and McPherson, M. (2000). Measuring National Power in the postindustrial age, Santa Monica, ca.: Rand Corporation.

United Nations. (2013). *Making the most of Africa's commodities: Industrializing for growth, jobs and transformation*. Addis Ababa: United Nations Economic Commission for Africa.

United Nations (2014). *General assembly adopts resolution calling upon states not to recognize changes in status of Crimea region*, 14 March.

Waltz, K. N. (2000). Structural realism after the cold war. *International Security, 25*(1), 5–51.

Wilson, D., & Purushothaman, R. (2003). *Dreaming with BRICs: The Path to 2050*. New York: Goldman Sachs, Global Economics Paper no. 99, 1 October.

Wohlforth, W. C. (1999). The stability of a unipolar world. *International Security, 24*(2), 7–8.

Zakaria, Z. (2008). *The Post American world*. New York: W. W. Norton & Company.

Chapter 4
China's Ascent: A Strategic Perspective of Its Vision

Jian Shi and Zeren Langjia

4.1 Introduction

New powers are rapidly rising while old powers are relatively declining. As a result, the global order is changing. Essentially, nonetheless, the old-world order is not global but Western-dominated. Seen in this light, the changing global order actually means a shift from the Western-dominated world order to a new and globally balanced international order where even developing countries (aspire to) have a say in how to govern a global order. In other words, non-Western and particularly developing countries want their voices heard and valued. They want to be creators of such a global order. In particular, emerging powers (e.g., China, Russia and India in Part II) are increasingly proactive in global issues with a view to reshaping and reorganizing the current international order. Consequently, to know how these countries view the current international order and what they intend to do is of crucial importance for better understanding the nature of the changing global order. To this end, this chapter focuses on China as an important branch of the emerging BRICS.

China's impressive emergence in this changing and globalizing world has recently attracted the wide attention, but the nature of its ascent, and its potential impact on world order, have been in the spotlight for decades. With regard to its status, China is divergently labeled as a general emerging power, a realist power (Mearsheimer 2001), a status-quo state (Johnston 2003), a superpower (Overholt 2002; Shi 2007), a fragile superpower (Shirk 2007), a regional power (Breslin 2009), a partial power (Shambaugh 2013a), a peaceful, pleasant and civilized lion (Cunningham 2014), and a major power or major country (Chen 2015). These epi-

J. Shi
Sichuan University, Chengdu, China

Z. Langjia (✉)
Institute of European Studies of Chinese Academy of Social Sciences, Beijing, China
e-mail: zeren.Langjia@qq.com

© Springer Nature Switzerland AG 2020
M. O. Hosli, J. Selleslaghs (eds.), *The Changing Global Order*, United Nations University Series on Regionalism 17,
https://doi.org/10.1007/978-3-030-21603-0_4

thets reflect variations in interpreting the nature of China as a power, but the commonality is that China is considered an increasingly influencial force challenging the current 'Western world order'. Meanwhile, scholars have interpreted China's ascent from various IR perspectives. For instance, Mearsheimer (2001) and Goswami (2013) underline an offensive realist perspective, while Kirshner (2010) prefers a classical realist viewpoint and Glaser (2011) prefers a non-pessimistic realist angle. Additionally, liberals believe in the China's potential for democratization (Xie and Page 2010; Roy 2009), and semi-optimistic liberals value economic interdependence and China's engagement in international organizations (Weede 2010; Hudda 2015). Nevertheless, while these scholars have contributed to IR theory,[1] it cannot be denied that there exists a wide gap in perception regarding China, within and outside the country. This chasm can only be straddled with a better understanding of China's strategic panorama. Mindful of this potentiality in bridging the chasms, but without assuming a position on China's peaceful rise, this chapter sheds light on China's resurgence by considering its related strategies: its vision of a world order, its focus on external partners, and its intention of national rejuvenation.

4.2 China's Ascendancy and Its Strategic Vision for a Twenty-First Century Order

To observe how China perceives the current world order contributes to an understanding of how the country positions itself in an envisioned world order. China's perception can also be influential in formulating China's strategies to accomplish its objectives. The following subsections analyze significant dimensions of China's vision of a potential world order.

4.2.1 China's Vision of a Twenty-First Century World Order: Harmony in Diversity?

The idea "harmony in diversity" or "harmonious yet different" (he er bu tong), which originally referred to a harmonious status of interpersonal relations in ancient China, was regularly emphasized during Jiang Zemin Administration and consequently regarded as an important principle by which international relations should abide. The concept became the core of the new China's international strategy, an important guiding principle of establishing a just, fair and new international order, and a potent weapon against hegemonism and power politics (Xia 2003, p.34). In a

---

[1] For why there is no Chinese school of international relations theory, see Yan (2016). Yan said, Chinese scholars are working to enrich modern IR theories with traditional Chinese thought, using modern methodology.

response to the party's principles and policies, Chinese academia has been over-whelmingly expressing the same parlance to justify the country's external behavior, which makes it difficult to fully prognosticate the intention and impact of China's reemergence, but apparently the term pays equal attention to the differences between international actors, i.e. their characteristics. China places much emphasis on "Chinese characteristics," but the Chinese ways are not necessarily compatible with others, as China sees the Western model as unsuitable for its own development, according to Wang (2011). Namely, while China denies the universality of the Western model, the country struggles contradictorily to realize a world order with Chinese characteristics.

In contrast, China continuously endeavors to convince others to believe in the benign nature of its resurgence. In the Chinese context, China's "Peaceful Rise"[2] has two direct implications and one indirect implication: first, China rises to become world power; second, China ascends to become a world power without major wars, without an enduring Cold-War confrontation; and third, the indirect meaning is that China needs to strive for maintaining the status of being world power, rather than imitate the powers who rose rapidly but fell quickly in modern history (Shi 2007, p.30). Nevertheless, Wang contends that Peaceful Rising is not a great diplomatic strategy because it requires planning for the world that also accommodates China as a means to enhance the legitimacy of its world leadership (Wang 2011, p.142). With regard to diplomatic theory, Wang argues that leading countries advance their own diplomatic conceptions that originate from the country concerned and that belong to the world (Wang 2011, p.142). The problem is that China's diplomatic theory is confined to remove doubt or reduce obstructions, and that Chinese diplomacy has a strong trace of domestic bureaucracy, with diplomacy considered to be an extension of domestic affairs (Wang 2011, p.142). However, the purpose of the peaceful rising narrative is to demonstrate that China can harmoniously coexist with other international actors.

4.2.2 China's Adaptive Mechanism of Learning from Others

With China's emergence, the country not only recognizes the importance of opening up to the outside world, but also progressively implements this in practice. Thus, the general perception (that China closes its door to external contact) perhaps needs updating. China was previously relatively isolated, and this has been regarded as a main cause of its economic lag. New China became aware of the mistake and has been trying to learn from it. Thus, China's acceptance or rejection of external influences remains a matter of degree. Over these decades, China has been transitioning from a passive acceptance of external influence to a kind of proactive rejection. To

---

[2] Zheng Bijian, former President Hu Jintao's senior advisor first posed the term 'China's Peaceful rise', which was later replaced by 'China's peaceful development' to "remove the challenging undertone of 'rise' and to dissuade adversarial reactions" (Luttwak 2012, p. 273).

absorb what is good and reject what is bad becomes an important principle. Among other qualities, adaptation is the main feature of China's attitude toward external influence. For instance, Maoism is an adapted version of Marxism and Leninism (Shi 2015, p.102).

Based on the principle of selectivity, China's rapid (economic) development has been benefiting from the experience and knowledge of Western development, rather than following an undifferentiated replication. As China becomes stronger, it develops more ambition to exert influence on the same international system that previously influenced China. Indeed, China's international interactions have evolved from being influenced by to actually influencing others. The current international system is considered the result of transforming the European international system into a global system, so China endeavors to transform the Asian international system and expand its influence in the global system.

Furthermore, China's increasing engagement in external relations has illustrated the global expansion of international system, and China's rise is also shifting the power base from the West to the East, which will inevitably influence the evolution of international norms (Shi 2007, p.32). In doing so, Chinese values, political orientation, and normative intentions can be exported around the world, and Zhou (2013) argues that international order is in the middle of this transition. China's confidence in a power transition and in a reconfigured world order is incremental but real, and it no longer compromises so readily regarding disagreements with other actors. These developments are reflected in China's somewhat hawkish attitudes in international affairs. Chung (2016) believes that China's rise has been evolving from its earlier position of adaptation to the international system to a new kind of assertiveness,[3] which may be problematic for some actors in the international system (2015, p. 154). China's 'assertiveness' thesis is an oft-discussed topic, particularly through the country's attitudes and responses towards international issues such as South China Sea (the issue is also briefly debated in Chap. 3, Sect. 3.6; Chap. 6, Sect. 6.1; Chap. 9, Sect. 9.1 of this Volume).

4.2.3 Actions Taken to Shape a New International Order

China's strategic view of international order radiates from the Asia-Pacific region. The Asia Infrastructure Investment Bank (AIIB) and the One Belt One Road policy (OBOR) reflect China's global strategy (Lu 2016), and also its view of international order in the twenty-first century (Sun 2016). Although recently attentive to relations with major powers, China is also aware of the necessity to cultivate relations with small countries and regions, so as not to follow the footsteps of US's diplomacy,

---

[3] Luttwak considers it as 'premature assertiveness'. For more detail, see (Luttwak 2012). In Chap. 1 of this volume, the author has also discussed about the relationship between the changing world order and the assertiveness of rising powers, arguing that the assertiveness of both China and Russia is increasing, though not in the same way.

because it was small countries such as Vietnam, Iraq, Afghanistan and even regional actors such as ISIL (rather than Germany, Japan and former Soviet Union) that exhausted the US (Zhang 2016, p.30). Neighboring countries are geopolitically significant for China. Additionally, China is clear about its strategic partnerships where it can give full play to its role. Now China is in a state of transition from a regional power to a global power, and its strategic interests are rapidly expanding with an outward orientation at the global level (Men 2016, p.4). The power transition narrative, to a large extent, approves of China's intention to expand its power at the global level.

However, many international actors hold an "illusion of Chinese power" (Shambaugh 2016, p. 147), which consciously or unconsciously intensifies China's sense of self-importance. As a result, they not only exaggerate the impact of China's rise but also blindly follow Chinese policies. For instance, China initiated the Asia Infrastructure Investment Bank (AIIB) and it was originally supposed to be just an Asian regional facility, but the UK, Italy and others immediately internationalized it by joining the AIIB. It is said that the AIIB initiative, including SCR, BRICS, and the SCO bank, was the result of the US refusal of China's demand to improve its currency (RMB) through the International Monetary Fund (IMF). For China the result was unexpected, and UK membership was "not just a surprise to allies in Europe and Washington. It also caught Beijing unawares" (Anderlini 2015). When asked about the rationale behind the decision, British diplomats and officials responded identically: "What did we have to lose by joining?" (Anderlini 2015). The answer not only sounds irresponsible for its allies, but also lacks strategic consideration. Besides, France and Germany also joined the AIIB, signaling an eastward shift of global power (Anderlini 2015). Nevertheless, the rush of new European membership spears to be somewhat arbitrary and perhaps reflects erroneous judgment. These countries seem to get carried away by economic interests without clear strategic awareness and objectives. To set up international institutions is a new try for China. Bearing in mind Xiaoping Deng's saying of crossing the river by feeling the stones, the country, as always, moves carefully, not least in a new field. This policy principle insinuates that when one desires to explore new territory, it might have to take a step-by-step approach. In this light, non-Asian (European membership in particular) membership of the AIIB and other Chinese-dominated international organizations boosts Chinese confidence in shaping a new world order.

4.2.4   From Traditional Values to National Politics and Foreign Policy Principles

In a response to China's lack of IR theories, its reversion to traditional philosophy (mainly relating to moral practices) became an instrument to guide and illustrate its external behavior. As Yan said, "the hope of Chinese IR theoretical study lies in rediscovering traditional Chinese IR thought" (Yan 2016, p. 256). China hopes to acquire insights from this ancient political thinking. Its ancient political values place strong emphasis on the moral practices of individuals, including those of monarchs and emperors, but moral doctrines often functioned to restrain the behavior of citizens rather than the behavior of officials in high administrative positions. Notwithstanding the impact of political values on individuals and their thinking, these values are not well integrated into institutional administration and external practices. Thus, moral principles and national institutional system proceed without much intersection.

Among others, Confucian Pacifism is "an alternative to the principle international theories" for Chinese scholars, but "Confucian rhetoric can be used to justify aggressive as well as defensive behavior" (Mearsheimer 2001). Obviously, according to Mearsheimer, Confucian Pacifism compensates for China's lack of international theories and even an excuse for disguising provocative behavior. However, it should be noted that the nature of Confucianism is mild. Due to this mildness, Chinese scholars frequently use Confucianism to justify China's international behavior (Yan 2010). Nevertheless, the problem that triggers disputes lies in whether China adheres to Confucianism in a strict manner, and how. Measheimer argues that Confucianism is not well practiced because it becomes just an excuse for China's "aggressive" and "offensive" acts. "Like liberalism in the United States, Confucianism makes it easy for Chinese leaders to speak like idealists and act like realists," but little evidence shows that "China is an exceptional great power that eschews realist logic and instead behaves in accordance with the principles of Confucian pacifism" (Mearsheimer 2001). Obviously, Mearsheimer takes it for granted that China surely follows in "Uncle Sam's footsteps," but it is unnecessarily correct as scholars such as Buzan (2010) believe in the potential for China's peaceful rise.

Notwithstanding that they are not essentially diplomatic instruments, these traditional values have influenced Chinese mentality and behavior. Above all, traditional cultural influence on people's routine behavior is remarkable. The ideas such as "To be a cut above the rest" and "conceal one's strengths and bide one's time" (tao guang yang hui) (i.e. avoidance of radiance) are heritages of Chinese traditional culture that have affected Chinese people from the grassroots to the top leaders. In particular, avoidance of radiance became an important Chinese external strategic instrument or principle in the 1990s and refers to a low-key behavioral model of self-cultivation that is gradually influencing Chinese external relations. In the 1990s, China mainly implemented a policy of "concealing its strengths and biding its time" and focused on economic development (Zhou 2012, p.11). In doing so, China's economic power did not threaten US security, and the US also benefited from bilateral economic cooperation. Consequently, the policy made it hard for the US to implement a comprehensive and intensive containment policy for China. Deng Xiaoping, the former Chinese Vice-Premier, proposed this policy in 1992, stating that China needed to "conceal its strengths and bide its time" for couple of years before becoming a sizeable political power. At the practical level, two aspects displayed the policy: first, China exercised restraint on security issues and avoided challenging the US position of advantage in the global system and in East Asia; and second, China proactively participated in international and regional economic systems and developed trade relations with East Asian countries (Zhou 2012, p.12). Admittedly, this low-key policy was deployed for full development without containment through reducing the vigilance of other powers.

Secondly, historical experience and the national situation have been exerting an effect on the motivation of Chinese external relations. Avenging "One Hundred Years' Humiliation" (bai nian chi ru) is regarded as a mission that every Chinese is told to undertake, and to make China better and stronger is the best way to seek vengeance on those who caused the humiliation (for related discussion, see also Chap. 3, Sect. 3.2). The country is eager to dismantle the dark part of its history imposed by Western and Japanese power politics, and this has motivated Chinese leaders to strive for its national dream of rejuvenating China. Likewise, the status quo of the previous national situation implanted people with an unforgettable memory: Luohou jiuyao aida. This literally means that one (referring to the China of yesteryear) will suffer from being beaten if it lags behind. Mao Zedong, previous President of China, once said that lagging behind leaves one vulnerable to attack, and the Chinese government frequently uses this saying to spur the country's people on to greater efforts.

Finally, some ancient principles relating to inter-state and interpersonal relations could be employed as guidelines for modern Chinese diplomacy. For instance, chun wang chi han literally means that if the lips are gone, the teeth will be cold. Seen from a perspective of international relations, this signifies that if one of two interdependent things falls, the other is in danger. Besides, the old saying yuan qin bu ru jin lin, (which means that a distant relative is not as good as a near neighbor), insinuates that relations with peripheral countries and regions are more favorable than those with far-off powers. Even though the term highlights the geographical distance, it still applies to current international relations.

It should be noted, however, that even those traditional values cannot be considered integrated but fragmented. Over time, increasing emphasis has been placed on these and other values for gaining momentum and guiding Chinese external relations. This is also a process of integrating the dispersed traditional thoughts into a systematic arrangement of diplomacy. In doing so, the country's international relations can become better systemized, regulated and operationalized.

4.3 China's Emergence and Its Strategic Centrality

A strategic focus on external partners is the second important factor for realizing a better understanding of China's ascent. China has been prioritizing the relations with major (developed) powers with top concern for the US. China has also been emphasizing relations with neighboring countries, focusing on binary situations in East Asia, especially where the US and China appear to be irreconcilable competitors. Also, China has been strengthening its relations with distant developing countries and regions with a view to consolidating the legitimacy of its rise.

4.3.1 Prioritizing Relations with Major Powers

Although changing over the time, Chinese external policies have a tradition prioritizing developed powers, not least with regard to economic cooperation. As Shi argues, "While China claims to be an advocate for a world order, relations with developed countries are a priority, as the nation itself wants to become a member of the club" (Shi 2015 p.105). In 2004, China introduced the idea of a "New Type of Major Country Relations." This refers to China's bilateral relations with other major powers such as the EU, Japan, Russia, India and especially the US. China pays great attention to these powers not only because they are capable of influencing on international system, its order and norms, but also because there are many conflicting interests between these actors in the Asia-Pacific region. The term "New Type of Major Country Relations" has diverse versions such as "New Type of Major Power Relations" and "New Type of Great Power Relations," but the Chinese phrase Daguo means big or major country. Besides, this foreign policy harkens back to the traditional model of power relations between nation states (with an exception for the EU), although China frequently and officially states that the new type of relationship differs from conventional and historical relations between powers such as US-Soviet Union, and that it will not contend for world hegemony or secure its fundamental rights through violence (Zhou 2013, pp.5–6). As always, China continuously reminds its partners of the cruelty of wars such as WWI and WWII, which brought great harm and damage to the countries and regions concerned. China reiterates its peaceful views of international relations, and emphasizes the benign nature of its rise. Nevertheless, it should also be noted that policies towards these major powers place less emphasis on political relations, in particular on high-politics areas, and strong economic cooperation has been a tradition.

4.3.2 The Case of US-China Relations

Among bilateral relations, China pays special attention to the US and its Asia-Pacific "pivot" or rebalancing strategy. The Sino-US relationship is one of the most important but also one of the most complicated bilateral relations in the world, which can influence the world order (Zhou 2013, p.4). Both countries are Pacific Ocean powers and have competing regional interests. The "New Type of Major Country Relations" between China and the US has the function of reducing and specifying the scope of bilateral (joint) actions through reaching a consensus on regional activity (Zhou 2013, p.7). Subconsciously, a power transition is believed to shift from the US to China, and China wants to influence this transition through a peaceful approach (Liu 2013a), but there is no consensus on whether a power transition in the current international system is underway. The subconsciousness also demonstrates, however, that China prioritizes its bilateral relations with the US.

China regards itself as a major power second only to the US and avoids following in the former Soviet Union's footsteps because, according to the evolutionary regularity of the international order, the position of the second largest power is often unstable (Liu 2013b). The ideal future world structure is to shift current "one superpower plus several big powers" to a "co-existence of a group of more or less equal powers" and then to "an integrated multi-power community" under the framework of the United Nations (Liu 2013b). Thus, it is obvious that China's strategic mentality focuses on major powers. Additionally, the US is an inevitable and constant subject in China's strategy. China attaches great importance to the US and pays much attention US actions in the world, particularly in the Asia-Pacific region, and the "US-China strategic coordination has the decisive influence on maintaining peaceful order in the East Asian region" (Gao 2014, p.38).

From a long-term perspective, the rise of China will be the top factor influencing US global power and signals power shift in the East Asian region, especially regarding Mainland China's control over the issue of Taiwan (Shi 2007, p.29), which is ascribed to China's rapid economic growth and proactive diplomatic activities. While US power comparatively decreases, Chinese power increases. This situation in international politics is regarded as an auspicious omen for China's ascent, especially in the (East) Asian regions. The most realistic position for China is to observe, estimate, and have a full understanding of US global power and its position in East Asian (Shi 2007, p. 30). By doing so, China can fully capitalize on this favorable opportunity and radiate its global strategy from East Asia.

Furthermore, China avoids head-on confrontation with the US to prevent any potential war and reinforce national security. "To prevent the US from being the single global hegemon is also part of China's diplomatic task," and China should propagandize multipolarity, which is not necessarily anti-American, although this position certainly weakens US hegemony in reality (Lv 2000, p.40). China worries that the US might become the single global hegemon, but the US regards itself as the only regional hegemon because no country can be a global hegemon (Mearsheimer 2001). This is a typical result of a security dilemma under realist logic, where countries would rather overestimate the power of their adversaries than to underestimate them. Therefore, to correctly and properly assess the power of rivals is also a process of normalizing international relations and removing mutual suspicion. The US was believed to use its superpower advantage to enhance its unipolarity and pre-emptive strategy, and to pursuit its strategic objectives even at the expense of wars that seriously harmed international security, world peace and stability (Xia 2003, p. 32). Nevertheless, the current situation represents a diminishment of US unipolarity, and a transition towards multipolarity between the US, Japan, Russia, Europe and China (Qin 2004, p.11). At least, according to Chinese media, China makes a great whoop and a holler about its role in shaping a new and multipolar world order. This is the same case for Russia. As André Gerrits argues in Chap. 5, multipolarity is an ambition of Russian (foreign) policy such as sovereignty and self-determination, which are closely related to Russia strategic interests.

The concept of strategic demarcation in the Asia-Pacific region, between China and the US, also demonstrates China's East Asian ambition: China wants the US to accept Chinese military (superiority) in "China's offshore area (with Taiwan's eastern coastline as the approximate demarcation line) and a peaceful reunification of the two sides of the Taiwan Strait, together with China's strategic space in a narrow but substantial span of the western Pacific;" and China will accept US "military superiority overall and in the central and western Pacific in particular, as well as predominant diplomatic influence in other regions" (Shi 2015, p.108). From his argument, three conclusions can be drawn: first, China regards the Asia-Pacific region as its strategically significant zone for exerting international influence; second, the Taiwan issue matters; and third, the US is an obstacle for China to become a regional hegemon, such that China wants to demarcate their respective spaces in the region. In other words, China wants the US to keep away from Chinese strategic space.

Since the 2008 global financial crisis, US-China relations shifted from a positive-sum game aimed at pursuing relative economic benefit to a zero-sum game of power competition and relative international influence (Gao 2014, p.35). It is also a shift from interest sharing with regard to economic cooperation, to interest conflict in the field of security and power relations. The nature of strategic objectives of the US and China in the region is changing. Bilateral strategic relations are becoming more competitive and replacing the compatibility and inclusiveness of economic benefits. As a result, it comes to be increasingly difficult for these two "tangled titans," though "inextricably tied together," to coexist – yet they must (Shambaugh 2013b).

4.3.3 Prioritizing Relations with Neighboring and Developing Countries

China has strong economic and security relations with neighboring countries and increasing economic cooperation with distant developing countries and regions. However, the security situation in East Asia is turbulent and changing due to various reasons: China's rise and its neighbors' apprehensiveness; the US pivot to the Asia-Pacific region; and neighbors' external reaction to these developments (Qi and Shi 2013, p.26). Simultaneously, China attempts to enhance trust and remove doubts, to confront the US through institutional balancing, to safeguard its rights through diplomacy while preparing for potential conflict (Qi and Shi 2013). China is developing its "greater neighborhood diplomacy" that includes Northeast Asia, Southeast Asia, South Asia, Central Asia, Western Asia and South Pacific region, and establishing a "New Type of Major Power Relations" with the US, Japan, Russia and India (Qi and Shi 2013, p.44–5). These prevailing policies are clearly based upon the great changes taking place in Asia-Pacific and other regions. Concurrently, China is also enhancing its diplomatic relations, economic cooperation, and political bonds with countries from these regions. After all, China's peaceful rise and power shift of world center depend on regional relationships.

China's foreign policy foci are also featured by cooperation on the "high-politics" fields of neighboring countries and on the "low-politics" sectors of distant partners. Due to regional non-homogeneity and China's scarcity of strategic resources, China can only take unbalanced development approach, i.e., concentrating on advantageous resources to first make breakthroughs in the areas where constraints are weak and where "investment" benefits are high (Du and Ma 2012, p.9). At the global level, China's strategic breakthrough is confined to the low-politics sectors through fully using the penetration power of economic instruments, but it should strengthen cooperation in the high-politics sectors with regional countries (Du and Ma 2012, p.9). Few countries in Asia are not experiencing tensions with China (Shambaugh 2016, p. 138), which makes it impossible for China to overlook its relations with countries in the region. Thus, China will endeavor to enhance its political and security bonds with its neighboring countries such as West and East Asian countries, who are of primary strategic significance for China, while keeping close economic relations with spatially far-distant countries and regions such as Latin America, Africa, Eastern and Central European countries, and Australia. Even though focusing on low-politics with the latter, it does not deny the potential political influence underneath the economic activities.

Without doubt, therefore, the core of China's strategic focus is on the Asia-Pacific region regarding its regional advantages, its limited political repercussion, and its peripheral security consideration, though China continues to emphasize bilateral relations with major countries and economies. China puts equal if not more stress on neighboring and other developing countries, for whom it is able to set an example, and upon whom it is able to maximize its impact. Apparently, the parallel model of cooperating both with developed and developing countries and regions better guarantees the ascent of China.

4.3.4   Overcoming East Asian Binary Situations: The US and China as Irreconcilable Competitors

During the post-Cold War period, a binary situation emerged with two economic and security centers in East Asia. China's ascendance ran up against the US "exposure plus containment" China policy. Also, East Asian countries developed a double bet policy regarding the US and China (Zhou 2012). The implications of the binary situation are profound not only for the US and China but also for other countries in the region. The US and China have developed divergent and incompatible strategic interests. Despite understanding their respective positions, the two powers are not open and sincere with each other. According to Yan's "Superficial Friendship Theory" the US and China are unwilling to face up to structural conflicts in their strategic interests, and they frequently conceal their differences by establishing a short-term and superficial friendship (Yan 2010).

For ASEAN and other East Asian countries, while relying on the US for security, are economically more dependent upon China. In 2015, the trade volume between China and ASEAN was 472.16 billion USD, which is almost 60 times of that of 1991 with only 7.96 billion USD (Song 2016). ASEAN is China's third largest trading partner after the EU (564.75 billion USD) and the US (558.28 billion USD). Without doubt, the trade volume between China and ASEAN became quite considerable, and they are economically interdependent. Besides, the geopolitical and geostrategic position of ASEAN countries could check the economic leverage of China, though the former bloc is economically not as strong as China. According to 2015 trade statistics, the US-ASEAN trade volume was much lower compared with that of China-ASEAN (asean.org), which roughly indicates China's increasing importance for ASEAN economically (while the US-ASEAN relationship is more political and strategic). In other words, the US-ASEAN political and security cooperation becomes the main obstruction in China-ASEAN relations. This situation attests to the binary reality of economy and security in East Asian.

4.4 China's Ascent and Its Strategic Intention

Strategic intention is an indispensable aspect for understanding China's rise. This section explores Chinese intentions of establishing international identity and expecting stronger presence of developing countries in the potential world order, of pursuing an exploitable multipolarity, reconstructing itself as the Asian regional hegemon, and envisaging Asia as the new world center.

4.4.1 Strengthening Its International Identity and Cultivating Developing Powers in the Twenty-First Century World Order

Along with its ascendance, China stresses its contribution to the international system as marked with Chineseness or Chinese characteristics or Chinese identity. To this end, much importance is attached to international system because it is believed to consist of international order, international actors, and international norms, but there is no consensus on standards that can be used to judge the changes in the international system (Yan 2010, p.13). Yan argues that international actors are mainly nation states and that international order is changing, so to initiate change in international norms is to initiate change in the international system. As a result, China is trying to influence on international norms such that international system will be more compatible with its development model. Nevertheless, it will be challenging because China often does not share the universality of values and norms, and yet is now struggling to influence international norms for itself and others. In other words,

China strives to set international norms with Chineseness that can work for others (mainly developing countries). Even though Chinese socialist values include the main components of current international norms such as freedom, equality and democracy, there are discrepancies derived from rival interpretations. China strives for, and insists upon, Chinese versions of these values, with a view to making others recognize and even acknowledge an international normative system marked by Chineseness.

Shi also argues that world order is mainly composed of three basic elements: the international distribution of power, the international normative system, and the transnational value system. Here, the relationship between China and future world order revolves around those three elements (Shi 2014, pp. 33–34). Shi contends that China is exponentially becoming involved and "entangled" in the outside world, which leads to the expansion of the international system. Shi further notes that China's rise continues to change the structure of international power, with repercussions for the international normative system. However, the relationship between China and the transnational value system is uncertain because China has made few contributions to the modern transnational value system such as freedom, social justice, ecological protection and economic growth (Shi 2014, pp.33–34). Shi also emphasizes that the historical challenge is whether China can really create a "Beijing Consensus" that is internationally and transnationally applicable and innovative. To meet the challenge, China is struggling to shake off its passive situation and take the initiative where it can dominate and exert more impact on international (value) system. Since 2004, the Beijing Consensus was promoted as a model of development, which is based on autocracy and state capitalism but without human rights, democratization and other conditions (Chap. 3, Sect. 3.6 of this Volume).

Regarding China's expectation of the enduring presence of developing countries in a potential world order, China emphasizes the different contexts between developed and developing worlds and the differences between China and other developing countries. First, Western scholars use the Westphalian state system to understand China's rise. "It has in fact been common for international relations scholars to use European history to explain East Asia," but "the nineteenth century German analogy for twenty-first century China is probably less useful than might appear at first glance" (Kang 2015, pp.31–2) because there were several similar sized powers in the former Europe, and there exists a power disparity between China and its neighboring powers. Second, there is also a gap between how Western countries and China perceive developing countries and regions, and between how they position the role of developing countries in the current international community. While the West regards China as a developing country, China sees itself as "a presumptive leader" of the developing world (Ferdinand 2011, p.86). China positions itself better than others with an ambition to set a good example for other developing countries (Yan 2012). Thus, while the West sees the relationship between developing countries as horizontal, China interprets this relationship as vertical.

In addition, China expects developing countries to contribute to international standards. China denies that Western standards are international standards, maintaining that international standards should take in the best standards of countries all over the world, including developed and developing countries, and that Chinese standards represent a part of international standards. Besides, China tries to improve the legitimacy of its interest demands by pulling to its side other developing countries (including African and Latin American countries), explaining that the Chinese development model is a better fit for developing countries. In doing so, China can make its voice heard in the international arena and influence the setting of international standards.

4.4.2   The Pursuit of an Exploitable Multipolarity: Reasoning and Challenges

China persistently advocates a multipolar order rather than unipolar and bipolar hegemonism, which is very much in alignment with its strategic interests. There are several reasons for China's preference for a multipolar world order. Firstly, multipolarity of world order approximates the democratization of international relations (Lv 2000, p.37; Xia 2003, p.32). This creates a wide and exploitable space for China to gain a foothold in Asia-Pacific region, thus stabilizing neighboring countries (Lv 2000, p.39). Secondly, it is provisionally unrealistic for China to surpass the US and to become a unipolar power. More importantly, it would be exceptionally challenging to maintain the status quo even if China becomes the unipolar power. Thirdly, multipolarity can largely contain the projection of US power and result in a kind of "balance of power." Fourthly, China is an emerging power in Asia, but the power gap between Asian countries is significant, which may turn China into a regional hegemon that will have a stronger say in many regionally disputable matters. Finally, a multipolar position results from China's strategic awareness, insightfulness and deployments, wherein regional stability benefits China's emergence. China distinctly maps out its strategic deployment, carefully looks for opportunity, and accurately locks its targets to minimize unnecessary losses and maximize strategic benefits. Besides, China is clear about making less effort where fewer opportunities exist and strengthening its inputs where it may have more chance to augment its interests. For instance, there is slight hope that Japan will stop allying with the US unconditionally because it is the basis for establishing Japan after WWII, and China does not look to Japan to be a good friend but rather a neighbor (Lv 2000, p.40). In this way, China will not squander much time on something in vain.

The Chinese multipolar view can also be elucidated from various challenges that it faces both internally and peripherally. Above all, China still needs to make much effort to improve its domestic development because most challenges are primarily domestic including sovereignty, territory, and security:

China will face some major challenges in the future: the changing shape of modernity; the persistent calls for national unification, territorial integration, and self-determination from those hostile to China's present political system; the leadership's ability to inspire an increasingly heterogeneous Chinese society; the necessity and difficulty of developing a new body of ethics for contemporary China; and the popular conservative nationalism and its possible echoes in the high political echelon (Shi 2015, pp.105–6).

These problems do not disappear automatically with the country's exponential economic growth. Conversely, it is undeniable that China's rapid economic development comes with heavy costs. For instance, China is currently facing serious problems of the environment and social justice that were often neglected when pursuing economic development. All this indicates that "China's fate will be primarily decided by its approaches to dealing with the bottleneck problems related to rapid economic development and the challenges it poses for social justice and environmental protection" (Shi 2015, p.106). Additionally, unlike the US, which has no dangerous foes in its own region, allowing it to patrol distant regions (Mearsheimer 2014), China cannot station military forces around the world and intrude into other regions, because it faces serious threats in Asia and because its relations with neighboring countries have been challenging.

4.4.3 China's Resurgence: A Return to Asian Regional Hegemony

The Asian-Pacific region is the most important external geopolitical environment and is of primary significance for China to get well along with neighboring countries. "The neighboring relations, especially in the Asian-Pacific region, are China's diplomatic task of prime importance" and China should advance its objective of exerting influence on neighboring countries to play the leading role in the region (Lv 2000, p.40). In response to this strategic ambition, "The Belt and Road" Policy was proposed to establish a regional and even global capital control system aimed at maintaining the long-term sustainable development of China (Li and Li 2015, p.59). However, China's strategic focus will be neighboring countries and developing countries, though it undeniably holds expectation of producing effect at the global level. After all, China still confronts various challenges in Asia. Although China may want to regain its hegemonic status in East Asia, "the other states in the region do not view China as a legitimate leader" and East Asian states have not achieved "truly stable relations to develop" (Kang 2015, p.43). Hence, the practical strategic positioning is also correspondent to its historical global status and its narrative of rejuvenating China. "China is one of the world's oldest civilizations and was an unquestioned hegemon in East Asia for centuries, and its rise in the twenty-first century is more a return to a place of centrality than anything new" (Kang 2015, p.31). Admittedly, historical memory is still stimulating and motivating China to pursue a kind of hegemonic status in the region.

4.4.4   Asia: China's Envisioned New World

While the relative decline of the US is believed to be unrelated to the shift of the world's center, the relative decline of Europe (without superpower potential) and the rise of Russia and East Asia are the main reasons behind this shift (Yan 2012, pp.8–9). According to Yan, a region needs to fulfill two conditions to become world center: first, the region must be an influential country at the global level with strong material power (especially military power) and cultural power (especially the power of ideas) that other countries can follow; and second, the world center should be situated at the region where international contradictions are concentrated (Yan 2012, p.6). Obviously, these two conditions drop a hint that China regards itself as an influential country in the world, and East Asia is a conflict-stricken region where China can hold the baton, so the world center is implicitly supposed to shift from Europe (or the West in general) to East Asia. Yan stresses that the rise China is the prerequisite for East Asia becoming the world center (Yan 2012, p.9). This means that China can raise East Asia's global influence up to a higher level than that of Europe. The argument also indicates that China still puts much emphasis on (traditional) nation-state power. Additionally, in a response to its lack of political influence, China is now attempting to transform its economic power into political influence. This is a significant challenge for China considering its territorial disputes with neighboring countries, which shrinks the space of its political impact. As a result, its political and strategic focus is on neighbors such as Pakistan, Burma and Mongolia.

Being an economic power in the region, however, is insufficient for maintaining its hegemonic position. In the long run, Chinese hegemony will depend on how much 'minxin' (the will of the people or the popular will) China can gain from its neighbors. Even if China dominates Asia and becomes a regional hegemon, it would be difficult for China to project its power to other regions such as Europe, the Middle East, or Latin America. Based on realist doctrine, regional domination offers "the best way to survive under international anarchy" (Mearsheimer 2001). In sum, regional domination is compatible with China's current multipolar narrative.

Apart from the strategic intentions mentioned above, the transformation of economic strength into political power can also motivate China's proactive global economic engagement. China has been strengthening its international identity and presence through playing strong economic roles in many parts of the world, which is eventually expected to consolidate China's voice in the international community. In doing so, economic power can be transformed into political strength. China's economic growth creates confidence and opportunities for China to be engaged in international affairs. However, China's international responsibility, political participation and global leadership are far from matching its economic status, and this mismatch restrains China from building more international legitimacy and from becoming a regional or global hegemon.

4.5 Conclusion

To conclude, China has been steadily expanding its external economic cooperation and progressively accentuating its global presence with a view to maintaining its advantageous position and materializing its national resurgence or rejuvenation. To this end, China continues to reinforce its defensive power while deliberately eschewing head-on collisions with major powers and peripheral countries. There is a slight possibility that China will initiate offensive and provocative actions, but it does not suggest that China's aspiration of shaping itself as a self-reliant power capable of safeguarding national interests and ruining hidden threats will not be relentless.

China is envisaging a twenty-first-century world order where emerging powers, especially China, play important roles. In a response to China's lack of IR theories, it turns to its traditional concepts to define its position. Regarding China's vision of a future world order, the imperceptible influence of traditional Chinese thought is an important factor explaining the behaviors of its foreign policy. Apart from learning from its tradition, China's external strategy takes lessons from the strengths and weaknesses of various IR perspectives rather than simply following a particular IR theory. In this challenge to IR theory, China advances its own worldview of a global order that has not yet taken full shape.

In terms of its strategic priorities, China pays special attention to three groups of external partners: first, major or developed powers; second, countries in its neighborhood; and third, other (distant) developing countries in Africa and Latin America. When the potential economic and political implications of the third group are taken into consideration, the strategic significance for China to influence world order becomes conspicuously noticeable and profound. Concurrently, the strategic significance of these countries and regions is also an important indicator of China's motivation to fortify its external relations and an influential principle for China to make decisions. China's coextending relations with major powers, adjacent countries, and other developing countries make its ascent more invincible.

While having an indispensable connection to its strategic vision, China's strategic intentions will continuously be in alignment with its misgivings about uncertainties in its foreign relations due to the capricious climate of international relations. In addition, the strategic intentions of Chinese foreign policies are based upon, and guided by, historical experiences, national interests, and strategic needs.

Therefore, while not denying theoretical contributions to understanding China's rise, its strategic position comes to the surface. Although China's economic ascendancy is an undisputable fact, both China and other international actors are under suspicion of excessively exaggerating and overestimating China's influence on the international community. In general, it should be noted that China has not yet realized its leadership potential due to its internal limitations, and due to its constrained and partial engagement in addressing global issues. So far, it does not act as an example for other international actors either. Nonetheless, there is no doubt that China aspires to forge a new globally balanced order where its own interests and preferences can be better protected. Moreover, seen in the light of this Volume, Chinese perspective is an important aspect of better understanding general influence of emerging powers on the changing global order.

Further Readings

Aggarwal, V. K., & Newland, S. A. (Eds.). (2015). *Responding to China's rise: US and EU strategies*. New York: Spinger.

Benedikter, R., & Nowotny, V. (2014). *China's road ahead: Problems, Questions, perspectives*. New York: Springer.

Klieman, A. (Ed.). (2015). *Great powers and geopolitics international affairs in a rebalancing world*. New York: Springer.

Luttwak, E. N. 2012, . *The rise of China vs. the logic of strategy*. Harvard University Press/The Belknap London/Cambridge, MA.

Mearsheimer, J. (2001). *Tragedy of great power politics*. New York/London: W. W. Norton & Company.

Sapelli, G. (2015). *Global challenges and the emerging world order*. New York: Springer.

Shambaugh, D. (2016). *China's future*. Cambridge/Malden: Polity Press.

Youtube Videos

Jacques, M. (2011). *Understanding The Rise of China*. YouTube, online video, https://www.youtube.com/watch?v=oT8ki6ciopI

Nye, J. (2012). *The Rise of China and American Power*. YouTube, online video, https://www.youtube.com/watch?v=BwWT0kbYSZs

Mearsheimer, J. (2012). *Why China Cannot Rise Peacefully*. YouTube, online video, https://www.youtube.com/watch?v=CXov7MkgPB4

References

Anderlini, J. (2015). UK moves to join China-led Bank a surprise even to Beijing. *Financial Times*, March 27.

Asean.org. (2016). *External trade statistics*, viewed 4 December 2016. http://asean.org/?static_post=external-trade-statistics-3

Breslin, S. (2009). Understanding China's regional rise: Interpretations, identities and implications. *International Affairs (Royal Institute of International Affairs 1944-), 85*(4), 817–835.

Buzan, B. (2010). China in international society: Is "peaceful rise" possible? *The Chinese Journal of International Politics, 3*(1), 5–36.

Chen, J. (2015). China-US: Obstacles to a "New Type of Major Power Relation". *The Diplomat*, viewed 12 December 2016. http://thediplomat.com/2015/04/china-us-obstacles-to-a-new-type-of-major-power-relations/

Chung, J. H. (2016). The rise of China and East Asia: A new regional order on the horizon? *China Political Science Review, 1*, 47–59.

Cunningham, Philip J. (2014). The roar of the metaphorical lion. China Daily.com.cn, 7 May, viewed 10 June 2019, http://www.chinadaily.com.cn/opinion/2014-05/07/content_17489407. htm

Du, D., & Ma, Y. (2012). International geostrategic studies of China's rise. *Journal of World Regional Studies, 21*(1), 1–16.

Ferdinand, P. (2011). China and the developing world. In D. Shambaugh (Ed.), *Charting China's future: Domestic and international challenges* (pp. 86–94). Oxon/New York: Routledge.

Gao, C. (2014). China's rise, structural evolution of its neighboring regions and its strategic adjustment. *International Economic Review*, (2), 32–48.

Glaser, C. (2011). Will China's rise Lead to war? Why realism does not mean pessimism. *Foreign Affairs, 90*(2), 80–91.

Goswami, N. (2013). Power shifts in East Asia: Balance of power vs. liberal institutionalism. *Perceptions, XVIII*(1), 3–31.

Hudda, N. (2015). Interpreting the rise of China: Realist and liberalist perspectives. *E-International Relations*, viewed 20 June 2017, http://www.eir.info/2015/04/03/interpreting-the-rise-of-china-realist-and-liberalist-perspectives/

Johnston, A. L. (2003). Is China a status quo power? '*International Security, 27*(4), 5–56.

Kang, D. C. (2015). China, hegemony, and leadership in East Asia. In V. K. Aggarwal & S. A. Newland (Eds.), *Responding to China's rise: US and EU strategies* (pp. 27–49). New York: Springer.

Kirshner, J. (2010). The tragedy of offensive realism: Classical realism and the rise of China. *European Journal of International Relations, 18*(1), 53–75.

Li, X., & LI, J. (2015). One belt and one road' and the reshaping of China's geopolitical and Geoeconomic strategy. *Journal of World Politics and Economics*, (10), 31–59.

Liu, F. (2013a). Transition of international system and China's positioning. *Review of Foreign Affairs*, (2), 1–16.

Liu, J. (2013b). World structure and China's peripheral security. *Journal of World Economic and Politics*, (6), 4–24.

Lu, D. (2016). Global view and strategy of contemporary China. *Scientia Geographica Sinica*, (36), 483–490.

Luttwak, E. N. (2012). *The rise of China vs. the logic of strategy*. London/Cambridge, MA: The Belknap Press of Harvard University Press.

Lv, J. (2000). A comment on multipolarity trend of world situation. *Scientific Socialism*, (3), 36–40.

Mearsheimer, J. (2001). *Tragedy of great power politics*. New York/London: W. W. Norton & Company.

Mearsheimer, J. J.. (2014). *Can China rise peacefully?* Viewed 1 December 2016. http://nationalinterest.org/commentary/can-china-rise-peacefully-10204?page=3

Men, H. (2016). Building a new type of international relations: China's responsibility and undertakings. *World Economics and Politics*, (3), 4–25.

Overholt, H. W. (2002). *The rise of China: How economic reform is creating a new superpower*. New York: W. W. Norton & Company.

Qi, H., & Shi, Y. (2013). China's peripheral security challenges and its pan-peripheral diplomatic strategy. *World Economics and Politics*, (3), 25–46.

Qin, Y. (2004). World order and China's peaceful rise. *Journal of Party Building*, (5), 11–12.

Roy, D. (2009). China's democratised foreign policy. *Survival: Global Politics and Strategy, 51*(2), 25–40. https://doi.org/10.1080/00396330902860769.

Shambaugh, D. (2013a). *China goes global: The partial power*. Oxford/New York: Oxford University Press.

Shambaugh, D. (2013b). Tangled titans: Conceptualizing the U.S.-China relationship. In D. Shambaugh (Ed.), *Tangled titans: The United States and China* (pp. 3–26). Rowman & Littlefield: Lanham.

Shambaugh, D. (2016). *China's future*. Cambridge/Malden: Polity Press.

Shi, Y. (2007). The US power, the rise of China, and World order. *Journal of International Studies*, (3), 28–32.

Shi, Y. (2014). The rise of China and world order. *Contemporary International Relations*, (7), 32–34.

Shi, Y. (2015). Rising China: Political leadership, foreign policy, and Chineseness. In V. K. Aggarwal & S. A. Newland (Eds.), *Responding to China's rise: US and EU strategies* (pp. 99–110). New York: Springer.

Shirk, S. L. (2007). *China: Fragile superpower*. Oxford: Oxford University Press.

Song, J. (2016). *China-ASEAN bilateral trade volume reaching 400 billion US Dollar in 2015*, viewed 4 December 2016. http://www.chinadevelopment.com.cn/news/zj/2016/07/1062590.shtml

Sun, Y. (2016). AIIB, OBOR and Chinese view of international order. *Journal of Foreign Affairs*, (1), 1–30.

Wang, Y. (2011). Surpassing peaceful rising: The necessity and possibility of China's implementation of inclusive rising strategy. *World Economics and Politics*, (8), 140–160.

Weede, E. (2010). The capitalist peace and the rise of China: Establishing global harmony by economic interdependence. *International Interactions: Empirical and Theoretical Research in International Relations, 36*(2), 206–213.

Xia, L. (2003). China's peaceful rising and its new concept of international strategy. *Journal of International Studies*, (6), 31–35, 201.

Xie, T., & Page, B. (2010). Americans and the rise of China as a world power. *Journal of Contemporary China, 19*(65), 479–501.

Yan, X. (2010). An analysis of uncertainty in Sino-US relations. *World Economics and Politics*, (12), 4–30.

Yan, X. (2012). The shift of world center and the change of international system. *Journal of Contemporary Asia-Pacific Studies*, (6), 4–21.

Yan, X. (2016). Why is there no Chinese school of international relations theory? (Appendix 3). In X. Yan, D. A. Bell, E. Ryden, & S. Zhe (Eds.), *Ancient Chinese thought, modern Chinese power* (pp. 252–259). Princeton/Oxford: Princeton University Press.

Zhang, Q. (2016). The essence of diplomacy and the strategic choices of rising powers. *Journal of Foreign Affairs*, (4), 1–34.

Zhou, F. (2012). The rise of China, change in East Asia situation and development direction of east Asian order. *Journal of Contemporary Asia-Pacific Studies*, (5), 4–32.

Zhou, F. (2013). Driving force, paths and prospects of new type of great power relations between China and the US. *Journal of Contemporary Asia-Pacific Studies*, (2), 4–21.

Chapter 5
Russia in the Changing Global Order: Multipolarity, Multilateralism, and Sovereignty

André Gerrits

5.1 Introduction

The foreign policy of any country, including major powers like Russia, is determined by multiple variables, some of which it can influence, but others it cannot. Some factors are of a domestic nature, while others relate to the international environment. None of these variables are fixed. They are dynamic and change over time. Domestic conditions not only relate to the political nature of the regime (authoritarian, democratic) and to the state of the economy, but also to deeper structural conditions like geography, culture and history. Material and immaterial power resources can also be relevant, from energy reserves and other material assets as deployable military forces, to less tangible, political assets as the willpower, the effectiveness and the legitimacy of political leadership.

The weight of international factors is more difficult to assess. The most important variable is of course the same combination of material and immaterial power of other states, including their economic, military and other resources. Power is relative and relational. It is not only about measurable assets but also about the extent to which states are able to generate desired outcomes. A country can enhance its regional or global influence through membership of international organizations and alliances. If we consider these domestic and international variables, we recognize why and how Russia's foreign policies have fluctuated so dramatically since the early 1990s. We understand why the foreign policy of president Boris Yeltsin (1991–2000) differed strongly from that of his successor, Vladimir Putin. And its also explains why Putin's first two terms as president (2000–2004, 2004–2008), contrasted with his third (2012–2018) and fourth (from 2012) ones.

A. Gerrits (✉)
Institute for History, Leiden University, Leiden, The Netherlands
e-mail: a.w.m.gerrits@hum.leidenuniv.nl

© Springer Nature Switzerland AG 2020
M. O. Hosli, J. Selleslaghs (eds.), *The Changing Global Order*, United Nations University Series on Regionalism 17,
https://doi.org/10.1007/978-3-030-21603-0_5

Yeltsin's domestic power resources were extremely limited. During the early 1990s Russia was in a deep crisis. The political leadership was extremely divided. The popularity of the president was low, and the power of the government was weak. For his re-election in 1996 president Yeltsin had to turn for support to Russia's powerful oligarchs. During the first decade after the Cold War Yeltsin's realistic foreign policy options were few. The United States was exceptionally powerful, a hyper-power in an essentially unipolar world. The Zeitgeist was uniquely universalist. The world seemed one, dominated by a superior, self-confident 'West' (the United States and the countries of the European Union). One could argue that the leaders of Russia did not carry many more options than a pro-Western foreign policy—and that was precisely what Yeltsin did during the first years of his presidency, in the interest also of his domestic reform agenda.

A decade later, the situation had changed profoundly. In the spring of 2000, after a brief but powerfully orchestrated media campaign, Putin was elected president of Russia. Within a remarkably short period of time, he managed to consolidate his personal power and strengthen Moscow's control over the country, including the unruly North Caucasus. Putin subdued, exiled and in the case of Yukos CEO Mikhail Khodorkovsky imprisoned the same oligarchs that had saved Yeltsin's re-election a few years earlier. In comparison with Yeltsin's, Putin's leadership was practically undisputed, legitimate, and effective. Putin's rule also benefited from changes beyond its control. Global economic growth drove the price of energy up. Russia was able to pay off its international debt and to build a substantial financial reserve. The political confidence of Russia's elite increased proportionally with the price of a barrel of Ural crude oil. Meanwhile in the United States, the sense of triumphalism that had followed the Cold War, had suffered from the terrorist attacks on 9/11 and the two wars the United States chose to start but could not decisively win, in Afghanistan and Iraq. The deepest financial crisis since the Great Depression (from 2008) added to the problems of the West. It undermined the image and prestige of Western powers and accelerated their further relative decline. In Europe the global financial crisis hit not only individual countries, but also dangerously undermined the process, if not the very idea of European integration. Europe turned inward, struggling with a persistent economic malaise, rising Euro scepticism, and a deepening crisis of confidence.

Russia was not immune to adverse global economic developments. The world financial crisis plunged the country into a depression, from which it recovered quickly though. The volatility of energy prices impacted the state budget positively for most of the 2000s, but negatively from 2013/2014. Consecutive presidential terms by Putin and Dmitri Medvedev (2008–2012) achieved little to improve the structural weakness and vulnerability of Russia's economy. Politics is short-term business though, and the combination of favourable domestic and international conditions boosted Russia's self-confidence and positively impacted on the country's foreign policy and international prestige. Russia acquired a more prominent and politically autonomous position within a global order that became gradually less liberal and less dominated by the West.

This contribution will zoom in on two related aspects of Russia's foreign policies within a changing global context: ideas about multipolarity and multilateralism. It begins by analysing the particular worldview of Russia's leaders, and key aspects of Russian foreign policy, revisionism, pragmatism and sovereignty. Subsequently it discusses how Russia's specific idea of multipolarity and its strategy of multilateralism relate to the country's core foreign policy ambition, that is to revise the global order by strengthening its own power and sovereignty?

A few words about foreign policy decision-making in Russia seem in order. Although we do not necessarily know more about the inner workings of the Kremlin today, than we did in communist times, it may be safely assumed that among the multiple institutions involved in the decision-making process, the office of the president is key. The Constitution gives the president 'leadership of the foreign policy of the Russian Federation'. The president defines the basic direction of foreign and security policies, approves the foreign policy and security doctrines, serves as commander-in-chief, and so forth. As important as the institutions of the state in Russia are, they are trumped by individuals and informal networks. During the Medvedev presidency, foreign policy decision-making prerogatives partially shifted with Putin to the prime minister's office. From Putin's return to the presidency, formal and informal politics converged again. Bobo Lo (2015, 13) probably rightly asserts that in Russian foreign policy 'all big decisions go through Putin in some form or other'.

5.2 How Russia Sees the World

The core of the foreign policy perspective by the Russian political elite is the integral link between the country's domestic order (including the interests of its supreme elite), its foreign policies and its global status. The overall foreign policy ambition, as James Sherr (2013, 96) defines it, is 'the creation of an international environment conducive to the maintenance of its system of governance at home' (italics in original). And national interest means regime interest. 'Only when Russia is strong and stands firmly on its own feet, will it be treated with respect', Putin emphasized in a campaign article before the presidential elections of 2012 (Putin, February 2012). Russia projects adequate sovereign power, i.e. hard power, or she will be at the mercy of other powers, thereby putting the sheer survival of the Russian state at risk. In other words, Russia is a great power or Russia is not! It is this simple but urgent lesson that Russia's leadership and foreign policy elite learned from the collapse of the Soviet Union and the deep crisis of most of the 1990s. Derzhavnost is the crucial notion. Derzhavnost has no equivalent in either the English language or in the Western tradition. The French étatisme comes closest, but even étatisme does not have the deep cultural connotation and the unique flavour that derzhavnost has in the Russian language: the crucially important combination of a strong state and a great power.

Global politics is nasty, brutish, and anarchic. This typical Hobbesian or realist view of world politics is broadly shared among politicians and scholars in Russia (Sergunin 2004; Tsygankov and Tsygankov 2003). Russian scholarship copies the theoretical divides of Western, especially American international relations research: realism, liberalism, and constructivism. Typically Russian features mostly concern the direction of foreign policy, rather than the analysis of global politics. In the early years of international relations discourse in Russia after 1991, the distinction between 'Atlanticism' and 'Eurasianism' was especially influential. The former orientation favoured the pro-Western policies of president Yeltsin and his minister of Foreign Affairs Andrei Kozyrev; the latter, shared by a larger and more heterogeneous but initially less influential group of scholars, emphasized the distinctiveness of Russian civilization and the need to balance between East and West. These scholars prioritized relations with the countries of the former Soviet Union over partnership with the West. Two decades later, Atlanticism has almost disappeared from foreign policy discourse in Russia; whilst Eurasianism in all its diversity blossoms. Eurasianism has deeply penetrated official discourse. It serves as an ideological driver for strengthening Russian influence in the Eurasian region (the former Soviet space) and for supporting policy initiatives as the Eurasian Union—a fundamental component of Putin's foreign policy strategy of multipolarity and great power balancing.

In the Russian realist interpretation domestic and international security are firmly linked. The narrative remained over the years, but the analysis partially changed. Russian realists agreed that the gravest threat to Russia's security initially came from within, from the country's deep internal crisis (Sergunin 2004; Tsygankov and Tsygankov 2003). That danger has now been averted, and the focus has shifted to old/new threats from without: instability along Russia's borders, cross-bordering crime and terrorism and, conspicuously present during Putin's presidency, the dangers that emanate from US or Western unilateralism and interventionism.

If the predominance of the realist interpretation of global politics is not particularly controversial among Russia scholars, more contentious are the normative drivers of Russian foreign policy. Honour is often mentioned. Andrei Tsygankov (2012) combines realist and constructivist perspectives, and explains Russia's varying approaches towards the West—cooperation, defensive reaction, and assertiveness—by its profound sense of honour. Russia is deeply concerned about its position among the world's great powers. Apart from honour, related concepts as status (Larson and Shevchenko 2014) and prestige (Donaldson et al. 2014, 383) are also considered as powerful logics of Russian foreign policy. It is imperative to add, though, that immaterial factors have driven Russian foreign policy in different directions. Yeltsin's cooperative strategy and Putin's confrontational policies can both be explained by these leaders' desire to seek global political status and to be accepted as an equal partner. (Larson and Shevchenko 2010, 63).

5.3 Revisionism

A foreign policy that intends to reach global pluralism or multipolarity aims to change international power relations. Is Russia a revisionist power? And if so, what does Russia aim to revise, and what does it want to remain?

Russian foreign policy undeniably has a revisionist aspect. It comes from the combination of its former great power status (a feature, with interruptions, of Russia's international position and self-perception from the early nineteenth century), its collapse and retrenchment during the 1990s, and its economic growth, political revival and growing presence in the international system from the early 2000s. Russia has a complex relationship with the global liberal order that reigned supreme after the Cold War. The Soviet Union was the ultimate outsider, a challenger of the liberal order per se. Post-communist Russia was in a more ambiguous position. Its trajectory went from initial adjustment to the socioeconomic and international-political features of the liberal international order, to the increasing emphasis on the special and unique nature of Russia and its interests, a separate pole in a pluralistic world order.

Yeltsin's early attempts to integrate more closely with the West and to adapt to the dominant liberal order are now generally considered in Russia as naive and harmful. It was a brief, contested but still a defining moment in Russia's recent history. In the early 1990s Russia adopted the institutions of liberal democracy, but not its rules, its standards. Russia became the archetypical example of a democracy with adjectives, like illiberal, managed or authoritarian democracy, while turning increasingly authoritarian. (Levitsky and Way 2010) Yeltsin's predominantly pro-Western strategy did not survive his first presidential term. From the mid-1990s Russia's foreign policy approach moved into a different direction, less reactive and submissive, and more firmly geared towards Russia's apparently unique global position and corresponding interests and ambitions. This foreign policy change is generally associated with Yeltsin's minister of Foreign Affairs from 1996–1998, Yevgeny Primakov and his emphasis on multipolarity. Multipolarity remained a cornerstone of Russia's foreign strategy ever since. It coexisted with different policies, from moments of rapprochement and cooperation with the West, especially during Putin's first (2000–2004) and Medvedev's only presidential term (2008–2012), to periods of antagonism and conflict, especially after the Crimea crisis (2014). The persistence of multipolarity reflects how Russia continues to see itself as a relative outsider from the West. The civilizational distinction between Russia and the West is routinely used in Russian discourse today. There are few other countries where Huntington's idea of a 'clash of civilizations' (Huntington 1996) is as popular and as frequently referred to by policy-thinkers and policy-makers, as Russia.

Russia's perceived revisionism is often discussed in the context of another, related feature of the post-Cold War global order, that of emerging powers—a notion that is often associated with the BRICS countries.[1] Russia has never been 'just' an emerging power though, neither economically nor politically. In relative economic terms Russia is a declining rather than an emerging power. Its economy has grown considerably over the last two decades, though not as impressive as most other emerging economies, and with serious lapses. With a Gross Domestic Product of slightly over 1.331 billion US dollars, Russia reached thirteenth in 2015 in the World Bank global ranking, the smallest of the original BRIC countries and far behind the United States (18.036 billion USD) and China (11.007 billion USD) (World Bank 2015).

Russia's longer-term economic prospects are mixed, but they do not seem to justify its ranking among the emerging markets of today. If Russia can be considered as an emerging power at all, it is not for its economic but for its political potential. And it is also for political reasons that the Russian leadership values its affiliation with the BRICS community. The BRICS are not an organization, not an alliance, but essentially a series of agreements among sovereign states. Partnership with the other BRICS countries does not in any way limit Russia's independence, but it adds to its international reputation. BRICS provides Russia with an important platform to present its ideas and ambitions about global reform.

Public relations is an important aspect of Russia's BRICS strategy. Putin as a leader may appeal to people around the globe, but Russia as a country has a weak international reputation. The BRICS story is one of the instruments used by the Russian leadership to strengthen its brand name. Around the time of the formalization of political cooperation by the BRICS countries, the Foreign Policy Concept of the Russian Federation promised that Russia would commit 'even more explicitly' to formats such as the G8 and BRIC, and to actively use 'these and other informal ways and structures for dialogue'. (Foreign Policy Concept of the Russian Federation, 2008) In Russia's latest Foreign Policy Concept (December 2016), BRICS is ranked among the partners with which Russia intends to further expand its ties, together with the United Nations, the Group of 20, the Shanghai Cooperation Organization and the Cooperation between Russia, India and China (RIC). In this edition the G8, from which Russia was removed after the Crimea crisis, was understandably absent.

The future political relevance of BRICS depends on a series of factors on which Russia has only limited leverage. It is China and not Russia who defines the geostrategic and financial weight of BRICS. Generally, the strategic interests of the BRICS diverge considerably. South Africa and Brazil are regional powers. They cherish modest global ambitions. India, the soon-to-be most populous country in the world, has wider ambitions, but its security agenda is still mostly filled with regional issues, especially its relations with Pakistan and China. Russia is as much a re-emerging or 'recovering' power (MacFarlane 2006), as it is an emerging one. She is a great

---

[1] The BRICs notion was coined by Jim O'Neill (2001), Goldman Sachs. It refered to what he saw as the four major emerging market economies: Brazil, Russia, India, and China. The idea of BRICs became increasingly politicized, which was also the major reason why in 2010 the Republic of South Africa 'joined' this loose association of states, which from then on was known as BRICS.

power not only by virtue of her size, nuclear arsenal, and energy resources, but also because she is the successor state to the super power Soviet Union. Russia inherited its most prestigious symbol of great power status, its permanent seat in the UN Security Council, from its predecessor. Russia is deeply involved in the political and economic architecture of the post-Cold War world. Russia, and the same goes for China, have benefited greatly from the wave of globalization from the early 1990s. In short, Russia's relationship with the West and with the liberal order that the United States built is too deep and too multifaceted to simply define Russia as a fully revisionist power. Russian foreign policy has evident conservative traits. Russia is a revisionist and a status-quo power. Russia has much to defend in the current global order. As Richard Sakwa (2016, 6) puts it, Russia is a neo-revisionist power, 'challenging the practices but not the principles of international order'. Russia's strategy is not so much about changing the international order, as it is about strengthening its role within this order.

5.4 Pragmatism

The Putin leadership consistently labels Russia's foreign policy as pragmatic, and many scholars tend to agree (Donaldson et al. 2014, 363; Kuchins and Zevelev 2012; Rowe and Torjesen 2009). In its dealings with other powers Russia makes little distinction on domestic order, political ideology or international orientation. For most of its post-communist history, Russia maintained good relations with Western democracies, non-Western countries, including most emerging powers, and outliers, like Syria and Iran. Did the annexation of the Crimea and the intervention in the Syrian war represent a break with Russia's relatively pragmatic and partial revisionist foreign policies?

Russia's decision to militarily intervene in the Crimea and to go to war in Syria came unexpectedly and they were crucial moments in Russia's recent foreign policy trajectory. Post-Communist Russia has not been a particularly war-prone country. Over the past two decades Russia has been much less involved in large-scale military conflict than the US and some of its allies, and never beyond the borders of the former Soviet Union. The intervention in Syria was a novelty, risky, and with unforeseen military and diplomatic consequences, but the political rationale of it matched with the longer-term ambitions of the Putin leadership (Allison 2013). The intervention reflected various key ambitions of Russian foreign policy. It qualified Russia to play a crucial role in the future of Syria, if not of the Middle East as a whole. It confirmed Russia's international presence, and as such it was another step towards the global multipolar order that Russia's aspires. And paradoxically it strongly supported the claim by the Russian leadership that external intervention and regime change (examples: Iraq 2003 and Libya 2011) were largely responsible for the violent chaos and conflict in the Middle East. Russia's intervention in the Syrian civil war was therefore aimed at the exact opposite: to save the Assad regime and to prevent the imminent collapse of the Syrian state. And it speaks to the sophistication of Russia's diplomacy that the negative consequences of Russia's intervention remained limited. Russia remains on relatively good terms with most countries in the region, including traditional adversaries as Israel and Iran, the Gulf States, and organizations as Hezbollah (Phillips 2016). Only relations with the United States and its European allies, whose relative passivity had encouraged Russia's to intervene, further soured. They reached a new low, a year after Russia's annexation of the Crimea.

The Crimea in the spring of 2014 was not the first instance of Russian uninvited military intervention in a neighbouring country, a former Soviet republic. In 1992 Russian troops had interfered in the armed conflict between Moldova and the break-away Transnistrian territory. As yet, they haven't left. In August 2008, Moscow sent troops into Georgia, after hostilities between Georgian government forces and Russia-backed local militias had broken out in the separatist region of South-Ossetia. Russia supported the quasi-independence of South-Ossetia and Abkhazia and its subsequent policies towards the Georgian regions came close to actual annexation (Gerrits and Bader 2015). But the military intervention in the Crimea, the referendum on its future status, and the formal incorporation of the peninsula into Russia was an even more blatant violation of international law. Never before had Russia formally annexed part of the territory of one of its neighbours. But was it an irrational move, a deviation from Russia's relatively pragmatic foreign policy tradition?

First, the annexation of the Crimea cannot be measured by foreign policy criteria only. There have been few foreign policy issues that were so much driven by domestic sentiments and concerns as the relationship with Ukraine and the future of the Crimea. And a from a domestic policy perspective, the occupation and annexation of the Crimea yielded significant profits. It further boosted the popularity of the Putin presidency.

Secondly, the diplomatic fall-out of the annexation of the Crimea was serious, but it remained mostly limited to Russia's relations with the West. Beyond the United States, Europe and its allies, the annexation of the Crimea had little diplomatic repercussions. It may have longer-term consequences though in Russia's relations with some of the countries in the former Soviet space. Russia's friends in the region showed only lukewarm support for the annexation of the Crimea (Dragneva 2016; Kropatcheva 2016). The reaction by Belarus, Armenia and Kazakhstan was not very different from their earlier refusal to recognize the independence of Abkhazia and South-Ossetia. Russian belligerence in its geopolitical environment unnerves the other former Soviet republics, especially those with substantial Russian minorities, like Kazakhstan.

Finally, returning to domestic issues again, the annexation of the Crimea occurred within a context of rising nationalism in Russia. The conservative and nationalist turn which Russian politics took after Putin's return to the presidency in 2012 is generally explained as the response by a cornered regime. Putin apparently felt threatened by mass protests against the outcome of the parliamentary and presidential elections in 2011–2012, and turned to nationalist rhetoric to boost his popular support. Nationalism played a classical role. It was supposed to provide the ruling elite with an instrument to raise its legitimacy, without addressing the protestors' real political grievances. Given also the rising tide of nationalism in Russia, the annexation of the Crimea was expected to receive strong support in Russian society, and it apparently did.

However, the new nationalism in Russia can also be explained differently, without questioning its strongly functionalist nature. It was the absence, rather than the presence of radical, state-sponsored nationalism which had distinguished political developments in Russia since the early 1990s. The political relevance of nationalism in post-communist Russia had remained remarkably low, given the deep economic crisis during most of the decade, the country's weakly developed political and social institutions, in combination with the unpopularity of the Yeltsin leadership and the relative openness of its political arena (Lieven 1999). Theoretically, post-communist Russia was an ideal candidate for Jack Snyder's thesis that early and partial democratization easily leads to nationalist conflict (Snyder 2000).

In this context, the rise of nationalism in Russian politics could also be interpreted not as a move into a radical or extremist direction, but as a 'catching-up' development, or perhaps as a 'return to normalcy' (Laruelle 2010). The Putin leadership allegedly perceives the relatively weak sense of national identity (Riasanovsky 2005, 231) among the Russian population as a political liability. As Putin put it in September 2013 before an international meeting of Russia specialists: '(Russia needs) to preserve (its) identity in a rapidly changing world (…) It is impossible to move forward without spiritual, cultural and national self-determination (…)' Putin stressed the civic, as against the ethnic nature of state sponsored nationalism. 'Nationalists must remember that by calling into question our multi-ethnic character (…), means that we are starting to destroy our genetic code. In effect, we will begin to destroy ourselves.' (Putin, September 19, 2013).

5.5   Multipolarity

Independence and self-determination are the most frequently professed norms of foreign policy by the Russian leadership. A 'highly restrictive interpretation of domestic jurisdiction and sovereign rights', as MacFarlane (2006, 49) puts it, determines Russia's interpretation of global politics and international relations. Sovereignty and non-intervention, or 'the primacy of international law' as the Russian leaders prefer to phrase it, is the crucial link between their domestic and foreign policies. It is the major logic of Russia's ambition to create a multipolar, a pluralist global order.

The Russian leadership claims to unequivocally support the principle of sovereignty, territoriality and non-intervention, but it does not always act accordingly. Russia rejects any interference into its own internal affairs and neither is it very demanding about the domestic political order, ideological viewpoints or even foreign policy orientations of its international partners. Different from the United States and some West European countries, and from the Soviet Union of course,

Russia has never been seriously engaged in the promotion abroad of its political values or domestic system. But there is one important exception, the countries of the Former Soviet Union. Russia is strongly focused on the internal and international developments of its neighbouring countries. Only in its 'Near Abroad' has Russia intervened militarily in the internal affairs of other countries, also for reasons of regime-change or to defend an authoritarian political order.[2]

Sovereignty and self-determination are also the cornerstones of what can be considered as Russia's main foreign policy ambition: a pluralistic or multipolar global order. In Russia's view multipolarity represents a global system, which consists of different geopolitical poles, each dominated by one or more leading powers. These powers are sovereign and equal, and they share a common responsibility for global peace and stability. Russia is meant to be one of these poles. Multipolarity appears in every major foreign policy document since the Cold War. It is Russia's answer to the post-Cold War global dominance of the United States and its tendency towards unilateralism, which Russia considers as a danger to global peace and as a threat to its own security.

Scholarship differs on the relationship between global multipolarity and stability. Some consider multipolarity as a relatively benign system, wherein states compete and cooperate with each other (Donaldson et al. 2014). Other scholars stress the geopolitical clarity and relative predictability of a bipolar system. Fewer actors are involved, and although their mutual relations may be antagonistic, they are also in balance (Mearsheimer 1990). Not surprisingly, most Western politicians, pundits and public opinion tend to associate current changes towards a more plural world order with uncertainty and danger. It is associated with the decline of the West and the emergence of new powers. Russia draws the opposite conclusion. Change towards multipolarity is seen as a prerequisite for global peace and security. It is the refusal by the West to accept the emerging reality of multipolarity and their attempts to contain other centres of power, which leads to growing global turbulence and insecurity (Foreign Policy Concept 2016).

Russian discourse on multipolarity has changed over time. During Yeltsin's first presidential term, America was too strong, and Russia's ambition to cooperate with the West still too powerful to seriously consider multipolarity as a realistic foreign policy option. This came from the second half of the 1990s, out of frustration with the continuing unilateralism of the United States and the meagre benefits that its pro-Western, accommodating foreign policy had brought Russia. President Putin never returned to Yeltsin's compliant policies, but especially in the early 2000s, after the terrorist attacks on New York and Washington, he adopted a relatively forthcoming and understanding attitude towards the West. He accepted the necessity of rapprochement and of cooperation with the United States. Russia's benign position

---

[2] At the time of writing reports about Russia's interference in the presidential elections in the United States are still too indeterminate to draw conclusions on the extent of involvement of the Russian leadership or on the strategic nature of the intervention.

lasted less than 3 years. The turning point was the American invasion of Iraq in March 2003. Throughout the 2000s, and especially after the crisis in Ukraine, which Russia blamed on the offensive policies by the United States and the European Union, the approach to multipolarity further developed; from a statement of purpose, it became a statement of reality. In Russia's 2016 Foreign Policy Concept multipolarity is presented as a geopolitical fact, with Russia as one of its 'civilization poles'. 'The world is currently going through fundamental changes, related to the emergence of a multipolar international system', the policy concept states. 'New centres of economic and political power' have arisen. 'Global power and development (…) is shifting towards the Asia-Pacific Region, eroding the global economic and political dominance of the traditional Western powers. The cultural and civilizational diversity of the world and the existence of multiple development models are clearer than ever.'

This reference to civilizational diversity brings in another aspect of Russia's multipolarity, namely its struggle against key ideational aspects of Western-led globalization. Russia's response to globalization is almost as diverse as the reality of globalization itself is. As an energy-exporting power Russia benefited enormously from the economic dynamism and deepening interconnectedness that are often associated with globalization. But globalization is also problematic for Russia.

As the loser of the Cold War, but also as an actor still in possession of significant power resources and thus suspended between great and middling power status, (Russia) has had to rebuild its political and cultural identity, its external security, and its domestic as well as international legitimacy in a situation characterized not only by the turbulence of the immediate historical past but also by the pressure exerted by the economic, political, and cultural forces of Western globalization. (Hedetoft and Blum 2008, 21).

With the brief exception of its first years of independence, Russia tried to resist unwelcome aspects of political, cultural and economic globalization, including the predominance of (Western) liberal democracy, the free market, the qualification of national sovereignty, in short: liberal internationalism. The Foreign Policy Concept of 2000 talked about Russia's firm intention to not only build multipolarity, but to also help to shape the 'ideology' behind it. (National Security Concept of the Russian Federation 2000). The 'national idea' that Putin has been pursuing since his return to the presidency in 2012, in combination with his emphasis on the supreme role of the state in Russia's economic development, are the key components of this ideological endeavour. Russia plays an important part in the proliferation of anti-liberal nationalism and state capitalism (Kurlantzick 2016), the two major ideational alternatives to globalization as we know it.

5.6 Multilateralism

Multipolarity and multilateralism are closely related in Russia's foreign policy strategy. Russia's multilateralism serves its ambition of multipolarity. Alternatively, the multilateralism that Russia prefers can only be fully realized in the context of a pluralistic and multipolar world order.

Multilateralism relates to states' policies towards regional and global institutions and organizations. Institutions stand for the rules and regulations which specify how states should interact with each other. Organizations give theses institutions an administrative structure and a degree of operational autonomy. Multilateralism enables countries to work together in a sustained and institutionalized manner, and it differs from integration, which involves the transfer and pooling of countries' sovereignty (Rowe and Torjesen 2009, 1). Few international organizations have sufficient means to enforce their member states to abide by the rules. Generally, the level of states' compliance depends on the extent to which states wish and are able to comply or not.

International Relations theorists differ on the relevance of international organizations in global politics (Hurd 2011). Not surprisingly, given their strongly state-centric view on foreign relations and global politics, realists tend to question the agency of international institutions and organizations. Generally, international organizations reflect the distribution of power at the global or regional level, John Mearsheimer (1994/95, 7) argues. They are based on the self-interest of powerful states and they have little autonomous impact on the behaviour of states. The role and relevance of international organizations is therefore determined by why and how states use them. And states 'use' them for a variety of self-serving purposes, as instruments to enhance their share of global or regional power, as forums for policy coordination, bargaining or the diffusion of norms and ideas, or as a means to raise their global or regional prestige. To put it simply, international institutions and organizations are what states make of them. Other scholars, especially liberal institutionalists, attach a wider importance to multilateralism.

Liberal institutionalists see the possibility of truly collaborative policies among states, which may produce 'common goods' that go beyond the interests and the capabilities of individual states (Hurd 2011; Rowe and Torjesen 2009, 2). They argue that realists underestimate the utility of international organizations, also to more powerful states. But even most institutionalist would agree that state interests reign supreme. In the end, states define the real-world significance of international institutions and organizations: 'International organizations (…) exist only because states that have created them, and their powers apply only to the extent that states consent to them' (Hurd 2011, 10).

Given the direction of Russian foreign policy in general, it is to be expected that Russia's approach towards international institutions and organizations comes close to the realist interpretation. In the perception of the Russian leadership, multilateralism should reflect Russia's sovereignty, its regional or global status and its special global role and responsibility. Russia's approach towards multilateralism is generally perceived as instrumental rather than principled. It largely depends on the power and influence that Russia is able to wield within the variety of multilateral arrangements it participates in. Bobo Lo (2015, 73) talks about Russia's 'qualified' multilateralism. Russia 'has observed the letter of multilateralism, while often ignoring its spirit.' Russia's instrumentalist attitude is not unique, but what makes Russia stand out, according to Lo, is the degree to which it exploits its position in multilateral organizations to project its influence, its perceived great power status. Robert Legvold also emphasizes the instrumental nature of Russia's multilateralism. For Russia's leaders multilateralism is not so much a foreign policy norm or principle, but a tool, a means of 'levelling the playing field' (Legvold 2009, 30). Other scholars accentuate the temporal shifts in Russia's multilateralism, from an essentially defensive posture during the 1990s to a more offensive one from the mid-2000s (Bond 2015, 189). Initially Russia aimed to use international organizations to restrain the West, especially in the Kosovo crisis in 1999–2000, and the interventions in Iraq in 2003. This strategy proved largely unsuccessful. Russia lacked the institutional power to effectively influence US decision-making through international institutions and organizations. Later, a more assertive and confident Russia used the same multilateral institutions to legitimize its own international ideas and unilateral behaviour, especially its war against Georgia in 2008 and the annexation of the Crimea in 2014.

More in detail, what are the key features of Russia's multilateralism, or 'multilateral diplomacy' as it is mostly referred to in Russian foreign policy discourse? First, Russia is a big but also 'lonely' power (Shevtsova 2010). Russia is not a member of any true alliance, except in its own neighbourhood. It has few real enemies or friends. There may not be many compelling reasons for Russia to ally up with or against other countries, but the country even seems reluctant to do so. In the immediate wake of the annexation of the Crimea, at a meeting of the National Security Council, president Putin explained it as follows: 'Russia is fortunately not a member of any alliance. This is also a guarantee of our sovereignty. Any nation that is part of an alliance, gives up part of its sovereignty.' (Putin, July 2014b).

Russia may be a lonely, but it is not an isolationist power. It is present in a wide range of international institutions and organizations, albeit it not, with a few exceptions, very prominently. Russia seeks cooperation, if possible on its own terms, but not integration. Integration would be in conflict with the higher goals of sovereignty and independence. In terms of real and effective engagement, Russia emphasizes a variant of multilateralism, 'great power multilateralism', which facilitates international coordination by leading powers, without questioning the primacy of national sovereignty.

Russia is especially eager to join influential, prestigious 'great power' clubs. The UN Security Council and the G8 (from which it was excluded after the annexation of the Crimea) are the prime examples. Permanent membership of the Security Council provides Russia with the influence and prestige that no other international organization can. It puts Russia on par with the United States and China. Russia understands international 'high' politics predominantly in 'plutocratic' or 'oligarchic' terms. (Lo 2015, 41) Global politics is all about relations among great powers.

For Russia, this is more than a statement of fact; it comes close to a normative assertion. Great powers have a special responsibility to ensure global stability. 'Russia attaches great importance to ensuring the sustainable manageability of global development', the Foreign Policy Concept of 2016 emphasizes, 'which requires collective leadership by the major states that should be representative in geographic and civilisational terms and fully respect the central and coordinating role of the UN' (Foreign Policy Concept of the Russian Federation 2016). Russia's ideas come close to the nineteenth century notion of the 'Concert of Europe'. Deeply shocked by the turbulences of the Napoleonic Wars (1803–15) the major leaders of Europe agreed on a mutual arrangement that would help to guarantee the stability on the continent. The Concert 'had a deeply conservative sense of mission', the historian Mark Mazower (2013, 5) opines. 'Based on respect for kings and hierarchy, it prioritized order over equality, stability over justice.' One should not stretch the comparison too far, but the parallel with Russia's approach to the role of great powers today is hard to avoid. 'Management by Great Powers' (Makarychev and Morozov 2011) may be fundamentally different from multilateralism as it is often understood, but it closely resembles Russia's preferred form of multilateralism. Given the complexity, the interdependence and the volatility of today's world, Russia's Great Power multipolarity does not seem very realistic though. Greater powers do not easily control or contain smaller states anymore. The restrictive and disciplinary decades of the Cold War are behind us.

Secondly, depending on its relative power capacity, Russia has a preference for bilateral over multilateral relations. The default position is multilateralism when possible, bilateralism or unilateralism when necessary. Russia's policies towards the European Union offer a good example. Moscow judged the EU's early strategy of integration (cooperation) through transformation as overly patronizing. What Brussels presented as partnership, Moscow perceived as an asymmetric, hierarchical relationship, which denigrated its status and questioned its sovereignty (Prozorov 2006, ix). From the end of the 1990s, the EU changed its strategy—not so much because of Russia's concerns, but because of a lack of results. The EU cut back on its transformative objectives. It finally aimed to deal with the Russia that was, not with the Russia that it wished to be. EU-Russian relations are deep and diverse, but they have always been problematic, especially at the highest political level. The European Union remains a strange animal to Russia. '(W)ithin the sovereign logic the very entity of the EU is conceived as problematic', as the Russian scholar Sergei Prozorov (2006, 81) phrases it, 'unsubsumable under any conventional definition, which makes dealing with "regular" foreign policy actors a preferable option.' If possible, Russia follows a divide-and-rule policy towards the EU. It is in its self-perceived interest to prevent a common European Russia strategy, whether it concerns energy security, sanctions or Europe's neighbourhood policy. Russia prefers to work with the EU member states on an individual basis, bilaterally.

Thirdly, Russia has a strong aversion against multilateralism in the sphere of political values and other normative issues, especially when they reach into the domestic affairs of countries. This approach is clearly reflected in Moscow's changed attitude towards the Organization of Security and Cooperation in Europe (OSCE) (Alberts 2016).

During the first phase of the Yeltsin presidency the OSCE was considered as the preferred institutional core of a post-Cold War European security architecture, as an inclusive alternative to NATO. The OSCE developed however in a direction that Russia did not want, but was unable to stop. As Russia saw it, the OSCE, especially through its various semi-autonomous institutions like the Office of Democratic Institutions and Human Rights (ODIHR), increasingly intervened into the internal affairs of its member states, Russia and the other countries in the former Soviet space in particular. The OSCE reported critically on the war against Chechnya and on elections in various post-communist countries. In the perception of Russia, Western countries had turned the OSCE into an instrument aimed against Russia and its interests in the region. Russia initially attempted to change the geographic and thematic direction of OSCE activities, but when that proved futile, it engaged in a more successful strategy of obstruction, of 'obstructive multilateralism' as it were. It succeeded to effectively marginalize the OSCE as an all-European institution.

After the annexation of the Crimea and the military conflict in the eastern part of Ukraine, Russia partly reconsidered its position towards the OSCE. It hesitantly accepted the presence of OSCE monitors in the region and participated in negotiations within the OSCE framework about the future status of eastern Ukraine. Lack of organizational alternatives, apart from summit meetings with the leaderships of Ukraine, France, Germany and the United States, and especially Russia's prevailing influence on the conflict (its enhanced 'institutional power' and agenda-setting capacity in the OSCE), explains Russia's more cooperative attitude.

Fourthly, there is a range of partial explanations why Russia's multilateralism is instrumental and conditional, rather than normative and principled. The bottom-line is power, or rather the lack thereof. To understand Russia's multilateralism and its approach towards international organizations 'institutional power' as defined by Michael Barnett and Raymond Duval (2005, 51) is a crucial variable. Institutional power is the extent to which states have the capacity to influence other states in indirect ways, especially through the rules and procedures of formal and informal institutions. In comparison with the United States, architect and linchpin of the liberal global order, with other leading Western powers, and increasingly also with China, Russia's capability to influence international organizations, and through these organizations the behaviour of other states is rather limited. Russia can adapt to the global order, which it did after the collapse of the Soviet Union, or it can try to balance within institutions (UN Security Council) or between institutions (OSCE versus NATO; the BRICS' New Development Bank versus the World Bank and the International Monetary Fund). But to challenge the liberal order, Russia needs more powerful partners, China in particular.

Also in the UN at crucial moments, Russia lacked the capacity to steer Security Council deliberations into the preferred direction. In the 1990s Russia repeatedly attempted to either prevent or reduce sanctions against Sadam Hussein's Iraq. It was of no avail. Russia saved Iran from sanctions a number of times, but eventually it concurred with the tougher approach by the United States and its European allies.

Russia's relations with Iran are important for economic and geopolitical reasons. After the US invasion had effectively destroyed Iraq as a regional power, Iran began to play an increasingly prominent role in the wider Middle East, its influence reaching as far as Central Asia and the Caucasus. Russia assisted Iran in the development of its nuclear industry, including the construction of the Busher power plant, and benefited from its revenues. Still, Russian-Iranian relations have always remained challenging. Russia may have had its own reasons to worry about Iran's nuclear ambitions, but in this dossier relations with its Western partners clearly trumped its links with Iran. Russia's equal participation made the P5 + 1 (Germany), plus the European Union, an acceptable format for nuclear negotiations with Iran. In 2015 all parties agreed on the Iran Nuclear Deal Framework, a reduction and redirection of Tehran's nuclear programme in exchange for the lifting of sanctions. The deal was one of the few complex and controversial agreements that Russia, the United States and the Europe Union reached since the annexation of the Crimea. In 2018 the United States abandoned the deal. It should be added that over the years neither Iran nor Iraq proved particularly grateful for Russia's efforts. At crucial moments they persisted in their uncompromising and confrontational behaviour, also against the expressed interests of the Russian Federation.

In March 2011 Russia abstained in the UNSC on the vote which established a no-fly zone over Libya, but it was ineffective to prevent Western powers from using the resolution as a go-ahead for a full military operation against the Qaddafi regime. It is not in Russia's or in any other permanent member state's interest to use its veto-power too frequently. Vetoes in the Security Council are 'rare' (Ferdinand 2013, 4). States neither want to isolate themselves, nor do they want to risk the devaluation of the Security Council as the world's highest, most powerful centre of decision-making. So when it comes to a vote in the Security Council, which in itself does not occur very often, Russia and China, who frequently coordinate their positions, rather abstain from voting than veto unwelcome decisions (Ferdinand 2013). All the more remarkable were their three vetoes in 2011 and 2012 against resolutions that called upon the Bashar al-Assad regime in Syria to refrain from military violence against its own people and, later, to step down. The vetoes were indicative of the deep aversion by the two powers against intervention into the domestic affairs of other countries, whether sanctioned by the Security Council or not.

And finally, and most importantly, when discussing Russia's engagement with multilateralism, a distinction needs to be made between its general strategy and its approach towards the countries in its immediate geopolitical environment, the countries of the Former Soviet Union.

5.7 Russia in its Geopolitical Neighbourhood

The post-Soviet countries have never been just 'abroad' for Russia. Referred to during the 1990s as the 'Near Abroad', Russia has always claimed special responsibility for its geopolitical environment (Donaldson et al. 2014; Lo 2015; Sherr 2013). Russia believes to have 'a legitimate right of intervention', as Lo (2015, xxi) puts it.

Different foreign policy rules apply. Russia's special relationship with the former Soviet republics not only stems from conventional security concerns, but also from a sense of entitlement that is based on a perceived common history and culture, and on Russia's predominant position in the region. In the wake of the war with Georgia, president Medvedev presented the five principles of Russian foreign policy, including the 'privileged interests' that Russia claims in regions, where 'there are countries with which we have traditionally had friendly cordial relations, historically special relations. We will work very attentively in these regions and develop these friendly relations with these states, with our close neighbours.' When asked if these regions bordered on Russia, Medvedev answered: 'Certainly the regions bordering (on Russia), but not only them' (The Economist, 1 September 2008).

Developments in the countries of the FSU, in Russia increasingly referred to as Eurasia, can have an immediate impact on the security of the Russian Federation. The former Soviet space is a geopolitically contested and volatile part of the world. The countries border areas of deep instability and conflict: the Southern Caucasus, the Middle East, Afghanistan and Pakistan. The FSU forms a shared neighbourhood with other major power, with the European Union in the West, and with China in Central Asia. Arguably Russia has extensive and legitimate interests in the region, not only traditional security interests, like political stability and controllable borders, but also economic interests, especially in the sphere of energy and energy transport.

Russia's policies in Eurasia go beyond traditional security interests though. They should be seen as parts of a larger geopolitical project. Russia aspires to create a strong, dynamic regional order under its own leadership, not only to serve its own economic interests, but also to build a block towards the global multipolar order it envisions.

Scholars present different interpretations of Russia's multilateral strategy towards its neighbouring countries. Legvold (2009, 32–33) talks about 'multilateralism in concentric circles'. He distinguishes between Russia's different but interrelated strategies towards the Former Soviet Union, other neighbouring countries, and the wider world. Julian Cooper opines that Russia's policy in the region cannot be characterized as one of multilateralism, not even in its 'great power form'. He prefers 'hegemonic bilateralism'. (Cooper 2009, 179) Another distinction is between reactive and competitive Russian multilateralism in the former Soviet space. (Allison 2004) Reactive multilateralism is primarily aimed against growing inroads by Western states and institutions in the region (especially affiliation with NATO and the European Union); while competitive multilateralism is focussed on building multilateral institutions which serve Russia's (and allegedly the other countries') political and economic interests. Both variants are present in Russia's policies towards the Former Soviet Union, agrees also Stina Torjesen. Although, as she adds, 'the timing of Russia's multilateral activities strongly points to the former' (Rowe and Torjesen 2009, 17; Torjesen 2009). Russian multilateralism in Eurasia is particularly aimed at keeping others out, she concludes. And Putin apparently agrees. Speaking to a conference of Russian ambassadors in July 2004, he warned against the risk of a 'vacuum' in international relation: '(were) Russia to abstain from an active policy in the Commonwealth of Independent States or even embark on a unwarranted pause, this would inevitably lead to nothing else but other, more active, states resolutely filling this political space' (Quoted in Adomeit 2007, 22).

Bobo Lo's (2015, 128) stresses that Russias policies towards the countries of the FSU have generally been more pragmatic than messianic, more defensive than offensive, and rather declining in terms of power and influence than increasing (See also Donaldson et al. 2014, 383; Rowe and Torjesen 2009, 14). Given the persistency with which the Russian leadership has expressed the priority of deepening bilateral and multilateral ties in the region, the actual level of integration is indeed disappointing. Too little resolve on the part of Russia cannot be the explanation, although also in its relations with other Eurasian countries Russia has shown more enthusiasm for bilateral over multilateral forms of cooperation. It is hesitancy by the other countries to join or further develop Russian-led organizations that mostly accounts for the lack of progress. The other republics are careful to engage too deeply in formalized cooperation with Russia. Experience with Russia's (past) imperial behaviour and its overbearing weight among the former Soviet republics are the major explanatory factors. Membership of multilateral organizations in the Former Soviet Union fluctuated with the degree to which the member states' leaderships felt the aspiration and had the capacity to widen or narrow their distance from Russia.

In December 1991 ten former Soviet republics joined Russia in the Commonwealth of Independent States (CIS). The CIS was the first multilateral institution in the former Soviet space. The CIS served its purpose as a means of policy coordination between Russia and the other members during the hectic and volatile times around the collapse of the Soviet Union, but it never developed into a real multilateral organization. Throughout the years, the share in world trade by the countries of the CIS remained marginal (with the exception of Russia's energy and arms exports) and mutual trade even decreased (Cooper 2009, 167). Security issues remained outside of the CIS framework. They are mostly discussed within the Collective Security Treaty Organization. The CSTO was established in May 1992 and has partly overlapping membership with the Shanghai Cooperation Agreement (SCO), which also includes major non-regional powers like China.

The first steps towards a free trade regime or customs union in the Former Soviet Union (FSU) were taken in October 2000. Russia, Belarus, Kazakhstan, Kyrgyzstan and Tajikistan established the Eurasian Economic Community. In 2006 they were joined by Uzbekistan. Moldova and Ukraine required an observer status in May 2002, followed in 2003 by Armenia. In the ambition of the Russian leadership the Eurasian Economic Community would progress towards a single economic space, a common market, and eventually a full supranational organization. And indeed, through various organizational stages and in different membership constellations, the Eurasian Economic Community eventually developed into a Eurasian Economic Union or just Eurasian Union, starting from January 1, 2015. In May 2014, Russia, Kazakhstan and Belarus (Armenia and Kyrgyzstan would join the Union later that year) signed the Treaty on the Eurasian Economic Union in Astana. At the occasion, Putin described the founding of the Union as an 'epoch-making' event (Putin, May 2014a).

It is too early to tell if the Eurasian Union represents a qualitatively new form of cooperation in the post Soviet space. The establishment of the Union was accompanied by reassurances, by Putin, and emphasises, especially by the Kazakh leader Nursultan Nazarbayev, that the treaty would neither limit nor violate any of the signatories' sovereignty. An early assessment of the institutional framework of the Union confirms that it is only weakly supranational and with minor infringements on the national authority of its members. The mode of decision-making remains firmly intergovernmental, and centred at the highest level of state authority (Dragneva 2016).

The Shanghai Cooperation Organization (SCO) was established in 2001, when Uzbekistan joined the member states of the original 'Shanghai Five' (1996), Russia, China, Kazakhstan, Kyrgyzstan, and Tajikistan. The SCO is different from any other multilateral organization in the former Soviet space, because it includes China. Russia and China seem to have partly diverging ambitions for the organization though. Whereas China sees the SCO primarily as a means to expand its economic influence in the Eurasian region; Russia positions it within the larger security context of its relationship with its powerful neighbour (Donaldson et al. 2014, 290). For the Russian leadership, security cooperation with China is a highly valuable component of its balance-of-power approach, its global multipolarity, which is primarily envisioned against the United States, its allies and their liberal world order.

Despite these diverging ambitions and notwithstanding Russia's historically unique junior position vis-à-vis China, the Russian leadership has repeatedly expressed its great appreciation of the SCO. Putin called the SCO his 'preferred model of multilateralism.' (Cited by Torjesen 2009, 182).

The key difference between Russia's engagement with multilateralism in general and its strategy towards the former Soviet republics is Russia's institutional power. The FSU is the only part of the world where Russia wields significant institutional power. Still, the discourse on special responsibilities and vital interests are not necessarily indicative of the level of influence which Russia is able to exercise over the countries in its neighbourhood. Russia's influence in the region remains contested, by outside powers like China and the European Union, but mostly by the partner-countries themselves. Mutual relations between Russia and the other republics of the former Soviet Union are diverse (as does their importance for Russia) and they are volatile. Some countries have generally been close to Russia, also for lack of alternatives (Armenia, Belarus, Tajikistan, and with reservations Kazakhstan); others keep their distance (Uzbekistan), and others again vacillated, pulling Russia closer and then pushing it away again, largely conditioned by the preferences of their leaderships (Georgia and Ukraine).

Paradoxically, Russia's predominance among the former Soviet republics has mixed consequences. It enables Russia to claim a leading role in the area, but it also makes the other countries cautious not to give up too much of their sovereignty. Russia's population is almost five times bigger than the numbers of the three other members of the Eurasian Union combined. Russia's area size is almost eight times larger. Russia's GDP is seven times bigger. At its inception, the Eurasian Union is a much more heterogeneous club of nations than the European Economic Community was in 1957. At that time, as the largest member of the Community, Germany's population share and GDP were 32% and 40% of the EEC's total, respectively.[3] Russia is simply too big and too powerful to be a comfortable partner for the countries in its neighbourhood.

5.8   Conclusion

The worldview of the current Russian leadership is simple and straightforward: Russia is a great power or Russia is not. With a reference to Russia's size and location, its unique history and culture, and massive economic and military resources Putin claims a prominent role for Russia in the global order today. Russia deserves a great power status. Actually, in order to survive, Russia needs to be a great power.

The foreign policy strategy which Russia's post-communist leadership developed from this worldview, has generally been pragmatic, relatively prudent and not particularly confrontational. Multipolarity is Russia's major foreign policy ambition. Russia believes in global politics that are based on the cooperation and if necessary on the competition between 'poles', led by equal, sovereign great powers. Russia aspires to be one of those poles.

Throughout the post-Cold War decades, Russia's idea on how global politics (should) work have largely remained constant; its foreign policies however evolved. Partly due to developments which were beyond Russia's influence and partially as a result of political and economic changes in Russia itself, the country's foreign policies became more self-confident, more assertive and more offensive, initially especially in its own environment but later also beyond its sphere of influence. The longer-term trends and ambitions of Russian foreign policy have not changed though, and neither have its remarkable paradoxes. Russia wants to revise the liberal global order and she wants to be a prominent part of it. Russia is a revisionist power, but with a strongly conservative streak. Russia demands the right to be included, but it also wants to stand apart. Russia is strongly in favour of multilateralism, but preferably a multilateralism for the few, for great powers only—Russia included.

---

[3] The inspiration to compare the Eurasian Union with the European Economic Community comes from Blockmans, Kostanyan and Vorobiov 2012, who also give the figures on Germany. The figures for the countries of the Eurasian Union come from different web sources, including the World Bank.

Further Reading

Russian foreign policy is the topic of a dazzling number of academic and policy-related studies. The interested reader may begin with the series of brilliant essays in Russian Foreign Policy in the Twenty-First Century and the Shadow of the Past, edited by Robert Legvold (2007). The book offers fascinating insights into the longer-term, historical continuities of Russian foreign policy. Robert Donaldson, Joseph Nogee and Vidya Nadkarni (2014, fifth edition) present a well-structured, balanced and chronological overview of Russia's international policies in The Foreign Policy of Russia. Changing Systems, Enduring Interests. The best study of Putin's foreign policies is Russia and the New World Disorder by Bobo Lo (2015). The book is topical, thorough and admirably objective.

References

Adomeit, H. (2007). *Inside or outside? Russia's policies towards NATO*. Paper delivered to the annual conference of the Centre for Russian Studies at the Norwegian Institute of International Affairs (NUPI) on "The Multilateral Dimension in Russian Foreign Policy", Oslo, October 12–13, Revised December 20, 2006.

Alberts, Hannah Claire (2016). *Russia's OSCE policy and the Ukraine crisis: Renewed interest, enduring approach*. Thesis master of global policy studies and master of arts. Austin: The University of Texas.

Allison, R. (2004). Regionalism, regional structures and security Management in Central Asia. *International Affairs, 80*(3), 463–483.

Allison, R. (2013). Russia and Syria: Explaining alignment with a regime in crisis. *International Affairs, 89*(4), 795–823.

Barnett, M., & Duvall, R. (2005). Power in international Politics. *International Organization, 59*(1), 39–75.

Blockmans, S., Kostanyan, H., & Vorobiov, I. (2012). *Towards a Eurasian economic union: The challenge of integration and unity*. Brussels: CEPS.

Bond, I. (2015). Russia in international organizations: The shift from defence to offence. In D. Cadier & M. Light (Eds.), *Russia's foreign policy. Ideas, domestic politics and external relations* (pp. 189–203). Houndmills/Basingstoke: Palgrave Macmillan.

Cooper, J. (2009). Russia's trade relations within the commonwealth of independent states. In E. W. Rowe & S. Torjesen (Eds.), *The multilateral dimension in Russian foreign policy*. New York: Routledge.

Donaldson, R. H., Nogee, J. L., & Nadkarni, V. (2014). The foreign policy of Russia. Changing systems, enduring interests. In *Armonk*. New York/London: M.E. Sharpe.

Dragneva, R. (2016). *The Eurasian economic union: Balancing sovereignty and integration*. Institute of European Law. Working Paper 10. University of Birmingham.

The Economist. *Medvedev on Russia's interest*. http://www.economist.com/blogs/certainideasofeurope/2008/09/medvedev_on_russias_interests

Ferdinand, P. (2013). *The positions of Russia and China at the UN Security Council in the light of recent crises*. European Parliament/Directorate-General for External Policies. Brussels.

The Foreign Policy Concept of the Russian Federation. (2008). http://en.kremlin.ru/supplement/4116

The Foreign Policy Concept of the Russian Federation. (2016). http://www.mid.ru/en/foreign_policy/official_documents//asset_publisher/CptICkB6BZ29/content/id/2542248

Gerrits, A., & Bader, M. (2015). Russian patronage over Abkhazia and South Ossetia: Implications for conflict resolution. *East European Politics, 32*(3), 297–313.

Hedetoft, U., & Blum, D. W. (2008). Introduction: Russia and globalization—A historical and conceptual framework. In D. W. Blum (Ed.), *Russia and globalization. Identity, security, and society in an era of change*. Washington, DC/Baltimore: Woodrow Wilson Center Press/The Johns Hopkins University Press.

Huntington, S. P. (1996). *The clash of civilizations and the remaking of world order*. New York: Simon & Schuster.

Hurd, I. (2011). *International organizations. Politics, law, practice*. Cambridge: Cambridge University Press.

Kropatcheva, E. (2016). Russia and the collective security treaty organisation: Multilateral policy or unilateral ambitions? *Europe-Asia Studies, 68*(9), 1526–1552.

Kuchins, A. C., & Zevelev, I. A. (2012). Russian foreign policy: Continuity in change. *The Washington Quarterly, 35*(1), 147–161.

Kurlantzick, J. (2016). *State capitalism. How the return of Statism is transforming the world*. New York: Oxford University Press.

Larson, D. W., & Shevchenko, A. (2010). Status seekers. Chinese and Russian responses to U.S. primacy. *International Security, 34*(4), 63–95.

Larson, D. W., & Shevchenko, A. (2014). Russia says no: Power, status and emotions in foreign policy. *Communist and Post-Communist Studies, 47*, 269–279.

Laruelle, M. (2010). *In the name of the nation. Nationalism and Politics in contemporary Russia*. New York: Palgrave Macmillan.

Legvold, R. (2009). The role of multilateralism in Russian foreign policy approaches. In E. W. Rowe & S. Torjesen (Eds.), *The multilateral dimension in Russian foreign policy*. New York: Routledge.

Levitsky, S., & Way, L. A. (2010). *Competitive authoritarianism. Hybrid regimes after the cold war*. New York: Cambridge University Press.

Lieven, A. (1999). The weakness of Russian nationalism. *Survival, 41*(2), 53–70.

Lo, B. (2015). *Russia and the new world disorde*r. London/Washington, DC: Chatham House/Brookings Institution Press.

MacFarlane, S. N. (2006). The 'R' in BRICs: Is Russia an emerging power? *International Affairs, 82*(1), 41–57.

Makarychev, A., & Morozov, V. (2011). Multilateralism, multipolarity, and beyond: A menu of Russia's policy strategies'. *Global Governance, 17*, 353–373.

Mazower, M. (2013). *Governing the world. The history of an idea*. London: Penguin Books.

Mearsheimer, J. (1990). Back to the future: Instability in Europe after the Cold War. *International Security, 15*(1), 5–56.

Mearsheimer, John (1994/95). The false promise of international institutions. International Security 19(3), 5–49.

National Security Concept of the Russian Federation. (2000). http://www.mid.ru/en/foreign_policy/official_documents//asset_publisher/CptICkB6BZ29/content/id/589768

O'Neill, J. (2001). *Building better economic BRICs*. Global Economics Paper No: 66. New York, etc., Goldman Sachs.

Phillips, C. (2016). *The Battle for Syria. International Rivalry in the New Middle East*. New Haven/London: Yale University Press.

Prozorov, S. (2006). *Understanding conflict between Russia and the EU. The limits of integration*. Houndmills/Basingstoke: Palgrave Macmillan.

Putin, V. (2012, February). *Russia and the changing world*. Moskovskiye Novosti February 27, 2012. Johnson's Russia List, 2012, 34.

Putin, V. (2013, September). *Meeting of the Valdai International Discussion Club*, 19 September. Retrieved from http://eng.kremlin.ru/news/6007

Putin, V. (2014a, May). *Putin: Peredacha polnomochnyi v EAEU ne osnachayet utratu suverenita*. https://ria.ru/economy/20140529/1009842639.html

Putin, V. (2014b, July). *Security council meeting. Vladimir Putin chaired a security council meeting in the Kremlin*. Retrieved from http://en.kremlin.ru/events/president/news/46305

Riasanovsky, N. V. (2005). *Russian identities. A historical survey*. Oxford: Oxford University Press.

Rowe, E. W., & Torjesen, S. (2009). Key features of Russian multilateralism. In E. W. Rowe & S. Torjesen (Eds.), *The multilateral dimension in Russian foreign policy*. New York: Routledge.

Sakwa, R. (2016). How the Eurasian elites envisage the role of the EEU in global perspective. *European Politics and Society, 17*(1), 4–22.

Sergunin, A. A. (2004). Discussions of international relations in post-communist Russia. *Communist and Post-Communist Studies, 37*, 19–35.

Sherr, J. (2013). *Hard diplomacy and soft coercion. Russia's influence abroad*. London: Chatham House.

Shevtsova, L. (2010). *Lonely power. Why Russia has failed to become the west and the west is Weary of Russia*. Washington, DC: Carnegie Endowment for International Peace.

Snyder, J. (2000). *From voting to violence. Democratization and nationalist conflict*. New York: Norton.

Torjesen, S. (2009). Russia as a military great power: The uses of the CSTO and the CSO in Central Asia. In E. W. Rowe & S. Torjesen (Eds.), *The multilateral dimension in Russian foreign policy*. New York: Routledge.

Tsygankov, A. P. (2012). *Russia and the west from Alexander to Putin. Honor in international relations*. Cambridge University Press.

Tsygankov, A. P., & Tsygankov, P. A. (2003). New directions in Russian international studies: Pluralization, westernization, and isolationism. *Communist and Post-Communist Studies, 37*, 1–17.

World Bank. (2015). *Gross domestic product* 2015. http://databank.worldbank.org/data/download/GDP.xls

Chapter 6
India as an Emerging Power: Understanding Its Meaning

Carina van de Wetering

6.1 Introduction

There has been a discussion about the rise of BRIC economies for over a decade. Chief economist for Goldman Sachs, Jim O'Neill, first coined the term in 2001, in reference to Brazil, Russia, India and China, asserting that their share of the world economy would grow substantially.[1] In particular, Asia attracted a lot of attention. Books multiplied about Asia's rise in general (Meredith 2007; Acharya 2007; Mahbubani 2008; Sharma 2009; Eichengreen et al. 2010; Jones and Steven 2014; Piccone 2016; Ogden 2017). The idea was normalised that India was one of these emerging powers. Indeed, India's newly gained great power status was "repeated ad nauseum in the Indian and often in global media" (Pant 2011: 14).[2] Epithets such as "emerging", "rising", or "surging" are attributed to India (Chacko 2012: 1). Rajan Menon refers to this as the "India Myth", which is rooted in portrayals of Asia's return to economic prominence, India as a democratic counterweight against China, and India's increasingly close relationship with the US in the last two decades (2014: 46). However, he does not analyze the larger debate regarding "rising India"

---

[1] A flurry of acronyms were introduced, such as "BRICS" with the inclusion of South Africa. Other grouping acronyms for growing economies were CIVETS: Colombia, Indonesia, Vietnam, Egypt, Turkey and South Africa; and MINT: Mexico, Indonesia, Nigeria, and Turkey

[2] An example of these discussions about India's rise and others was a video produced by the European Union to appeal to young voters, but which was quickly retracted after criticism of racist imagery of an aggressive kungfu-fighter and turbaned knife-wielder. The video seemed to imply that the EU should remain strong against China, India and Brazil through its own enlargement. As it said: "The more we are, the stronger we are" (See The Guardian 2012).

C. van de Wetering (✉)
The Institute of Political Science, Faculty of Social and Behavioural Sciences, Leiden University, Leiden, The Netherlands
e-mail: c.c.van.de.wetering@fsw.leidenuniv.nl

© Springer Nature Switzerland AG 2020
M. O. Hosli, J. Selleslaghs (eds.), *The Changing Global Order*, United Nations University Series on Regionalism 17,
https://doi.org/10.1007/978-3-030-21603-0_6

any further. Others are also interested in the identification process of India as a rising power, but they are interested in India's domestic beliefs or foreign policy discourse (Miller 2016; Wojczewski 2018).

The question here is how India came to be understood as an emerging power during the last two decades. What this chapter shows is that we should problematise this understanding and not take it for granted. The representation of India's emergence assumes that India is experiencing large economic growth, expanding its military and pursuing a larger role in the world. These assumptions are based on realist theory, a perspective that has dominated IR scholarship for a long time and remains substantial within the field, which argues that India's rapid economic growth will help it to become a great power on the grounds that "wealth and military power go hand-in-hand" (Cohen and Dasgupta 2010: x).[3] As discussed in the first chapter, realism suggests that every state has the same self-interested behaviour; all states want to survive the anarchical nature of the international system. Nevertheless, a unipolar power or a few great powers can dominate the international system due to a varying distribution of capabilities.

"Rising powers" are often formulated by realists as challengers within the international system, in other words, a rising-as-a-revisionist power.[4] As Randall Schweller argues, the more strength and richess a state acquires, the more influence it wants to gain out of self-interest (1999: 3). Hence realists predict that, "as states grow wealthier and more powerful, they not only seek greater-world-wide political influence (control over territory, the behaviour of other states, and the world economy) commensurate with their new capabilities; they are also more capable of expanding their interests and, if necessary, of waging large-scale, hegemonic wars to revise drastically or overthrow entirely the established order" (Schweller 1999: 3). Some realist authors, including Schweller, also find that it can vary in how dangerous rising powers can become. Not all rising states are revisionists; it depends on whether the states demonstrate revolutionary aims in combination with sufficient means for overthrowing current power relations (Schweller 1999: 25; Johnston 2003: 6, 49; Schweller 2015). About the BRIC countries, Schweller indeed argues: "[T]oday's emerging powers appear only modestly dissatisfied with the current international order. They seek only limited territorial changes and, for the most part, prefer peaceful to violent means to achieve their aims" (2015).

Nevertheless, it assumes that "emerging" powers are still interested in gaining military, political and economic advantages. The assumptions about a rising power preclude other understandings of India by setting a limit upon what can be said. The discussion about the nature of India and the relationship with others should not be treated as natural facts. The underlying presuppositions should be denaturalised and

---

[3] "It is only a slight exaggeration," William Wohlforth once stated, "to say that the academic study of international relations is a debate about realism" (Wohlforth 2008: 131). Even though realism is currently somewhat less dominant, it has co-opted other theories in the past, such as neoliberalism.

[4] Hostile tendencies of rising powers are, for instance, further explored in Robert Gilpin, War and Change in World Politics (1981), John Mearsheimer, The Tragedy of Great Power Politics (2001), and Randal Schweller "Managing the rise of great powers: history and theory" (1999).

hence interrogated. Drawing on the theories in the first chapter, I will initially make use of a social constructivist approach. As discussed in Chap. 1, social constructivism proposes that each subject and object, including a house, a statue, or country, or international organisation, is always shaped by human interpretation (Hopf 1998: 182). According to Alexander Wendt, one of the most prominent social constructivists, social phenomena have no fixed meanings as they are produced through dialogue and discourse between individuals and groups (1999: 1). This approach argues that we do not objectively assess a situation, but we interpret and make sense of it within a framework of meanings attached to, for instance, objects, subjects, facts, identities, and interests. This does not mean that constructivists deny facts or events, but they argue that the meanings attained can become meaningful in various ways. Indeed, "[o]nce constructed, each of these objects has a particular meaning and use within a context" (Fierke 2010: 179). What makes them social constructs is how they are "imbued with social values, norms, and assumptions rather than being the product of purely individual thought or meaning" (Fierke 2010: 179). They are a product of inter-subjective interactions between people.

Hence, this chapter discusses the understanding of India's "emergence". First, it will go through some recent political and economic developments in India. It shows how these facts can be viewed in different ways by making use of social constructivism. Then it will show how this interpretation is embedded within a larger debate on rising Asia and the declining US. Lastly, post-positivist insights of Chap. 2 are included to problematise the debate itself.

6.2 Political and Economic Development

As mentioned above, India is presented as a growing economic power which experienced military and political gains in the last two decades. The representation of India's emergence can be substantiated by developments in recent years. However, these accounts should not be taken for granted and should be interrogated.

With regard to India's economy, it is often argued that India is a "rising economic power" due to its steady increase in economic growth since 1991 (Tellis 2007: 239). The narrative maintains that Prime Minister Narasimha Rao and Manmohan Singh liberalised India's centrally planned economy in 1991 after the fiscal crisis at the start of the 1990s. Instead of import substitution, exports were promoted through the removal of quota and customs duties on imports. Trade barriers such as industrial licensing were removed and tariffs were lowered, while tax rates were reduced and the rupee devalued. Prime Minister Rao promoted more foreign direct investment (FDI) by introducing change in the banking sector, interest rates, and convertibility of the rupee (Kant Jha 1994: 1042; Das 2006).

Indeed, since India put in place its market reforms, India's economy has surged forward with 6% annually from 1992 until 2006, with a rise per capita GDP of $1255 to $2732 in the period 1978–2003 (Sharma 2006: 170). Mid-2000s the annual rate of GDP grew even more strongly by an average of more than 8% in 2004 until 2008

(Gupta et al. 2018: 26). In particular, the services exports increased due to the IT industry (Schaffer 2009: 37). With the global economic crisis in 2008, there was a slowdown in economic growth, with growth remaining below 5% from 2012 until 2014, but it bounced back exceeding 7% per year in 2014–2016 with merely a few temporary setbacks. At the same time, India's per capita income nearly doubled to $5350 in 2013 (Menon 2014: 46, 50). Fittingly called, "India's growth story", the World Bank narrates that economic growth has become more durable and stable for the services and industry sectors (See the World Bank report by Gupta et al. 2018: 18).

There is also the understanding that India is rising in terms of military greatness. As Stephen Cohen and Sunil Dasgupta write: "Whether emerging, rising, or an Asian 'giant,' there is some expectation that India's new affluence will enable it to deploy vastly improved armed forces. This expanded military capability will enable it, then, to play a larger role in world affairs, notably in Asia" (2010: ix). India had already a large arms market and its defence budget also grew substantially. In 2000 India had the second largest arms market in the world with imports of $4.8 billion dollars (Lansford 2002: 133). India's arms market continues to boom. Israel, the United States and the Soviet Union are now important arms suppliers (Menon 2014: 54). India's defence budget grew from 11.8 billion in 2000, to 20 billion in 2009, and more than doubled again in 2013 with $47 billion (Cohen and Dasgupta 2010: 16; Menon 2014: 53). In the last few years, Prime Minister Narendra Modi's government, elected in 2014, increased the budget again, even though it remains a relatively small percentage of the GDP as rates continue to stay at 2–3% (Riedel 2015: 168).

Does this then allow India to qualify for the epithet "emerging power"? Can we problematise these claims? There are indeed challenges. Even though poverty levels were reduced from 45% in the early 1980s to 27.5% in 2004–2005, India's poverty rates are still very high in absolute numbers (Sharma 2009: 139). The major benefactors of improvement are the middle class and businesses. 300–400 million Indians are still living in very poor circumstances subsisting on a maximum of $1.25 each day.[5] In fact, there has been an inability to create manufacturing jobs. Economic growth is not driven by manufacturing or foreign direct investment, but by its service sector such as the IT sector (Sharma 2006: 170).[6] Since the Green Revolution, large-scale reforms have also been lacking in the large rural sector due to a shifting focus to other sectors, while the agricultural sector accounts for 25% of its GDP (Sharma 2009: 149).

Also, an "infrastructure deficit" surfaced, because India did not invest enough resources in infrastructure, such as sanitation systems, bridges, roads, airports, and reliable electricity supply (Sharma 2009: 147; Menon 2014: 49). There are also

---

[5] When the Bharatiya Janata Party (BJP) waged the "India Shining" election campaign through various advertisement channels in 2004 in order to celebrate the success of economic advances, the Indian population was thus not hailed into this self-understanding as critics were quick to point out the large inequalities.

[6] Foreign direct investment to India is much lower than in other BRIC countries. In order to attract foreign direct investment, Menon argues that more changes are necessary regarding subsidies on basic products, overregulation due to rigid labor laws, protection of certain sectors including agriculture and services, and tax evasion (2014: 49–50).

underinvestments within the public sector, including in food, health, sanitation and education for the poor, which affect people's living conditions (Drèze and Sen 2013: 8).[7] For instance, India's literacy rate is 74% on average, while large economies such as China and Indonesia achieve rates of 90%. In fact, in India's rural areas these rates are much lower (Menon 2014: 49). There are also other structural constraints, such as good governance. There is dissatisfaction within Indian society about corruption amongst Indian government officials which was, for instance, exposed in the Commonwealth Games through substandard building construction and inexplicably high bills for equipment (Chadda 2012: 141).

Additionally, it is mistaken to presume that India did not undergo any large developments in the past. Contrary to recent years, poverty rates were very high during colonial rule: 70% lived in sheer poverty confronted by malnutrition. Life expectancy was merely 30 years old (Sharma 2016: 193). Also, there were much higher illiteracy rates. Undeniably, from 1950 until 1980 there was an economic growth rate of 3.5%, also called the slow "Hindu rate of growth", but this was "a very large step forward compared with the near-zero growth (and at times even economic decline) that occurred in the colonial days" (Dreze and Sen 2013: 3). That said, the Indian government could have undertaken more activities to increase the GDP in order to keep up with the population growth.[8] With the increase of economic growth, according to Jagdish Bhagwati and Arvind Panagariya, living conditions could be altered through the accumulation in wealth (2013: 18).

India has thus gone through large economic developments in the last two decades, but the developments have been uneven. With regard to India's military, its recent increasing capacities can also be interrogated. At the start of the 1990s, according to Akhtar Majeed, India already had the Third World's largest military-industrial complex consisting of thirty-three factories, nine public sectors organisations, and thirty-four research and development organisations which were all owned by the Ministry of Defence (1990: 1087). In the 1980s, India's military capacity expanded to become the fourth largest army in the world, totalling 960,000 men on active duty, behind China, the Soviet Union and the US (Wood and Vaagenes 1984: 725). Defence spending was at an unprecedented percentage of the GDP in the 1980s, namely 5%, while it was normally around 2–3% (Cohen and Dasgupta 2010: 16). There was thus an estimated increase of Indian military expenditure from less than a billion in 1950 to 3.7 billion in 1980 (Wood and Vaagenes 1984: 728).

Before then, the level of investment went back and forth. Indian capacity decreased in the 1950s, but the Sino-Indian War of 1962 was a clear watershed for Indian defence. During this war China invaded India over a border issue, which led to a program of military modernisation, starting with the mountain divisions, as

---

[7] There have been some different developments. The Food Security Bill was passed in 2013 which provided three-quarters of the rural population and 50% of the urban population with 5 kilos of grain for each person per month at lower prices (Sharma 2016: 197)

[8] In the 1980s, Prime Minister Rajiv Gandhi also implemented modest liberal reforms by lowering taxes and tariffs, which increased the growth to 5.6%. Yet, his policy reinforced a corrupt regime which created a fiscal crisis in the 1990s (Das 2006).

India's priorities shifted away from an army based on its former colonial military organisation (Thakur 1993: 836–837). To achieve this, India initially received support from the US for its mountain divisions until the Indo-Pakistan war of 1965 erupted. Especially from the 1970s onwards, when India signed the 1971 Indo-Soviet Treaty of Friendship and Cooperation, the Soviet Union became a major donor until the very end of the Cold War (Cohen and Dasgupta 2010: 8, 20).[9]

Also, India's "greatness" can be challenged in terms of its lack of military direction since its independence. India pursued ad-hoc decision making in the absence of a coherent strategic culture (See for a further discussion Bajpai 2002: 246; Subrahmanyam and Monteiro 2005: i; Sagar 2009: 812; Pant 2011: 16–20; Chaudhuri 2014: 258). A well-known account was prepared by George Tanham at the RAND National Defense Research Institute for the US government who stressed that "India has great ambitions for a position in the world", but it should articulate a more "coherent strategic identity" in order to be accepted by other large powers (1992a: 129). In his opinion, so-called Hindu cultural traits, India's diversity, its insular geography, and its ancient past affected its current political-military strengths (1992b: 11–13). As Harsh Pant cogently summarises: "He [Tanham] argued that his lack of long-term planning and strategy derives from India's historical and cultural development patterns. These include the Hindu view of life as largely unknowable, thereby being outside man's control, and the Hindu concept of time as eternal, thereby discouraging planning" (2011: 15).[10] Nevertheless, this account is often dismissed, because Tanham's analysis lacks methodogical rigour and displays ethnocentrism by putting too much emphasis on cultural traits.

Other authors explore different reasons for the lack of strategy (Pant 2011: 15).[11] For instance, Cohen and Dasgupta argue that India was "arming without aiming", because of several reasons: the threats within the region were regarded as manageable by the leaders, economic development was favoured over military expansion, and the use of armed forces was rejected as part of its colonial past (Cohen and Dasgupta 2010: xii). In 1947 civil-military relations were reformed, because the Indian army was seen as the last supporter of the British Raj. Accordingly, the Indian army was marginalised with the establishment of civilian-led control by the Ministry of Defence (Pant 2011: 16–17). Also, there is a role to play for the Indian Foreign Service (IFS), an exclusive group with a stringent admission process, which dominates foreign policy-making through the Prime Minister's office, the Ministry of External Affairs (MEA) and other diplomatic posts. According to Miller, their presence leads to more individualistic and ad-hoc decision-making, especially since the IFS is understaffed and subsequently has very large responsibilities (Miller 2016: 232–233).

---

[9] Since the end of the Cold War, the military relationship changed, because the Russian Federation had not the means to supply all the required equipments

[10] The reference to the importance of India's cultural traits can also be found in a report by Rodney Jones prepared for the Defense Threat Reduction Agency (2006: 4–9).

[11] See for different views, for instance, the compilation of essays by George Tanham and commentaries of Indian scholars (1996).

Some authors identify strategic thinking in the past. As Rudra Chaudhuri argues, "There is an imagination that guides India. It can loosely be called non-alignment" (2014: 259).[12] A prominent figure within Indian politics and leader of the Indian Congress Party, Prime Minister Jawaharlal Nehru (1947–1964) promoted non-alignment as part of India's foreign policy. The non-alignment approach stood for the absence of military alliances with another country, especially with countries of the Western and the Communist bloc. Non-alignment did not always entail neutrality since a country could take sides on issues which divided the superpowers. For instance, India signed the 1971 Indo-Soviet treaty (Appadorai and Rajan 1985: 40; Thakur 1997: 27). Instead, non-alignment stood for non-involvement in quarrels that were of little interest to the non-aligned (Sagar 2009: 803–804). As Prime Minister Jawaharlal Nehru declared in the Lok Sabha, the House of the People, on 9 December 1958: "When we say our policy is one of non-alignment, obviously we mean non-alignment with military blocs. It is not a negative policy. It is a positive one, a definite one and, I hope, a dynamic one. But, in so far as the military blocs today and the Cold War are concerned, we do not align ourselves with either bloc" (In Appadorai and Rajan 1985: 40).

However, non-alignment is currently regarded as a weak strategy. According to Chaudhuri, non-alignment "irk[s] contemporary elites, irritate[s] those commentators narrowly in search of national 'stature'" (2014: 259). Krishnaswamy Subrahmanyam sees non-alignment as an overarching strategy, but it is not well-applied (Bajpai et al. 2014: 6). In realist terms, India's aim was disruptive by showing its dissatisfaction with the world order and questioning its legitimacy, but it was unwilling to risk change by strong means (Schweller 1999: 24; 2015). Indeed, after nearly 50 years of relative Indian Congress Party dominance, these visions of India's identity were seen as too idealistic amongst the Bharatiya Janata Party (BJP) coalition governments: India should face geopolitical realities and show more military strength (Chacko 2012: 168).[13] There is still a focus on "strategic autonomy", however. A 2012 strategy document on Indian foreign policy, entitled "Non-alignment 2.0" was published by several independent scholars and policy makers to formulate a vision for the coming few years (Khilnani et al. 2012). The document aimed for "strategic autonomy": "NonAlignment [sic] will no longer be limited to avoiding becoming a frontline state in a conflict between two powers. It will instead require a very skilful management of complicated coalitions and opportunities" as there are new "hubs of power" alongside China and the US (Khilnani et al. 2012: 9).

Nevertheless, meanings such as "rising" or "emerging" can still be attached to India's identity in the last few years. After the election of Prime Minister Narendra Modi from the BJP in 2014, he was seen as more activist by putting a personal stamp on foreign-policy making, while he aimed for a larger role for India in the

---

[12] See also van de Wetering (2016a). The book argues that there are four continuous themes that are coined with regard to US-India relations, including the non-alignment theme.

[13] According to Chacko, these assumptions can also be found in Indian foreign policy literature; quite a few authors argue that India should have a more realist foreign policy, such as Mohan and Pant (2012: 2–3)

region through its perceived great power status. He was pragmatic with regard to, for instance, the United States (Mohan 2015; Gupta and Mullen 2018: 4).[14] US President Barack Obama and the Prime Minister met several times in order to discuss Asian-wide issues, including China. In the joint statement of June 2016, entitled The United States and India: Enduring Global Partners in the twenty-first century, the two governments said that the US continued to see India as a "Major Defense Partner" and their defence relations "as an anchor of stability" through sharing military technology. Also, they were "priority partners in the Asia-Pacific" through continued cooperation of their fleets (2016). An example is the Malabar maritime exercises amongst India, the US, and in some instances, Japan, which were conducted close to islands claimed by China in the South and East China Sea.[15] Similarly, President Donald Trump continued to refer to India as a "Major Defense Partner" by welcoming the country as a "leading global power and stronger strategic and defense partner" (2017: 46–47). Continuing with the Malabar maritime exercises in the Indian Ocean, both US administrations have been concerned with threatening actors within the region, especially with China (Obama 2015: i; Trump 2017: 25).

This shows that India's apparent emergence can be questioned through developments in its economy, military and interference in global politics. Nevertheless, India continues to be presented as a "rising" power. The next section discusses how one interpretation became more dominant than the other.

6.3 Rising and Declining Powers Debate

As will be shown below, India came to be understood as a "rising power" due to a concern with Asia's rise and US decline. The meanings about "rising India" and "US decline" were brought into existence through interactions amongst people, either through language or practice (Wetering 2018: 150–151, 153). For instance, Rajan Menon signals that the interest in India in part "stems from analyses that portray India's and China's resurgence as part of a shift that is ineluctably returning the center of global economic power to Asia" (2014: 46). At the same time, the declinist debate about US demise resurfaced as well (Joffe 2009).

The declinist debate is not a recent phenomenon in the US. During the early Cold War, the US was represented as losing its military and scientific superiority since the Soviet Union was the first to launch a satellite, Sputnik. Kennedy therefore complained during his presidential campaign in 1960: "American strength relative to that of the Soviet Union has been slipping, and communism has been

---

[14] Prime Minister was initially seen as more proactive. This has become less the case, but he remains pragmatic concerning particular issues, as mentioned above.

[15] This region was articulated as important to the Obama administration, which was evident by the Pivot to Asia plans, by strengthening its collaboration with Japan, Australia and others.

advancing steadily in every area of the world" (In Joffe 2009).[16] Other countries were also regarded as up and coming, such as Japan (Kahn 1971; Vogel 1979). In the 1980s the narrative of US economic declinism emerged again. In fact, according to Samuel Huntington, "In 1988 the United States reached the zenith of its fifth wave of declinism since the 1950s" (1988: 76).[17] The political economy literature began to analyze the "fading American economic hegemony" and "[t]hese themes were picked up in more popular and policy-oriented writings" (Huntington 1988: 76). One of the most well-known works in political economy was Paul Kennedy's The Rise and Fall of the Great Powers (1987) in which he argued that the United States will suffer "imperial overstretch" if it does not have the strong economy and the power to maintain it (1987: 515).[18]

Also, India was already presented as a significant country during the Cold war as part of Nehruvian thinking within Indian politics. As a nationalist, Nehru conceived India as a great state with a claim to a long history which preceded the struggle against the British. He adhered to a state directed economic system, skepticism of US pressure, and a measure of idealism to act in the international well-being as long as it did not interfere with India's vital interests. Nehru thus took an idealistic internationalist stance which aimed for peace and harmony through which all countries were treated equally, while interference was met with criticism. Specific policies reflected non-alignment, self-reliance, non-violence and nuclear non-proliferation (Ogden 2011: 4–6). These were not the only Indian world views; his daughter, Prime Minister Indira Gandhi (1966–1977 and 1980–1984) took a more militant and realpolitical viewpoint, while there was the emergence of less tolerant Hindu nationalism under the Bharatiya Janata Party, but India's greatness was accepted across the board in India (Cohen 2002: 36–42).[19] As Chris Ogden argues, "Over the

---

[16] There were more discussions about US decline. Joffe elaborates: "In the late 1950s, it was the Sputnik shock, followed by the 'missile gap' trumpeted by John F. Kennedy in the 1960 presidential campaign. A decade later, Richard Nixon and Henry Kissinger sounded the dirge over bipolarity, predicting a world of five, rather than two, global powers. At the end of the 1970s, Jimmy Carter's 'malaise' speech invoked 'a crisis of confidence' that struck 'at the very heart and soul and spirit of our national will'" (2009).

[17] Others agree that there was again a lively declinist debate in the 1980s. G. John Ikenberry argued: "In recent years no topic has occupied the attention of scholars of international relations more than that of American hegemonic decline. The erosion of American economic, political and military power is unmistakable" (1989: 375).

[18] Other scholars were also concerned with the decline of the US, especially in the literature on international regimes and hegemonic stability theory, based on realist and liberal insights. It discusses whether the stability of a regime and economic openness is most likely dependent on a single dominant power. For instance, Robert Gilpin writes about America's declining economic and political position in American Policy in the Post-Reagan era, while Stephen Krasner discusses the decline in US external economic power and domestic constraints (Gilpin 1987: 65; Krasner 1977).

[19] There are more viewpoints. See, for instance, Bajpai (2002, 2014) who discusses that there are three main schools of thought: Nehruvians, hyperrealists, and neoliberals and three smaller schools, including Marxism, Hindu nationalism and Ghandianism. Stephen Cohen looks at four schools that shape Indian foreign policy-making, namely classical-Nehruvian, militant Nehruvian, conservative realism and Hindu revivalism (2002). Rahul Sagar lists four visions, namely moral-

last 60 years, an aspiration to achieve Great Power status has become a normalised feature of Indian foreign policy" (Ogden 2011: 10).

What makes the rising and declining powers debate different from the previous ones is that the focus shifted to include and legitimise the role of more large non-Western countries, particularly Asian countries, as evidenced by discussions of scholars, politicians and others. Already in December 1997 during the Kyoto climate conference, India and China's started both to be constructed as key developing nations, but also as large, growing economies which would become important polluters in the twenty-first century (Wetering 2016: 104).[20] These constructions became more salient after 2000. From the start of the 2000s onwards countries were articulated as "emerging" or "rising" in an increasingly multipolar world, as evidenced by BRIC terminology in 2001 and the establishment of BRIC summits in 2009, while since the mid-2000s, the US was again represented as a country in relative decline. Especially, China was mentioned, which was also highlighted in popular magazines, such as Time magazine and Der Spiegel that referred to China as a rising power or as a competitor to the US already in 2005 (Time magazine 2005; Der Spiegel 2005).[21]

Even though China was often mentioned, there was discussion of a larger overhaul. In The Post-American World Fareed Zakaria writes that in the twenty-first century US will not dominate the global arena, and therefore, "[t]his is not a book about the decline of America, but rather about the rise of everyone else" (2008 and 2011: 1). Other authors also said more about US decline or the changing world order. Kennedy revisits his 1987 arguments, proclaiming that fiscal deficits and military overstretch were finally undoing the US global position and meant that there was a "global tectonic power shift, toward Asia and away from the West" (2009). Charles Kupchan also argues that the world will not be dominated by one power as the world will not have a new great power with a universal order; it will become multipolar and politically diverse (2012: x).[22] Similarly, Amitav Acharya introduces the notion of multiplex world in which global governance will become more decentered as the US guided international system will coexist with different institutions and ideas (2014, 2017).

---

ists, Hindu nationalists, strategists and liberals (2009: 801). Thorsten Wojczewski, however, argues that post-Nehruvianism and its counterhegemonic discourse, the hyper-nationalist dsicsourse, are more suitable, to discuss Indian foreign policy (2018: 2).

[20] Smaller Asian countries, including Hong Kong, Singapore, South Korea and Taiwan were already articulated as Asian Tigers. Several of these East Asian economies were affected by the Asian financial crisis of 1997.

[21] In 2011 there were the Munk debates, biannual series of debates on major policy issues which took place in Canada, entitled: "Be it resolved, the twenty-first century will belong to China" with Niall Ferguson, David Daokui Li, Henry Kissinger, and Fareed Zakaria. The former two were on the yes-side and the latter two on the no-side (Munk debates 2011). China was also discussed within US politics. For instance, the Obama administration said it "welcomes the rise of a stable, peaceful, and prosperous China" (Obama 2015: 24)

[22] The viewpoint of US decline was sometimes also challenged. See Stephen Brooks and William Wohlforth (2008) and Robert Kagan (2012).

India began to be articulated as "rising" (See Cohen 2002; Ganguly 2003; Panagariya 2010; Waheguru et al. 2013; Gordon 2015; Pant and Joshi 2015). For instance, Arvind Panagariya's India: The Emerging Giant (2010) gives an account of India's strong economic growth, while in The US Pivot and Indian Foreign Policy Harsh V. Pant and Yogesh Joshi refer to the decline of the US and rise of China with India "as an economic growth story" hedging its bets by maintaining relations with both (2015: 15). Already in the early 2000s some authors saw the potential of India. Both Stephen Cohen's India: Emerging Power (2002) and Sumit Ganguly's India as an Emerging Power (2003) gave an overview of India's domestic situation and also its role in regional and international politics. According to Cohen, India is "becoming a major power" as India will become increasingly important to the United States for its technology revolution and nuclear issues (2002: 1). Ganguly also writes that India has some features that "undergird its strategic significance in the region and beyond" such as its substantial military, and democratic and stable institutions, and a growing economy with a few highly ranked sectors (2003: 1).

Within the debate, it has become common-sensible to talk about India as a great and emerging power. Often China and India's economies are compared. President Obama said at a fundraising event in San Francisco in 2011: "We were seeing changes around the world – countries like China and India rising". He continued: "So I think we understood that we were going to have to adapt in some fundamental way in order to make sure that our kids and our grandkids ended up inheriting the kind of America that we inherited" (Obama 2011). In fact, China and India's growing economies was already increasingly articulated by the Bush administration in the mid-2000s.[23] As President Bush stated in 2006:

> The American economy is preeminent, but we cannot afford to be complacent. In a dynamic world economy, we are seeing new competitors like China and India, and this creates uncertainty, which makes it easier to feed people's fears. So we're seeing some old temptations return. Protectionists want to escape competition, pretending that we can keep our high standard of living while walling off our economy (2006).

As part of the declinist debate, President Bush's world view thus encompassed a warning for the US to take seriously its competitors. It was assessed that India would be the fourth most "capable concentration of power after 2015" following the United States, The European Union, and China (Congress 2005).

Within the debate, there are still distinctions made between India and China. China's "revisionist" rise was particularly debated. For instance, Aaron Friedberg writes: "[I]f we permit an illiberal China to displace us as the preponderant player in this most vital region, we will face grave dangers to our interests and our values throughout the world" (2011: 8).

Earlier, Friedberg constructed Asia as "ripe for rivalry" (1993/1994).[24] In comparison, India is not presented as a revisionist country that challenges the super-

---

[23] This also reflects Robyn Meredith's ideas in The Elephant and the Dragon, in which she argues that India's approach was more "slow-but-steady" while China's was a "rocket-like rise" (2007: 11).

[24] However, there is more stability in Asia than assumed by International Relations theories. For

power within or outside Asia. During most of the 1990s, India was not mentioned as a player of significance within Asia, but it was soon constructed as a potential partner of the US or regarded as a stable yet hesitant world power (See, for instance, Kang 2003: 60; Acharya 2003/2004: 150; Menon 2014: 46; Wetering 2016: 180–183). In fact, "rising" India was regarded as a counterweight against China as US-India relations improved after the Cold War (Menon 2014: 46). India continued to be constructed as an "emerging" and "benign" country as part of the debate.

6.4   Debating the Debate

We described constructions of "rising India" and "declining US" and how they are embedded within the debate. However, these constructions can be further unpacked. The rising and declining powers debate presupposes a particular international order. Boundaries are not merely drawn concerning our understanding of what constitutes as "rising" or "in decline", but they also delineate what the "international", the "system", and "order" are.

What is unfortunate is that particular social constructivist theories are not entirely self-reflexive to analyze this further, because particular strands of social constructivism, similar to other strands within IR, take at a minimum anarchy as the organizing principle of the international order for granted, either by accepting that there is no overarching authority or by adding a more concrete constellation (Sjoberg 2017: 328). For instance, Alexander Wendt agrees with realists that anarchy is an essential feature within the international system, even though it can vary through states' interactions (1992). This leads him to argue that the interaction between states lead to three logics of anarchy, a Hobbesian, Lockean or Kantian view, in which actors are enemies, rivals or friends respectively (Wendt 1999: 246–247). However, we can find eclectic conceptions of the political order when looking, for instance, more up close at several Indian scholars, including Angadipuram Appadorai with his emphasis on harmony through addressing global inequities and the rejection of neo-imperialism (Mallavarapu 2018).

Especially within postcolonial and feminist studies, questions are raised about how IR scholarship, and realist scholars in particular, define and explain the workings of global politics through their knowledge production (Chowdry and Nair 2004; Tickner 2013; See Hobson 2014 for an extensive account). As part of the larger debate, the authority of IR scholars helps to produce a particular understanding of the international order. Even though they often takes anarchy for granted, it ironically privileges a Eurocentric/US-centric order, and therefore, the presence of a hierarchy of states rather than anarchy (Barkawi and Laffey 2002: 110; Chowdry and Nair 2004: 3–4; Bially-Mattern and Zarakol 2016: 630–631). For instance,

---

instance, David Kang discusses that various International Relations scholars, including realists, institutionalists and constructivists, base their theoretical assumptions and predictions on an "expansionist and revisionist China" (2003: 63)

countries are constructed to be in need of development to "rise" to Eurocentric standards based on capitalism or modernism. There are thus advanced states and those that are lagging behind, by which the latter are singled out in order to achieve progress within the international order (See also Blaney and Inayatullah 2008 or Smith 2004: 505). Accordingly, racial, gendered and class-based divisions are made invisible within this order as if there is an equal level playing field for all, even though hierarchy is achieved by the demarcation of groups (See also Chowdry and Nair 2004: 6).[25]

Overall, the debate is based on the acceptance of the US as a leader in a liberal-order led world. This has been a relatively successful construction (Ikenberry 2018: 7–8). As Amitav Acharya argues, this myth about the U.S.-led liberal order has continued throughout its history, even more so during the Cold War, which led to a "US-UK-West Europe-Australasian configuration" after the WWII (2014: 37). The debate should thus not be seen as a dialogue, but as a discursive struggle between different meanings articulated by policy-makers, the media, scholars, by which a particular narrative was more successfully articulated and normalised than the other (Wojczewski 2018: 36–37). As Thorsten Wojczewksi puts it in reference to Ernesto Laclau and Chantal Mouffe's seminal writings on discourses, discourses of global powers shifts constitute "a hegemonic struggle over meanings and identities triggered by the dislocation of the existent discursive order" (2018: 34).

6.5   Conclusion

This chapter does not want to take for granted India's "rise", but it wants to show that India's "emergence" is constructed as part of a larger debate. It shows how some "facts" about India's military, foreign policy and economy can become more salient than others. These facts are often taken for granted, while they should be interrogated. As the constructivists argue, social phenomena and situations are produced through dialogue within the media, academia and politics. The fact that India can be presented as a growing economic power that made military and political gains makes more sense within the larger rising and declining powers debate which moved beyond declinist debates in the US and India's discussions about their greatness. What is less articulated is that India's economy could also be portrayed as not very strong, that it is still confronted with poverty and other social deficiencies, and that it experienced large economic growth in the past. Indeed, the meaning of "emerging" or "rising" is attached to India so as to constitute India's rise as a recent

---

[25] The IR discipline itself can be seen as ethnocentric, gendered and reproductive of non-West IR communities at the periphery and a western community at the core. This is, for instance, even visible in terms of citation practices, in which scholars associated with the US and Western-Europe received higher citation rates by authors in the US and Western-Europe, and in the periphery (Tickner 2013: 631–632).

and important phenomenon. Similarly, it could be argued that India made military advancements in the past and its strategic outlook remains unclear.

However, this Chapter also highlights how these assertions can be further interrogated. Scholars, politicians, journalists and others are not innocent bystanders, but by repeating the meanings of "rise" and "decline" they also produce this knowledge. Particular strands of social constructivism are less adept at questioning the knowledge production by taking the anarchical system for granted, but feminist and postcolonial theories have analyzed the international order. The rising and declining powers debate appears to be part of a particular understanding of the international order, which is much more hierarchical than often discussed by realist scholars and other IR scholars. The so-called decline of the US also serves as a reminder of this: it is constructed as globally prominent position, while India should strive to become more similar to the US. Indeed, the understanding of India as an "emerging" power within the rising and declining debate also enables India to take more action on the global stage, which is an angle that can be further explored for Prime Minister Modi but also other "emerging" powers.

Further Readings

Chowdry, G. (2004). In S. Nair (Ed.), *Power, postcolonialism and international relations: Reading race, gender and class*. Abingdon: Routledge.
Malone, D. M., Mohan, C. R., & Raghavan, S. (2015). *The Oxford handbook of Indian foreign policy*. Oxford: Oxford University Press.
Miller, M. C. (2016). The role of beliefs in identifying rising powers. *The Chinese Journal of International Politics, 9*(2), 211–238.
van de Wetering, C. (2016). *Changing US foreign policy toward India: US-India relations since the cold war*. New York: Palgrave Macmillan.
Wojczewksi, T. (2018). *India's foreign policy discourse and its conceptions of world order: The question for power and identity*. Abingdon: Routledge.

References

Acharya, A. (2003). Will Asia's past be its future? *International Security, 28*(3), 149–164.
Acharya, A. (2007). *Asia rising: Who is leading?* London: World Scientific Publishing.
Acharya, A. (2014). *The end of American world order*. Cambridge: Polity.
Acharya, A. (2017). After liberal hegemony: The advent of a multiplex world order. *Ethics & International Affairs, 31*(3), 271–285.
Appadorai, A., & Rajan, M. S. (1985). *India's foreign policy and relations*. New Delhi: South Asian Publishers Private Ltd.
Bajpai, K. (2002). Indian strategic culture. In M. R. Chambers (Ed.), *South Asia in 2020: Future strategic balances and alliances* (pp. 245–305). Carlisle: Strategic Studies Institute.
Bajpai, K. (2014). Indian grand strategy: Six schools of thought. In K. Bajpai, S. Basit, & V. Krishnappa (Eds.), *India's grand strategy: History, theory, cases* (pp. 113–150). New Delhi: Routledge.

Bajpai, K., Basit, S., & Krishnapa, V. (2014). Introduction: India's grand strategic thought and practice. In B. Kanti, S. Basit, & V. Krishnapa (Eds.), *India's grand strategy: History, theory, cases* (pp. 1–28). New Delhi: Routledge.

Barkawi, T., & Laffey, M. (2002). Retrieving the imperial: Empire and international relations. *Millennium: Journal of International Studies, 31*(1), 109–127.

Bhagwati, J., & Panagariya, A. (2013). *Why growth matters: How economic growth in India reduced poverty and the lessons for other developing countries.* New York: Public Affairs.

Bially-Mattern, J., & Zarakol, A. (2016). Review essay: Hierarchies in world politics. *International Organization, 70*(3), 623–654.

Blaney, D., & Inayatullah, N. (2008). Internatonal relations from below. In C. Reus-Smit & D. Snidal (Eds.), *The oxford handbook of international relations.* Oxford: Oxford University Press.

Brooks, S. G., & Wohlforth, W. C. (2008). *World out of balance: International relations and the challenge of American primacy.* Princeton: Princeton University Press.

Bush, G. W. (2006, January 31). *Address before a Joint Session of the Congress on the State of the Union. The American Presidency Project.* Retrieved from: http://www.presidency.ucsb.edu/ws/?pid=65090

Chacko, P. (2012). *Indian foreign policy: The politics of postcolonial identity from 1947 to 2004.* London: Routledge.

Chadda, M. (2012). India in 2011: The state encounters the people. *Asian Survey, 52*(1), 114–129.

Chaudhuri, R. (2014). *Forged in crisis: India and the United States since 1947.* London: Hurst.

Chowdry, G., & Nair, S. (2004). Introduction: Power in a postcolonial world: Race, gender, and class in international relations. In G. Chowdry & S. Nair (Eds.), *Power, postcolonialism and international relations: Reading race, gender and class.* Abingdon: Routledge.

Cohen, S. P. (2002). *India: Emerging power.* Oxford: Oxford University Press.

Cohen, S. P., & Dasgupta, S. (2010). *Arming without aiming: India's military modernization.* Harissonburg: R.R. Donnelley.

Congress. (2005, November 16). *The US-India "Global Partnership": How significant for American interests? Hearing before the Committee on International Relations.* House of Representatives, 109th Congress. Retrieved from: http://commdocs.house.gov/committees/intlrel/hfa24598.000/hfa24598_0f.htm

Das, G. (2006). The India model. *Foreign Affairs, 85*(4), 2–16.

Der Spiegel. (2005). *China gegen USA. Kamp um die Welt von Morgen.* Retrieved from: http://www.spiegel.de/spiegel/print/index-2005-32.html

Drèze, J., & Sen, A. (2013). *An uncertain glory: India and its contradictions.* Princeton: Princeton University Press.

Eichengreen, B., Poonam, G., & Kumar, R. (2010). *Emerging giants: China and India in the world economy.* Oxford: Oxford University Press.

Fierke, K. M. (2010). Constructivism. In T. Dunne, M. Kurki, & S. Smith (Eds.), *International relations theories: Discipline and diversity* (2nd ed., pp. 177–194). Oxford: Oxford University Press.

Friedberg, A. L. (1993/1994). *Ripe for rivalry: Prospects for peace in a multipolar Asia. International Security, 18*(3), 5–33.

Friedberg, A. L. (2011). *A contest for supremacy: China, America and the struggle for mastery in Asia.* New York: W.W. Norton & Company.

Ganguly, S. (Ed.). (2003). *India as an emerging power.* London: Frank Cass Publishers.

Gilpin, R. (1981). *War and change in world politics.* Cambridge: Cambridge University Press.

Gilpin, R. (1987). American policy in the post-Reagan era. *Daedalus, 116*(3), 33–67.

Gordon, S. (2015). *India's rise as an Asian power: Nation, neighbourhood, and region.* Washington, DC: Georgetown University Press.

Gupta, S., & Mullen Randi, D. (2018). Introduction. In Gupta (Ed.) *Forum: Indian foreign policy under Modi: New brand or just repackaging? International studies perspectives.* Retrieved from: https://doi.org/10.1093/isp/eky008

Gupta, P. et al. (2018, March). *India development update: India's growth story*. The World Bank. Retrieved from: http://www.worldbank.org/en/news/press-release/2018/03/14/india-growth-story-since-1990s-remarkably-stable-resilient

Hobson, J. M. (2014). *The Eurocentric conception of world politics. Western international theory* (pp. 1760–2010). Cambridge: Cambridge University Press.

Hopf, T. (1998). The promise of constructivism in international relations theory. *International Security, 23*(1), 171–200.

Huntington, S. P. (1988). The US- decline or renewal? *Foreign Affairs, 67*(2), 76–96.

Ikenberry, G. J. (1989). Rethinking the origins of American hegemony. *Political Science Quarterly, 104*(3), 375–400.

Ikenberry, G. J. (2018). The end of liberal international order? *International Affairs, 94*(1), 7–23.

Joffe, J. (2009). The default power: The false prophecy of America's decline. *Foreign Affairs, 88*(5), 21–35.

Johnston, A. I. (2003). Is China a status quo power? *International Security, 27*(4), 5–56.

Jones, R. W. (2006). *India's strategic culture*. Federation of American Scientists. Retrieved from: https://fas.org/irp/agency/dod/dtra/india.pdf

Jones, B. D., & Steven, D. (2014). *The risk pivot. Great powers, international security, and the energy revolution*. Washington, DC: Brookings Institution Press.

Kagan, R. (2012). *The world America made*. New York: Alfred A. Knopf.

Kahn, H. (1971). *The emerging Japanese superstate*. London: A. Deutsch.

Kang, D. C. (2003). Getting Asia wrong. The need for new analytical frameworks. *International Security, 27*(4), 57–85.

Kant Jha, N. (1994). Reviving US-India friendship in a changing international order. *Asian Survey, 34*(12), 1035–1046.

Kennedy, P. (1987). *The rise and fall of the great powers: Economic change and military conflict from 1500 to 2000*. New York: Vintage Books.

Kennedy, P. (2009, January 14). American power is on the wane. *The Wall Street Journal*. Retrieved from http://online.wsj.com/article/SB123189377673479433.html

Khilnani, S. et al. (2012, February 29). *Nonalignment 2.0: A foreign and strategic policy for India in the Twenty First Century*. Centre for Policy Research. http://www.cprindia.org/research/reports/nonalignment-20-foreign-and-strategic-policy-india-twenty-first-century

Krasner, S. D. (1977). US commercial and monetary policy: Unravelling the paradox of external strength and internal weakness. *International Organization, 31*(4), 635–671.

Kupchan, C. (2012). *No one's world: The west, the rising rest, and the coming global turn*. Oxford: Oxford University Press.

Lansford, T. (2002). The great game renewed? US-Russian rivalry in the arms trade of South Asia. *Security Dialogue, 33*(2), 128–140.

Mahbubani, K. (2008). *The new Asian hemisphere: The irresistible shift of global power to the east*. New York: Public Affairs.

Majeed, A. (1990). Indian security perspectives in the 1990s. *Asian Survey, 30*(11), 1084–1098.

Mallavarapu, S. (2018). The sociology of international relations in India: Competing conceptions of political order. In G. Hellman (Ed.), *Theorizing global order. The international culture and governance* (pp. 142–171). Frankfurt: Campus Verlag.

Mearsheimer, J. J. (2001). *The tragedy of great power politics*. New York: W.W. Norton & Company.

Menon, R. (2014, October 23). The India myth. *The National Interest*. Retrieved from: http://nationalinterest.org/feature/the-india-myth-11517

Meredith, R. (2007). *The elephant and the dragon: The rise of India and China and what it means for all of us*. New York: W.W. Norton & Company.

Miller, M. C. (2016). The role of beliefs in identifying rising powers. *The Chinese Journal of International Politics, 9*(2), 211–238.

Mohan, C. R. (2015). *Modi's world: Expanding India's sphere of influence*. India: HarperCollins Publishers India.

Munk Debates. (2011, June 17). *Be it resolved, the 21st century will belong to China*. Retrieved from http://www.munkdebates.com/debates/China
Obama, B. H. (2011, April 21). *Remarks by the President at a DNC event*. The White House. Retrieved from: https://www.whitehouse.gov/the-press-office/2011/04/22/remarks-president-dnc-event
Obama, B. H. (2015, February). *National security strategy*. Retrieved from http://nssarchive.us/wp-content/uploads/2015/02/2015.pdf
Obama, B. H. (2016, June 7). *Joint statement—The United States and India: Enduring global partners in the 21st century*. The American Presidency Project. Retrieved from http://www.presidency.ucsb.edu/ws/index.php?pid=117903
Ogden, C. (2011). International "aspirations" of a rising power. In D. E. Scott (Ed.), *Handbook of India's international relations* (pp. 3–13). London: Routledge.
Ogden, C. (2017). *China and India: Asia's emergent great powers*. Cambridge: Polity Press.
Panagariya, A. (2010). *India: The emerging giant*. Oxford: Oxford University Press.
Pant, H. V. (2011). Indian strategic culture: The debate and its consequences. In D. E. Scott (Ed.), *Handbook of India's international relations* (pp. 14–22). London: Routledge.
Pant, H. V., & Joshi, Y. (2015). *The US pivot and Indian foreign policy: Asia's evolving balance of power*. New York: Palgrave Macmillan.
Piccone, T. (2016). *Five rising democracies: And the fate of the international liberal order*. Washington, DC: Brookings Institution Press.
Riedel, B. (2015). *JFK's forgotten crisis: Tibet, the CIA, and the Sino-Indian war*. Washington, DC: Brookings Institute.
Sagar, R. (2009). State of mind: What kind of power will India become? *International Affairs, 85*(4), 801–816.
Schaffer, T. C. (2009). *India and the United States in the 21st century: Reinventing partnership*. Washington, DC: Center for Strategic & International Studies.
Schweller, R. L. (1999). Managing the rise of great powers: History and theory. In A. I. Johnston & R. S. Ross (Eds.), *Engaging China: The management of an emerging power* (pp. 1–31). New York: Routledge.
Schweller, R. L. (2015). *Rising powers and revisionism in emerging international orders*. Valdai Institute Publication. Retrieved from: http://valdaiclub.com/a/valdai-papers/valdai_paper_16_rising_powers_and_revisionism_in_emerging_international_orders/
Sharma, S. D. (2006). Asia's challenged giants. *Current History, 105*(690), 170–175.
Sharma, S. D. (2009). *China and India in the age of globalization*. Cambridge: Cambridge University Press.
Sharma, S. D. (2016). Which way India? The Bhagwati–Sen debate and its lessons. *India Quarterly: A Journal of International Affairs, 72*(2), 192–199.
Sjoberg, L. (2017). The invisible structures of anarchy: Gender, orders, and global politics. *Journal of International Political Theory, 13*(3), 325–340.
Smith, S. (2004). Singing our world into existence: International relations theory and September 11. *International Studies Quarterly, 48*(3), 499–515.
Subrahmanyam, K., & Monteiro, A. (2005). *Shedding Shibboleths: India's evolving strategic outlook*. New Delhi: Wordsmiths.
Tanham, G. K. (1992a). Indian strategic culture. *The Washington Quarterly, 15*(1), 129–142.
Tanham, G. K. (1992b). *Indian strategic thought. An Interpretive Essay*. RAND Retrieved from http://www.rand.org/content/dam/rand/pubs/reports/2007/R4207.pdf
Tanham, G. K., Bajpai, K., & Mattoo, A. (1996). *Securing India: Strategic thought and practice*. New Delhi: Manohar Publications.
Tellis, A. J. (2007). What should we expect from India as a strategic partner? In H. Sokolski (Ed.), *Gauging US-Indian strategic cooperation* (pp. 231–258). Carlisle: Strategic Studies Institute.
Thakur, R. (1993). The impact of the Soviet collapse on military relations with India. *Europe-Asia Studies, 45*(5), 831–850.
Thakur, R. (1997). India in the world: Neither rich, powerful, nor principled. *Foreign Affairs, 76*(4), 15–22.

The Guardian. (2012). *European Commission criticised for "racist" ad*. Retrieved from: https://www.theguardian.com/world/2012/mar/06/european-commission-criticised-racist-ad

Tickner, A. (2013). Core, periphery and (neo)imperialist international relations. *European Journal of International Relations, 19*(3), 627–646.

Time Magazine. (2005). *China's new revolution. Remaking our world, one deal at a time*. Retrieved from http://content.time.com/time/covers/0,16641,20050627,00.html?

Trump, Donald J. (2017, December). *National security strategy*. Retrieved from https://www.whitehouse.gov/wp-content/uploads/2017/12/NSS-Final-12-18-2017-0905.pdf

van de Wetering, C. (2016). *Changing US foreign policy toward India: US-India relations since the cold war*. New York: Palgrave Macmillan.

van de Wetering, C. (2018). A narrative for cooperation with rising India: An analysis of a US think tank. In S. S. F. Regilme & J. Parisot (Eds.), *American hegemony and the rise of emerging powers: Cooperation or conflict* (pp. 149–168). Abingdon: Routledge.

Vogel, E. F. (1979). *Japan as number one: Lessons for America*. Cambridge: Harvard University press.

Waheguru, S. S., Mehta, P. B., & Jones, B. D. (2013). *Shaping the emerging world: India and the multilateral order*. Washington, DC: Brookings Institution Press.

Wendt, A. (1992). Anarchy is what states make of it: The social construction of power politics. *International Organization, 46*(2), 391–425.

Wendt, A. (1999). *Social theory of international politics*. Cambridge: Cambridge University Press.

Wohlforth, W. C. (2008). Realism. In C. Reus-Smit & D. Snidal (Eds.), *The Oxford handbook of international relations* (pp. 131–149). Oxford: Oxford University Press.

Wojczewksi, T. (2018). *India's foreign policy discourse and its conceptions of world order: The question for power and identity*. Abingdon: Routledge.

Wood, G. L., & Vaagenes, D. (1984). Indian defense policy: A new phase? *Asian Survey, 24*(7), 721–735.

Zakaria, F. (2008/2011). *The post-American world*. New York: W.W. Norton & Company.

Chapter 7
Africa in the Changing Global Order: Does African Agency Matter in Global Politics?

Fridon Lala

7.1 Introduction

The discourse concerning Africa's position in the international system has experienced a significant shift in the last two decades, from *The Hopeless Continent*[1] to *The Rising Star.*[2] In 2001, Tony Blair, Britain's Prime Minister at that time, during his speech to the annual Labour party conference called on the international community to back a partnership for Africa through joint forces and initiatives around the New African Initiative:

> The state of Africa is a scar on the conscience of the world. But if the world as a community focused on it, we could heal it. And if we don't, it will become deeper and angrier. (Tony Blair 2001)

Almost two decades later, the African continent is ranked among the emerging regions that are challenging the orthodoxy of the global governance architecture.

The post-Cold War era of multipolarity and shifts in global governance has opened doors for emerging economies and created space for intergovernmental organisations. Wyck (2016), describes a recent shift from ideological differences to economic differences between developed and developing countries. This has spurred a departure from the previous East-West global division towards a new North-South one. Acharya (2017) describes the twenty-first-century world as being "politically and culturally diverse, but economically and institutionally interlinked" as *multiplex world*. The term 'multiplex world' is defined as a world of interconnectedness and

---

[1] *See,* The Economist: Hopeless Africa at: https://www.economist.com/leaders/2000/05/11/hopeless-africa

[2] *See,* The Economist: Hopeful Africa at: https://www.economist.com/special-report/2013/03/02/a-hopeful-continent

---

F. Lala (✉)
School of Public Policy, Central European University in Budapest, Budapest, Hungary
e-mail: fridonlala@gmail.com

© Springer Nature Switzerland AG 2020
M. O. Hosli, J. Selleslaghs (eds.), *The Changing Global Order*, United Nations
University Series on Regionalism 17,
https://doi.org/10.1007/978-3-030-21603-0_7

interdependence, offering a variety of systems and institutions (Acharya 2017). The author illustrates such multiplexity by looking at the case examples of Trump and Brexit, which have shown that there are different variations of the world order even within the West not just between the West and East as it is generally assumed.

The denouement of the global power asymmetry and the rise of nations from the global South, especially China, opened new avenues for the African continent and increased its role in global politics. Political reforms coupled with rapid economic growth – fueled by South-South Cooperation (SSC) – have strengthened tremendously Africa's position as a global player. Cooperative initiatives, such as BRICS and IBSA, have been central in this re-conceptualization and reinterpretation of the changing global order. Besides boosting its economic growth and amplifying its political weight, such incidents of SSC offered greater opportunities for equal partnerships by strengthening the principle of sovereignty and discouraging the interference into African domestic affairs. Sovereignty remains a key global value which, in the case of Africa, had long been undermined by the intrusion of external powers. The 'African Renaissance'[3] led by Thabo Mbeki pursued ownership of the continent's development agenda, policy autonomy and challenged the Western hegemony. Driven by the ideology of *'African solutions for African problems'*, leading African politicians at the time aimed to end the long-term humiliation and colonial domination they had endured, instead seeking a relationship with their former colonizers and outside powers, not of paternalism, arrogance, and neo-colonialism, but of equal partnership (Landsberg 2011). Unlike traditional Western donors, emerging powers construe their ties to Africa in terms of South-South solidarity, shared identities and historical past, inequality and inherently incommensurate structures of international order.

The new multilateral global order has shifted the focus of the international order onto the world's regional groups and regional organizations. The rise of Africa is manifested with the birth of the African Union (AU), the New Partnership for Africa's Development (NEPAD) and many other pivotal regional organizations which offered Africa a platform to participate internationally, coordinate its development programs and assure solidarity among African nations in global negotiations. This stronger form of multilateralism enabled Africa to pursue higher goals. Africa is gradually taking its seat at the table and is re-negotiating its place in the global system by successfully contributing in international negotiations.

Being home to some of the poorest regions in the world,[4] Africa has long pushed for reorienting development strategies and has been the frontrunner in shaping the global normative framework on this. African nations harshly criticized the Bretton

---

[3] The concept date back to Cheikh Anta Diop's book *Towards the African Renaissance: Essays in Culture and Development,* 1946–1960.

The concept has been further popularised by former South African President Thabo Mbeki meaning the right of African people to determine
their own future.

[4] *See,* 2015's research from the Oxford Poverty and Human Development Initiative at:
http://www.ox.ac.uk/news/2015-01-07-world%E2%80%99s-poorest-regions-countries-you-wouldn%E2%80%99t-expect

Woods twins, The International Monetary Fund (IMF) and The World Bank (WB) regarding the impact of their structural adjustment programs on developing countries, especially in Africa. The institutions are critiqued for representing the interests of the wealthy western economies. Their programs and financial orthodoxies are claimed to be inappropriately developed and applied on the continent, considering Africa's development needs. In this regard, the BRICS countries established The New Development Bank as an alternative for developing countries. Moreover, Africa has been insisting on the reform of the United Nations system and pushing for a UN focus towards development issues, as well as demanding the greater representation of African countries on the UN Security Council (UNSC). Out of the five UN Regional Groups, The African Group is the largest one with 54 members and 28% of the votes in the UN General Assembly.

This chapter is a continuation of the section on the rise of new powers in the changing global order. The chapter analyses Africa's position in contemporary geopolitical and economic affairs, focusing on African agency and its role played in multilateral negotiations. It demonstrates an emergence of African agency in the multilateral fora in the domains of peace, security, climate change, and in shaping the global normative framework. The chapter starts by looking at African agency in international relations (IR) discourse, with a focus on the birth and rise of the AU as the continent's prime intergovernmental institution. It illustrates how the AU has come to be a voice for Africa, and its ability to exercise agency internationally in such cases as the UN system reform, African Common Position on Climate Change, AU-EU partnership and Doha Development Agenda. It also looks at the rise of the South Africa (SA) as the regional hegemon and continental giant.

7.2 African Agency

Traditional international relations (IR) theory has come under severe criticism for its narrow Eurocentric view of the African continent. They are seen to misapprehend the continent's reality and history (Brown 2006; Faleye 2014; Chipaike and Knowledge 2018). For many pundits, Africa has been ignored and marginalised within the IR discipline as well as subjectively studied by being an object of generalisation. As a non-Western actor, Africa is placed as the region at the periphery by mainstream IR studies (Brown 2006; Cornelissen et al. 2012; Acharya and Buzan 2007; Dunn and Shaw 2001; Warner and Shaw 2018; Chipaike and Knowledge 2018). According to Blaauw (2014), this is a result of the theory's focus on the power of states. Therefore, IR theory has tended to concentrate on great powers, portraying Africa as less institutionally functional in the traditional sense (Blaauw 2014). However, Brown (2006) argues that what is under attack is neorealism and not, by and large, IR theory as a whole (See Chap. 1 on *Traditional IR Theories*). There are other elements of Westernized IR theory that, in the era of growing multilateralism, new powers and non-state actors, have discerned the need for a more global approach to IR scholarship (See Chap. 2).

New power dynamics in a multipolar world gave rise to the concept of agency in the IR discourse. Andreasson (2013: 144), defines agency as the "ability of states as the primary actors in the international system, to generate and deploy a range of capabilities (hard and soft) in the pursuit of their national interest". Cargill (2013: 65) defines agency as "the capacity, as a matter of deliberate policy, to exert political influence externally". As shown by these two examples agency is variously delineated among authors and the lack of a common definition presents difficulties in evaluating the significance of agency in international politics. Regardless of its multifarious definitions, economic sanctions and military power are often seen to be the most pivotal instruments to exercise real power in foreign policy. Yet, smaller countries lacking one or two of the abovementioned instruments can still have an impact through the formation of coalitions and effective multilateralism (See Chap. 3).

Most of the existing literature on African agency is state-centric and focuses on extroversion, the role of external agencies in the continent. Nevertheless, questions on how African agency interacts, cooperates and competes with superpowers in the multipolar global system have been predominant issues in IR discussions. Brown (2012: 1891), defines African agency in four spheres: "that exercised by collective, intergovernmental organizations including the African Union and sub-regional intergovernmental bodies; that exercised by national states; the agency of state-based actors acting on behalf of national states; particularly state leaders and their representatives; and non-state actors". The period 1998–2008 saw the burgeoning of African diplomacy. Emerging African nations organised themselves in order to build a continental order. The birth of the AU, NEPAD and a few other successful African initiatives represent the pinnacle of this victorious decade for African diplomacy. While both articulating a continental outlook, most importantly, there was a demand for an equal partnership with world powers. Landsberg (2011), describes it as a relationship based on "the principles of mutual respect, equality, responsibility and accountability, responsiveness and an equitable world order" (p.7). According to the author, Africa wanted a partnership with its former colonisers and great powers, not paternalism or neo-colonialism. Moving away from a relationship of dependency, where African nations could have their own agendas and identify their own needs and priorities rather than having them imposed by outsiders (Landsberg 2011).

Over the last two decades, Africa's participation and engagement in global diplomacy has grown tremendously. The continent has played a pivotal role in the fields of climate change, world trade, migration, security, and terrorism. It has been successful in creating new allies and ties with emerging powers, as well as prevailing and strengthening its old relations with western partners. The following section provides an overview of the AU, as the most significant regional body in Africa and its role in coordinating common African interests in multilateral organisations. It introduces you to the cases of the UN reform system, African Common Position on Climate Change, AU-EU partnership and Doha Development Agenda. In these cases, the agency is evaluated as is the ability to act in order to change outcomes or rules. The African choice of being more than just a passive receiver.

7.3   African Union

Contemporary geopolitical and economic dynamics have shifted the focus of the international order onto regional groups. In this context, Africa's newfound influence is centered upon the African Union (AU), which is the continent's prime intergovernmental institution. The AU has emerged as Africa's preeminent platform to participate internationally, promoting unity among African nations in global negotiations. As the continent's foremost multilateral institution the AU is the main organizer, promoter, protector and defender of the continent's political, socio-economic and environmental interests.

In 2018, the AU marked 17 years since its establishment on May 26, 2001. Building on the Pan-African legacies of its predecessor, the Organisation of African Unity (OAU), the AU shifted and expanded its focus and mission towards new foundations, based on strong normative commitments such as constitutional democracy and the rejection of mass atrocity. The AU is the most significant instrument of African international agency, comprising 55-member states. The aims of the organisation are for a peaceful, prosperous and integrated Africa and it plays a pivotal role in the key areas of justice, migration, security & peace, and international affairs. The current chair, Paul Kagame, recently announced extensive structural and financial reforms. Kagame has emphasised the focus on political affairs and Africa's global representation (AU 2018).

In March 2018, the AU enacted the African Continental Free Trade Area (AfCFTA), the world's largest free trade zone in terms of member countries, which was ratified by nearly all its member states.[5] According to African leaders, the AfCFTA will strengthen Africa's position in global trade. The Chairperson of the African Union Commission, H.E. Moussa Faki said: "AfCFTA will make Africa one of the largest economies in the world and enhance its capacity to interact on equal terms with other international economic blocs." For the Kenyan President Uhuru Kenyatta "The African CFTA means an end to poverty." For the AU, the AfCFTA is a flagship project of its Agenda 2063. Comprised of seven aspirations,[6] Agenda 2063 is a roadmap for continental development, setting a number of achievable ambitions. It is a strategic framework for the socio-economic transformation of the continent, pledging a path to growth and sustainable development. Agenda 2063 was adopted on the occasion of the golden jubilee of the OAU, in 2015. It builds on the Pan African vision of "An integrated, prosperous and peaceful Africa, driven by its own citizens, representing a dynamic force in the international arena" (Agenda 2063 2015).

Since its foundation in 2001, the AU has played a crucial part in the domestic and foreign policy affairs of the continent. The Union is the central coordinating mechanism promoting peace and security, integration, and economic development within the continent. Several new institutions have been established by AU playing a key role in African politics in areas of representation, accountability, governance etc. In

---

[5] Nigeria, the largest economy in the continent did not join the agreement

[6] *See,* Agenda 2063 at: http://www.un.org/en/africa/osaa/pdf/au/agenda2063.pdf

a synchronous manner, the AU has been the main advocate of African interests at the international level. The AU has gained more legitimacy through its vital strategic partnerships, such as its relationship with the United Nations. The AU has been pushing for the reform of the UN system and insisting that the UN focus on development problems. Additionally, the AU has played a vibrant role in demanding African representation not only in the UN but also in the WB, IMF, and World Trade Organization (WTO). The Common African Position (CAP) on the Post-2015 Development Agenda, launched in 2014, is another fruitful initiative steered by the AU, which brought together the African Union Commission, UN Economic Commission, UNDP, and Regional Bureau for Africa and African Development Bank. This is an opportunity for Africa to effectively address development issues and participate in the global community's efforts to achieve the SDGs. The CAP prioritises structural transformation for inclusive and people-centered development in Africa (UNECA 2014). In terms of peace and security, the AU is the main mechanism used to steer conflict prevention negotiations, including intervening in cases of an unconstitutional change of government that could threaten armed conflict. (de Waal 2017).

7.3.1   AU, the Voice of Africa

Murithi (2012) identifies the AU as 'a voice of Africa'. Further, the author claims that the world is also waking up to this fact. This was reflected in President Obama's decision to give a speech at the African Union in Addis Ababa in 2015; the first time in history, an American President had addressed the Union. According to the UN Office of the Special Adviser on Africa, the AU has been effective as a leader and coordinator, ensuring that African nations increasingly speak with one voice on global matters. Agenda 2063 adopted by the AU affirms the importance of speaking with one voice and maintaining collective action when it comes to promoting common African interests globally. The AU also uses NEPAD, an umbrella framework, to help coordinate its continent-wide programs (UN-OSSA 2018). NEPAD is an example of the AU's persistence in trying to regain control of continental economic development policies, especially from the WB and IMF (Murithi 2012). Furthermore, Anthony Mothae Maruping, an AU Ex-Commissioner for Economic Affairs, stated that the continent played an important part in drawing up the post-2015 development goals, all due to the AU's success in organizing African voices in international issues (ECDPM 2015). Murithi (2012), asserts that the AU is the continent's leading norm entrepreneur and has established "norms to guide the behavior of its member states" (pp.664).

7.3.2   Ezulwini Consensus

Being unrepresented in the Security Council, Africa has been leading the calls for reform of the UN system. In this regard, the AU member nations agreed on a common position known as 'Ezulwini Consensus'.[7] The common position stressed the need for third world representation in the UN system. A proposal to expand the Security Council to 26 seats was submitted by the AU during the 2005 debate on UN reform. Five of the extra seats were foreseen to be permanent and 6 nonpermanent (Zondi 2013). However, the key demand of the AU was a veto right for all permanent members (Welz 2013). Following strong resistance from other UN member states, the AU launched negotiations with the G4 and successfully reached an agreement. The two groups came up with a joint proposal, which included two African countries having a permanent seat. However, the new G6 (G4 and two African countries) would not have a veto right, as was initially requested by the AU. Unfortunately, there arose a stalemate among the African nations as to who should represent them in the UNSC (Welz 2013). The two permanent seats foreseen for the African countries therefore remained empty as the nations could not reach a consensus in delegating two representatives. However, Zondi (2013) highlights the importance of the African Common Position in this process and the African courageousness in demanding greater representation in UN decision-making. According to the author, the process showed that if given permanent seats, the African nations represented would expect the same privileges as the five other permanent members.

7.3.3   Africa in Global Climate Governance – The Common Position on Climate Change

Climate change is one of the main talking points in contemporary global governance strategy. Having appreciated the gravity of the climate change challenge unfolding across the African continent, the AU adopted its own Declaration on Climate Change and Development in 2007. Two years later, AU member countries reached a consensus and agreed upon a common stand ahead of the Copenhagen Conference on Climate Change in 2009. The 'African Common Position on Climate Change' was a result of the AU's belief that the lack of a coordinated stance on global warming by African governments had previously placed serious limitations on Africa's ability to negotiate on this topic. Making the point that although Africa accounts for a very small proportion of global greenhouse gas emissions it is being impacted disproportionately by its negative effects. The common position therefore demanded compensation from more developed nations for the damages caused by climate change across the-continent.

---

[7] See, http://www.un.org/en/africa/osaa/pdf/au/cap_screform_2005.pdf

Apropos to the African Common Position, Zondi (2013) highlighted the crucial role of SA during the Copenhagen conference. As the negotiations over climate change stagnated because of the different positions of the US and China. Thanks largely to SA's facilitating efforts through the BASIC discussion group the 'Copenhagen Accord' was eventually successfully ratified (Zondi 2013). The Copenhagen Conference further demonstrated the capability of African nations to act as one, pursue common policy, and shape global negotiations.

Africa continues to be actively involved in global climate governance in various forms. The continent demonstrates an ongoing commitment and engagement to deal effectively and efficiently with the risks posed by climate change through the AU, and other associated institutions and mechanisms. For instance, the African Ministerial Conference on the Environment (AMCEN), a permanent forum where African ministers of the environment discuss matters of relevance to the environment of the continent, has been a central platform for presenting the African Common Position in the United Nations Framework Convention on Climate Change (UNFCCC).

7.3.4   AU – EU Strategic Partnership

According to the International Crisis Group (2017), the EU strengthened its long-term partnership with the AU starting from renaming their summit from Africa – EU to AU – EU. Through a strategic partnership with EU, such as aligned agendas on peace and security, migration, and terrorism, the AU is clearly gaining international power. In 2017, the fifth AU – EU Summit took place in Abidjan. The two sides agreed on a set of global priorities and discussed the progress of the Roadmap 2014–2017, which was launched during the previous Summit held in 2014. Among different priorities, priority number five states to "achieve common positions in global fora and international negotiations and jointly address global challenges" (EU-Africa Summit 2014). In May 2018, Brussels hosted the ninth high-level meeting between the Commissions of the two unions. According to the European Commission, both sides have adopted concrete actions measures to address global issues in key areas such as peace and security, migration, job creation, and agriculture. European Commission President Jean-Claude Juncker said: "The future of the world depends on the good cooperation between Europe and Africa", while his counterpart, African Union Chairperson H.E. Moussa Faki added: "Multilateralism is the only response to today's global challenges in an increasingly polarised world". These two sentences gave unequivocal and succinct indication regarding the importance of multilateralism as a platform for exercising agency for Africa, and its role in the future globalised world.

7.3.5   WTO – Doha Development Agenda

The WTO offers another key example of how African nations have exercised agency in multilateral negotiations. The continent has been proactive and engaged in the Doha Development Agenda (DDA) discussions, negotiating and proposing trade rules. During the DDA negotiations, African nations demanded accountability from advanced countries, urging them to live up to their commitments to global development (Lee 2013). By taking advantage of DDA's consensus decision-making process, African leaders insisted on the fulfilment of development promises made by major countries. Sharman (2007) argues that weak countries develop their resistance strategies by using the same rhetoric of the superpowers and WTO development discourse is an opportunity's dispenser for developing countries to raise their voice. Lee (2013) reasons the African capability in WTO due to the opportunity of exercising discursive power. As the international economic governance shifted its discourse towards development, African countries had the chance to refuse any agreements that did not foresee development outcomes. By using these DDA institutional and structural advantages and by establishing strategic partnerships with other members within WTO, African agency pushed forward their agenda and influenced WTO's processes. Besides negotiating process, some African countries also participate in various WTO bodies. According to Apecu (2013), the General Council, Committee on Trade and Development and the TRIPS Council are the ones where the African members are highly represented.

7.4   South Africa (SA)

The scholarly discourse on regional powers and regional hegemons has increased vis-à-vis the endless debate on emerging powers. Regional powers are considered an essential link of today's global governance chain. The tremendous progress of the post-apartheid SA has positioned the nation as a regional hegemonic power. The political and institutional reforms of SA's iconic president Mandela, who became the nation's first black president, laid the foundations for this new regional leadership. A change of regime, from segregationist and supremacist to a democratic system which valued and promoted human rights and equality, came with the great support of the international community. From an economic perspective, the 1994 democratic transition boosted the nation's economic performance, especially when compared to the previous decade (1984–1993) which was "the poorest ten-year growth performance since the Second World War" (Plessis and Smit 2006; 3). During the period 1996–2011, SA's dollarized GDP skyrocketed from around $140 billion to over $400 billion (Carrol 2017). SA beats developing nations in terms of fast industrialisation and has the most sophisticated economy on the continent (Kingah and Uberti 2016). Furthermore, SA is also a major source of FDI in Africa. According to UNCTAD (2013), South Africa was the second-most important investor in Africa (from developing nations) in 2012 after Malaysia. SA is also ranked as the most technologically advanced nation in Africa. According to the Global Innovation Index, SA continues to maintain the top spot among all economies in the region (Dutta, Lanvin and Wunsch-Vincent 2018).

In the political realm, SA has been a pioneer of African politics and diplomacy. The nation championed the African Agenda; promoting good governance, political stability, and economic prosperity on the continent. SA's determined efforts were paramount in erecting the current continental order as well as maintaining peace and security. During the presidency of Thabo Mbeki, SA was at the vanguard of the African Renaissance. Mbeki's vision was to embrace African identity and empower African people. He insisted on the right of African people to determine their own future, pushing a development agenda and challenging the Western hegemony. With Mbeki acting as the chief architect of NEPAD, the Pan-African Parliament (PAP), the African Peer Review Mechanism (APRM) and the birth of the AU, SA paved the way for its regional leadership. The launch of such institutions, masterminded by Mbeki, represented a milestone in African history. SA became the first African nation to chair the AU, setting the tone of its hegemonic power. The nation's focus and proactive engagement in the continent helped Africa to grease the wheels in global politics. Moreover, SA emerged as a middle power in the international order, characterised by its soft power (Soko and Balchin 2016).

In June 2018, SA was elected to serve as a non-permanent member on the United Nations Security Council (UNSC) for the term 2019–2020, which will be nation's third term, having previously served in 2007–2008 and 2011–2012. SA received an overwhelming level of support from other UN member states and its African counterparts. Its candidature was nominated by the Southern African Development Community (SADC) and endorsed by the AU, being the only African nation backed by the regional body, according to Human Rights Watch.[8] Its membership in elite clubs such as the G20 and BRICS, strengthens the nation's prestige and enhances its regional and global influence. Multilateral bodies and strategic partnerships have given SA the opportunity to raise the African voice at the international level. Its engagements and efforts are building blocks in the processes of regional economic integration, peace, and security in the continent. Many pundits identify SA as the African spokesman.

When it comes to bilateral relations with the continent, SA has been a longstanding strategic partner for both, western and eastern powers. According to the European Commission's data, the European Union remains committed as SA's most important development partner, providing for 70% of all external assistance funds, including Foreign Direct Investments.[9] All trade programs are under EU – SADC EPA (Southern African Development Community, Economic Partnership Agreement). Among SADC EPA nations, SA is the EU's largest trading partner as it is recognized

---

[8] *See* the post at: https://www.hrw.org/news/2018/06/11/south-africa-secures-seat-un-security-council-third-time

[9] *See*, EU Commission 2018 at: http://ec.europa.eu/trade/policy/countries-and-regions/countries/south-africa/

as being the strongest of sub-Saharan Africa's economies.[10] The basis of EU – SA relations is underpinned by the Trade, Development and Cooperation Agreement (TDCA)[11] of 1999, which is affirmed by the Multiannual Indicative Programme between SA and EU for the period of 2014–2020.[12] Politically, there is a range of dialogues, regular Presidential summits and Ministerial meetings and regular SA-EU Political and Security Committee meetings. The EU's partnership abets SA to push its agenda forward in aligned areas of common interest including; peace and security, energy and innovation, migration, human rights etc., as well as to increase its influence in the global fora.

Similarly, SA is India's largest trading partner on the continent due to SA's developed markets (Taylor 2014). According to the United Nations Economic Commission for Africa (2015), SA was India's top exporter for the period of 2014–2015. Their long history of partnership dating back to the 1960's is built upon South-South cooperation. In April 2018, the first ever India – South Africa Business Summit took place in Johannesburg. The High Commission of India in Pretoria announced that this summit sought to maximize the potential of the economic and commercial partnership between the two nations. SA has been successful in establishing beneficial bilateralism with other BRICS nations as well. In September 2018, Chinese President Xi Jinping agreed to pump $14 billion into SA.[13] Russian President Vladimir Putin expressed his idea on organising the very first Russian-African summit during 2018 BRICS Summit in Johannesburg. SA's strategic partnership with Russia lies in the area of foreign politics, in particular within the UN and BRICS.

Throughout the years, Pretoria has also developed a solid partnership with Washington. Carrol (2017) ranks SA as the US' main African trading partner. The two nations also share common areas of interest when it comes to regional security, trade and investment, and public health. John Kerry, a former US Secretary of State, in his speech during the meeting with South African Foreign Minister Maite Nkoana-Mashabane stated:

> South Africa is playing an increasingly important global role, a very important leadership role on the continent of Africa, and, we are pleased to say, an important cooperative role together with the United States. (John Kerry 2015)

However, under the Trump administration, the US – SA relationship has somewhat faltered. President Trump has been apathetic in maintaining partnerships with the African continent and has lacked a clear foreign policy towards Africa. He has been criticized for the delays in filling key diplomatic positions such as the Assistant Secretary for African Affairs, who has just been appointed in July 2018, and the position of the US Ambassador to South Africa. The post of US ambassador to SA

---

[10] *See*, EU Commission 2018 at: http://ec.europa.eu/trade/policy/countries-and-regions/regions/sadc/

[11] *See* TDCA at: https://eur-lex.europa.eu/legal-content/EN/TXT/?uri=LEGISSUM:r12201

[12] *See* MIP at: https://ec.europa.eu/europeaid/node/96850

[13] *See* https://www.thesouthafrican.com/three-major-agreements-just-signed-by-china-and-south-africa/

has been vacant since 2016. Recently, Lana Marks, a handbag designer has report-edly been chosen by Donald Trump as the next US ambassador to SA.[14]

Despite all the above-mentioned points, SA's assumed regional leadership has not gone uncontested by its neighbors. Scholvin (2018) suggests that examples of such contestation can be both intentional and unintentional and can be variously interpreted as arising from processes of hard balancing, soft balancing, rejection of followership, and a disregard of leadership (p. 3). But, does SA have the material capabilities to fulfil the criteria of a regional hegemon and to exert influence and leadership? Leadership can be exercised through hard and soft power, as well as a combination of the two, which is known as smart power (See Chaps. 1, 2 and 3). Let us then evaluate SA's leadership ambitions through the prism of these leadership determinants. In terms of hard power i.e. assessing the nation's military capabilities, SA has one of the strongest and largest militaries on the continent. SA is ranked 33rd on Global Firepower's 2018 World Military Strength Rankings, notably above European nations such as Switzerland, Norway, and the Netherlands (Global Firepower 2018). In economic terms, SA has been considered as one of the biggest African economies. SA's stock exchange is Africa's largest and among the top 20 in the world. The nation is also steadily recovering from the low economic growth rates of 2015/2016. GDP growth increased from 1.3% in 2017 to 1.4% in 2018, and economic forecasts predict growth rates of up to 2% by 2020. According to the WB, this would contribute to a wider economic rebound for emerging markets and devel-oping economies, and to overall global growth (WB 2018). Soft power is deter-mined by a nation's political value, culture and foreign policy. SA has been revered for its ideal of Ubuntuism which it has adopted in its approach to foreign policy and is built around the core values of freedom, human rights, equality, and justice. SA was also one of the forerunners in implementing the Rome Statute of the International Criminal Court (ICC) and was the first nation on the continent to enact the Statute into domestic law (Kingah and Quilicioni 2016). SA further showed its cultural leadership by organizing successfully one of the biggest events worldwide, The FIFA World Cup 2010. SA also remains the most technologically advanced nation in Africa, an indicator of the nation's smart power. However, SA's 'golden decade' came to an end after Mbeki's resignation.[15] The African giant and spokesman declined in global standing and lost its pole position in the continent. Its preeminent regional position has subsequently waned and been challenged by other sub-Saharan nations such as Nigeria, Angola, Kenya and Ethiopia. According to Scholvin (2018), from the perspective of IR realism this is to be expected as secondary powers are

---

[14] See, The Guardian: https://www.theguardian.com/us-news/2018/oct/02/lana-marks-trump-us-ambassador-south-africa

[15] *See*, The New York Times: https://www.nytimes.com/2018/02/14/world/africa/zuma-south-africa-legacy.html;

The Telegraph: https://www.telegraph.co.uk/news/worldnews/africaandindianocean/south-africa/11684492/South-Africas-long-walk-to-decline.html;

fin24:https://www.fin24.com/BizNews/numbers-dont-lie-sa-moving-backwards-under-zumas-leadership-20160902-3 likely to pursue competitive or even confrontational policies vis-à-vis regional hegemons.

From the economic perspective, Nigeria overtook SA as the largest sub-Saharan African economy in terms of overall GDP since 2014. IMF affirms Nigeria as Africa's largest economy with estimated GDP of $376.3 billion in 2017. The list of top African economies looks different when wealth is measured by GDP per capita. From this perspective, Nigeria is ranked 15 in the continent (IMF 2018). Country's size, economic upswing and military capabilities are main indicators of Nigeria's influence in the region. Nigeria is ranked 4 in terms of military strength in Africa by GFP 2018. Also, the nation was one of the largest contributors to UN peacekeeping missions in past years. However, the number declined greatly, from 2968 people in 2015 to 455 in 2018 (UN 2018). Nigeria's economic potential has earned her consideration for inclusion in the N-11 or Next 11[16] emerging countries (Adetula 2014). Considering all the factors, Nigeria's continental and international influence is rising gradually and the nation is long contesting SA's hegemonic power in the region. Undoubtedly, part of the continent's rise discourse and the tectonic shift of its position in global politics is attributed to Nigeria's recent rise.

Other contributing factors to SA's decline include; some misguided foreign policy decisions taken by Jakob Zuma's administration, the rise of xenophobia in the country, economic stagnation, growing inequality, and rising unemployment. Soko and Balchin (2016), add to this list SA's mismanagement of the crisis in Zimbabwe, which represented one of its most glaring failures according to the authors. SA has been also criticised for its inability to integrate its global aspirations into a concrete set of foreign policies. According to Kingah and Umberti (2016), SA lacks a clear and coherent strategy or commonly defined goal in order to operationalise a leadership role in the international system. There are no attempts in public diplomacy to pursue a harmonious agenda that the nation should follow at the global level. "… coherent national, regional and global vision for itself remains to be reliably confronted" (Kingah and Umberti 2016; 221).

Yet, SA has recorded significant achievements and has been the African frontrunner in global politics and multilateral fora for a long time. The country led Africa through some of its crucial periods and transformations, carrying successfully the mantle of the leadership. Through its strategic partnerships and its membership in clubs such as the G20, BRICS, and IBSA, SA has been the leading African voice in the global arena and has constantly pushed and contributed to the reconfiguration of the international architecture. In 2018, under the theme 'BRICS in Africa', SA hosted the tenth annual BRICS summit. The BRICS leaders declared that they will join efforts to strengthen multilateralism and push for a fairer, more equal, more democratic and more representative world order. Furthermore, SA has reawakened under the new presidency of Cyrill Ramaphosa, beginning with fighting corruption which has been one of his top priorities. Regarding the question of regional

---

[16] Next Eleven is a term coined by Jim O'Neill of Goldman Sachs including countries that have the potential for attaining global

competitiveness based on their economic and demographic settings.

hegemony, the rise of secondary powers and hegemonic contestations may in fact turn out to be a positive step towards the reinforcement of the African voice beyond the borders of the continent.

7.5 Conclusion

Gauging African agency and answering squarely whether it matters or not is an uphill struggle. Two main obstacles that one encounters in the evaluation of African agency are the lack of a common definition and its multifaceted role. As demonstrated in this chapter the AU, the main institutional agent on the continent, plays a dual role. On the one hand, the Union builds unity among its nations and coordinates domestic policies, on the other the organization has been advocating globally for African interests since its foundation. However, African agency is an incontrovertible fact and its significance is increasing gradually. Various African actors exercise agency at different levels, from individual states, like SA through its bilateral agreements and strategic partnerships, to intergovernmental organizations. In all cases, the structural organization of the relevant institutions is crucial to the process of exercising agency.

The continent has long pushed for realigning development strategies and has been the frontrunner in shaping the global normative framework in this regard. Africa has rightly earned its laurels from international studies pundits for advancing the concepts of fairness and equality in the new global order through pro-active participation in global negotiations. Furthermore, Africa has been the leader among developing nations in representing their interests in the international fora. Africa has been championing the reconfiguration of the international architecture, aiming for an equilibrium between growth and development and calling for an open and participatory global community. Africa has also been revered for its role in refashioning today's multilateralism. Allying with emerging powers, the continent is known for its contribution in shaping modern multilateralism whilst promoting the development agenda. Through regional mechanisms, such as the AU, which successfully emerged as the continent's prime intergovernmental institution, Africa has been at the forefront of the processes of UN system reform, global climate governance, peace, security, and trade negotiations. Again, since signing the world's largest free trade zone (CFTA), Africa is progressively securing its seat at the top table. Likewise, Africa plays a crucial role in global governance systems that seek to reduce inequalities and bring about global stability.

> We expect the billion Africans who in the past decade have already experienced the fastest growth the continent has ever seen to become the fastest two billion, and Africa' s GDP to increase from \$2 trillion today to \$29 trillion in today' s money by 2050…The process will not be complete by 2050, but Africa is set to be the final beneficiary of this revolution. (Charles Robertson 2012)

In other words, in the book *The Fastest Billion: The Story Behind Africa's Economic Revolution,* Charles Robertson believes that by 2050, the continent will produce more GDP than the US and Eurozone combined do today.

Further Readings

Alden, C., & Large, D. (2018). *New directions in Africa-China studies.* Abingdon: Routledge.

Brown, W., & Harman, S. (2013). *African agency in international politics.* Abingdon: Routledge.

Ebert, H., & Flemes, D. (2018). *Regional powers and contested leadership.* Cham: Palgrave Macmillian.

Robertson, C. (2012). *The fastest billion: The story behind Africa's economic revolution.* London: Renaissance Capital.

Taylor, I. (2014). *Africa rising? BRICS – Diversifying dependency.* Woodbridge: James Currey.

References

Acharya, A. (2017). After liberal hegemony: The advent of a multiplex world order. *Ethics & International Affairs, 31*(03), 271–285.

Acharya, A., & Buzan, B. (2007). Why is there no non-western international relations theory? An introduction. *International Relations of the Asia-Pacific, 7*(3), 287–312.

Adetula, V. (2014). Nigeria's rebased economy and its role in regional and global politics. *E-International Relations.* [online] Available at: https://www.e-ir.info/2014/10/13/nigerias-rebased-economy-and-its-role-in-regional-and-global-politics/

Agenda 2063: The Africa we want. (2015). *African Union Commission. [online] Available at: https://au.int/sites/default/files/documents/36204-doc-agenda2063_popular_version_en.pdf. Accessed 6 September 2018*

Andreasson, S. (2013). Elusive agency: Africa's persistently peripheral role in international relations. In W. Brown & S. Harman (Eds.), *African agency in international politics.* Abingdon: Routledge.

Apecu, J. (2013). The level of African engagement at the World Trade Organization from 1995 to 2010. *Revue internationale de politique de développement, 4*(2), 29–67.

Au.int. (2018). *Home|African Union.* [online] Available at: https://au.int/. Accessed 5 Sept 2018.

Blaauw, L. (2014). Challenging realists international relations theory: Soft balancing and agency in the international relations of African states. *Afro Asian Journal of Social Sciences, 5*(5.2), 2229–5313.

Blair, T. (2001). *Full speech at the Labour Party conference.* [online] Available at: https://www.independent.co.uk/news/uk/politics/tony-blairs-speech-full-text-5363384.html. Accessed 10 Aug 2018.

Brown, W. (2006). Africa and international relations: A comment on IR theory, anarchy and statehood. *Review of International Studies, 32*(01), 119–143.

Brown, W. (2012). A question of agency: Africa in international politics. *Third World Quarterly, 33*(10), 1889–1908.

Cargill, T. (2013). Back to business? UK policy and African agency. In W. Brown & S. Harman (Eds.), *African agency in international politics.* Abingdon: Routledge.

Carrol, A. (2017). *Forging a new era in US-south African relations.* [online] Washington: The Atlantic Council. Available at: http://www.atlanticcouncil.org/images/Forging_a_New_Era_in_US-South_African_Relations_1128_web.pdf. Accessed 3 Sept 2018.

Chipaike, R., & Knowledge, M. (2018). The question of African agency in international relations. *Cogent Social Sciences, 4*(1), 1–16.

Cornelissen, S., Cheru, F., & Shaw, T. (Eds.). (2012). *Africa and international relations in the 21st century*. Chippenham: Palgrave Macmillian.

de Waal, A. (2017). The emerging global order, multilateralism and Africa. In *Background paper for African union annual mediators' retreat*. Cambridge, MA: World Peace Foundation.

du Plessis, S., & Smit, B. (2006). Economic growth in South Africa since 1994. In *Economic policy under democracy: A ten year review*. Stellenbosch: University of Stellenbosch.

Dunn, K., & Shaw, T. (Eds.). (2001). *Africa's challenge to international relations theory*. London: Palgrave Macmillian.

Dutta, S., Lanvin, B., & Wunsch-Vincent, S. (2018). *Global innovation index 2018*. [online] Geneva: Cornell University; INSEAD; WIPO. Available at: https://www.globalinnovationin-dex.org/gii-2018-report. Accessed 25 Aug 2018.

ECDPM. (2015). *Interview with H.E. Anthony Maruping* [video]. Available at: https://www.you-tube.com/watch?v=RvLBuPoPdYM. Accessed 3 Sep 2018.

EU-Africa Summit. (2014). *Roadmap 2014–2017*. Brussels.

Faleye, O. (2014). Africa and international relations theory: Acquiescence and responses. *Journal of Globalization Studies, 5*(2), 81–90.

Global Firepower. (2018). *2018 military strength ranking*. [online] Available at: https://www.glo-balfirepower.com/countries-listing.asp. Accessed 6 Aug 2018.

International Crisis Group. (2017). *Time to reset African union-European Union relations*. Africa report no 255. [online] Brussels: International Crisis Group. Available at: https://d2071an-dvip0wj.cloudfront.net/255-time-to-reset-african-union-european-union-relations.pdf. Accessed 24 Aug 2018.

International Monetary Fund. (2018). *World economic outlook*. [online] Available at: http://www.imf.org/external/datamapper/datasets/WEO. Accessed 2 Sept 2018.

Kerry, J. (2015). Remarks with South African Foreign Minister Maite Nkoana-Mashabane. (2015). [Speech] https://2009-2017.state.gov/secretary/remarks/2015/09/246970.htm. U.S. Department of State, Washington, DC.

Kingah, S., & Quiliconi, C. (2006). *Global and Regional Leadership of BRICS Countries*. Cham: Springer.

Kingah, S., & Umberti, S. (2016). How South Africa the spine for global leadership. In S. Kingah & C. Quilicioni (Eds.), *Global and regional leadership of BRICS countries*. Cham: Springer.

Landsberg, C. (2011, September 14). *Fractured continentally, undermined abroad: African agency in world affairs*. Paper presented to the seminar African Agency: Implications for IR Theory, London. Available at: https://www.open.ac.uk/socialsciences/bisa-africa/files/africanagency-seminar4-landsberg.pdf. Accessed 13 Aug 2018.

Lee, D. (2013). African agency in global trade governance. In W. Brown & S. Harman (Eds.), *African agency in international politcs*. Abingdon: Routledge.

Murithi, T. (2012). Briefing: The African union at ten: An appraisal. *African Affairs, 111*(445), 662–669.

Office of the Special Adviser on Africa (OSAA). (2018). [online] Available at: http://www.un.org/en/africa/osaa/. Accessed 9 Sept 2018.

Scholvin, S. (2018). Contestation in sub-Saharan Africa: The foreign policies of Angola, Kenya and Nigeria Vis-à-Vis South Africa. In H. Ebert & D. Flemes (Eds.), *Regional powers and contested leadership*. Cham: Palgrave Macmillian.

Sharman, J. (2007). The agency of peripheral actors: Small state tax havens and international regimes as weapons of the weak. In J. Hobson & L. Seabrooke (Eds.), *Everyday politics of the world economy* (pp. 45–62). Cambride: Cambridge University Press.

Soko, M., & Balchin, N. (2016). South Africa's quest for leadership in Africa: Achievements, con-straints and dilemmas. In S. Kingah & C. Quilicioni (Eds.), *Global and regional leadership of BRICS countries*. Cham: Springer.

The World Bank. (2018). *South Africa economic update*. [online] Washington: The World Bank. Available at: http://pubdocs.worldbank.org/en/798731523331698204/South-Africa-Economic-Update-April-2018.pdf. Accessed 17 Aug 2018.

UNCTAD. (2013). *World investment report 2013*. [online] Geneva: United Nations. Available at: http://unctad.org/en/PublicationsLibrary/wir2013_en.pdf. Accessed 2 Sept 2018.

United Nations Economic Commission for Africa. (2014). *Common African position on the post-2015 development agenda*. [online] Available at: https://sustainabledevelopment.un.org/index.php?page=view&type=400&nr=1329&menu=35. Accessed 13 Aug 2018.

United Nations Economic Commission for Africa. (2015). *AFRICA-INDIA facts & figures*. Available at: https://www.uneca.org/sites/default/files/PublicationFiles/africaindia_ff_17oct_rev4.pdf

United Nations Peacekeeping. (2018). *Troop and police contributors*. [online] Available at: https://peacekeeping.un.org/en/troop-and-police-contributors. Accessed 19 Nov 2018.

van Wyck, J. (2016). Africa in international relations: Agent, bystander or victim? In P. Bischoff, K. Aning, & A. Acharya (Eds.), *Africa in global international relations: Emerging approaches to theory and practice*. Abingdon: Routledge.

Warner, J., & Shaw, T. (Eds.). (2018). *African foreign policies in international institutions*. New York: Palgrave Macmillan.

Welz, M. (2013). The African union beyond Africa: Explaining the limited impact of Africa's continental organization on global governance. *Global Governance, 19*(3), 425–441.

Zondi, S. (2013). Common positions as African agency in international negotiations: An appraisal. In W. Brown & S. Harman (Eds.), *African agency in international politics*. Abingdon: Routledge.

Part III
Regional Organisations in Global Affairs

Chapter 8
The Rise of Regions: Introduction to Regional Integration & Organisations

Joren Selleslaghs and Luk Van Langenhove

8.1 The Field of Regionalism, Regional Cooperation and Regional Integration in International Relations

One of the main challenges facing modern societies today is that they have rapidly become increasingly interconnected. A crucial aspect of this are the increased inter-actions across borders among citizens, society, markets and the state (Thakur and Van Langenhove 2006). Behind the forces of globalization, states have now been joined on the international stage by a plethora of other public and private actors. Among these new influential actors, particularly since the post-WWII era and even more increasingly so since the end of the Cold War, have been the rise and prolifera-tion of regional organizations (ROs), which have largely been created in response to dealing with new transnational political and economic governance concerns able to permeate between state borders.

In the study of regional organizations, scholars have stressed the importance of distinguishing between the concepts of regionalism, regional cooperation, regional sub-systems or sub regional systems and regional integration (Van Langenhove 2011). Regional integration could be seen as 'an end process', as Nye (1968: 856–858) claims, whereas "terms and concepts such as regional cooperation, orga-nization, regional systems, and regional subsystems may help describe steps on the way towards regional integration, but they should not be confused with the resulting condition". For instance, regional cooperation represents the interaction of states within a region towards specific areas of policy concern. More on this will be

J. Selleslaghs (✉)
Faculty of Governance and Global Affairs, Leiden University, The Hague, The Netherlands
e-mail: selleslaghs.joren@gmail.com

L. Van Langenhove
Institute of European Studies, Free University of Brussels (VUB), Brussels, Belgium

© Springer Nature Switzerland AG 2020
M. O. Hosli, J. Selleslaghs (eds.), *The Changing Global Order*, United Nations University Series on Regionalism 17,
https://doi.org/10.1007/978-3-030-21603-0_8

addressed in the proceeding parts of this chapter. Additionally, as is evident from a practical standpoint, some regions also include sub-regions within the broader regional ambit, and institutions are grounded on such specific sub regions, i.e. sub-systems within a region. For example, within the broader framework of Latin America (OAS-CELAC) there exist sub-regional organizations in the Caribbean (CARICOM), Central (SICA), and Southern America (CAN-MERCOSUR-UNASUR). Sub-regional systems are also evident in Africa and within the broader framework of the African Union (AU). Akin to the sub-regional systems noted above in Latin America, ECOWAS, SADC, CEMAC, IGAD, and to a certain extent the Arab Maghreb Union, are some examples of sub-regional systems within Africa (and the AU).

There has been, and still is, much debate over what exactly constitutes a region, how the boundaries of a region may be drawn, and how regional projects are to be operationalized (Van Langenhove 2011; Fawcett 2016). This matter is complicated further due to that fact that those attempting to define a region often find that they are not clearly defined, but have burred boundaries and are prone to adaptation and change. According to Fredrik Söderbaum and Timothy Shaw, this problem of definition has been further "exasperated by the various, and often competing, qualitative and quantitative approaches to regionalization seeking to understand and measure its processes" (Söderbaum and Shaw 2003: 5–6). In light of these theoretical burdens, competing approaches, and problems of defining regionalism and regionalization, it is perhaps most constructive for the purposes of this chapter to maintain a more open definition. To this end, following the arguments put forth by Louise Fawcett, it may simply be put that with respect to an increase in regional interaction and activity, "regionalism refers to policies and projects", whereas "regionalization refers to processes" (Fawcett 2016) and regionalization refers to "processes of regional cooperation" (Telò et al. 2015: 36). A similar definition has been put forward by both Morgan (2005) and Van Langenhove (2011) who distinguish between regional projects (or dreams), regional processes (the acts that put the dreams into practice) and the regional products (the institutionalization of the integration into treaties and organizations as well into flows of goods, capitals, services and people).

In recent years, regional integration is usually defined as "a concept used by policymakers and social scientists to refer to the strengthening of interconnections between neighbouring states" (Van Langenhove 2011: 48). From a historical point of view, it is not an entirely new concept, as the first forms of regional integration date back as early as the nineteenth century (Selleslaghs 2014).[1] Yet it is in recent history that regional organizations have been created all over the world, one more known than the other. Scholars such as Dicken (2007: 189) have closely studied the genesis and evolution of regional cooperation/integration systems and speak of four different "waves of regionalism" each with its own characteristics. The first "wave"

---

[1] A number of trade agreements were established in Europe such as the customs unions between the Austrian and Nordic states.

dates back to the nineteenth century and lasted until the First World War. It was a period characterized by a large variety of regions and regional communities which were interconnected to one another by means of alliances, pacts, unions etc. However, as Jönsson et al. (2000: 22–23) explained: "in the revolutionary year of 1848, the idea of a unified Europe gained a broader following". Yet, the outbreak of World War I prohibited any such political project to be properly executed. Also in other continents, regionalism dates back (at least) to the nineteenth century. In Latin America for example, Simon Bolivar played a key role in developing a sense of Latin American (or 'Pan-American') shared identity against the Spanish conquistadores (Sommer 1991).

The second wave mostly covers the *interbellum* period and ends in the mid 1960's. It is characterized by a period in which, according to Fawcett (2009: 18) "material calculations, the power balance, security and pursuit of (state) interests are central". Three main types of regional integration efforts can be identified in this period (Fawcett 2009; Mendel University 2018). First, so called 'multipurpose' institutions like the League of Arab States (LAS) and the Organisation of American States (OAS). Second, regional security alliances, most notably NATO, but also the Warsaw Pact and the Rio Pact fall into this category. As Fawcett (2009:18) explains: "these alliances owed their rationale more to the evolving Cold War system and corresponding attempts by the superpowers to consolidate their respective spheres of influence, and as such constituted a blow to multilateralism". Finally, the third type of regional integration efforts were more economic in nature, and envisaged regional (macro-)economic harmonization and integration. Europe led the way in this category with the creation of the European Community (EC) in 1958, followed by other regional economic integration efforts which made the global order "filled with proposals for NAFTA, PAFTA, LAFTA… and more" (Fawcett 2009: 8).

It was also in this period that most European nations were still colonial powers and organized their geopolitical influence sphere by means of regional bonds (Söderbaum 2016). For example, the British Empire created the Southern African Customs Union (SACU) in order to structure and organize its colonial territories in Southern Africa and the French created the CFA Franc Zone (CFA) in francophone Africa which still characterizes regionalism in Western Africa today (Niemann 2001: 69).

However, as Van Langenhove (2011: 52) noted, the third (until the 1970s) and fourth (current) waves of regionalism are the ones that are studied mostly, as they attract much attention by truly *challenging* the actual Westphalian World Order which (still) is dominated by sovereign nation states. Whereas the third wave of regionalism is often referred to as "old" regionalism, the fourth wave is referred to in the study of "new regionalism". In old regionalism studies, scholars look at the regional blocs that began to emerge during the 1950s and 1960s: the European Economic Community (EEC) most notably, but also the Latin American Free Trade Area (LAFTA), the Central American Common Market (CACM), and the Andean Pact (AP) were examined (Warleigh-Lack and Rosamond 2010: 994). Even if most scholarly attention was oriented towards the European continent, some literature also emerged on regionalist tendencies in the developing world, most notably Latin America and Africa. Here, scholars mostly studied how regional cooperation schemes could provide a structural solution to economic development and even nation-building (Söderbaum 2016). For example, Raul Prebisch, the Executive Secretary of the United Nations Economic Commission (ECLA) believed that economies of scale and liberalized intra-regional trade would ultimately provide the necessary economic growth for the continent (Prebisch 1959). Hence (old) regionalism in the developing world provided a different rationale for regional (economic) integration than it did on the European continent: it was not so much about avoiding war but more about economic development and cooperation to solve shared regional governance issues.

Shifting our attention towards "New regionalism", the break-down of the Berlin wall and the end of the bi-polar world order was a decisive moment nearing the end of the 80s, as newly independent states were left in "political uncertainty and instability" (Söderbaum and Van Langenhove 2005: 255). Furthermore, as globalization accelerated at a high pace, more and more countries began to look for regional cooperation schemes in order to counterbalance the wide-ranging effects of worldwide economic interdependence[2] (Söderbaum and Van Langenhove 2005: 256). This led to the creation (or evolution of pre-existing ones) of so-called "New regionalist" cooperation/integration schemes as the EU and MERCOSUR. Following Hettne et al. (1999: 7–8) and de Melo and Panagarriya (1995), this new regionalism can be defined by contrasting it with the old regionalism: (1) new regionalism is a truly worldwide phenomenon and not so (2) Eurocentric anymore, (3) it has broader and more comprehensive aims than the rather narrowly defined defensive and economical oriented aims of old regionalism and encompasses political, cultural and social aspects too and finally (4) the process of integration can be driven or initiated "from below" instead of "from above".

Since the turn of the millennium, various scholars[3] have offered new concepts and approaches to study regionalist movements around the world which has led Söderbaum (2016) to suggest a new, *fifth* wave of regionalism: namely 'Comparative Regionalism'. According to Söderbaum (2016: 30), defining characteristics of the current wave of regionalism include:

> the war on terror, the responsibility to intervene and protect, changing understandings of government and governance, a multilayered or "multiplex" global order, the rise of the BRICS and emerging powers, recurrent financial crises and the persistent pattern of overlapping and crisscrossing regional and interregional projects and processes in most parts of the world.

---

[2] According to Van Langenhove (2011: 48) the Westphalian world order has three built in deficiencies that make it difficult to come to just and efficient global governance schemes that also contribute towards the creation of new regionalist cooperation schemes: the differences in size of states that challenge the principle that all states are equal; the differences in wealth and power that allow some states to dominate others; and the non-binding aspects of the multilateral system.

[3] See for example Riggirozzi and Tussie (2012) in which the authors propose the concept of "post-neoliberal regionalism" or Acharya (2014) who proposed "converging regions" and Baldersheim et al. (2011) introducing the concept of "networking regions".

In addition, contemporary "Comparative" regionalism acknowledges the increasing multidimensionality and multilayered nature of regionalism, where state and non-state actors, institutions and processes interact heavily at both national, regional (so called 'inter-regionalism, see Chap. 9 in this volume) and the global level (Söderbaum 2016). Contemporary "Comparative" regionalism also identifies new policy fields in which regionalism is expanding, such as: gender and social policy, migration, science policy, environmental governance etc (Söderbaum 2016). Other scholars from their side try to bring the academic literature on regionalism further by focusing on so called "fringe regionalisms" in which they argue that regionalism scholars have overly emphasized "intergovernmental negotiations and their plans to configure and reconfigure a region delineated by the exclusionary amalgamation of pre-defined nation-states" (Mattheis 2019: 2). According to Mattheis (2019), scholars have an 'obsession' with formal institutions and territorial delineations when analyzing regions, and suggest to explore other types of regional movements. More specifically, Mattheis makes the case that scholars should study more 'marginal regions'and seemingly 'marginal spaces'. Such as for example the Sahara and the Caucasus, as regions are (also) built on "the cross-border practices of non-state actors, informal institutions rooted in states' peripheries and alternative, overlapping sources of legitimacy and identity" (Mattheis 2019: 2).

To summarize, today's world (map) is characterized by a "complex landscape of hundreds of regional groupings"[4] and "contrary to the world of states, that world of supra-national regions does not resemble a jig-saw-puzzle, but looks more like a 'spaghetti bowl' as the regional groupings are overlapping and sometimes nested" (Van Langenhove 2011: 55). For instance, in Latin America, there are various (overlapping) regional integration systems actually active, which made Mark Keller come up with the phrase: "alphabetic soup of regional integrations" in order not to "confuse the jumble of acronyms and abbreviations of the region's multilateral organizations".[5]

8.2 Classification of Regionalism, and Regional Organisations

Regional cooperation and integration systems can vary in depth, level, or stage. Various ways of classification exist, depending on the discipline (political science/ political economy etc.) and/or variables one adopts. A commonly referred classification is the one created by Kritzinger-van Niekerk (2005). Kritizinger-van Niekerk

---

[4]For a complete overview of all the regional integration agreements signed in the world, have a look at UNI-CRIS (2018) "Regional Integration database" [online] available at http://www.cris. unu.edu/riks/web/arrangement [Accessed 13 January 2018].

[5]Full details: R. Glickhouse (2012) "Explainer: An Alphabet Soup of Regional Integration Organizations" [online] available at http://www.as-coa.org/articles/explainer-alphabet-soup-regional-integration-organizations/ [Accessed 13 January 2018].

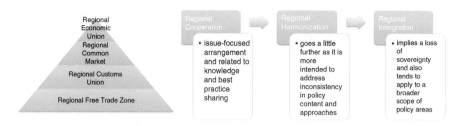

Fig. 8.1 Different typologies of regional integration/cooperation modes, authors' own creation based on Heinonen (2006) and Kritzinger-van Niekerk (2005)

(2005: 6) distinguishes three levels of regional integration depending on the scope of activities and loss of sovereignty: regional cooperation, regional harmonization and truly regional integration (also see Fig. 8.1). Whereas regional cooperation is a rather "issue-focused arrangement" and related to knowledge and best practice sharing, regional harmonization goes a little further as it is more intended to address inconsistency in policy content and approaches. Integration finally implies a loss of sovereignty, and also tends to apply to a broader scope of policy areas. From a more economic perspective, H. Heinonen (2006) proposes a different typology of regionalism, focusing on the issue areas covered by regional agreements.[6]

For Heinonen (2006) (also see as early as Balassa 1961), the first type of regional integration is a free trade zone, which takes place when trade restrictions between the party member states are removed. Secondly, when member states also have a common external trade policy towards third parties/countries, it is called a customs union. Thirdly, when next to trade barriers also a free movement of services, capital and labor is permitted between the member states, the phase of a common market is achieved. Finally, when economic and monetary policies are also decided upon by a supranational institution, it is called an economic union. Most of the regional integration systems are of the first stage (e.g. NAFTA and ASEAN) and arguably only one is in the final phase of a common market/economic union: the European Union.[7]

In an effort to 'quantify' regionalism, scholars usually look at the number of regional agreements registered with the World Trade Organization (Caporaso 2002; Börzel 2010b). Using these data, it would appear that since the end of the Cold War, regionalist movements have surged considerably around the globe (up to five times the number that there were pre-1989). However, upon closer look at the data, scholars have revealed that reality is more nuanced, as more than half of the registered accords are only put into force at the time being and a considerable amount (about

---

[6] H. Heinonen (2006). *Regional Integration and the State: The Changing Nature of Sovereignty in Southern Africa and Europe.* Interkont Books, Helsinki, p. 68. B. Balassa (1961) *The Theory of Economic Integration*, R.D. Allen & Unwin, Crows Nest, 304p.

[7] For a list and brief description of current regional arrangements and membership of regional organizations by country, see the UNU-CRIS Regional Integration Knowledge System at http://www.cris.unu.edu/. The most important counter-argument for not including the EU in the classification of "Economic Union" is that it is no unified fiscal zone (yet).

40%) of them have no more than two members (Börzel 2011). Finally, when apply-ing the more economic oriented classification of regionalism, scholars such as Börzel (2010a, b) have indicated that despite an apparent numerical increase in regional integration systems around the world, the vast majority of these still remain "shallow" as 90% of the cases are Free Trade Areas and, only nine customs unions, six common markets and four economic unions.

8.3   Regional Organisations

A core manifestation of regionalism is the creation of regional organizations, be it supra-national or intergovernmental in nature. Yet, despite the most recent fourth wave of "New Regionalism" and claims for a regionalization of the world order, no notable new regional organizations have been created since the end of the Cold War. In contrast, prominent regional organisations which already existed before the Cold War continue to exist and evolve (Börzel 2011). In fact, of the more than 50 'mul-tiple issues' regional organizations that exist to date, only 16 were established after 1990 (Börzel 2011). Indeed, Börzel (2011) 'demystified' the argument that since the Cold War, a watershed of new regionalisms and regional integration systems would have been created as a consequence of a new 'global order'. Instead, and more of interest to the research presented in this volume, regionalism goes back a long time and can be grouped in various 'waves', making it a recurrent and 'eclec-tic' aspect of international affairs, likely to continue evolving in the (near) future.

8.4   Studying Regionalism and Regional Integration Through Standard IR Lenses and Related Research Challenges

Regional integration is a growing, but nascent scholarship which received a signifi-cant boost after the Cold War as demonstrated by Börzel and Risse (2016a, b) in the Oxford Research Handbook on Comparative Regionalism. By showing the so-called Google n-grams chart frequencies of the term "regional integration" in all Google Books, the authors argue that very little scholarly activity has been recorded until 1960, that a slow increase from 1960 to 1990 can be seen but that it grew expo-nentially since the fall of the Berlin Wall. Today, the field is ever-growing, with renowned scholars and book titles such as Katzensteins (2005) "A world of regions", Hettne et al. (1999) "Globalism and the New Regionalism", "Theories of New Regionalism" by Söderbaum and Shaw (2003) and Van Langehove's (2011) "Building Regions: the Regionalisation of the World Order" in which it is argued that "we are approaching a "world of regions" (Katzenstein 2005: 12) and that "regions are now everywhere across the globe and are increasingly fundamental to the functioning of all aspects of world affairs from trade to conflict management, and can be said to now constitute world order" (Fawn 2009: 5).

Within International Relations literature, various theoretical approaches exist that help explain regionalist tendencies. According to the Oxford Handbook on Comparative Regionalism, four major theoretical perspectives on regionalism exist, drawing on (neo-)realism, (neo)liberal institutionalism, (neo)functionalism and social constructivism (Börzel and Risse 2016a, b). While they do offer important insights, these schools of thought are less appropriate to study broader and deeper forms of regionalism which involve the delegation of political authority across a wider range of issues, for which insights of Area Studies, and (EU) integration studies are also required (Börzel et al. 2016; Acharya 2005). As such, it is very difficult to explain the exact rationale and outcomes of regionalism around the world by drawing just on one theoretical approach. In what follows, we will nonetheless provide a brief overview of how major International Relations theories have tried to explain the different forms and outcomes of regionalist movements around the world. This section draws on the Sage Handbook of International Relations (Carlsnaes et al. 2013), the Oxford Handbook on Comparative Regionalism (Börzel and Risse 2016a, b) and the Palgrave Reader on Theories of New Regionalism (Söderbaum and Shaw 2003). It goes beyond the scope of this chapter to provide elaborate information on the different theoretical models, but if the reader wishes to find out more about theories on regionalism, the above mentioned volumes can be a good starting point. Another refreshing (and newer) academic piece of work in this regard is the one by Parthenay (2019) titled 'a Political Sociology of Regionalisms – a Perspective for a Comparison'. In this work, he proposes to make use of a political sociology approach to understand better the drivers behind regionalism and its outcomes. This new approach stresses the importance of looking at regionalism as an "international social phenemonon which […] results from the complex interplay between actors, representations and varied temporalities" (Partenay 2019: 61). Such an approach holds great potential, as in today's regionalism various non-state actors increasingly define the outlook of regionalism. In order to trace the exact reasons why regionalism is shaped and performing in a particular manner, it thus merits to analyze more closely the exact preferences of various interest groups and the way non-state actors shape (inter)regionalism. The first type of approaches to analyze regionalism is commonly referred to as 'rationalism' and focuses on the (potential) economic or material gains from regionalism. It is argued that, in a globalized world, economies of scale, customs harmonization and economic collaboration to attract more foreign direct investment and trade is what drives regionalism (Börzel and Risse 2016a, b; Börzel et al. 2016). States may either seek membership in regional institutions (such as the European Economic Community) or can create their own regional group (such as NAFTA) in order to generate the especially interesting (economic) external effects related to regionalism (Börzel and Risse 2016a, b). Rationalist approaches refer to (neo-)realism and (neo-)liberalism and "are based on rational choice and take the interests, ideas and identities of actors (which are seen as self-interested egos)" (Söderbaum 2003: 12). As such, (neo-)realists focus on power (politics), security and national interests, while (neo)liberalists focus more on the role of institutions and regional cooperation schemes as a way to achieve collective goods on a regional basis (Söderbaum 2003, also see Mansfield and Milner 1999 or Fawcett 2016). Liberal intergovernmentalist approaches from their side claim that "governments act as rational actors pursuing domestic goals and interests (Moravcsik 1995: 53). It is believed that regional integration is the result of an active interstate 'bargaining' and can best be analyzed as a 'process of collective choice through which conflicting interests are reconciled' (Börzel and Risse 2016a). Yet from their side, domestic interest groups which are not related to the state/government apparatus may try to circumvent them by forming transnational alliances and try to leverage on their national governments by influencing regional policy outcomes and institutional reforms (Moravcsik 1997, as listed in Börzel 2011, also see Moravcsik and Schimmelfennig 2009).

Contrary to the rationalist beliefs, (neo-)functionalists explain regionalism more as a way of technocratic problem-solving across borders (Börzel 2011; Börzel and Risse 2016a, b). An important scholar in this school of thought is Haas (1967) who introduced the concept of 'functional spill-over'. Functional spill-over refers to the mechanism that once states have conferred particular power or political authority to a supranational/regional entity in regards a particular policy area, this will lead to a 'snow-ball effect' in the transfer of powers to make the supranational/regional institution perform well in that particular policy area. Similarly, it is explained by means of functional spill-over that when regional cooperation or integration is started in one particular area (e.g. cooperation on border control), in order to be effective, further cooperation and integration is always required and the delegation of power from the member states to the regional organization increases incrementally (e.g. next cooperation illegal immigration is also required, then a shared visa policy is established, a joint Asylum Agency, etc.). Interesting in this regard is the impact that Brexit might have on this way of thinking. Instead of 'an ever closer union', Brexit shows the clear limitations of the European regional integration project. From a theoretical perspective, (neo-)functionalists seem to be revisiting their fundamentals as some have argued that "it is not surprising to observe the EU showing some signs of disintegration as most of the many efforts of trans-national regional integration since the Second World War have exhibited similar symptons" and as a consequence thereof "the neo-functionalist theory of regional integration may then become a disintegration theory" (Parthenay 2019: 16–17).

Constructivist approaches emphasize the importance of studying (collective) identities, norms and discourses in order to understand the rationale behind regionalism. As Söderbaum and Shaw (2003: 27) state "regions come to life as we talk and think about them". However, as Börzel (2011: 19) explains: "it is unclear whether collective identity is a precondition for, or an indicator of regional integration (…) pundits of European integration argue to what extent the EU has built a common identity and what it is based upon while the sense of community is weaker in North America, Africa, the Middle East or Asia, the question remains whether this is because states are so diverse with regard to their political systems, societal structures and cultures that there is no demand for (stronger) common institutions, or are regional institutions simply not strong enough to breed a community?" Constructivist approaches also emphasize regional awareness, norms and identity (building) in order to explain why regionalism in a particular part of the world is organized in a particular manner. As an example, Acharya (2005) explains that ASEAN structures reflect very well the regional culture of 'informal consensus-building' and 'organizational minimalism' as opposed to 'western models of legalized institutions'. Whereas these explanations help understand particular cases of regionalism and to a certain extent allow the usage of knowledge typically gathered in Area Studies, scholars often criticize constructivism for not being able to offer more systematic and mainstream explanations for the existence of regionalism around the globe (Börzel 2011).

Whereas the above mentioned theories and approaches help explain important features of regionalism, no theory in itself can explain the complex phenomenon of regionalist tendencies and their outlooks in various parts of the world. Why for example, do the African Union and the Andean Community resemble to a large extent the institutional outlook of the European Union, whereas UNASUR and ECOWAS do not? Why has the South-East Asian integration system of ASEAN not led to a shared ASEAN identity whereas the Central American System (SICA) – arguably- has? The preceding paragraphs make it clear that its extremely difficult, if not impossible for even three or four theoretical lenses of International Relations to effectively evaluate regional processes. When studying regions, limiting one's theoretical tenets to one, or even two schools of IR theory severely limits explanatory power. Instead, regions entail elements from all schools of IR theory, i.e. realism, liberalism and constructivism, including their sub-schools or sub-theories (such as neorealism, structural realism, neoliberalism, etc.) (De Lombaerde and Schulz 2009). Therefore, a more objective and inclusive approach is advised when analysing regionalism and regional integration. Such an approach is grounded on analytical eclecticism as proposed by Sil and Katzenstein (2010: 411–431). Analytical eclecticism allows for a unique combination of the different explanatory theories. In fact, factors or variables from the different (sub-)schools of mainstream theories can be included in a unified analytical framework; i.e. liberals' focus on economic gains from cooperation, combined with for example constructivists' focus on the foundational ideas of long-lasting peace.

8.5   The Conceptual Challenge

In addition to the theoretical complexity and challenges faced when studying regions and regional integration from an IR perspective, scholars of this field also encounter various conceptual challenges. First of all, and as already briefly touched upon in the beginning of this chapter, there is a wide range of definitions of region, regional integration, regionalism, regionalization and related concepts in the academic literature (De Lombaerde et al. 2010: 735–736, Mattheis 2014). Definitions of regionalism and regions often contradict one another, and for numerous scholars it remains extremely complex to understand what exactly it is that they are studying.

Take for example the definitions put forward by Van Langenhove (2003) and Joseph Nye (1971).

According to Nye (1971) a region is "a limited number of states linked together by a geographical relationship and by a degree of mutual interdependence".

Whereas Van Langenhove (2003) argues that:

> Calling something a region is done because it emphasises that that geographical area with its attached social community and/or system is not a state while at the same time it can have some statehood properties. As such one can say that in principle every geographical area in the world (with its social system) that is not a state can be considered as a region if to some extent statehood properties can be attributed to it. So, regions can be defined as what they are not: they are not sovereign states. But they have some resemblance of states.

For Van Langenhove (2003), regions are thus much more than just geographic realities and should not only be defined by their surface or boundaries. They are a clear illustration of what Searle (1995, also see Ruggie 1993) has called 'institutional facts': those portions of the world that are only 'facts' by human agreement. For instance, for a piece of paper to count as a five euro bill one needs the existence of 'money' and a set of conventions about the value of that bill as well as a 'market' to trade it. Searle (1995) has labelled these facts 'institutional' because they require people and human institutions for their existence. As pointed out by Paasi (2002: 805), this holds for regions too: although being a geographical area, a region does not exist without people and their 'belief' in the existence of that region. A region is thus always an institutional fact and therefore also an idea. And because regions are ideas (be it with a geographical component), they are being talked about. As such, and in line with a social constructivist point of view, they argue that it is not because regions exist that they can be discussed. Instead it is because they are being discussed that they start existing. In other words, a region is always constructed through discourse. In such a view, the concept of 'region' can be regarded as a linguistic tool used by actors to talk about a geographical area that is not a state. Accordingly, one may say that in principle every geographical area in the world that is not a state has the potential to be considered as a region. For instance, a region can have its own regional innovation policy (just as there exist national innovation policies). Or it can raise taxes and have its own budget for the provision of certain public goods. Regions can also possess symbols or institutions (such as a flag or a parliament) that one normally associates with states. The concept of region seems therefore to be used in everyday language by people in order to refer to geographical spaces that whilst not being a state do look to some extent as if they are a state. Talking of regions can thus be regarded as a linguistic tool used to refer to something that is not a state but has some resemblances to a state. Such an interpretation of what a region truly is has considerable consequences for the way in which regions, and the interactions amongst them, should be studied. As regionalism is not interpreted as a mere result of negotiations between states, so should the state not be the sole (explanatory) variable in the analysis of (inter)regionalism. Yet, today, as Mattheis (2019:12) righteously puts it: "the interregionalism and comparative regionalism subfields find themselves coming face-to-face with the challenge of conceptual shortcomings in relation to space due to the nature of their object of study".

It is also important to understand the linkage between the conceptual problem and the problem of comparability in empirical research. As De Lombaerde et al. (2010: 740) explain: "if the absence of sovereignty combined with supra- nationality are considered essential characteristics of a region, then it might be reasonable to compare the EU with SADC in order to study, for example, how national constitutional courts deal with regional rule making (…) however, if the capacity to influence decision-making in the area of trade at the global level (WTO) is considered an essential characteristic of a region (in the sense of a regional economic power), then it probably makes more sense to compare the EU with e.g. MERCOSUR". As such, the way in which regions are identified and conceptualized also defines the way in which they are -or can be- compared with each other.

8.6   Empirical Challenges

Finally, also various empirical challenges exist when studying regionalism and regional integration processes. In fact, two broad approaches to the study of regions exist (De Lombaerde et al. 2010). The first is to study single cases with an emphasis on understanding the historical processes of the case (i.e. regionalism as a dependent variable). This is called 'idiographic research' and characterized by the use of various qualitative research methods (De Lombaerde et al. 2010). The second approach is to study multiple cases in order to track general trends and explanations on the various facets of region building/regionalism (i.e. regionalism as an independent variable) (De Lombaerde et al. 2010). In between these two alternatives stands the comparative case-study method. A combination of both approaches is often feasible and, also desirable in order to improve the quality of comparative work in this area (De Lombaerde et al. 2010, also see King et al. 1994).

In addition, for some scholars, the EU is often attributed as a model 'power', or 'prime example' of regionalism/regional integration (Jetschke 2009: 407–426, Mattheis 2014). As such, there has also been a tendency within EU studies during the recent decade to consider the EU as a polity in its own right (De Lombaerde et al. 2010). As a consequence, it is argued that the EU could only be studied as a specific/new type of political system, and it would be very difficult to compare it with other types of regionalism efforts (i.e. the $N = 1$ problem) (De Lombaerde et al. 2010, also see Parthenay 2019).

8.7   Concluding Remarks

This first section of the chapter on regionalism has shown that the often argued 'rise in regionalism' since the end of the Cold War does not constitute a new phenomenon (Börzel 2011; Börzel and Risse, eds. 2016). In fact, it can be argued that regionalism is eclectic (i.e. occurring in different waves) as it oscillates between more intense and less intense periods of regional integration activity. Regionalist movements can at least be traced back to the 19th century and today we are experiencing its fifth wave also referred to as 'comparative regionalism'. What is distinct about regionalism in the twenty-first century is the extent to which it draws on existing forms and the importance it has in structuring the global politico-economic order (Börzel 2011). Therefore, as shown in section two, today's world (map) is characterized by a complex landscape of hundreds of regional groupings[8] and "contrary to the world of states, that world of supra-national regions does not resemble a jigsaw-puzzle, but looks more like a 'spaghetti bowl' as the regional groupings are overlapping and sometimes nested" (Van Langenhove 2011: 55). Regionalism has attracted considerable academic scholarship since the end of the Cold War. However, to date various conceptual and theoretical challenges still exist on what exactly constitutes a 'region' and how best to compare one with another (most notably the EU with other schemes). In addition, scholars are involved in a heated debate on the place of regions in world politics: are we moving towards a 'regionalized world order' such as Van Langenhove (2005) argued or are regions rather 'stumbling blocs' for effective global governance? With this chapter, we join scholars such as Acharya (2015) and Börzel (2011: 26–27) who argue that "there is not one dominant form of regionalism and it nonetheless has become part of a global governance script, in which region-building does not only feature as a successful and legitimate way to foster peace and prosperity but which sees regions as the fundamental, even driving force of world politics".

Further Readings

Acharya, A. (2007). The emerging regional architecture of world politics. *World Politics, 59*, 629–652.

Börzel, T., & Risse, T. (2016). *The Oxford handbook of comparative regionalism* (560p). Oxford: Oxford University Press.

Keohane, R. (2005). *After hegemony: cooperation and discord in the world political economy* (320p). Princeton: Princeton University Press.

Söderbaum, F., & Shaw, T. (Eds.). (2003). *Theories of new regionalism, a Palgrave reader* (225p). Basingstoke: Palgrave.

References

Acharya, A. (2005). Do norms and identity matter? Community and power in Southeast Asia's regional order. *The Pacific Review, 18*(1), 95–118.

---

[8] For a complete overview of all the regional integration agreements signed in the world, have a look at UNI-CRIS (2018) "Regional Integration database" [online] available at http://www.cris.unu.edu/riks/web/arrangement [Accessed 13 January 2018].

Acharya, A. (2014). *Constructing a security community in Southeast Asia: ASEAN and the problem of regional order* (314p). Basingstoke: Routledge.

Acharya, A. (2015). Foreword. In M. Telò, L. Fawcett, & F. Ponjaert (Eds.), *Interregionalism and the European Union: A post-revisionist approach to Europe's place in a changing world* (pp. xx–xxvi). Routledge.

Balassa, B. (1961). *The theory of economic integration* (304p). London: R.D. Allen & Unwin.

Baldersheim, H., et al. (2011). *The rise of the networking region: The challenges of regional collaboration in a globalized world* (192p). Burlington: Ashgate Publishing, Ltd.

Börzel, T. A. (2010a). *The transformative power of Europe reloaded: The limits of external Europeanization* (KFG Working Papers). Freie Universität Berlin, 11, Berlin, 31p.

Börzel, T. A. (2010b). Comparative regionalism: European integration and beyond. In W. Carlsnaes et al. (Eds.), *Handbook on international relations* (2nd ed., pp. 503–530). London: Sage.

Börzel, T. (2011) *"Comparative regionalism, a new research agenda"*, KFG Working Papers, Berlin, Freie Universität Berlin, Berlin.

Börzel, T. A., & Risse, T. (2016a). The EU and diffusion regionalism. In M. Telo et al. (Eds.), *The European Union and interregionalism. Controversial impact and drivers of regionalism* (pp. 51–67). Aldershot: Ashgate

Börzel, T. A., & Risse, T. (2016b). *The Oxford handbook of comparative regionalism* (560p). Oxford: Oxford University Press.

Börzel, T., Goltermann, L., & Striebinger, K. (2016). *Roads to regionalism: Genesis, design, and effects of regional organizations*. Basingstoke: Routledge.

Caporaso, J. (2002). Comparative regional integration. In W. Carlsnaes, T. Risse, & B. Simmons (Eds.), *Handbook of international relations*. Los Angeles: Sage.

Carlsnaes, W., Risse, T., & Simmons, B. A. (Eds.). (2013). *Handbook of international relations*. Sage. ISO 690.

De Lombaerde, P., & Schulz, M. (Eds.). (2009). *The EU and world regionalism: The makability of regions in the 21st century* (297p). Surrey: Ashgate Publishing, Ltd.

De Lombaerde, P., et al. (2010). The problem of comparison in comparative regionalism. *Review of International Studies, 36*(3), 731–753.

De Melo, J., & Panagariya, A. (Eds.). (1995). *New dimensions in regional integration* (473p). Cambridge: Cambridge University Press.

Dicken, P. (2007) *Global shift: Making the changing contour of the world economy* (5th ed., 599p). London: Sage.

Fawcett, L. (2009). *Regionalism in world politics, past and present* (18p). Oxford: University of Oxford.

Fawcett, L. (2016). *International relations of the Middle East* (424p). Oxford: Oxford University Press.

Fawn, R. (2009). 'Regions' and their study: Wherefrom, what for and whereto? *Review of International Studies, 35*(S1), 5–34.

Glickhouse, R. (2012). *Explainer: An alphabet soup of regional integration organizations* [online]. Available at http://www.as-coa.org/articles/explainer-alphabet-soup-regional-integration-organizations/. Accessed 13 Jan 2018.

Haas, E. B. (1967). The uniting of Europe and the uniting of Latin America. *Journal of Common Market Studies, 5*(4), 315–343.

Heinonen, H. (2006). *Regional integration and the state: The changing nature of Sovereignty in Southern Africa and Europe* (68p). Helsinki: Interkont Books.

Hettne, B., Inotai, A., & Sunkel, O. (Eds.). (1999). *Globalism and the new regionalism (p. xvii)*. London: Macmillan.

Jetschke, A. (2009). Institutionalizing ASEAN: Celebrating Europe through network governance. *Cambridge Review of International Affairs, 22*(3), 407–426.

Jönsson., et al. (2000). *Organising European space* (216p). London: Sage.

Katzenstein, P. J. (2015). *A world of regions: Asia and Europe in the American imperium* (320p). Ithaca: Cornell University Press.

King, G., Keohane, R., & Verba, S. (1994). *Designing social inquiry* (264p). Princeton: Princeton University Press.

Kritzinger-van Niekerk, L. (2005). *Regional integration: Concepts, advantages, disadvantages and lessons of experience*. Washington, DC: World Bank.

Mansfield, E. D., & Milner, H. V. (1999). The new wave of regionalism. *International Organization, 53*(3), 589–627.

Mattheis, F. (2014). *New regionalism in the South – Mercosur and SADC in a comparative and interregional perspective* (308 P). Leipzig: Leipziger Universitätsverlag.

Mattheis, F. (2019). *Fringe regionalism*. Switzerland: Palgrave Macmillan.

Mendelu University. (2018). *Security activities of selected regional institutions* [online]. Available at https://is.mendelu.cz/eknihovna/opory/zobraz_cast.pl?cast=69580. Accessed 13 Oct 2018.

Moravcsik, A. (1995). Liberal intergovernmentalism and integration: A rejoinder. *Journal of Common Market Studies, 33*, 611.

Moravcsik, A. (1997). Taking preferences seriously: A liberal theory of international politics. *International Organization, 51*(4), 513–553.

Morgan, K. (2005). Sustainable regions: Governance, innovation and sustainability. In *New regionalism in Australia* (pp. 27–48). Aldershot: Ashgate.

Moravcsik, A., & Schimmelfennig, F. (2009). Liberal intergovernmentalism. *European Integration Theory, 2*, 67–87.

Niemann, M. (2001). Unstated places—Rereading southern Africa. In *Theory, change and southern Africa's future* (pp. 58–82). London: Palgrave Macmillan.

Nye, J. S. (1968). Comparative regional integration: Concept and measurement. *International Organization, 22*(4), 855–880.

Nye, J. S. (1971). *Peace in parts: Integration and conflict in regional organization* (210p). New York: Little, Brown.

Paasi, A. (2002). Place and region: Regional worlds and words. *Progress in Human Geography, 26*(6), 802–811.

Parthenay, K. (2019). *A political sociology of regionalisms*. Springer.

Prebisch, R. (1959). Commercial policy in the underdeveloped countries. *The American Economic Review, 49*(2), 251–273.

Riggirozzi, P., & Tussie, D. (2012). The rise of post-hegemonic regionalism in Latin America. In *The rise of post-hegemonic regionalism* (pp. 1–16). Dordrecht: Springer.

Ruggie, J. (1993). Territoriality and beyond: Problematizing modernity in international relations. *International Organization, 47*(1), 139–174.

Searle, J. R. (1995) *The construction of social reality* (241p). New York: Simon and Schuster.

Sil, R., & Katzenstein, P. (2010). Analytic eclecticism in the study of world politics: Reconfiguring problems and mechanisms across research traditions. *Perspectives on Politics, 8*(2), 411–431.

Selleslaghs, J. (2014). *"Managing global interdependence on the central American isthmus: EU-Central America interregional relations"*, UNU-CRIS working papers (Vol. 8). Bruges: United Nations University Institute on Comparative Regional Integration Studies.

Söderbaum, F. (2003). Introduction: Theories of new regionalism. In *Theories of new regionalism* (pp. 1–21). London: Palgrave Macmillan.

Söderbaum, F. (2016). Old, new, and comparative regionalism. In T. A. Börzel & T. Risse (Eds.), *The Oxford handbook of comparative regionalism* (pp. 16–41). Oxford: Oxford University Press.

Söderbaum, F., & Shaw, T. (Eds.). (2003). *Theories of new regionalism, a Palgrave reader* (225p). Basingstoke: Palgrave.

Söderbaum, F., & Van Langenhove, L. (2005). Introduction: The EU as a global actor and the role of interregionalism. *European Integration, 27*(3), 249–262.

Sommer, D. (1991). *Foundational fictions: The national romances of Latin America* (418p). Berkeley: University of California Press.

Telò, M., Fawcett, L., & Ponjaert, F. (2015). Interregionalism and the European Union. A post-revisionist approach to Europe's place in a changing world. London: Routledge.

Thakur, R., & Van Langenhove, L. (2006). Enhancing global governance through regional integration. *Global Governance: A Review of Multilateralism and International Organizations, 12*(3), 233–240.

UNU-CRIS. (2018). *Regional integration database* [online]. Available at http://www.cris.unu.edu/riks/web/arrangement. Accessed 13 Jan 2018.

Van Langenhove, L. (2003). *Theorising regionhood* (UNU-CRIS e-Working Papers, W-2003/1). United Nations University Institute on Comparative Regional Integration Studies, Bruges, 38p.

Van Langenhove, L. (2011). *Building regions: The regionalization of world order* (198p). Burlington: Ashgate Publishing Ltd.

Warleigh-Lack, A., & Rosamond, B. (2010). Across the EU studies–new regionalism frontier: Invitation to a dialogue. *JCMS: Journal of Common Market Studies, 48*(4), 993–1013.

Chapter 9
The European Union: Integration, Institutions and External Relations in a Globalised and Regionalised World

Joren Selleslaghs, Mario Telò, and Madeleine O. Hosli

9.1 EU-Driven Interregionalism or Region-to-Region Diplomacy

In a world caught between global pressures and local pushback, regional dynamics come to the fore. As complex webs of power, interaction and identity, regions represent critical spaces of governance in a de-centred world. Voluntary forms of regional governance offer states and peoples the opportunity to better manage security concerns, reap the economic gains of globalisation, express more fully cultures and identities, and project influence in world affairs. This is a fundamental rationale for the EU's own peace and development in the twenty-first century. This is why we will promote and support cooperative regional orders worldwide, including in the most divided areas.

Federica Mogherini, High Representative of the Union for Foreign Affairs and Security Policy/Vice-President of the Commission, EU Global Strategy (2016).

In the early phases of the European integration process, the European Communities (EC) did not yet have an outspoken external profile. The EC and its institutions, including what is now the European Commission, were not very relevant in international politics, as international relations and representation were very much managed by individual member states, also within the Cold War framework

J. Selleslaghs
Faculty of Governance and Global Affairs, Leiden University, The Hague, The Netherlands
e-mail: selleslaghs.joren@gmail.com

M. Telò
Free University of Brussels (ULB), Brussels, Belgium
e-mail: mtelo@ulb.ac.be

M. O. Hosli (✉)
Institute of Security and Global Affairs, Leiden University, The Hague, The Netherlands
e-mail: m.o.hosli@fgga.leidenuniv.nl

© Springer Nature Switzerland AG 2020
M. O. Hosli, J. Selleslaghs (eds.), *The Changing Global Order*, United Nations University Series on Regionalism 17,
https://doi.org/10.1007/978-3-030-21603-0_9

(Allahverdiyev 2008). The limited external relations the EC did entertain, were largely restricted to former European colonies and almost exclusively oriented on trade and development relations (Dinan 1999).[1] But when assessing the EU's external relations and the EU's clout in international politics at the beginning of the twenty-first century, the situation had drastically changed. The EU, since the implementation of the Lisbon Treaty, has its own High Representative of the Union for Foreign Affairs and Security Policy (High Representative), its own diplomatic services (the 'European External Action Service', EEAS), has established a worldwide network of about 141 delegations/representations[2] and signed numerous cooperation and association agreements with different states and regions globally.[3] Today, the EU is by many seen as a new kind of global power and its ambition is to assert its weight in international politics even more prominently in the future, as the recently developed and adopted Global Strategy (EEAS 2016) has shown. An important aspect of the EU's external relations, next to bilateral patterns of interaction, is its so-called 'interregional' relations, notably with other regional entities (Söderbaum and Van Langenhove 2005). In fact, the EU's interregional approach has gradually achieved an important position in the history of European integration and specifically in regards to its external relations management. Before providing a more detailed account of this particular way of conducting external relations, this chapter will provide an overview of the scholarly research efforts on interregionalism and their place within scholarship on European Foreign Policy. The third and final section of this chapter then provides an analysis of the main *rationale* behind EU-driven interregionalism, its current formats and outreach activit, as well as its strategic place within today's EU foreign policy as encompassed in the 2016 Global Strategy.

9.2   European Foreign Policy Studies and Interregional Relations

In the early days of European integration, the creation of the EC was in itself an act of foreign policy and did not lead (yet) to actual patterns of coordinated 'European' foreign policy (Keukeleire and Delreux 2014). It was only in the 1970s, with the establishment of European Political Cooperation (EPC) that first actual steps towards coordination in member states' foreign policies took place. With the signing of the Maastricht Treaty in 1992, the EU started to develop an –essentially

---

[1] For more information on the history of the EC and the EU's external relations, e.g. see Dinan (1999).

[2] Respective information can be found at http://eeas.europa.eu/delegations/ [Accessed 17 January 2018].

[3] With such agreements, the EU also aims to spread its values and beliefs on human rights and democratic governance, economic liberalization and privatization, acting as a 'norm entrepreneur'. For an overview of all respective agreements: http://www.consilium.europa.eu/policies/agreements?lang=en [Accessed 1 April 2018].

intergovernmental- Common Foreign and Security Policy (CFSP) in the framework of which all member states would start coordinating their diplomatic actions and 'uphold a common position' in international home affairs and environmental cooperation, the EU, and its delegations abroad, gradually started to be recognized as an international actors, to be considered notably in areas of 'traditional' foreign policy. In the first decade of the new millennium, treaty changes allowed for considerable advances regarding CFSP coordination: the Treaty of Nice created the Political Security Committee (PSC) in which Brussels-based diplomats from all member-states would weekly gather (at ambassadorial level) to develop and monitor the EU's external relations and the Treaty of Lisbon created the actual post of a High Representative, supported by the EEAS (and with this, further building on the HR function that the Treaty of Amsterdam had already introduced). A further important step, implemented with the Treaty of Lisbon, was the establishment of a 'semi-permanent' presidency of the European Council, which would represent the EU and its member states at the highest diplomatic level (e.g. within the G20 and at the United Nations General Assembly, UNGA). The EEAS, a new administrative service that would work under the High Representative and be the motor for policy formulation and implementation on external action, was gradually implemented. As a consequence of these developments, seen over the time span of about the last five decades, European integration not only reflects foreign policy behavior of European states, but increasingly also defines and shapes European foreign policy (Keukeleire and Delreux 2014). The EU representations abroad have been transformed into EU delegations and have de facto surpassed the size of the embassies of several member states in third countries. Also within important international fora and organizations, including the (UNGA, the EU seems to increasingly speak with 'one voice' (e.g., Jin and Hosli 2013; Jin 2014); ambassadors and representatives of the delegations then gradually develop into 'focal points' to turn to when aiming to discover the positions of the EU in given (foreign) policy domains. As the EU is increasingly recognized as a 'diplomatic actor', it is also increasingly studied by scholars in international relations and foreign policy analysis (e.g., Koops and Macaj 2015). In fact, the scholarship on the EU's external relations has more or less followed the same (historical) evolution as its practice: at first, scholars focused on whether or not (1) the EC or EU was 'present' as a diplomatic actor, followed by the question (2) what kind of 'actor' in international relations it is, and more recently (3) the focus shifted to its 'effectiveness' or 'performance' of international affairs (Hardacre and Smith 2009). For an overview of EU foreign policy analysis e.g. see Hardacre and Smith (2009), Koops and Macaj (2015) or Drieskens (2017). In EU FPA scholarship, a first key debate revolved around the question of 'presence' and 'actorness', that is the EU's capacity to act externally (Schunz 2018). Actorness examines the external context of EU action ('opportunity'), its own 'presence', as well as its 'capability', that is, "the internal context of EU external action" (Bretherton and Vogler 2006: 29). In early work on this topic, Cosgrove-Sacks and Twitchett (1970) introduced the concept of 'actorness' to describe the EC's capacities and policies in the international realm, distinct and independent from the policies of its member states. According to Sjöstedt (1977: 7), actorness should be defined as 'the ability to work actively and deliberatively in relation to other actors in the international system'. Central in the debate on the EC's 'actorness' were aspects that would define the EC's own 'actorness', exceeding the real of the foreign policies of its member states (see e.g. Jupille and Caporaso 1998; Bretherton and Vogler 1999). Whereas actorness in stricto senso only indicates whether or not the entity could act externally in a given context, EU foreign policy analyis scholars started to increasingly question the capacity of the EU to act. This second phase of research, in the 1990s and the beginning of the new millennium, recognized that the EU is indeed an 'actor' of its own of international affairs, but scholars now explored what kind of 'actor' it constitutes: a civilian power or 'soft power Europe' (Telò 2005), normative power (Manners 2002), ethical power (Aggestam 2008), transformative power (Leonard 2005), market power (Damro 2012), 'civilian power with teeth' (Schmalz 2005) or an 'integrative power' and active promotor of 'effective multilaterlism' within other international institutions such as the UN and NATO (Koops 2011). Yet, no systematic analysis of the actual impact of the EU's 'actorness' was conducted, while over the most recent decade, the academic debate slightly moved away from pure 'the nature of the beast' discussions and instead started focusing on "the actual extent of EU actorness and especially effectiveness in international politics" (Niemann and Bretherton 2013, 262). Referring to it as the 'effectiveness turn' (Drieskens 2017: 1539), scholars are now less focused on studying the real activities and policies of EU external action (both as regards CFSP and so-called 'external aspects of internal policies'), but rather focus on the EU as a 'diplomatic actor', scrutinizing its 'performance' in global affairs (e.g., Keukeleire and Delreux 2014 or Koops and Macaj 2015; Blavoukos and Bourantonis 2017). However, according to Mayer (2008: 8–11) and Keuleers et al. (2016:1–2), recent EU foreign policy analysis has tended to be rather 'Eurocentric', as "most scholarship and policy discourse about the future of European foreign policy remains too self-absorbed, looking at Europe through European eyes in a well-shaped European mirror". More specifically, according to Keuleers et al. (2016: 15): "a very large majority of recent work on EU foreign policy focuses on the institutional underpinnings and intentions of EU external action, whereas only a very small share of articles is focused on the impact, relevance or perception of the EU's policy in a particular state or region". Another often overlooked aspect of EU foreign policy making in the EU foreign policy analysis literature, however, is its interregional relations – an aspect we will now focus on.

Over the last decades, numerous scholarly attempts were made to define the real value of interregionalism as a (new) way of conducting (EU) international relations or a potential 'building bloc' in an (increasingly) multilayered global governance architecture (Baert et al. 2014). As Gaens (2012: 15) noted: "scholars are currently engaged in a heated debate on the definitions and theoretical implications of the interaction of regions, and on the actual importance and potential future impact of interregionalism within the international order". Some scholars see the ever increasing relations and interactions between (supra-national) regions as a sign that we are moving towards a new world order which is no longer dominated by nation states as is the case in the actual Westphalian world order (Van Langenhove 2011). They see regions as the 'building blocks' in a 'new age of empires' (Verhofstadt 2008) as the Westphalian nation state world is being challenged by the raising tide of globalization. In addition to the debate on the exact role of interregionalism in today's global order is the debate on the 'nature of the beast'. The concept of 'interregionalism' itself is still theoretically "unclear and shifting" as Söderbaum and Van Langenhove (2005: 257) have stated. In addition, there is discussion as regards the driving forces that led to its emergence. In his book 'The European Union and interregionalism: Patterns of engagement' Doidge (2011) proposes an overall analytical framework that combines the insights of different schools if international relations, to understand why an interregional dialogue was called into life (also see Telò et al. 2015). By building further upon previous work by Hänggi et al. (2006) and Rüland (2001), Doidge (2011) argues that interregional relations serve one or several of the following five functions: (1) balancing, (2) institution building, (3) rationalizing, (4) agenda-setting and (5) collective identity building. Regarding the first function, which is very much in line with realist perspectives, interregionalism is often seen as a way to 'balance' the different international actors in the global powerplay as they defend their (strategic) interests and look for geopolitical/geo-economic partners to further strengthen their own position. Instead, the second and third functions are both extracted from the institutionalist school of thought and stress the importance of institutions and agreements that can oversee the implementation of decisions to deal with a particular policy matter (2). The rationalizing function (3) emphasises the importance of interregional platforms as important 'clearing houses' in which various diplomatic actors can find common ground and potentially, solutions for the management of shared or (inter)regional governance challenges. In the same trend, Doidge (2011) argues that interregionalism "can also serve as a mechanism to first create consensus on a lower level of the global governance structure before introducing these common positions to the agendas of multilateral fora in a concerted manner" (4). Finally, interregionalism can serve the process of identity formation: as 'a self' engages with an identifiable 'other' (Gilson 2005: 46), it "allows the regional identity to be formed through differentiation from the other and/or through the interaction and the mutual exchange with the partner(s)". Turning the attention to the EU, scholars such as Rüland (2006) usually argue that EU-driven interregionalism serves three major (interlinked) goals. First of all, by pursuing interregional dialogues and interaction, the EU promotes and actively contributes to the development of other regional integration schemes. Secondly, in doing so it also contributes to the EU's quest to become an internally, as well as externally, recognized international actor. By serving as a 'blueprint' or 'best-practice' for many other regions globally, it legitimises and asserts its power on the international stage, which also strengthens its identity as a meaningful political actor at home (Rüland 2006). Thirdly, interregionalism also serves as a method to promote and defend the EU's interests abroad. More specifically, interregionalism is particularly useful for "achieving gains the EU has been unable to reap through more traditional multilateral and bilateral channels" (Aggarwal and Fogarty 2005: 342). The next section will focus on reasons for the EU to have engaged increasingly in interregional foreign policy.

9.3 The EU's Choice for Interregional Relations: A Consistent Answer to Manage Global Interdependence

It can hence be stated that the EU has, over time, gradually embraced interregional dialogues as a foreign policy tool in order to develop and deepen its external relations with other parts of the world and to simultaneously assert itself on the global level. However, the EU has other foreign policy tools at its disposal. So why does it embark on interregional approaches to pursue its goals? Former European Commissioner for External Relations Patten (2000), might provide an answer: "as a regional organization, it makes sense to deal with others on a regional basis. Interregionalism, therefore, is seen as providing a natural answer to managing global interdependence" (quoted in Shaw and Cornelissen 2012: 76).

The EU may have chosen to develop interregional relations for a variety of reasons (e.g., Söderbaum et al. 2005; Telò et al. 2015). First, interregionalism has an important impact on regional integration and the worldwide development of regionalism. As interregional dialogue and cooperation requires two (or more) regions to have a coherent and well-functioning regional organization and system, it is likely to considerably contribute to the development of such schemes. This is exactly what the EU seems to strives for, as Söderbaum et al. (2005: 370) argue: "Europeans firmly believe that regional integration and regionalism can enhance peace, prevent conflict, support regional economic convergence and promote cross border problem solving and the better use and management of natural resources" (Söderbaum et al. 2005: 370). Even though it is true that de facto the European model of integration cannot (always) serve as a 'blueprint' for other regional integration processes globally, it appears to still be a component of EU external strategy that the broader concept and phenomena of regionalism and regional integration may lead to stability, peace and security in a region (e.g., Zepter 2008: 463). Or as De Flers and Regelsberger (2005: 317) stated: "the logic of interregional cooperation derives from the successful European model". Next to promoting and developing regionalism, EU external action also seems advocate interregionalism, with this 'legitimising' itself as a (global) actor in international relations (Hardacre and Smith 2009). Further building on such reflections, according to Söderbaum et al. (2006), the EU pursues interregional relations for one, or a combination of, the following three factors: (i) the promotion of liberal internationalism; (ii) building the EU's identity as a global actor; and (iii) the promotion of the EU's power and competitiveness.

According to these authors, the promotion of liberal internationalism is a core reason why the EU as an entity advocates more distinctive and deeper EU interregional relations. Important substantive areas that can be subsumed under the label 'liberal internationalist' encompass, for example, international solidarity, human rights, global poverty eradication, sustainable and participatory development, (inclusive) democracy and the 'human' benefits of economic interdependence (Smith 2004). The categorisation is largely in line with the 'civilian power Europe' vision, seeing the EU as an actor aiming to promote and defend 'universal values', such as the rule of law, democracy, equality and human rights at the global stage, based on peaceful means (e.g., Söderbaum et al. 2006). As these are values and norms closely related to the EU's own integration project, it is argued that through the wider promotion of regionalism and the relationships between one regional entity and another globally, such values are well defended and promoted on the international level. Building on this, Söderbaum et al. (2006: 372) argue that the EU also uses interregionalism to strengthen the EU's power and the promotion of its interests globally. Accordingly, an additional goal is "to strengthen the EU's political power" and to "defend its legitimate economic and commercial interests in the international arena as it has started to appear more frequently in the justification of its foreign policy and external relations" (Söderbaum et al. 2006: 372). This 'turn to power' can arguably also be traced back in the so-called 'Lisbon agenda' for socio-economic modernization, which already signalled the EU's increased emphasis on strengthening its economic power position, as it prescribed that the EU should strive to become "the world's most competitive knowledge–based society while at the same time maintaining its social welfare system"(Söderbaum et al. 2006; European Council 2000: 2). Accordingly, different aims seem to underly the EU's attempts to promote interregionalism.

9.4 A Snapshot of Contemporary EU-Driven Interregionalism

Accordingly, interregionalism has gradually become an element in the ways the EU has been striving to conduct its externa relations. Aggarwal and Fogarty (2005: 327–346) even state that the EU is the "patron saint of interregionalism" in international (economic) relations. But what are the current patterns of EU interregional relations? Figure 9.1 provides an overview of most of the regional organizations or settings with or through which the EU engages in interregionalism.[4] If one transposes this overview to a world map, it is clear that EU interregionalism in fact covers a large part of the globe. Yet, according to Söderbaum et al. (2005: 279) "interregionalism is particularly strong in the EU's external policies towards Latin America, where the EU has interregional partnerships with the most relevant subregions, such as the Andean region, Central America and, above all, Mercosur".

---

[4]For more on EU-Africa relations, e.g., see Farrell (2005); on EU-Asia relations, e.g., see Gilson (2005). On EU-Latin America relations, see García (2014).

Fig. 9.1 Overview of EU interregional cooperation, partnerships and policies

Simultaneously, several states, and sometimes even supra-national regional integration schemes, are a part of different regional settings and interregional dialogues;
hence, there is overlap. However, as the overview also demonstrates, interregionalism is not always a tool resorted to by the EU in dealing with other regions globally.

This is particularly true as regards its relations with North America (if one
excludes 'NATO' as potentially being a manifestation of so-called 'hybrid interregionalism', where a security organisation interacts with interregional patterns of
collaboration). With regard to the North American case, Aggarwal and Fogarty (2006:
80) in fact state that "even as the EU pursued interregional strategies towards many
other ill-defined and weakly institutionalized 'regions', it avoided an interregional
approach toward its most important commercial partner". Yet, with the negotiations
on the Transatlantic Trade and Investment Partnership (TTIP), some authors
have argued that the EU approach somewhat changed and indeed turned to patterns
of interregionalism, as this scheme can neither be called 'bilateral' nor 'multilateral'. Accordingly, for this kind of interregional activity, scholars such as Telò et al.
(2015) have put forward the term "hybrid interregionalism".

9.5   Current Priorities in EU-driven Interregionalism: Insights Based on the 2016 Global Strategy

In order to have a good understanding of the contemporary strategic value and scope of interregionalism for the EU, the Global Strategy (2016: 10) as well as its implementation action plans provide valuable insights. In fact, it the strategy states that this type of "cooperation is a fundamental rationale for the EU's own peace and development in the twenty-first century. This is why we will promote and support cooperative regional orders worldwide, including in the most divided areas". The Global Strategy then continues to further outline why regions matter (EEAS 2016: 32):

> Regional orders do not take a single form. Where possible and when in line with our interests, the EU will support regional organisations. We will not strive to export our model, but rather seek reciprocal inspiration from different regional experiences. Cooperative regional orders, however, are not created only by organisations. They comprise a mix of bilateral, sub-regional, regional and inter-regional relations. They also feature the role of global players interlinked with regionally-owned cooperative efforts. Taken together these can address transnational conflicts, challenges and opportunities. In different world regions, the EU will be driven by specific goals. Across all regions, we will invest in cooperative relationships to spur shared global responsibilities.

Interestingly, the Global Strategy does not leave out specific regions when assessing the EU's relationship with different continents. For example, the section on the Middle East and Africa, which includes the Gulf Cooperation Countries (GCCs), mentions (EEAS 2016: 35–36):

> We will deepen dialogue with Iran and GCC countries on regional conflicts, human rights and counter-terrorism, seeking to prevent contagion of existing crises and foster the space for cooperation and diplomacy.
>   In light of the growing interconnections between North- and sub-Saharan Africa, as well as between the Horn of Africa and the Middle East, the EU will support cooperation across these sub-regions. It means systematically addressing cross-border dynamics in North and West Africa, the Sahel and Lake Chad regions through closer links with the African Union, the Economic Community of Western African States (ECOWAS) and the G5 Sahel. Finally, we will invest in African peace and development as an investment in our own security and prosperity. We will intensify cooperation with and support for the African Union, as well as ECOWAS, the Inter-Governmental Authority on Development in Eastern Africa, and the East African Community, among others. The Economic Partnership Agreements can spur African integration and mobility, and encourage Africa's full and equitable participation in global value chains.

Instead of emphasizing the EU's strategic –bilateral- relationship with the U.S., the Global Strategy also highlights stronger Atlantic interaction through an interregional platform, i.e. NATO (EEAS 2016: 20–36):

> The EU will invest further in strong bonds across the Atlantic, both north and south. A solid transatlantic partnership through NATO and with the United States and Canada helps us strengthen resilience, address conflicts, and contribute to effective global governance. NATO, for its members, has been the bedrock of Euro-Atlantic security for almost 70 years.

An area which has traditionally received considerable EU interregional attention is Latin America. For this region, the Global Strategy states:

> The Union will expand cooperation and build stronger partnerships with Latin America and the Caribbean, grounded on shared values and interests. It will develop multilateral ties with the Community of Latin American and Caribbean States (CELAC) and with different regional groupings according to their competitive advantage. We will pursue a free trade agreement with Mercosur, (…) and invest in deeper socio-economic connections with Latin American and Caribbean countries through visa facilitation, student exchanges, twinning, research cooperation and technical projects.

In view of ASEAN, the Global Strategy (2016: 36) explicitly mentions:

> the EU will deepen its economic diplomacy in the region, working towards ambitious free trade agreements with strategic partners such as Japan and India, as well as ASEAN member states, with the goal of an eventual EU-ASEAN agreement. We will help build maritime capacities and support an ASEAN-led regional security architecture.

Finally, even in the 'high north' of the globe, the Global Strategy foresees an interregional partnership: "in the Arctic, a low-tension area, with ongoing cooperation ensured by the Arctic Council, a well-functioning legal framework, and solid political and security cooperation" (EEAS 2016: 40). Accordingly, the Global Strategy presents interregionalism as an important strategy to enhance relations between the EU and various regional integration schemes, while it aims to strengthen patterns of regional stability on the global level.

9.6   Conclusions

The first part of this chapter has focused on the ways in which interregionalism has gradually been adopted in EU foreign policy strategies, alongside the EU's gradual strengthening of foreign policy coordination between its member states. We then provided an overview of the interregional relations encompassed in more recent EU external and demonstrated how it is a core of the 2016 Global Strategy. We also demonstrated how EU institutionalisation in foreign affairs and external relations, notably with the creation of the post of High Representative of the Union for Foreign Affairs and Security Policy and its supporting EEAS, in the framework of the Lisbon treaty, has provided an additional impetus for the EU to engage in multilateral and in interregional relations. EU interregionalism is shown to encompass different strategies and rationales, among them the defense of the EU's economic and strategic interests globally and ways to strengthen its core values on the international level, via patterns of interregional collaboration, to support fundamental goals such as respect for the rule of law, democracy and human rights. Clearly, next to patterns of bilateral and multilateral foreign policy, interregionalism can constitute a strong diplomatic, as well as geo-political and strategic tool reinforcing the EU's ambition to ensure a multilateral, rules-based world order (EEAS 2016). The intensity of EU inter-regional relations varies across continents, but clearly, as our chapter has shown, interregionalism is an important element in the ways the EU interacts with other regions and regional integration schemes, complementing and strengthening patterns of EU bilateral and multilateral diplomacy.

Further Readings

Keukeleire, S., & Delreux, T. (2014). *The foreign policy of the European Union.* Basingstoke: Palgrave Macmillan, 408p.
Söderbaum, F., & Van Langenhove, L. (2005). The EU as a global actor and the role of interregionalism. London: Routledge, 262p.
Telò, M., Fawcett, L., & Ponjaert, F. (2015). *Interregionalism and the EU.* Abingdon: Routledge.

References

Aggestam, L. (2008). Introduction: Ethical power Europe? *International Affairs, 84*(1), 1–11.
Aggarwal, V. K., & Fogarty, E. A. (2005). The limits of interregionalism: The EU and North America. *Journal of European Integration, 27*(3), 327–346.
Aggarwal, V., & Fogarty, E. (2006). The limits of Interregionalism: The EU and North America. In Söderbaum & V. Langenhove (Eds.), *The EU as a global power: The politics of interregionalism* (pp. 79–99). Routledge.
Allahverdiyev, V. (2008). *Interregionalism as a foreign policy tool of the EU: The cases of ASEM and EU-ASEAN partnership.* Master thesis, Central European University, Budapest.
Baert, F., Scaramagli, T., & SöDerbaum, F. (Eds.) (2014). Intersecting interregionalism. *Regions, global governance, and the EU.* Dordrecht/Heidelberg: Springer.
Blavoukos, S., & Bourantonis, D. (2017). *The EU in UN politics actors, processes and performances.* Basingstoke: Palgrave Macmillan.
Bretherton, C., & Vogler, J. (1999). *The European Union as a Global Actor.* Routledge.
Bretherton, C., & Vogler, J. (2006). Conceptualizing actors and actorness. *The European Union as a Global Actor, 2,* 12–36.
Cosgrove-Sacks, C., & Twitchett, K. J. (Eds.). (1970). *The new international actors: The United Nations and the European economic community.* Macmillan.
Damro, C. (2012). Market power Europe. *Journal of European Public Policy, 19*(5), 682–699.
De Flers, N. A., & Regelsberger, E. (2005). The EU and inter-regional cooperation. In C. Hill & M. Smith (Eds.), *International relations and the European Union* (pp. 317–347). Oxford: Oxford University Press.
Dinan, D. (1999). *Ever closer union: An introduction to European integration.* Boulder/London: Lynne Rienner Publishers.
Doidge, M. (2011). *The European Union and interregionalism: Patterns of engagement.* Surrey: Ashgate.
Drieskens, E. (2017). Golden or gilded jubilee? A research agenda for actorness. *Journal of European Public Policy, 24*(10), 1534–1546.

EEAS. (2016). *Shared vision, common action: A stronger Europe, a global strategy for the European Union's foreign and security policy*. Brussels: Publications Office of the European Union.

European Council. (2000). *Lisbon strategy for growth and jobs*. Brussels: Publications of the European Union.

Farrell, M. (2005). A triumph of realism over idealism? Cooperation between the European Union and Africa. *Journal of European Integratio, 27*(3), 263–283.

Gaens, B. (2012). The rise of interregionalisms: "The case of the European Union's relations with East Asia". In *The Ashgate research companion to regionalisms* (pp. 69–91). Burlington: Ashgate.

García, M. (2014). The European Union and Latin America: 'Transformative power Europe' versus the realities of economic interests. *Cambridge Review of International Affairs, 28*(4), 621–640.

Gilson, J. (2005). New interregionalism? The EU and East Asia. *European Integration, 27*(3), 307–326.

Global Strategy. (2016). *Shared vision, common action. A dtronger Europe: A global strategy for the European union's foreign and security policy*. June.

Hänggi, H., Roloff, R., & Rüland, J. (Eds.). (2006). *Interregionalism and international relations*. London: Routledge.

Hardacre, A., & Smith, M. (2009). The EU and the diplomacy of complex Interregionalism. *The Hague Journal of Diplomacy, 4*(2), 167–188.

Jin, X. (2014). *European Union representation at the United Nations: Towards more coherence after the Treaty of Lisbon*. PhD dissertation, Leiden University, 202p.

Jin, X., & Hosli, M. O. (2013). Pre- and post-Lisbon: European Union voting in the United Nations general assembly. *West European Politics, 36*(6), 1274–1291.

Jupille, J., & Caporaso, J. A. (1998). States, agency, and rules: The European Union in global environmental politics. *The European Union in the world community, 17*, 157–182.

Keukeleire, S., & Delreux, T. (2014). *The foreign policy of the European Union*. Basingstoke: Palgrave Macmillan.

Keuleers, F., Fonck, D., & Keukeleire, S. (2016). Beyond EU navel-gazing: Taking stock of EU-centrism in the analysis of EU foreign policy. *Cooperation and Conflict, 51*(3), 345–364.

Koops, J. A. (2011). *The European Union as an integrative power: Assessing the EU's' effective multilateralism' with NATO and the United Nations* (Vol. 16). Brussels: ASP/VUB Press/UPA.

Koops, J., & Macaj, G. (Eds.). (2014). *The European Union as a diplomatic actor*. Springer.

Koops, J., & Macaj, G. (Eds.). (2015). *The European Union as a diplomatic actor*. Basingstoke: Palgrave Macmillan.

Leonard, M. (2005). Europe's transformative power. *CER Bulletin, 40*, 1–2.

Manners, I. (2002). Normative power Europe: A contradiction in terms? *JCMS: Journal of Common Market Studies, 40*(2), 235–258.

Mayer, H. (2008). The long legacy of Dorian Gray: Why the European Union needs to redefine its role in global affairs. *Journal of European Integration, 30*, 7–25.

Niemann, A., & Bretherton, C. (2013). EU external policy at the crossroads: The challenge of actorness and effectiveness. *International Relations, 27*(3), 261–275.

Rüland, J. (2001). *ASEAN and the European union: A bumpy inter-regional relation*, Bonn, Zentrum für Europaeische Integrationsforschung (ZEI), Discussion Paper C95.

Rüland, J. (2006). Interregionalism: An unfinished agenda. In H. Hänggi, R. Roloff, & J. Rüland (Eds.), *Interregionalism and international relations* (pp. 295–313). London: Routledge.

Schmalz, U. (2005). Die Entwicklung der Europäischen Sicherheits- und Verteidigungspolitik 1990–2004. In J. Varwick (Ed.), *Die Beziehungen zwischen NATO und EU. Partnerschaft, Konkurrenz, Rivalität?* (pp. 45–59). Opladen: Budrich-Verlag.

Shaw, T. M., & Cornelissen, S. (2012). *The Ashgate research companion to regionalisms*. Burlington: Ashgate.

Sjöstedt, G. (1977). *The external role of the European Community* (Vol. 7). Gower Publishing Company, Limited.

Smith, M. (2004). Between two worlds? The European Union, the United States and world order. *International Politics, 41*(1), 95–117.

Söderbaum, F., & Van Langenhove, L. (2005). *The EU as a global actor and the role of interregionalism.* London: Routledge.

Söderbaum, F., Stålgren, P., & Van Langenhove, L. (2005). The EU as a global actor and the dynamics of Interregionalism: A comparative analysis. *European Integration, 27*(3), 342–366.

Söderbaum, F., Stålgren, P., & Van Langenhove, L. (2006). *The EU as a global player: The politics of interregionalism.* London/New York: Taylor and Francis Group.

Telò, M. (2005). *Europe: A Civilan power?* Basingstoke: Palgrave Macmillan.

Telò, M., Fawcett, L., & Ponjaert, F. (2015). *Interregionalism and the European Union: A post-revisionist approach to Europe's place in a changing world.* London: Routledge.

Van Langenhove, L. (2011). *Building regions: The regionalization of world order.* Burlington: Ashgate.

Verhofstadt, G. (2008). *The financial crisis: Three ways out for Europe.* Gütersloh: Bertelsmann Stiftung, 12p.

Zepter, B. (2008). Reflections on regionalization in Europe: Lessons for Asia? *Asia Europe Journal, 5*, 455–464.

Chapter 10
The Shanghai Cooperation Organisation

Giles Scott-Smith

10.1 Introduction

The Shanghai Cooperation Organisation (SCO) is an intergovernmental organization founded in Shanghai on 15 June 2001 by six countries: China, Russia, Kazakhstan, Kyrgyzstan, Tajikistan and Uzbekistan. Established to ensure the security of the Central Asian region in the post-Soviet era, in its early years it was interpreted in many studies as little more than an extension of Russian foreign policy interests, but recently it is clear that the initiative has shifted to Beijing. In 2015 its membership was expanded for the first time with the addition of India and Pakistan, and this was formalised at its 2016 summit. Including the two new members means the SCO represents 45% of the world's population and 19% of world GDP. As Russia and China further develop their cooperation, the SCO is now "increasingly viewed by governments across the world as an organization reflecting the political and economic ascendancy of the Eurasian region" (Savic 2016). This chapter outlines the origins and purposes of the SCO, and its position in relation to other post-Soviet regional entities that have been formed since 1991 under the heading of the Commonwealth of Independent States (CIS), such as the Collective Security Treaty Organisation (CSTO) and the Eurasian Economic Union (EAEU). The question is to what extent these formations are beginning to represent an inter-connected, multi-layered regional governance structure for Eurasia that could have consequences within a changing global order.

G. Scott-Smith (✉)
Leiden University, Leiden, The Netherlands
e-mail: g.scott-smith@hum.leidenuniv.nl

© Springer Nature Switzerland AG 2020
M. O. Hosli, J. Selleslaghs (eds.), *The Changing Global Order*, United Nations University Series on Regionalism 17,
https://doi.org/10.1007/978-3-030-21603-0_10

10.2   Russia and China: The SCO Core

The SCO was created by the original Shanghai Five group (the SCO six minus Uzbekistan), which came together in the mid-1990s as a measure to secure national borders in post-Soviet Central Asia. This was made official with the 1996 Shanghai Treaty and the Agreement on Deepening Military Trust in Border Regions and the 1997 Agreement on Reduction of Military Forces in Border Regions. Uzbekistan joined in 2001, at the time of the creation of the SCO itself. The main impulse behind the Organisation was the prevention of post-Soviet state collapse in Central Asia, in particular through radical insurgencies (often fuelled by religious extremism) that could threaten stability. NATO military intervention against Serbia in 1999 also raised fears in Russia that Kosovo could come to represent an unraveling of Moscow's influence in its near-abroad. These concerns were further heightened by the post 9/11 entry of US forces into Central Asia as part of the wider context to Operation Enduring Freedom in Afghanistan. From the beginning, the protection of sovereignty was the aim – that is, the post-Soviet Russian sovereign right to determine how and when to respond to threats in the Central Asian space (Hussein 2013).

In referring to Russia's outside pressures, attention must also be given to China. Due to the fractious past between the two powers, particularly in the 1960s and 1970s, it would be tempting to interpret the SCO as a bottle containing two large scorpions. Russian ambition could never match rising Chinese productivity and wealth, and fractious border disputes lingered on (Donaldson et al. 2014). However, the decline of ideologically-driven foreign policy and the rise of nationalisms eager to establish their reach, influence and legitimacy in their immediate neighbourhoods – particularly in opposition to ongoing encroachments and assumptions of hegemony by the United States – have enabled Moscow and Beijing to find each other on a potentially level playing field via the SCO. The Organisation's early agreements meant that China has for the first time committed to sending its military forces beyond its borders in times of emergency, and military cooperation has deepened since then. The disputed Russia-China border issues were all resolved by 2005, marking a significant step towards full bilateral normalization. In recent years the relationship has been marked by a new phase of multi-level cooperation, with the two powers signing Strategic Partnerships in 2012 and 2014. The latter, confirmed shortly after the introduction of sanctions by the US and EU in response to the Russian annexation of Crimea, indicates a new determination to establish an alternative set of norms for international transactions outside of those maintained by the US-led post-WW II global order (see Chap. 4 by Jian Shi and Zeren Langjia, 'China's Ascent').

Whereas it is often assumed that post-Soviet Russia operates on a short-term, impulsive basis in contrast to China's more patient long-term build-up of resources, the recent developments point to a more balanced, shared world-view between the two. Since WW II China has showed flexibility in aligning with major partners in response to outside pressures, be that with the Soviet Union against the United States (1950s) or with the United States against the Soviet Union (1970s). In the

1980s this was abandoned in favour of a non-aligned posture that allowed for greater independence, but in the 2010s various scholars and think tanks have begun to advocate for an alliance policy in order to strengthen China's strategic position. These positions were fuelled by the Obama administration's Pivot (or Rebalance) to Asia and the sense that the United States was looking to obstruct Chinese ambitions through the revival of a string of alliance relationships across the Asia-Pacific. One of the principal results of this trend, especially since the arrival of Xi as leader in 2013, is the rapidly developing bilateral relationship with Russia, although non-alignment continues to be the official outlook (Zhang 2012).

The evolution of the Russia-China relationship and the place of the SCO within that context should be seen in the context of China's so-called New Diplomacy, which has been focused on re-crafting its relations with its Asian neighbors to ensure a 'peaceful rise' (Qi and Shi 2013). Active since 1978 and the arrival of Deng Xiaoping as leader, New Diplomacy has had several dimensions: the New Security Concept, which takes a broad view of security beyond military goals and which aims to generate a post-Cold War environment through multilateral dialogue, cooperation, and institution-building; the New Development Approach, which looks to promote a coordinated economic strategy based on mutual benefits for all partners; and the overarching Chinese conception of a Harmonious World, which respects the existence of multiple civilizations and encourages their interaction in the interests of peace and prosperity (Fei 2010: 2–4). To a Western-orientated reader these ambitions sound vague and suspiciously like a cover for great power ambitions, and there is definitely an aim in the background to respond to the previously dominant economic and military power of the US and the normative power of the EU with a new conception of global order that is China-centred. From this perspective, the relationship with Russia is fundamental to moving beyond the Cold War dynamic of the Washington-Beijing-Moscow power triangle. The 1997 Russian-Chinese Joint Declaration on a Multipolar World and the Establishment of a New International Order stated emphatically "the multipolarization of the world" as a central aim, and the importance of the United Nations through which this can be promoted (China-Russia 1997). The discourse of the SCO is likewise saturated with the Chinese view of a Harmonious World created through dialogue, cooperation, and trust. From this perspective, the China-Russia relationship is a response to American *exceptionalism* as much as it is to American hegemony, where exceptionalism refers in this case to the United States acting in ways that set it outside the very rule-based system that it enforces on the behavior of others. By adopting the rhetoric of harmony across all activities, China (and by extension the SCO) seeks over time to shift attention away from the alleged goals of the Chinese (and Russian) regimes and more towards the perception of the United States not as the bringer of peace and prosperity but as a major source of global instability.

Alliances possess particular characteristics: they are formed by states; they represent a formal or informal form of security cooperation; they are generally directed against an external threat, with a limited appliance internally (Liska 1962; Walt 1989; Snyder 2007). In this regard the China-Russia relationship has not formally attained the level of an alliance, although it exhibits some key elements. The joint naval manouevres in the South China Sea in September 2016, announced soon after the Permanent Court of Arbitration in The Hague ruled against Chinese territorial claims in the region in July, pointed to an increasing mutual recognition of each other's immediate security interests. US and EU sanctions against Russia in the Crimea and a very visible US military presence in the Baltics to strengthen NATO's resolve have irritated Moscow, similar to how US naval operations in the South China Sea, not to mention the outbursts of President Trump and Secretaries of State Rex Tillerson and Mike Pompeo on the matter, have irritated Beijing (*Washington Post* 2017). If an alliance requires an external threat, the mutual determination to push back against the United States could provide it. However, this would have been more likely had Hillary Clinton been elected, since at the time of writing the actual relationship between Trump and Putin is shrouded in a haze of opaque transactions that make it impossible to judge how that will develop. Finally, beyond the mutual rejection by Moscow and Beijing of US dominance, scholars are generally in agreement that the SCO does not and cannot represent a full security alliance, because that is not its intention. Instead it represents "a new type of looser, more informal, and flexible alignment system" that falls outside of traditional definitions of alliances in IR theory, reflecting the criss-crossing systems of linkages and ties that have come to define post-Cold War global order (Tugsbilguun 2008: 100). For some, the SCO has been an "enigma", not fitting into any neat definition of a regional organization (Zeb 2006: 51). Talk of a 'Nato of the East', common in Western circles in the mid-2000s, probably not only misses the point but also avoids the fact that NATO itself is struggling to maintain its credibility and common value system amongst its 28 members (CSS 2009; Wilkins 2012).

10.3   Regional Governance

The SCO should therefore be seen in the wider context of Eur-Asia's rising prominence in global governance structures. Global order has long been framed in terms of a 'Westphalian system' based on territorial integrity, state sovereignty, and a system of international law built around these foundations. The onset of globalisation in terms of cross-border flows of finance, information, and crime, and the loss or 'pooling' of national sovereignty in supranational and international organisations, pointed towards a post-Westphalian (or, for some, 'Westfailure') system in the 1990s (Strange 1999). The rise of Asia has now brought on discussion of a potential 'Eastphalia system' emerging, supplanting Western norms and introducing new structures of governance that will at least overlap with and potentially surpass existing entities. Although it remains contested whether a defined set of "Asian power, principles, and practices" can be clarified, and whether major powers such as China and India (not to mention Japan) can actually coalesce around such a common worldview, the Eastphalian concept does correctly point to the need to investigate the contours of this new era (Fidler 2010: 3).

In terms of economic governance, the Bretton Woods institutions have adapted slowly to incorporating rising powers and are now being faced with a more crowded institutional field as other parties organize separately. The G20's Financial Stability Board, established in 2009 to facilitate and coordinate financial regulation, "is now considered as the fourth institutional pillar of global economic governance (along with the World Trade Organization, International Monetary Fund and World Bank)" (Madhur 2012: 819). Next to this should be placed the New Development Bank of the BRICS, founded in 2015, and the official opening of the Asian Infrastructure and Investment Bank in early 2016. The latter introduced a new player in multilateral economic development with, for the first time, Beijing acting as the undisputed lead power (Chin 2015). The SCO should be seen in the context of this expanding non-Western post-Cold War architecture.

In the first place, the SCO has become an important element in the infrastructure that has been built up by Moscow to stabilize the post-Soviet space in political, economic, and security terms, alongside the Commonwealth of Independent States (CIS) and its security (CSTO) and economic (EAEA) components. The CSTO's more formal security agreements, involving a collective security clause and a deployable rapid reaction force, make it part of the inner ring of Moscow's concentric security system, with the SCO, involving larger partners such as China and now India, occupying a more outlying position. The Russian impulse has always been to use these arrangements to secure its influence and prevent other powers from encroaching on its designated sphere of influence. For this reason, the Russian recognition of multipolarity and multilateralism should be seen as an extension of Russian nationalism with both an offensive (raise influence in multi-polar world) and defensive (retake the initiative in Central Asia) purpose. Despite their apparent congruence, multipolarity and multilateralism are "seldom straightforward" from a Russian perspective (see Chap. 5 by André Gerrits, 'Russia in the Changing Global Order'). Since the mid-2000s the preference has been to interpret multipolarity as a concert of great powers that recognizes and rehabilitates Russian influence, leaving little room for actual multilateral mechanisms to develop (Kuhrt 2014: 139; Makarychev and Morozov 2011). The EAEU has been described as a "counterhegemonic institution" in its attempt to both mimic the apparatus of and exclude the EU from influencing the Russian sphere of influence, but it remains to be seen to what extent Russian hegemony can be really embedded by means of using the EAEU to satisfy the interests of key groups within its economic space (Kirkham 2016). Likewise, Russian efforts to tie the CSTO to the SCO have met with Chinese resistance due exactly to Beijing's unwillingness to be caught in a web of Russian-inspired security guarantees (de Haas 2007: 60).

The SCO is predominantly an intergovernmental institution, with a great emphasis placed on its annual summits of state leaders. Its central body is the Council of Heads of State, which meets annually to determine the organization's priorities and further its agenda of cooperation. With working languages in Russian and Chinese, the Council is supported by a hierarchical apparatus that includes the Council of Heads of Government (which approves the budget), the Council of Foreign Ministers and other ministerial meetings in specific policy fields, and a Secretariat (located in

Beijing). An SCO Studies Center is located in Shanghai under the leadership of Professor Pan Guang, but it remains to be seen how far this means the Organisation is developing an in-house think tank apparatus.[1] In 2002 the SCO issued a Charter, outlining its purpose and governing apparatus. The Charter emphasizes the value of the Organization for building trust, ensuring regional stability, and promoting economic, social, and cultural integration amongst its members. The Council of Heads of State also decides on membership applications from other states. From 2004 several states joined the annual SCO summits as official observers: Afghanistan, Armenia, Azerbaijan, Belarus, Cambodia, Iran, Mongolia, and Nepal. A separate group, known as Dialogue Partners, was also created, currently including Turkey and Sri Lanka. Iran has long shown a strong interest to join as a full member in order to withstand pressure from the United States, but both China and Russia have been wary of such a move. The nuclear deal with the United States in 2015 did not immediately change this, and it is unclear at the time of writing whether the possibility of Iranian membership has been improved by President Trump's reneging on that deal in 2018. New members must not face any UN sanctions, or be involved in armed conflicts.

Normative studies in IR have tended to operate according to a Western bias, treating regional organisations that don't conform to established modes of operation or that lack democratic foundations less seriously (Bailes and Dunay 2007; Bailes 2007). If the European Union is presented as the benchmark for regional integration (Zielonka 2008; Jetschke 2009), the SCO will always fall short. Thus the Organization is regarded as relevant more "for the nurturing of relationships and the building of mutual trust" than for a "narrow collective-action problem-solving function generally ascribed to international organizations" (Prantl 2013: 163). It is often interpreted as a forum for both managing and overcoming issues of tension between Moscow and Beijing, in the process reassuring their Central Asian neighbours through this superpower rapprochement. The Declaration on the Establishment of the Shanghai Cooperation Organization from June 2001 does list an ambitious list of policy areas where "effective cooperation" is aimed for (politics, economics, science, culture, education, energy, environment, communications, "and other fields"), and also declares a desire for "a democratic, fair and rational new international and political order." The document is laden with references to confidence building, trust, and the "Shanghai spirit".[2] Such statements contributed to both the level of skepticism of the SCO's actual importance, and the sense that it was 'hiding' its real intentions behind pleasant-sounding window-dressing. Regionalism, from an orthodox normative standpoint, can only succeed if it is based on a sense of common values. Thus a recent collection of essays on the SCO has maintained that

> countries and peoples that share common values usually find it easier to cooperate than those who do not. In addition, a lack of common values, that is, a lack of a common discourse or vision for what one wants to get out of the relationship, often leads to misunderstandings, of a cultural if not political nature. (Fredholm 2013: 16)

---

[1] See http://www.wise-qatar.org/pan-guang
[2] Available online at http://eng.sectsco.org/documents/

However, these approaches miss the point that European-style integration is not the goal. Mutual recognition is more important in a Central Asian context than transparency or democratic accountability. The SCO's aim is to "occupy political space" and ensure that a highly vulnerable region in the Russian and Chinese backyard does not fall into political and/or economic collapse. Likewise, the SCO offers a mechanism for the Central Asian states to interact with their powerful neighbors from positions of outward equality, strengthening their status and political regimes. SCO decision-making is based on consensus, which explains the gradual development of the organization over the last 20 years. Decision-making outside of the heads of state summits has expanded, indicating incremental steps towards using the SCO as a diplomatic system through which common interests can slowly be framed (de Haas 2007: 58). The acceptance of new members in particular has been a carefully monitored issue, and the admission of both India and Pakistan in 2016 indicated a major step forward in this regard (Prantl 2013: 168, 175).

10.4   Two Challenges

The SCO is now evolving into a new phase of maturity as an international organization with a growing level of global recognition. Nevertheless, it faces significant challenges if it is to achieve the status it appears to be asking for. Firstly, there is the extent to which it can develop into an effective diplomatic platform for new policy areas beyond counter-terrorism and security. Secondly, it is still in doubt how far it will contribute to the political and economic stabilization of Afghanistan in the longer term.

10.4.1   Regional Policy Cooperation

In terms of specific areas of policy cooperation, the SCO has always been based on a security agenda that focuses on the so-called 'three evils' of terrorism, separatism and extremism, and these have been extended into related fields such as combating illicit narcotics and arms trafficking and illegal migration. To coordinate this among the members, a Regional Anti-Terrorism Structure (RATS) was set up in 2001, its executive committee based in Tashkent, Uzbekistan, and its operational base in Bishkek, Kyrgystan. In January 2016 Yevgeny Sysoyev, the deputy director of the Russian Federal Security Service (FSB), was appointed the director of RATS. The website indicates regular meetings with diplomatic representatives in the Central Asian region, including the UN, the EU, and Japan, and a rolling update of news on terrorist attacks around the world that evidently look to align RATS activities with other counter-terrorism initiatives in the West and elsewhere.[3] During the mid-2000s, Vladimir Putin pushed an agenda that sought to use the SCO to balance US power and stressed that the United States was not required for Eurasian security. Threatened by Western-supported regime changes in Georgia in 2003, Ukraine in 2004, and Kyrgystan in 2005, and negotiating the increasing presence of US military forces in the Central Asia region following 9/11 and the onset of Operation Enduring Freedom in Afghanistan, the SCO asserted its primacy as the organization legitimately tasked with ensuring Central Asian security. This was evident in the declaration issued at its 2005 summit in Astana (Kazakhstan), which both called for the US presence in the region to be temporary, and fully supported the repressive measures taken by Uzbek leader Karimov against the political protests in Andijan earlier that year (Human Rights Watch 2005).

> We support the efforts of the international coalition engaged in the antiterrorist operation in Afghanistan and we will continue doing so. Today, we note the positive trend of internal political stabilization in Afghanistan. A number of the SCO member states have provided their ground infrastructure for temporary deployment of military contingents of the coalition participating states, as well as their territory and air space for military transit in the interest of the antiterrorist operation. Given the completion of the active military phase of the antiterrorist operation in Afghanistan, the member states of the Shanghai Cooperation Organization deem it necessary for the relevant participating states of the antiterrorist coalition *to set a deadline for the temporary use of said infrastructure and presence of their military contingents in the territory of the SCO member states.* (Declaration 2005)

This message was backed with full-scale military exercises conducted by the Russian and Chinese armed forces in August 2005.

Following this mid-2000s period of Russian belligerence, Beijing began to take more of a leading role within the SCO, in line with its general development as a leading global power and the transition of its leadership's world-view from caution to an increasing self-confidence. In line with this development, the SCO has been central for expanding the application of a wide view of security into other policy fields, and using these initiatives to expand its network of partnerships beyond the Central Asian region. In July 2006, at the SCO's Shanghai summit, Vladimir Putin initiated the SCO's Energy Club, with the purpose of uniting energy-producing and consuming states, coordinating energy strategies, and strengthening energy security. At the center of this arrangement lies Russia as a major energy source and China as the world's second-largest consumer of oil and natural gas, with SCO members holding 25% of known oil reserves, 50% of gas reserves, 35% of coal and around 50% of all uranium. The potential of these vast holdings in the ground have often been talked up (Movkebaeva 2013). Yet the Russian-hosted SCO website (not the site of the SCO's secretariat) admitted in early 2015 that economic integration and energy infrastructure "remains the least developed area in the organization's activities". Ongoing global economic instability placed heavy reliance for its recov-

---

[3]The website does include information of RATS activities but lacks background information, http://ecrats.org/en/. Sysoyev, then with the FSB, announced in November 2015 that 7000 of the estimated 30,000 foreign fighters with Islamic State were from the post-Soviet region, see http://www.interpretermag.com/tag/yevgeny-sysoyev/

ery "on the economic growth pace in China and India", and that an integrated energy plan "would also have a positive impact on the world economy in general" (SCO Energy Club 2015). Interesting in this regard is that part of the delay came from the perceived need for all SCO members to take part, in line with the Organization's functioning according to consensus. Since Uzbekistan's resistance to the original proposal effectively blocked its advance, Russia has since shifted to a more flexible arrangement that sees the Energy Club not as an SCO 'closed shop' but as a platform for wider regional development. Here again one can note a shift in approach of the SCO from the Russian-orientated mid-2000s to the more flexible China-led 2010s, but it has been slow in coming, and it continues to be riven with competitive antagonisms. Russia's wish to dominate the regional energy sector and dictate terms through its quasi-state entities such as Gazprom has met resistance from among others Turkmenistan (not an SCO member), and a regional contest has been ongoing as to whether Russia could somehow incorporate major Chinese gas supply deals with both Turkmenistan and Kazakhstan into a greater regional whole.

In this context the Turkmenistan-Afghanistan-Pakistan-India (TAPI) gas pipeline, construction of which began in late 2015, should be seen as an important initiative to create a more dynamic, cross-regional energy market, bringing in new players. Supplementing existing oil and gas deals between Kazakhstan and India, it will also position Afghanistan as a key transit state. In a similar vein, in 2017 Turkey became the first non-SCO member state to chair the Energy Club, a clear sign that outside powers are now being admitted as partners in key SCO sectors. Turkey's future stance is potentially ground-breaking for the future development of the SCO. A dialogue partner with the Organization since 2012, in 2013 President Erdogan issued statements suggesting he was interested in orientating Turkey more towards the SCO than the EU. Not taken seriously at the time, Erdogan made similar statements in 2016 which were interpreted as a sign to the EU that the westward course of Turkish foreign and domestic policy was not guaranteed. Some have even speculated about Ankara swapping NATO for SCO membership. Turkey's key location for east-west pipelines escalated in the 1990s with the expansion of the Caspian Sea region's oil and gas production, but now the emphasis has moved from the US-backed Baku-Ceyhan and Nabucco projects that aimed to bypass Russian sources, to the South Stream/Turkish Stream pipelines that would bring Russian gas direct to European markets. The power balance in the region has shifted, closely connected to the shifting energy infrastructure, and Turkey's entry into the Energy Club is significant for this reason (Chulkovskaya 2017).

The SCO Business Club and Interbank Consortium have previously struggled to make any headway in terms of integration. The mercantilist outlook of most of the SCO member-states makes it difficult to achieve win-win deals, and suspicions and rivalries continue to obstruct the (Russian) ambitions for a genuine 'single market'-type economic space. However, the chances for success may be changing as Putin's aim for a Eurasian economic space is gradually coinciding with Beijing's aims for the Silk Road Economic Belt to become a vast development corridor across the Eurasian continent. Initially seen as another sign of an inevitable clash of interests between the two powers, in May 2015 Xi Jinping called for combining the two during a visit to Moscow, and Putin followed up by declaring a "great Eurasian partnership" during a conference in St. Petersburg in July 2016. The sense is that Russian regional ambitions are being re-framed in order to accommodate and benefit from the rising economic power of China – whereas few nations trusted Russian motives, Beijing seems more attuned (at least on the surface) to a mutually beneficial development agenda for all parties involved, as expressed through the aims of the Asian Infrastructure and Investment Bank (AIIB). For Beijing, Russia is part of the trajectory of the Silk Road Economic Belt across the Eurasian landmass to Europe. For Russia, the Belt is a new means with which to potentially entice European business eastwards (OSW 2016).

These Central Asian shifts may herald a new phase of development for the SCO, which after all has provided the platform for mutual trust-building between the two powers in the sensitive field of security, and in doing so laying the ground for other initiatives. Looking for greater recognition as an international organization, the SCO achieved observer status at the UN General Assembly in December 2004, and memoranda of understanding were signed with the CIS and the Association of South-East Asian Nations (ASEAN) in 2005. At the 2014 summit held in Astana, the only representatives of other international organizations attending were from the UN's Economic and Social Commission for the Asia-Pacific (UNESCAP) and the Russian-led Commonwealth of Independent States and Eurasian Economic Union. In terms of inter-regionalism, therefore, it is taking time for the SCO to be recognized as a legitimate partner. However, the study of inter-regional interaction has largely focused on the status of the European Union as a key normative actor in setting the agenda for inter-regional activity. Yet as a recent study has argued, "the emergence of a more diverse international system marks the end, or dilution, of 'exceptionalism' and questions notions of US and/or EU global leadership and power" (Baert et al. 2014: 2). The lack of credibility given to the SCO by diplomatic observers can also indicate a lack of recognition of the changing international system and the fading of the EU's leading role as catalyst and model. While the SCO is definitely a convenient platform through which Russia and China can exert their influence over the Central Asian region, both its gradual interlocking with other fora such as the EAEU and its careful expansion of membership point to the need to take it more seriously in inter-regional terms. Lacking the credibility and the prestige accorded to other new international fora such as the G20 or the BRICS has allowed the SCO to develop out of the spotlight. The 2016–2020 Action Plan for regional development, the ambitious Silk Road initiative, the founding of the AIIB, and other Chinese-led development plans such as the China-Pakistan Economic Corridor will continue to integrate the vast Eurasian regional economy and strengthen cooperation. If in the future the SCO does develop a common agenda together with the BRICS, it could mean a further shift in the balance of global governance.

10.4.2   *Afghanistan*

Afghanistan was a priority for all SCO summits in the 2010s. The current SCO member states share mutual concerns about radical Islamic terrorist networks, separatist movements, human trafficking and drug trafficking, with Afghanistan being the main source of the global heroin trade. In many ways, Afghanistan represents the porous borders that the SCO was founded to police, and one source of the 'three evils' that the SCO is meant to combat. The Afghani government has been represented as a guest at SCO summits since 2005, enabling at least some top-level discussion on the security situation. Despite logical expectations (Khan 2009), relations between NATO and the SCO have never developed. The US-led Enduring Freedom security operation from late 2001 relied on Central Asian acquiescence for logistics, but the deployment of NATO's International Security Assistance Force in Afghanistan from 2003 to December 2014 did not lead to any substantial coordination or even liaison with the SCO powers. Cautious advice from security experts that NATO could seek closer relations with the SCO and the CSTO have not been reciprocated (NATO 2020, 2010). As the withdrawal of NATO forces approached, the country was upgraded to observer status at the SCO summit in 2012, suggesting that the Organisation could begin to upgrade its involvement. At the time, President Karzai also courted the SCO in an effort to obtain alternative support with a US exit approaching (Anand 2012). Yet the SCO has remained reticent about entering the security vacuum militarily, instead concentrating on bolstering Afghan authorities and economic development in order to secure national 'self-reliance'. In many ways this has shadowed the continuing NATO presence in the form of its Resolute Support Mission that runs from January 2015 to at least 2020, which interacts with Afghanistan as an equal partner responsible for its own security, providing advice, training and infrastructure assistance.

Russian regional jealousies mean that Afghanistan falls more under the Moscow-directed CSTO than the Russia-China SCO, and Beijing has so far seen no reason to challenge that assumption. Nevertheless, Chinese investments in Afghanistan far exceed Russia's, and the experience of the Red Army there in the 1980s means that Russian interests fade out beyond improved border controls among SCO members. For the SCO, Afghanistan is largely dealt with from the perspective of the RATS, and several Cooperation Programs to Counter Terrorism and Separatism have been run by its members, the most recent through 2016–2018. For these reasons, the SCO's main contribution to the Afghan situation could be in using its diplomatic network to normalize relations between Kabul and its regional neighbors, thus keeping the door open for Afghan involvement in regional infrastructure (Sharma 2015). Afghan involvement in the TAPI is a clear example of this. Once again, as with Turkey and the Caspian, US-led pipeline plans from the 1990s are now being revived, but now in the context of a different regional and international order.

The potential game-changer for this Afghan impasse is the arrival of India and Pakistan as SCO members in 2016. This adds a new twist, since it remains to be seen how the traditional alignments of Russia-India and China-Pakistan may allow for a more effective approach to Afghanistan. The admittance of these two nations was delayed for several years because of these great power rivalries and the contradictory, antagonistic ambitions of the two South Asian states. While India had donated $2bn in aid to Afghanistan up to 2013 in order to stabilize the country, Pakistan has been a source of Afghan radicalization. Attempts to improve economic ties and create new levels of interdependence through the South Asian Association for Regional Cooperation (SAARC) have not succeeded in tempering Indian-Pakistani suspicions since its founding in 1985. Once again, a change in approach can be noticed since the arrival of Xi Jinping to power in 2013, as Chinese-Indian rapprochement was a central item on his agenda. The arrival of India, the world's largest democracy, does add a welcome layer of extra legitimacy to the SCO's club of post-communist authoritarian regimes. Yet India, one of the champions of non-alignment during the Cold War, is also moving in various directions. It has developed close relations with the US through the 2006 nuclear deal, and the idea of a formal link with NATO has been proposed. At the same time, India has taken the EAEU seriously, looking for a possible free trade deal, and has already coordinated diplomatically with Russia and China through the BRICS. The SCO will therefore be one of several paths that India is looking to take to enhance its position as an international power-broker and 'rising power' (see Chap. 6 by Carina van de Wetering, 'India as an Emerging Power'). Expectations should not be too high for a full India-China rapprochement, but the Organization itself is now enhanced for providing another opportunity for constructive diplomatic engagements between these two rivals (Stobdan 2016).

10.5   Conclusion

A recent study of the SCO rightly commented that "Analysts have difficulty in determining exactly what the Shanghai Cooperation Organization (SCO) is, what it does, and how it functions" (Blank 2013: 39). The entry of India and Pakistan as members has vividly illustrated how opaque the requirements for membership actually are, and what is actually agreed at the time of acceptance. The (largely US-based) talk of a 'NATO of the East' that was common in the mid-2000s has now dimmed, and instead a stream of (largely Eurasian-based) studies are pointing to the SCO moving into a new phase of maturity as a regional organization showing traits both of effective governance and inter-regional recognition. Despite the lack of clarity, an analysis of the last 20 years does indicate three significant phases in the SCO's development: The 1990s brought its formation as a necessary initiative to secure borders and reduce tensions across the post-Soviet space; the 2000s saw Moscow attempt to direct the SCO as a tool to oppose US hegemony; the 2010s – and particularly the arrival of Xi in 2013 – have witnessed the emergence of China as the dominant force, turning the SCO in the direction of its own long-term development agenda and challenging the assumptions and norms of the Western-led global order. Russia's international posturing is an effort to hide the fact that it is second-best even in its own Central Asian backyard. As one Russian commentator has put it,

attempts to compete with China within the SCO are also doomed to failure, since for China the SCO is a matter of foreign strategy and for Russia it is a matter of prestige. Therefore, Moscow either has to agree to the position of second player (as it does now), or to spend much of its resources on real rivalry. (Teploukhova 2010: 83)

In this situation, it serves Putin's interests to massage the message and give the impression of a new great power alliance emerging from the Eurasian heartland. But the EAEU-Silk Road 'merger' of 2015–2016 cannot fully hide the ongoing tensions between the two powers (Wilson 2016). It is not surprising that the SCO has been put forward as another example in the many case studies on regionalism and inter-regional dynamics in recent years, as the developments across Eurasia do ask for serious interpretation and analysis (Gatev and Diesen 2016). In terms of what it has achieved, it remains in the category of 'regional cooperation', as opposed to 'har-monization' or 'integration' (see Chap. 8 by Joren Selleslaghs and Luk van Langenhove, 'The Rise of Regions'). Yet the Organisation should not be narrowly interpreted according to the normative models used in Western-based IR. The SCO's principal achievement may be the construction of a discursive screen of great power cooperation, behind which Moscow and Beijing can find a modus operandi for their ongoing Great Game in Central Asia. Criticisms of unfulfilled ambition, lack of transparency or failure to achieve much institutional integration beyond military exercises therefore apply the wrong rubrics for evaluation. The existence of mutual trust, a fundamental requirement in Western-based understandings of regional coop-eration, is a factor largely absent in the case of the SCO. In this context of fractious or absent levels of trust, the real question is how Russia's declining power relative to China's rise will continue to be successfully masked by the Organization's out-ward presentation of brotherhood and unity.

Further Readings

Börzel, T., & Risse, T. (2016). *The Oxford handbook of comparative regionalism*. Oxford: Oxford University Press.
Fredholm, M. (Ed.). (2013). *The Shanghai cooperation organization and Eurasian politics: New directions, perspectives, and challenges*. Copenhagen: Nordic Institute of Asian Studies.

References

Anand, V. (2012). *SCO summit and Afghanistan: Looking for regional solution*. Vivekanada International Foundation.

Baert, F., Scaramagli, T., & Söderbaum, F. (Eds.). (2014). *Intersecting interregionalisms: Regions, global governance and the EU*. Dordrecht: Springer.

Bailes, A. (2007). The Shanghai Cooperation Organization and Europe. *The China and Eurasia Forum Quarterly, 5*, 13–18.

Bailes, A., & Dunay, P. (2007). The Shanghai Cooperation Organisation as a regional security institution. In A. Bailes, P. Dunay, P. Guang, & M. Troitskiy (Ed.), *The Shanghai cooperation organization* (SIPRI Policy Paper 17).

Blank, S. (2013). Making sense of the Shanghai Cooperation Organization. *Georgetown Journal of International Affairs, 39*. Available online: http://journal.georgetown.edu/the-shanghai-cooperation-organization-by-stephen-blank/. Accessed 15 June 2017.

Chin, G. (2015). Asia infrastructure investment Bank: Governance innovation and prospects. *Global Governance, 22*, 11–15.

Chulkovskaya, Y. (2017). Will Turkey leave NATO? *Al-Monitor*. Available online: http://www.al-monitor.com/pulse/originals/2017/01/russia-turkey-erdogan-putin-membership-shanghai-sco-eu.html#ixzz4VpaDHNL5. Accessed 30 Jan 2017.

CSS Analyses in Security Policy. (2009). *Shanghai Cooperation Organisation: An anti-western alignment?* 66. Available online: http://www.css.ethz.ch/content/dam/ethz/special-interest/gess/cis/center-for-securities-studies/pdfs/CSS-Analyses-66.pdf. Accessed 1 June 2017.

de Haas, M. (2007). *The Shanghai Cooperation Organization: Towards a full-grown security alliance?* Netherlands Institute of International Affairs.

'Declaration by the Heads of the Member States of the Shanghai Cooperation Organization.' (2005). Available online: http://eng.sectsco.org/documents/. Accessed 1 June 2017.

Donaldson, R. H., Nogee, J., & Nadkarni, V. (2014). *The foreign policy of Russia: Changing systems, enduring interests*. Armonk/London: M.E. Sharpe.

Fei, G. (2010). *The Shanghai Cooperation Organization and China's new diplomacy*. Discussion papers in diplomacy, Netherlands Institute of International Relations Clingendael.

Fidler, D. (2010). Introduction: Eastphalia emerging? Asia, International Law, and Global Governance. *Indiana Journal of Global Legal Studies, 17*, 1–12.

Fredholm, M. (2013). Too many plans for war, too few common values: Another chapter in the history of the great game or the guarantor of central Asian security? In M. Fredholm (Ed.), *The Shanghai cooperation organization and Eurasian politics: New directions, perspectives, and challenges* (pp. 3–19). Copenhagen: Nordic Institute of Asian Studies.

Gatev, I., & Diesen, G. (2016). Eurasian encounters: The Eurasian economic union and the Shanghai cooperation organisation. *European Politics and Society, 17*, 133–150.

Human Rights Watch. (2005). Burying the truth: Uzbekistan rewrites the story of the Andijan massacre. *17*: 66–68.

Hussein, I. (2013). The Shanghai framework and Central Asia: Chop Suey governance? In E. Kirchner & R. Dominguez (Eds.), *The security governance of regional organisations* (pp. 243–272). London: Routledge.

International Legal Materials. (1997). China-Russia: Joint declaration on a multipolar world and the establishment of a new international order. *36*, 986–989.

Jetschke, A. (2009). Institutionalizing ASEAN: Celebrating Europe through network governance. *Cambridge Review of International Affairs, 22*, 407–426.

Khan, S. (2009). Stabilization of Afghanistan: U.S.-NATO regional strategy and the role of SCO. *China and Eurasia Forum Quarterly, 7*, 11–15.

Kirkham, K. (2016). The formation of the Eurasian economic union: How successful is the Russian regional hegemony? *Journal of Eurasian Studies, 7*, 111–128.

Kuhrt, N. (2014). Russia and Asia-Pacific: From 'Competing' to 'Complementary' regionalisms? *Politics, 34*, 138–148.

Liska, G. (1962). *Nations in alliance: The limits of interdependence*. Baltimore: Johns Hopkins Press.

Madhur, S. (2012). Asia's role in twenty-first century global economic governance. *International Affairs, 88*, 817–833.

Makarychev, A., & Morozov, V. (2011). Multilateralism, multipolarity and beyond: A menu of Russia's policy strategies. *Global Governance, 17*, 353–373.

Movkebaeva, G. (2013). Energy cooperation among Kazakhstan, Russia, and China within the Shanghai Cooperation Organization. *Russian Politics and Law, 51*, 80–87.

NATO 2020: Assured Security, Dynamic Engagement: Analysis and Recommendations of the Group of Experts on a New Strategic Concept for NATO. (2010). Available online: https://www.nato.int/cps/en/natohq/official_texts_63654.htm?selectedLocale=en#members. Accessed 21 Sept 2018.

OSW. (2016). *Russia's Greater Eurasia and China's New Silk Road: Adaptation instead of competition.* Available online: https://www.osw.waw.pl/en/publikacje/osw-commentary/2016-07-21/russias-greater-eurasia-and-chinas-new-silk-road-adaptation. Accessed 1 June 2017.

Prantl, J. (2013). The Shanghai cooperation organization: Legitimacy through (self-) legitimation? In D. Zaum (Ed.), *Legitimating international organizations* (pp. 162–178). Oxford: Oxford University Press.

Qi, H., & Shi, Y. (2013). China's peripheral security challenges and its pan-peripheral diplomatic strategy. *World Economics and Politics, 3*, 25–46.

Savic, B. (2016). Behind Russia and China's 'Special relationship'. *The Diplomat, 7.* Available online: http://thediplomat.com/2016/12/behind-china-and-russias-special-relationship/. Accessed 30 Jan 2017.

'SCO Energy Club.' (2015). Available online: http://infoshos.ru/en/?idn=13913. Accessed 30 Jan 2017.

Sharma, R. K. (2015). SCO's role in Afghanistan: Prospects and challenges. *Mainstream 53.* Available online: http://www.mainstreamweekly.net/article5721.html. Accessed 15 June 2017.

Snyder, G. (2007). *Alliance politics.* Ithaca: Cornell University Press.

Stobdan, P. (2016). *SCO: India enters Eurasia.* Institute for Defence Studies and Analyses. Available online: http://www.idsa.in/policybrief/sco-india-enters-eurasia_pstobdan_140616. Accessed 1 June 2017.

Strange, S. (1999). The Westfailure system. *Review of International Studies, 25*, 345–354.

Teploukhova, M. (2010). Russia and international organizations in the Asia-Pacific: Agenda for the Russian Far East. *Security Index, 16*, 77–87.

Tugsbilguun, T. (2008–2009). Does the Shanghai Cooperation Organisation represent an example of a military alliance? *Mongolian Journal of International Affairs, 15–16*, 59–107.

Walt, S. (1989). *The origins of alliances.* Ithaca: Cornell University Press.

Washington Post. (2017). *Is Trump ready for war in the South China Sea, or is his team just not being clear?* Available online: https://www.washingtonpost.com/news/worldviews/wp/2017/01/24/is-trump-ready-for-war-in-the-south-china-sea-or-is-his-team-just-not-being-clear/?utm_term=.cf9074ad178c. Accessed 1 June 2017.

Wilkins, T. (2012). *'Alignment', not 'Alliance'* – The shifting paradigm of international security cooperation: Toward a conceptual taxonomy of alignment. *Review of International Studies, 38*, 53–76.

Wilson, J. (2016). The Eurasian economic union and China's silk road: Implications for the Russian–Chinese relationship. *European Politics and Society, 17*, 113–132.

Zeb, R. (2006). Pakistan and the Shanghai cooperation framework. *The China and Eurasia Forum Quarterly, 4*, 51–60.

Zhang, F. (2012). China's new thinking on alliances. *Survival, 54*, 129–148.

Zielonka, J. (2008). Europe as a global actor: Empire by example? *International Affairs, 84*, 471–484.

Chapter 11
ASEAN as a Conflict Manager: Lukewarm Mediation

Fathania Queen and Ying-Hsien Sheng

11.1 Introduction

The regional security of ASEAN has already been a main concern since the early stage of its formation. The political milieu of the 1960s very much explains the impetus why states in Southeast Asia decided to form ASEAN. It was a very significant decade for the new states in the region as most of them had just come out of the throes of colonialism (Caballero-Anthony 2005). Since then, the member states of ASEAN have been trying to keep the stability for the sake of regional security. Until the late 1990s, the ASEAN's efforts in maintaining a peaceful relationship with its members and with states beyond Southeast Asia has made ASEAN an important actor in the bigger international arena of the Asia-Pacific (Caballero-Anthony 2005). ASEAN had no institutional or formal means of dispute settlement until the adoption of the Treaty of Amity and Cooperation (TAC) in 1976. The TAC offers specific guidelines in the field of conflict management particularly in connection with the peaceful settlement of disputes (Ramses Amer 2015). Thus, mediation is not something new for ASEAN in terms of conflict management. In that official document, the option of mediation has already been stated as part of ASEAN conflict management framework. It had at least laid down the principle that disputes between and among ASEAN states were to be settled bilaterally and/or preferably within the region to the extent possible and without outside interference (Caballero-Anthony 2005). It can be seen from here that the member states would prefer to lean more on ASEAN as the closest formal entity in the region to help find the way out.

F. Queen
Leiden University, Leiden, The Netherlands
e-mail: fathania_queen@yahoo.co.id

Y.-H. Sheng (✉)
Hakka Affairs Council, Taichung City, Taiwan
e-mail: insengirl@gmail.com

© Springer Nature Switzerland AG 2020
M. O. Hosli, J. Selleslaghs (eds.), *The Changing Global Order*, United Nations
University Series on Regionalism 17,
https://doi.org/10.1007/978-3-030-21603-0_11

Generally, international mediation activities include managing international conflicts on interstate (between countries) and intrastate (between governments and groups challenging their power) levels (Vuković 2014). As our world has grown more globalized, so has our "complex interdependence." Due to this interdependence, states are more likely to reduce the number of interstate conflicts (Kirsten Elliott 2012). That helps explain why the number of interstate conflicts has dropped while intrastate conflicts has risen pretty dramatically. 'Not only in my village, but in other places, there is no family who has not lost a relative. This is the reality,' he said. This disastrous comment came from Samsul who has witnessed conflict in Aceh since his birth in 1979. In 2003, when this interview was conducted, he explained that he was unable to go back to the village where he was raised owing to the violent conflict that was still raging at that time (Development 2003). This commentary is from just one of the people who have experienced one of the many intrastate conflicts that have been going on in Southeast Asia. Of these global intrastate conflicts, geographically, Asia has the highest in number throughout the years.

Based on the Uppsala Conflict Data Program (UCDP) database, almost half of the Asian intrastate conflicts took place in Southeast Asia, which comprises only 10 countries. Of the 44 countries that make up the continent of Asia, Southeast Asian countries do not account for even half of them (Countries Listed By Continent 2016). Southeast Asian intrastate conflicts account for 48% of the total number of conflicts in Asia. When we know these facts, it is expected to wonder how these conflicts were resolved. As a primary conflict manager in the region, therefore, ASEAN undoubtedly should take responsibility both in theory and practice.

The article by laid out the argument that even if bilateral talks were more common in terms of conflict management in Southeast Asia, mediation has been the most effective method of bringing the parties towards a mutually acceptable agreement and thus resolving the conflict (DeRouen and Bercovitch 2011). In line with its popularity in practice, mediation has also been considered the most efficient method of managing conflicts through peaceful means in the academic literature (Vuković 2015a, b, c).

One way to look at the threat posed by internal conflict in the region is to consider the potential for increased involvement by regional organisations. As what has been explained in the Chap. 8 in this volume; the number of the regional organization started to arise since the post-World War II era and their roles in global order have become more recognizable. The major organisation in the region capable of assuming such a role is the ASEAN (Moller et al. 2007). Nevertheless, ASEAN, despite being a successful organisation that has somehow managed to achieve regional peace and stability, has rarely got involved as a mediator in solving the conflicts (Kamarulzaman et al. 2002). Of all the mediation processes that were conducted in Southeast Asia between 1976 and 2014, ASEAN as an institution was involved fewer than five times.

For most regional organisations, choosing and determining which mechanisms are feasible and relevant is dependent on their respective institutional capacity. Regional organisations eventually develop their own mechanisms for conflict management that are deemed appropriate to their own setting (Caballero-Anthony

1998). ASEAN had no institutional or formal means of dispute settlement until the adoption of the TAC in 1976. The option of mediation is stated as part of ASEAN's conflict management framework under article 14–16 of TAC (Treaty of Amity and Cooperation in Southeast Asia Indonesia 1976).

ASEAN is a growing regional organisation aimed at establishing an economically viable but also 'politically secure community'. This goal is defined as creating a 'cohesive, peaceful and resilient region with shared responsibility for comprehensive security' (Ropers 2012). From here, the question remains one of how ASEAN has responded as a formal institution to conflicts in its region, most of which have been protracted. As mentioned above, the mediation option is stated within the ASEAN framework. However, a gap still exists in the extent to which ASEAN has been proactive as a conflict manager in the region, leading to the main question of this chapter: What are the factors that explain the dynamic of ASEAN's involvement as a mediator in intrastate conflicts?

In continuing this research, the next part will explain the previous studies on regional and international organisations as mediators before talking about ASEAN as a conflict manager in the region. Then, the fifth chapter will provide an analysis of the three chosen cases: the Cambodia conflict (1991–1997), the Aceh conflict (1976–2005), and the East-Timor conflict (1976–1999). The conclusion chapter will wrap up the whole discussion along with recommendations relative to the topic.

11.2 International and Regional Organisations as Mediators

Mediation is defined by Bercovitch et al. as a process of conflict management where disputants seek the assistance of, or accept an offer of help from, an individual, group, state, or organisation to settle their conflict or resolve their differences without resorting to physical force or invoking the authority of the law (Wilkenfeld et al. 2005). Moving on from here, the concept of international mediation in general refers to mediation activities conducted by various international actors with the aim of managing international conflicts on interstate and intrastate levels (Vuković 2014). These two understandings are needed since the main concern of this chapter is the implementation of international mediation concept in the realm of intrastate conflicts.

In the contemporary world, international organisations have become very active participants in the search for mechanisms and procedures conducive to peacemaking and conflict resolution. The end of the Cold War freed them from the pre-existing bipolar constraints and allowed them to refine their conflict management role, specifically in the context of mediation (Vukovic 2013). Moreover, the work of Frazier and Dixon on analysing the effectiveness of different types of conflict managers, laid out the evidence that among all types of actor (states, coalitions and international organisations), international organisations appear to perform better than the others (Vukovic 2013).

Regional organisations such as the European Union (EU), the Organization of American States (OAS), the African Union (AU), ASEAN and the Arab League, all adhere to the principles of negotiation and mediation as their preferred means of resolving conflicts (Jackson and Bercovitch 2009). As stated earlier, ASEAN has the TAC mediation option as its first official conflict mechanism, which generates the expectation that mediation can be actively implemented as part of its role as a conflict manager. From the broader perspective, this mediation development phenomenon somehow illustrates well the concept of a two-tier conflict resolution system – a global regional peacemaking system – which then encourages regional organisations or groupings of states to assume primary responsibility for conflict management activities within their geographical area (Jackson and Bercovitch 2009).

11.2.1 Expectations of Regional Organisations

In international mediation, there is no universal default for its implementation. One important note about regional organisations is that each has its background, context of culture and experience that shape its overall strength as a conflict manager (Zartman 2002). The OAU, for instance, was created in order to enhance the maintenance of non-violent relations within the African region and thereby protect each state from the others. In pursuing this condition, the OAU requires that member states adhere to the principle of 'peaceful settlement of disputes by negotiation, mediation, conciliation, or arbitration' (Zartman 2002). Owing to these commonalities, regional organisations are well placed as suitable actors to be mediators. They are expected to affect the responsiveness and cohesiveness of organisations in moments of crisis. Geographically, they are well positioned to understand such conflicts owing to their knowledge of the region (Fretter and Bercovitch 2004). Another factor that causes regional organisations to be regarded as relatively more effective mediators is that neighbouring states have more to lose from an ongoing war than other states. From here it is possible to expect mentally regional organisations to react faster and be more willing to mediate than other states so that the effects of conflict will not spill over on to other member states (Gartner 2011).

11.2.2 Limitations of Regional Organisations

Carrying this expectation as conflict managers, regional organisations do face certain limitations. A previous study about the UN as a mediator by Bercovitch, Fretter, et al. argued that, despite the benefits a regional composition and common history can afford, regional organisations operate under many of the same organisational constraints and resource limitations as the United Nations (UN) (Fretter and Bercovitch 2004). In the same article, they explained that the effectiveness of the UN depends on the political will and resources of its member states. They stressed:

"Some of the UN leverage derives from its institutional standing and the kind of norms it exemplifies, but beyond that UN mediation is hampered considerably by lack of resources" (Fretter and Bercovitch 2004). Further, the United Nations does not have the independent means to impose the will of international community upon the parties to a conflict (Akashi 1995). On top of that, some regional organisations have undertaken classic peacekeeping involving the use of force without legal authorization. On certain occasions, they are even tools of powerful states to pursue their own national interest. The much more powerful states may invade the weaker ones to advance their interests. As a result, the interests of the small, weaker states are largely ignored in the current anarchic international system (Siyabonga Hadebe 2011).

11.2.3 ASEAN as a Conflict Manager

The reactions and activities of ASEAN in the context of conflict management have been analysed by several scholars. Previous academic research laid out some important themes about how ASEAN has responded to conflicts in the region. Michael Leifer, a prominent Southeast Asian scholar, once argued that security, and hence peace, has been addressed by ASEAN primarily through developing a culture of intra-mural dialogue and consultation based on close working relationships between ministers and officials and an adherence to common norms; not through invoking formal legal mechanisms for dispute settlement (Leifer 1999). On the other hand, looking through the official framework of ASEAN, this organisation has already adopted the Treaty of Amity and Cooperation (TAC), which was the first dispute settlement mechanism available (Phan 2013). In understanding TAC, Askandar et al. stated that ASEAN's ability to combine the TAC principles with the more tacit and passive approach of avoiding conflict, dampening it, or postponing dealing with it for an indefinite period, has made ASEAN different from other regional organisations (Kamarulzaman et al. 2002). Under TAC, the option of mediation is clearly explained in articles 14–16.[1]

---

[1] Article 14: To settle disputes through regional processes, the High Contracting Parties shall constitute, as a continuing body, a High Council comprising a Representative at ministerial level from each of the High Contracting Parties to take cognizance of the existence of disputes or situations likely to disturb regional peace and harmony. Article 15: In the event no solution is reached through direct negotiations, the High Council shall take cognizance of the dispute or the situation and shall recommend to the parties in dispute appropriate means of settlement such as good offices, mediation, inquiry or conciliation. The High Council may however offer its good offices, or upon agreement of the parties in dispute, constitute itself into a committee of mediation, inquiry or conciliation. When deemed necessary, the High Council shall recommend appropriate measures for the prevention of a deterioration of the dispute or the situation. Article 16: The foregoing provision of this Chapter shall not apply to a dispute unless all the parties to the dispute agree to their application to that dispute. However, this shall not preclude the other High Contracting Parties not party to the dispute from offering all possible assistance to settle the said dispute. Parties to the dispute should be well disposed towards such offers of assistance.

Moreover, although that treaty with its strong registration of the sanctity of national sovereignty has been extolled as a model code of conduct for regional relations, its provision for dispute settlement, involving the establishment of a High Council, has never once been invoked but has remained totally dormant (Leifer 1999). Michael Leifer argued that the strong reluctance to invoke that provision of formal intra-mural dispute settlement could well be highly contentious and divisive and therefore self-defeating in terms of the limited security purpose of the association, which is, above all, about conflict avoidance and management (Leifer 1999).

One ASEAN practitioner argued that the secret of its success is its 'system of consultations' identified as 'the ASEAN Way' in dealing with regional problems (Leifer 1999). Relating to this thought, Askandar et al. explained that ASEAN principles dictate restraint, thus ASEAN does not resort to coercive means to address conflict (Kamarulzaman et al. 2002). Self-restraint is also a product of positive relationships nourished among the member states through the exercise of ASEAN values such as consultation and consensus. Since the assurance of no security threats among them, each state is supposed to concentrate within its own intrastate conflict on having 'preventing the conflict from internationalising' as the goal. However, it has been argued that the conventional strategy no longer works well. ASEAN now faces intrastate conflicts that can be internationalised more easily than before through human rights, spill-over and environmental channels (Kamarulzaman et al. 2002).

Despite ASEAN having been concerned with security and peace since its formation, it has never been effectively responsible for regional peacemaking as opposed to helping to keep the peace through exercising a benign influence on the overall climate of regional relations (Leifer 1999). Kay Moller stated that ASEAN tends to enhance sovereignty as a regional strategist confirmed: 'Divisive issues are simply passed over for later resolution – or until they have been made either irrelevant by time and events' (Moller et al. 2007). Kathrin Rupprecht in her article about conflict management in Southern Thailand and Mindanao explained that there have been no official statements by ASEAN on the conflicts at hand or their progression. Neither country called upon ASEAN's capacity as a mediator at that time, either. Then she argued that even though it has not played a proactive role in managing the separatist insurgencies in Southern Thailand or Mindanao so far, it still provides an intergovernmental platform that has, at least in theory, the capacity to influence the two conflicts (Rupprecht 2014).

With regard to the underlying norm of ASEAN conflict management, the ASEAN Way became another important theme discussed among scholars. There are various interpretations of the ASEAN Way. Amitav Acharya, understood the ASEAN Way as a process of identity building that relies upon the conventional modern-specific modes of socialisation and decision making that are prevalent in Southeast Asia. Logan Masilamani and Jimmy Peterson stated that the ASEAN Way helped to bring about flexibility and a multi-dimensional approach to conflict resolution over political issues. Besides, they mentioned further that there has been a movement away from the ASEAN Way to "flexible-consensus building" over time (Logan Masilamani and Jimmy Peterson 2014). Another interpretation was from Haacke, who summed up the ASEAN Way as a normative framework the role of which in mediating disputes, is to guide interaction and underpin a process of identity construction (Caballero-Anthony 1998). In general, previous studies perceived the ASEAN Way as the region's first and foremost principle, with perhaps the greatest influence over security and conflict management, towards protection of sovereignty (Nishikawa 2007).

Beverly Loke argued that TAC is a validation and reflection of the ASEAN Way, which is, again, shorthand for a regional norm that can be characterised by a focus on consultation and consensus (Phan 2013). In relation to this, Hao Duy Phan argued that the consensus rule should not be applied too rigidly. Consensus may work in other areas of cooperation or may have worked in the past, but it may just as likely now become an obstacle in the way of employing and monitoring dispute settlement mechanisms (Phan 2013). ASEAN is also identified as taking an alternative form in such a way that it acts as an umbrella body for individual (bilateral, trilateral or quadripartite) attempts among member states to manage disputes, rather than acting as a firm collective body that undertakes and imposes collective action (Nishikawa 2007). ASEAN has never developed a collective approach owing to its general underlying principle of non-interference (Kamarulzaman et al. 2002). On the contrary, in terms of responding to new challenges in conflict management, some practitioners such as the Malaysian Deputy Minister Anwar Ibrahim have, proposed that ASEAN adopts a more flexible implementation of its non-interference principle. However, such an idea has yet to gain much support from member states in general (Kamarulzaman et al. 2002) (Table 11.1).

Table 11.1 The ASEAN WAY and its interpretations

The ASEAN WAY	
General understandings	A system of consultations.
	Dealing with its regional problems.
	The greatest influence over security and conflict management, towards protection of sovereignty.
Various interpretations	A set of rules and norms designed to influence state action and improve interstate relations.
	A process of identity building.
	Bring about flexibility and a multi-dimensional approach to conflict resolution over political issues.
	Mediating disputes, guiding interaction and underpinning a process of identity construction.
Common features	Mentally: identity building and construction.
	Practically: regional problem-solving management.

Source: Data collected and compacted by the authors

11.3   Three Cases: Analysed

The main theoretical framework that will be used in this chapter is the contingency model.[2] This was chosen because it illustrates the evolution of mediation decision making and conflict management behavior (Houston and Bercovitch 2000). There are three stages identified under this model: antecedent, current and consequent stages. This chapter focuses only on the first stage since the key concern here is to find out the factors behind the existence of mediation in ASEAN.

The antecedent stage is composed of three major contextual dimensions: pre-existing (conditions of a conflict that come before any intervention), concurrent (various attributes a mediator may possess), and background mediation contextual conditions (factors resulting from previous experiences with mediation). In this chapter, the pre-existing and concurrent dimensions are used as the framework for further analysis in finding the key factors of ASEAN's mediation dynamic. The variables under the pre-existing dimension that are used for this analysis are state sovereignty and non-interference as common principles, conflict intensity, presence of a valid spokesman and impartiality. From the concurrent dimensions, the indicator is the leverage from mediator.

The third dimension is considered owing to the fact that there is a lack of mediation experience on the part of ASEAN to which this chapter can refer. The adoption of TAC in 1976 is the touchstone of the analysis owing to the fact that it was the first ever official written mechanism for ASEAN's conflict management. Within this part, the chapter tries to describe the findings of the three chosen cases: the Cambodia conflict, the Aceh conflict and the East Timor conflict (Fig. 11.1).

This paper will use three cases to support the analysis: the Cambodia conflict, the Aceh conflict and the East Timor. These conflicts were chosen as they diverge on the dependent variable, which in this research refers to the dynamic of ASEAN mediation (active mediation, passive mediation and non-mediation). In the Cambodia conflict, ASEAN became an active mediator. For the Aceh conflict, ASEAN was a passive mediator, merely involved in a mediation effort led by other actors. In the East Timor conflict ASEAN showed no response in the capacity of mediator. These three cases took place between 1976 and 2014. The year 1976 was chosen as the touchstone because TAC was created in that year. From all the intrastate conflicts that happened during that timeframe, this paper narrows its focus to the ones that experienced mediation efforts in general. These three cases were derived from this specific category – ones where mediation took place – in order to be further analysed through the five hypotheses laid out in the previous section. The cases of Cambodia and Aceh were chosen because the UCDP data showed these to be two of the three cases for which ASEAN got involved in the mediation process. East Timor was selected because it was under the high intensity category and started in 1976.

---

[2]The contingency approach has its roots in the social-psychological theories of negotiation as developed by Sawyer and Guetzkow and modified by Druckman. This paper refers to the contingency models by Bercovitch and Houston (2000) which is the modification and combination of contingency model by Bercovitch and Gochman for the purpose of depicting the evolution of mediation decision making and conflict management behavior.

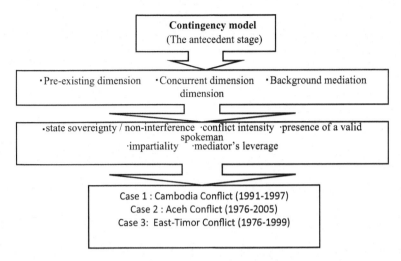

Fig. 11.1 Main theoretical framework and three conflict cases. (Source: Data collected and compacted by the authors)

11.4   Cambodia Conflict (1991–1997)

11.4.1   Use of the Non-interference Principle Argument

As the situation worsened, Deputy Prime Minister of Malaysia Anwar Ibrahim acknowledged that ASEAN's non-involvement in the reconstruction of Cambodia had contributed to the deterioration and final collapse of national reconciliation (Peou 1998). This signified the intention to challenge the principle of non-interference that all member states had been upholding. It was the first time that the idea of a 'more constructive intervention' in Cambodia's affairs was openly advocated (Peou 1998). ASEAN decided to use its mediation framework to help pacify the instability in the country, which had just reached the end of the intense war with Vietnam. This consensus did not formulate that easily. In the first meeting after the overthrow of Prince Ranariddh, ASEAN's foreign ministers jointly committed to the principle of non-interference in internal affairs but opposed Hun Sen's use of force. It was at the next meeting of the ASEAN Regional Forum (ARF) and its dialogue partners – the US, Japan, Russia, China and the European Union – that they concluded that ASEAN's involvement was crucially needed in this situation.

ASEAN constructed its mediation effort by appointing three foreign ministers – Ali Alatas (Indonesia), Domingo Siazon (Philippines) and Prachuab Chayasan (Thailand) – as mediators (Peou 1998). ASEAN insisted that the act of sending delegations did not constitute a violation of non-interference. Indonesia's Foreign Minister Ali Alatas articulated: 'We don't want to interfere but we have the right and the duty, as ASEAN foreign ministers, to discuss what are the implications of this (Acharya 2009). It was not the first time that the Association had tried to intervene in a member state's problem. Within the same year, Malaysia's Foreign Minister

Abdullah Badawi, as Chair of ASEAN's Standing Committee, visited Yangon to persuade the military junta to hold talks with opposition leader Aung San Suu Kyi (*ASEAN and the Question of Cambodia* 2007).

11.4.2   Conflict Intensity

Since the conflict first erupted among the two prime ministerial factions after the election conducted by United Nations Transitional Authority in Cambodia (UNTAC), more clashes occurred. One of the most shocking events was a grenade attack in March 1993 that killed civilians, including foreigners. The ASEAN members remained acutely aware of the threat Cambodia's internal problems posed to their security. When the conflict between Hun Sen and Ranarridh escalated in early 1997, several ASEAN leaders – Indonesia's President Soeharto and Thailand's Prime Minister Chaovalit Yongchaiyudh – travelled to Cambodia to urge restraint and reconciliation between the two sides. On 8 July 1997, after the coup, Indonesia suggested convening a special ASEAN Foreign Ministers Meeting to discuss the crisis. The meeting produced the following agreement: while reaffirming commitment to the principle of non-interference in the internal affairs of other states, the ASEAN foreign ministers decided that, in the light of the unfortunate circumstances that had resulted from the use of force, the wisest course of action would be to delay the admission of Cambodia into ASEAN until a later date (Acharya 2009). The struggle in Cambodia at that time was more than a military attack; it had escalated to extreme violence. As Brad Adams[3] reported: "I and many of my colleagues at the UN human rights office had the unforgettable experience of digging up the bodies of men stripped naked to their underwear, handcuffed behind their backs, blindfolded, and shot in the head (Adams 2007). In 1996, when the fighting between the two factions became even more intense, it reached Cambodia's western provinces bordering with Thailand (Peou 1998).

11.4.3   Presence of a Valid Spokesman

ASEAN's member states were quite active in reacting to the situation in Cambodia. Indonesia called an emergency AMM (Aceh Monitoring Mission) with a view towards intervention: 'The ASEAN countries stand ready to contribute their efforts to the peaceful resolution of the situation in Cambodia (Jones 2010). Most other member states made similar comments about what was happening in Cambodia. Surin Pitsuwan, then Vice Foreign Minister of Thailand, explained: "ASEAN had invested quite a bit of energy, resources and emotion into helping Cambodia return to national reconciliation. We thought that was a successful story that we could

---

[3] Briad Adams was Asia Director of Human Rights Watch at that time.

quote." Ali Alatas, who led ASEAN's Troika mission, also expressed a view on Cambodia: "I felt the least danger of interference. Indonesia felt that. It was entitled to pick up the broken pieces and try to get it (back together) (Jones 2010). Even though the initiation came more from the supply side – ASEAN as an institution in this case – and less from the demand side – the Hun Sen side – it was good enough for ASEAN mediation to take place.

11.4.4   Impartiality

On 19 July 1997, ASEAN's Troika team arrived in Phnom Penh to talk with Hun Sen for the first time. The second meeting took place in August. The intention of the mediation was to end the power struggle between Prince Norodom Ranariddh and Hun Sen (Rieffel 2010). It was somewhat difficult at first for Hun Sen to accept mediation from ASEAN. When ASEAN decided to postpone Cambodia's membership, he threatened to withdraw Cambodia's application: "I am afraid of joining ASEAN because of ASEAN interference in internal affairs (Acharya 2009). However, in the end, Hun Sen accepted ASEAN as a mediator on condition that it refrained from interfering in Cambodia's internal affairs and respected its role of strict neutrality (Peou 1998). Even so, at the beginning of mediation, Hun Sen still showed reluctance towards ASEAN delegates, as Ali Alatas expressed: "Hun Sen was livid with rage. He gave a half-hour criticism of me when I first met him. He said, 'This is foreign interference! This is against ASEAN's own principles! What are you doing here? You have nothing to do with what is happening to Cambodia! I don't want to become a member of ASEAN, not with that kind of organization (Jones 2011). Aside from threatening to withdraw the application, he claimed that China would continue providing aid with its non-interventionist stance (Jones 2011).

   Another fact that should be noted was that alongside ASEAN offering its assistance as a mediator, Ung Huat, Cambodia's foreign minister at that time, also invited ASEAN's presence. The mutual understanding and consent existed for ASEAN to play its role as a mediator (Rieffel 2010). Moreover, King Norodom Sihanouk gave his blessing to the ASEAN Troika mission during an audience in Phnom Penh on 17 July 1997 (Rieffel 2010). Hun Sen's threat to withdraw Cambodia's application to join ASEAN did not continue, as, in the end, he agreed with his foreign minister that joining ASEAN should continue to be a high priority foreign policy objective for Cambodia (Rieffel 2010). As the mediation process proceeded, at the second meeting Hun Sen kept criticising ASEAN for interfering in Cambodia's internal affairs. The mediation process did not continue as Hun Sen rejected the group's peace plan. The ASEAN proposal called for an end to the fighting, for a caretaker government to be installed to prepare for new elections and for Hun Sen to share power until the elections took place. Ali Alatas said both the ousted co-prime minister, Prince Norodom Ranariddh, and Cambodia's monarch, King Norodom Sihanouk, were in favour of the ASEAN plan. It finally stopped there as Ali Alatas explained: "ASEAN will only assist in trying to contribute if all sides want that. This is why, as of this moment, our efforts stop and we will return and report to the ASEAN foreign ministers" (ASEAN halts Cambodia mediation 1997).

11.4.5   Mediator's Leverage

During the conflict, Cambodia did not become a member of ASEAN. For ASEAN, the coup interrupted the timetable for enlarging the association to include all 10 regional states – Brunei, Cambodia, Indonesia, Laos, Malaysia, Myanmar, the Philippines, Singapore, Thailand and Vietnam (*ASEAN and the Question of Cambodia* 2007). Cambodia was granted 'observer status' in 1994 and ASEAN countries followed this up by providing technical assistance to facilitate the transition to full membership. However, it was suspended owing to the worsening of the political situation in Cambodia (Peou 1998). Being aware of this condition, at an emergency meeting of ASEAN Foreign Ministers in July 1997, a decision to postpone Cambodia's membership was taken but without challenging Phnom Penh's existing observer status (*ASEAN and the Question of Cambodia* 2007). This membership postponing became the trigger for Hun Sen to accept mediation, although at first he threatened ASEAN by saying that he would withdraw his membership application. Even though Hun Sen rejected the peace plan offered by ASEAN, ASEAN did not change its mind about not letting Cambodia become a member until it achieved political stability. It also supported a UN decision to leave Cambodia's seat vacant until such a time (Peou 1998). Threatened by international economic sanctions and denial of ASEAN membership, Hun Sen was forced to accept new elections in 1998 (Weatherbee 2005).

ASEAN and its member states created their engagement in building the new government of Cambodia. Besides postponing Cambodia's membership as a button push for Hun Sen to accept mediation, ASEAN warned long before about investments developed there. Widyono explained that Malaysia made major investments into areas like logging, tourism, entertainment and services. Mahathir even put personal effort into persuading top Malaysian companies to invest. Singaporean interests also rushed to invest in tourism. By 1996, 59% of all foreign investment in Cambodia came from ASEAN. In total, ASEAN businesses had invested over $2 billion in Cambodia by 1997 (Jones 2011). When the conflict started to emerge, in May 1996, ASEAN appointed Malaysia's foreign minister to counsel 'against any escalation of violence' between the factions, warning that open hostilities would force ASEAN to leave Cambodia alone. Other member states such as Singapore, Indonesia and the Philippines expressed similar concerns about what was happening in Cambodia at that time. In February 1997, Suharto along with other Indonesian delegations visited Cambodia to restate their demands for stability and the Philippines publicly articulated fears about Cambodia's readiness for ASEAN membership following a grenade attack on a Sam Rainsy Party rally in March 1997 (Jones 2011).

Other actors outside Southeast Asia started to get involved in the Cambodia conflict. The US suspended aid to Cambodia, which became a serious threat for Cambodia since it represented 70% of the state budget. Then US Secretary of State Madeleine Albright emphasised that foreign aid was now conditional upon ASEAN's intervention, stating that 'cooperation with ASEAN mediation is essential if Cambodia is to fully rejoin the international community' (Jones 2011).

11.5 Aceh Conflict (1976–2005)

11.5.1 Use of the Non-interference Principle Argument

Up until the fall of the Soeharto regime, the Indonesian government reacted to the situation using its military. When *Gerakan Aceh Merdeka* (GAM)/Free Aceh Movement launched guerrilla operations in 1989, President Soeharto imposed *Daerah Operasi Militer* (DOM)/Military Operation Area, which increased the death toll from previous years. During this time, the media was also restricted, which meant that people outside the region were less aware about the ongoing conflict (Large and Aguswandi 2008). ASEAN did not make any significant move in terms of helping to puzzle out the conflict.

After the fall of the Soeharto regime, President Habibie started democratic reforms, ended restrictions on free media and lifted Aceh's designation as a Military Operation Area. *Tentara Nasional Indonesia* (TNI)/Indonesian National Army chief General Wiranto issued a public apology on 7 August 1998 following the exposure of human rights violations in Aceh (Large and Aguswandi 2008). These changes brought a new approach in responding to the Aceh conflict. Mediation by an external actor took place when Abdurrahman Wahid became president, replacing Habibie. In 1999 President Wahid approached the Henri Dunant Centre with a view to offering its good offices in negotiating a peace deal in Aceh (Daly and Higgins 2010). When the approach from the Indonesian government became more open than before in considering the involvement of external actors, ASEAN was not really visibly involved to begin with. ASEAN member states did not discuss the Aceh conflict in the Ministerial Meeting deeply enough to consider the mediation option. ASEAN saw the Aceh conflict as an internal problem that Indonesia needed to resolve. What it was concerned about was the sovereignty, territorial integrity and national unity of Indonesia. In 1999, when the option of Acehnese independence was emerging, Senior Minister Lee Kuan Yew stated: "No country in Southeast Asia will recognise it and nobody wants and nobody sees any benefit in the breaking up of Indonesia." Foreign Minister Syed Hamid Albar stated in 1999: "Malaysia wanted to see Indonesia return to normal, its economy revived and Indonesia's integrity as a nation defended at all times." He also urged Indonesia to restore peace saying that violence could undermine stability in Southeast Asia. Moreover, during the Ministerial Meeting in Phnom Penh in 2003, they pledged 'to deny the separatist movement access to means of violence through, among all, preventing arms smuggling into Aceh province' (Tan 2003).

11.5.2   Conflict Intensity

The conflict escalated significantly in the period following the return of the trained GAM guerrillas in mid-1989 from Libya to Aceh. It enormously strengthened the capability of the movement (Oishi and Baikoeni 2015). In 1999, during Habibie's presidency, the conflict intensified after Regional Autonomy Law was introduced in Aceh. Well-publicised massacres of civilians by security forces in north and central Aceh took place in May and July. Year by year after that, the conflict caused an increasing death toll in Aceh. In 2002, the Cessation of Hostilities Agreement (CoHA) was signed. However, it did not last long. The Indonesian government responded by declaring a state of emergency and launching a massive military campaign that severely weakened GAM (Pan 2005). Based on the UCDP (Uppsala Conflict Data Program) database, the intensity dramatically increased from 2002 to 2004 with the number of deaths rising from 466 to 907 (UCDP – Government of Indonesia – GAM n.d.). As the fighting became more intense, GAM's capacity was weakened both militarily and economically. In May 2003 the Indonesian army launched an operation aimed at ending the conflict by dismantling GAM. It had a significant effect on the rebel group as the number of casualties within the organisation grew, morale declined and public support dropped (Schiff 2014).

11.5.3   Presence of a Valid Spokesman

Indonesia was perceived a heavyweight in the region, with no state willing to make an issue with it (Oishi and Baikoeni 2015). Since the early stages, ASEAN and its member states had restrained their intention to intervene owing to the non-interference principle they held. The fact that Indonesia had been a leading peace-maker who several times had initiated talks about ongoing conflicts in the region made it more difficult to see other states as able to take over the mantle of peacemaker (Oishi and Baikoeni 2015). Aceh was never really brought to the discussion table except – as was explained in the previous section – to restate the importance of Indonesian sovereignty. Some of the member states such as Thailand and the Philippines were watchful towards the situation in Aceh and in 2003 they were prepared to send monitors to Aceh. In general, though, they were not willing to criticise Indonesia in terms of how it was reacting to the conflict (Smith 2003).

There was a light change in terms of understanding the conflict resolution in the region. Before the annual ASEAN Ministerial Meeting was held in Manila in July 1998, reports about Thailand's proposal for a 'constructive intervention' policy emerged. It was renamed 'flexible engagement' a month later. Thailand proposed two main points: discussion within ASEAN member states needed to be more open and frank; and a broad set of domestic issues where 'interference' was justified needed to be set out, especially where they impacted on bilateral, regional and extra-regional relations. Thailand here can be seen as an initiator in bringing about a newer understanding of how to be more involved in managing existing intrastate conflicts. However, it was only the Philippines at that time who supported Thailand. It did not get enough support to further discuss this possible transformation of non-interference (Caballero-Anthony 2005). There was no one to persuade the conflicting parties to have ASEAN as a mediator because – as the next chapter will discuss – GAM did not see ASEAN as an impartial actor suitable to be a mediator even if Indonesia once considered seeking help from ASEAN.

11.5.4 *Impartiality*

As the conflict evolved, President Habibie sought help from the international community in responding to the Aceh conflict. The first choice was ASEAN but GAM rejected that idea based on the assumption that ASEAN would not be impartial, leaning instead towards the government and putting pressure on the organisation's leadership for concessions (Oishi and Baikoeni 2015). GAM then proposed having the UN as a mediator, but this was unacceptable to the Indonesian government as it had just experienced the UN-supervised referendum in East Timor in August 1999 (Oishi and Baikoeni 2015).

11.5.5 *Mediator's Leverage*

During the conflict period, the Indonesian government received unfortunate sanctions, though not from ASEAN. In October 1992 the US imposed sanctions on Indonesia to ban military aid and suspended the International Military Education and Training (IMET) programme. Within Bill Clinton's tenure (1993–2001) the bilateral relations between Indonesia and the US came to their lowest point. In January 1997 Clinton even announced the 'Clinton's List', which detailed Indonesia as one of the countries classified as not yet or non-democratic in Asia (Oishi and Baikoeni 2015). In the last round of mediation effort led by Martti Ahtisaari, he used a directive strategy to move the negotiation forward. At the beginning, he ruled out the independence option from the parameters of the negotiation and imposed the option of 'special autonomy' as proposed by the Indonesian government. During the negotiation, he stated: "Do not waste my time if you just come to my place to curse each other. You come here for a solution, not for condemnation. If you keep talking about the idea of independence, please leave my room and never come back […] I will use all of my muscles to influence Europe and the world not to support you. You will never get independence" (Large and Aguswandi 2008). Towards the end, he offered some conditions that might benefit GAM such as the logistic support of the Finnish government and involvement of the European Union in the proposed Aceh Monitoring Mission (AMM) (Oishi and Baikoeni 2015).

11.6   East-Timor Conflict (1976–1999)

11.6.1   Use of the Non-interference Principle Argument

In responding to the situation in East Timor, it was the UN that took immediate action rather than ASEAN. In January 1976, the UN special envoy to East Timor, Signor Vittorio Winspeare Guicciardi, conducted a round of talks. These were attended by UN Secretary-General Dr. Kurt Waldheim and representatives from Indonesia, Portugal, Australian and FRETILIN. Afterwards Winspeare flew to Jakarta and held talks with President Suharto and then went on to East Timor for discussions with pro-Indonesian groups. He also tried to arrange a visit to FRETILIN bases but it was considered too insecure. However, the talks brought no concrete results. Later, in March, Portugal proposed to arrange talks involving Australia, Indonesia and FRETILIN. These did not happen, since the Indonesian government rejected the idea by arguing that Portugal no longer had any authority to act in the name of the people of East Timor (UCDP- Government of Indonesia – FRETILIN n.d.).

ASEAN member states supported Indonesia's invasion of East Timor materially and diplomatically. Since it started during the Cold War period, ASEAN was still holding on to the anti-communist perspective, perceiving the struggle in East Timor as a 'communist' threat. When Indonesia invaded and faced international condemnation, other ASEAN countries rallied behind Indonesia by arguing that Indonesia had to do it for national security reasons (Kamarulzaman et al. 2002). A journalist in East Timor wrote a note before his death describing how "visions of Chinese sampans, Hanoi dhows and Russian cruisers riding at anchor in Dili harbor were sufficient for ASEAN states, countering communist insurgencies to see the threat as real and applaud its removal". This note illustrated the common fear about the possible emergence of a radical state in the midst of the Indonesian archipelago, which encouraged them to keep backing Indonesia (Carey 1996).

When East Timor received more attention from the international community in the wake of the Santa Cruz massacre, the UN was continually hosting talks between the Indonesian and Portuguese governments. In 1995, the UN hosted negotiations on the East Timor issue between the Indonesian and Portuguese foreign ministers. These negotiations, led by the UN secretary general, resulted in an agreement between the two foreign ministers to have further meetings with all Timorese groups—from pro-independence to pro-Indonesia—in the coming months. In the next 3 years, the UN actively hosted talks between the Indonesian and Portuguese governments on behalf of East Timor, which finally led to the option of referendum in 1999 (Jamal 2001).

As for ASEAN, there was still no official public comment regarding how Indonesia was handling the East Timor conflict even after the Cold War had ended. Until the UN-sponsored ballot in August 1999, ASEAN adhered to its long-standing position that East Timor was an internal affair of Indonesia (Weatherbee 2005). ASEAN leaders persistently used the argument of non-interference. Thai Prime Minister Chuan Leekpai said: "East Timor is none of our business. It is a consensus among the ASEAN countries that they will not interfere in each other's internal affairs. We should not get involved". It was only after Indonesia gave its nominal permission for INTERFET to enter Indonesia that ASEAN started to participate. Thailand and the Philippines made battalion-sized contributions to INTEFRET. The presence of ASEAN uniformed troops had a political and military significance, but it needs to be noted that they were national contingents dedicated to an international force, not acting as an ASEAN force (Weatherbee 2005).

11.6.2 Conflict Intensity

Since 1976, the situation in East Timor had brought many casualties, most of which were not able to be officially documented. Beyond some scattered and often journalistic work, no systematic account of Indonesian casualties in the war in East Timor exists (Klinken 2005). The UCDP dataset recorded only the intensity of the conflict between 1992 and 1999. Based on this source, the number of deaths increased from 1994 until 1997. The total number of casualties at 1999 was 201.

The Santa Cruz massacre in 1991 awakened the uninformed public about what was really going on in East Timor. Based on previous research by van Klinken,[4] there were about 3600 Indonesian deaths during the East Timor struggle between 1975 and 1999. Forty percent of these casualties were East Timorese irregulars (not including unregistered civilians, forced to assist the Indonesian military in combat situations). The rest (about 2100) were mostly Indonesians from hundreds of different units around the country, while some were East Timorese regulars (Klinken 2005). This is only the number of military force casualties, not including civilians. East Timor was almost certainly Indonesia's bloodiest arena since the war for independence. For the Indonesians, most of the war was a counterinsurgency operation, classified as low-intensity conflict (Klinken 2005). This conflict is considered one of the greatest bloodlettings in modern history compared to the total population. The consequence of this conflict led to the deaths of around 200,000 civilians in East Timor, caused by massacre, forced starvation and disease. In addition, Indonesian forces engaged in torture, rape and forced relocation on a massive scale (Albert et al. 1999).

---

[4] Gerry van Klinken is a research fellow at the Royal Netherlands Institute of Southeast Asian and Caribbean Studies (KITLV), (www.kitlv.nl).

11.6.3 Presence of a Valid Spokesman

Despite Indonesia proclaiming East Timor part of Indonesia in 1976, the situation in East Timor was still full of struggle, which unfortunately was muted worldwide. Even so, there was no single actor from ASEAN's member states who proposed the mediation option to resolve the case. The situation in East Timor was never part of ASEAN's discourse (Weatherbee 2005). Other ASEAN countries except Singapore rallied behind Indonesia by emphasizing that Indonesia had to do it for national security (Dupont 2000). Singapore always showed abstention regarding intervention by bigger powers during General Assembly Meetings in 1975 and 1976. Even so, Singapore never publicly criticized Indonesia's invasion. By 1977, Singapore made a U-turn regarding East Timor by voting against UN Resolutions condemning Indonesia. This change can be attributed to Indonesian pressure, both public and private. The CIA analysis reportedly said that Indonesia would suspend intelligence exchanges with Singapore as well as closing Indonesian airspace to Singapore military aircraft. Moreover, according to Australian Ambassador Woolcott's secret cablegram to Canberra from Jakarta (30 January 1976), Ali Murtopo told Lee Khoon Choy (Singapore's then senior minister of state for foreign affairs) that "Indonesia would not forget for two hundred years what Singapore had done" (Ortuoste, Timor-Leste and ASEAN: Shaping Region and State in Southeast Asia 2011).

The shock of the Santa Cruz massacre, which took place at the end of the Cold War, finally woke up the international community. It also affected the dynamic within ASEAN's discussions. Since the ASEAN–EU Ministerial Meetings in 1992, the discussions had been marked by debates between Indonesia and Portugal over the East Timor issue. In the ASEAN Regional Forum, the Europeans and the Australians repeatedly raised the issue even though it was never reflected in the ARF's public statements (Severino and Severino 2006). Whereas the pressure from actors outside the region was increasing, none of the member states were powerful enough to initiate mediation by ASEAN. The conflicting parties did not see ASEAN as an option anymore, especially for the FRETILIN side, since the UN was more active in helping out and Portugal put a serious concern in their agenda for them to do something about it.

11.6.4 Impartiality

Before the invasion, FRETILIN (Revolutionary Front for an Independent East Timor) considered gaining support from ASEAN as an institution. The FRETILIN leadership declared that it would welcome 'fact-finding' missions from ASEAN, Australia and New Zealand as well as observers from other nations and the press to assess the situation in East Timor. It was stated in FRETILIN's Press Statement on 16 September 1975 that "regional stability is of utmost importance for the development of the South East Asian Nations, therefore, now and in the future, we will strive to promote friendship and cooperation between ourselves and the countries of the region. ASEAN is a factor of stability and a driving force of regional cooperation. East Timor would greatly benefit from integration into ASEAN after independence" (Dunn 2004). However, during the Cold War period, most of the member states of ASEAN considered them a 'communist threat' and did not respond until the invasion had already taken place.

Since the conflict went on for almost two decades, the vast majority wanted and many actively campaigned for UN intervention to end the Indonesian military occupation of their homeland (Terrall 2004). Not long after the invasion took place, the UN Secretary-General appointed a special envoy for East Timor to hold talks with the Indonesian government and FRETILIN. These, however, did not bring any significant result as the visit to the FRETILIN base was cancelled owing to security concerns. After the Santa Cruz massacre and Portugal holding the EU presidency, more talks were conducted by the UN between Portugal, who represented East Timor, and the Indonesian government. East Timor became part of the EU's foreign policy agenda, which became the conflicting factor in its relationship with ASEAN (McCloskey and Hainsworth 2000).

11.6.5   *Mediator's Leverage*

ASEAN as an institution was weak in terms of resources and expertise, especially during the Cold War period. The intention to jump into resolving the conflict was distracted at this time since member states all supported Indonesia because they wanted to 'maintain ASEAN', implying that they did not want political differences to scuttle the new organisation. Indonesia also argued that it had an obligation to help the East Timorese. As Indonesia was the biggest country in the region and the frontline state, ASEAN members indicated that they would only act upon its request (Ortueste 2011). In term of resources such as sanctions or rewards, ASEAN was not capable of providing them, as the conflict was never on the ASEAN agenda for discussion.

11.7   Case Comparison: Analysis

In the previous section, the three cases have been observed in the context of their evolution over the years and how they have been resolved by using the five indicators. With this in mind, this section analyses the findings in order to find the related factors to explain the dynamic of ASEAN involvement as a mediator in intrastate conflicts.

11.7.1 Use of the Non-interference Principle Argument

The use of non-interference principle gave impact to the existence of mediation by ASEAN. All three conflicts occurred during different eras; the Aceh conflict during the Cold War, Cambodia at the end of the Cold War and East Timor in the post-Cold War period. ASEAN member states did not use the non-interference argument when responding to the East Timor conflict during the Cold War due to a common understanding – among the majority of them – that East Timor could develop into a communist threat for the region. When the Cold War ended, ASEAN began to react differently, using the principle of 'non-interference' as the magic phrase to justify inaction in resolution processes.

Despite the Aceh conflict beginning during the Cold War, ASEAN did not perceive it as a communist threat and from the beginning reacted to the conflict as Indonesia's internal problem. In doing so, they utilised the principal of non-interference as justification for not intervening. Albeit they did insert the Aceh conflict into their annual meetings, but what they highlighted was only a concern for Indonesia's sovereignty by restating that there should not be any separation within Indonesia region. As for the Cambodia conflict, ASEAN did not consider that their actions contradicted with the non-interference principle, arguing that it was part of their duty as ASEAN foreign ministers to observe the implications of what has occurred and react accordingly. Through this observation, it could be seen that when non-interference was not put on the discussion table, the mediation from ASEAN was more likely to occur.

It is interesting to note that the argument of non-interference was replaced by taking action as part of their duty as ASEAN foreign ministers when responding to Cambodia conflict. The similar argument never applied in the other two cases. From here it can be determined that the non-interference principle is flexible in its practice. It depends on the perception of ASEAN as an institution in understanding the dynamic of a particular conflict.

11.7.2 Conflict Intensity

Within these three cases, the Cambodia case could be considered as less intense than the other two, though it did still indicate characteristics of intense conflict. However, the Aceh and East Timor conflict suffered more than Cambodia in terms of the length and resolution process that required several attempts before a final agreement was reached. It took two NGOs to bring the Aceh conflict to its final resolution. Although the intensity of the conflict escalated over its course, it did not change ASEAN's consideration to put more effort into becoming mediator. As for the East Timor conflict, they did not consider intensity as a sufficient indicator to intervene. This was especially due to the context of the Cold War era, since the majority of member states had similar justifications for supporting Indonesia's action towards East Timor situation. Even once the Cold War ended, intensity still was not considered a touchstone for them to initiate mediation effort as the closest regional entity.

In the Cambodian case, intensity was one of the main considerations when selecting Troika to mediate. There were several attacks ongoing in the country and the violence was considered extreme, almost reaching the border with Thailand. However, in comparison with the other two cases, the element of high intensity could not be a consistent indicator for ASEAN to be a mediator. If this element were significantly considered, ASEAN would put more effort in initiating mediation to resolve the more intense Aceh and East Timor conflicts, just as they did in Cambodia.

11.7.3   Presence of a Valid Spokesman

The mediation in Cambodia began with the Deputy Prime Minister of Malaysia Anwar Ibrahim challenging the non-intervention principle of ASEAN in responding to the emerging conflict. Not long after that, the Indonesian Foreign Minister called an emergency AMM meeting. Despite the fact that the mediation option did not occur until the later ARF (ASEAN Regional Forum) encouraged ASEAN to get involved, the speed with which the meeting was called indicates that this is a primary trigger the mediation option existed. The initiator from ASEAN to get ASEAN more involved in the resolution of the Aceh conflict was not as strong as in Cambodia conflict. Indonesia was perceived as a leading peacemaker in the region, and none of the other actors could replace such a position in a conflict that was occurring in Indonesia. However, there were some member states who were cautious about ASEAN involvement in the Aceh conflict, particularly the Philippines and Thailand. The willingness to get involved was visible but was not strong enough for the mediation to occur; it resulted only in the two countries sending unarmed delegates to monitor the situation in Aceh. As a final agreement was reached between the two conflicting parties, ASEAN showed its involvement by becoming part of Aceh Monitoring Mission (AMM) along with the EU.

Here it can be seen that the willingness was there but that none of the member states were powerful enough to become the Valid Spokesman and gather other member states to create another 'Troika' for Aceh until the two NGOs – HDC (Henry Dunant Centre for Humanitarian Dialogue) and CMI (Crisis Management Initiative) – became the leading mediators in this case. Even though Singapore was brave enough to be different from the other member states by responding to Indonesia's action in East Timor, it was not powerful enough to be an initiator and propose mediation during the Cold War. When the Cold War ended, Singapore did not pursue its perspective of not supporting what Indonesia had done in East Timor anymore. It also needs to be noted that Indonesia was more capable of pressuring Singapore – just as the Indonesian government did under Soeharto presidency to Singapore – rather than Singapore towards Indonesia if Singapore just acted alone. No actor can force others to follow the official framework of ASEAN so initiative from related actors is crucially needed. There are three different kinds of actor in this context: member states who are not one of the conflicting parties; conflicting party who is part of ASEAN member states and conflicting party who is not part of ASEAN member states. So, reflecting from what have been found in those three cases, there needs to be at least one additional support coming from different side of conflict for the Valid Spokesman, in order to have ASEAN mediation possible to take place. Just like what happened in Cambodia, ASEAN as an institution had the Valid Spokesman that encouraged the creation of Troika but for ASEAN mediation to finally take place at that time, Troika needed to get support which they did receive from the Prince Ranariddh side. It was only with Hun Sen ASEAN faced difficulty to implement its mediation effort.

11.7.4 Impartiality

In general, from the observation of these three cases, ASEAN was never really perceived by both conflicting parties as an impartial mediator. In the Cambodian case, it was Hun Sen's side that was having difficulty in accepting ASEAN as a mediator, but more because of the non-interference principle. He kept arguing that ASEAN should not be present because it indicated the intention to intervene in Cambodia's own issue. So for Hun Sen, the idea of mediation itself was disagreeable. However, the other side still perceived ASEAN as a potential mediator, and Ung Huat as the foreign minister agreed to use ASEAN as mediator. The mediation in the end existed because Hun Sen was in the weakest position once the King of Cambodia and another side of the conflicting party, Prince Ranariddh, agreed on having ASEAN as a mediator. Due to other pressures and leverage – which will be discussed in the next section – Hun Sen accepted the presence of ASEAN. Impartiality of ASEAN in this case was weak since only one side of parties fully agreed in accepting ASEAN as a mediator. The lack of trust from Hun Sen was demonstrated at the end of the mediation when he rejected the proposal from ASEAN which caused the delegates from ASEAN to stop their efforts. Although Prince Ranariddh's side agreed on the proposal, Hun Sen kept his argument that he would not accept it.

ASEAN was actually once considered by Indonesian government to be the mediator during the Habibie presidency. However, GAM did not consider ASEAN impartial enough to be a mediator, arguing that ASEAN would favour the Indonesian government. When Jusuf Kalla was trying to find a way in resolving the Aceh conflict, ASEAN was not inserted into his consideration as the potential mediator. Neither did GAM who from the very beginning had no trust towards ASEAN to be a mediator.

For East Timor, ASEAN was only once to be considered as an actor that might help to resolve the conflict: before the attack from Indonesian government started. When the UN started to intervene, ASEAN faded away as an alternative option as mediator. In addition, most member states were having similar voice with Indonesia in combating the communist threat, which in this case was how they perceived East Timor during the Cold War. Even after the Cold War ended, ASEAN was being more pushed away as the UN became more active in resolving the conflict by hosting the dialogue between Indonesian government and Portugal on behalf of East Timor. These two actors were seen to be more impartial and for East Timor, Portugal was more reliable due to the fact that Portugal's government put East Timor into their own government agenda. The UN put its effort in East Timor mediation numerously which can indicate the conflicting parties kept perceiving the UN as a trusted third party.

11.7.5 Mediator's Leverage

ASEAN as an institution did not have any leverage that could act as the factor for conflicting parties to consider ASEAN as a mediator. For Aceh case, in term of resources, there was nothing to offer from ASEAN that could attract conflicting parties to choose ASEAN as a mediator. Regarding expertise, in comparison with Cambodia case when the Troika was created intentionally to mediate, in this case ASEAN did not have the capacity to do so because it was never really discussed in any forum.

It was similar to what happened in the East Timor case. ASEAN did not have the capacity to encourage the conflicting parties to come to the mediation table under ASEAN leadership. When the UN held the position as a mediator, ASEAN was never really considered a mediator anymore. Unlike in the Cambodia case, the leverage from ASEAN could be seen in two forms: the postponement of membership and the possibility of drawing the investments by ASEAN member states in Cambodia. The investments were more valuable as Cambodia relied on the foreign investment for its economic stability during that period of time. The leverage from ASEAN was a significant factor for especially Hun Sen in accepting ASEAN presence in Cambodia. If ASEAN did not have such leverage, it was less likely that Hun Sen would reconsider rejecting ASEAN and also withdraw the ASEAN membership application (Table 11.2).

11.8 Conclusion

Given the fact that ASEAN has been existing for more than three decades as of this year, it aroused the question of how ASEAN as an institution has maintained and handled the potential conflicts in the region throughout these years. As explained in this chapter, Southeast Asia has experienced almost half of the total percentage of intrastate conflicts in Asia since the middle of the twentieth century. ASEAN as the closest formal entity in the region is expected to have a role as conflict manager, and becoming a mediator is a big part of it. Why a mediator? As discussed earlier,

Table 11.2 Five indicators for case comparison

Indicators	Non-interference principle	Conflict intensity	Valid spokesman	Impartiality	Mediator's leverage
Similarities of three cases	"Critical juncture" (The Cold War) played important roles.	Both the *Aceh and East Timor conflict* suffered in terms of the length and resolution process.	There needs to be one additional support coming from different side of conflict for the Valid Spokesman.	ASEAN was never perceived by both conflicting parties as an impartial mediator.	ASEAN did not have any leverage that could act as the factor for conflicting parties to consider it as a mediator.
Differences of three cases	ASEAN reacted to the *Aceh conflict* as Indonesia's internal problem, so they used this principle as justification for not intervening.	It took two NGOs to bring the *Aceh conflict* to its final resolution.	The Philippines and Thailand were particularly cautious about ASEAN involvement in the *Aceh conflict.*	GAM rejected to seek help from ASEAN and proposed having the UN as a mediator originally in responding to the *Aceh conflict.*	In the *Aceh conflict,* there was nothing to offer from ASEAN, especially when the U.S. imposed sanctions on Indonesia.
	ASEAN used this principle to respond to the *East Timor conflict* after the Cold War to justify inaction in resolution processes.	ASEAN did not consider intensity of the *East Timor conflict* as a sufficient indicator to intervene, especially due to the context of the Cold War era.	Singapore was different from the other member states by responding to Indonesia's action in *East Timor*.	Both ASEAN and the UN were seen to be more impartial, Portugal was more reliable because Portugal's government put *East Timor* into their own government agenda.	In the *East Timor conflict*, ASEAN did not have the capacity to encourage the conflicting parties under ASEAN leadership.
	This principle was replaced by taking action as part of their duty as ASEAN foreign ministers when responding to the *Cambodia conflict.*	The *Cambodia conflict* was less intense than the other two. It was not a consistent indicator for ASEAN to be a mediator.	ASEAN's member states were more active in reacting to the *Cambodia conflict.* They stood ready to contribute efforts to the peaceful resolution in Cambodia.	Two different voices in the *Cambodia conflict.* Yet, the mediation in the end existed.	The leverage from ASEAN could be seen in two forms: (1) the postponement of membership. (2) the possibility of drawing the investments by ASEAN member states in *Cambodia.*

Source: Data collected and compacted by the author

mediation has been considered as the most effective method in bringing conflicting parties to a mutually acceptable agreement. However, ASEAN has shown inconsistency in playing its role as mediator.

As the main concern of this chapter is to find out the factors that explain the dynamics of ASEAN's role as mediator, we have tried to show there is a correlation between several possible factors. Among the five factors that have been laid out, the ones that are most significant are the use of the non-interference argument in considering mediation, the presence of a Valid Spokesman and the leverage of ASEAN as a mediator.

As can be seen in the Cambodian conflict, ASEAN member states argued that the mediation was not considered as intervening unlike in the other two cases – the Aceh Conflict and East Timor conflict – where the non-interference principle became the rhetoric boundary for ASEAN mediation to exist. It shows contrasting implications when it was used or not used towards the occurrence of mediation. Especially in the context of regional organisation, in which any decision depends on the collective voice of member states and when most of them argue for certain action as intervention, that would tend to be the representation of ASEAN as an institution.

The second factor which is the presence of a Valid Spokesman who could present the option of ASEAN mediation did provide significant impact. In the Aceh conflict and East Timor conflict, there was a lack of presence of a Valid Spokesperson who could gather the member states to agree on implementing a mediation effort. In contrast to the Cambodia conflict, Indonesia's Foreign Minister at that time called an emergency meeting in regards to this case and the majority of member states who had a similar view, pushed them to agree on hosting a mediation team from ASEAN for Cambodia. From both sides of the conflict, there was a lack of initiators and a concern about ASEAN's ability to be impartial. Based on these apprehensions, they were reluctant to have ASEAN mediate the conflicts.

The third factor is the leverage that ASEAN can bring in terms of rewards, sanctions, and expertise. In the Cambodia conflict, the leverage of ASEAN was influential in bringing the conflicting parties, especially Hun Sen, into agreeing to have them act as the mediator. ASEAN used its leverage by sanctioning Cambodia through postponing its application to become an ASEAN member state and also through threatening Cambodia that ASEAN member states would withdraw their investments in Cambodia. These leverages were quite successful to push Hun Sen into accepting ASEAN as the mediator, even though he had no trust in ASEAN at that time. In terms of expertise, ASEAN had the capability to create mediation team, which did not happen in the Aceh conflict and the East Timor conflict.

The other two factors – conflict intensity and impartiality – played less of a role in influencing the practice of ASEAN mediation in general. Unfortunately, this chapter could suggest that the intensity of conflict was not included as an indicator. Due to the fact that the conflict that ASEAN got involved in was the Cambodia conflict which was less intense than the other two cases. The impartiality was less significant in comparison to the other three factors, because mediation still took place as in the Cambodia conflict, even though one side of the conflicting parties did not trust ASEAN as an impartial mediator; but mediation still took place. Lastly, it can be concluded that the five possible factors discussed above had a variety of levels of influence towards the dynamics of ASEAN mediation.

It is hoped that this paper can be a fruitful contribution to previous studies about ASEAN as a regional conflict manager and also as a basis for future research in the context of the potential of ASEAN as an effective mediator. Picturing ASEAN in that position does not mean that ASEAN will be suggested to be the only mediator to resolve conflict in the region. Nonetheless, the intention is to have ASEAN become more aware of its potential role to act as a mediator that might be a significant support structure in the context of international conflict resolution.

Further Readings

Amer, R. (2009). The Association of Southeast Asian Nations' (ASEAN) conflict management approach revisited: Will the charter reinforce ASEAN's role? *Austrian Journal of South-East Asian Studies*

Collins, A. (2013). *Building a people-oriented security community the ASEAN way*. London: Routledge.

Oishi, M. (2016). Introduction: The ASEAN way of conflict management under challenge. In M. Oishi (Ed.), *Contemporary conflicts in Southeast Asia. Asia in transition* (Vol. 3). Singapore: Springer.

References

1976 Treaty of Amity and Cooperation in Southeast Asia. (2016, March). Retrieved from ASEAN: http://www.aseansec.org/1217.htm

Acharya, A. (2009). *Constructing a security community in Southeast Asia*. New York: Routledge.

Adams, B. (2007, July 27). *Cambodia: July 1997: Shock and aftermath*. Retrieved May 10, 2016, from Human Rights Watch: https://www.hrw.org/news/2007/07/27/cambodia-july-1997-shock-and-aftermath

Akashi, Y. (1995). The limits of UN diplomacy and the future of conflict mediation. *Survival: Global Politics and Strategy, 37*, 83–98.

Albert, M., Chomsky, N., & Shalom, S. (1999, October). *East timor questions & answers*. Retrieved May 10, 2016, from Chomsky.info: https://chomsky.info/199910__02/

Amer, R. (2015). Intra-state conflicts: Can the Association of Southeast Asian Nations (ASEAN) play a role? *Hiroshima Peace Research Journal, 2*, 97–121.

ASEAN and the question of Cambodia. (2007). *Strategic comments*, 1–3.

ASEAN halts Cambodia mediation. (1997, July 19). Retrieved May 10, 2016, from CNN Interactive: http://edition.cnn.com/WORLD/9707/19/cambodia/

Caballero-Anthony, M. (1998). Mechanisms of dispute settlement: The ASEAN experience. *Contemporary Southeast Asia, 20*, 38–66.

Caballero-Anthony, M. (2005). *Regional security in Southeast Asia: Beyond the ASEAN way*. Singapore: Institute of Southeast Asian Studies.

Cambodia: July 1997: Shock and Aftermath. (2007, July 27). Retrieved May 10, 2016, from Human Rights Watch: https://www.hrw.org/news/2007/07/27/cambodia-july-1997-shock-and-aftermath

Carey, P. (1996). *East Timor: Third World colonialism and the struggle for national identity*. London: Research Institute for the Study of Conflict and Terrorism.

Countries Listed By Continent. (2016, May 14). Retrieved from World Atlas: http://www.worldatlas.com/cntycont.htm

Daly, B., & Higgins, N. (2010). Resolving armed conflict: The Acehnese experience of mediation. *US-China Law Review, 55*, 4–5.

DeRouen, K., & Bercovitch, J. (2011). *Unraveling internal conflicts in East Asia and the Pacific: Incidence, consequences and resolutions*. Plymouth: Lexington Books.

Development, C. A. (2003, June 23). *Campaigning for human rights and peace in Aceh – interview with Samsul Bahri*. Retrieved May 14, 2016, from Reliefweb: http://reliefweb.int/report/indonesia/campaigning-human-rights-and-peace-aceh-interview-samsul-bahri

Diehl, P. F., & Greig, J. M. (2012). Providers of mediation. In *International mediation*. Cambridge: Polity Press.

Dunn, J. (2004). *East Timor: A rough passage to independence*. New South Wales: Longueville Media.

Dupont, A. (2000). ASEAN's response to the East Timor crisis. *Australian Journal of International Affairs, 54*, 163–170.

East Timor Profile – Timeline. (2015, February 17). Retrieved May 10, 2016, from BBC News: http://www.bbc.com/news/world-asia-pacific-14952883

Elliott Kirsten. (2012). *The international problems behind intrastate conflict: Spillover effects and mass atrocities*. Retrieved June 12, 2014, from http://www.ualr.edu/kxelliott/Writing%20Samples/KirstenElliott_IR_IntrastateConflict.pdf

Framework for a Comprehensive Political Settlement of the Cambodia Conflict. (1991, October 23). Retrieved May 10, 2016, from United Nations Peacemaker: http://peacemaker.un.org/cambodiaparisagreement91

Fretter, J., & Bercovitch, J. (2004). International organizations and regional conflicts. In *Regional guide to international conflict and management from 1945 to 2003*. Washington, DC: CQ Press.

Gartner, S. S. (2011). Signs of trouble: Regional organization mediation and civil war agreement durability. *The Journal of Politics, 73*, 380–390.

Hadebe Patrick Siyabonga. (2011). *The limitations of regional organizations and hegemonic states in international peacekeeping and security: The case of the South African military intervention in Lesotho in 1998*. Retrieved June 12, 2017, from http://www.academia.edu/1330093/The_Limitations_of_Regional_Organizations_and_Hegemonic_States_in_international_peacekeeping_and_security

Houston, A., & Bercovitch, J. (2000). Why do they do it like this? An analysis of the factors influencing mediation behavior in international conflicts. *The Journal of Conflict Resolution, 44*, 170–202.

International, A. (1997). *Kingdom of Cambodia: Arrest and execution of political opponents*. Retrieved May 10, 2016, from http://www.refworld.org/pdfid/3ae6a98428.pdf

Jackson, R., & Bercovitch, J. (2009). *Conflict resolution in the twenty-first century-principles, methods, and approaches*. Michigan: University of Michigan Press.

Jamal, T. (2001, December). *Indonesia – East Timor (1975–2001)*. Retrieved May 10, 2016, from Research and Action for Peace: http://ploughshares.ca/pl_armedconflict/indonesia-east-timor-1975-2001/

Jones, L. (2010). *ASEAN's unchanged melody? The theory and practice of 'Non-Interference' in Southeast Asia*. Retrieved May 13, 2016, from https://www.hitpages.com/doc/5151323410399232/17/

Jones, L. (2011). *ASEAN, sovereignty and intervention in Southeast Asia*. London: Palgrave Macmillan.

Kamarulzaman, A., Bercovitch, J., & Oishi, M. (2002). The ASEAN way of conflict management: Old patterns and new trends. *Asian Journal of Political Science*. https://doi.org/10.1080/02185370208434209.

Klinken, G. V. (2005). *Indonesian casualties in East Timor, 1975–1999: Analysis of an official list*. Retrieved May 10, 2016, from http://cip.cornell.edu/DPubS?service=Repository&version =1.0&verb=Disseminate&view=body&content-type=pdf_1&handle=seap.indo/1132335834#

Large, J., & Aguswandi. (2008). *Reconfiguring politics: The Indonesia-Aceh peace process*. Retrieved May 10, 2016, from Conciliation Resources: http://www.c-r.org/accord/ reconfiguring-politics-indonesia-aceh-peace-process

Leifer, M. (1999). The ASEAN peace process: A category mistake. *The Pacific Review., 12*, 25–38.

Masilamani, L., & Peterson, J. (2014). The "ASEAN Way": The structural underpinnings of constructive engagement. *Foreign Policy Journal, 2*, 1–21.

McCloskey, S., & Hainsworth, P. (2000). *The East Timor question: The struggle for independence from Indonesia*. London: Tauris.

Moller, F., DeRouen, K., Bercovitch, J., & Wallensteen, P. (2007). The limits of peace: Third parties in civil wars in Southeast Asia, 1993–2004. *Negotiation Journal, 23*, 373–391.

Nations, T. U. (2003). *United Nations transitional authority in Cambodia*. Retrieved May 10, 2016, from United Nations Peacekeeping: http://www.un.org/en/peacekeeping/missions/past/ untac.htm

Nishikawa, Y. (2007). The 'ASEAN Way' and Asian regional security. *Southeastern Political Review, 12*, 1.

Oishi, M., & Baikoeni, E. Y. (2015). Ending a long-standing intrastate conflict through internationalisation: The case of Aceh in Indonesia. In M. Oishi (Ed.), *Contemporary conflicts in Southeast Asia: Towards a new ASEAN way of conflict management* (pp. 19–44). Singapore: Springer.

Organizing Your Social Sciences Research Paper: Types of Research Designs. (n.d.). Retrieved April 2016, from USC Libraries: http://libguides.usc.edu/writingguide/researchdesigns

Ortuoste, M. (2011). Timor-Leste and ASEAN: Shaping region and state in Southeast Asia. *Asian Journal of Political Science, 19*, 1–24.

Pan, E. (2005, September 15). *INDONESIA: The Aceh Peace Agreement*. Retrieved May 10, 2016, from Council on Foreign Relations: http://www.cfr.org/indonesia/ indonesia-aceh-peace-agreement/p8789#p5.

Peou, S. (1998). *Diplomatic pragmatism: ASEAN's responses to the July 1997 coup*. Retrieved May 10, 2016, from Concilliation Resources: http://www.c-r.org/downloads/Accord%20 Cambodia_Diplomatic%20pragmatism.pdf.

Pettersson, T. (2015). *Armed conflict by conflict type and year*. Retrieved May 14, 2016, from Department of Peace and Conflict Research: http://www.pcr.uu.se/ digitalAssets/66/66314_1armed-conflict-by-region-1946-2014.pdf

Phan, H. D. (2013). Procedures for peace: Building mechanisms for dispute settlement and conflict management within ASEAN. *Journal of International Law and Policy, 20*(1), 47–73.

Rieffel, L. (2010). *Myanmar/Burma: Inside challenges, outside interests*. Washington, DC: Brookings Institution Press.

Ropers, N. (2012). Insider mediation as a tool of collaborative security: Trends, discourse, and insights from Asia. *International Studies, 49*, 189–205.

Rupprecht, K. (2014). Separatist conflicts in the ASEAN region: Comparing southern Thailand and Mindanao. *ASEAS-Austrian Journal of South-east Asia Studies, 7*(1), 21–40.

Schiff, A. (2014). Reaching a mutual agreement: Readiness theory and coalition building in the Aceh peace process. *Negotiation and Conflict Management Research, 7*, 57–82.

Severino, R., & Severino, C. (2006). *Southeast Asia in search of an ASEAN community: Insights from the former ASEAN secretary-general*. Singapore: ISEAS Publishing.

Simons, K. (2003). *Sovereignty and responsibility to protect*. Retrieved from Peace Magazine: http://peacemagazine.org/archive/v19n1p23.htm

Smith, A. L. (2003). Indonesia's Aceh problem: Measuring international and domestic costs. *Asia-Pacific Security Studies, 2*, 1–4.

Tan, A. (2003, July 1). *CO03025|The Acehnese conflict: Transnational linkages, responses and implications.* Retrieved May 10, 2016, from RSIS Publications: https://www.rsis.edu.sg/rsis-publication/rsis/579-the-acehnese-conflict-transna/#.Vzn6Wfl97IU

Terrall, B. (2004). *The UN in East Timor: Lessons for Iraq?*

Treaty of Amity and Cooperation in Southeast Asia Indonesia, 24 February 1976. (1976, February 24). Retrieved May 8, 2016, from Association of Southeast Asian Nations (ASEAN): http://www.asean.org/treaty-amity-cooperation-southeast-asia-indonesia-24-february-1976/

UCDP – Government of Indonesia – FRETILIN. (n.d.). Retrieved May 10, 2016, from Uppsala Conflict Database Program: http://ucdp.uu.se/#/statebased/720

UCDP – Government of Indonesia – GAM. (n.d.). Retrieved May 10, 2016, from Uppsala Conflict Data Program (UCDP): http://ucdp.uu.se/#/statebased/794

Vukovic, S. (2013). *Analysis of multiparty mediation processes.* Doctoral dissertation, Doctoral dissertation, University of Leiden.

Vuković, S. (2014). International mediation as a distinct form of conflict management. *International Journal of Conflict Management, 25,* 61–80.

Vuković, S. (2015a). *International multiparty mediation and conflict management: Challenges of cooperation and coordination.* Oxford: Routledge.

Vuković, S. (2015b). *International multiparty mediation and conflict management: Challenges of cooperation and coordination.* New York: Routledge.

Vuković, S. (2015c). Soft power, Bias and manipulation of international organizations in international mediation. *International Negotiation, 20,* 414–443.

Weatherbee, D. E. (2005). *International relations in Southeast Asia: The struggle for autonomy.* Maryland: Rowman and Littlefield.

Wilkenfeld, J., Young, K., Quinn, D., & Asal, V. (2005). *Mediating international crisis.* New York: Routledge.

Zartman, I. W. (2002). Mediation by regional organization: The OAU in Chad and Congo. In J. Bercovitch (Ed.), *International mediation.* New York: Palgrave Macmillan.

Chapter 12
Regionalism in Latin America: Eclectic, Multi-faceted and Multi-layered

Joren Selleslaghs, José Briceño Ruiz, and Philippe de Lombaerde

12.1 Introduction

Regionalism in Latin America is a complex phenomenon. This chapter will argue that after a sequence of various waves of regionalization efforts, Latin-American regionalism has become multi-layered, multi-faceted and eclectic. It is characterized by a large set of different arrangements, both formal and informal in nature and structure, and various regimes and regional institutions currently coexist (Malamud and Gardini 2012). This diversity is actually not a novelty in Latin American regionalism. In the 1960s, 1970s and 1980s, large Latin American regional schemes (e.g. LAFTA or LAIA) already coexisted with sub-regional blocs such as the Central American Common Market and the Andean Pact. A similar situation is observed nowadays, when regional spaces (such as CELAC) co-exist with sub-regional initiatives like Mercosur, the Andean Community, ALBA or the Pacific Alliance. What has been different in the last decade is the emergence of regional projects with primarily a political goal, examples of which include UNASUR and CELAC. At the same time, with respect to regional economic integration, an ideological fragmentation occurred due to the different views on globalization and economic development in the Pacific Alliance, Mercosur and ALBA. As we will discuss in this chapter, it is

J. Selleslaghs (✉)
Faculty of Governance and Global Affairs, Leiden University, The Hague, The Netherlands
e-mail: selleslaghs.joren@gmail.com

J. B. Ruiz
Faculty of Economical and Social Sciences, University of the Andes,
Mérida, Venezuela
e-mail: bricenoruiz@unam.mx

P. de Lombaerde
Neoma Business School, Rouen, France
e-mail: philippe.de-lombaerde@neoma-bs.fr

© Springer Nature Switzerland AG 2020   223
M. O. Hosli, J. Selleslaghs (eds.), *The Changing Global Order*, United Nations
University Series on Regionalism 17,
https://doi.org/10.1007/978-3-030-21603-0_12

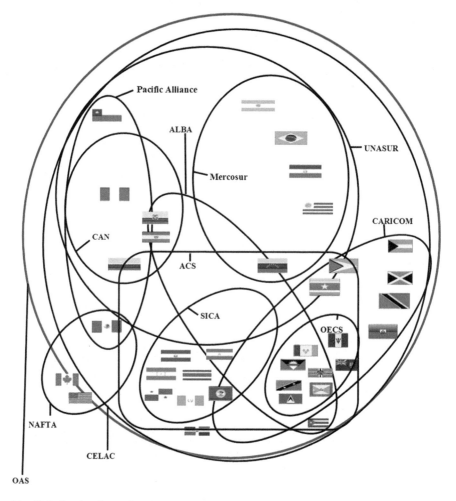

Fig. 12.1 Overlapping regionalisms in the Americas. (Source: Elaborated by the authors of this chapter)

the result of a large variety of different drivers and influential factors, both endogenous as well as exogenous, that resulted in what Glickhouse (2012) has labelled "the alphabet soup of Latin American regionalism", visualized in Fig. 12.1.

Regionalism as a political project has been present in Latin American politics since its early days after independence. The economic dimension was not absent in various regionalist projects in the nineteenth and early twentieth century though (see Rivarola Puntigliano and Briceño Ruiz 2013). One could mention the so-called Family Pact, proposed by the Mexican Lucas Alamán in 1830 with the goal of establishing a network of trade agreements among the Hispanic American republics. In 1909, Argentine economist Alejando Bunge proposed the creation of a Southern Custom Union that would include Argentina, Chile, Uruguay, Bolivia, Paraguay and even Brazil. After World War II, under the leadership of Raúl Prebisch

and the Economic Commission for Latin America (ECLA), the economic dimension became the core of Latin American regionalism. The project of setting up a
Latin American Common Market was discussed and negotiated in the 1950s and led
to the creation of LAFTA in 1960. A sub-regional bureau of ECLAC was established in Mexico City, one of its goals being to foster initiatives of economic integration for Central America. As a result, a Multilateral Treaty of Free Trade and
Economic Integration was subscribed in 1956 and later a General Treaty of
Economic Integration was signed in 1958 that eventually led to the creation of the
Central American Common Market in 1960.

Thus, regionalism is a crucial element of Latin American and Caribbean international policies to the point that regional integration and cooperation, and the benefits
thereof, are also explicitly referred to in various Latin American constitutions, as is
the case of Brazil (1988), Peru (1993), and Bolivia (2009) (which adds the integration with indigenous peoples of the world). Colombia (1991) and Venezuela (1999),
also being part of the Caribbean, refer in addition to the promotion of regional integration with this region (Rettberg et al. 2014: 16). However, rather than going
through a process of enlargement, deepening and/or 'spill-over' effects as happened
in Western Europe, no single regional organization has come to dominate Latin
American (or South American) regionalism[1] and its pervasiveness and cast has
changed over time. As new organizations were created, old ones were reconstructed
and reframed, leading in turn to different waves or stages of regional cooperation
(Rosenthal 1991:10) and to the superposition of various layers (Bianculli 2010: 4).

In this chapter, we will provide a critical account of the different phases, drivers
and limitations of Latin American regional integration and cooperation efforts, as
well as a structural overview of today's most *well-known* regional (integration and
cooperation) organizations. Section one first reflects on the definition of the 'Latin
American region' and will argue that due to a variation in possible geo-political and
geo-economic interpretations of the 'region', different visions –and consequently
outcomes of- regional integration efforts have been generated. Section two gives an
overview of the various waves of Latin American regional integration efforts. In
section three, a selection of today's most *well-known* Latin American regional organizations or cooperation schemes are presented in order to empirically show how
multi-faced and multi-layered the Latin American regional architecture really is.
The fourth section then moves to the identification and explanation of important
drivers/factors that characterize and influence Latin American regionalism. Whereas
the endogenous factors relate to issues of ideology, political cycles of major Latin

---

[1] However, this is not only the Latin American case. Regionalism in Africa includes a myriad of
economic and security organizations. There is not a single bloc in the whole Pacific Rim or in the
whole Asian continent. The Association of South East Asian Nations (ASEAN) is being transformed by new initiatives such as the Regional Comprehensive Economic Partnership that include
China, Australia, New Zealand and India or the almost disappeared Transpacific Partnership
(TPP). The idea of a single regional project that has widened and deepened has as empirical evidence just the European Union, that certainly became hegemonic in Western Europe, despite the
existence of the European Free Trade Association (EFTA) or the Council of Europe in the field of
Human Rights.

American countries (i.e. Brazil, Argentina, Venezuela etc.), the exogenous factors are more related to changes in the global political economy and the (changing) geopolitical global order. Finally, in section five, reflections are provided on how the authors believe Latin American regionalism will likely evolve in the (near) future and suggestions for further readings are provided.

12.2   Latin America: A/One Region?

Before delving into the particular ways in which regionalism has advanced in Latin America, a question is worth asking: what defines it as a/one region? (Bianculli 2010: 3) The traditional characterization of Latin America as a region relies on a combination of geographical, historical, cultural and linguistic criteria. In this sense, Latin America refers to the area comprised between the Rio Grande, as the demarcation line with the United States of America in the north, and the southernmost tip of South America – the region known as *Tierra del Fuego* (Bianculli 2016), characterized by their use of two official Latin languages (Spanish and Portugese), next to a number of indigenous languages. As such, the region 'Latin America' is composed of 21 countries today, starting with Mexico, all the way down to Chile/Argentina in the south. Contemporary understandings of regions, however, emphasize that one should move beyond issues of geography (Hurrell 1995). Indeed, regions are "socially constructed and politically contested space[s] between the national and global levels" in which political unity and regional cooperation is based on a shared set of politico-social preferences, homogeneities and, ultimately, solidarity (Bianculli 2016: 155).

These ideas are crucial to understand Latin America as a region. Ideas about regional unity and solidarity go back to the early nineteenth century when most of the countries in the region became independent. Simón Bolívar was a leading figure in the promotion of regional unity among the new nations. In the Letter of Jamaica, published in 1815 during his exile in the British territory, Bolivar called for convening a Hispanic American congress in Panamá that was eventually held in 1826. Similar Congresses were held in Lima (1846–47), Santiago (1856) and Lima (1864–65) (see Briceño Ruiz 2014). Although external threats were the reasons that led to convene those congresses, the identity issue was also a crucial variable. For Bolívar, the idea was to create a Confederation of the former Spanish territories, excluding the United States and Brazil (the latter due to its monarchical form of government). However, Brazil was invited to Panama and to the further congresses of Lima and Santiago, invitations that it always rejected. This was not the only case: Venezuela in the 1840s took distance from regional initiatives and Argentina did likewise after 1850 (Briceño Ruiz 2014). Uruguay and Paraguay were never enthusiastic in participating in those initiatives. This shows that already in the nineteenth century there was a coexistence of forces that highlighted common interests and identities to foster regional unity and forces that were skeptical about it.

Notwithstanding those facts, the idea of promoting regional agreements never disappeared in Latin America. In reality a long-term historical analysis shows that variables such as identity, economic development, or the search for political autonomy vis-à-vis the major global powers have been the reason behind Latin American regionalism (Briceño Ruiz 2014). However, more recently various regional projects have been proposed and/or implemented in the region, based on different– views on the desired scope of the project (be it geographically or in terms of policy areas) and on its ideological foundations. The diversity reflects the vastness of the Latin American subcontinent. Regions such as Central America are particularly differentiated not only due to the level of development of their countries but also because there is a sort o "myth" of Central America as single nation that has never disappeared. This explains why Central America did not originally participate in LAFTA in the 1960s and a seperate own regional scheme was created: The Central American Common Market. The Andean Pact emerged as a response of mid-size Latin American countries to the shortcomings of LAFTA, in particular the unequal distribution of the gains of economic integration. Nevertheless, LAFTA, the CACM and the Pact shared a similar approach to regional economic integration based on ECLAC's ideas of regional industrialization and economic nationalism. The scenario was not too different from the wave of economic regionalism that was developed since the late 1980s and early 1990s: a regional Latin America scheme (LAIA-ALADI) coexisted with sub-regional schemes such as SICA, the Andean Pact and Mercosur. All of them shared a similar economic approach, the so called open regionalism, in which the goal was to use economic integration as a mechanism for a better insertion into the global markets. This scenario was modified to some extent in the last decade of regionalism (described as post-liberal or post-hegemonic). Especially, in the sphere of economic integration various regional schemes such as the Pacific Alliance, Mercosur and ALBA have emerged that seem incompatible with one other. Mercosur remained as a trade agreement but complemented with new policy initiatives in areas such as productivity, social policy and education, a reason why in some circles it began to be described as a "new Mercosur". ALBA was described as anti-capitalist, anti-imperialist and contrahegemonic initiative (Briceño Ruiz 2014). The Pacific Alliance is an example of open regionalism that aims at fostering free trade and deep (economic) integration. These schemes are based on different logics of regionalism, but contradictory as it might seem, this diversity in the economic sphere was accompanied by the promotion of new regional initiatives in the field of political and functional cooperation, examples of which are UNASUR and CELAC. In the following section, we will look at how these different visions and interpretations of what defines Latin America as a/one region have led to the configuration which is in place in the region today.

12.3 Competing Views on Regionalism in Latin America Leading to a Complex Regional Institutional Configuration

One of the divides that exist in the views on regionalism in Latin America is about whether countries should strive towards *hemispheric* wide-regionalism, also including the United States and Canada, or quasi-hemispheric (i.e. Latin American) regionalism, on the one hand, or some form of smaller-scale sub-continental regionalism (also called sub-regional integration), on the other (Bianculli 2016). Exemplar for the viewpoint on hemispheric regionalism in the Americas is the long series of 'Pan-American conferences' which had as objective to promote the creation of formal multilateral institutions to deal with issues such as democracy, human rights, trade, development and security (Bianculli 2016). Right after World War II, it gained institutional expression with the creation of the Organization of American States (OAS) (Bianculli 2016). In the 1990s, on the initiative of the US, the Summits of the Americas continued this tendency, until the proposal to create a Free Trade Area of the Americas (FTAA) was abandoned in 2006 in a context of rising opposition, especially in South America.

More recently, the creation of the Community of Latin American and Caribbean States (CELAC) in 2010 in which all Latin American (and Caribbean countries) are members and from which the United States (and Canada) are excluded, can also be interpreted – at least in part – as a further expression of US skepticism, anti-imperialism (Dabène 2009) or even anti-Americanism (Fawcett and Serrano 2005). Quasi-hemispheric arrangements further include the Latin American Integration Association (LAIA/ALADI) (see below) and the Economic System of Latin America (SELA), created in 1975. These four arrangements can be considered as the framework – both politically and economically – within which sub-regional initiatives have been developed. These latter are sometimes compatible with the former in a multi-level governance logic, but they can also be considered as expressions of a distinct vision on regionalism which is opposed to hemispheric continentalism.

On the other side of the spectrum is the view that Latin America is composed of different (sub-) regions which can also be traced back to the beginning of the nineteenth century, when many new sovereign states emerged (Vivares and Dolcetti-Marcolini 2016). The South American independence leader Simón Bolívar envisioned various (geo-)political unions that would ensure the independence of the newly created sovereign states vis-à-vis the European powers – in particular Spain – (Chasteen 2008). In 1825, Bolivar proposed the Federation of the Andes. In a similar way, in 1823 various provinces and territories joined forces to create a 'Federal Republic of Central America', and in South America similar movements came about by means of 'The United Provinces of South America' and 'The United Provinces of the Rio de la Plata'. Yet, as Bianculli (2016: 3) explains: " these early attempts for political unification failed to produce any form of institutional political cooperation at the regional level as opposing preferences and rivalries deepened, still they planted the seed of regional unity, an idea that has since permeated the intellectual community in Latin America".

12.4   Different Waves of Regionalism

The literature on the history of Latin American integration is unwieldy. There seems to be a consensus that modern regionalism takes off after WWII and usually distinct "waves", phases or periods are considered, although there is no convergence as to the number and length of these periods. The first wave, labeled "early" or "old" regionalism, spans approximately the timeframe of 1950 to the mid-1980s in which pioneers as Raul Prebisch and CEPAL laid the foundations of what has later been called "Latin-American structuralism" (Saad-Filho and Johnston 2005; Moncayo et al. 2012). As Bianculli (2010: 5) explains: "the main objective was not so much political in nature, but rather focused on economic cooperation, namely to promote the constitution of a regional market to allow for the enlargement of national markets and the development of national industries, while at the same time reducing the region's economic and political dependence on advanced industrial economies and improving the region's terms-of-trade". It became possible thanks to a growing consensus on the role of the State in the economy and the validity of the industrialization through import substitution development model. In this phase, the following three important regional integration schemes/institutions were created: the Central American Common Market (1960), the Latin American Free Trade Association (1960) (which would be replaced by LAIA in 1980), and the Andean Group (Bianculli 2010). The latter was created in 1969 and envisaged a common external tariff, as well as harmonization on industrial policies (Bianculli 2010). As such, CACM succeeded in agreeing on a common external tariff (CET) covering more than 98% of extra-regional trade, whereas the Andean Pact countries agreed on a common investment regime. Yet, the overall poor economic record of the first phase of regional integration schemes, in combination with the political turmoil related to the debt crises in the early 1980s, led to a relatively standstill in terms of further Latin American regionalist projects (Bianculli 2010). It was only with the structural reforms and *apertura* programs (including trade and investment liberalization) in the late 1980s and 1990s that a new phase of regional dynamism started (Bianculli 2010).

This second wave is associated with the "new" or "open" regionalism (De Lombaerde and Garay 2008). Mercosur (1991), NAFTA (1992), the Association of Caribbean States (1994) and the Group of Three (1995) were created, while several intra-regional FTAs were signed, and the FTAA negotiations were launched in 1994. Already existing groupings were re-engineered: CACM was turned into the Central American Integration System (SICA) in 1991, while the Andean Group became the Andean Community (CAN) in 1996. In both cases the process was deepened and the agenda was broadened. These developments clearly led to higher levels of intra-regional trade and investment, but this was not necessarily translated into the desired economic growth, poverty reduction and inequality reduction.

By the 2000s, these new organizations of 'open regionalism' that promoted above anything regional free trade of goods and services, showed signs of exhaustion and leftist coalitions came to power in many countries, seeking new national development strategies with a stronger social component (Bianculli 2010). The regional counterpart consisted of a new phase of regionalism, which has been labeled as post-hegemonic (Tussie and Riggirozzi 2012) or "post-liberal" regionalism (Sanahuja 2012), especially in South America. In fact, all regional integration efforts responded to political, social, and economic circumstances inherent to the regional context and were influenced by global tendencies of regional integration in the first decade of the twenty-first century (Dabène 2012): a rejection of competitive bilateralism of the USA and the poor fit of the European model to the new post-hegemonic realities, produced the ALBA-TCP (2004–2006), the CELAC (2010), and UNASUR (2004). Central American countries continued to sign bilateral FTAs, as well as the countries that more recently created the Pacific Alliance (2012) as a return to the open regionalism. However, recent developments in Southern America in the years 2016–2018, following political changes in Argentina and Brazil, have put these developments again in a different light.

The successive waves of regionalism have led to a complex landscape of regional integration and cooperation system systems, organizations and mechanisms which are often overlapping and sometimes even contradicting each other. This section provides a brief overview of a selection of regional arrangements in Latin America and looks at their (1) history and members, (2) institutions and mechanisms, (3) policy areas in which they are active and (4) limitations to the current framework and/or 'deeper' integration. By doing so, this section main message is to empirically show how multi-faceted and multi-layered the contemporary Latin American regional architecture is. This section is organized in two sub-sections, in compliance with the two major visions on regionalism in Latin America: i.e. hemispheric regionalism (i.e. spanning the whole continent) or quasi-hemispheric regionalism (i.e. Latin American, or Latin-American and Caribbean), on the one hand, and regionalism on a more '(sub-)regional' level (i.e. in Central America and/or South America and/or its subregions), on the other. Six regional organizations are described, Dabène (2009) and Garzón (2015) are both examples of sources that might offer a more comprehensive overview, with an historic perspective, of all regional organizations and integration systems in Latin America.

12.4.1   (Quasi-) Hemispheric Cooperation Projects (OAS – CELAC)

Latin America oscillates between (quasi-) hemispheric and sub-regional regionalism. In this section, we first present two instances of the former: the OAS and CELAC.

12.4.1.1 OAS

History and Members

The Organization of American States (OAS) is arguably the oldest regional organization in the American continent (Meyer 2018). It was founded in 1948 in Bogota, Colombia and signed by the United States and 20 Latin American nations to serve as a forum for addressing issues of mutual concern (OAS 2017). Over time, the organization expanded to include all 35 countries of the Western Hemisphere (also Canada). The main objective of the Organization, as stipulated in Article 1 of the Charter, is to achieve "an order of peace and justice, to promote their solidarity, to strengthen their collaboration, and to defend their sovereignty, their territorial integrity, and their independence" (OAS 2017: 1).

Institutions and Mechanisms

The OAS is composed of a variety of councils, committees, and other institutional organs, some of which are purely intergovernmental, others supranational in nature (Meyer 2018: 3–8). There are three primary bodies, however, that are responsible for setting and carrying out the agenda of the OAS: the General Assembly, the Permanent Council, and the General Secretariat. The General Assembly is the principal policymaking organ of the OAS. It meets annually to debate current issues, approve the organization's budget, and set policies to govern the other OAS bodies. The Permanent Council meets regularly throughout the year at the organization's headquarters in Washington, DC and runs the organization. The General Secretariat, directed by the Secretary-General and the Assistant Secretary-General, is the permanent body charged with implementing the policies set by the General Assembly and the Permanent Council. In addition to these three organs, the OAS also includes a juridical arm (the Inter-American Juridical committee and the Inter-American Commission on Human Rights) and various specialized, more thematically oriented, agencies such as the Pan American Health Organization, the Inter-American Commission of Women, The Inter-American Institute for Cooperation on Agriculture etc. (Meyer 2018: 3–8).

Policy Areas

The organization's areas of focus have also shifted over time, evolving in accordance with the priorities of its member states (Meyer 2018). Today, as detailed in the 2014 "Strategic Vision of the OAS", the OAS concentrates on four broad objectives: democracy promotion, human rights protection, economic and social development, and regional security cooperation (OAS 2014). It carries out a wide variety of activities to advance these goals, often providing policy guidance and technical assistance to member states (OAS 2014). In regards to democracy promotion, the

Inter-American Democratic Charter, signed in 2001, is particularly noteworthy (Cooper and Legler 2006). The charter asserts that the peoples of the Americas have a right to democracy and their governments have an obligation to promote and defend it (Meyer 2018). The OAS developed a set of instruments (including technical assistance, electoral observatory missions etc.) to ensure full compliance of its member states with this Charter. In the area of human rights protection, the Inter-American Court of Human Rights has been very active in promoting and protecting human rights in the Western Hemisphere. Advancing integral development is done by means of shared 'investment projects' and politico-economic policy convergence and dialogue. Finally, security cooperation mostly relates to fighting illicit drugs and related organized crime, as well as (home ground) terrorism.

Limitations

According to various foreign policy analysts, the dominant role of the United States within the OAS has been both the organizations' strength and major weakness (Meyer 2018). As the context of power asymmetry between the US and Latin American countries is increasingly reducing (because of economic growth, diversified commercial and diplomatic relations and/or global geopolitical trends), more and more Latin American countries argue(d) to move away from the OAS as the main hemispheric cooperation project in the political sphere and instead work through regional cooperation schemes such as CELAC which includes all of Latin America and the Caribbean but excludes the United States (and Canada).

12.4.1.2 CELAC

History and Members

CELAC was originally created after the third Latin America and Caribbean Summit on Integration and Development (CALC) held in Caracas, Venezuela (2011). It builds further on the Rio Group (1986), itself a further development of the Contadora Group (1983). It is one of the youngest regional institutions in Latin America. All Latin American (and Caribbean) countries are member of the organization, which has at its core objective to promote regional dialogue and cooperation with a balance between political, economical, social and cultural themes. CELAC can therefore best be seen as a forum for dialogue and consensus on non-institutionalized policies, and which, in stark contrast to the OAS or UNASUR (see below), does not have either a constitutive treaty nor does it constitute an international organization in stricto senso (Sanahuja et al. 2015: 32). Scholars have referred to CELAC as 'an experiment in revisionist multilateralism by Latin American countries', which seeks to construct a new (alternative) narrative of priorities embodied by the 2020 Agenda and the idea to replace the (US dominated) OAS (Sanahuja et al. 2015; Orozco et al. 2016).

Institutions and Mechanisms

CELAC main mechanism was the Troika, a group of three countries that led by Pro Tempore Presidency, exercised annually: Chile 2012, Cuba 2013, Costa Rica 2014, Ecuador 2015, Dominican Republic 2016 and El Salvador in 2017 (EU-LAC Foundation 2017). The troika became a quartet in 2013 that include the Pro Tempore Presidency, the previous Pro Tempore Presidency, the future Presidency Pro tempore and a representative of CARICOM. The Pro tempore Presidency supervises and organizes regular Summits of the Heads of State and Government, Meetings of Ministers of Foreign Affairs, Meetings of National Coordinators as well as specialized meetings and Extended Troika gatherings on a wide range of topics/policy areas. CELAC has no permanent secretary and works in an intergovernmental nature only: its declarations are non-binding and all decisions are adopted by consensus of all 33 member states.

Policy Areas

CELAC is active in a wide range of policy areas which covers several economic, social and environmental levels, science and technology and the management of the risk of disasters (Sanahuja 2015: 32). CELAC's agenda encompasses dialogues among 30 sectors and 21 thematic axes, as identified in the Costa Rica Action Plan for the CELAC Presidency in 2014, even though in most aspects the focus is on designing consensual agendas rather than defined (controversial) policies or initiatives (Sanahuja 2015: 32). According to the former president of Ecuador, Raphael Correa, CELAC currently focuses on the five following main topics (Correa 2016: 1–2): first, reducing extreme poverty and inequality: 68 million Latin American and Caribbean people live in destitution or extreme poverty. Second: CELAC needs to focus on collaboration in education, science, technology and innovation. Currently, the region invests 0.78% of GDP in research and development, CELAC aims to double this investment over the next 5 years, to increase it to at least 1.5 % of GDP by 2020. The third objective is related to the environment and climate change, as "failure to pay royalties for the use of patented products means prison" and "it is essential to declare climate change mitigation technologies global public goods and ensure that they are freely accessible". The fourth objective is financing for development, infrastructure and connectivity and the fifth objective relates to developing and enhancing 'our synergy' in which it is argued that the countries defend the same principles which need to be actively promoted and withheld in the entire region (Correa 2016: 1–2).

Limitations

Directly related to its young age, CELAC encounters difficulties regarding the (political) legitimacy/meaningfulness of its process and the credibility of its output. In fact, the lack of a permanent Secretary's office and the system of decision making by consensus have led to "the form of paralysis characteristic of zombie or minimum common denominator multilateralism" (Rinke and Schnekener 2012: 24) which CELAC has attempted to compensate through the proliferation of special declarations (28 so far) and plans of action that are impossible to all follow/execute (up to 30 in 2017). As CELAC was driven by the joint leadership of Mexico and Brazil (arguably also Venezuela), it remains to be seen what the impact will be of the recent political developments in these countries on the course of CELAC.

12.4.2 Sub-regional Integration and Cooperation Systems (SICA, CAN, MERCOSUR and UNASUR)

Next to the hemispheric or quasi-hemispheric schemes, Latin America counts several sub-regional cooperation or integration and cooperation groupings. We will present the three arguably historically most important cases (SICA, CAN, Mercosur), together with the recently created UNASUR. This means that a number of regional arrangements will not be discussed here. These are, first, the ones at the "borders" of Latin America: the North American Free Trade Area – NAFTA – created in 1991 (involving Mexico) and the Caribbean arrangements (CARICOM, created in 1973, and the Organization of Eastern Caribbean States, created in 1981). Other arrangements that will not be discussed include: the Amazon Cooperation Treaty Organization (ACTO), the Association of Caribbean States (ACS), ALBA, and the Pacific Alliance. The ACS is related to the idea of the "Greater Caribbean", based on common social, cultural and economic roots. The ACS focuses on cooperation, trade, transport, sustainable tourism and disaster management. ALBA is according to its manifesto an anti-imperialist and anti-capitalist initiative that strives for self-determination, autonomy and sovereignty of the American peoples, even if it also adopts a dose of pragmatism vis-à-vis the USA (Cusack 2018). ACTO was created in 1978 by Bolivia, Brazil, Colombia, Ecuador, Guyana, Peru, Surinam and Venezuela in order to protect the sovereignty of these countries in the Amazon region, protect the environment, and stimulate sustainable development. Finally, the Pacific Alliance was created in 2011 between Chile, Colombia, Mexico and Peru as a regional integration initiative to remove trade barriers and enable closer economic cooperation between these four founding members (Villareal 2016).

12.4.2.1 Central America: The Central American Integration System (SICA)

History and Members

Central America has a rich history in terms of regional cooperation and integration. As early as 1823, the countries of the Central American isthmus sought regional cooperation and integration, at the time by means of 'the United Provinces of Central America'. However, it was only in 1991, with the signing of the Tegucicalpa protocol, when the current SICA, or Central American Integration System, was created as we know it today. The initial members were most countries of the Central American isthmus: Costa Rica, El Salvador, Guatemala, Honduras and Nicaragua. In a later stage, Panama (1991), Belize (2000) and the Dominican Republic (2013) also joined SICA (Selleslaghs 2014).

Institutions and Mechanisms

The Central American Integration System is characterized by a high-level of institutionalization (Selleslaghs 2014: 10–12). The four most important Central American Regional Integration bodies as created by the Tegucigalpa protocol of December 1993 are the Summits of Central American Presidents, the Central American Court of Justice, the Central American Parliament (PARLACEN) and the Secretary of Central American Economic Integration (SIECA). The meeting of Presidents is for the Central American Regional Integration System the supreme organ where all presidents of the member states meet every 6 months and define the overall integration strategy and process. The SICA administration can be regarded as the spill for deeper regional integration and has the constitutive role to ensure the efficient execution of the decisions adopted in the Meetings of Presidents. Next to the General Secretariat (SG SICA), it consists of an executive committee (CE-SICA), a consultative committee (CC-SICA), the SIECA and more than hundred other secretariats and specialized institutions such as SECMCA, SCAC, SISCA, SITCA etc.[2]

Policy Areas

As a consequence of the vast amount of specialized institutions/regional organizations active in Central America's regional integration system, it seems that almost no policy area is left out of potential integration/regional cooperation efforts. As an indication, the official website of SICA's head secretariat (SG-SICA 2017) identifies not less than 43 "Integration topics" in which regional advances have been

---

[2] For a complete overview, start at the SICA (2017) "Homepage" [online] accessible at http://www.sica.int/

made. These topics include Foreign Relations and Security Issues, Social Policy, Public Health, Housing, Fishing and Aquiculture, Air Navigation, Micro and Small Enterprise, Telecommunications, Water Resources, University Education etc.

Limitations

The Central American Integration Systems runs into different limitations and challenges, not the least on an institutional level, but there is also a lack of high-level political will for further (political) integration as there are still various inter-state conflicts that block or at least hamper deeper integration (Selleslaghs 2014). As was briefly noted above, there exist a wide variety of institutional bodies and organizations. In fact, no one really knows how many Central American regional organizations and secretariats really exist, estimates go from 42 up to 100, which is seen by many scholars as well as policy makers as a sign of institutional naivety at best, bureaucratic perversity at worst (SICA 2017; Selleslaghs 2014). Yet, most (institutional) criticism is directed towards a particular institution: the Central American Parliament (PARLACEN) as its democratic legitimacy is challenged by many.

12.4.2.2 South America: Andean Community (CAN)

History and Members

The Andean Community (CAN) was first established in 1969 by all members of the Andean region (Venezuela, Colombia, Ecuador, Peru and Bolivia). First created under the name of 'the Andean Pact', it had the ambition to establish considerable regional integration in the Andean region, inspired by he European Union. In 1996, with the signing of the Trujillo Protocol, the Andean Pact was upgraded into the the Andean Community under which the 'Andean Integration System (AIS) with the various institutions as listed below were created. However, over the last decades, several countries decided to change their membership status of this organization (notably Chile, Venezuela and –potentially-Ecuador).

Institutions and Mechanisms

Various regional institutions and official bodies have been created over time in the Andean region. These institutions are both intergovernmental as well as supranational (community-like) in nature. Currently, the main intergovernmental institutions are the Andean Presidential Council (APC), which is the highest level official body, the Andean Council of Foreign Ministers (ACFM), and the Commission of the Andean Community (Communidad Andina 2017). The APC is composed of the Presidents of each member state and has an annual rotating presidency. The Commission is made up of the member states' ministers of trade. In addition, the

CAN is also composed of a General Secretariat (with headquarters in Lima, Peru) and an Andean Community Court of Justice (Quito, Ecuador). The General Secretariat, and more specifically its Secretary-General is the 'driver' of Andean integration (Communidad Andina 2017).

Policy Areas

CAN consists of 27 (official) thematic committees and ad hoc groups that cover a wide array of policy areas. Whereas CAN's initial focus was on economic integration and the creation of a customs union/unified economic market, over the years it shifted to focus more on policy convergence on socio-developmental and political themes such as human rights, natural disasters, education, health care, culture, telecommunications, support for SME's and tourism (Communidad Andina 2017).

Limitations

After more than four decades now, it has been argued that the Andean nations engaged in the process of regional integration more rhetorically than through concerted action (Malamud 2013). In fact, as identified by many scholars analyzing the Andean Integration system, the implementation of agreements and action plans has been insufficient due to a variety of reasons ranging from the institutional weaknesses, over the lack of incentives to deepen regional integration, to the existence of different opinions in regards to (national) development plans and economic approaches which do not match on a regional level (Laugier 2014; Dominguez 2015). The withdrawal of Venezuela from CAN in 2006, the creation of ALBA, the clash of economic and political projects between Peru and Colombia on one side and Bolivia and Ecuador on the other, the establishment of the Pacific Alliance as well as the Bolivian submission of the incorporation protocol as a member of Mercosur (see below) have produced not only considerable setbacks for the CAN regional integration system but have also led to –persistent- existential questioning of the regionalist efforts in this particular area of South America (Malamud 2008). In fact, voices for a 'new design of regional integration in the South American space' have become more apparent as limitations to CAN became more visible with the turn of the century (Dominguez 2015).

12.4.2.3   The Southern Common Market (MERCOSUR)

History and Members

Mercosur, also known as MERCOSUL in Portuguese (acronym of Mercado Comun del Sur, Common Market of the South) is a regional integration scheme established in 1991 under the treaty of Asuncion. Essentially economic in nature, it were especially Brazil and Argentina who wanted to create a regional common market in order to stimulate their (national) economies by means of larger intra-regional trade flows amongst the constituting members and a better integration in the international market (Mercosur 2019). MERCOSUR was originally composed of four countries: Argentina, Brazil, Paraguay and Uruguay. In a later stage, Venezuela (2012) and Bolivia (2016) joined the integration scheme as well.[3]

Institutions and Mechanisms

Mercosur has a largely intergovernmental DNA, with the The Common Market Council (CMC), composed of the constituting member states' presidents, as its main decision making body. In addition, Mercosur is composed of a Common Market Group (composed of the ministries of Foreign Affairs), the Mercosur Trade Commission, a General Secretariat (headquarters in Montevideo, Uruguay), an Economic and Social Consultative Forum, a Joint Parliamentary Commission, a Permanent Review Court and an Administrative Labour Court (see Pena and Rozemberg 2005 for full descriptions). Decisions are made on a consensual basis.

Policy Areas

From the onset of its creation, the scheme's principle objective was "to promote a common economic space that would generate trade and investment opportunities through the competitive integration of national economies into the international market" (Mercosur 2017:1). Yet, overtime, Mercosur's activity range expanded to cover other policy areas as well, including nuclear non-proliferation, cooperation in the area of higher education, science and technology, energy (especially bio-fuels), migration, the fight against drugs, related organized crime, social policy and the integration of production (Mercosur 2017).

Limitations

The challenges Mercosur faces are mostly of an institutional and political nature (Meissner 2016). In fact, Mercosur depends highly on (the relationship between) two of its core member states: Argentina and Brazil. As these two countries (and their relationship) are characterized by recurrent tension and (economic) instability, so is the Mercosur regional integration process. In addition, Mercosur's 'commu-

---

[3]Venezuela was temporarily suspended from MERCOSUR's membership in December 2016 for failing to comply with membership requirements, in particular the incorporation of several Mercosur decisions and norms into Venezuelan legislation. In April 2017 the Mercosur Democratic Clause was activated due to the Venezuelan Supreme Court's decision to suspend the powers of the National Assembly further limiting participation of Venezuela in the MERCOSUR system.

nity' legislation is only limited implemented at the national and domestic level, as argued by Doctor (2013).

12.4.2.4 The Union of South American Nations (UNASUR)

History and Members

UNASUR is a relatively new regional organization in which the countries of CAN, Mercosur as well as Chile, Guyana and Suriname are seated. It was officially launched by the 12 constituting Southern American nations in May 2008 and has as its core objective to "prioritize political dialogue, social policies, education, energy, infrastructure, financing and the environment, with a view to eliminating socio-economic inequality in South America" (Cancilleria 2018:1). But while Mercosur represents only five South American countries (Argentina, Brazil, Uruguay, Paraguay and Venezuela), UNASUR with twelve, aims to unite the whole Southern Western hemisphere. Just as importantly, UNASUR sets aside any attempt at economic integration –the area in which Mercosur arguably came short– and is merely oriented towards creating a sort of a shared –regional- political identity at the world stage (Riggirozzi and Grugel 2015).

Institutions and Mechanisms

UNASUR is an intergovernmental organization with no supranational institutions (Nolte and Comini 2016). Yet, it has a General Secretariat, based in Ecuador, which prepares and follows up the working of the 12 'Sectorial Councils' and as such covers a large variety of issue areas. Some authors argue that the system of Sectorial Councils is conducive to a "variable geometry" of integration and to cooperative regional governance (Nolte 2014). In addition to the permanent secretariat and sectorial councils, UNASUR's supreme bodies are the Council of Heads of State and Government and the Council of Ministers of Foreign Affairs. In addition, a Council of Delegates, 4 Specialized Working Groups (Natural Disasters, Settlement of Disputes in Investments, South American Citizenship) and a Citizen Participation Forum are also part of the UNASUR institutional set-up. Within UNASUR, the focus is on consensual political cooperation, sovereignty of its Member States and selective cooperation by the member countries in areas of common interest (without the obligation to participate in all areas) (Nolte 2014: 23).

Policy Areas

UNASUR is a regional governance project based not on economic integration but on social policies, political cooperation and a defence of democracy (Riggirozzi and Grugel 2015). A concrete example of the latter are its activities related to elections:

UNASUR has an electoral council and regularly organizes electoral missions to exchange information and continuous improvement of the member states' electoral processes and establish cooperation between electoral bodies. Of the twelve sectorial councils, the following three are the most well-known and active ones: South American Defense Council; South American Council of Education; South American Council on Health; South American Council on the World Drug Problem and the South American Council of Infrastructure and Planning (COSIPLAN and its technical forum "IIRSA") (Cienfuegos and Sanahuja 2010).

Limitations

The most important potential limitation UNASUR faces is the difficulty in regards to potential overlap/conflict with other regional governance schemes in South America. UNASUR was initially seen as an umbrella organization under which both Mercosur and CAN could come together, along with countries in South America not represented by either of these two regional entities, but its role was limited (Pimenta and Arantes 2014). Brazil, which was the initiator of both MERCOSUR and UNASUR, claims that it is possible for the different organizations to be complementary to each other, but it is a difficult balance to maintain. Yet, (other) scholars have recently demonstrated that the institutional structure of UNASUR is not the result of some distorted design or organizational defect (Nolte and Comini 2016). Instead, it responds to "the – sometimes contradictory – interests of the organization's designers" and "UNASUR is not merely another instance of institutional chaos or another piece of spaghetti in the bowl, but rather the result of a conscious decision to add a further layer to the institutional architecture of South America" (Nolte 2016: 4). In addition, as is rightly observed by various scholars and commentators, UNASUR is above anything a political organization in which various countries with the same (rather left-winged, in contrast to the more right-winged CELAC and/or Pacific Alliance) political and economical affiliation could find eachother to collaborate on issues of regional governance, it remains yet to be seen what would be the future of such a regional cooperation scheme once governments change and (even 'light') regime changes happen. It will be telling in this regard what the more pragmatic and (more rightwinged) centrist new president of Ecuador (Lenin) position will be on UNASUR, the country that hosts its headquarters.

12.5   Concluding Remarks: The Future of Latin American Regionalism

This chapter provided an overview of how regionalism has been defined and shaped in Latin America over time. As became clear from this chapter, regionalism in Latin America has not converged in a single initiative or towards one dominant integration system (also see Bianculli 2010, 2016). In fact, different regionalist moves or "waves" and a complex set of both endogenous and exogenous factors have led to a proliferation of different regional organizations with overlapping memberships, geographic reaches and governance agendas. Regionalism in Latin America can therefore probably best be labeled as eclectic, multi-faceted and multi-layered.

Whether the overlapping of regional organizations is harmful or beneficial ultimately depends on what the involved actors make out of it (Nolte and Comini 2016: 561). In this context, each Latin American actor seems to choose the regionalist governance model that best fits its own national interests (regionalism "à la carte"). However, pundits like Laura Gomez Mera have a different approach to the issue. For them, the proliferation of regional schemes, especially in the field of economic integration, "could encourage self-interested behavior and competition among actors and regimes, ultimately undermining the success of cooperative initiatives (Gomez-Mera 2015: 20) The overlapping of regional schemes and institutions could as a consequence lead to cross-institutional political strategies such as "forum shopping", "regime shifting" or "strategic inconsistency" that has the potential to erode interregional unity and cohesion (Gomez-Mera 2015).

Various scholars also argue that the Latin American regional architecture will likely stay multifaceted and multilayered:" the trend may be not towards amalgamation or a single converged regional bloc, but towards greater diversity of hybrids with mutually fuzzy boundaries, arranging component pieces in ever new combinations underpinned by increasingly intense regional relations" (Tussie 2009:185–186). However, more pessimistic observers argue that "the presence of segmented and overlapping regionalist projects is not a manifestation of successful integration but, on the contrary, signals the exhaustion of its potential" (Malamud and Gardini 2012: 117). For them, regionalism in Latin America should be understood as 'little more than a series of disappointments' (Malamud and Gardini 2012). Various scenarios for the future of Latin American regionalism lay thus open. These scenarios are characterized by a more or less fragmented region, more or less institutionalized forms of regionalism, more or less effective institutions, more or less regional mobilization of resources, compatible with more or less government intervention in the economy, showing more or less external political actorness of the region, etc. Rather than attaching probabilities to the distinct scenarios, let us have a look at some of the driving forces that are shaping and will likely shape the future of regionalism in Latin America. These drivers are both exogenous and endogenous.

As regards the exogenous drivers, these have been present all along the history of Latin American regionalism. The end of the Cold War and the increasing integration and globalization in the 1990s, for example, are usually portrayed as the dividing line between the 'old' and the 'new' regionalism (Bianculli 2010). Thus, as Bianculli (2010:4) explains: "whereas the 'old' regionalism of the 1960s and 1970s was a devise to promote industrialization through high tariffs and protectionist measures and thus reduce dependency on the international economy, the new regional schemes were part and parcel of the effort to open national and regional markets in response to the accelerated transnationalization of trade and production processes". Today, other exogenous factors might lead to new types of regionalism, including the shift of economic gravity towards Asia-Pacific, the rise of China (also in Latin America), the emergence of a new security agenda and political changes in key countries such as the USA, UK etc. Even if the EU will no longer be seen as a global integration model due to Brexit, it is likely that it will continue to be available as a partner in regional cooperation projects and, even more importantly, that it will continue to be a potential counterpart for inter-regional dialogue, given the multiple coinciding policy preferences that exist between the two regions, if e.g. South America strengthens its extra-regional actorness. The de facto diversification of its external economic relations is a contributing factor in this respect.

Indeed, the increased importance of Asia-Pacific, and especially China, in Latin America's external economic relations strengthens its negotiation position vis-à-vis the US and the EU, even if these markets will continue to be important over the coming years. Diversification of exports reduces the vulnerability of the Latin America, certainly if China and India continue to show high growth rates as they currently do (ECLAC 2016). However, the expansion of trade with China has also led to a re-'primarization' of the exports of the region and thus more vulnerability (Sanahuja 2015). This might well lead to renewed calls for industrial and technological policies and intra-regional economic cooperation and integration.

Endogenous factors include the difficult economic situation the region is going through, with overall average negative growth rates for South America over the last couple of years (notably 2015–2016) (ECLAC 2016). At the same time, the divergence between the performances between South America, on the one hand, and Central America/Mexico, on the other, points to structural differences between the respective sub-regions, making regionalism at the hemispheric scale less straightforward. The speed and strength of economic recovery will also be an important factor in predicting political stability in the region. It remains to be seen how political cycles and events will play out in South America, especially in key countries like Brazil, Argentina and Venezuela, and their impact on developments in Mercosur, UNASUR, CELAC and potentially new regionalist schemes.

Further Readings

Malamud, A., & Gardini, G. L. (2012). Has regionalism peaked? The Latin American quagmire and its lessons. *The International Spectator, 47*(1), 116–133.

Nolte, D. (2014). *Latin America's new regional architecture: A cooperative or segmented regional governance complex?* Robert Schuman Centre for Advanced Studies Research Paper, RSCAS 2014/89, 34p.

Vivares, E., & Dolcetti-Marcolini, M. (2016). Two regionalisms, two Latin Americas or beyond Latin America? Contributions from a critical and decolonial IPE. *Third World Quarterly, 37*(5), 866–882.

References

Bianculli, A. C. (2010). *Trade governance in Latin America. Interest articulation and institutions across negotiations in Argentina and Chile.* Doctoral dissertation, Universitat Pompeu Fabra, 370p.

Bianculli, A. C. (2016). Latin America. In T. A. Börzel (Ed.), *The Oxford handbook of comparative regionalism* (pp. 154–178). Oxford: Oxford University Press.

Briceño Ruiz, J. (2014). Los congresos hispanoamericanos en el siglo XIX: identidad, amenazas externas e intereses en la construcción del regionalismo. *Revista de Relaciones Internacionales de la UNAM, 118,* 131–170.

Cancilleria. (2018). *Union of South American Nations, UNASUR* [online]. Available https://www.cancilleria.gob.ec/union-of-south-american-nations-unasur/. Accessed 13 Oct 2018.

Cienfuegos, M., & Sanahuja, J. A. (2010). Una región en construcción: UNASUR y la integración en América del Sur. *CIDOB,* Barcelona, 412p.

Communidad Andina. (2017). *Portal de la Comunidad Andina.* Accessible at http://www.comunidadandina.org

Cooper, A., & Legler, T. (2006). *Intervention without intervening?: The OAS defense and promotion of democracy in the Americas.* New York: Palgrave Macmillan.

Correa, R. (2016). *Correa outlines CELAC priorities* [online]. Available https://videosenglish.telesurtv.net/video/344215/correa-outlines-celac-priorities/aspx. Accessed 13 Jan 2018.

Chasteen, J. (2008). *Americanos: Latin America's struggle for Independence.* Oxford: Oxford University Press, 240p.

Cusack, A. (2018). *Understanding ALBA: The Progress, problems, and prospects of alternative regionalism in Latin America and the Caribbean.* Brookings Institution Press.

Dabène, O. (2009). *The politics of regional integration in Latin America: Theoretical and comparative explorations* (258p). Basingstoke: Palgrave.

Dabène, O. (2012). *La gauche en Amérique latine, 1998–2012* (464p). Paris: Presses de Sciences Po.

De Lombaerde, P., & Garay, L. J. (2008). El nuevo regionalismo en América Latina. In P. De Lombaerde, S. Kochi, & J. Briceño Ruíz (Eds.), *Del regionalismo latinoamericano a la integración interregional* (pp. 3–35). Madrid: Fundación Carolina – Siglo XXI.

De Lombaerde, P., & Schulz, M. (Eds.). (2009). *The EU and world regionalism: The makability of regions in the 21st century* (297p). Surrey: Ashgate Publishing, Ltd.

Doctor, M. (2013). Why bother with inter-regionalism? Negotiations for a European Union – Mercosur agreement. *Journal of Common Market Studies, 45*(2), 281–314.

Dominguez, R. (2015). *EU foreign policy towards Latin America* (185p). New York: Springer.

ECLAC. (2016). *Preliminary overview of the economies of Latin America and the Caribbean* (133p). Santiago de Chile: ECLAC.

EULAC Foundation. (2017). *The Carribbean in the European Union- Community of Latin American and Caribbean States Partnership* (126p). Hamburg.

Fawcett, L., & Serrano, M. (Eds.). (2005). *Regionalism and governance in the Americas: Continental drift* (284p). New York: Springer.

Garzón, J. F. (2015) *Multipolarity and the future of regionalism: Latin America and beyond* (GIGA Working Papers, No. 264, 34p).

Glickhouse, R. (2012). *Explainer: An alphabet soup of regional integration organizations* [online]. Available at http://www.as-coa.org/articles/explainer-alphabet-soup-regional-integration-organizations/. Accessed 13 Jan 2018.

Gomez-Mera, L. (2015). International regime complexity and regional governance: Evidence from the Americas. *Global Governance, 21,* 19–42.

Hurrell, A. (1995). Explaining the resurgence of regionalism in world politics. *Review of International Studies, 21,* 331–358.

Khazeh, K., & Clark, D. P. (1990). A case study of effects of developing country integration on trade flows: The Andean pact. *Journal of Latin American Studies, 22*(1–2), 317–330.

Laugier, G. P. (2014). Presentacion en el Cuadragésimo Quinto aniversario de suscripcion del Acuerdo de Cartagena, Lima, 4p.

Malamud, A. (2008). *The internal agenda of Mercosur: Interdependence, leadership and institutionalization. Los nuevos enfoques de la integración: más allá del regionalismo* (pp. 115–135). Quito: FLACSO.

Malamud, A. (2013). *Overlapping regionalism, no integration: Conceptual issues and the Latin American experiences* (EUI Working Papers RSCAS, pp. 1–12).

Malamud, A., & Gardini, G. L. (2012). Has regionalism peaked? The Latin American quagmire and its lessons. *The International Spectator, 47*(1), 116–133.

Manzetti, L. (1993a). The political economy of privatization through divestiture in lesser developed economies. *Comparative Politics, 25*, 429–454.

Manzetti, L. (1993b). *Institutions, parties, and coalitions in Argentine politics* (382p). University of Pittsburgh Press.

McCrossan, P. (2015). *The political economy of EU interregionalism*. Doctoral dissertation, Dublin City University, 274p.

Meissner, K. (2016). Interregionalism re-loaded: Assessing the EU-MERCOSUR negotiations. *St Antony's International Review, 11*(2), 95–120.

Mercosur. (2017). *Mercosur in brief*. Online accessible at: https://www.mercosur.int/en/about-mercosur/mercosur-in-brief/

Mercosur. (2019). *Mercosur in brief*. Online accessible at: https://www.mercosur.int/en/about-mercosur/mercosur-in-brief/

Meyer, P. J. (2018). *Organization of American States: Background and issues for Congress* (27p). Washington, DC: Congressional Research Service.

Moncayo, E., De Lombaerde, P., & Guinea Ibáñez, O. (2012). Latin American regionalism and the role of UN-ECLAC, 1948-2010. In C. Auroi & M. Helg (Eds.), *Latin America 1810–2010. Dreams and legacies* (pp. 359–386). London: Imperial College Press.

Nolte, D. (2014). Latin America's new regional architecture: a cooperative or segmented regional governance complex?. Robert Schuman Centre for Advanced Studies Research Paper, RSCAS 2014/89, 34p.

Nolte, D. (2016). The Pacific Alliance: Nation-branding through regional Organisations. *GIGA Focus Lateinamerika, 04*, 13p.

Nolte, D., & Comini, N. (2016). UNASUR: Regional pluralism as a strategic outcome. *Contexto International, 38*(2), 545–565.

OAS. (2014). Resolution on strategic vision with a view to adapting the organization to the challenges of the 21st century. E-370/14, Washington, DC, 3p.

OAS. (2017). *Who we are* [online]. Available http://www.oas.org/en/about/who_we_are.asp. Accessed 13 Jan 2018.

O'Keefe, T. A. (1996). How the Andean pact transformed itself into a friend of foreign enterprise. *International Law, 30*, 811–823.

Orozco, G., Dominguez, R., & Carrera, M. (2016). *The matrix of regional governance in Latin America* (12p). Academia.edu.

Pena, C., & Rozemberg, R. (2005). *Una aproximación al desarrollo institucional del MERCOSUR: sus fortalezas y debilidades* (Occasional Paper ITD= Documento de Divulgación ITD; n. 31) (Vol. 31). BID-INTAL.

Perales, J. R. (2003). A supply-side theory of international economic institutions for the Mercosur. In F. Laursen (Ed.), *Comparative regional integration. Theoretical perspectives* (pp. 75–101). Aldershot: Ashgate.

Pimenta, G. F., & Arantes, P. C. (2014). *Rethinking integration in Latin America: The "Pink tide" and the post-neoliberal regionalism*. FLASCO-ISA joint international conference, 20p.

Puntigliano, A. R., & Briceño-Ruiz, J. (Eds.). (2013). *The resilience of regionalism in Latin America* (Autonomy and development, 273p) New York: Springer.

Rettberg, A., De Lombaerde, P., Lizarazo Rodríguez, L. and Ortiz-Riomalo, J. (2014). *Rights, free trade, and politics: The strategic use of a rights discourse in the negotiation of free trade agree-*

ments (FTAs). Available at HYPERLINK https://doi.org/10.2139/ssrn.2428668. Accessed 8 June 2019. [online].

Riggirozzi, P., & Grugel, J. (2015). Regional governance and legitimacy in South America: The meaning of UNASUR. *International Affairs, 91*(4), 781–797.

Rinke, B. y Scheneckener, U. (2012). Informalisation of world politics? Global governance by clubs. In T. Debiel, et al. (Eds.), *Global trends 2013. Peace, development, enviroment* (pp. 21–35). Bonn: Development and Peace Foundation.

Rosenthal, G. (1991). Un Informe Crítico a 30 años de Integración en América Latina. *Nueva Sociedad, 113*, 60–65.

Saad-Filho, A., & Johnston, D. (2005). *Neoliberalism: A critical reader* (268p). Chicago: University of Chicago Press.

Sanahuja, J. A. (2012). *Regionalismo post-liberal y multilateralismo en Sudamérica: El caso de UNASUR*. Anuario de Integración Regional de América Latina y el Caribe, pp. 19–72.

Sanahuja, J. A. (2015). *The EU and CELAC: Reinvigorating a strategic partnership*. Hamburg: EU-LAC Foundation, 85p.

Sanahuja, J. A., et al. (2015). *Beyond 2015: Perspectives and proposals for development cooperation between the European Union and Latin America and the Caribbean* (134p). Hamburg: EU-LAC Foundation.

Selleslaghs, J. (2014). *The EU's role and interest in promoting regional integration in Central America* (30p). Bruges: UNU-CRIS.

SG-SICA. (2017). *SG-SICA en Breve* [online]. Available https://www.sica.int/sgsica/sgsica_breve. aspx. Accessed 13 Jan 2018.

SICA. (2017). *Instancias regionals del SICA* [online]. Available https://www.sica.int/sica/instituciones.aspx. Accessed 13 Jan 2018.

Tussie, D. (2009). Latin America: Contrasting motivations for regional projects. *Review of International Studies, 35*(S1), 169–188.

Tussie, D. & Riggirozzi, P. (2012). *The rise of post-hegemonic regionalism. The case of Latin America* (203p). Dordrecht: Springer.

Villareal, M. A. (2016). The Pacific Alliance: A trade integration initiative in Latin America. In *Congressional research service* (pp. 7–5700).

Vivares, E., & Dolcetti-Marcolini, M. (2016). Two regionalisms, two Latin Americas or beyond Latin America? Contributions from a critical and decolonial IPE. *Third World Quarterly, 37*(5), 866–882.

Chapter 13
An Analysis of Regional Integration in South Asia

Indraneel Baruah

13.1 Introduction[1]

There is an inherent paradox when discussing South-Asia as a region, which is widely considered as one of the least integrated regions on the planet. As per statistics of the World Bank, in economic terms, South Asia is the fastest growing region in the world, but at the same time the least integrated. In other words, South Asian countries are witnessing rapid economic growth individually, whereas as a region, it languishes. This trajectory is due to hostility, and lack of mutual trust amidst countries within the region. More on this in the proceeding sections of this chapter, which seeks to reveal why this is the case, and how regional integration might be materialised in South Asia. Most notably, one factor which is crucial for the integration of almost any region is the cooperation between the two key regional players. Part II of this edited volume specifically focuses on regions, regional organisations, and regional integration in general, and sheds light on regional processes across the globe. Preceding chapters have asserted that one of the principal 'shifts' in today's changing global order is one towards regions, as the IR world is steadily moving towards multipolarity, from American unipolarity after the Cold War. Consequently, this led scholars and commentators to postulate we are now moving towards a 'world of regions' (Acharya 2007, 2014a, b; Acharya and

[1] Harsh V. Pant helped refine this chapter by providing an insightful review, who is professor of International Relations in the Defence Studies Department, and the India Institute at King's College London. He is Non-Resident Fellow for the US-India Policy Studies at the Center for Strategic and International Studies, Washington, DC. This chapter draws modestly from the MSc thesis: Baruah, I. (2016). An Analysis of South Asia in Light of Regional Integration: An investigation of the conflict in Kashmir and prospects for international mediation, thesis, The Hague, viewed on 2 July 2018, Leiden University Thesis Repository.

I. Baruah (✉)
Faculty of Governance and Global Affairs, Leiden University, The Hague, The Netherlands
e-mail: I.Baruah16@gmail.com

© Springer Nature Switzerland AG 2020
M. O. Hosli, J. Selleslaghs (eds.), *The Changing Global Order*, United Nations University Series on Regionalism 17,
https://doi.org/10.1007/978-3-030-21603-0_13

Johnston 2007; Katzenstein 2005). Additionally, major players like China, and Russia are assertively working to strengthen control in their respective regions, as Chaps. 4 and 5 have demonstrated. Moreover, international trade blocs such as BRICs, FTAs involving the EU, and regional sub-systems within a region (for e.g. MERCOSUR, and BIMSTEC, SASEC in the context of South Asia) have also come to the fore of scholarly and practical attention.

The current chapter analyses regional integration in South Asia, and utilises: a) the regional organisation, i.e. the South Asian Association for Regional Cooperation (SAARC); and b) sub-regional systems or organisations, i.e. BIMSTEC (Bay of Bengal Initiative for Multi-Sectoral Technical and Economic Cooperation) and SASEC (South Asia Subregional Economic Cooperation) for analysis. As the forthcoming paragraphs indicate, South Asia as a region is far from integration. It can be argued that regional members are experiencing a challenging time in materialising, or rather maintaining regional cooperation to begin with. The role of India in the region is imperative, as is the relationship between the regional powers India and Pakistan. The conflict in Kashmir has led to consistent tensions between the regional powers, and have ultimately played a major role in impeding regional cooperation, and integration in South Asia. Another notable aspect is the limitations of the power asymmetry and superior resources of India within the region. Despite being the most powerful state in the region, at least in the traditional realms of military and economic power or hard power, New Delhi faces persistent challenges to unilaterally take the lead in South Asian regional integration. This sheds light on the importance of soft and smart power in the current era of the information age, where the better or more attractive 'story' or 'narrative' as percieved by the wider world prevails. Furthermore, as the name of the regional organisation itself suggests, the institution was established with the very purpose of 'regional cooperation'. It has also been revealed previously in this volume and elsewhere that regional cooperation is characterised by the cooperation amidst states within a region in specific policy areas of mutual concern. Furthermore, cooperation can be assessed as a step towards regional integration, which is the goal or end-result of the wider process of regionalism.[2] In addition, recent developments such as the role of external actors, such as China's involvement within the region, bilateral relations between China and Pakistan, the involvement of the United States and its complex and changing policies towards India and Pakistan further complicate the overall regional scenario in South Asia. Furthermore, Afghanistan being a part of South Asia, along with Pakistan are sensitive areas in terms of security and terrorism, which is yet another significant issue inhibiting regionalism (also the complex bilateral dynam-

---

[2] Integral conceptualisations have been established in the early years of the scholarly pursuit of the study of regions. For a representative agenda of topics and articles illustrating the rubrics of competing, overlapping and cognate terms such as regionalism, regional cooperation, regional organisation, regional movements, regional systems, etc., see Nye, JS Jr. 1968, International Regionalism: Readings, Boston: Little, Brown and Co. See also, Haas, E. (1970). The Study of Regional Integration: Reflections on the Joy and Anguish of Pretheorizing. *International Organization*, 24(4), 607-646.

ics between Pakistan and Afghanistan). Evidently, South Asia as a region is quite complex, which demands attention owing to its developmental potential, and because it's the most populated region on the planet.

In terms of a theoretical framework for studying regions, this chapter will acknowledge the relevance, as well as challenge the validity of mainstream (mainly positivist) schools of IR theory. Furthermore, it will propose a holistic theoretical approach to study regional integration in South-Asia, and other regions in general. This can be labelled as "analytical eclecticism", which essentially supplements the theoretical framework by allowing, or enabling theories from multiple schools of IR thought (more on this in the forthcoming sections). Clearly, there are several forces, or elements from the three major schools (and sub-schools) of IR at play in South Asia. Although realism and liberalism have been demonstrated as singularly lacking salience in analysing the region, one cannot argue about their relevance in IR. Constructivism is also clearly at play, as identities, norms, values, religion, etc. occupy a dominant position in South Asian regional politics. It is also useful to note that theories have their pros and cons, and the wiser option seems to select the relevant aspects of all and combine them in a smart power strategy. In other words, how do the IR theories consisting of Realism, Liberalism and Constructivism roughly correspond with a "smart power" strategy? Smart power can be broadly defined as a strategy that selectively combines elements of hard and soft power to attain policy objectives (Nye 2009, p.160–163). Individually, soft power is the power of attraction, the likeable qualities of a nation or entity, the moral authority of a nation's foreign policy, and the crucial characteristic of being liked and respected by (most) members of the international community (Nye 1990, 2008; Tharoor 2012). Hard power pertains to the military or economic strength of a nation, and focuses solely on the coercive or authoritative utility of power. Singularly, more often than not, neither is able to effectively attain desired policy objectives in a salient manner.

As this chapter aims to demonstrate, the investigation of SAARC by re-approaching the phenomenon of regional integration can reveal important lessons for other regions, and the concept of regional integration. In other words, SAARC can be positioned as a unique model for regionalism and regional integration, based on which other regions and regional organisations can draw insights from. Outright hostility, or lack of cooperation and trust between key regional players severely impedes regional integration. This is a generalisable observation, with evidence from theory and practice. For example, bilateral tensions between Brazil and Argentina led to the creation of additional overlapping institutions in Latin America, further complicating the regional scenario (see Chap. 12). In addition, any serious discussion in Europe about an exit by either France or Germany undoubtedly raises tensions in Brussels. Essentially, the relations between the two regional powers are fundamental for regional integration. The current chapter aims to substantiate the main hypothesis about regional integration, which can be stated in more than one way. For instance, regional power rivalry, or lack of cooperation between key regional players severely impedes regional integration. It can also be derived that for regional integration to materialise, cooperation between key regional players is vital.

Or, only after initial cooperation and reciprocal committment between key regional players within a region, does incremental cooperation, and integration efforts lead to fruition. A crucial element of the above hypothesis is the partnership between key regional players. Again, it is extremely difficult to imagine the EU project, without the cooperation between the continental powers of France and Germany. Or a peaceful Scandinavia back in the day, during the antagonistic periods between Sweden and Denmark. Contrastingly, in South-Asia, the lack of cooperation between India and Pakistan seems to have impeded regional integration, and severely handicapped the process at its very roots. Thus, an argument can be made that manifesting cooperation between the regional powers may lead to regional integration of South Asia. But for this to happen, the resolution of the Kashmir conflict is key. Nevertheless, in lieu of the past and present dynamics in Kashmir, as well as the overall nature of bilateral relations between the regional powers, South Asia as a region is highly unlikely to witness integration, at least anytime soon. Consequently, sub-regional organisations such as SASEC and BIMSTEC have gained attention.

The structure of this chapter is as follows: The introduction presented an overall outline of the chapter's content. The first section briefly outlines the concept of regional integration, and evaluates the South-Asian region. It also outlines the theoretical framework within the tenets of international relations theory, which guides this study. The second section will briefly address the Kashmir conflict, which is a root cause of the hostility between India and Pakistan. The next section compares other regions across the globe such as Europe, North America, and South East Asia with South-Asia, whilst utilising similar factors (or independent variables). The fourth section sheds light on sub-regional organisations, i.e. SASEC and BIMSTEC. The fifth and final section examines the pre-requisites of regional integration in South-Asia, and draws conclusions.

13.2   Concept of Regional Integration and its Application in South Asia

The concept of regional integration has been addressed in sufficient detail in preceding chapters, most notably in Chaps. 8, 9, and 12. Therefore, to avoid repetition, this chapter shall refrain from delving into too much detail about the conceptual particularities. Whilst studying regions in general, semantic issues spark up and debates ensue as to what consists of a region, how regional boundaries are drawn up, and how regions are operationalised.[3] In general, regions can be conceptualised as a "cluster of states that are proximate to each other and are interconnected in spatial, cultural, and ideational terms in a significant and distinguishable manner" (Paul 2012, p.4). It is useful to note the geographical element is crucial in this definition. Another key element which has been deemed relevant to study regions is the distinct

---

[3] For a clearer and broader perspective on regions, see for instance, Van Langenhove, L. (2013) Building Regions.

institutional forms manifest in a region (Katzenstein 2005, p.12). Nevertheless, such problems pertaining to what constitutes a region, and the definition of regional boundaries is avoided whilst evaluating South-Asia. This is mainly because the borders of the South-Asian region have been established with the conception of the regional organisation SAARC. Therefore, South-Asia comprises of its eight constituent states: Afghanistan, Bangladesh, Bhutan, India, Nepal, Maldives, Pakistan, and Sri Lanka.

13.2.1 Theoretical Framework

It is extremely difficult, if not impossible for one, or two different theoretical tenets of IR to effectively evaluate regional processes. In other words, neither of the three main schools of IR thought, i.e. realism, liberalism, and constructivism (and their sub-schools) singularly lack adequate salience in addressing regional integration, especially in the South Asian context. Therefore, theoretical innovation is vital, which is also the primary divergence from the extant literature currently available on South Asian regionalism. Thus, in terms of a theoretical framework for studying regions, this chapter advocates a holistic theoretical approach to study regional integration, i.e. "analytical eclecticism", which essentially supplements the theoretical framework by allowing theories from multiple schools of IR thought. It must be acknowledged at the outset that analytic eclecticism is problematic to an extent vis-à-vis its relevance with South Asia. Indeed, liberal-institutionalism is the weakest link within the research tradition of analytic eclecticism pertaining to South Asian regionalism. The SAARC region's lack of institutionalisation means liberal-institutionalism has low salience within the region (low intra-regional trade and absence, or utility of institutions). In addition, although realism and constructivism undergird regional integration, due to the role of interests and power in the context of South Asian regionalism, neither of them singularly supply a sound theoretical basis for understanding regionalism. A blend of constructivism and realism, or what might be called a constructivist-realism might be a basis for an explanation (Chap. 6), which would count as a mid-range theory. Nevertheless, although liberal-institutionalism is the weakest link, it cannot be discounted, as evidence from practice indicates. This is manifest from the very existence of SAARC and SAFTA. Discounting the shortcomings, their sheer existence demonstrates some degree (or intent) of liberal-institutionalism. Moreover, analytical eclecticism is applicable to South-Asia because it can be used as a strategy for theoretical innovation, as the complex links between power, interests, and norms defy analytical capture by any one paradigm (Katzenstein and Okawara 2002). Consequently, proponents of an eclectic approach postulate more variables should be considered for analysing empirical puzzles, rather than striving for parsimonious and often incomplete explanations (Hlatky 2012). Furthermore, analytic eclecticism can be defined as comprising an intellectual stance supporting efforts to complement, engage, and selectively utilise theoretical constructs embedded in contending research traditions to build complex arguments that bear on substantive problems of interest to both scholars and practitioners (Sil and Katzenstein 2010).

Therefore, one must adopt a nuanced perspective in terms of IR theory, when studying regions and regional integration, as limiting the theoretical framework to one, or even two schools of IR theory severely limits the theoretical outreach. Thus, an argument can be made that a much larger, and stronger theoretical net is required for a holistic approach, which allows the inclusion of variables from multiple schools of IR theory. Analytical eclecticism allows for a unique and natural division of labor approach, as realist tenets mainly address the likelihood of war, conflict, or stability. Liberalism focuses on economic gain from cooperation, institutions, and the conditions which lead to peace and stability. Constructivism addresses identities, norms, values, religion, etc. which also occupy a dominant position in regional politics (Wendt 1992). As per Wendt, constructivists also focus on the foundational ideas of long-lasting peace and the emergence of pluralistic security communities. This facilitates a sort of 'division of labour' approach. Such a multi-paradigmatic approach seems apposite in evaluating regions, which can guide the theoretical framework by including variables linked with different IR theories. Such an approach also allows theoretical insights and variables to be strung together in one overarching framework. In general, regions are redolent of inter-state rivalry (or cooperation), regional competition based on national interests, (free) trade, cultural and human exchange, the exchange of ideas and opinions, and in some cases supranationalist cooperation in specific issues based on either common identity, and/or consensus. On a similar vein, some of the key fundamental aspects of integration itself is based on liberal principles, such as increased trade, preference for institutions, and free movement of people. Furthermore, ideational factors on decision-making, consensus building, or simply cooperation on specific matters include multiple perspectives from a variety of groups and actors within a state and region. These naturally fall under constructivist premises, like norm formation and advocacy, identity, etc. Therefore, it can be agreed upon that regions entail a fully functioning regional international system of states, which naturally entails all elements of IR theory, and cannot be plausibly explained by one, or two overarching theories. It is also useful to note that most theories have their pros and cons, and the better option seems to select their positively relevant aspects and combine them in a smart power strategy. Smart power can be broadly defined as a strategy that selectively combines elements of hard and soft power to attain policy objectives (Nye 2009, 2011). It can be added that a smart power strategy considers the perspectives, needs, and interests of all parties concerned, and considers the big picture, and the ability to act with others.

Soft power is the power of attraction, the likeable qualities of a nation, the moral authority of its foreign policies, and the crucial quality being liked and respected by the international community (Nye 1990, 2004, 2008). Soft power is especially significant in today's information age that has made information easily accessible, which a couple decades ago was exclusive for heads of states, high level statesmen, businessmen, and the likes. Coined by Joseph Nye in the late 1980s, the term soft power pertains to the ability of a country to persuade others to do what it wants without force or coercion (Nye 2004). The US may have dominated other countries, but it has also excelled in projecting soft power, with the help of its companies, foundations, universities, churches, and other institutions of civil society. American culture, ideals, and values have been extraordinarily important in helping Washington attract partners and supporters. Nevertheless, in accordance with Nye, the limits of soft power must also be acknowledged, as it tends to have diffuse effects on the outside world and is not easily wielded to achieve specific policy outcomes. Recently, the term has also been used in changing and influencing social and public opinion through relatively less transparent channels and lobbying through powerful political and non-political organisations. Nye insists that with soft power, 'the best propaganda is not propaganda', further explaining that during the Information Age, credibility is the scarcest resource. Essentially, soft power is singularly unable, or rather insufficient to attain policy objectives, and hence must be used as part of strategy of smart power that combines soft and hard power. Nye's core message is that American (and global) security hinges as much on winning hearts and minds as it does on winning wars. In contrast, hard power is the use of military and economic means to influence the behaviour or interests of other political actors. This form of political power is often aggressive, and is often most effective when imposed by one political actor upon another of lesser military and/or economic ability. Nye posits the term as the ability to use the carrots and sticks of economic and military might to make others follow your will. Here, "carrots" are inducements such as the reduction of trade barriers, the offer of an alliance or the promise of military protection. On the other hand, "sticks" are threats including the use of coercive diplomacy, the threat of military intervention, or the implementation of economic sanctions. Ernest Wilson (2008) describes it as the capacity to coerce another to act in ways in which that entity would not have acted otherwise. Nye advocates that successful states need both hard and soft power – the ability to coerce others as well as the ability to shape their long-term attitudes and preferences. Singularly, neither soft nor hard power is unable to attain a nation's desired political outcomes.

The international relations, or foreign relations amongst South Asian states within the region has been documented by several experts (Ganguly 2006; Chari et al. 2003; Paul 2010; DeVotta 2015; Bose and Jalal 2011; Hagerty 2005; Shastri and Wilson 2013). Regional politics has mostly been grounded on India-Pakistan dynamics, as both regional powers give precedence to domestic priorities. Consequently, most interaction between states in the region are at least to a certain extent pre-occupied by this bilateral rivalry between the regional powers. It must be noted that this is not a unique phenomenon, and is reminiscent of any or every region of the globe. Furthermore, the hegemonic perception of India owing to its superior military, economy, territory, population, culture, etc. has not necessarily enabled New Delhi to take a unilateral lead in regionalism. The bilateral relationship between the regional powers India and Pakistan has severely impeded regionalism. In addition, the Kashmir conflict can be traced as a root cause of the antagonism between the regional powers. The justification of actions, or unilateral claims of both India and Pakistan towards Kashmir is unconvincing to say the least. In varying degrees, both New Delhi and Islamabad seem guilty on certain accounts in lieu of the conflict in Kashmir. Extremist and violent Jihadist views on Kashmir seem to be beyond the reach of any political party, Indian or Pakistani. On Pakistan's account, there are countless instances of state sponsored (mainly by ISI) terrorist activities and cross-border violations of established ceasefire lines. On India's account, there is violation of human rights, and harassment of the local populace by police and the armed forces. It is difficult to picture regional cooperation, or integration in such a scenario. In sum, South Asia as a region is far from integration.

13.3   Kashmir: The Inception of Problems Between India and Pakistan

The conflict in Kashmir is one of the most severe and intractable conflicts on earth, which has plagued India-Pakistan relations, and impeded regional integration of, and wider regional cooperation in South Asia. India and Pakistan bypassed international norms and developed nuclear weapons owing to the protracted and enduring conflict in Kashmir. In order not to digress from the main topic, this chapter avoids delving into the intricacies concerning Kashmir. Scholars have delved deep into the conflict in Kashmir, and numerous aspects of the bilateral relations between India and Pakistan, and its impact on South Asia (Ganguly 2013, 2016; Cohen 2013; Ganguly and Thompson 2011; Schofield 2003; Hakeem 2014; Davis 2011). Kashmir has been described by experts as a hardy perennial in the catalog of international disputes, often serving as a kind of metaphor for the broader problems that plague India and Pakistan (Schaffer and Schaffer 2005). In essence, both regional powers singularly claim Kashmir, and do not seem to be willing or able to permanently resolve this issue.

For Pakistan, the Kashmir issue is rooted at the core identity of the Pakistani state. When Pakistan was conceived, it was meant to be the homeland for the Muslim populace of the subcontinent. Islamabad's objective to bring the territory of Kashmir under its ambit is not just a matter of territory, but more importantly, of identity, and a distinct form of nationalism. The very idea of Pakistan was conceived of as Kashmir being a part of it. Form India's perspective, Kashmir is not just a matter of gaining territory for New Delhi, but also a part of the secular Indian identity, and nationalism. Thus, in the most crucial aspects, India and Pakistan's perspectives' of Kashmir was, and still is essentially the same. Both countries see is as a zero-sum game, in which one's loss is perceived as the others win, and vice-versa.

An additional observation is that although there certainly exists zero-sum dynamics on an ideational level, but the same cannot be said on a territorial level, evident from India's actions. Albeit as a sign of goodwill, India has ceded strategically critical territory such as the Haji Pir Pass which it conquered in the 1965 war, and ceded considerable territory in the Sindh that was captured in the Western sector during the 1971 war with Pakistan. Territorially, India was prepared to cede ground in some parts of Poonch and Gilgit in 1947 and 1948 following Pakistan's attack in October 1947. Partition was the only solution, which not only the Nehru-led dispensation was ready to concede, but also the UN Commission had come to concur with this conclusion. The Pakistanis also rejected a partition-cum-plebiscite solution in 1947–1948. Furthermore, the Simla Agreement of 1972 made the LoC (Line of Control) de facto boundary, which India believed should be the basis of a final settlement and the conversion of the LoC in to a border or de jure boundary. The most contested area is the Valley of Kashmir, which is strategically important, because critical rivers such as the Jhelum flow through the valley.[4] Evidently, India has been ready to make compromises, whereas Pakistan apparently has not been ready to do the same. In sum, Pakistan regards Kashmir as part of its Muslim identity and nationalism, whereas India regards it as a part of its secular identity and nationalism. In addition, there have been efforts at reconciliation, on and off operations of diplomatic missions, trade, people-to-people exchange, etc. However, the complexities and unfortunate interactions between the two South Asian powers seem to have overshadowed any attempts at reconciliation.

Nevertheless, as indicated earlier, India and Pakistan seem to be losing a unilateral claim and moral authority on Kashmir. Due to both states' actions, the Kashmiri populace have experienced an inhumane and tragic fate. Moreover, since New Delhi and Islamabad have acquired nuclear weapon arsenals, and in lieu of complex relations concerning the United States and China, international will to get involved is very minimal, or rather non-existent. In addition, Pakistan advocates internationalisation of the conflict, and India regards it as a bilateral issue, as stated in the Simla Agreement signed bilaterally between India and Pakistan in 1972. In a notable contribution, Sumit Ganguly (2004) demonstrates the erosion of singular claims of both India and Pakistan. In case of the former, the erosion of secularity and meddling of elections in the 1980s; for the latter, the atrocities, plight, and eventual break-up of East from West Pakistan meant that sympathy towards Kashmir was not based solely on religion (Widmalm 2014). The Kashmir conflict has led to violent engagement between India and Pakistan, and stands as a severe impediment to regional integration in South-Asia and human development of around two billion people. The prospects of regional development and growth in South-Asia is negligible, unless a positive peace[5] between the regional powers is ascertained. In other words, for South-Asia to emerge from the developing world, the resolution of the Kashmir conflict seems vital.

Furthermore, despite India's secular commitment of Kashmir's future to "be settled by a reference to its people" (Wirsing 1994, p.54) certain past actions of the government have contributed to erode a genuine claim, and has accentuated popular mistrust. For instance, the special provision of Kashmir as prescribed in the Indian constitution was eroded, and electoral rigging, non-functional democracy, and repression by the Indian state reinforce the Kashmiri people's claim for the right to

---

[4] Interestingly, and oddly enough, the Indus Waters Treaty represents one of the few success stories in broader India-Pakistan relations.

[5] For details, see Galtung, J. (1969) pp. 167–191.

self-determination (Ganguly 2013; Sheikh 1965; Lockwood 1969; Baba 2012; CIA 1964, Special Report). Since 1980s, the residents of the Kashmir Valley have been involved in rebellion and violence against Indian occupancy, with tacit support from Pakistan's intelligence agencies and militant groups. What is required for resolving Kashmir is the consideration of "enlightened self-interest"[6] on behalf of both India and Pakistan. A total reversal and complete overhaul of stereotypical perceptions is needed. Furthermore, UN Security Council resolutions also endorsed the will of the Kashmiri people as the final dispensation, which was to be determined via a plebiscite or referendum. It is useful to consider the facts pertaining to a plebiscite, as India is obliged to hold a plebiscite in Kashmir under UN auspices only after Pakistan's withdrawal of its forces from Kashmir, including PoK (Pakistan occupied Kashmir). India is mandated to draw down forces only after Pakistan does so, and New Delhi can retain the presence of police forces to maintain law and order under UNSCR 47 in 1948.[7] From India's perspective, Pakistan did not undertake the actions mandated by the UN. Arguably, Pakistan's continued usage of state sponsored terrorism in the Kashmir region (and beyond) has contributed to the worsening situation, and hasn't helped with pacifying India's doubts either. India made efforts on several occasions to demonstrate good will, amidst hopes for reconciliation. For instance, after the 1971 war, along with a considerable amount of territory, many thousands of POWs were released who committed ghastly war crimes in Bangladesh.[8] Nevertheless, as mentioned before, the acrimonious complexities and antagonism between the Indian and Pakistani States and their defence institutions overshadow the question of reconciliation.

13.3.1   Westphalian Roots, or Eastphalian Dynamics

From the above sections, it can be inferred that Kashmir is a colossal mess, and this conflict has plagued India-Pakistan relations since the advent of independence, and the very inception of these two states. In the post-colonial order of the subcontinent, nuclear warfare capable states who recently gained independence in the late 1940s (as compared to mid -seventeenth century in Western Europe, 1648 to be precise with the signing of the Peace of Westphalia) are much reluctant, or directly dismiss the idea of sharing, or giving up their sovereignty in the quest for regional development. It is essentially an embryonic Westphalian system, as the utmost importance is given to sovereignty and territorial integrity. This has indeed led to the

---

[6]This term was used by renowned scholars in different scenarios, but it can be asserted that this applies in the South Asian regional context. This term is borrowed from Collier, P. (2007), The Bottom Billion, Oxford: Oxford University Press; and Stiglitz, J. (2015). The Great Divide, New York: W.W. Norton & Company, Inc.

[7]S/RES/47(1948).

[8]Among several other examples, see International Crimes Tribunal. (2013) ICT[2]-BD Case No. 03 of 201.

characterisation of the scenario in South Asia as Eastphalia (Fidler and Ganguly 2010). Additionally, national interests in South-Asia supersedes the will towards integration. Be it regionalism, or regional integration, or cooperation within a region, a crucial aspect of 'integration' is sharing sovereignty by partly conceding (or pooling in, or combining) the authority of national or individual decision-making powers. This is the inherent logic behind supranationalism, liberal institutionalism, and inter-governmentalism (as manifest in the EU). The unanimous preference for the containment of sovereignty can be illustrated via the consistent decisions made by policy makers in New Delhi and Islamabad over the past decades, which have often given precedence to missile production and arms race, as compared to basic issues such as health care, education, and poverty eradication, among others (although in varying degrees). In addition to regional politics being dictated by India-Pakistan relations, the rise of sub-regional systems or organisations, and the involvement of key international players in the regional dynamics of South Asia is noteworthy. Notably, the involvement of China and US is particularly interesting.

13.3.2 Future Power Dynamics

The South Asian regional context demonstrates power asymmetry does not guarantee regional control. In other words, India's superior military, economic, cultural, and demographic capacities have proved insufficient to unilaterally endorse and materialise regional integration. Although this lesson is drawn from the South Asian context, it can be argued that it is valid for other regions too. The establishment of communication, trust, cooperation, and consensus are vital elements to share unilateral decision-making power, and combine them into a joint enterprise. Furthermore, it can be argued that the hard power approach adopted by both India and Pakistan has proved insufficient for unilateral attainment of desired policy objectives. Therefore, it seems reasonable to postulate that future modes of power, i.e. smart power, by combining soft and hard power could be essential prerequisites for regional integration in South-Asia. As part of a smart strategy to utilise soft power, states can for instance deploy public diplomacy to import its image to change hearts and minds, as well as to indirectly influence the recipient country's government. Furthermore, the conversion of soft power only as top-down government initiatives is insufficient to obtain desired outcomes. Equally important are bottom-up approaches which include wider civil society networks, transnational NGOs, and civil-society actors. Potential avenues in this direction are universities, educational and cultural exchanges, sports (cricket, hockey), film and television, regional entertainment contests, think-tanks, etc. Besides government initiatives and policies that aim at regional integration and cooperation, people and civil society at large need to be involved in a region building process, in order to attain a sufficient level of success.

In addition, India's superior military, economic, demographic, and geopolitical endowments are a consistent source of concern for South-Asian states, especially from a Westphalian perspective. Scholars posit hegemonic states as necessary, who must lead the production of global (in this case, regional) public goods because smaller states lack the incentives or the capacity (Nye 2011, p.214). This is also relevant in regional contexts where such conditions apply, as hegemony on a regional level can be arguably less intimidating than on a global level. In addition, regional hegemonies can be constrained by institutional rules and frameworks. Scholars demonstrate the potential in international institutions to solve problems of coordination and free riding in the period after hegemony (Snidal 1985; Keohane 1984). This is relevant in the context of South-Asia, vis- a-vis SAARC. For instance, it is aptly argued that although American power after WWII rested on a network of institutions that constrained it, but also increased its power to act with others (Ikenberry 2006). This is an important point in assessing power of nations in the current international system (Slaughter 2009). As South-Asian states perceive India as a hegemony, the alternative is strengthening the regional institutional capacity of SAARC. Therefore, to accentuate integration of the entire region of South Asia (SAARC), or sub-regional integration (SASEC, BIMSTEC), India being the perceived regional hegemony ought to deploy a smart power strategy to effectively foster cooperation, and eventually integration.

13.3.3 Comparison of Regional Processes

The following parts of this chapter briefly compares South Asia with other regional processes across the globe, whilst utilising common indicators (or independent variables). This will be particularly useful to draw insights for the phenomenon of regional integration. These are as follows:

Sovereignty and Regional Decision Making It is often (aptly) argued that European nations in the current era of global politics have moved beyond the traditional convention of the Westphalian system, which heeds utmost importance to sovereignty and territorial integrity of states. Such criteria seemed relevant, as the peace of Westphalia was signed in 1648 to end centuries of warfare and hostilities owing to land, identity, religion, and power, among others. In other words, the peace of Westphalia was established so that nascent European nation states begin to respect each other's borders and territorial integrity. The Westphalian system was and still is a success story, as it prevailed for centuries, until the inception of the European Union project. With the EU, European states commenced to share, or pool in their decision-making capacities, starting with the economic domain. Furthermore, with more members joining in, and the adoption of a single market, currency, bank, parliament, court and the establishment of the multiple interlinked EU institutions led to decision making on a consensual basis. In simple terms, European countries 'pooled in' their individual or unilateral decision making authority, by transferring decision making on a supranational basis, which is a core element of regional integration and regionalism in general (see Chap. 9 for details about EU history and institutions). Nevertheless, this does not apply to the South-Asian regional context. Furthermore, it is also relevant in South East Asia, which is considered a steadily progressing region towards integration, owing to effective cooperation. Nevertheless, in ASEAN, the importance of territorial integrity and sovereignty is documented at the core of its constitution, as members strictly adhere not to engage in the domestic affairs of one another. An argument can be made that third world countries in Asia are reluctant to share decision making authority. Arguably, the relatively recent attainment of independence from colonial empires in the mid or late twentieth century have likely led to a higher regard for sovereignty and territorial integrity. Western European states have enjoyed sovereignty and obtained experience as well as expertise in statecraft. Since 1648 these states have had the time to experiment with the notions, tools, and concepts of statehood and statecraft. In stark contrast, the past, present, and future trajectory of the third world regions seems vastly different. This point can be substantiated by the texts documented in the core of constitutional documents of regional organisations such as SAARC, and ASEAN for instance. Respect for domestic issues, and strict non-interference have been established as the core fundamental, or definitional elements of these charters.

Basic Objectives These denote the fundamental purpose of a particular regional organisation, for which it was established to begin with. In other words, although different regional organisations around the globe entail distinct historical backgrounds, characteristics, region specific dynamics, and a set of conflicts or complexities amidst member states, it can be argued that regional organisations are established to maintain peace and order in a region, deepen economic and political interdependence, and present an opportunity for cooperation and consensus building among regional neighbours. It can be postulated that such basic objectives of regional organisations are sort of universal, at least theoretically. Although some regional organisations may differ from others in structure, (colonial) history, level of institutionalism, institutional frameworks, budget, and decision-making processes among others, basic principles essentially remain the same. For instance, Wong (2012) opines that the EU's basis of economic integration as a means towards political reconciliation and integration is not very relevant to ASEAN's culture of non-interference in the context of newly independent states, who guard their sovereignty in the face of disputes regarding territorial claims (such as coup d'état in Thailand, and sensitivities pertaining to South-China sea, among others). But this does not mean EU and ASEAN were established for very different reasons. In other words, it can be inferred both these organisations, and SAARC, were established to facilitate cooperation for mutual benefits, to institutionalise economic and political interdependence among members, to increase people to people contact, and facilitate social progress. The system for this may differ from one political culture and context to the other, or from one organisation to the other, but it is arguably based on similar ideas or principles. Most regional institutions, movements towards regional cooperation, and regional integration are generally envisaged for economic growth and prosperity of the countries in respective regions. The EU, NAFTA, MERCOSUR, ASEAN, and so on were all established to increase regional economic output, and political cooperation. SAARC is South Asia was similarly formulated for increasing regional economic output, and to facilitate regional political cooperation.

Regional Dynamics These pertain to a range of elements which are relevant for examining any regional context. One of the most important variables or indicator is the official position of leaders and the governments of key regional players within a region, vis-a-vis regional integration. This applies for regions where key regional players share peaceful relations whilst promoting economic cooperation and trade (Europe, North America, South East-Asia), as well as regions with acrimonious or outright hostile relations amidst regional players (South-Asia, Latin America, Middle-East). This factor or variable can be operationalised, or analysed via examining relevant policy documents, official press releases, and national strategy or approaches in the regional and international systems. Public opinion towards integration is also an important element, which can be examined by evaluating the domestic public opinions as well as official position of countries (and their populations) in a region. Furthermore, international opinion towards integration can also be a useful indicator, depending on existing surveys and research. This variable is an exogenous factor which can be examined (operationalised) by evaluating the proaction and reaction of key international players. Regional dynamics and its relation to regional integration is also manifest in Latin America, which has a long history of institutionalisation, in addition to the multi-faceted and multi-layered nature of the regional architecture. The all-encompassing regional organisation is the Community of Latin American and Caribbean States (CELAC), which includes all 33 Latin American and Caribbean countries. Additional sub-regional cooperation systems include: Central American Integration System (SICA), Community of Andean Nations (CAN), Mercado Comun del Sur, Common Market of the South (MERCOSUR), Caribbean Community (CARICOM), and UNASUR, a relatively new regional organisation in which the countries of CAN, Mercosur, Chile, Guyana and Suriname are seated. Nevertheless, the most noteworthy aspect of Latin American regional integration (akin to South Asia) is the impact of regional power rivalry on regional integration. For instance, MERCOSUR is highly dependant on the bilateral relationship between the two regional powers and core members, i.e. Argentina and Brazil. Similar to bilateral relations which are characterised by recurrent instability, consequently, the same is the case for the MERCOSUR regional integration process.

Nature of Bilateral Relations Relations between key regional players can be essentially seen as an extension of the definition of (intra) regional dynamics. This variable can be operationalised by examining in detail, the bilateral relations between key regional powers. It can be postulated that regional integration in South Asia is severely hindered by the protracted rivalry between the two regional powers of India and Pakistan. This chapter asserts regional integration of South Asia can only be ascertained with the easing of tensions between India and Pakistan, and the peaceful resolution of the conflict in Kashmir, which is the root cause. In other words, regional integration of South Asia, and any other region largely depends on the bilateral relations between key regional players. In case of South-Asia, it concerns India and Pakistan relations, in Europe it concerns Franco-German relations, in North America it mainly concerns Canada and the US, in Latin America, the relations between Argentina and Brazil, for example.

Institutional Frameworks and Mechanisms These are integral for regional integration. Although national priorities remain significant, regional institutional structures have a remarkable impact on community, or society building within a region. This variable is operationalised by evaluating the distinct regional organisations, and the relevant political fora on a regional (or sub-regional) basis. The institutional architecture of the EU is noteworthy,[9] which has established a plethora of institutions for different purposes, e.g. common market, regulations, a bank, parliament, council, commission, defence & foreign policy, among many others. Such institutionalisation has led, or rather inspired ASEAN to develop under its ambit, distinct regional institutions for specific purposes. Examples of the establishment of ASEAN institutions are: AICHR in 2009, ASEAN Human Rights Declaration in 2012, ASEAN Commission on the Rights of Minorities in 2010, and Committee of Permanent Representatives from the ASEAN member states. Consequently, scholars have indicated that this can be attributed to the EU's reference as a 'model power' (Jetschke 2009; Zielonka 2008; Lenz 2008; Jokela 2009). In terms of institutionalisation, the EU project has been rather exemplary in the institutional design of ASEAN, and offers insights for SAARC, and beyond. It is redolent of scholarly analyses that intraregional trade within SAARC is not as significant, or even comparable to EU, NAFTA, ASEAN, or MERCOSUR. As per the World Bank (2018), with intra-regional trade at less than 5% of total trade, South Asia is the least integrated region in the world, dwarfed by South East Asia's 25%, East Asia's 35% and Europe's 60%. The extensive intraregional trade in the EU is supplemented by distinct institutional frameworks and mechanisms. The institutions in Brussels also provide a common platform for communication and interaction. In contrast, SAARC has so far been unable to take full advantage of its region-wide FTA, i.e. SAFTA, and prefers free trade strictly on a bilateral, rather than a multilateral basis. In other words, SAFTA has been unable to contribute towards significant increase in intra-regional trade. It can thus be inferred that effective supranational regional institutions are fundamental for regionalism.

Additional features of ASEAN institutionalisation include the summit meetings twice every year; designation of Foreign Ministers of member states as the ASEAN Coordinating Council; Chairmanship for high-level ASEAN bodies; and the formation of the Committee of Permanent Representatives to ASEAN, based in Jakarta, the de facto capital of the organisation, akin to Brussels for the EU. Similarly,

---

[9]Although this is an intense topic and many in Brussels would disagree, the above-mentioned statement is made in this chapter for the purpose of simplification. Moreover, the supranational institutions of the EU, despite their imperfections and flaws, still can be characterised as the most advanced manifestation of regional integration.

SAARC too has manifested a certain level of institutionalisation, i.e. designated yearly summits (although not evident in practice), a secretariat, standing committee, technical and action committees, etc. Some notable agreements include: South Asia Preferential Trade Agreement (SAPTA) signed in 1993, and the South Asian Free Trade Agreement (SAFTA) signed in 2004. Nevertheless, for these to work at par with advanced regional organisations such as EU, deeper institutionalisation is vital. For instance, as is the case with EU and ASEAN, there is no committee or council of SAARC permanent representatives based in the de facto capital of Kathmandu. Member states can thus cut off diplomatic ties in lieu of bilateral conflicts, as redolent of India and Pakistan relations as SAARC members. Without permanent representatives in the de facto capital, it is difficult to maintain consistent communication for matters pertaining to regional concern. Moreover, the boycotting and cancellation of summits are a common occurrence in South Asia.[10]

Furthermore, as it is widely believed that the EU functions on its doctrine of a rules-based organisation which strictly adheres to the rule of law as compared to ASEANs norm based culture of mutual dialogue and consensus building. This is owing to the existence of distinct legal institutions in the EU, which addresses issues of regional concern, which are lacking in SAARC, and ASEAN. Although there is a commitment to a more formalised structure in the ASEAN Charter, research outputs differ as to ASEAN's value in promoting regional integration and further institution building, as its mandate and influence are limited (SIPRI 2008, p.9). Therefore, although institutions are deemed important, "ASEAN patterns of inter-state cooperation are looser and less regulated than the EU's codified methods of decision making" (Murray 2010, p.312). The same can be said about SAARC, and Mercosur for that matter. In addition, too many institutions in a region can also contradict the very purpose of regionalism. There are noteworthy references to the complex regional architecture in Latin America, characterised by a "complex landscape of hundreds of regional groupings" and "contrary to the world of states, that world of supra-national regions does not resemble a jig-saw-puzzle, but looks more like a 'spaghetti bowl' as the regional groupings are overlapping and sometimes nested" (Van Langenhove 2013, p.55). Furthermore, the several overlapping regional and sub-regional organisations in Latin America led to Mark Keller's phrase "alphabetic soup of regional integrations" in order not to confuse the jumble of acronyms and abbreviations of the region's numerous organisations (Glickhouse 2012). Therefore, regional states must strive for the right balance pertaining to the number and function of (sub) regional institutions.

Economic integration is a crucial aspect of regional integration in any region, which entails tangible economic benefits for regional members. This is summed up by the former Secretary-General of ASEAN, who posits, "like Europe, a regional consciousness in ASEAN must first aim at the integration of the regional economy" (Severino 2008, p.111). Economic integration is a very basic objective of regional

---

[10] The summit is automatically postponed or cancelled even if one member country skips the event. See The Indian Express (2016).

integration, as indicated earlier. Nevertheless, the level of integration depends on the organisation itself, along with region specific dynamics. It can be inferred the EU maintains significant levels of intraregional trade owing to its advanced institutions and supranational capacity to support intra-regional trade. A common parliament, bank, monetary policy, and regular meetings of representatives of member states makes this possible. This is peculiar in the context of SAARC, as countries in the region have individually maintained consistent economic growth over the past years, but with negligent growth in the "per capita" aspect. In fact, it can be argued that per capita and HDI are more plausible indicators of a country's economic health rather than gross income, which does not equitably represent important aspects. SAARC countries are individually witnessing high economic growth, especially compared to economic stagnation and crisis in Europe (and North America). States in South Asia mainly prefer to deal on a bilateral basis, or via sub-regional systems. Although ASEAN has been effective in generating increased intraregional trade, it is not as significant as EU, as most manufactured products are exported to developed nations outside ASEAN (Ruland and Jetschke 2008). In contrast, the EU's commitment to mutually agreed upon economic policies complements the single market and the common currency, the euro, and market and regulatory mechanisms are key features of economic integration (Murray 2010). One of the significant benefits of economic integration is an increase in intra-regional trade. This has been personified as a major success of the EU, a lack of success for SAARC, and a somewhat emerging success for ASEAN (as it lacks a singular or common economic ideology).[11] Following Europe, the regional scenario in North America can also be characterised as advanced, at least in the economic realm. It might be useful to note the initial idea was a free trade agreement between the US and Canada, which culminated in 1988, after which Mexico was also included (Fawn 2009). Furthermore, the existence of only three countries in the region have arguably made dialogue and consensus building relatively easier, as compared to eight (SAARC), ten (ASEAN), or twenty-eight (EU). Although an economically integrated and developed region, North America cannot be compared to EU on equal terms, owing to the latter's multitude of supranational institutions, and the sheer number of states, who have a stake and vote on policy making. Notably, proposals to deepen integration of North America, notably political integration, NAFTA-plus, or steps towards a supranational union like the EU, were rejected by the US (Fox and Allyn 2008). The key insight here is: without the cooperation or consent of the key regional player, i.e. US in this case, deeper political integration at a supranational level was not possible.

---

[11] Nevertheless, a counter argument can be presented, that due to independence of national policy making, while at the same time maintaining regional cooperation, ASEAN countries in SE Asia were fairly unscathed by the economic crisis that plagued the Western world. The financial crisis hit Europe particularly hard and it took a while to recover as compared to the United States, South East Asia, or even South Asia. Nonetheless, this a different topic, and owing to the topic under scrutiny, regional institutions and mechanisms are vital for a regional organisation.

International or External Support This is the final factor to be examined in this study for the comparison of regions. Notably, the success behind the institutionalisation, and economic advancement of Europe is also largely owed to the material and moral support from the US after World War II. It can be postulated that for external support to materialise in practice, there should also be tangible material benefits for the providers of such support. For instance, the US established the Marshal aid program and opened its previously protectionist economy to include Western and Central European states as more and more of these states were falling under the Soviet bloc. Compared to Europe, South East Asia received minimal economic incentives, characterised notably as "hubs and spokes" (Ikenberry 2004; Calder and Fukuyama 2008). This is on point, as before the second World War the US viewed national sovereignty (newly gained) as so sacrosanct, that it even refrained from signing the League of Nations. It is useful to note two factors: a) the United States adopted such drastic measures to not share its newly gained sovereignty, which can be traced to Westphalian roots (an important factor when comparing both EU and NAFTA with SAARC); and b) The United States decided to share national sovereignty, and opened its previously protectionist economy due to its own self-interest, as more and more central and eastern European states were entering the Communist domain. Consequently, in stark contrast, after the second world war, the US founded a range of institutions such as the UN, OECD, IMF, OAS, NATO, as well as supported Europe to create the European community. These were all systems for mutual governance and support. Most notably, what happened was a total reversal of previously protectionist trade policy. With the founding of the GATT, the American economy drastically helped the European economy. The important question is how was this done, the answer to which pertains to national sovereignty. In other words, decision makers in Washington transformed the 11th Commandment, i.e. national sovereignty. Similarly, a total reversal of security policy is also manifest, as Washington decided to position 100,000 troops in Europe for more than 40 years immediately after the war.[12] The purpose of this description is to demonstrate the impact of external support on regional processes or organisations. Compared to countries in the EU, the regional member states within the regional organisations SAARC, and ASEAN (and Mercosur) received limited external support.

---

[12] This can be inferred from numerous sources, and basic historical research and process tracing. To review one such source, in lecture form, see Collier, P. (2008). The Bottom Billion, TED Talk. Available at: https://www.ted.com/talks/paul_collier_shares_4_ways_to_help_the_bottom_billion

13.4 Regional Dynamics in South Asia: The Rise of Sub-Regional Organizations

At the time when SAARC was conceived, neither India nor Pakistan was too eager about joining the organisation, and eventually ended up as members owing to the initiatives of the other regional states. In short, from India's perspective, it was an agenda of the smaller countries of the region to try and gang up against their giant neighbour. From Pakistan's perspective, the organisation could be used by India as a means to further its own ends (Dash 2008; Saez 2012). It can be argued that the surge in regional integration studies is a significant development in IR literature, and in international studies in general. Almost every country today is now virtually a member of at least one regional institution (and/or sub-regional institution). The existing literature contains several remarkable studies which examine the regional scenario in South-Asia (Hagerty 2005; Francois et al. 2009; Dossani et al. 2010; Shastri and Wilson 2013; Razzaque and Basnett 2014). These comprehensive studies comparatively utilise theories of trade, security, great-power influence, and domestic political theories to examine South-Asia. One study evaluates SAARC beyond economic integration to present a detailed appraisal of cooperation in environmental security, human welfare, and cooperation in security matters (Ahmed 2013). Another volume examines human development and well-being, and reveals in light of the current trajectory, the alarming impact on the region, as well as the wider international community (Najam and Yusuf 2013). These studies consistently argue that any progress towards regional integration in South-Asia hinges on the cooperation between India and Pakistan. This demonstrates the importance of cooperation between the regional powers to manifest integration, and the adverse impact in its absence. At the same time, it is useful to acknowledge the debate on regional integration in India and the broader South Asian region has moved on from being too focused on the Indo-Pak matrix. In the current context, it is increasingly becoming more about sub-regional initiatives such as BIMSTEC, BBIN and SASEC, China's role in South Asian economies and sub-regional cooperation (its bilateral relations with South-Asian states, as well as sub-regional initiatives such as BCIM), and its relationship with Pakistan. The debate on how New Delhi and Islamabad have addressed regional concerns, and who can be blamed for what, is an endless one, with little to no prospects of settlement in the foreseeable future. Consequently, policymakers in South Asia (except Pakistan) have realised they are losing out. As per certain senior policy makers in Delhi, Dhaka and Colombo for instance, the line that India-Pakistan cooperation is essential for regional cooperation is no longer strongly held.

Subsequently, sub-regional organisations in South-Asia have attained the limelight, which can be of two types: (1) sub-regional systems which only include South Asian (SAARC) members, such as the Bangladesh, Bhutan, India, Nepal (BBIN), and the South Asia Subregional Economic Cooperation (SASEC) program; and (2) sub-regional systems which include a mixture of South Asian (SAARC) members, and external Asian member states who are also part of their own regional frameworks. Examples of the latter category include the Bay of Bengal Initiative for Multi-Sectoral Technical and Economic Cooperation (BIMSTEC), which is a cross-regional international organisation involving a group of countries in South Asia (SAARC) and South East Asia (ASEAN), comprising of: Bangladesh, India, Myanmar, Sri Lanka, Thailand, Bhutan and Nepal. Another example is the Bangladesh–China–India–Myanmar Forum for Regional Cooperation (BCIM). In lieu of the word limit, it seems reasonable to briefly discuss two sub-regional organisations involving South Asia, one from each of the above categories, i.e. BIMSTEC and SASEC.

BIMSTEC This forum was established in 1997, mainly with Thailand's initiative, in pursuit of its Look West policy, which matched the Look East policy visions of both India and Bangladesh in the early 1990s, and offered the four South Asian members (other than Sri Lanka, an island country) a potential land route, or bridge to southeast Asia. A catalyst for this trajectory can be traced back to the impediments of regionalism via SAARC, owing to the India-Pakistan relationship. BIMSTEC can be characterised as a hybrid between "supra-structure" and "infra-structure" institution. It displays the following characteristics of supra-structure institutions: there are intergovernmental institutions whose decisions are based largely on consensus, most of their agreements are non-binding, their summits often involve heads of state/government and they usually have somewhat weak standing secretariats (ADB 2010). However, BIMSTEC also displays characteristics of an infra-structure institution in that it is of a much more functional nature than SAARC and focuses almost exclusively on economic matters (it eschews any political or security agenda, apart from counter-terrorism). BIMSTEC has set economic development squarely at the top of its agenda. One of the key areas of cooperation is the BIMSTEC FTA, which provides for liberalisation not just of merchandise trade, but also of services and investments. Negotiations on the FTA are premised on the Framework Agreement signed in 2004. Another area of cooperation is developing cross-border infrastructure. As per the BIMSTEC website, 14 thematic areas have been recognised as areas of cooperation. BIMSTEC's main policy making bodies are the periodic summits of heads of state or government, and two sets of ministerial meetings, one consisting of foreign ministers, the other of trade and economic ministers. The BIMSTEC secretariat is located in Dhaka, Bangladesh.

SASEC This forum was launched by ADB in 2001 to support the South Asia Growth Quadrilateral set up by the four SAARC members in the eastern part of South Asia (i.e. Bangladesh, Bhutan, India, and Nepal). Maldives and Sri Lanka joined as members in 2014, and Myanmar joined in 2017. SASEC mainly follows a project-based approach aimed at building confidence among countries involved by demonstrating tangible results. Participating countries have identified the priority sectors of (i) Transport; (ii) Trade Facilitation; (iii) Energy; and (iv) Economic Corridor Development. Transport connectivity has emerged as the major sector of emphasis, given the landlocked nature of two of the four countries, and the northeastern region of India. SASEC's two-tiered structure consists of a Country

Advisers Meeting (CAM) consisting of finance ministers, and sector working groups consisting of senior sectoral officials. Since it does not have a distinct secretariat of its own, it is often better described as a program rather than an institution. The ADB base in Manila serves as the *de facto* secretariat. As per data from official records on its website, SASEC as of May 2019 is involved in 54 projects worth 12.51 billion USD. It has also received technical assistance grants in 79 projects with an estimated value of 103.50 million USD from ADB, which has provided a forum for enhancing cooperation among the member countries and have helped identify and prioritise multiple transport corridors and develop subregional infrastructure projects. An institutional issue that has constrained SASEC is the absence of foreign ministries in the CAM, which causes difficulties in obtaining endorsement for the processing and implementation of projects.

13.5   Conclusions: Insights Pertaining to the Pre-Requisites of Regional Integration

This chapter examines regional integration in South Asia, and attempts to outline why there has been no integration so far. Furthermore, it examined the bilateral relations between the two regional players, India and Pakistan, briefly investigated the Kashmir conflict, and compared different regions across the globe. Subsequently, it derives hypotheses, or arguments that regional integration of the South-Asian region, or any other region for that matter, requires the cooperation, and good will of the key regional players. To substantiate this statement, the chapter presented a comparison of other regions such as Europe, North and South America, and South East Asia, and how regional integration is materialised and maintained in practice. Furthermore, similar indicators, factors, or independent variables were applied to study the conditions of regional integration in South Asia, to that of other regions. These are namely: state sovereignty, basic objectives, regional dynamics, nature of bilateral relations between regional powers, institutional frameworks and mechanisms, economic integration, and international or external support. This chapter rejects the overarching capacity of mainstream or positivist schools of IR theory, i.e. (neo) realism and liberalism, to effectively study regional phenomena. Instead, a more nuanced argument is made in terms of theoretical innovation. In other words, an eclectic theoretical framework is proposed to study regional integration in South Asia, and beyond. This is mainly because (neo) realist, as well as liberal schools of IR thought have proved insufficient to examine regional integration in South Asia. The superior economic and military capabilities have not enabled India to unilaterally endorse regional integration. Furthermore, the sheer asymmetry in terms of size of territory, population, cultural influence, etc. have also proved insufficient to materialise regional integration. Hence, the importance of soft and smart power is highlighted as future modes of power.

One of the objectives of this chapter is to present a critical outlook on regional integration, by highlighting the importance of cooperation between key regional players. All regions which are integrated economically, or militarily, or both, require the cooperation between key regional players. For instance, regional integration in Europe is difficult to imagine without the cooperation between France and Germany. The EU project came to fruition largely owing to the collaboration between the continental powers, who decided to put an end to centuries of warfare, and focus on economic growth, peace, and prosperity. It is rather difficult to imagine the EU project without the cooperation between France and Germany to mutualise their coal and steel industries. Similarly, NAFTA is difficult to imagine without the consent and cooperation of either US, or Canada, and ASEAN might not have been a success story without the cooperation between key players such as Indonesia and Thailand, for example. Furthermore, the overlap of institutions or 'alphabetical soup' of institutions denote the numerous institutions in Latin America, which ultimately contradict their very purpose. In addition, the regional rivalry between Brazil and Argentina have severely impacted regional integration most notably in Mercosur. Therefore, this chapter argues that for regional integration to manifest, the cooperation, and partnership between key regional players is essential. Furthermore, outright hostility and rivalry between regional powers, or the presence of a protracted or intractable conflict between the regional players further diminishes the odds for cooperation, or integration. In other words, it is difficult to imagine the integration of a region, or even cooperation in a region where the regional powers are engaged in perpetual belligerence and antagonism. Under such circumstances, sub-regional organisations, and external actors come to the light, for e.g. BBIN, SASEC, BIMSTEC, and BCIM, in addition to the involvement of China (string of pearls) and US (Afghanistan and Pakistan) in South Asia.

Following Europe, the regional scenario is highly advanced in North America. Although an economically integrated region, it cannot be compared to EU on equal or fair terms, owing to the latter's multitude of effective supranational institutions, and the sheer number of states, who have a stake and vote on policy-making. South East Asia is increasingly becoming known as a region moving towards integration, and is particularly impressive considering its economic integration. With the establishment of the 'ASEAN way of diplomacy', which is grounded on non-interference in domestic affairs and respect for territorial integrity has been a success story at large. The economic gains have been significant, as economic power in the changing global order is shifting towards Asia in general, as other chapters from this volume have demonstrated. Nevertheless, despite ASEAN's recognition as an economic power, or even a conflict manager, its level of integration cannot be compared to EU. The brief comparisons between EU, SAARC, NAFTA, MERCOSUR and ASEAN, and consistent praise for EU institutions does not imply that SAARC, or other regional organisations must learn from the EU. Instead, the EU is, or should be perceived as a model power. In addition, almost all regional organisations actively look for solutions to distinct problems of collective action and policy coordination between member states (Rosamond 2005; Rosamond and Alex 2011; Camroux 2010, 2011). These problems are faced in all regions, and most notably in Europe itself. For example, the complexities manifest in Belgium (Wallonia) pertaining to the CETA – FTA between the EU and Canada.

In accordance with Joe Nye, the future modes of power which can help garner cooperation in, and integration of South-Asia lies in smart power, which is a strategy consisting of a well-balanced combination of soft and hard power. This chapter postulates that for South Asia (SAARC) to become a developed, industrialised and a positively peaceful society, the conflict between India and Pakistan needs resolution as a prerequisite. An argument can be made that regional integration can be characterised as a movement, which entails both governmental as well as societal elements. States and decision makers (top-down approach) work in tandem with the wider civil society actors and their networks (bottom-up approach) in achieving preferred outcomes. This study posits the prerequisites of regional integration in South Asia are: positive peace between the regional powers, resolution of the Kashmir conflict, institutional development of SAARC, soft and smart power in the international relations of South-Asia.

Operationally, this study has found the debate on South Asian regionalism has moved on from being too focused on the Indo-Pak matrix. Additional factors have come to the fore, such as America and China's role in South Asian countries, and sub-regional organisations (BCIM, SASEC). Thus, sub-regional initiatives such as BBIN, BIMSTEC, SASEC, BCIM have gained attention from scholars as well as practitioners. This chapter sought to demonstrate that the regional scenario in South Asia is quite complex, and hinges on the most part, upon the bilateral relations between India and Pakistan, at least in terms of SAARC. Nevertheless, considering regional political dynamics, the assertive involvement of China and the US, and sub-regional organisations have come to fore. The protracted conflict in Kashmir is an underlying cause, but no external or internal entity has been able to either resolve or predict the end of this catastrophic conflict so far. The pessimist observer would imply that things are to keep going on for the foreseeable future as they have been in the past, since the advent of independence. The nihilist will demand that there will be no peace between India and Pakistan, and the fight will continue till the bitter end, or culminate in nuclear warfare. The optimist observer would assert that only time can heal, and help resolve the Kashmir conflict, which will ultimately lead to regional cooperation, and eventual integration. It took European nation states hundreds of years since the treaty of Westphalia, to share their sovereignty and develop supranational institutions. Optimistic observers would perhaps hope that future leaders will take the appropriate and necessary initiatives for a peaceful and prosperous regional order in South Asia.

Further Readings

Abdullah, A. Y. (2011). *South Asian hope SAARC, will it survive?* Dhaka: Life and Hope Foundation.

Ahmed, N. (1999). *Trade liberalization in Bangladesh: An empirical investigation*, A Ph.D. Thesis, University of Sydney, Australia.

Batliwalla, C.J. (1987). *Financial cooperation in South Asia. ADB/EWC Symposium on regional cooperation in South Asia*, Asian Development Bank, Manila, Philippines.

de Mel, D. (2011). *Trade facilitation issues in South Asia.* Kathmandu: South Asia Centre for Policy Studies (SACEPS).

Hill, C. W. L. (2007–2008). *International business.* Fifth Edition.

Govindan, K. (1996). A South Asian preferential trading arrangement: Implications for regional trade in food commodities. *Journal of Economic Integration, 11*(4), 478–491.

Guru-Gharana, K. K. (2000). *Macro-Economic modeling of South Asian economies with Intra-SAARC trade link . Final report- submitted to south Asian network of economic institutes.* Nepal: IIDS.

Hossain, M. M., & Vousden, N. (1996). *Welfare effects of a discriminatory trading area in South Asia* (Economic division working paper # 96/9). Canberra: Research School of Pacific and Asian Studies, Australian National University.

Naqvi, S. N. H., et al. (1988). Possibilities of regional trade expansion: A link model for Pakistan, India, Bangladesh and Sri Lanka. In H. W. Singer et al. (Eds.), *Challenges of south -south cooperation, (part II)*. New Delhi: Asia Publishing House.

Quantification of Benefits from Economic Cooperation in South Asia. (2008). Report prepared under Asian Development Bank Technical Assistance TA 4780. Page no 55–59.

References

Acharya, A. (2007). The emerging regional architecture of world politics: A review essay. *World Politics, 59*(4), 629–652.

Acharya, A. (2014a). Global International Relations (IR) and regional worlds: A new agenda for international studies. *International Studies Quarterly, 58*(4), 647–659.

Acharya, A. (2014b). *Constructing a security community in Southeast Asia: ASEAN and the problem of regional order.* London: Routledge.

Acharya, A., & Johnston, A. I. (2007). Comparing regional institutions: An introduction. In A. Acharya & A. I. Johnston (Eds.), *Crafting cooperation. Regional International institutions in comparative perspective* (pp. 1–31). Cambridge: Cambridge University Press.

Ahmed, Z. S. (2013). *Regionalism and regional security in South Asia: The role of SAARC.* Surrey: Ashgate Publishing.

Asian Development Bank. (2010). *BIMSTEC transport infrastructure and logistics study TA completion reports November 2010*, viewed on 25 July 2017, https://www.adb.org/projects/documents/bimstec-transport-infrastructure-and-logistics-study

Baba, N. A. (2012). Democracy and governance in Kashmir. In N. A. Khan (Ed.), *The parchment of Kashmir.* New York: Palgrave Macmillan.

Bose, S., & Jalal, A. (2011). *Modern South Asia: History, culture, political economy.* London: Routledge.

Calder, K. E., & Fukuyama, F. (Eds.). (2008). *EastAsian multilateralism: Prospects for regional stability.* Baltimore: Johns Hopkins University Press.

Camroux, D. F. (2010). Interregionalism or merely a fourth-level game? An examination of the EU-ASEAN relationship. *East Asia, 27*(1), 57–77.

Camroux, D. F. (2011). Interregionalism, a critique: The four levels of EU-ASEAN relations. In A. Warleigh-Lack, N. Robinson, & B. Rosamond (Eds.), *New regionalism and the European Union*. London: Routledge.

Central Intelligence Agency. (1964, April 22). *Sheikh Abdullah and the Kashmir Issue*, Special Report. https://www.cia.gov/library/readingroom/docs/DOC_0000283431.pdf

Chari, P., Cheema, P., & Cohen, S. (2003). *Perception, politics and security in South Asia: The compound crisis of 1990*. London: Routledge Curzon.

Cohen, S. (2013). *Shooting for a century: The India-Pakistan conundrum*. Washington, DC: Brookings Institution Press.

Dash, K. (2008). *Regionalism in South Asia: Negotiating cooperation, institutional structures*. London: Routledge.

Davis, Z. (2011). *The India-Pakistan military standoff: Crisis and escalation in South Asia*. New York: Palgrave Macmillan.

DeVotta, N. (2015). *An introduction to South Asian politics, routledge*. London: Taylor & Francis.

Dossani, R., Sneider, D., & Sood, V. (2010). *Does South Asia exist?* Stanford: Walter H. Shorenstein Asia-Pacific Research Center.

Ernest, J. W. (2008). Hard power, soft power, smart power. *The Annals of the American Academy of Political and Social Science, 616*(1), 110–124.

Fawn, R. (2009). *Globalising the regional, regionalising the global: Volume 35. Review of international studies*. Cambridge: Cambridge University Press.

Fidler, D., & Ganguly, S. (2010). India and Eastphalia. *Indiana Journal of Global Legal Studies, 17*(1), 147–164. Article 7. Available at: http://www.repository.law.indiana.edu/ijgls/vol17/iss1/7.

Fox, V., & Allyn, R. (2008). *Revolution of hope: The life, faith, and dreams of a Mexican president*. New York: Penguin Group USA.

Francois, J., Rana, P., & Wignaraja, G. (2009). *National strategies for regional integration: South and East Asian case studies*. London: Anthem Press.

Galtung, J. (1969). Violence, peace, and peace research. *Journal of Peace Research, 6*(3), 167–191.

Ganguly, S. (2004). *The Kashmir question: Retrospect and prospect*. London: Routledge/Frank Cass.

Ganguly, S. (2006). *South Asia*. New York: New York University Press.

Ganguly, S. (2013). *Conflict unending: India-Pakistan tensions since 1947*. New York: Columbia University Press.

Ganguly, S. (2016). *Deadly impasse: Indo-Pakistani relations at the dawn of a new century*. Cambridge: Cambridge University Press.

Ganguly, S., & Thompson, W. (2011). *Asian rivalries: Conflict, escalation, and limitations on two-level games* (Stanford security series). Stanford: Stanford Security Studies.

Glickhouse, R. (2012). *Explainer: An alphabet soup of Regional Integration Organisations*. Washington, DC: Americas Society/Council of the Americas, 22nd March [online], viewed on 17 April 2017. http://www.as-coa.org/articles/explainer-alphabet-soup-regional-integration-organizations/

Hagerty, D. T. (2005). *South Asia in world politics*. Lanham: Rowman & Littlefield Publishers.

Hakeem, A. (2014). *Paradise on fire: Syed Ali Geelani and the struggle for freedom in Kashmir*. Markfield: Kube Publishers.

Hlatky, S. V. (2012). Strategies and mechanisms of regional change. In T. V. Paul (Ed.), *International relations theory and regional transformation* (pp. 283–298). New York: Cambridge University Press.

Ikenberry, G. J. (2004). American hegemony and East Asian order. *Australian Journal of International Affairs, 58*(3), 353–367.

Ikenberry, G. J. (2006). *Liberal order and imperial ambition: Essays on American power and international order*. Cambridge: Polity Press.

International Crimes Tribunal. (2013). ICT[2]-BD Case No. 03 of 2013 Judgement Summary. Chief Prosecutor Vs Mir Quasem Ali. Website: www.ict-bd.org. 1. International Crimes

Tribunal-2 (ICT-2). [Tribunal constituted under section 6 (1) of the Act No. XIX of 1973]. Old High Court Building, Dhaka, Bangladesh. ICT-BD Case No. 03 of 2013. [Charges: crimes against Humanity and aiding & complicity to commit such crimes as specified in section 3(2) (a)(g)(h) of the Act No. XIX of 1973] viewed on 27 July 2017, http://www.ict-bd.org/ict2/ ICT2%20judgment/Mir%20Quasem-judge-02.pdf

Jetschke, A. (2009). Institutionalizing ASEAN: Celebrating Europe through network governance. *Cambridge Review of International Affairs, 22*(3), 407–426.

Jokela, J. (2009). The European Union as an international actor: Europeanization and institutional changes in the light of the EU's Asia policies. In B. Gaens, J. Jokela, & E. Limnell (Eds.), *The role of the European Union in Asia: China and India as strategic partners* (pp. 37–53). Franham: Ashgate.

Katzenstein, P. J. (2005). *A world of regions: Asia and Europe in the American imperium*. Ithaca, NY: Cornell University Press.

Katzenstein, P. J., & Okawara, N. (2002). Japan, Asian-Pacific security, and the case for analytical eclecticism. *International Security, 26*(3), 153–185.

Keohane, R. O. (1984). *After hegemony: Cooperation and discord in the world political economy*. Princeton: Princeton University Press.

Lenz, T. (2008). *Problematizing the EU's model export to Mercosur: Strategies and motivations*. Paper presented at the GARNET conference on the European Union in International Affairs, Brussels, 24–26 April.

Lockwood, D. E. (1969). Sheikh Abdullah and the politics of Kashmir. *Asian Survey, 9*(5), 382–396.

Murray, P. (2010). Comparative regional integration in the EU and East Asia: Moving beyond integration snobbery. *International Politics, 47*(3–4), 308–323.

Najam, A., & Yusuf, M. (2013). *South Asia 2060: Envisioning regional futures*. London: Anthem Press.

Nye, J. S., Jr. (Ed.). (1968). *International regionalism: Readings*. Boston: Little, Brown and Co.

Nye, J. S., Jr. (1990). Soft power. *Foreign Policy*, (80), 153–171.

Nye, J. S., Jr. (2004). *Soft power: The means to success in world politics*. New York: PublicAffairs.

Nye, J. S., Jr. (2008). Public diplomacy and soft power. *The Annals of the American Academy of Political and Social Science, 616*(1), 94–109.

Nye, J. S., Jr. (2009). Get smart: Combining hard and soft power. *Foreign Affairs, 88*, 160–163.

Nye, J. S., Jr. (2011). *The future of power*. New York: PublicAffairs.

Paul, R. B. (2010). *Routledge handbook of South Asian politics: India, Pakistan, Bangladesh, Sri Lanka and Nepal*. London: Routledge.

Paul, T. V. (2012). *International relations theory and regional transformation*. New York: Cambridge University Press.

Razzaque, M., & Basnett, Y. (Eds.). (2014). *Regional integration in South Asia: Trends, challenges and prospects*. London: Commonwealth Secretariat.

Rosamond, B. (2005). Conceptualising the EU model of governance in world politics. *European Foreign Affairs Review, 10*(4), 463–478.

Rosamond, B., & Alex, W. L. (2011). *Studying regions comparatively: Back to the future?* London: Routledge.

Ruland, J., & Jetschke, A. (2008). 40 years of ASEAN: Perspectives, performance and lessons for change. *The Pacific Review, 21*(4), 397–409.

S/RES/47. (1948). viewed on 27 July 2017, Available at: http://www.un.org/en/ga/search/view_ doc.asp?symbol=S/RES/47(1948).

Saez, L. (2012). *The South Asian Association for Regional Cooperation (SAARC): An emerging collaboration architecture*. Hoboken: Taylor & Francis.

Schaffer, H. B., & Schaffer, T. C. (2005). Kashmir: Fifty years of running in place. In Crocker, Hampson, & Aall (Eds.), *Grasping the Nettle: Analysing the cases of intractable conflicts* (pp. 295–318). Washington, DC: United States Institute of Peace Press.

Schofield, V. (2003). *Kashmir in conflict: India, Pakistan and the unending war*. London: I.B. Tauris.

Severino, R. (2008). *ASEAN* (Southeast Asia background series 10). Singapore: Institute of Southeast Asian Studies, ISEAS.

Shastri, A., & Wilson, A. (2013). *The post-colonial states of South Asia: Political and constitutional problems*. Hoboken: Taylor and Francis.

Sheikh, M. A. (1965, April 1). Kashmir, India and Pakistan. *Foreign Affairs, 43*(3). https://www.foreignaffairs.com/articles/asia/1965-04-01/kashmir-india-and-pakistan; https://www.foreignaffairs.com/issues/1965/43/3

Sil, R., & Katzenstein, P. (2010). Analytic eclecticism in the study of world politics: Reconfiguring problems and mechanisms across research traditions. *Perspectives on Politics, 8*(2), 411–431.

Slaughter, A. M. (2009, January/February). America's edge: Power in the networked century. *Foreign Affairs, 88,* 94–113.

Snidal, D. (1985). The limits of hegemonic stability theory. *International Organization, 39*(4), 579–614.

Stanley Foundation and Stockholm International Peace Research Institute (SIPRI) and the Swedish School of Advanced Asia Pacific Studies of The Swedish Foundation for International Cooperation in Research and Higher Education. (2008). *Challenges to effective multilateralism: Comparing Asian and European experiences*. Sigtuna.

Tharoor, S. (2012). *Pax indica: India and the world in the 21st century*. New Delhi: Allen Lane.

The Indian Express. (2016). *SAARC summit postponed after India's boycott*, viewed on 16 July 2018, http://indianexpress.com/article/india/india-news-india/saarc-summit-postponed-after-indias-boycott-3054721/

The World Bank. (2018). *Intra regional trade South Asia*, viewed on 1 September 2018, http://www.worldbank.org/en/news/infographic/2016/05/24/the-potential-of-intra-regional-trade-for-south-asia

Van Langenhove, L. (2013). *Building regions: The regionalization of world order*. Burlington: Ashgate Publishing.

Wendt, A. (1992). Anarchy is what states make of it: The social construction of power politics. *International Organization, 46*(2), 391–425.

Widmalm, S. (2014). *Kashmir in comparative perspective: Democracy and violent separatism in India*. London: Routledge/Curzon.

Wirsing, R. G. (1994). *India, Pakistan and the Kashmir dispute*. New York: St Martin's Press.

Wong, R. (2012). Model power or reference point? The EU and the ASEAN charter. *Cambridge Review of International Affairs, 25*(4), 669–682.

Zielonka, J. (2008). Europe as a global actor: Empire by example? *International Affairs, 84*(3), 471–484.

Part IV
International Organisations and Global Governance 2.0

Chapter 14
Global Governance 2.0

Amy E. P. Kasper

14.1 Introduction

As previous chapters have discussed, the idea of a 'global order' is constantly shifting in relation to the pressures and influences of its environment. Within the current environment, processes of globalisation have contributed to increased discussion on the idea of 'global governance' as a new means of structuring the global order. But what is global governance? And what exactly is its relationship to globalisation? In the first part of this chapter we will briefly discuss these key conceptualisations, examining the current setting shaping our ideas of global governance, as well as the key actors and theories involved. Then in the second and third sections of this chapter, we will expand this analysis to a discussion on the competing philosophies behind governance structures and what this means for the changing world order, providing several case studies of the impact of globalisation on different levels of governance. Finally the chapter will conclude by outlining the implications of this analysis and engaging in a brief discussion on how the international community may adapt to an increasingly globalised world.

A. E. P. Kasper (✉)
Leiden University, The Hague, the Netherlands
e-mail: amy.eileenll@gmail.com

© Springer Nature Switzerland AG 2020
M. O. Hosli, J. Selleslaghs (eds.), *The Changing Global Order*, United Nations University Series on Regionalism 17,
https://doi.org/10.1007/978-3-030-21603-0_14

14.2 What Is Global Governance?

14.2.1 Defining Global Governance and Globalisation

The term 'global governance' is a relatively new term, having first entered the International Relations lexicon in the early 1990s (Hofferberth 2016, p. 2). According to some scholars, it "emerged as a result of the inadequacy of either the classical realist or functional paradigms to explain the post-Cold War global order" (Lennox 2008). The concept behind global governance is not new, with roots in Wilsonian philosophy and the Peace of Westphalia; but after the end of the Cold War, it expanded into its own domain as part of the "end of history" idea, whereby humanity was assumed to have rejected communism and to instead be pursuing an increasingly democratic order (Fukuyama 1989). Yet the essence of global governance is often shrouded in vagueness and theoretical complexity. We may build a working definition of this concept by deconstructing it and examining the word governance:

> Governance is the sum of many ways individuals and institutions, public and private, manage their common affairs. It is a continuing process through which conflicting or diverse interests may be accommodated and co-operative action taken. It includes formal institutions and regimes empowered to enforce compliance, as well as informal arrangements that people and institutions either have agreed to or perceive to be in their interest. (Hägel 2011)

This oft-cited definition not only serves as a foundation for our understanding of governance, but also provides a roadmap for how to analyse global governance as a concept.

Firstly, governance is complex, made up of a variety of approaches and structures. Governance does not imply government; instead it is a collaborative effort of a multitude of actors, both public and private, which have a stake in the common interest. Secondly, it is a continuing project. Governance is a fluid, ever-changing endeavour, which adapts to meet the needs and challenges of its environment. Therefore when we discuss global governance, we are expanding this basic definition to include all actors within a global context. This includes both states and non-state actors, such as intergovernmental organisations (IGOs), regional entities, multinational corporations (MNCs), and nongovernmental organisations (NGOs). Due to the enhanced communicative technologies characteristic of this current wave of globalisation, countless such stakeholders may now participate in global governance, beyond formalized arrangements. In theory, this creates an international platform for collaboration, promoting creative endeavours and the pooling of resources and talent required to effect change. The reality, as we will see, is a bit more complex.

The concept of global governance is applied inconsistently, at times as a policy notion, at times as an analytical tool, and at times as empirical condition, or in other words a term used to describe the current state of international relations (Hofferberth 2016, p. 2). As Matthias Hofferberth (2016) notes, from its very inception, global governance semantically entailed and continues to entail today a wide range of different meanings, including the activities of actors engaged in world politics, the conceptual tools and the ontology to intellectually grasp these, and the paradigmatic description thereof as a new type of world politics. (p. 2)

This flexibility in meaning may be viewed as either a weakness or a strength. On the one hand, as Lawrence Finkelstein comments, global governance "appears to be virtually anything" (Finkelstein 1995, p. 368), a 'spaghetti bowl' which makes it difficult to know what is excluded from its scope. On the other hand, it is useful to have a term with such wide breadth, since it is relating a reality which is similarly all-encompassing. However in order for the term to have any utility, some boundaries must be established for its meaning. Different authors will conceptualise global governance differently according to their analytical needs; this chapter will use Finkelstein's suggestion that global governance be limited to an activity, and that when discussing those institutions which play a role in effecting global governance, we shall reference them as actors which implement governance (Finkelstein 1995, p. 368). Therefore we will also use Finkelstein's broad definition of global governance as "governing, without sovereign authority, relationships that transcend national frontiers. Global governance is doing internationally what governments do at home" (Finkelstein 1995, p. 369).

Any discussion of global governance must also include an appreciation for the current wave of globalisation, which has made its application and realisation possible. Globalisation, while a common buzzword in modern society, describes a cyclical process within the international system which has manifested itself repeatedly in the past. As a defined concept, globalisation has existed since the nineteenth century, yet it was not until the 1960s that it truly came into vogue as a topic of discussion (Crockett 2011). While much in our current society is popularly attributed to the forces of globalisation, it is a notoriously difficult process to define. This is partly related to the vastness of the concept and the many different manifestations which it takes.

For the purposes of this chapter, perhaps the most useful definition of globalisation is as the "growing interconnectedness reflected in the extended flows of information, technology, capital, goods, services, and people throughout the world" (Stefanachi 2011). This definition is complemented by that of Dr. Nayef R.F. Al-Rodhan and Ambassador Gérard Stoudmann, who describe globalisation as "a process that encompasses the causes, course, and consequences of transnational and transcultural integration of human and non-human activities" (Al-Rodhan and Stoudmann 2006). Previous examples of globalisation from history include Alexander the Great's Hellenic world in the 300s BCE, and the burgeoning Western European fascination and exchange with Southeast Asia in the fifteenth century (Pieterse 2006). Both movements facilitated an exchange of language, culture, products, and knowledge between previously disconnected societies. The current wave of globalisation has been described as an 'accelerated' movement, because of its utilisation of new technologies to more rapidly foster international exchange and connectivity (Pieterse 2006). Modern globalisation, even more than past cycles, is not restricted to one area of human society. Rather it encompasses political, economic, technological, and social spheres, and spurs the intertwining of these spheres so that it is now increasingly difficult to isolate one from another.

14.2.2 Actors Involved

As previously mentioned, due to the impact of globalisation on realising a full conception of global governance, governance is no longer restricted to the state as the main actor. Indeed now any individual with a mobile phone may contribute to a global discussion on the topic. The most commonly cited instance of this is the Arab Spring, in which mobile technology was utilised to connect and mobilise public revolutions. However there are still some actors which play a more prominent role in global governance. These include states, intergovernmental organisations (IGOs), regional entities, multinational corporations (MNCs), and nongovernmental organisations (NGOs). In this section we will briefly describe the relevance of each of these actors, grouped by whether they are public or private bodies.

Within the public sector, the international community comprises states, IGOs, and regional integration schemes, such as those discussed in Chap. 8 of this volume. Some have speculated that the state will fade from its position as the dominant actor in the international system, but if such a change were to come about it would require an extended evolution from the current environment. The nation-state continues to be the primary unit for identity, security, and sovereignty on a structural level, particularly according to realist and neorealist scholars (Krasner 2009). However the nation-state has been joined by IGOs, which serve as mechanisms for the realisation of global governance. Institutions such as the United Nations, the World Bank, the G20, and the International Criminal Court allow for management of issues which, due to globalisation, are now transnational. One example of this is Interpol, which allows for the detection and prosecution of transnational criminal organisations. Additionally, regional integration schemes, such as the European Union, UNASUR, ASEAN, the African Union, and the Arab League occupy an increasingly prominent position on the world stage. The European Union, for example, continues to explore the lengths to which regional entities may aggregate sovereignty and address cross-border issues in an efficient manner.

But while governance has typically been under the purview of the public sector, global governance also includes private sector institutions in a collaborative effort to address common issues. In broad terms of categorisation, this typically includes NGOs and MNCs. NGOs, while not named as such until after the creation of the United Nations, have long held a great deal of influence over policymakers. Religious institutions, scientific societies, and cultural associations are just a few examples of NGOs throughout history which have facilitated organisation within civil society. Like intergovernmental institutions, they have seized upon the connective capability of globalisation to expand greatly in number and scope in the past 50 years. Now, according to some estimates, there are at least 1.5 million operating in the U.S. alone (Bureau of Democracy, Human Rights and Labor 2016), and it is estimated that worldwide there are approximately 40,000 NGOs which have international operations (Nelson 2007). This includes a number of NGO coalitions which have joined forces in order to amplify their collective voice, such as Oxfam International, and large NGOs such as the Bill & Melinda Gates Foundation and MSF (Doctors Without Borders) (Bolton and Nash 2010).

MNCs, or companies which operate in more than one country, are also nothing new, though they have similarly expanded in the past century. It is estimated that there are approximately 35,000 companies which operate internationally, with the top 100 controlling about 40% of world trade, and the top 500 controlling an astonishing 70% (Business Dictionary 2017). Their involvement in governance is somewhat controversial, with many pointing to their financial self-interest and poor record on protecting human rights (Amnesty International 2017). However they also have greater capacity than public institutions or privately-funded NGOs to effect change. It is for this reason that recent years have seen an increase in public-private partnerships (PPPs), defined by the Center for Strategic and International Studies as

> an approach to solving development problems through a coordinated and concerted effort between government and nongovernment actors, including companies and civil society, leveraging the resources, expertise, or market efforts to achieve greater impact and sustainability in development outcomes. (Runde 2013)

Such partnerships have received 'overwhelming' enthusiasm over the past few decades (Linder and Rosenau 2000), being hailed as engines for productive synthesis and innovative collaboration. While this has yet to be empirically tested, it is undeniable that the expanding international presence of NGOs and MNCs is shifting the global governance landscape, giving rise to "network diplomacy," whereby coalitions of states, commercial actors, and NGOs coordinate to pursue mutual goals (Bolton and Nash 2010).

14.2.3   Global Governance, Globalisation, and IR Theory

Recalling Hofferberth's observation that global governance may be conceptualised in widely different manners, it is also clear that one's definition of global governance is tied to one's preferred theoretical paradigm. The idea of global governance as a policy notion, or a means of ordering the international community, is grounded in liberal IR theory, with roots in Wilsonian and Kantian philosophical traditions. Realist interpretations of the current world order may instead treat global governance as an empirical condition, a manifestation of globalisation's impact on traditional forms of governance. Finally constructivists may treat the concept of global governance as an analytical tool, by which they may observe the interaction and construction of transnational identities. In this section, we will briefly apply these three main schools of IR theory to an examination of global governance and globalisation.

Global governance and globalisation have strong ties to liberal IR theory, which first gained pre-eminence in the latter half of the twentieth century after the end of the Cold War. Within a liberal paradigm, the more interconnected human societies are through common markets and institutions supporting their common interests, the more likely the international system will be characterised by creative collaboration and a lessening of conflict (Watson 2004). Therefore globalisation is viewed as a tool for positive change, as it facilitates the development of institutionalisation. Vilde Wikan has even claimed that "neoliberalism is the main driver of globalisation and that globalisation itself can be seen as both the effect of, and the move towards, global neoliberalism" (2015). Additionally, an entire subset of liberal theory, neoliberal institutionalism, is devoted to the concept of global governance, maintaining that international institutions are the key to maintaining peace within the international system (Richardson 2010). This expands the traditional liberal emphasis on the role of the economy as a driving force in the global order. The idea is that the more ties between nations, whether they be economic, political, or social, the less likely it is that those nations will engage in conflict (Richardson 2010).

 Globalisation through a realist lens is often seen as facilitating the continuation of colonisation, albeit a less overt or direct sense. It is a tool which powerful nations employ to exploit and subjugate their less powerful neighbours. The current wave is not far removed from those previously spurred through imperial forces. Some authors note that there are two faces to globalisation, and that one's level of privilege impacts whether globalisation is viewed as a force for good or ill (Milanovic 2003). Similarly, the expansion of global governance as vested in international institutions, from a realist perspective, represents the extended monopolisation of authority by the most powerful states in the international system. Therefore it does not present a significant departure from previous iterations of the world order (Mearsheimer 1994, p. 13). However, some realists also view the effects of globalisation as a threat to traditional conceptions of the state, primarily in relation to territoriality and sovereignty. Another concern is that "although other IR paradigms point to the increasing interdependence of states as contributing to a new global order, realists such as Waltz (1998) have said that rather than growing interdependence of states, we are witnessing the increasing inequality of states" (Lennox 2008). This statement demonstrates the common, yet unproved, assumption among liberal theorists in particular that interdependence will lead to a more just, equal world. Instead, Waltz emphasises the "centrality of the state and importance of power and self-interest in the international realm" (Lennox 2008). Thus even interdependence cannot override states' willingness to use a globalized system for their own self-interest.

In contrast to the realist view of the state as the primary actor within the international system, constructivists view the state as a constructed institution, "no more than a complex set of social functions" (Lennox 2008). In the same way, power, accountability, legitimacy, and sovereignty are considered to be social constructs, and therefore open to interpretation and variation depending on the context. In this sense, constructivists are more open to the idea of a changing world order than realists, being less bound to traditions of governance (Stefanachi 2011, p. 318). Within the constructivist paradigm, what links individuals and groups is common interests, needs, and identities. Therefore the development of transnational perceptions of mutual interest spurs the expansion of global governance. These transnational perceptions are in turn developed through increased globalisation, as constructivists maintain that identity and interest are the products of international interaction. Global governance, therefore, is not necessarily a strategic move to minimise transaction costs, but rather is the natural outgrowth of ongoing interactions between actors (Lennox 2008). Constructivists do not view any particular system of global governance as permanent; instead they emphasise the importance of context and the "temporal-spatial dependency of any structure" (Lennox 2008). As Lennox shares, this conceptualisation of global governance as an analytical tool provides the term with "an intersubjective dimension and a more expansive understanding of how international institutions help to construct 'actors, interests, and social purposes that state-centred theories cannot" (Lennox 2008).

These three main schools of IR theory therefore contribute different, complementary nuances to our understanding of global governance. A full examination of global governance and globalisation would ideally hold all three perspectives in balance. It is important to recognise, however, the liberal impetus behind much of the Western conversation on global governance, and to recall the recent history of this theoretical paradigm.

14.2.4 What Does This Mean for Traditional Governance/ Sovereignty?

Beyond a conceptual and theoretical understanding of global governance, this chapter also aims to familiarise the reader with how globalisation both enables an integrated world order but also impedes some more traditional aspects of local or state governance. A key discussion on this front is the tension between global governance and state sovereignty.

Global governance implies that sovereignty is dispersed amongst various stakeholders, as outlined previously; therefore the push in the past century for a more integrated global system has already challenged the singular authority once enjoyed by the state. Globalisation has pushed this trend even further; as Jens Bartelson shares, "Globalisation entails the increasing volume, velocity and importance of flows within and across borders of people, ideas, goods, money, and much else, thus challenging one of sovereignty's basic principles: the ability to control what crosses borders in either direction" (Bartelson 2009).

However aside from merely seeing the dissipation of sovereignty, the current global order is characterised by various competing types of sovereignty, each linked to a different actor exercising a particular kind of authority. This can be a confusing system, as sovereignty is a highly complex concept with a multitude of definitions.

To simplify the discussion, this chapter has selected four relevant conceptualisations of sovereignty to define, chosen as they represent the interaction of the four different categories of actors involved in global governance. These include 'real sovereignty', 'public sovereignty', 'pooled sovereignty', and 'de facto sovereignty'.

The idea of sovereignty first became a popular topic of discussion in Europe in the sixteenth and seventeenth centuries, developed by Hobbes and Bodin to establish the legitimacy of a strong, centralised authority. This notion of sovereignty therefore became attached to the head of state, often a monarch, and was imbued with both divine and legal authority (Krasner 2009). At the same time, the Peace of Westphalia established a system whereby states respected the sovereignty of neighbouring states, bringing to an end the interventions which had characterised the European continent for centuries (Kissinger 2014, p. 31). Partly thanks to this success, this became the primary conception of sovereignty for many years, and later came to be known as 'real/titular sovereignty,' with the latter referring to the powers of a monarch which would later be divested from those of the centralised governing authority (Krasner 2009). The idea of real sovereignty is today vested in the nation-state. It includes some notion of territorial borders, being "closely related to the preservation of the country's territorial integrity, independence, and security and to the provision of the rights and freedoms of man and citizen" (Kokoshin 2014). Because of this it is directly challenged by globalisation's blurring of borders; some have even said that globalisation "attacks" the idea of sovereignty (Kokoshin 2014).

With the development of representative democracies in the seventeenth and eighteenth centuries, a new form of sovereignty slowly emerged, which has had several designations but for this paper shall be labelled 'public sovereignty.' This is the idea that the ultimate sovereignty of a nation lies with its citizens. Democracy by definition adheres strongly to public sovereignty, as the word comes from the Ancient Greek term dēmokratía, meaning "rule of the people" (Crockett 2011), but it is not exclusive to it. Even non-democracies can recognise that their authority comes from the consent of their citizens. Public sovereignty may be wielded by NGOs, in particular those which comprise membership, but it is much more than this. The interaction of the public in governance has grown in the past 50 years through the introduction of information communication technology (ICT). Public sovereignty is a cornerstone of democracy. Its belief in the power of the people assumes that the public is well-educated and informed on the issues. While this may or may not be accurate, many have viewed the current wave of internet-supported globalisation as a force for good, as it distributes educational resources and spreads a greater awareness of other peoples and cultures (The Economist 2001).

The emergence of international institutions has led scholars to discuss another level of sovereignty: 'pooled sovereignty.' In this conceptualisation, individual authorities give up some piece of their independence to a greater body, which through aggregating the authority from each of its members gains the license to dictate certain norms and laws. Both IGOs and regional entities are examples of bodies which exercise pooled sovereignty. This is a tenuous and still developing notion of sovereignty, with the European Union providing the most ambitious experiment in its application. It should be noted that pooled sovereignty schemes are facing backlash and challenges to their legitimacy, most notably amongst its standard bearers such as the United Nations, the International Criminal Court, and the European Union; it is therefore an important area for further study.

Finally, the proliferation of MNCs has given rise to another relevant conceptualisation of sovereignty: 'de facto sovereignty' (Kapfer 2006). As the name suggests, this concept eludes to the 'real' power to accomplish one's goals, often supported by MNCs' financial power. As such corporations are large enough to influence policies and be heard at the highest levels of governance, they diminish the real sovereignty of nation-states (Nye 1974). The interaction of MNCs in governance is controversial; they are simultaneously able to accomplish more than a state necessarily could on its own (e.g. Tesla) but also tend to push for their own financial interests, benefitting a few rather than the whole of society. With financial incentives to promote international cooperation and prosperity, MNCs inhabit and blur boundary lines, enjoying de facto sovereignty because of their economic influence. In some cases they act in lieu of a government, taking security measures to protect their employees, and advocating on behalf of their interests at the national and international level (Kapfer 2006).

It should be emphasised that these are merely four possible conceptions of sovereignty, and that there is a great deal of literature identifying further and more nuanced means of defining the concept. Already it is clear that global governance in a globalised environment is an ambitious endeavour and a complex juggling act of different interests.

Complicating this further, not everyone has the same idea of what global governance should look like. In the following section, we will examine the various actors and types of sovereignty further, while adding yet another layer of comparison between authoritarian and democratic views of a constructed world order.

14.3 Whose Global Governance?

Next we will move toward a more concrete discussion on the implementation of global governance, while leaving the discussion of specific institutions involved to the other chapters in this section. Instead, this next section will take a broader view on the interaction of different approaches to global governance, and what this means for building a cohesive world order. Although the diverse theories and views toward the global order are numerous, this chapter will simplify the discussion to the conflict between authoritarian and democratic visions for global governance, which correspond to liberal and realist theories. These differing perspectives will also be compared through several brief case studies on the ways in which globalisation impacts various actors' ability to enact governance.

14.3.1 Liberal Democratic Order

After the end of the Cold War, the advancement of neo-liberal institutionalist theory gave rise to new ideas about how to address the evils of inequality and lack of development around the world. Previously in this chapter we briefly alluded to the belief that globalisation would result in the increased democratisation and equality of the global order (Dalpino 2001). Democratic structures of governance accompanied by free market capitalism were seen as a valuable tool for correcting these inequalities and advancing norms of human rights and freedom of speech throughout the world (Milanovic 2003). The democratic West pursued integration with authoritarian regimes in the belief that this would organically encourage them closer to democratic systems (Walker 2016). Even staunchly authoritarian systems, such as China or Russia, "were expected slowly but inevitably to liberalise politically as their economies grew and their middle classes developed" (Walker 2016).

Globalisation, in turn, was seen as a valuable tool for this integration, enabling the promotion of Western liberal and democratic norms (Dalpino 2001). In the United States, one popular view was that "creating an international order in which more people are free and prosperous is profoundly in America's self-interest. In a world of market democracies, America and Americans are likely to be both more prosperous and more secure" (Daalder and Lindsay 2003). As a Brookings Institute piece shares, "in regions lacking a widespread and overt commitment to democracy, Western policymakers and nongovernmental groups trying to promote greater political liberalisation have placed their faith in the indirect effects of globalisation" (Dalpino 2001). These indirect effects included economic interdependence, which would create common interests across borders, and the development of international institutions to facilitate cooperation and exchange (Ikenberry 2011).

Therefore in a Western liberal view, global governance is a means and an end in itself, creating a world system characterised by multilateralism, integrated markets, and a rule-based order built on shared liberal norms and ideals. Coming from its liberal IR roots, it holds the view that the more democratic the international community is, the less likely it is to slip into another major conflict. This notion of global governance also prioritises "universal principles of individual rights and common humanity," even at the expense of state sovereignty (Ikenberry 2011). This system was originally constructed on the foundation of the Westphalian system designed in 1648, but in the twentieth century became linked to the United States' hegemony and formalised through a steady stream of treaties and conventions (Ikenberry 2011).

However, in recent years the endurance of this vision of the world order has been questioned. Academics have begun to turn away from viewing globalisation as a panacea for political dysfunction, and democracy globally is stagnating. Freedom House's 2017 annual Freedom in the World report described a world in which "A total of 67 countries suffered net declines in political rights and civil liberties in 2016, compared with 36 that registered gains. This marked the 11th consecutive year in which declines outnumbered improvements" (Puddington and Roylance

2017). This trend has led many academics to discuss a "democratic recession" (Diamond 2015). Recent publications have included articles such as "Why Promoting Democracy is Smart and Right", but they are increasingly joined by others such as "Democracy in Decline?" and "Is There Any Future for Democracy?" These appear to have sprung from a realisation that the forces of globalisation and investments into global governance have not significantly strengthened the ability of democratic states to spread liberal norms. Instead, "the past decade has seen the rise of tribalism and nationalism; an increasing focus on the "other" in all societies; and a loss of confidence in government, in the capitalist system, and in democracy" (Kagan 2017). This will be demonstrated further through the case studies in the following section.

Thus the future of this vision of global governance is unclear. Many believe that the foundations of the liberal world order are secure and will endure no matter the changes in state governments or political ideologies; that the institutions binding the world together are already too powerful to unmake. However, this view has met challenges from a competing vision of a globalised world order originating from the more authoritarian corners of the world, but growing in popularity within some Western nations, as well.[1]

14.3.2 Realist Authoritarian Order

The authoritarian perspective on global governance is more in line with realist IR theory than liberal, with an ultimate view towards the balance of power on the global stage. From the perspective of authoritarian regimes such as China, Russia, Venezuela, Iran, and Saudi Arabia, the push for globalisation is an attempt by the West to impose their values and culture onto the rest of the world (Walker 2016, p. 50). And indeed, with the open discussion of globalisation as a tool to spread democracy, they have good reason to be suspicious. In reaction, these countries have come to share a common objective of "containing the spread of democracy," which they pursue through building their own systems of global governance (Walker 2016, p. 50). In this way, they may protect their individual sovereignty rather than see it absorbed in pooled sovereignty schemes which do not adequately represent their interests.

Christopher Walker at the National Endowment for Democracy has written of Russia's "antidemocratic toolkit," a counter to the use of soft power in the Western world. It includes "government-organised nongovernmental organisations (GONGOs), "zombie" election monitoring, foreign aid and investment, and both traditional- and new-media enterprises" (2016, p. 51). In this endeavour globalisation has enhanced their capability to spread these practices both domestically and internationally (Walker 2016, p. 50). In addition, authoritarian regimes have built

---

[1] See Uri Friedman's piece, "Donald Trump Issues a Scathing Rejection of 'Globalism'". *The Atlantic*, 25 September 2018.

their own IGOs to facilitate an ideologically illiberal mode of global governance. These include the Eurasian Economic Union (EEU), the Collective Security Treaty Organisation (STO), and the Shanghai Cooperation Organisation (SCO), among many others. These enable them to spread norms counter to those of the Western liberal sphere, while still allowing them to benefit from increased cooperation with similar countries. The SCO cooperation between two major powers, China and Russia, also reflects their "shared interest in keeping Western (primarily U.S.) economic, political, and military influence out of the region" (Shevtsova 2015). Through these tools, authoritarian regimes prioritise norms of 'state sovereignty,' 'civilisational diversity,' and "the defense of 'traditional values' against liberal democracy" (Walker 2016, p. 52). As a result, regional organisations are embracing shifting missions, and non-Western powers are increasingly looked to as international patrons (Walker 2016).

The effectiveness of this approach is also reflected in a trend reported by Freedom House, where a large share of the decline in political rights and civil liberties has taken place in countries already labelled 'not free' (Walker 2016, p. 53). In other words, authoritarian countries have not significantly democratised in response to increasing globalisation and interdependence with liberal nations, but have instead become even more repressive. This has of course been influenced by numerous factors and is not a solid indicator of the success or failure of either approach to global governance. It does, however, weaken the assumption following the end of the Cold War that globalisation and the creation of a global system of governance would necessarily lead to a liberal world order.

14.4   Case Studies

These warring conceptualisations of global governance may be found on the political, social, and economic level, influencing states' cooperation and dialogue with one another. Adding to this ideological struggle is the impact of intensified globalisation. In this section we will briefly examine three cases where the struggle between democratic and authoritarian visions for governance manifests, and the ways in which they are influenced by globalisation. These cases will focus on three of the actors involved in global governance: IGOs, civil society, and MNCs.

14.4.1   Norm-Building Through IGOs

When it comes to conceptualisations of the global order, IGOs are the front line. We have already discussed the ways in which IGOs may promote either liberal or illiberal ideals, but in this section we will provide some further discussion on what this looks like in practice.

As mentioned previously, after the end of the Cold War Western liberal nations tended to believe they had arrived at the "end of history," wherein humanity had reached "the end point of mankind's ideological evolution and the universalisation of Western liberal democracy as the final form of human government" (Fukuyama 1989). Democratic nations eagerly supported the expansion of pooled sovereignty schemes as a means to proliferate liberal norms and democratic values throughout the world (Dalpino 2001). However recent research has concluded that this is not always a successful strategy.

Institutions such as the European Union and United Nations explicitly champion the spread of liberal norms, such as "protecting and promoting human rights, the rule of law and democracy, recognising that they are interlinked and mutually reinforcing and that they belong to the universal and indivisible core values and principles of the United Nations" (United Nations 2009, p. 1). But studies have shown that institutions tend to promote democratic values when they exist in a region where there is already a powerful constituency of democratic nations, whether that be because they are the majority or because they hold the most economic power (Dalpino 2001). At the same time, institutions including an equal number of democratic and nondemocratic states, or those where authoritarian regimes are predominant, tend to avoid discussing democratic norms and values in their negotiations. Evidence of this may be found in an examination of institutions in Asia, where "the diversity of political regimes has largely kept democracy and human rights off the table in the Asian-Pacific Economic Cooperation (APEC) group and the Association of Southeast Asian Nations (ASEAN)" (Dalpino 2001). Additionally, it is striking that in the charter of the Union of South American Nations (UNASUR), it primarily asserts "unlimited respect" for state sovereignty, with its purpose articulated as "regional integration and global rebalancing, which is to be based on respect for national sovereignty" (Global Americans 2016). It is only later that it mentions "unlimited respect for human rights," and its mandate on monitoring elections is explicitly designed to accompany a state's electoral commission, resulting in a pro-government bias that removes them as an independent arbiter of fair and just elections (Global Americans 2016).

This analysis supports the classic realist perspective expressed by Mearsheimer that international institutions are merely tools of the most powerful states, used to further their interests and survival (2001). In this view, 'world order' is not created for its own sake, for ideals of peace and prosperity. Instead "the configuration of the system, in other words, is the unintended consequence of great-power security competition, not the result of states acting together to organise peace" (Mearsheimer 2001, p. 64). Globalisation has allowed for the expansion of IGOs on a massive scale, turning them into some of the most important actors in global governance. However the Western liberal world still often takes the (as-yet unproven) relationship between IGOs and democratisation for granted, believing that such schemes will automatically promote democratic norms because of their representative structure. This results in a mismatch between two competing ideologies regarding the purpose of IGOs. As Walker et al. observe, Western liberals end up disadvantaged in an arena where their more authoritarian counterparts take the competition for power more seriously. (Walker et al. 2016).

14.4.2   ICTs and Public Sovereignty

Civil society[2] is an increasingly important actor in global governance schemes, as it wields influence on decision-making at both the state and international level. The United Nations, among others, has specifically called out the importance of strengthening civil society as a means of improving global governance (Cardoso 2003; Ishkanian 2007). Globalisation and the prevalence of ICTs has made it easier than ever for citizens to participate in governance, providing increased access to information and enabling the organisation of grassroots movements. Civil society has been described as the "frontline fighters" in the promotion of democracy, and countless billions have been invested in building robust civil societies in former socialist and developing nations to advance liberal norms (Ishkanian 2007).

However the involvement of civil society in global governance is far from straightforward, and certain elements of globalisation complicate their inclusion further. Civil society depends upon an engaged, well-informed citizenry. Some have argued that with the ability to find an inexhaustible amount of information on the internet, it is easier for citizens to be educated, informed participants in governance. Indeed, a free internet has commonly been assumed to open closed societies and hasten the demise of authoritarian regimes (Kurlantzick 2010). But this ignores the existence of psychological biases influencing how individuals process information. For instance, the availability heuristic details how individuals will believe something is more prevalent than it really is, based on how salient the issue is to them personally (Madigan 2013). A common example is the undue fear assigned to shark attacks as opposed to car accidents, even though the chances of being killed in a car accident is about 700 times greater than the chances of being killed in a shark attack (Dew 2016). This heuristic coupled with the evolution of news on the internet, where bias and 'fake news' hinder the ability of citizens to be reliably informed voters, presents a concerning trend. With an open, capitalist media informing the public on current events, a dynamic that has also increased with globalisation, some are asking whether democracy "can survive the internet" (Balz 2017).

This dynamic begins at the local level, but in the current interconnected environment it does not take long for it to reach the level of international governance as well. Take for example the prevalence of referendums throughout the EU; such tools are increasingly used to acknowledge and attempt to institutionalise the power of the public (Leyland 2017). This is a classic example of Putnam's two-level games theory, wherein negotiators must not only negotiate with their counterparts, but also with their home public (Putnam 1988). In a truly democratic vision of global governance, civil society would continue to grow and hold more authority; but how does this work if the public is misinformed?

---

[2] For the purposes of this discussion, the term 'civil society' is used to indicate the public, including individuals, grassroots movements, and NGOs.

Authoritarian structures, on the other hand, are built upon the tight control of information. It was once thought that globalisation would impede their ability to manage channels of information, but in some cases it has been seen that regimes are able to use the internet and communications technology to more easily monitor and intercept activists (Barysch 2013). This adds to a dynamic where citizens may be unaware of the specific extent to which the government may be involved in curating what they see online, so they may develop the incorrect perception that their society is more open and free than it is. Two specific examples of this trend include China, where citizens are involved in local governance but largely trust national decisions to the authorities (Ervine 2011). Additionally with the creation of lavishly funded media organisations such as the CCTV, China is able to spread its messaging not just throughout its own country, but throughout the entire globe. Another example of this trend may be observed in Cuba, where the regime "seeks to guide and channel the growth of the Internet so that like other media its primary impact is to serve the political goals of the revolution" (Kalathil and Boas 2001). This is textbook propaganda, employing new technologies and the dissemination capabilities of the internet. As Foreign Policy contributor Peter Pomerantsev summarises, "Why fight the information age and globalisation when you can use it?" (Pomerantsev 2015).

Beyond being impeded by the tight control of information, civil society structures in authoritarian countries have recently been demonstrated to not always be the champions of democracy they were once thought to be. Recent research on the true impact of civil society on authoritarian regimes has come to the surprising conclusion that rather than present a challenge to the status quo, a robust civil society may serve as a legitimisation tool for authoritarian governments (Lewis 2013). This is because:

> Civic associations, regardless of whether they are church societies or sports clubs, will reproduce elements of the political context in which they exist and will structure themselves accordingly. Where associational contexts are dominated by state-centralised, patron–client tendencies, then associations, too, become sites for the potential replication of those vertical ties. (Lewis 2013, p. 328)

The endpoint of this comparison is simply that the effects of globalisation on information dissemination and the development of civil society is not straightforward, and that globalisation does not inherently promote a liberal democratic vision of global governance. Instead, the current trend shows democratic systems struggling to find a balance between an engaged citizenry and controlling the preponderance of hysteria and false information, while authoritarian regimes are able to more easily disseminate propaganda and monitor the activities of their citizens – as well as interfere in information dispersion and influencing of public opinion in other countries, as seen in the recent American and European elections.

14.4.3   MNCs and Economic Globalisation

Finally, no discussion on global governance would be complete without reviewing the role of MNCs. International companies have been a powerful force on the global stage for centuries, and de facto sovereignty has always rested in individuals or enterprises which have the financial means to carry out their objectives (Nye 1974). Due to the capitalist nature of such corporations, their involvement in the global community has traditionally been viewed as a tool for liberalisation, both economic and political. As Anne-Marie Slaughter has observed, this results from an erosion of the state's authority, weakening the state's power to regulate within its borders "both because people can easily flee their jurisdiction and because the flows of capital, pollution, pathogens, and weapons are too great and sudden for any [state] to control" (Slaughter qtd. in Adolf 2011). Hence it is assumed that as countries open their borders to economic exchange, they are also opening their borders to the infiltration of liberal ideas and norms. As the current wave of globalisation has allowed for the expansion of MNCs like never before in history, many have assumed that this porosity of borders will contribute to the spread of liberal ideals, which will in turn spur the democratisation of the international community (Adolf 2011).

However, since the end of the Cold War there has been a great deal of research on whether there is a correlation between economic and political liberalisation, and the results have been inconclusive. It appears, instead, that the extent to which states liberalise politically depends a great deal on their cultural and economic conditions (Adolf 2011). One study has even found that "trade openness and portfolio investment inflows negatively affect democracy. The effect of trade openness is constant over time while the negative effect of portfolio investment strengthens. Foreign direct investment inflows positively affect democracy, but the effect weakens over time" (Li and Reuveny 2003, Abstract.). Therefore the relationship between economic globalisation and political liberalisation appears to be negligible, at best.

A corresponding area of research examines whether MNCs prefer to invest in democratic or authoritarian markets; the findings demonstrate that while democratic markets do tend to receive more investment, hybrid or authoritarian regimes are still able to attract significant resources (Stølan 2012). Indeed,

> Some argue that the successful model of economic development, combining an open economy with a closed political system, has made regimes such as Russia's and China's more attractive in a political world characterised by the competition between democratic and authoritarian regimes. (Hayoz 2012, p. 23)

And since, as mentioned previously, the 500 largest MNCs represent 70% of world trade, their investments not only represent the financial priorities of the global market, but also act as a means by which authoritarian governments may bolster their authority (Kapfer and Champion 2013). For instance, Wen-Chin Wu's 2014 research on trade openness in authoritarian countries demonstrated that "dictators in labor-abundant countries expand trade to neutralise democratisation threats initiated by rising inequality," and that in the end economic globalisation appears to strengthen authoritarian regimes (Wu 2015, p. 790). From an ideological perspective, it is also the case that MNCs typically share a realist philosophy with authoritarian regimes; while one is primarily concerned with self-interest and the balance of power, another is primarily concerned with turning a profit.

This de facto sovereignty exercised by MNCs concerns many Western liberal progressives, who fear that corporate interests will result in the manipulation of multilateral organisations, such as the WTO, to "protect profits at the expense of social, health, safety, and environmental standards" (Moravcsik 2010). Additionally, sceptics have argued that "while globalisation promotes opportunity for growth and increase in wealth, it has also increased the socio-economic disparity between people, making nations less democratic and progressively more ruled by the wealthy multi-nationals" (Crockett 2011). This poses a challenge to the democratic view of global governance, wherein the international community organises to protect liberal norms such as human rights. As MNCs over the past decade have most often led, rather than followed, global governance efforts,[3] their de facto sovereignty may in some ways be complementary to an authoritarian view of the world order (Detomasi 2014).

14.5   What Does This Mean for the International Community?

These three broadly defined cases illustrate how, far from strengthening and promoting democratisation, globalisation has exacerbated existing challenges to democratic systems. IGOs do not necessarily promote liberal norms, the public is not always a champion for democracy, and economic globalisation does not inherently lead to political liberalisation. Concurrently, authoritarian regimes have proved to be far more resilient and adaptable to a globalised system than was previously assumed. Rather than seeing the 'end of history,' it is now apparent that authoritarian regimes and strategies of governance will continue to play an important role in the global community for some time to come, particularly considering the forecasted rise of China as a world leader.

Thus when discussing the implementation of global governance, it is clear that there is still a crucial debate on the purpose, norms, and structure of the international community. This conflict may be seen most clearly in institutions such as the United Nations, which despite their foundation in Western liberal norms and explicit promotion of democracy, in practice are far from democratic. Instead, "it is commonly witnessed that the elite wealthy countries always have the final say in conflicts or important issues that are discussed, which ends up swaying the domestic politics of less developed countries to their favour" (Crockett 2011).

A constructivist view toward global governance may be helpful moving forward, explaining how the evolution of the world order is a continual struggle between

---

[3] Such as in the areas of intellectual property, labour standards, environmental standards, and sovereign debt-rating agencies.

liberal and realist perspectives and priorities. It is crucial to understand that the current system of global governance is not permanent. International institutions and dynamics are constantly shifting, and their changes may be hailed as a natural evolution of the world order, rather than presenting an upset to the foundations of liberal thought.

This does not remove but rather highlights the importance of thoughtful discussions on how best to structure the international community moving forward. John Ruggie, former deputy secretary general of the United Nations, has shared that "postwar institutions, including the United Nations, were built for an international world, but we have entered a global world. International institutions were designed to reduce external frictions between states; our challenge today is to devise more inclusive forms of global governance" (Fonte 2011). Global Governance 2.0, it appears, has yet to be developed.

14.6 Conclusion

This chapter aimed to provide a definitional and theoretical foundation for the concepts of global governance and globalisation, along with a practical examination of what their evolution means for our understanding of the current global order. The ensuing comparison between democratic and authoritarian perspectives and capabilities in terms of governance structures will hopefully inspire readers to carefully weigh the implications of not only the current global environment, but also to extrapolate those challenges which will continue to develop in coming years.

The world is unlikely to retreat to a less globalised system, even if it does slow the steady march of increased interconnectedness. Therefore it is worth examining how well our current systems of governance are equipped to handle a world very different from those of previous centuries, and to study their continuing evolution.

Further Readings

Held, D., & McGrew, A. (1993). Globalization and the liberal democratic state. *Government and Opposition, 28*(2), 261–288. Retrieved from https://doi.org/10.1111/j.1477-7053.1993.tb01281.x.

Jentleson, B. (2018, September 9). That post-liberal international order world: Some core characteristics. *Lawfare*. Retrieved from https://www.lawfareblog.com/post-liberal-international-order-world-some-core-characteristics

Köksal, E. (2006). *The impact of multinational corporations on international relations – A study of American multinationals*. Middle East Technical University. Retrieved from http://citeseerx.ist.psu.edu/viewdoc/download;jsessionid=AF50951F32E856AF9B5DF084360711DA?doi=10.1.1.633.5124&rep=rep1&type=pdf

Mcdonald, P. J., & Sweeney, K. (2007). The Achilles' heel of liberal IR theory? Globalization and conflict in the Pre-World War I era. *World Politics, 59*(3), 370–403. Retrieved from http://www.jstor.org/stable/40060163

Slaughter, A.-M. (2004). *A new world order*. Princeton/Oxford: Princeton University Press.

Ştefanachi, B. (2011). Globalization and identities – A constructivist approach. In *The scale of globalization. Think globally, act locally, change individually in the 21st century* (pp. 312–318). Ostrava: University of Ostrava. ISBN 978-80-7368-963-6. Retrieved from http://conference. osu.eu/globalization/publ2011/312-318_Stefanachi.pdf

References

Adolf, R. G. (2011, October 14). Do economic globalization and political freedom go together? *Asian Politics & Policy, 3*(4), 569–609.

Al-Rodhan, N., & Stoudmann, G. (2006). *Definitions of globalization: A comprehensive overview and a proposed definition* (1st ed.). Geneva Centre for Security Policy.

Amnesty International. (2017, March). Corporations. In *What we do*. Retrieved from www. amnesty.org/en/what-we-do/corporate-accountability/

Balz, D. (2017, April 22). A scholar asks, 'Can democracy survive the Internet?' *The Washington Post*.

Bartelson, J. (2009, March 2). Is there a global society? *International Political Sociology, 3*(1), 112–115.

Barysch, K. (2013, October 21). Is the internet really good for democracy? *World Economic Forum*. Retrieved from www.weforum.org/agenda/2013/10/is-the-internet-really-good-for-democracy/

Bolton, M., & Nash, T. (2010, May). The role of middle power-NGO coalitions in global policy: The case of the cluster munitions ban. *Global Policy, 1*(2), 172–184.

Bureau of Democracy, Human Rights and Labor. (2016, March). *Fact sheet: Non-Governmental Organizations (NGOs) in the United States*. HumanRights.gov. Retrieved from www.human-rights.gov/dyn/2016/01/fact-sheet-non-governmental-organizations-ngos-in-the-united-states/

Cardoso, F. H. (2003, January 2). Civil society and global governance: High level panel on UN-Civil Society. In *Global Policy Forum*. Retrieved from www.globalpolicy.org/un-reform/31820.html

Crockett, S. (2011, August 27). Has globalization spread democracy around the world? In *E-international relations students*. Retrieved from www.e-ir.info/2011/08/27/has-globalization-spread-democracy-around-the-world/

Daalder, I. H., & Lindsay, J. M. (2003,January 1). The globalization of politics: American Foreign Policy for a new century. *Brookings Institution*. Retrieved from www.brookings.edu/articles/the-globalization-of-politics-american-foreign-policy-for-a-new-century/

Dalpino, C. E.. (2001, September 1). Does globalization promote democracy? An early assessment. *Brookings Institution*. Retrieved from www.brookings.edu/articles/does-globalization-promote-democracy-an-early-assessment/

Detomasi, D. (2014, March 28). The multinational corporation as a political actor: 'Varieties of capitalism' revisited. *Journal of Business Ethics, 128*(3), 685–700.

Dew, D. (2016, September 13). Fear of immigrants and sharks: From stories to statistics. *The Gazette*. Retrieved from www.thegazette.com/subject/opinion/guest-columnists/fear-of-immigrants-and-sharks-from-stories-to-statistics-20160913

Diamond, L. (2015, January). Facing up to the democratic recession. *Journal of Democracy, 26*(1), 141–155.

Ervine, P. (2011, Feburary 4). Can China be defined as an Authoritarian State? *E-International Relations Students*. Retrieved from http://www.e-ir.info/2011/02/04/can-china-be-defined-as-an-authoritarian-state/

Finkelstein, L. (1995). What is global governance? *Global Governance, 1*(3), 367–372.

Fonte, J. (2011, October 3). Sovereignty or submission: Liberal democracy or global governance? *Foreign Policy Research Institute*. Retrieved from www.fpri.org/article/2011/10/sovereignty-or-submission-liberal-democracy-or-global-governance/

Fukuyama, F. (1989). The end of history? *The National Interest*. Retrieved from https://ps321. community.uaf.edu/files/2012/10/Fukuyama-End-of-history-article.pdf

Global Americans. (2016). Global Americans report: Tracking Latin American foreign policies and human rights. UNASUR/CELAC. *Latin America Goes Global*. Retrieved from http:// latinamericagoesglobal.org/files/LAGG-final-report.pdf, pp 11.

Hägel, P. (2011). *Global governance*. Oxford Bibliographies. Retrieved from http://www.oxford-bibliographies.com/view/document/obo-9780199743292/obo-9780199743292-0015.xml

Hayoz, N. (2012). Globalization and discursive resistance: Authoritarian power structures in Russia and the challenges of modernity. In *Waiting for reform under Putin and Medvedev* (pp. 19–37). London: Palgrave Macmillan UK.

Hofferberth, M. (2016, January 19). *'Confusion is a fundamental state of mind' – On the peculiar intellectual career of global governance in international relations*. Texas: University of Texas, San Antonio, USA. Retrieved from https://doi.org/10.1057/palcomms.2015.44.

Ikenberry, G. J. (2011). The future of the liberal world order: Internationalism after America. *Foreign Affairs*.

Ishkanian, A. (2007). Democracy promotion and civil society. In M. Albrow, M. Glasius, H. K. Anheier, & M. Kaldor (Eds.), *Global civil society 2007/8: Communicative power and democracy* (Global civil society – Year books, pp. 58–85). London: SAGE.

Kagan, R. (2017, January 24). The twilight of the liberal world order. *Brookings Institution*. Retrieved from www.brookings.edu/research/the-twilight-of-the-liberal-world-order/

Kalathil, S., & Boas, T. C. (2001, August 6). The internet and state control in authoritarian regimes: China, Cuba, and the Counterrevolution. *Carnegie Endowment for International Peace*. Retrieved from http://firstmonday.org/article/view/876/785

Kapfer, S. (2006, April 7). Multinational corporations and the erosion of state sovereignty. *Brigham Young University*. Retrieved from http://pol.illinoisstate.edu/downloads/conferences/2006/ Kapfer2006.pdf

Kapfer, S., & Champion, B. (2013, September 20). The growing power of multinational corporations. *Brigham Young University Journal of Undergraduate Research*. Retrieved from http:// jur.byu.edu/?p=6205

Kissinger, H. (2014). *World Order*. New York: Penguin Press.

Kokoshin, A. A. (2014). Providing Russia with real sovereignty in the contemporary world. *Herald of the Russian Academy of Sciences, 84*(6), 449–455. Translated from Russian by Alekseev, B.

Krasner, S. D. (2009, November 20). Think again: sovereignty. *Foreign Policy*. Retrieved from http://foreignpolicy.com/2009/11/20/think-again-sovereignty/

Kurlantzick, J. (2010, May 9). Is the internet good for democracy? A debate. *Newsweek*. Retrieved from www.newsweek.com/internet-good-democracy-debate-70215

Lennox, V. (2008). Conceptualising global governance in international relations. *University of Ottowa*. Retrieved from www.e-ir.info/2008/10/03/ conceptualising-global-governance-in-international-relations/

Leyland, P. J. (2017). Referendums, constitutional reform and the perils of popular sovereignty. *The Italian Law Journal*, January 2017 Special Issue.

Lewis, D. (2013, July 30). Civil society and the authoritarian state: Cooperation, contestation and discourse. *Journal of Civil Society, 9*(3), 325–340.

Li, Q., & Reuveny, R. (2003, January). Economic globalization and democracy: An empirical analysis. *British Journal of Political Science, 33*(1), 29–54.

Linder, S. H., & Rosenau, P. V. (2000). Mapping the terrain of the public-private policy partnership. In *Public-private policy partnerships*. Cambridge: Massachusetts Institute of Technology.

Madigan, J. (2013, April 15). The availability heuristic is always on. *Psychology Today*. Retrieved from www.psychologytoday.com/blog/mind-games/201304/the-availability-heuristic-is-always

Mearsheimer, J. (2001). *The Tragedy of Great Power Politics*. New York: W.W. Norton & Company.

Mearsheimer, J. (1994). The false promise of international institutions. *International Security, 19*(3), 5–49.

Milanovic, B. (2003, March 4). The two faces of globalization: Against globalization as we know it. *World Bank,* Washington, DC, USA.

Moravcsik, A. (Jan 2010). Affirming Democracy in International Organizations. In Goldstein, Joshua and Pevehouse, Jon (eds.) *Global Challenges in 2030.* Retrieved from www.princeton.edu/~amoravcs/library/goldstein.pdf

Multinational Corporation (MNC). (2017). BusinessDictionary.com. Retrieved from www.businessdictionary.com/definition/multinational-corporation-MNC.html

Nelson, J. (2007). The operation of Non-Governmental Organizations (NGOs) in a world of corporate and other codes of conduct. In *Corporate social responsibility initiative.* Cambridge, MA: John F. Kennedy School of Government/Harvard University.

Nye, J. S. Jr. (1974, October). Multinationals: The game and the rules: Multinational corporations in world politics. *Foreign Affairs.* Retrieved from www.foreignaffairs.com/articles/1974-10-01/multinationals-game-and-rules-multinational-corporations-world-politics

Pieterse, J. N. (2006). *Globalization goes in circles: Hybridities east-west.* Santa Barbara: University of California.

Pomerantsev, P. (2015, June 23). Beyond Propaganda: How authoritarian regimes are learning to engineer human souls in the age of Facebook. *Foreign Policy.* Retrieved from https://foreignpolicy.com/2015/06/23/beyond-propaganda-legatum-transitions-forum-russia-china-venezuela-syria/

Puddington, A., & Roylance, T. (2017). Freedom in the World 2017. Populists and Autocrats: The Dual Threat to Global Democracy. *Freedom House.*

Putnam, R. D. (1988). Diplomacy and domestic politics: The logic of two-level games. *International Organization, 42*(3), 427–460.

Richardson, J. L. (2010). The ethics of neoliberal institutionalism. In *The Oxford handbook of international relations.* New York: Oxford University Press.

Runde, D. F. (2013, October 25). The future of public-private partnerships: Strengthening a powerful instrument for global development. *Center for Strategic & International Studies (CSIS).* Retrieved from www.csis.org/analysis/future-public-private-partnerships-strengthening-powerful-instrument-global-development

Shevtsova, L. (2015, April). Forward to the past in Russia. *Journal of Democracy, 26*(2), 22–36.

Ştefanachi, B. (2011). Globalization and identities – A constructivist approach. In *The scale of globalization. Think globally, act locally, change individually in the 21st century* (pp. 312–318). Ostrava: University of Ostrava. Retrieved from http://conference.osu.eu/globalization/publ2011/312-318_Stefanachi.pdf

Stølan, R. (2012, June). *Political regimes and FDI: An empirical analysis of the attractiveness of hybrid regimes for multinational companies.* Trondheim: Norwegian University of Science and Technology, Master's Thesis.

The Economist. (2001, September 27). *Globalization and its critics.* Retrieved from http://www.economist.com/node/795995

United Nations. (2009, September 11). *Guidance note of the secretary general on democracy.* Retrieved from www.un.org/democracyfund/Docs/UNSG%20Guidance%20Note%20on%20Democracy.pdf

Walker, C. (Jan 2016). The hijacking of "soft power". *Journal of Democracy, 27*(1), 49–63.

Walker, C., Plattner, M., & Diamond, L. (2016, March 28). Authoritarianism goes global. *The American Interest.* Retrieved from www.the-american-interest.com/2016/03/28/authoritarianism-goes-global/

Watson, G. (2004). Liberalism and globalisation. *Asia Europe Journal, 2*(2), 167–173.

Waltz, K. (1998). Globalisation and Governance. *Political Science and Politics, 32*(4), 693–700.

Wikan, V. (2015, March 21). What is 'Neoliberalism', and how does it relate to globalization? *E-International Relations Students.* Retrieved from www.e-ir.info/2015/03/21/what-is-neoliberalism-and-how-does-it-relate-to-globalization/

Wu, W.-C. (2015). When do dictators decide to liberalize trade regimes? Inequality and trade openness in authoritarian countries. *International Studies Quarterly., 59*(4), 790–801.

Chapter 15
The United Nations Security Council: History, Current Composition, and Reform Proposals

Madeleine O. Hosli and Thomas Dörfler

15.1 Introduction

The lack of formal reform of the Security Council seems puzzling against the tremendous shifts in global order since its establishment. Consider the following example: In 1945, the Security Council consisted of 21.6% of the general membership (11 Council members, 51 UN member states), this ratio decreased to 12.8% in 1965 (15 Council members, 117 UN member states) and further to only 7.8% today (15 Council members, 193 UN member states). Yet, other international institutions have proven able to adapt to these changes through the admission of new members in the World Trade Organization, adapting voting weights in the International Monetary Fund or introducing new patterns of weighted voting in the European Union (EU).

Even though many states vociferously demand a more 'equitable representation' and criticize the P5 dominance, so far, none of the reform proposals, ranging from adding new permanent members, expanding solely the number of non-permanent members to intermediate models of reform have yet obtained the necessary majorities. Over 10 years ago, Bruce Russett already noted that "[t]he politics and politicking [of Security Council reform](…) all boil down to this: a coalition of minorities has always been able to defeat any such proposal even before it could be brought to a vote. Each member might accept certain kinds of changes, but any package always seemed to carry a poison pill to which the status quo was preferable" (2005).

M. O. Hosli (✉)
Institute of Security and Global Affairs, Leiden University, The Hague, The Netherlands
e-mail: m.o.hosli@fgga.leidenuniv.nl

T. Dörfler
University of Potsdam, Potsdam, Germany
e-mail: tdoerfler@uni-potsdam.de

© Springer Nature Switzerland AG 2020
M. O. Hosli, J. Selleslaghs (eds.), *The Changing Global Order*, United Nations University Series on Regionalism 17,
https://doi.org/10.1007/978-3-030-21603-0_15

The chapter explores how the Security Council has reacted to the changing global order both in terms of formal institutional reform and more informal ways of granting more influence to rising and established powers through increasing informalization, reforming its working methods, or institutional innovation. We argue that while the various camps have not found any bridging position that avoids the 'poison pill' of Council reform, those members who have been denied membership have not walked away. Instead, these members use various avenues to influence the Council's politics over international peace and security even though the current permanent members continue to dominate the Council. At the same time, the Council has tried to increase its procedural legitimacy, one main criticism of UN Member States (Binder and Heupel 2014), by various initiatives, including working methods reform and institutional design.

The chapter proceeds as follows. Next, we explore the tremendous shifts in global power and how the changing nature of conflicts has presented a challenge to the current system of global governance. In the third section, we analyze the political, structural and theoretical obstacles to a formal Security Council reform. In the fourth section, we study what alternative routes nonmembers and non-permanent members have taken and how those members can influence Council proceedings without (permanent) membership. In a fifth section, the chapter explores how the Security Council has reacted to the vociferous calls for reform by developing novel working methods, relying on committee governance in the field of sanctions and the increasing the participation of experts. We find that the ways in which the Council has reacted to shifts in the global order as well as changing patterns of conflict, even though the membership of the Council has not yet been altered, could get more attention in both practice and academic background analysis.

15.2 The Changing Global Order & the Changing Nature of Armed Conflict

The current setup of the Security Council looks increasingly anachronistic against the tremendous shifts in military, economic and diplomatic global power since the San Francisco conference over 70 years ago. In contrast to the time of the UN's foundation, global power has been redistributed among nations. Many smaller and middle-sized countries are rising powers, 'emerging economies' or among the so-called 'Next Eleven'. These states seek a greater role in shaping the institutions of global governance. Yet, the relation between military, economic and political weight is less defined than at the UN's creation and thus, it is less clear which states should take crucial decisions about international peace and security on behalf of all UN members. Especially the emerging nations Brazil, India, South Africa, but also others such as Nigeria, Pakistan or Argentina, demand greater representation in the Security Council.

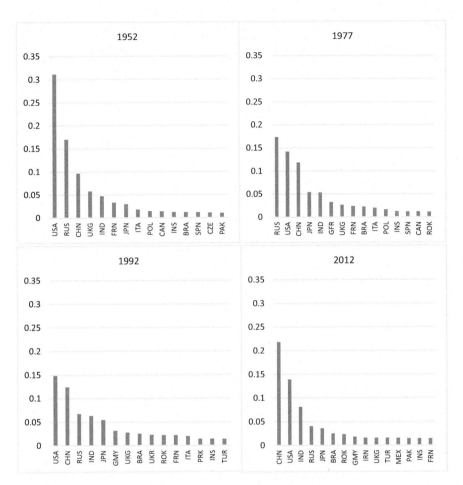

Fig. 15.1 The Changing Global Order, Material Capabilities of States from 1952 to 2012
Note: CINC 5.0 Scores, as discussed in Singer, D. J. (1987). Reconstructing the Correlates of War Dataset on Material Capabilities of States, 1816–1985. *International Interactions, 14*, 115–132

When pondering over the shifts in national capabilities (see Fig. 15.1) based on the Correlates of War dataset as an indicator for changing global power, we can observe these tremendous shifts. While France and the UK had been among the top 6 of most capable nations in 1952, they only rank at top 10 and top 15 respectively in 2012. Notably, the four candidates for new permanent membership (Brazil, Germany, India, and Japan) as well as other middle-sized countries (South Korea, Iran, Turkey, Mexico, Pakistan, Indonesia) have higher national capabilities than the UK and France (Mahbubani refers to the latter as 'yesterday's powers', 2016). A similar picture is revealed for other economic measurements, for instance, GDP (Mahbubani 2016). Mahbubani argues that this is the reason that the UK and France have not used the veto in the post-Cold War period. In fact, both countries have essentially lost the legitimacy to veto decisions and their use of veto power would trigger a "political explosion" among the wider UN membership (Mahbubani 2016). Still, the material capabilities also show how two world powers, China and the United States by far exceed the capabilities of other states, and China has even overtaken the US in the age of globalization (see Chap. 4 in this volume). The picture is different for Russia, though being a permanent member and nuclear power, it is not an economic global power (see Chap. 5 in this volume).

But how do these relational shifts in global power translate into shifts in global order? How do these constituent parts form a different global order than in 1945? Certainly, the processes of growing economic interdependence and globalization have triggered state efforts towards international solutions to cooperation problems (Keohane 1984). Processes of legalization (Abbott et al. 2000) have created an international sphere that is more and more regulated. States now operate in an increasingly dense fabric of institutions and global norms that has given rise to regime complexes and frequent institutional interaction (Keohane and Victor 2011; Raustiala and Victor 2004). Most institutions share governance competence with other organizations, sometimes with considerable overlap. Increasingly, global governance is characterized by informal ways of governance (Stone 2011).

Against this background, notably, none of the powers aspirant for permanent membership in the Security Council are major global military powers. This situation is different compared to 1945 when the permanent members – the victorious nations of World War II – were those who should keep peace (Jones 2016). Yet, these established and rising powers have accumulated economic and diplomatic capacities. Consider for instance, the conflict over the Iran nuclear program. Germany, even though not a permanent member and for most of the time, not even an elected Council member, has played a major role in the EU3 (UK, France and Germany) and later in the P5+1 (plus Germany) format for negotiating with Iran. In this context, Brazil and Turkey co-initiated a nuclear fuel swap deal with Iran by in 2010, which demonstrated their ambition and possibilities for engaging in international diplomacy, even though the United States did not welcome this initiative. However, the picture is different for the African representation. Neither South Africa nor Nigeria, even though they are important actors, have the diplomatic or economic standing of other aspirant nations. And even among African states, their aspirations are far from being undisputed (Jones 2016). Thus, in any reform proposal, Africa would be overrepresented, provided that capabilities are the dimension of comparison.

Beyond these fundamental changes in global order, the changing nature of armed conflict, the surge of terrorism and foreign fighters, the proliferation of nuclear weapons and the persistence of intra-state conflicts are presenting a serious challenge to the Council efforts in preserving international peace and security. The changing nature of armed conflict has prompted influential academic debates about its quality and extent. Mary Kaldor argued that, in the context of globalization, a new type of conflict, the *new war*, has emerged that is "blurring the distinction between war (usually defined as violence between states or organized political groups for political objectives), organized crime (violence undertaken by privately organized groups for private purposes, usually financial gain), and large-scale violations of human rights (violence undertaken by states or politically organized groups against individuals)" (Kaldor 2012). This type of conflict is different from *old wars* that had been fought up until the first half of the twentieth century (Kaldor 2012). Münkler identified three distinct features of the new wars: The "asymmetricalization of war", the "privatization of war" referring to loss of the state monopoly of violence and an increasing role of non-state actors where the state recedes, and the "de-militarization of war" referring to the emergence of private militias and rebel groups instead of regular armies as well as the targeting civilians and civilian infrastructure, blurring the distinction between combatants and non-combatants (Münkler 2012). However, the new wars thesis has been criticized from a number of quarters. One major critique was that it created an arbitrary boundary between old and new wars were none should be drawn. Others cautioned against reducing conflict dynamics to economic aspirations of warring parties (on this debate see Mello (2010)).

One remarkable finding of the data-driven conflict research is the tremendous decline in interstate wars, which have been responsible for most battle-related deaths during the first half of the twentieth century (Ramsbotham et al. 2016). Indeed, in 2014, the Uppsala Conflict Data Project (UCDP)[1] recorded only one interstate war (India – Pakistan), while all 39 other violent conflicts occurred in domestic conflict settings (Pettersson and Wallensteen 2015). Yet, the 2014 Ukraine crisis or the dispute over the denuclearization of the Korean Peninsula illustrates that inter-state conflicts have not ceased to exist and that realist arguments about state power in the international system are still relevant (Ramsbotham et al. 2016, on power politics see Chap. 3 in this volume).

In the area of peace operations, besides the noticeable surge in size and mandates of peacekeeping missions after 1990, there is an increasingly complex link between Council-mandated peacekeeping missions which are operated and staffed by regional organizations (Stagno Ugarte 2016), for instance the EU in Mali, NATO in Afghanistan (see Chap. 16 in this volume), the G5 Sahel Joint Force, as well as hybrid peace operations (Tardy 2014) such as the UN/African Union mission in Darfur. This complexity helps the UN join forces with regional actors, but also leads to new complexities in terms of the management of missions and operations on the ground (Williams 2016).

The nature of intra-state conflict, which is increasingly considered as a threat to international peace and security, also seems to be changing. Sebastian von Einsiedel (2017), for example, identifies three major conflict trends in recent years. First, he notes the emergence of organized crime as a major factor in making intrastate wars increasingly "intractable and messy". Making up for superpower support, rebel groups increasingly engage in the shadow economy, conflict economies, natural resource exploitation and illicit markets (Einsiedel 2017). Second, states increasingly interfere in domestic conflicts abroad, which both prolongs these conflicts and makes them more deadly (Einsiedel 2017). The UCDP recorded a record high in

---

[1] http://ucdp.uu.se/

internationalized domestic conflicts: A third of all intrastate conflicts are subject to foreign support for one or more conflict parties (Pettersson and Wallensteen 2015). Third, the world is witnessing an increase in jihadi terrorism, in terms of a ten-fold increase in terrorist incidents, a steady and accelerating increase in Salafi-jihadist fighters since the late 80s, as well as a steep increase in the number of terrorism-related deaths (Einsiedel 2017). In fact, UN peacekeepers operate in areas vulnerable to terrorism and increasingly become the target of terrorist attacks (Einsiedel 2017). Moreover, a Soufan Group report estimated that the number of foreign terrorist fighters who have traveled to Syria and Iraq to fight for ISIL is as high as 31,000 individuals from over 86 countries (Barrett et al. 2015). But also groups such as Boko Haram, Al-Qaida and the Taliban have posed a threat to peace, often operating across borders (Einsiedel 2017). In addition to challenges related to Iran and DPRK nuclear programs, there is a growing concern about the proliferation of weapons of mass destruction to non-state actors (Heupel 2008). Taken together, this has posed new challenges to the UN and led to changes in terms of peace operations over time. Most notably, the range and scope of peacekeeping missions have expanded, allowing for more possibilities for peacekeepers 'on the ground'.

All of this implies that in the context of the changing global order, and changing challenges to UN member states, the United Nations had to adapt its range and scope of activities considerably. Accordingly, the Security Council faces new challenges that are urgent and important but fundamentally different from those facing the UN when the organization was established.

15.3 Obstacles to the Unfulfilled Promise of Security Council Reform

In return for their acceptance of the 'Yalta formula', which enshrined the P5 veto privilege, small and middle-sized countries were promised a conference for reviewing and revamping the UN Charter within 10 years of its adoption (Article 109 (3) UN Charter, see Luck 2008; Rensmann 2012). Indeed, the underprivileged rather preferred a formal and comprehensive review of the collective security system with a view to abolishing the paralyzing veto privilege. Yet, the Cold War realities prevented such a conference from being convened. In fact, the struggles over the setup and role of the Security Council in San Francisco and the time after mirror the contradictory interests of UN Member States on the question of its fundamental reform ever since (Luck 2008).

What are the political hurdles for reforming the Security Council's composition? The core obstacle is that not all states will equally profit from Council expansions, while some states fear that they might be worse off. The political preferences among UN Member States diverge along three dimensions (see Table 15.1). First, the UN Member States fundamentally disagree over the seat categories for any additional Council seats. On the one hand, three groups of states prefer to add new permanent

Table 15.1 Major reform proposals for the security council (by seat categories)

	Total seats	Permanent seats (current)	Permanent seats (proposal)	Non-permanent seats
Group of four	25	5	6 (no veto)	14
				No immediate re-election
Uniting for consensus	25	5	–	20
				Immediate re-election possible
African group	26	5	6 (veto)	15
				1 additional NP for Africa
L69	27	5	6 (veto)	16
				1 additional NP for Africa
				1 additional NP for small island developing states

Source: Dörfler, T., & Hosli, M. O. (2013). Reforming the United Nations Security Council: Proposals, Strategies and Preferences. In B. Reinalda (Ed.), *Routledge Handbook of International Organization* (pp. 377–390). Milton Park, Abingdon, Oxon: Routledge, with additions based on Swart, L. (2013). Reform of the Security Council: 2007–2013. In L. Swart & E. Perry (Eds.), *Governing & Managing Change at the United Nations: Security Council Reform from 1945 to September 2013* (pp. 23–59). New York, NY

members to the Council. Among these is the *Group of Four* (G4) proposal, which champions Brazil, India, Germany and Japan and two African countries as candidates for permanent membership. Similarly, the *African Group* proposal, representing more than fifty states, favors both expanding the permanent and non-permanent seat categories. A third group, considerably overlapping with the African Group, is the *L69*, which includes Brazil and India, some African countries and the small island states. It suggests a solution similar to the African model. The *Uniting for Consensus* (UfC) group represents a smaller, but vocal opposition to the expansion of permanent seats and instead favors to add more non-permanent seats. This group mainly comprises of the regional rivals of the G4 states, including Italy, Argentina, Colombia, Pakistan, the Republic of Korea, and Spain, among others. Their opposition is mainly driven by the fact that they would go away empty handed while their larger regional rivals might obtain the privileged permanent seats.

Second, any system of Council expansion requires allocating new seats, usually among regional groups, which creates a distribution problem. Fundamentally, every group needs to benefit from an expansion (why region A, if not region B?). The proposed models consider a size between 25 and 27 seats. The difference between the G4 proposal and the African proposal is that the African Group suggests an additional non-permanent seat for Africa. The L69 adds another non-permanent seat for small island states.

Third, the question of the veto divides many states, while three lines of thinking prevail. One group favors expanding the veto to potential new permanent members (African Group, L69). Yet, critics argue that this will further diminish the prospects of conflict resolution and is widely seen as an unrealistic proposal. A different – sober – assessment of the reform prospects does neither suggest extending the veto nor restricting the existing P5 veto privilege (G4). A third line of thinking argues that the existing veto privilege should be restricted to certain situations, excluding for instance grave violations of human rights or genocide. Indeed, even one permanent member has suggested this recently (Security Council Report 2015, see section 14.6 below).

The permanent members have a vested interest in the status quo. Because all "declining powers and regional blocs can prevent any diminution of their representation on the Council", Security Council reform is "inevitably 'additive' in nature" (US Permanent Mission to the UN 2007). The ideal solution for the US would be a "smallest possible expansion" and in particular "no extension of veto" with the goal of "maintaining our arithmetic advantage in UNSC voting" (US Permanent Mission to the UN 2007). Yet, the US also noted that "[t]he real danger is that, as the membership of the Council has not been updated to reflect geopolitical realities, new rising powers as well as their friends and allies might come to view the Council's role as illegitimate. This, in turn, could undermine the willingness of countries to abide by its resolutions" (US Permanent Mission to the UN 2007). Accordingly, the two European permanent members France and the UK have voiced cautious support for Council expansion with a few new permanent and non-permanent members. Yet, China, Russia and the US remain hostile to any change in Council composition.

Since 2005, some countries have suggested creating an interim or intermediate model of expansion, based on the idea of longer-term renewable Council seats, potentially with some sort of review of its feasibility after an initial period. Yet, while some states – including Germany and Japan – seem willing to at least engage with the idea, it has been criticized in other quarters (Swart 2013, 2015).

How can we account for the apparent lack of consensus? To what degree is the 'structural situation' (Russett 2005) presenting an institutional hurdle for the unfulfilled promise of Security Council reform? In essence, any reform of the Council's composition, seat categories or veto privilege requires amending articles 23 and 27 of the UN Charter. There are two principle avenues to do this, either through a GA resolution or convening a review conference. Essentially, both require a *two-thirds majority* and need to be ratified by two-thirds of the UN membership and *all five permanent Council members*. This provision is a high hurdle. To date, the UN Charter has been amended three times based on article 108 in 1965, 1968 and 1973, whereas so far, article 109 has never been applied (Witschel 2012a, b).

The failure of Security Council reform has triggered many commentators to dig into an analysis of this issue. Erik Voeten, based on an institutionalist account, argues we should look at the Council within its strategic context. The Council is designed to provide the public good of international peace and security while lacking the capacities for preventing unilateral action. As, he argues, the availability of outside options curtails the power of some permanent members over others, this shows that what really matters is 'real world' power (in the form of outside options), not formal institutional power (2008). Accordingly, he concludes that the 'benefits of clever constitutional engineering' are likely to be marginal compared to the status quo (2008). Alexander Thompson argues that the key function of the Council is one of 'strategic information transmission'. It is relevant for all UN Member States precisely because of its small size, diversity and the veto power of states that often withstood the interests of the most powerful states. Expanding the Council risks reviving Cold War paralysis without enhancing its 'political usefulness' (2009). Barry O'Neill – relying on the Shapely-Shubik model of voting power – looks into potential shifts in voting power by adding more seats with or without veto power and adaptations of the majority threshold (1997). He concludes that granting more seats to members without veto can actually decrease a state's individual power and that a new member only makes a difference (in actual voting power) if it has a different position than already existing members do. In all his scenarios, the increase in members leads to a decrease in the probability that a resolution is adopted (O'Neill 1997).

Hosli et al., using social choice theory and models of voting power, demonstrate that the 1965 expansion of the Council to fifteen members has already reduced the probability of Council agreement. The various reform proposals discussed in recent years would all lead to a further reduction in action probability of the Council, in particular proposal foreseeing new veto rights (2011). Combined with member state priorities, Council reform amounts to 'squaring the circle' (Hosli et al. 2011). Using Coleman's index of the "Power of a Collectivity to Act", Hosli and Dörfler further find that the steep increase in UN membership reduced prospects for achieving the necessary majorities for Charter amendment in the General Assembly tremendously and in a non-linear fashion (2017). In fact, membership growth combined with the high hurdle for Charter reform has decreased the possibilities for finding consensus, regardless of member states' negotiation positions (Hosli and Dörfler 2017).

Conversely, the reform proposals are strikingly mute when it comes to the question of what Klabbers calls 'instrumental' versus 'political rationality' or 'effective managerial capability' versus 'political deliberative quality' (2010). This implies a tradeoff between effectiveness and inclusiveness. Yet, none of the reform proposals address how an enlarged Council would not undermine the post-Cold War levels of Council effectiveness and seem to imply that political rationality will automatically lead to 'better' outcomes.

15.4 Alternative Routes & Influence 'Without' (Permanent) Membership

Whilst the Council's composition has not formally changed, despite the remarkably changing global order, states eager to join the Council have not disengaged or discontinued to cooperate (see for instance Voeten 2008). Despite the fact that the states calling most vociferously for Security Council reform have not yet achieved a constitutional reform, they exhibit astonishingly high rates of compliance with Council decisions even though these are hardly enforceable (Mahbubani 2016, see also Chap. 18 in this volume). Hence, in this section, we analyze how non-members and non-permanent members can affect Council negotiations even though they do not have (much) formal powers. Already in 1997, Ian Hurd noted that the increasing informal role of nonmembers of the Council has "blurred the practical distinction between member and nonmember" (Hurd 1997).

Let us first explore the role of the non-permanent members within the Council. A notable descriptive observation is that both those states that strive for a permanent representation and their UfC rivals are represented in the Council as non-permanent members regularly (see Fig. 15.2). In fact, Japan has served on the Council more than 35% of the time since the end of the Cold War. The other Asian candidate for permanent membership, India, has been on the Council 15% of the time since 1990. Regional contenders also spent considerable years on the Council (Pakistan 22%, Indonesia 15%, Republic of Korea 15%, Malaysia 15%). In the Western European and Others Group (WEOG) group, Germany has served almost 22% of the time since 1990, but even its rivals Spain (22%) and Italy (19%) have served considerable time. In Latin America (GRULAC), both Brazil (30%) and Argentina (30%) have been on the Council in almost one-third of all post-Cold War years, followed by Chile (22%), Colombia (15%), and Mexico (15%). Both the African Group (AG) and Eastern European Group (EEG) seemingly follow a rotational model of Council tenure. Of the African members, a number of countries and those ambitious for permanent seats including South Africa, Rwanda, Angola, Egypt, Gabon and Morocco have each spent 15% of the time as Council members, with Nigeria slightly more (22%). Africa, in contrast to other regions shows a more equitable form of representation, which is due to the rotational logic of assigning seats within the Group. In the EEG, only Ukraine and Romania have served twice since 1990. A large and often forgotten group of more than 60 UN member states has not yet been elected to the Council. Even though the G4 countries and members of the UfC prefer different models of Council expansion, the wider UN membership seems to have found a system of distributing non-permanent seats that mirrors the influence of respective states in the international system quite well.

In their analytical and data-driven approach based on Council elections from 1970 to 2005, Vreeland and Dreher find that "there appears to exist a compromise between the demands of powerful countries to win elections more frequently and (…) giving each country its turn" (Vreeland and Dreher 2014). Statistically, the turn-taking is robust across all regions, modified by the notion that more powerful states take turns more often. The authors also observe that a state's involvement in intra-state or interstate wars lowers its election probability, while contributions to peacekeeping operations increases it. In addition, there is little evidence of great power mingling with the results, as for instance US aid or multilateral lending do not significantly increase the likelihood of obtaining a temporary seat on the Council (Dreher et al. 2014; Vreeland and Dreher 2014). Yet, if turn-taking is an influential norm, we should ask if elected members actually represent their regions. In fact, Lai and Lefler demonstrate that even though regions tend to have a higher voting coincidence, the regional non-permanent members do not have higher similarity with their region than with others. In other words, the elected members do not represent the same preferences as their regions (with the exception of the WEOG group) (Lai and Lefler 2016). This finding resonates with findings of Vreeland and Dreher that

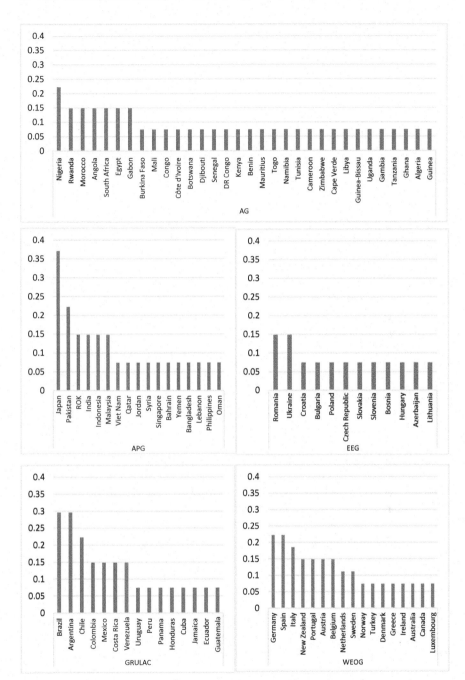

Fig. 15.2 Years served on UNSC (percent of years since 1990)

Note: Own calculations based on UN Security Council membership data, available at: http://www.un.org/en/sc/members/ and years of accession, available at: http://www.un.org/en/member-states/

the current institutional design does not incentivize the pursuance of regional interests. Accordingly, they suggest to hold regional election rather than General Assembly (UNGA) elections and to abolish the re-election prohibition to increase accountability of E10 regional representatives (Vreeland and Dreher 2014).

Certainly, the current permanent members have a tight grip over Council decision-making. The five powers have two considerable advantages vis-à-vis the elected members as enshrined in the UN Charter (Einsiedel et al. 2016). First, the permanent members enjoy a veto right and therefore, no substantive Council decision can pass without their approval or at least acquiescence. Second, they enjoy the advantage of permanency, which gives them access to institutional memory over previous practice and procedures whereas the elected members have no such privileges (Krisch 2008; Sievers and Daws 2014). A notable consequence of the P5 dominance is the emergence of the penholder system. In essence, France, the UK and the US each 'hold the pen' on certain agenda items and reserve the right of drafting a prospective resolution. After P3 consultations that draft resolution would be exclusively negotiated within the P5 (incl. China and Russia) and only presented to the wider Council once a compromise has been found leaving little time and room for maneuver before putting the resolution to a vote (Einsiedel et al. 2016).

How, if at all, can the non-permanent Council members then yield influence beyond their (lack of) formal voting power? Based on a case study of the recent Australian Council membership, Langmore and Farrall (2016) argue that Australia had been instrumental in adopting a resolution on the downing of MH17. At the same time, however, they note the failure of Australia to succeed in desired UN sanctions reform and the mixed results of Australian efforts to obtain Council decisions to improve the humanitarian access in Syria. They also note that knowledge about previous practice is valuable (Langmore and Farrall 2016). Overall, Australia "had had the greatest impact of any elected members during the past decade" (2016). In a similar account, Thorhallsson notes that non-permanent members can become influential through acquiring necessary knowledge about the Council's procedures, diplomatic skills, leadership and coalition-building. Several episodes of Nordic non-permanent members serve to illustrate these means of influence (Thorhallsson 2012). In this context, these commentators have also pointed to the importance of institutional memory, or 'necessary knowledge for a small state to become influential' in the Council (Thorhallsson 2012). Moreover, Langmore and Farrall argue that a non-profit organization named *Security Council Report*, which provides reporting and forecasting of Council decision processes on all agenda items, is a major and influential source of institutional memory for non-permanent members and non-members (2016). Notably, many of the states ambitious for Council membership contribute to the funding of this organization.[2] However, these descriptive accounts lack suitable theoretical underpinning and cannot answer *how exactly* these factors translate into influence in some instances and not in others.

---

[2] See http://www.securitycouncilreport.org/about-security-council-report.php

The rationalist Council literature is slowly starting to take informal institutional opportunities and constraints more seriously. Based on the logic of focal points in coordination situations (Schelling 1960), a recent study has shown how and under what conditions precedent and doctrine affect the collective choice of strategically behaving states in the Security Council. Gehring, Dorsch and Dörfler show that precedents provide focal points that allow for finding collective decisions in coordination situations despite diverging preferences (2017). They also find that the logic of a staged response to crisis situations provides institutional constraints that drive skeptical members to agree with previously undesired measures. They illustrate these effects with the Council's decision-making on key terrorism decisions on Libya (1992) and 9/11, which was influenced by an emerging Council doctrine on terrorism (2017).

There is also a growing theoretical literature on the Council's characteristics from a constructivist perspective. Johnstone, for instance, regards the Security Council as an 'interpretative community' whose decisions are influenced by a 'justificatory discourse' and an exchange of legal arguments. In this way, the 'power of the better argument' may provide an avenue for smaller states to influence Council decisions beyond realist notions of material power (Johnstone 2003, 2008). More recently, the concept of 'international practices' has drawn the attention towards how power is enacted in the Security Council. For instance, Adler-Nissen and Pouliot explain the Council intervention in Libya in 2011 by the logic of claiming competence, social negotiation and transforming those into non-coercive influence (Adler-Nissen and Pouliot 2014). While both rationalist and constructivist approaches have focused on the permanent members, these studies suggest that precedents and informal practice could be equally available to non-permanent members, provided that they accumulated sufficient knowledge about previous practice. In fact, Ralph and Gifkins (2017) argue that 'penholding', an informal practice that distributes the privilege of drafting a resolution on an agenda item ('holding the pen') mostly among the Western permanent members, constitutes such an international practice and becomes an influential pattern of Council diplomacy. This study shows that smaller elected members could exploit the power-generating effects of penholding for negotiating humanitarian access in Syria. However, they cannot explain how exactly this practice exerts influence and why the permanent members yield to that influence.

Although several ambitious states are deprived of an equal representation in the Council and their efforts to increase their formal representation have been unsuccessful so far, these states have not been disenfranchised (Hosli and Dörfler 2015) and – quite to the contrary – have tried to increase their representation and influence in more informal ways without Council membership (for an early contribution, see Hurd 1997; also Prantl 2010). Overall, both the potential candidates for permanent seats as well as their regional counterparts show a high level of commitment to collective security, either through their contributions to peacekeeping missions, within informal groups of states or within the Peacebuilding Commission (PBC).

The states that are most eager to be more permanently represented on the Council are major providers of UN peacekeepers (see Fig. 15.3). A large share of UN peace-

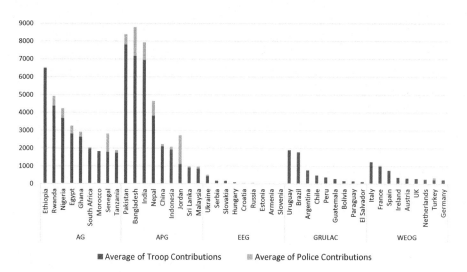

Fig. 15.3 Troop contributing countries (5-year average, 2011–2016)
Note: Own calculations based on the IPI Peacekeeping Database, available at http://www.providingforpeacekeeping.org/contributions/

keeping contingents is contributed by India and Pakistan, which together with Bangladesh have formed the top three troop-contributing countries (TCC) from 2011 to 2016. Nigeria is among the top seven (ca. 4100) and South Africa and Brazil are also contributing significantly ranking among the top 15 with 1000–2000 troops annually. Among the UfC, Italy and Argentina are notable contributors. Over the last 5 years, China has sent 2000 peacekeepers, a notable change in policy. Germany and Japan support UN peacekeeping in the lower hundreds. Yet, Germany shoulders major responsibilities within the NATO contingents in Afghanistan and EU training missions in Northern Africa. As concerns Japan, its share of the UN budget exceeds those of four of the five permanent members, namely the UK, France, the Russian Federation and China. Also, Germany's exceeds the former three financial contributions.

Despite these descriptive results and the fact that the Council has institutionalized regular briefings with the TCCs since 1994 (Security Council Report 2014), the literature offers little analysis into whether or not and if yes, to what degree TCCs could affect Council deliberations. In theory, troop contingents provide leverage to obtain concessions through threats of non-participation or withdrawal (Gowan 2016). Cursory evidence suggests that TCCs have extracted some Council concessions, for instance, the European members have during the UNIFIL/Lebanon negotiations (Novosseloff 2015), Argentina, Brazil and Chile as concerns peacekeeping in Haiti (MINUSTAH), Ethiopia as sole troop contributor in Sudan/Abyei (UNISFA) or Tanzania and South Africa as regards the "Force Intervention Brigade" in DRC (MONUSCO) (Gowan 2016).

The states that are denied a change in formal Council composition are granted representation in the Peacebuilding Commission (PBC), a subsidiary organ of both the UNGA and the Security Council, with the aim to prevent relapse of conflict in post-conflict situations. The PBC consists of members elected by the UNSC, UNGA and ECOSOC, in addition to five of the top ten TCCs and five of the top ten contributors to the regular and voluntary budgets (A/RES/60/180 of 30 December 2005). Hence, the current configuration includes aspirant nations such as India, Pakistan, Argentina, Brazil, Nigeria, South Africa, Germany and Japan. However, the commission's track record has been criticized in many quarters and shortcomings identified in the 2010 and 2015 Reviews of the peacebuilding architecture. Since then, the reform of the peacebuilding architecture towards more tangible results has gained new momentum and is one of the key objectives of Secretary-General Antonio Guterres (Security Council Report 2017).

The increasing reliance on informal groups of states ('Groups of Friends') has presented an additional avenue for non-members to ease the "structural constraints" (Prantl 2005) of the rigid Council. Informal groups of states have formed diplomatic initiatives that compete with or complement Security Council governance and provide a means to enhance the efficiency of security governance from actors outside of the Security Council. When the Council is unable to act on a situation, states can act outside and later return to the Council for granting ex-post legitimacy for action. Groups of Friends affect Security Council governance by limiting P5 preponderance and decoupling solving a crisis from the legitimizing (enforcement) measures. In essence, Groups of Friends constitute an instance of 'informal' governance and allows for interaction and influence of non-members without any granting them formal membership rights (Prantl 2005). In turn, informal groups of states help to bridge the gap between the institutional status quo and the shifting global order and transforms the Council without altering its current structure (Prantl 2005). Thus, participation as a member of an informal group of states in a situation of particular interest has low costs and risks and provides a viable alternative to affecting the Council without changing the formal Council configuration (Hurd 1997; Prantl 2005, for a recent contribution see Whitfield 2016).

15.5 Informal Institutional Innovation and the Reform of Working Methods

Beyond the level of formal reform, the Council has not remained idle. Instead, driven by proactive members, it has developed several informal and innovative ways of addressing pressing global governance issues in international peace and security (see already Hurd 1997). One element of this strategy is the intensive linking up with regional organizations in the framework of peace missions, including with the EU and with the African Union. In their intriguing analysis of GA debates, Binder and Heupel find that even though the Council does not suffer from a 'legitimacy crisis', the general membership associates its perceived 'legitimacy deficit' mostly with a lack of procedural legitimacy rather than its performance or interpretation of its mandate (Binder and Heupel 2014). They conclude that "the challenge for Security Council reform will be to introduce meaningful procedural reforms while assuring that these reforms enhance rather than hamper the ability of the Council to act decisively when it comes to maintaining or restoring international peace and security" (Binder and Heupel 2014). At the same time, a whole range of small-sized states has not much to gain from an expanded Security Council and no realistic prospects of getting a seat on an enlarged Council, while these members are the most affected by the Council's interventions. Accordingly, these states have a vested interest in a reform of the Council's working methods (Wenaweser 2016).

Several states, mainly those that neither have stakes in an expanded Council nor in obtaining temporary membership, have championed the reform of Council working methods from the quarters of the General Assembly. The reform of working methods does not require any amendments to the Charter, not even to the 'provisional rules of procedure', which have remained unaltered since 1982. In fact, many Council practices are entirely informal. Non-represented countries have lobbied continuously for more inclusive and transparent working methods and have achieved at least gradual change towards a more integrative and transparent Council (Lehmann 2013). A notable group is *Accountability, Coherence and Transparency* (ACT), a successor of the Small-Five (S5) initiative. This initiative champions a number of reforms for greater inclusion of non-members, among others more regular briefings, a more equitable penholder system and committee chairmanship and a transparent and competitive selection process of the Secretary-General. This new initiative explicitly is not related to the issue of Security Council reform because many states seemingly would reject any formal GA decision on working methods, fearing that this might foreclose their prospects for a comprehensive institutional Council reform (Wenaweser 2016).

On the basis of working methods, three recent models suggest that the veto should be voluntarily restricted, two from outside the Council (ACT 'code of conduct', The Elders' proposal) and one from inside (French proposal). All three initiatives revolve around the idea that the veto should not apply when genocide, crimes against humanity and war crimes on a mass scale are committed in a conflict. The French proposal is the most concrete and stipulates that more than 50 states need to request the Secretary-General to make such an assessment. While both the French initiative and the ACT proposal have gained considerable support, and France and the UK have pledged not to use the veto in cases of mass atrocities, the other permanent members oppose the initiative because it encroaches on their UN Charter enshrined veto right. In addition, it remains unclear what kind of Council measures (e.g. sanctions or the use of force) would be considered as an appropriate response to such norm violations (Security Council Report 2015).

There also has been some movement from within the Security Council's 'Informal Working Group on Documentation and Other Procedural Questions' to adapt the working methods and Council practices, typically driven by non-permanent members. The Council increasingly codifies its working methods in what is called 'Note 507' and Japan led the difficult process of drafting the most recent version (S/2017/507, see Security Council Report 2018). Some of the innovations that derived from inside the Council were to increasingly consider thematic areas of work (e.g. Women, Peace and Security), hold wrap-up sessions, horizon-scanning meetings, Council meetings with civil society (termed 'Arria-formula' meetings after the Venezuelan ambassador who invented the format), Council visiting missions and increasing the use of consensus-based informal decisions (presidential statements, presidential press statements).

Another example and an intriguing aspect of changing Security Council governance is the emergence of *committee governance* within its sanctions regimes, which created a form of rule-based governance even though the same member states take all the actual decisions. Early on, Council diplomats and observers have noted that with the imposition of sanctions on Iraq in 1990, the Council shifted from "politico-military" towards a "legal-regulatory" form of decision-making (Malone 2006). Hence, Council members take politically-driven decisions in the Council but resort to bureaucratic decision-making on the bulk of the implementation decisions in its sanctions committees (Conlon 2000). For instance, two diplomats of the Yugoslavia sanctions committee noted that "[t]he record (sic!) of the Sanctions Committee's deliberations are full of references to previous cases which the Committee Members considered to constitute a precedent" (Scharf and Dorosin 1993). In their theoretically-driven analysis, Gehring and Dörfler argue that the Council's sanctions regime represents a highly institutionalized polity that shapes state behavior including the behavior of the great powers. They demonstrate that the steady stream of implementation decisions in the committees creates demand for rules, either because the consensus requirement threatens to cause stalemates or because laissez-faire approaches would create legitimacy problems. Even though this effect was not entirely intended, committee governance enhances procedural legitimacy, because it makes decisions more consistent and predictable though it does not rule out politically driven decisions (Gehring and Dörfler 2013).

Another intriguing feature of Security Council governance is the turn to experts since the late 1990s. Within its sanctions regimes, the Council now creates Panels of Experts (Farrall 2009) as a standard practice. These panels serve as the 'eyes and ears' of the Council on the ground. Within its thematic agendas on Counter-terrorism and proliferation of weapons of mass destruction to non-state actors, it has created larger expert panels (CTED and 1540 Expert Panel). Second, the creation of the Office of the Ombudsperson within the ISIL (Da'esh) and Al-Qaida sanctions regime is a rare instance of delegation to independent agents within the Council. The Ombudsperson is mandated to provide recommendations on the delisting of terror suspects, which are difficult to overturn (Gehring and Dörfler 2013). Third, in the non-proliferation cases of Iran and North Korea, the Council has utilized two transgovernmental networks of domestic regulatory experts (Eilstrup-Sangiovanni 2009) in the highly technical field of nuclear and ballistic missile related export control. The Nuclear Suppliers Group and the Missile Technology Control Regime provided export denial lists that were simply taken up by the Council and served as easily available focal points for agreement among Council members with different preferences. Accordingly, Council decisions tend to increasingly be embedded into networks of informal and formal governance, involving experts and representatives of many UN member states, even if these are not formally represented as permanent or non-permanent members of the Council.

15.6   Conclusion

The changing global order created new conditions for the Security Council to operate in. Simultaneously, the nature of conflicts has changed tremendously over time in terms of types of war and conflict, challenges such as terrorism and new forms of threats to societies. Increasingly, peace missions involve complex patterns of collaboration with regional organizations, aiming to create synergies and exploit benefits of joint operations. Even though the membership composition of the Security Council has not yet been altered, the institution has reacted to global shifts in power and conflicts in important ways.

Formal reform of the Council, in practice, is a difficult enterprise. As Bruce Russett, Barry O'Neill and Thomas Sutterlin (1997: 17–26) pointed out, any proposal to change the composition of Security Council needs to strike careful and intertwined balances, such as "the balance between practicality and vision," the balance "between power (or effectiveness) and legitimacy (or justice)," and, perhaps most importantly, the "balance of interests". When the United Nations was founded, the members of its Security Council and the permanent members in particular were to have the responsibility to secure and enforce peace. However, to fulfill this task, the member states represented in the UNSC also needed to have the resources to do so. Initially, this reasoning led to the creation of permanent seats for those UN member states that would be able to fulfill this task. Clearly, in today's world, the distribution of power and influence is quite different from what it was just after World War II. Accordingly, since the creation of the UN in 1945, there has been a debate about who should be represented as Council members. The discussion on possible reform of this institution became even more intensive after the end of the Cold War, when the Security Council had overcome superpower blockade, which created new possibilities for global action.

Due to the diverse nature of UN membership, common notions of fairness or shared values and linked to this, the decision on who should 'legitimately' be represented in the Council, are hard to come by. In combination with the high institutional hurdle for change, adapting the composition of the Security Council therefore constitutes a considerable challenge and explains why there appears to be a seemingly endless debate on Security Council reform.

However, the debate about the (failure of) Security Council reform overshadows the gradual change in how the Council operates. In fact, Security Council of today is very different to the Security Council 25 years ago, even though its composition remains the same. While formal representation is not inclusive and certainly biased, given today's global power distribution and the dominance of the current permanent members, Council decision-making is increasingly embedded into new forms of informal governance in which experts and representatives of various nations not formally represented in the Council do have a 'voice'. This system is far from ideal, but at least avoids some of the largest drawbacks of the lopsided ways in which the Security Council formally represents today's structures of global governance. Further reforming the working methods of the Council, driven by its own members, and creating institutional novelties may be a promising avenue to find answers to current global governance challenges and to make its members more accountable, its decisions more transparent and its impact greater.

Further Readings

Einsiedel, S. V., Malone, D. M., & Stagno Ugarte, B. (Eds.) (2016). *The UN Security Council in the twenty-first century*. Boulder: Lynne Rienner Publishers. [Chapters 8 & 38].
Hosli, M. O., & Dörfler, T. (2017). Why is change so slow?: Assessing prospects for United Nations Security Council reform. *Journal of Economic Policy Reform, 19*(2), 1–16.
Rittberger, V., Zangl, B., & Kruck, A. (2012). *International organization* (2nd ed.). Basingstoke: Palgrave Macmillan.

References

Abbott, K. W., Keohane, R. O., Moravcsik, A., Slaughter, A.-M., & Snidal, D. (2000). The concept of legalization. *International Organization, 54*(3), 401–419.
Adler-Nissen, R., & Pouliot, V. (2014). Power in practice: Negotiating the international intervention in Libya. *European Journal of International Relations, 20*(4), 889–911.
Barrett, R., Berger, J., Ghosh, L., Schoenfeld, D., el-Shawesh, Skinner, P. M., et al. (2015). *Foreign fighters: An updated assessment of the flow of foreign fighters into Syria and Iraq*. New York.
Binder, M., & Heupel, M. (2014). The legitimacy of the UN Security Council: Evidence from recent general assembly debates. *International Studies Quarterly, 59*(2), 238–250.
Conlon, P. (2000). *United Nations sanctions management: A case study of the Iraq Sanctions Committee, 1990–1994*. Ardsley: Transnational Publishers.
Dreher, A., Gould, M., Rablen, M. D., & Vreeland, J. R. (2014). The determinants of election to the United Nations Security Council. *Public Choice, 158*(1), 51–83.
Eilstrup-Sangiovanni, M. (2009). Varieties of cooperation: Government networks in international security. In M. Kahler (Ed.), *Networked politics: Agency, power, and governance* (pp. 194–227). Ithaca: Cornell University Press.
Einsiedel, S. v. (2017). *Civil war trends and the changing nature of armed conflict* (Occasional Paper 10). Tokyo.
Einsiedel, S. v., Malone, D. M., & Stagno Ugarte, B. (2016). Conclusion. In S. v. Einsiedel, D. M. Malone, & B. Stagno Ugarte (Eds.), *The UN Security Council in the twenty-first century* (pp. 827–876). Boulder: Lynne Rienner Publishers.
Farrall, J. M. (2009). Should the United Nations Security Council leave it to the experts? The governance and accountability of UN sanctions monitoring. In J. M. Farrall & K. Rubenstein (Eds.), *Sanctions, accountability and governance in a globalised world* (pp. 191–214). Cambridge: Cambridge University Press.
Gehring, T., & Dörfler, T. (2013). Division of labor and rule-based decision making within the UN Security Council: The Al-Qaeda/Taliban sanctions regime. *Global Governance, 19*(4), 567–587.
Gehring, T., Dorsch, C., & Dörfler, T. (2017). Precedent and doctrine in organisational decision-making: The power of informal institutional rules in the United Nations Security Council's activities on terrorism. *Journal of International Relations and Development, 42*(1), 1–29.

Gowan, R. (2016). The security council and peacekeeping. In S. v. Einsiedel, D. M. Malone, & B. Stagno Ugarte (Eds.), *The UN Security Council in the twenty-first century* (pp. 749–770). Boulder: Lynne Rienner Publishers.

Heupel, M. (2008). Combining hierarchical and soft modes of governance: The UN Security Council's approach to terrorism and weapons of mass destruction proliferation after 9/11. *Cooperation and Conflict, 43*(1), 7–29.

Hosli, M. O., & Dörfler, T. (2015). The United Nations Security Council: The challenge of reform. In D. Lesage & T. van de Graaf (Eds.), *Rising powers and multilateral institutions* (pp. 135–152). Basingstoke: Palgrave Macmillan.

Hosli, M. O., & Dörfler, T. (2017). Why is change so slow?: Assessing prospects for United Nations Security Council reform. *Journal of Economic Policy Reform, 19*(2), 1–16.

Hosli, M. O., Moody, R., O'Donovan, B., Kaniovski, S., & Little, A. C. H. (2011). Squaring the circle? Collective and distributive effects of United Nations Security Council reform. *The Review of International Organizations, 6*(2), 163–187.

Hurd, I. (1997). Security council reform: Informal membership and practice. In B. M. Russett (Ed.), *The once and future security council* (pp. 135–152). New York: St Martin's Press.

Johnstone, I. (2003). Security council deliberations: The power of the better argument. *European Journal of International Law, 14*(3), 437–480.

Johnstone, I. (2008). Legislation and adjudication in the UN Security Council: Bringing down the deliberative deficit. *American Journal of International Law, 102*(2), 275–308.

Jones, B. D. (2016). The security council and the changing distribution of power. In S. v. Einsiedel, D. M. Malone, & B. Stagno Ugarte (Eds.), *The UN Security Council in the twenty-first century* (pp. 793–813). Boulder: Lynne Rienner Publishers.

Kaldor, M. (2012). *New and old wars: [organized violence in a global era]* (3rd ed.). Cambridge [u.a.]: Polity Press.

Keohane, R. O. (1984). *After hegemony: Cooperation and discord in the world political economy.* (1st edn. Princeton: Princeton University Press.

Keohane, R. O., & Victor, D. G. (2011). The regime complex for climate change. *Perspectives on Politics, 9*(01), 7–23.

Klabbers, J. (2010). Reflections on the politics of institutional reform. In P. G. Danchin & H. Fischer (Eds.), *United Nations reform and the new collective security* (pp. 76–93). Cambridge: Cambridge University Press.

Krisch, N. (2008). The security council and great powers. In A. V. Lowe, A. Roberts, J. Welsh, & D. Zaum (Eds.), *The United Nations Security Council and war: The evolution of thought and practice since 1945* (pp. 133–153). Oxford/New York: Oxford University Press.

Lai, B., & Lefler, V. A. (2016). Examining the role of region and elections on representation in the UN Security Council. *The Review of International Organizations, 61*(04), 703.

Langmore, J., & Farrall, J. M. (2016). Can elected members make a difference in the UN Security Council? Australia's experience in 2013–2014. *Global Governance: A Review of Multilateralism and International Organizations, 22*(1), 59–77.

Lehmann, V. (2013). *Reforming the working methods of the UN Security Council: The next ACT.* New York: Friedrich-Ebert-Stiftung, Global Policy and Development.

Luck, E. C. (2008). Principal organs. In T. G. Weiss & S. Daws (Eds.), *The Oxford handbook on the United Nations* (pp. 653–674). Oxford: Oxford University Press.

Mahbubani, K. (2016). Council reform and the emerging powers. In S. v. Einsiedel, D. M. Malone, & B. Stagno Ugarte (Eds.), *The UN Security Council in the twenty-first century* (pp. 157–173). Boulder: Lynne Rienner Publishers.

Malone, D. M. (2006). *The international struggle over Iraq: Politics in the UN Security Council, 1980–2005.* Oxford: Oxford University Press.

Mello, P. A. (2010). Review article: In search of new wars: The debate about a transformation of war. *European Journal of International Relations, 16*(2), 297–309.

Münkler, H. (2012). Old and new wars. In M. D. Cavelty & V. Mauer (Eds.), *The Routledge handbook of security studies* (pp. 190–199). Milton Park/Abingdon/Oxon/New York: Routledge.

Novosseloff, A. (2015). Expanded United Nations Interim Force in Lebanon (UNIFIL II). In J. A. Koops, N. MacQueen, T. Tardy, & P. D. Williams (Eds.), *The Oxford handbook of United Nations peacekeeping operations* (pp. 767–778). Oxford: Oxford University Press.

O'Neill, B. (1997). Power and satisfaction in the security council. In B. M. Russett (Ed.), *The once and future security council* (pp. 59–82). New York: St Martin's Press.

Pettersson, T., & Wallensteen, P. (2015). Armed conflicts, 1946–2014. *Journal of Peace Research, 52*(4), 536–550.

Prantl, J. (2005). Informal groups of states and the UN Security Council. *International Organization, 59*(03), 559–592.

Prantl, J. (2010). The role of informal negotiation processes in breaking deadlocks: The UN Security Council. In A. Narlikar (Ed.), *Deadlocks in multilateral negotiations: Causes and solutions* (pp. 188–209). Cambridge: Cambridge University Press.

Ralph, J., & Gifkins, J. (2017). The purpose of United Nations Security Council practice: Contesting competence claims in the normative context created by the responsibility to protect. *European Journal of International Relations, 23*(3), 630–653.

Ramsbotham, O., Woodhouse, T., & Miall, H. (2016). *Contemporary conflict resolution: The prevention, management and transformation of dedly conflicts* (4th ed.). Malden: Polity Press.

Raustiala, K., & Victor, D. G. (2004). The regime complex for plant genetic resources. *International Organization, 58*(02), 277–309.

Rensmann, T. (2012). Reform. In B. Simma, D.-E. Khan, H. Mosler, G. Nolte, A. Paulus, & N. Wessendorf (Eds.), *The charter of the United Nations: A commentary* (3rd ed., pp. 25–69). Oxford: Oxford University Press.

Russett, B. (2005). Security council expansion: Can't, and shouldn't. In E. Zedillo (Ed.), *Reforming the United Nations for peace and security* (pp. 153–166). New Haven: Yale Centre for the Study of Globalization.

Russett, B., O'Neill, B., & Sutterlin, J. (1997). Breaking the Restructuring Logjam. In B. M. Russett (Ed.), *The once and future security council* (pp. 153–169). New York: St Martin's Press.

Scharf, M. P., & Dorosin, J. L. (1993). Interpreting UN sanctions: The rulings and role of the Yugoslavia Sanctions Committee. *Brooklyn Journal of International Law, 19*(1), 771–827.

Schelling, T. C. (1960). *The strategy of conflict*. Cambridge, MA: Harvard University Press.

Security Council Report. (2014). *Security council working methods: A tale of two councils?* (Special Research Report 1). New York.

Security Council Report. (2015). *The Veto* (Research Report 3). New York.

Security Council Report. (2017). *The peacebuilding commission and the security council: From cynicism to synergy?* (Research Report 5). New York.

Security Council Report. (2018). *Security council working methods: Provisional progress*. New York.

Sievers, L., & Daws, S. (2014). *The procedure of the UN Security Council* (4th ed.). Oxford: Oxford University Press.

Stagno Ugarte, B. (2016). Collaborating with regional organizations. In S. v. Einsiedel, D. M. Malone, & B. Stagno Ugarte (Eds.), *The UN Security Council in the twenty-first century* (pp. 475–490). Boulder: Lynne Rienner Publishers.

Stone, R. W. (2011). *Controlling institutions: International organizations and the global economy* (1st ed.). Cambridge: Cambridge Univ. Press.

Swart, L. (2013). Reform of the security council: 2007-2013. In L. Swart & E. Perry (Eds.), *Governing & managing change at the United Nations: Security council reform from 1945 to September 2013* (pp. 23–59). New York: Center for UN Reform Education.

Swart, L. (2015). *Timeline UN Security Council Reform: 1992–November 2015*. New York. http://centerforunreform.org/sites/default/files/Timeline%20November%202015%20final.pdf

Tardy, T. (2014). Hybrid peace operations: Rationale and challenges. *Global Governance, 20*(1), 95–118.

Thompson, A. (2009). *Channels of power: The UN Security Council and U.S. statecraft in Iraq.* Ithaca: Cornell University Press.

Thorhallsson, B. (2012). Small states in the UN Security Council: Means of influence? *The Hague Journal of Diplomacy, 7*(2), 135–160.

US Permanent Mission to the UN. (2007). USUN views on security council reform (07USUNNEWYORK1225_a).

Voeten, E. (2008). Why no UN Security Council reform?: Lessons for and from institutionalist theory. In D. Bourantonis, K. Ifantis, & P. I. Tsakåonas (Eds.), *Multilateralism and security institutions in an era of globalization* (pp. 288–305). London/New York: Routledge.

Vreeland, J. R., & Dreher, A. (2014). *Political economy of the United Nations Security Council: Money and influence.* Cambridge: Cambridge University Press.

Wenaweser, C. (2016). Working methods: The ugly duckling of security council reform. In S. v. Einsiedel, D. M. Malone, & B. Stagno Ugarte (Eds.), *The UN Security Council in the twenty-first century* (pp. 175–194). Boulder: Lynne Rienner Publishers.

Whitfield, T. (2016). Groups of friends. In S. v. Einsiedel, D. M. Malone, & B. Stagno Ugarte (Eds.), *The UN Security Council in the twenty-first century* (pp. 491–505). Boulder: Lynne Rienner Publishers.

Williams, P. D. (2016). *Global and regional peacekeepers* (Discussion Paper Series on Global and Regional Governance). New York.

Witschel, G. (2012a). Article 108. In B. Simma, D.-E. Khan, H. Mosler, G. Nolte, A. Paulus, & N. Wessendorf (Eds.), *The charter of the United Nations: A commentary* (3rd ed., pp. 2199–2231). Oxford: Oxford University Press.

Witschel, G. (2012b). Article 109. In B. Simma, D.-E. Khan, H. Mosler, G. Nolte, A. Paulus, & N. Wessendorf (Eds.), *The charter of the United Nations: A commentary* (3rd ed., pp. 2232–2241). Oxford: Oxford University Press.

Chapter 16
NATO in a Changing World

Roger A. Tosbotn and Eugenio Cusumano

16.1 Introduction

International organisations, built on fragile intergovernmental compromises and characterised by the presence of multiple veto players, are notoriously poor at adapting to a changing global order.[1] This is especially the case for a multinational military alliance like NATO. Military organisations are large bureaucracies steeped in tradition and characterised by hierarchy, *esprit de corps*, and relative insulation from external society. Cognitive biases and organisational parochial interests have often made military organisations slow to adapt to evolving threats. For this reason, militaries are renowned for always preparing themselves to 'fight the last war'. Military cultures shape, and often hinder, the ability of military organisations to transform in order to meet new challenges.

As a Cold-War military alliance which has outlived the enemy it was created to confront, NATO has faced strong pressure to change in order not to fall into obsolescence. The collapse of the Soviet Union turned the prospect of a large-scale combat in Eastern Europe into a ghost of the past. Consequently, NATO has been forced to embrace an array of new tasks, such as peacekeeping, combatting terrorism, and conducting counterinsurgency and state-building missions. As epitomised by operation ISAF in Afghanistan, the Alliance had to choose between going out of area or

---

[1] See Chap. 1 by Buck and Hosli for an introduction of the global order as such.

R. A. Tosbotn (✉)
Brussels, Belgium
e-mail: r.a.tosbotn@umail.leidenuniv.nl

E. Cusumano
Leiden University, Leiden, The Netherlands
e-mail: e.Cusumano@hum.leidenuniv.nl

© Springer Nature Switzerland AG 2020
M. O. Hosli, J. Selleslaghs (eds.), *The Changing Global Order*, United Nations University Series on Regionalism 17,
https://doi.org/10.1007/978-3-030-21603-0_16

going out of business. At the same time, NATO enormously increased in size, welcoming 12 new Eastern European states. This resulted in the need to both incorporate new member armed forces into the Alliance force structure and incorporate their national interests and threat perceptions in transatlantic security policies.

The challenges arising from this enlargement and from conducting out of area operations severely strained the capabilities and cohesion of the Alliance, which faced frequent criticism for its allegedly ineffective conduct in Afghanistan and the lack of effective burden sharing across members. Russia's invasion of Crimea and covert support for the civil war in Ukraine provided NATO with a much welcome opportunity to refocus on its original mission of deterring Russian attacks. Based on Article 5 of the NATO treaty, any direct attack against a member would amount to an attack against the Alliance as a whole.[2] As NATO members together enjoy a clear military superiority vis-à-vis Russia or any other opponent it is widely agreed that a direct invasion of a member state remains unlikely. However, as the likelihood of a conventional military confrontation diminishes, NATO members have instead found themselves having to deal with new 'hybrid' forms of warfare: a mixture of military and non-military societal destabilisation tools that could disrupt the functioning of a member state without directly amounting to an act of war, that still obliges the Alliance as a whole to respond. Due to the difficulty to attribute them to a specific actor, cyber-attacks figure prominently in the panoply of hybrid war strategies.[3]

This chapter examines NATO's response to the emergence of cyberspace as a new domain of military action. As it requires types of expertise that armed forces often do not have within their ranks. Adapting to the threats emanating from cyber space is an especially hard challenge for multinational military organisations like NATO. Consequently, choosing to specifically analyse NATO's adaptation to cyber threats allows for particularly interesting insights to be made of the Alliance's evolving role in the global order. As we show in the ensuing analysis, NATO's role conception played a key part in shaping the Alliance's response to the ongoing revolution in information technology. By conducting a quantitative and qualitative content analysis of NATO documents, we show that NATO's unique role conception has shaped a specific conceptualisation of cyber-attacks, which have been seen primarily as a tool of Russian hybrid warfare. Increasingly prominent in NATO discourses, the emphasis on preparedness against cyber operations has been used strategically by the Alliance to showcase its enduring relevance and advocate a refocusing of NATO towards its original purpose.

This chapter is divided as follows. Section 16.1 will provide an overview of NATO's structure and evolution over time. Section 16.2 will draw on existing scholarship on military change as a source of insight into the role played by role conceptions in shaping the military organisations' ability to adapt to new challenges. Section 16.3 will rely on evidence from content analyses to illustrate how cyber threats have been conceptualised in NATO doctrine and strategic communication.

---

[2] Article 5: https://www.nato.int/cps/ic/natohq/topics_110496.htm

[3] See Chap. 20 by Meerts for the changing nature of warfare, and the increasing prominence of negotiation as a means to resolve conflict.

Section 16.4 will analyse the findings of the content analysis, showing how NATO's organisational culture(s) has played a key role in shaping the Alliance's framing of and response to cyber threats. The conclusions will outline the theoretical and policy implications of this study, fleshing out some broader insights into how international security organisations adapt to technological, geostrategic, and societal changes.

16.2 The Evolution of NATO

After the collapse of the Soviet Union, the North Atlantic Treaty Organization faced the worst possible scenario for an international military alliance: the disappearance of the threat it was originally designed to stand against. As famously argued by Lord Ismay, NATO was created to "keep the Soviet Union out, the Americans in, and the Germans down".[4] Since its creation in 1949, NATO had been the main guarantor of territorial defence for its European member states against the existential threat posed by the Soviet Union and its Warsaw Pact allies. To be sure, the fall of the Iron Curtain clearly vindicated NATO's success in deterring the Soviet Union and contributing towards its downfall. At the same time, however, the end of the Cold War raised strong doubts about the need to maintain NATO's costly organisational apparatus at a time when public requests for peace dividends translated into large cuts in all member states' defence budgets. As a result, NATO was in danger of becoming a victim of its own success.

To be sure, the civil wars caused by the disintegration of the former Yugoslavia showed that the European continent still needed a provider of collective defence, supporting those that espoused the maintenance of NATO, which launched operations Deliberate Force and Allied Force against Serbia in 1995 and 1999 and the ensuing peacekeeping operations IFOR and KFOR (Kaplan 2004) Since 1999, however, the increasing unlikelihood of conflict in Europe cast new doubts over NATO's lasting utility.

These dilemmas did not stain the prestige of what was widely credited as the most successful military alliance in history, epitomised by the eagerness of the newly independent Eastern European states to join NATO. As a result, the organisation continued to grow, welcoming Poland, Czechia and Hungary in 1999, and Bulgaria, Estonia, Latvia, Lithuania, Romania, Slovakia and Slovenia in 2004 (Kaplan 2004). However, the lack of a clearly recognisable opponent, the European Union's willingness to develop an independent Common Security and Defence Policy, and Washington's concern that NATO was only encouraging European states to free-ride on US military power all fuelled scepticism about the organisations' enduring indispensability (Hofmann 2015; Auerswald and Saideman 2014). NATO was therefore confronted with the choice of either going out of area, projecting military power outside the Euroatlantic region, or going out of business.

---

[4] Lord Ismay, NATO declassified: https://www.nato.int/cps/en/natohq/declassified_137930.htm

In this context, the 9/11 attacks on US soil were the first occasion in which NATO's collective defence clause contained in Article 5 was invoked.[5] The ensuing occupation of Afghanistan provided the first occasion for NATO to go out of area. Operation International Security Assistance Force (ISAF) saw the participation of all member states, albeit at different levels and capacities. The US global war on terrorism, however, also widened the rift between member states, some of which (most notably France and Germany) did not participate in the 2003 invasion of Iraq, conducted by an ad-hoc coalition of the willing. At the same time, many NATO members' participation in operation ISAF became increasingly underwhelming. As argued by Rynning (2013, see also Auerswald and Saideman 2014) the force activation processes required by the expansion of operation ISAF beyond Kabul were 'an exercise in frustrated diplomacy' that saw NATO commit too few forces to meet the minimum force requirements. As repeatedly stressed by ISAF commander general McChristal, insufficient manpower caused the Taliban to gain the upper hand, putting NATO forces at risk of defeat (Cusumano 2015). The inability to deploy sufficient boots on the ground forced NATO to resort to strategies that undermined the conduct of counterinsurgency and stability tasks, such as the substantial outsourcing of operations to private military and security contractors (Cusumano 2017; Krahmann 2016).

The limited contributions made by European NATO members to ISAF also raised new doubts over the utility of the Alliance and the commitment of many European members, which consistently fell short of their obligations to increase their defence budgets and commit sufficient troops to Afghanistan. Frustration with insufficient burden sharing and scepticism over NATO's enduring utility have been repeatedly voiced by US President Donald Trump, who explicitly dismissed NATO as obsolete.[6] Against the backdrop of NATO's suboptimal performance in its first large-scale operation out of area, Vladimir Putin's Russia assertiveness,[7] vocally denounced by Eastern European member states, showed that traditional tasks such as deterrence and the territorial defence of Western Europe are still far from unnecessary. This was especially the case after the February 2014 Russian invasion of Crimea and the ensuing covert support for the civil war in Eastern Ukraine, which provided new arguments for NATO to refocus on the original task it had successfully accomplished in its first 40 years of existence. Refocusing on its original tasks eased NATO's failed search for a new purpose and identity, increasing the cohesion and credibility of the Alliance.[8]

In spite of Russia's resurgence as a potential major threat to European security, the possibility of large-scale tank battles in Western Europe remain a ghost of the

---

[5] After The Attacks: THE ALLIANCE; For First Time, NATO Invokes Joint Pact With U.S. Daley, Suzanne (2001). New York Times.

[6] http://www.independent.co.uk/news/world/americas/us-politics/donald-trump-not-know-much-nato-alliance-wolf-blitzer-cnn-obsolete-a7702201.html

[7] See Chap. 5 by Gerrits on Russia's role in the Changing Global Order

[8] See Chap. 3 by De Wijk on Power Politics for an analysis on the Russian annexation of Crimea in 2014

past. Due to the disparity in military capabilities between Russia and the collective might of all of NATO's members, confrontation moved to the theatre of hybrid war: a mixture of military and non-military societal destabilisation tools that could disrupt the functioning of a member state without amounting to an armed attack triggering the Washington's treaty collective defence clause. Consequently, while NATO found in Russia a familiar opponent, the policy responses identified as appropriate in tackling the Kremlin's renewed assertiveness were somewhat different (Cusumano and Corbe 2017). Cyber defence was identified as one of these responses.

16.3   Role Conceptions and NATO'S Search for a New Role

After the Constructivist turn in International Relations brought to the fore the awareness that the security environments in which states are embedded are not only material, but also institutional and cultural, military change scholarship also began to conceptualise the interests and goals of military organisations as "a function of its culture".[9] Below, we present the role of a specific element of organisational culture – role conceptions – as an intervening variable shaping the evolution of NATO and informing its willingness to embrace cyber defence as a new task.

Role conceptions can be understood as an organisation's understanding of itself: both in terms of what or who it is, and also of how that manifests into a role. This understanding is associated with a range of tasks, expectations, and responsibilities. Role conceptions guide an organisation in identifying its core competences, distinguishing between which activities should be considered as part of its core missions and which ones should be discarded as peripheral (Cusumano 2014; Vennesson et al. 2009). Consequently, NATO's role conception provides especially important insights into understanding the organisation's search for new competences after the end of the Cold War and the reasons it embraced cyber defence as an additional responsibility.

As discussed in the section above, NATO's attempt to show its enduring utility after the end of the Cold War by conducting peace enforcing and state-building operations did not lead to the desired results. Such missions only obtained half-hearted support from Alliance members, and were identified as ill-suited for combat-oriented multinational military organisations like NATO to perform. Against this backdrop, Russia's renewed assertiveness has presented NATO with the oppor-

---

[9] Elizabeth Kier, "Culture and French Military Doctrine Before World War II" in Katzenstein 1996: 187. See also Theo Farrell, Culture and Military Power, *Review of International Studies* (Vol. 24 (1998) 407–416. For instance, military culture has been used as an explanation for both restraint and excess in the use of force. See Jeffrey W. Legro, *Cooperation Under Fire: Anglo-German Restraint During World War II* (Ithaca, NY: Cornell UP 1995); and Isabel V. Hull, *Absolute Destruction: Military Culture and the Practices of War in Imperial Germany* (Ithaca, NY: Cornell UP 2005)

tunity to refocus on its preferred, traditional role: deterring Russia. In 2017, however, this task requires new strategies and technological capabilities. Russian attempts to destabilise NATO are likely to take a hybrid form rather than consisting of the use of conventional military capabilities. Consequently, cyberspace has been identified as a new battlefield NATO forces should prepare for.

But how exactly do role conceptions affect the way military organisations change? As argued by Berger, cultures and role conceptions generate cognitive biases within organisations. This is because information that resonates with organisations' preferences and reinforces existing beliefs and role conceptions is readily assimilated. On the other hand, information that challenges existing images and beliefs tends to be ignored, rejected, or distorted (1994: 24–25).

In addition, an organisations' behaviour is often path-dependent. By decreasing the importance of existing capabilities, disruptive military innovations may translate into a loss of resources, power, and career prospects for many of those at the high-end of the military hierarchy, who may have a vested interest in preserving traditional military doctrines (Allison 1971; Halperin 1974; Posen 1984; Wilson 1989). Consequently, change in military organisations often occurs slowly and incrementally. Organisational theory, in sum, maintains that bureaucracies seek to protect the capacities they deem central to what they consider to be their mission, and express indifference or even resistance to those capacities they see as peripheral or irrelevant.

The way to fundamentally challenge the dominant beliefs that underpin an organisation's role conceptions is through intense external shocks. Essentially, when the repertoire of tool kits, habits, skills and styles within an organisation culture is unable to provide solutions by drawing from its bank of historical narratives, a space opens where alternative solutions to these narratives can be presented. This can serve as a catalyst for change, both in the short and longer-term perspective (ibid: 106–112). One would expect a dominant culture within an organisation to resist change and new ideas, unless faced with dramatic events, traumatic experiences, or external shocks. This is especially true for an organisation imbued with conservative military cultures and run by rigid defence bureaucracies like NATO.

To be sure, arguing that NATO displays single, monolithic culture and role conception is to some extent a simplification. Transnational military alliances are characterised by the coexistence of different cultures. Becker and Malesky (2017), for instance, argue that a dichotomy can be found within NATO members' strategic cultures, which can be identified as either "Atlanticist" or "Europeanist". Assessing the competitive relationship between these two cultures provides an important insight into the member states' levels of military spending and participation in NATO operations (ibid.). Generally speaking, however, NATO displays an aggregate role conception that should inhibit change. Fundamentally new ideas would serve as fundamental challenges to the existing, prevailing beliefs that can ultimately undermine the Alliance's role conception. Therefore, one would normally expect outside pressure to cause, at best, a mild alteration of ideas and identity unless there are extraordinary incidents that shake the foundations of the beliefs and values of NATO. In short, a big defence alliance like NATO, is expected to be resistant to change, and therefore adapt only slowly and incrementally, unless there are critical junctures that spike the need for radical change (Tosbotn 2016: 6).

When it occurs, change is likely to be filtered by existing cognitive scripts and bureaucratic politics, which are likely to shape an interpretation of existing threats that is compatible with the role conception and parochial interests of the organisation. This tendency is clearly illustrated by NATO's conceptualisation of cyber security and the innovations it requires.

16.4 Transatlantic Security in Cyberspace

As explained in the last section, military organisations are slow and resistant to change. Global political landscapes and threat environments, by contrast, often evolve very quickly.[10] While NATO was engaged with the search for a new role, the possibilities offered by the internet revolution started to translate into new national and international security challenges. How has NATO adapted to the cyber revolution? Several NATO countries, spearheaded by the United States, have understood the need to train personnel in cyber security and operations, improve inter-organisational (cyber) security, and the intra-organisational systems of the member states. Some countries have already taken on leading roles as hubs for knowledge in this area. This has been achieved through increased spending and the foundation of cyber centres and sophisticated, national cyber programmes. Estonia, for instance, which experienced a large-scale cyber-attack in 2007, hosts the Cooperative Cyber-Defence NATO Centre of Excellence (CCDCOE), which actively assists all member states in confronting cyber threats by providing training, conducting research, and helping them to develop their own cyber doctrine.

The recent increase in spending on cyber defence, follows a long line of re-conceptualisation and collective learning about cyber. This is trace-able when examining official NATO communication in the period of 2002–2016. "Cyber" has developed from a being a concept in its 'infancy' stage in the early 2000s, to the highly sophisticated concept it is today. The two most prominent findings of a content analysis of NATO documents are that it has expanded significantly to include new, more complex associations such as energy grids, critical infrastructure, various types of attacks, new forms of cooperation, resilience, and industry-related threats. Secondly, the perceived 'enemy', or 'projector of these threats' has changed from being an unspecified subject, to 'non-state' actors, 'state actors', and an indistinguishable mixture of the two. Currently, as this chapter shows, Russia is usually identified as the cyber enemy *par excellance*. In NATO official communication, associations between cyber and Russia can be frequently found.[11]

---

[10] See Chap. 14 by Kasper on Global Governance 2.0, particularly subchapter 13.2, on the position of Authoritarian regimes in the global order.

[11] See for example: http://www.nato.int/docu/review/2017/Also-in-2017/nato-priority-spending-success-cyber-defence/EN/index.htm

16.5 Content Analysis

One way of examining how an organisation or entity view the importance of a concept, is to examine their outward communication. As forcefully stressed since the beginning of the Constructivist turn in international relations, foreign policy is 'made' by language (Wæver 1995). Consequently, the study of discourses and speeches has gained increasing prominence in foreign policy analysis and security studies (see for instance Pashakhanlou 2017). Content analysis is defined as 'a technique for making inferences by systematically and objectively identifying characteristics of specified messages' (Holsti 1969: 25).

Qualitative and quantitative examinations can determine how the language used in large bodies of texts reveals trends that relate to ideas and identity, and thus also role conceptions in any given context (Eriksson and Giacomello 2006, 2007, 2014). Content analysis tries to establish the frequency (or relative prominence) of a concept, phrase, or word, within a given corpus of documents. In addition to measuring the frequency, it examines specific keywords' relationship to other terms, as well as creating a baseline that lets us compare and contrast change and frequency over time (Palmquist et al. 1997). Relational content analysis goes deeper into the relationships between concepts discovered in a given corpus, providing information about the semantics of concepts. In effect, this enables the inference of the characteristics within a quantity of communication documents by looking at the associations related to a given word, phrase, or concept (Holsti 1969). Consequently, content analysis provides an ideal methodological tool to assess how NATO's role conception has shaped the alliance's conceptualization of, and response to, cyber security challenges.

Qualitative and quantitative content analyses were carried out on a corpus consisting of official NATO documents issued from 2002 to 2016. These documents are primarily NATO summit communiques, as well as keynotes from high officials at NATO. Applying content analysis to political communication allows us to see how NATO projects its own image outwards, and therefore how it sees its own position vis-à-vis a problem. In this case, cyber defence. The data used for the content analysis in this chapter, is based on the data in Tosbotn (2016),[12] with the addition of the NATO summit communiqué released after the NATO Warsaw summit in July 2016 (Chart 16.1)

As evident in Graph 1, the frequency in use of the word "cyber" ranks third in mentions behind "Russia" and "terrorism". We still see, however, that "Russia" is the main concern of NATO's official communication. The discourse from 2002–2016 is consistently dominated by "Russia" in a context of collective defence, deterrence, and a range of other incidents that occurred in this time-period. The spikes in mentions of "cyber" and "Russia" in Graph 1, correspond well with the cyber-attacks in

---

[12] The corpus list, the scripts used in the analyses, and the full analyses themselves are available in the annexes of Tosbotn, Roger (2016) NATO and Cyber Security: Critical Junctures as Catalysts for Change.

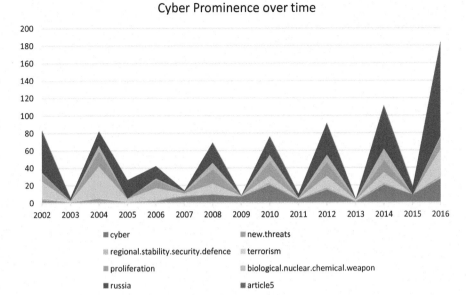

Chart 16.1 Cyber Prominence over time

Estonia (2007), Georgia (2008) and Ukraine (2014). Considering NATO's core objectives of collective defence, in the context of an international military alliance, one would assume these attacks to be perceived – at the very least – as strong warning signals of an emerging new, hybrid method of warfare being adopted by the traditional, Russian enemy. Moreover, if these attacks were perceived as the precursors for further similar incidents, they would have served as shocks to the culture of NATO, which at the time had a lacking understanding and organisational capacity to deal with attacks made in the cyber domain. These shocks, in turn, would be expected to spur movements within the mechanisms of change within NATO (Chart 16.2).

As illustrated in Graph 2, we see that the spikes of "cyber" and "Russia" correlate within the corpus of documents used. Additionally, the steady increase over time of the blue trend line tells a story of a concept that has seen an increasing importance from NATO's point of view in the same time-period.

The spikes in the chart, which correspond strongly with the attacks in Estonia, Georgia, and Ukraine, have exerted pressure on NATO to adapt and prepare. NATO, however, lacked the pre-agreed upon solutions to deal with these challenges. NATO's traditional role conception, grounded on deterring Russia, has played a prominent role in framing cyber-attacks and shaping its own response thereto.

The findings further illustrate that the conceptualisation of "cyber" over time, changed drastically. In the cases of 2007 and 2008, "cyber" becomes linked with terms like "collective defence", In the following years, from 2008 to 2010, the term "cyber" was associated with power grids, banking systems, government services, and IT infrastructure, as a result of a richer association of the concept based on

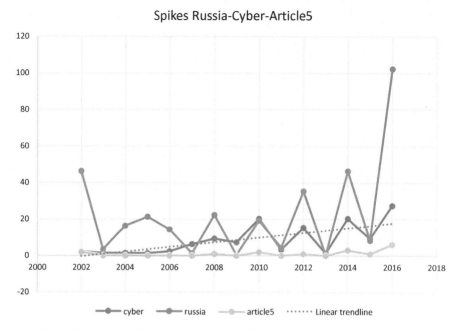

Chart 16.2 Spikes in mentions of Russia-Cyber-Article5 over time

experiences in countries with strong NATO relations. Moreover, in 2014, "hybrid" warfare became a new addition to the concept. The enlargement of the "cyber" concept reflects its dynamic nature: cyber space provides a plethora of opportunities to inflict damage on an opponent. Each new case study illustrated this in different ways. In Estonia, the whole digital government structure was made essentially useless while under cyber-attack in 2007. In Georgia, the country's ICT and communications services were paralysed, and in Ukraine, the abovementioned weaknesses were exploited alongside a take-over of large portions of the Ukrainian media services, in conjunction with a more traditional ground invasion, that rendered the Ukrainians defenceless during the initial annexation.

16.6   Russia, A New Old Enemy

The pervasiveness of "Russia" as a main concern, is easily explained. It is connected to the very identity of the alliance; deterring Soviet aggression was the core reason for the creation of NATO. As the issue of cyber security was linked to NATO's publicised role of constraining Russia, new opportunities arose. By identifying cyber-attacks as a threat associated with Russia, the organisation began to more forcefully reorient itself towards its original purpose, mobilising the resources, personnel, and political will to keep its members safe. There is now a plethora of instances where Russia has been linked to NATO's discussions on, and conceptualisation of, "cyber" space. While in the period of 2002–2005, dialogue in matters related to cyber security was hailed as a great opportunity for NATO-Russian cooperation, the tune has changed drastically in the 12 following years. In NATO's 2007 and 2008 speeches, London and Brussels respectively, "cyber-attacks" and "cyber security" became increasingly associated with collective defence against Russia. Russian cyber-attacks on Estonian governmental infrastructure in 2007, for instance, spurred a change in NATO's conceptualisation of "cyber". Not only was cyberspace becoming an arena where the enemy could interrupt service, but it could also have severe economic and infrastructural impacts. In direct response to the 2007 cyber-attack, in 2008 NATO responded by building the Cooperative Cyber Defence Centre of Excellence, in Tallinn, Estonia. However, this did little to prevent Russia from effectively employing hybrid warfare to achieve a quick and smooth victory in the 2008 Russo-Georgian war. In the period of 7–12 of August 2008, Russian forces mixed information warfare, conventional warfare, and cyber warfare, to gain the upper hand in strategic communication by disabling host servers, hacking the Georgian government, largely toppled the Georgian's ability to communicate during the war.

Yet further definitive proof the merger of the two conceptions of cyber space, and collective defence against Russia, came in the NATO CCDCOE publication titled "CYBER WAR IN PERSPECTIVE: Russian aggression against Ukraine", and the 2014 and 2016 NATO summit communiques. The former document openly and explicitly links historical Russian attitudes towards its neighbouring countries with regards to specific instances of cyber warfare, with an emphasis on the Russian annexation of Crimea. Moreover, the work links strategic culture with communications and the integration of cyber warfare in Russia's strategic arsenal. The publication ends by discussing the prospects of a cyber escalation by Putin in Ukraine, in the chapter "What's next for Putin in Ukraine: Cyber Escalation?" which builds on the wide range of cyber warfare tactics employed by the Russian's involvements in the country. Firstly, the vast amount of denial of service attacks and website defacements of Ukrainian public sector and resistance sites. Secondly, via cyber espionage, through cell phone network disruptions, targeted propaganda, and the controlling of information flow. Lastly, the harder types of attacks, which interrupted or disabled power grids for civilians and military fighters alike (Geers 2015: 13; Giles 2015: 23–26). These documents epitomise how NATO's conceptualisation of cyber-attacks as a threat associated with Russia has grown more and more explicit over the years.

In September 2014, roughly 6 months after Russia's invasion of Ukraine, NATO held a summit in Wales. The growing tension on the Eastern borders of NATO is well-reflected in the resulting communique. Moreover, the decreasing amounts of resistance to including, and expanding on NATO's own cyber capabilities as a key part of its planning, and inclusion into day-to-day operational processes is apparent. In essence, there was enshrined in the communique a broad acceptance of the concept of cyber as a key component in the future of the defensive work of the alliance as shown in the extract below:

As the Alliance looks to the future, **cyber threats and attacks** will continue to become more common, sophisticated, and potentially damaging. To face this evolving challenge, **we have endorsed an Enhanced Cyber Defence Policy**, Contributing to the fulfillment of the **Alliance's core tasks**. The policy reaffirms the principles of the indivisibility of Allied security and of prevention, detection, resilience, recovery, and defence. It recalls that the fundamental cyber defence responsibility of NATO is to defend its own networks, and that assistance to Allies should be addressed in accordance with the spirit of solidarity, emphasizing the responsibility of Allies to develop the relevant capabilities for the protection of national networks. Our policy also recognises that international law, including international humanitarian law and the UN Charter, applies in cyberspace. **Cyber attacks can reach a threshold that threatens national and Euro-Atlantic prosperity**, security, and stability. Their impact could be as harmful to modern societies as a conventional attack. We affirm therefore that cyber defence is part of NATO's core task of collective defence. **A decision as to when a cyber attack would lead to the invocation of Article 5 would be taken by the North Atlantic Council on a case-by-case basis**.

This paragraph from the communique serves as an excellent summary of several developments in NATO communiques in the 2002–2016 period. It recognises cyber threats and attacks as a growing part of what NATO must defend against, presents political decisions of enhancing policies, connects the cyber defence to the core tasks, and justifies doing so in explicit detail. Furthermore, it talks about the international legal framework surrounding cyber, mentions some of the threats inherent to cyber-attacks, and finally affirms that cyber-attacks *could* lead to an invocation of the Article 5 in the NATO charter.

The Warsaw summit communique, released in 2016, presents several paragraphs that link cyber-attacks and cyber defence with the protection of important critical infrastructure. What is more, the hybrid nature of warfare is emphasised as a key reason for an increased focus on cyber defence and intra-organisational cooperation to build resilient systems and responses within NATO. One of the most prominent changes in conceptualisation from the earlier period (2002–2007) to the more recent period (2008–2016) is a development towards conjoining the two concepts of 'Russia' and 'cyber', or 'hybrid warfare', and linking it with the original mission of NATO which is collective defence and regional stability:

from state and non-state actors; from military forces and from terrorist, **cyber, or hybrid attacks. Russia's aggressive actions, including provocative military activities in the periphery of NATO territory and its demonstrated willingness to attain political goals by the threat and use of force**, are a source of regional instability, fundamentally challenge the Alliance, have damaged Euro-Atlantic security, and threaten our long-standing goal of a Europe whole, free, and at peace.

This has culminated in an increased intra-organisational political will to improve the structures within the organisation to deal with, and increase the overall resilience(s) that affects the national and collective defence, "(…) including hybrid and cyber threats". By furthermore recognising cyberspace as a core domain of operations, "in which NATO must defend itself as effectively as it does in the air, on land, and at sea.", the conceptualisation of cyber has reached a point where there is no longer a teetering between identifying threats, different types of actors, and mapping out means of cooperation, and arriving at a consensus about *what cyber is*, but rather it has gone from implicitly calling out Russia for coordinating cyber-attacks in 2010 (Tosbotn 2016: 27), to explicitly pointing to Russia's aggressive actions in Ukraine – both on the ground and in cyber space – as a main reason for the organisation to modernise and take on greater capacity to serve its core purposes of defending its member states.

16.7   NATO'S Role Conception as an Intervening Variable: An Analysis

New technologies such as the internet revolution have reshaped the global order and threat environment, thereby compelling international military organisations like NATO to adapt.

As the previous section demonstrated, NATO's conceptualisation of the challenges arising from the cyber space has become increasingly tightly linked to the threat posed by Russia. To be sure, this is to some extent an obvious response to Russia's own military conduct, which has comprised cyber-espionage and cyber-sabotage in both Ukraine and Georgia. However, NATO's interpretation of threats in the cyberspace has also been deeply informed by its traditional role conceptions and organisational interests. Conducting counterinsurgency and stability operations out of area challenged NATO's effectiveness and cohesion, leading to widespread scepticism of the organisation's ability to tackle missions it was not originally designed for and reinforcing the criticism about NATO's obsoleteness. Conceptualising cyber defence as part of NATO's collective defence against Russia provides the possibility for NATO to strengthen its credibility and internal cohesion and attract new support by refocusing on its original purpose of providing deterrence and collective defence. The cognitive predispositions of high-ranking NATO military officers and civilians may have further increased the connection between cyber threats and Russia that is presently found in NATO discourses. As widely held by cognitive psychology, individuals tend to cope with uncertainty by drawing on past experience and relying on historical analogy. Such a tendency has been widely documented in the scholarship on military organisations and foreign policy decision-making (Van Evera 1984; Snyder 1984; Jervis 1968). Interpreting cyber threats as challenges coming from Russia allowed NATO decision-makers to cope with uncertainty, by categorising cyber security as just a novel element of a somewhat familiar challenge, and identifying an appropriate response at least partly based on traditional military means (Chart 16.3).

As summarised by the chart above, NATO's role conception can be fruitfully conceptualised as an intervening variable which has shaped the organisation's response to the cyber revolution. Cognitive scripts based on historical experience and NATO's vested interest in showing its enduring relevance in countering future challenges have shaped an interpretation of cyber threats as part of the organisation's traditional role of protecting its member states from Russia.

Chart 16.3 NATO's role conception as an intervening variable

While the connection that is presently found between cyber-attacks and the defence against Russian aggression is partly explained by the Kremlin's sponsorship of acts of cyberespionage and sabotage, cyber security is actually a much broader challenge that includes defence against a number of other perpetrators of hostile acts in the cyber space, ranging from Chinese hackers to non-state actors using the internet as a tool for recruitment and propaganda such as the Islamic State of Iraq and the Levant (ISIL) and criminal networks. Such issues, however, received much less prominence in NATO discourses as they were seen as peripheral to NATO's key role. Consequently, NATO's role conception was key in shaping a specific interpretation of cyber defence that revolves around deterring Russia and preparing against its attempts to destabilise NATO member states and allies by hybrid means.

16.8   Conclusions

The finding that NATO's role conception shaped its response to novel challenges such as cyber defence resonates with a large strand of institutionalist and constructivist scholarship and has broader implications for the study of how international organisations respond to the changing global order. Most notably, our study shows that organisations' role conceptions are key to explaining the way they interpret and conceptualise existing challenges. Organisational cultures and interests are a key intervening variable shaping the ways in which they respond to changes in the global order. Consequently, studying the organisational culture of different institutional actors provides important insights into the future evolution of international security cooperation and global politics at large.

A comparative analysis of different organisations' conceptualisations of the threats posed by the internet revolution would provide more precise insights into the role of organisational cultures in general and role conceptions specifically in shaping policy responses. For instance, a comparison between NATO and the European Union, which has recently dedicated increasing attention to strengthening the resilience of its member states' critical infrastructure against cyber-attacks, would be an important source of insight into the importance of role conceptions in shaping international organisations' response to novel challenges relative to other factors.

Further Readings

Gaddis, J. L. (1986, Spring). The long peace: Elements of stability in the postwar international system. *International Security, 10*(4), 99–142. MIT Press.
Gross-Stein, J. (2013). Building politics into psychology: The misperception of threat. In L. Huddy, D. O. Sears, & J. S. Levy (Eds.), *The Oxford handbook of political psychology* (second ed.). Oxford: Oxford University Press.
Jervis, R. (1976). *Perception and misperception in international politics.* Princeton: Princeton University Press.
Jervis, R. (1988, Spring). War and misperception. *The Journal of Interdisciplinary History, 18*(4), 675–700. The origin and prevention of major wars, MIT Press.
Kissinger, H. (1994). *Diplomacy.* New York: Simon & Schuster.
Kissinger, H. (2014). To settle the Ukraine crisis, start at the end. *Washington Post.*
Matlock, J. (2014). Ukraine: The price of internal division. *Peace Magazine.*
Morgenthau, H. (1978). *Six principles of political realism.* New York: Alfred A. Knopf.
Morgenthau, H. *The future of diplomacy.*

References

Allison, G. T. (1971). *Essence of decision. Explaining the Cuban missile crisis.* New York: Harper and Collins.
Auerswald, D. P., & Saideman, S. M. (2014). *NATO in Afghanistan: Fighting together, fighting alone.* Princeton: Princeton University Press.
Becker, J., & Malesky, E. (2017). The continent or the "grand large"? Strategic culture and operational burden-sharing in NATO. *International Studies Quarterly, 2017*(61), 163–180.
Berger, T. (1994). *Cultures of antimilitarism.* Baltimore: John Hopkins University Press.
Cusumano, E. (2014). The scope of military privatization. Military role conceptions and contractor support in the United States and the United Kingdom. *International Relations, 29*(2), 219–241.
Cusumano, E. (2015). Bridging the gap. Mobilisation constraints and contractor support to US and UK military operations. *Journal of Strategic Studies, 39*(1), 94–119.
Cusumano, E. (2017). Resilience for hire? NATO contractor support in Afghanistan examined. In E. Cusumano & M. Corbe (Eds.), *A civil-military response to hybrid threats* (pp. 101–122). Basingstoke: Palgrave Macmillan.
Cusumano, E., & Corbe, M (Eds.). (2017). *A civil-military response to hybrid threats.* Basingstoke: Palgrave.
Daley, S. (2001, September 13). After the attacks: THE ALLIANCE; for first time, NATO invokes joint pact with U.S. *New York Times.* Accessed 24 Oct 2017, from: http://www.nytimes.com/2001/09/13/us/after-attacks-alliance-for-first-time-nato-invokes-joint-defense-pact-with-us.html

Eriksson, J., & Giacomello, G. (2006). The information revolution, security, and international relations: (IR)relevant theory? *International Political Science Review, 27*(3), 221–244.

Eriksson, J., & Giacomello, G. (2007). *International relations and security in the digital age.* New York: Routledge Publishing.

Eriksson, J., & Giacomello, G. (2014). International relations, cybersecurity, and content analysis. In *The Global Politics of Science and Technology-Vol. 2.*

Farrell, T. (1998). Culture and military power. *Review of International Studies, 24*, 407–416.

Geers, K. (2015). *Cyber war in perspective: Russian aggression against Ukraine.* Tallinn: NATO CCD COE Publications.

Giles, K. (2015). Russia and its neighbours: Old attitudes, new capabilities. In *Chapter 2 in cyber war in perspective: Russian aggression against Ukraine.* Tallinn: NATO CCD COE Publications.

Halperin, M. S. (1974). *Bureaucratic politics and foreign policy.* Washington, DC: Brookings Institution.

Hoffman, S. (2015). *European security in NATO's shadow.* Cambridge: Cambridge University Press.

Holsti, O. R. (1969). *Content analysis for the social sciences and humanities.* Reading/Homeland: Addison- Wesley.

Hull, I. V. (2005). *Absolute destruction: Military culture and the practices of war in Imperial Germany.* Ithaca: Cornell University Press.

Jervis, R. (1968, April). Hypotheses on misperception. *World Politics, 20*(3), 454–479.

Kaplan, L. S. (2004). *NATO united, NATO divided: The evolution of an alliance.* Westport: Praeger.

Katzenstein, P. J. (1996). *The culture of national security: Norms and identity in world politics.* New York: Columbia University Press.

Kier, E. (1996). "Culture and French military doctrine before world war II". The Culture of National Security Norms and Identity in World Politics, 186–215,

Krahmann, E. (2016). NATO contracting in Afghanistan: The problem of principal-agent networks. *International Affairs, 92*(6), 1401–1426.

Legro, J. W. (1995). *Cooperation under fire: Anglo-German restraint during world war II.* Ithaca: Cornell University Press.

Palmquist, M., Carley, K., & Dale, T. (1997). Applications of computer text analysis: Analyzing literary and nonliterary texts. In *Roberts "Text analysis for the social sciences: Methods for drawing statistical inferences from texts and transcripts"* (pp. 171–189). Mahwah: Lawrence Erlbaum.

Pashakhanlou, A. (2017). Fully integrated content analysis in international relations. *International Relations.* https://doi.org/10.1177/0047117817723060.

Posen, B. R. (1984). The sources of military doctrine. Cornell University press Rynning, Sten 'ISAF and NATO: Campaign innovation and organizational adaptation'. In T. Farrell, F. Osinga, & J. A. Russell (Eds.), *Military adaptation in Afghanistan.* Stanford: Stanford University Press, 2013.

Snyder, J. (1984, Summer). Civil-military relations and the cult of the offensive, 1914 and 1984. *International Security, 9*(1), 108–146.

Tosbotn, R. A. (2016). *NATO and cyber security: Critical junctures as catalyst for change.* Leiden University Repository. https://openaccess.leidenuniv.nl/handle/1887/42987

Van Evera, S. (1984, Summer). The cult of the offensive and the origins of the first world war. *International Security, 9*(1), 58–107.

Vennesson, P., Fabian, B., de Chiara, F., & Schroeder Ursula, C. (2009, July). Is there a European way of war? Role conceptions, organizational frames, and the utility of force. *Armed Forces & Society,35*(4), 628–645.

Wæver, O. (1995). Securitization and Desecuritization. In *On security* (pp. 46–87). Columbia University Press.

Wilson, J. Q. (1989). *Bureaucracy: What government agencies do and why they do it.* New York: Basic Books, University of Michigan.

Chapter 17
The Role and Effectiveness of the G20

Jaroslaw Kantorowicz

> *There is virtually no major aspect of the global economy or*
> *international financial system that will be outside of the groups'*
> *purview.* (G20 2008, p. 28)
> Paul Martin (the first chair of the G20)

17.1 What Is the G20 and How Did It Emerge?[1]

In 2009, in the midst of the global financial crisis, the Group of 20 (hereinafter G20) replaced the G7/G8 as a 'premier forum for international economic cooperation' (G20 2009b, paragraph 19), recognising a crucial role the G20 played in containing the contemporary economic turmoil (Cooper 2010, p. 741). Although the G20 was brought to the spotlight and became a focal actor during the crisis of 2008–2010, its history can be traced back to the late 1990s. A series of financial crises in developing and emerging economies during the late 1990s (such as in Brazil, Russia, and South-East Asia), through their global and cross-border nature, evidenced that the G7/G8 was an obsolete mode of governance unable to effectively respond to global economic challenges (G20 2008, p. 9; Kirton 2000, p. 153). In response, G7 finance ministers and central bank governors proposed broadening the cooperation on crucial economic issues among 'systematically significant economies', realising that dealing with global financial fluctuations requires a more representative forum (Callaghan 2013a, p. 4; G20 2008, p. 8). The inaugural meeting of the new forum was organised in Berlin in 1999, assembling representatives of 20 significant

---

[1] It is acknowledged that parts of this chapter are based on my input to the report 'The European Union's Role in International Economic Fora. Paper 1: The G20' commissioned by the European Parliament. Detailed references to the report are given in the 'Recommended readings' section.

J. Kantorowicz (✉)
Leiden University, Leiden, The Netherlands
e-mail: j.j.kantorowicz@fgga.leidenuniv.nl

© Springer Nature Switzerland AG 2020
M. O. Hosli, J. Selleslaghs (eds.), *The Changing Global Order*, United Nations
University Series on Regionalism 17,
https://doi.org/10.1007/978-3-030-21603-0_17

economies and marking the establishment of what came to be known as the G20. For some political commentators, the launch of the G20 signified a 'tectonic shift' from a system of international co-operation based on supremacy of the most developed countries (G7/G8), to a regime of more inclusive co-operation reflecting the increasing role of emerging economies in the global economic order (G20 2008, p. 9; Beeson and Bell 2009, p. 68).

At the outset, the G20 operated as an informal forum, convening finance ministers and central bank governors from 20 significant industrialised and emerging economies (G20 2008, p. 5). This setup prevailed until 2008 – a year which constituted another turning point in the history of the G20. The Lehman Brothers' bankruptcy and the following near collapse of the global financial system in 2008 put unparalleled pressure on political leaders of advanced economies to take immediate action. It was widely recognised that piecemeal, national policy actions, however innovative and bold, would not be sufficient to stabilise the ensuing financial market meltdown. In reaction, President Barack Obama, following consultations with Nicolas Sarkozy and José Manuel Barosso, called for a special G20 meeting in Washington in November 2008, elevating the G20 to the level of heads of state or government (Kirton 2008) and vesting it with the role of reforming global financial regulation and institutions. This organisational shift significantly changed the role of the finance ministers and central bank governors, who prior to 2008 were the most crucial part of the G20. Since these meetings of state leaders are currently at the apex of the G20 hierarchy, ministers and central bankers meet in order to prepare the ground for the leaders' summits and implement the subsequent negotiated commitments (Henley and Blokker 2013, p. 22).

It is evident from this concise historical overview that the creation and upgrade of the G20 to the leaders' summit was in reaction to severe crisis events. As economic turbulences are currently less pronounced and recovery is underway, the G20 has seemingly evolved from a forum for the abrupt response to economic crises to a forum for international co-operation in multiple policy areas. In other words, the G20 has transformed from a 'crisis committee' to a 'steering committee' (Cooper 2010). This drift has inevitably led to the expansion of the G20's agenda. While initially the G20 mainly concentrated on financial regulation reforms (strengthening supervision of banks, hedge funds, and over-the-counter markets), and balanced economic growth, now it is not uncommon for the G20 to discuss anti-corruption measures, climate change, aid and development, and issues related to transnational terrorism.

Most interest in the G20, both scholarly and popular, revolves around the following questions: 'How and why did the G20 become a leader in global economic governance?' and 'Is the G20 effective?'. Without pretence of being exhaustive, this chapter tackles these questions and gives some possible responses. In what follows, this chapter gives a concise overview of the institutional design of the G20, since both the preference for using the G20 during the global financial crisis and its effectiveness have been largely determined by its institutional structure. In Sect. 17.4 the chapter describes the relationship between the G20 and other international financial institutions (IFIs) and standard setting bodies (SSBs). Without the institutional capacity and resources, the G20 is doomed to cooperate with international bodies, yet this cooperation has mutual gains. Special attention is paid to the close relationship between the G20 and the Financial Stability Board (FSB) – a catalyst of the G20's decisions. Section 17.5 examines in more detail the products (commitments) of the G20, using this lens to assess the effectiveness of the group. In the final section, this chapter provides both a concise summary and several arguments for and against further institutionalisation of the G20.

17.2 G20 Institutional Design: The Power of Informality

As its name suggests, the G20 consists of 20 permanent members, which regularly send representatives to meetings at various diplomatic levels. Formally, the G20 is comprised of the 19 'systematically significant' countries in the world (see Table 17.1), plus the European Union. Since no rules for admitting new members

Table 17.1 Categories of G20 participants

Permanent members	IO's and international bodies	Guest countries
The European Union and 19 member states: – Argentina, Australia, Brazil, Canada, China, France, Germany, India, Indonesia, Italy, Japan, South Korea, Mexico, Russia, Saudi Arabia, South Africa, Turkey, the UK, and the US Note that France, Germany, and Italy are part of the EU, which is also formally a member of the G20.[a]	Consensus has seemingly emerged to invite chairs/directors/presidents of the following organisations: Financial Stability Board (FSB), International Labour Organisation (ILO), International Monetary Fund (IMF), Organisation for Economic Co-operation and Development (OECD), United Nations (UN), World Bank (WB), World Health Organisation (WHO; starting from the German presidency in 2017), and World Trade Organisation (WTO).	The practice has emerged of issuing standing invitations to Spain (referred to as a 'permanent invitee'), two African countries chairing the African Union and New Partnership for Africa's Development, chairs of Association of Southeast Asian Nations (ASEAN), and the Global Governance Group (G3). On top of that, the country holding the presidency issues two additional invitations on an ad hoc basis (usually important countries from the region where the G20 Summits are organised).

Source: Amtenbrink et al. (2015, p. 17)

[a]The fact that EU has its own representation, which is separate from the representation of four EU member states (EU-4: France, Germany, Italy, the UK), may be somewhat confusing. Nonetheless, EU law gives some rough guidance regarding the EU and EU-4 involvement at the G20. To what extent EU-4 can act independently depends on whether topics discussed fall within the scope of exclusive or shared competences. If topics discussed at the G20 meetings concern exclusive EU external competences the EU member states can't take individual positions. In case of shared competences unilateral actions of EU-4 may be pre-empted if the competence has already been exercised by the EU. In areas where the EU-4 retained competences the member states are in principle prevented from taking positions that compromise EU objectives. For a more comprehensive discussion on the EU participation in the G20, see Amtenbrink et al. (2015, pp. 38–51). The EU and its external relations are discussed more in depth in Chap. 9 of this book.

have been set, membership in the G20 seems to be fixed at 20 (Jokela 2011, p. 8). In practice, however, membership and participation in the G20 meetings is much more complex.

To soften the exclusive membership rule, the G20 has established an informal practice of inviting designated international organisations (IOs) and guest countries to participate in meetings as so-called outreach participants (Amtenbrink et al. 2015, p. 8). Invites to outreach participants are issued by the acting presidency, after consultation with and approval from all G20 permanent members (Jin-seo 2010). Overall, as Table 17.1 suggests, there are three types of participants at the G20 meetings. One should note therefore that those actors participating in the G20 goes far beyond 20, and is in effect closer to 32–33 'members'. Nonetheless, final decision-making seems to be an exclusive right of the 20 permanent members, with the remaining participants having merely a consultative role. For some, the status of outreach participant reflects 'the practice of granting 'observer status' to non-members in international organisations' (Henley and Blokker 2013, p. 15).

An important discussion touching upon membership concerns the G20's legitimacy. For some, the fact that the G20 formally includes only 20 permanent members (10% of the total number of countries) and lacks formal criteria for membership causes it to have 'representational illegitimacy' (Vestergaard 2011, p. 26; Wouters and Geraets 2012, p. 6). This argument is particularly valid if one realises that the G20 addresses global issues which concern and target a wide array of actors beyond its immediate membership, thus making the G20 irreducible to its individual members (Viola 2015, p. 94). Another problem concerns the definition of the 'systematically significant' economies. The most straightforward way of capturing economic significance is through the volume of the gross domestic product (GDP). From Table A1 in the appendix, it can be seen that three countries – the Netherlands, Spain, and Switzerland – could have a strong case to be included as a part of the G20 based on their aggregate GDP. One should note, however, that Spain received the status of a permanent invitee and the Netherlands is indirectly represented by the EU. Thus, Switzerland emerges as the only 'systematically significant' economy left out of the G20 table. There is an apparent trade-off between offering membership to only economically powerful countries and having a continentally balanced representation at the G20.

For some other commentators and researchers, the G20, by representing a heavy economic weight, provides for 'input legitimacy' (Vestergaard and Wade 2012, p. 260). The permanent members of the G20 alone represent roughly 2/3 of the world's population, approx. 90% of global GDP, roughly 80% of global trade and 84% of all fossil fuel emission (Van Ham 2012, p. 1). The weight of the G20 countries is particularly visible in financial markets. In 2012, the G20 members 'accounted for 90% of the world banking system, 81% of global market capitalisation, and 94% of global bond markets', thus roughly 90% of global finance (Noelle 2015, p. 5).

The discussion of legitimacy is further fuelled by the informality of the institutional arrangement of the G20. It is of note that the G20 is not an international organisation *per se,* as it does not fulfil the definitive criteria set by the International

Law Association (see International Law Association 2004, p. 4). The G20 is an informal forum of states and non-state actors (EU) with neither legal basis (legal personality), nor a permanent secretariat (Nasra and Debaere 2016, p. 213). The G20's decisions are not binding as it relies on soft governance mechanisms, such as peer pressure and 'naming and shaming', to enforce agreements. Given this informal setting, some experts define the G20 as a *de facto* international forum with a special agenda of discussion (Giovannini et al. 2012, p. 17). Others describe the G20 as a 'club' or a 'network' (Wouters and Ramopoulos 2012, p. 14) due to the fact that the G20 is not governed, nor constrained, by a charter, nor does it apply fixed membership criteria or decision-making procedures.[2] One must further stress that the objectives of the G20 are not specified in a single authoritative document, resulting in its rather fluid working agenda (Angeloni and Pisani-Ferry 2012, p. 13; Callaghan 2013b, p. 3).

The informal setting and open-ended operational procedures of the G20 have been and still are widely challenged by scholars, non-governmental organisations, and the broader public (Åslund 2009; Der Spiegel 2010; Vestergaard 2011; Vestergaard and Wade 2012). One point of criticism is that in the absence of official rules and procedures, it is very difficult for non-member states to influence the G20 agenda (Viola 2015, p. 104).

Informality, however, has its advantage, as it enables reaching consensus on global economic issues 'quickly, flexibly, and effectively' (Cameron 2011, p. 14). As argued by Viola (2015), this institutional informality may result in more policy experimentation and entrepreneurship at the G20 as compared to more formal organisations, such as the IMF and WB. Furthermore, as expressed in the Cannes Summit Declaration (G20 2011a, paragraph 90), this 'power of informality' has been welcomed by G20 leaders. In that same Declaration the heads of state subsequently underscored that the G20 is 'a Leader-led and informal group and it should remain so' (paragraph 91), thereby implicitly rejecting the plan to impose any institutional straightjacket on the G20 (Wouters and Ramopoulos 2012, p. 23).

Although a set of stringent rules does not exist, the G20 has worked out a certain practice of governance, which is followed for the most part in non-crisis circumstances. After Canada's presidency in the G20 from 1999–2001, it was decided that the G20's chair/presidency would rotate annually in a pre-defined sequence among the permanent members (G20 2008, p. 22). The annual rotation determined that each year a country from a different country grouping (see Table 17.2) would be responsible for hosting the G20 summit and the majority of other accompanying meetings. Based on this practice, in the period from 2001–2006, the presidency was consecutively held by Canada (group 1) in 2001, India (group 2) in 2002, Mexico (group 3) in 2003, Germany (group 4) in 2004, China (group five) in 2005, and Australia (again group 1) in 2006 (Amtenbrink et al. 2015, p. 19). Some deviations to this orderly practice were observed at the height of the global financial crisis, when the US organised summits in Washington in 2008 and in Pittsburgh in 2009.

---

[2] The G20 policy manual, an internal document establishing a set of procedural rules (G20 2008, p. 23), is unfortunately not publicly available.

Table 17.2 G20 country grouping

Group 1	Group 2	Group 3	Group 4	Group 5
Australia	India	Argentina	France	China
Canada	Russia	Brazil	Germany	Indonesia
Saudi Arabia	South Africa	Mexico	Italy	Japan
U.S.	Turkey		UK	South Korea

Source: G20 (2008, p. 130)
Note: The EU is the only permanent member of the G20 which is excluded from the presidency rotation

Table 17.3 Organisation of the agenda-setting process

Finance track	Sherpas' track
Framework for strong, sustainable, and balanced growth	Employment
International financial architecture reform	Energy
Financial regulation	Development
Financing for long-term investment/international tax items	Trade
	Anticorruption

Source: Çanacki (2013) and G20 (2015c)

Moreover, due to pressing circumstances, summits were convened twice in both 2009 and 2010 (London and Pittsburgh in 2009, and Toronto and Seoul in 2010).

A country holding the G20 chair sets up a provisional secretariat or steering committee, which coordinates the G20's operations and arranges the majority of its meetings (Çanacki 2013; Wouters and Geraets 2012, p. 10; Amtenbrink et al. 2015, p. 19). The acting chair is a part of a 'revolving three-member management group of past, present, and future chairs', the so called Troika, which is supposed to 'ensure continuity in the G20's work and management across years' (Wouters and Geraets 2012, p. 10). Crucially, a chairing country assumes a leading role in the agenda-setting process. Given that the G20 agenda is dominated by pre-determined issues related to macroeconomic conditions, international financial institutions, regulations, and supervision, a chairing country can shape roughly 30% of the agenda (Se-jeong 2010).

The agenda-setting process and deliberations are organised within two so-called tracks, referred to as the Finance and Sherpas' tracks. The latter, which gathers leaders' personal representatives, is devoted to discussing broad issues, which fall beyond international finance and economic growth (see Table 17.3). Within the Finance Track, after an initial meeting of the deputies, finance ministers, and representatives for the central banks, the agenda is further discussed and shaped during the meetings of finance ministers and central bank governors (hereinafter ministerials) under the leadership of the acting chair. Ministerials are vital inasmuch as they formulate the agenda for the leaders' summits and are tasked with guaranteeing the implementation of agreements reached in prior summits. As of 2008, when the G20 was upgraded to heads-of-state level, a convention was developed whereby ministerials are subordinated to the leaders' summits. The Sherpas' Track, in turn, consists of several meetings organised throughout the year, where non-financial issues, such as employment, energy, and climate change, for instance, are discussed. Yet the Sherpas' responsibilities go beyond these meetings, as they are 'tasked by their leaders to negotiate the summits documents on their [leaders'] behalf' (G20 2015a), resulting in Sherpas being involved in the testing of ideas for reforms and in forging agreement at the highest political level. Remarkably, no official documents are released after the Sherpas' meeting, in contrast to the ministerials, after which communiqués or other types of documents are issued (Amtenbrink et al. 2015, p. 21).

Summits, ministerials, and Sherpas' meetings are the primary, but not the only, venues organised within the G20. A new phenomenon at the G20 is the launch of so-called sectoral ministerial meetings. Examples of such meetings are the G20 Meetings of Labour and Employment Ministers, Meetings of G20 Trade Ministers, G20 Meetings of Agriculture Ministers, and the informal G20 Meetings of Foreign Ministers (Amtenbrink et al. 2015, p. 21). Detailed information on participants in these kinds of meetings is nonetheless rather scarce. According to Wouters and Geraets (2012, p. 8), this 'broadening of the agenda [and] proliferation of sectoral ministerial meetings increases the degree of actor informality within the G20 setting'.

Moreover, both the Finance and Sherpas tracks are supported by a multitude of working groups and task forces providing assistance, technical analysis, and recommendations for the ministerials and the Sherpas's meetings (G20 2015b). These working groups and task forces are held on specific thematic issues and are comprised of officials nominated by their respective governments, accompanied by delegates from the guest countries, IOs, and engagement groups (Amtenbrink et al. 2015, p. 21). These additional meetings are usually co-chaired by representatives from one advanced and one emerging country of the G20 (G20 2015b).

Overall, the annual G20 program consists of a series of meetings, such as working group/task forces, ministerials, and sectoral ministerial meetings, which culminate and work toward the leaders' summit at the end of each year. Consequently, one could think of the G20 as a linear process of forging the agenda for the leaders' meeting, in which the main commitments along with action plans and other strategic documents are agreed upon and published via communiqués or declarations.

17.3   G20 as an Orchestrator

Without capacity and resources of its own, the G20 uses a wide range of international bodies to extend its own reach as a key player in global economic governance. It must rely on other bodies for technical expertise, coordination, and implementation of reforms on the ground. Eccleston et al. (2015, p. 301) postulates that the G20 engages in what is described as 'network relationships' with a wide array of international institutions, such as IFIs and SSB.[3] There is no legal mechanism of delega-

---

[3] The SSBs are independent regulatory and supervisory authorities. Their goal is to define good practices and guidelines which companies and supervisors operating in financial industry should follow.

tion which obliges independent international bodies to cooperate with the G20. They do so voluntarily, as they realise that cooperating with the G20 may provide an opportunity to augment their own global position and, hence, increase their influence. The G20 via its powerful and encompassing membership may provide the highest political endorsement to rules set by international bodies, thereby strengthening them in fulfilling their own mandate. This was the case, for instance, with the OECD tax transparency agenda, whereby the G20 endorsement of these rules increased their global impact (Eccleston et al. 2015, pp. 306–311). Moreover, the G20 has been instrumental toward building a consensus for the IMF quota reform, which led to an increase in the IMF's financial strength. Through this, the G20 contributed to reinforcing the credibility and legitimacy of the IMF, which was somewhat impaired after a series of unsuccessful reforms in late 1990s. Overall, cooperation between the G20 and international bodies results in mutual gains. The G20 generates political endorsement for the activities of international bodies. In return, these institutions provide their know-how, as well as implement and oversee G20 commitments, without which the G20 would be nothing but a 'toothless talking shop' (Vestergaard 2011, p. 29).

Viola (2015) describes the G20 as an orchestrator able to enlist and coordinate its work through intermediaries, such as IFIs, SSBs, and private industry regulators. Orchestration as a mode of governance is characterised by indirect and soft governance instruments, and is triggered when command-and-control devices to exert power and coercive mechanisms of enforcement are missing (Viola 2015, p. 90). As depicted in Fig. 17.1, G20 governance can be illustrated through the so-called orchestrator-intermediary-target model. Intermediaries provide that which the G20 lacks, i.e. necessary regulatory capacity to carry out the governance agenda targeted at states and financial market actors. Overall, this practice, developed within the G20 process and referred to as 'tasking', is structured so that the G20 assigns tasks to the IFIs, SSBs, and private industry regulators related to specific issues, and requires them to report back in the forthcoming G20 meeting.

Governance through orchestration, as opposed to hierarchy or delegation, for instance, has several additional advantages (Viola 2015). It allows member states to preserve control over regulations without having to create a supranational institution to impose sovereignty and control costs, stemming from principle-agent relations. Moreover, a non-binding character and soft governance style is most suitable

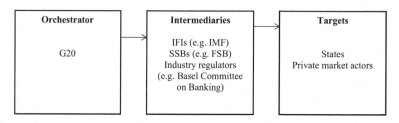

Fig. 17.1 Orchestrator-intermediary-target (O-I-T) model. (Source: Viola 2015, p. 97)

in situations where preferences for regulations are quite heterogeneous among participants. This seems to be the case with G20 members, which are very diverse economically, institutionally, and culturally, and hence have divergent interests regarding the details of reforms.

Some further describe the G20's governance as a triangular system where the G20, located at the apex, is supported by two notable intermediaries, the FSB and the IMF (Angeloni and Pisani-Ferry 2012, p. 15; Van Ham 2012, p. 5). Others, mainly in reference to the 'Finance Track', highlight the prominent role of the FSB, which functions as an 'agent' of the G20, translating commitments agreed upon in the summits into tangible actions. Nolle (2015, pp. 9–13) further implies that there is an understanding within G20 governance that international bodies, including the IMF, defer and report to the FSB on selected issues, making it along with the G20 'the biggest player in fixing the global financial system'.

The FSB is the key player in pushing forward the G20 agenda, and its role expands in parallel with the role played by the G20. The FSB's predecessor, the Financial Stability Forum (FSF), was established in 1999 to promote global financial stability and serve as technical support to the G20, although its membership was limited to the finance ministers and central bankers from the G7. A weak institutional structure, vague mandate, inability to encourage compliance, and a small staff made the FSF rather passive in achieving its main objectives (Viola 2015, p. 109). At the London Summit in 2009, when crisis was unfolding and leaders were pressured to respond rapidly, they decided to strengthen the mandate of the FSF and convert it into the FSB (G20 2009a, paragraph 15). For some, the creation and reinforcement of the FSB were the key institutional innovations of the G20 in the aftermath of the financial crisis.

Under the current institutional setup, the FSB's role is to coordinate the work of the multitude of IFIs and SSBs toward effective financial reforms, facilitate the exchange of information, identify gaps in financial regulations, and monitor compliance with reforms by national governments and regulators (for a full list of the FSB objectives see Article 2 of the FSB Charter). The FSB's membership is broader than that of the FSF. Apart from finance ministers and central bankers from 20 members of the G20, the FSB also hosts representatives from Hong Kong, the Netherlands, Singapore, Spain, and Switzerland, which all are large players in the global financial system. The FSB's membership further extends to the major IFIs, such as the IMF and the WB, and the SSBs, such as the Basal Committee on Banking Supervision (BCBS), the International Organisation of Securities Commissions (IOSCO), and the International Association of Insurance Supervisors (IAIS).

At the 2011 Cannes summit, the G20 further strengthened the FSB's resources and institutional capacity, institutionalising it as a permanent and legal organisation (G20 2011b, paragraph 16). Although the FSB has twice as many employees as the FSF, some argue that the staff of around 24 full-time employees could be further expanded (Lyngen and Simmons 2013, p. v). It needs to be stressed that the FSB is not legally subordinate to the G20 as its agent, yet it fulfils the G20's requests and regularly submits reports before the G20 meetings. Some of the main achievements of the FSB in recent years have been to develop (at the request of the G20) policy tools to address global systematically important financial institutions (G-SIFI) or set principles for sound compensation practices and credit rating agencies.

For some, the institutional overhaul and strengthening of the FSB signifies a paradigm shift from financial rulemaking in a rather decentralised, technocratic, and independent fashion, to coordinating and, to some extent, politicising the financial reform agenda (Gradinis 2013). One should note that the Plenary Committee, the FSB's key decision-making authority, is comprised of political appointees, such as finance and treasury ministers. According to Gradinis (2013, p. 166), 18 out of 70 members of the FSB are politicians, leading to direct interaction between elected politicians and independent regulators in the sphere of financial regulation. Arguably, these political appointees are the most crucial members of the FSB, as the remaining participants (the central bankers and national regulators) regularly meet in other fora, which are purely technocratic and in which political participation is excluded, such as, for instance, the BCBS or IOSCO. Thus, that which distinguishes the FSB from other SSBs is precisely the presence of the politicians. As argued by Gradinis (2013), this is the first time that political appointees, via the FSB, are able to directly drive the global financial regulation reform agenda.

According to Lyngen and Simmons (2013, p. iii), 'by forming the FSB, the G20 deepened connections between the technocratic world of international financial regulators such as the BCBS and the political world of the finance ministers of countries that are members of the G20'. As a result, politicians are now effectively responsible for most decisions affecting the functioning of the most important financial institutions, and are in the position to better control the SSBs. It remains to be seen whether this model of governance is effective and to what extent time inconsistency problems and public choice motives can be contained.[4]

17.4   The G20'S Products and Effectiveness

How are decisions and agreements reached by the G20, and what do they consist of? In principle, decisions are reached by consensus (mutual agreement), whereby all G20 countries are equal in formulating the veto (G20 2011b, paragraph 31; Debaere and Orbie 2013, p. 318; Bertoldi et al. 2013, p. 7). Formal voting does not take place, however, and the whole process relies on deliberations aimed at preference aggregation.

---

[4] As indicated by Lyngen and Simmons (2013), the FSB seems to be driven by politics, and consequently it may take on many somewhat unrelated regulatory projects. Given its limited staff, the FSB is arguably overcommitting. One should further note that similar to the G20, the FSB has rather limited enforcement capability. It relies on soft governance methods, such as peer review process and 'naming and shaming'. Some criticism can be also raised regarding the fact that the FSB pays no attention to problems faced by emerging or developing markets.

The core documents negotiated and ultimately formed during the G20 leaders' summits are leaders' communiqués. They are developed gradually throughout the year during ministerial and Sherpas' meetings. In the end, the leaders' summit frequently serves only to assign to them political weight. Nonetheless, the most contentious issues, on which agreement can't be reached, are left for the leaders to resolve (Callaghan 2013a, p. 6). When there is a disagreement regarding the formulation of the commitments, common practice is to use wording from the previous communiqué (Callaghan 2013a, p. 6).

Communiqués comprise a set of commitments, which are negotiated and agreed upon in secrecy. Commitments can be of various nature and accuracy and may prescribe different time horizons for compliance. Commitments may concern, for instance, establishing policies and rules, reaching targets, following action plans and principles, and endorsing initiatives by other IOs.

The G20 Research Group at the University of Toronto has been aggregating and classifying all G20 commitments publicised in the leaders' communiqués since 2008. In the period of 2008–2015, the G20 'produced' around 1.6 thousand commitments, although many of these were duplicates. For instance, each year G20 members commit to abstaining from enacting protectionist trade measures.[5] Nevertheless, tracing the evolution of the number of commitments should give a good indication whether the G20 agenda is expansionist. As illustrated in Fig. 17.2, although a tendency has been for the number of communiqués to expand, the recent

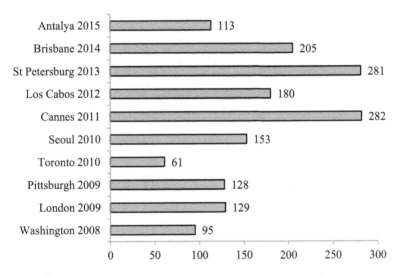

Fig. 17.2 Number of commitments per summit. (Source: Own figure based on data provided by the G20 Research Group)

---

[5] In March 2017, for the first time since 2008 the commitment to free trade principle in the G20 ministerial communiqué has been omitted. This might be a warning sign of a new wave of protectionist measures (Urban 2017).

Fig. 17.3 Commitments aggregated by policy areas issued in the period 2008–2015. (Source: Own figure based on data provided by the G20 Research Group)

summit in Antalya generated only slightly more than 100 commitments, which is comparable to the number of commitments issued in the period 2008–2010. The most abundant were communiqués issued after the summits in Saint Petersburg and Cannes, nearing 300 commitments. Roughly six times fewer commitments were found in the communiqués issued after the Toronto summit.

The commitments are concerned with various issues ranging from macroeconomic policy and financial matters to crime, corruption and transnational terrorism. By and large, the largest amount of commitments falls under the category of 'macroeconomic policy' (23%). The second most prevalent category has been 'financial regulation' (16%), and the third has been 'development' (11%). Others which are still moderately popular are commitments related to reforms of 'international financial institutions' (7%), 'trade' (7%), 'energy' (6%) and 'employment and labour' (6%). For shares of commitments in other policy areas, see Fig. 17.3. Over the last years, a departure has been observed from commitments concerning 'financial regulations' and reforms of 'international financial institutions', to a more diversified set of commitments with 'development' emerging as a dominant category (see Table A2 in the appendix). This trend is underscored if one compares the frequency of words used in the communiqué after the Washington summit in 2008 with those used in the communiqué issued after the Hangzhou summit in 2016 (see Fig. 17.4). Whereas the former is dominated by words such as 'financial', 'international', and 'regulators', the latter is full of words such as 'growth', 'development', and 'support'.

This seems to be a natural shift given that the G20 was first and foremost called upon to contain the global financial crisis and redesign the global financial architecture in the years 2008–2010, and hence its efforts were predominantly focused on regula-

Fig. 17.4 Word clouds of the communiqués issued after the 2008 Washington (left) and the 2016 Hangzhou (right) Summits. Note: Word clouds were generated after removing all punctuation and stopwords (such as, for instance, 'a', 'the', 'and') from communiqués, and performing stemming to ensure that different forms of the word are converted to the same stem

tions concerning financial market and institutions. Contemporarily, as the economic situation stabilises and financial markets reforms are completed or in the implementation phase, there is more scope for diversification and expansion of the agenda. The risk of this expansion is that the G20 may lose focus and undermine its ability to coordinate and sustain regulatory efforts in any one area (Viola 2015, p. 113).

The number of commitments and their heterogeneity by no means allows one to gauge the effectiveness of the G20. As counterfactual analysis is not feasible (what the outcome would have been in the absence of the G20) and clear objectives with respect to which the effectiveness of the G20 could be examined are missing, the 'second-best' means of measuring the G20's effectiveness is via compliance with the G20's own commitments.

The G20 Research Group checked for compliance with 164 high priority commitments issued in the period of 2008–2015. These commitments cover all key policy areas, such as macroeconomic policy, financial reform, development issues, IFIs, trade, etc. The following coding scheme for compliance was conceptualised was each priority commitment: 1 captures full or nearly full compliance with a commitment; 0 means inability to commit or a work in progress; lastly −1 signifies complete or nearly complete failure to implement a commitment (Kirton et al. 2014, p. 17). This system of coding enables us to construct compliance scores, detailing average compliance for all selected commitments, for every single G20 member state, summit, and policy area. Theoretically, the score varies between 1, meaning full compliance with all priority commitments, to −1, indicating complete incompliance with all priority commitments. A positive score signifies that, on average, there is some compliance with commitments, while a negative score indicates that non-compliance prevails (Angeloni and Pisani-Ferry 2012, p. 26). A higher compliance score signifies greater effectiveness of the G20.

Table 17.4 summarises the compliance scores distributed by summits for the entire G20 as well as for country groupings, such as the G20 advanced and emerging economies, G7, EU-4 (France, Germany, Italy, and the UK), EU-3 (excluding the UK), and the EU itself. The average compliance score for the entire G20 in the period 2008–2015 amounts to roughly 0.45, which means that the G20 complied with roughly half of all commitments, indicating moderate overall effectiveness of the G20 in fulfilling its commitments.

As shown in Table 17.4, there is a clear variation in the compliance scores, and thus effectiveness, between the summits. The greatest scores are recorded for the Washington (one should note, however, low number of priority commitments from this summit), Cannes, Los Cabos, and Antalya Summits, while the lowest scores are found in the case of the London, Pittsburgh, and Toronto Summits. This analysis slightly contradicts the common perception concerning the summits' outcomes. For example, the G20 Summit in London in 2009 was proclaimed to be a great success (Jokela 2011, p. 6), contrary to the abovementioned results. Why would we observe such as huge misalignment between the general perception and actual outcomes? The commitments of that particular Summit may have been very crucial but at the same time overly ambitious, and their execution turned out to be difficult in practice. Although there are no clear trends over time, it appears that in the years 2009–2010 compliance was somewhat weaker than in the period that followed.

One should further note that there is a clear difference in efficacy between the advanced and emerging economies of the G20, with advanced economies regularly outperforming emerging countries. The largest disparity in compliance was observed after the summit in London, and the smallest after the Antalya summit. A positive tendency is therefore observed of narrowing the gap in compliance between advanced

Table 17.4 Compliance with main G20 commitments by summits

	N = 164	G20	G7	G20 Advanced	G20 Emerging	EU-4	EU-3	EU	St. dev.
Washington 2008	4	0.67	0.88	0.88	0.43	1.00	1.00	1.00	0.49
London 2009	6	0.23	0.50	0.51	−0.04	0.65	0.53	0.60	0.45
Pittsburgh 2009	15	0.24	0.42	0.43	0.00	0.47	0.46	0.38	0.47
Toronto 2010	14	0.28	0.55	0.55	0.04	0.62	0.56	0.57	0.35
Seoul 2010	37	0.50	0.62	0.65	0.34	0.71	0.69	0.82	0.25
Cannes 2011	17	0.54	0.66	0.66	0.42	0.74	0.69	0.85	0.24
Los Cabos 2012	18	0.57	0.61	0.65	0.49	0.56	0.48	0.75	0.20
St.Petersburg 2013	19	0.44	0.55	0.56	0.31	0.66	0.63	0.63	0.22
Brisbane 2014	17	0.42	0.56	0.56	0.25	0.55	0.48	0.75	0.33
Antalya 2015	17	0.55	0.64	0.64	0.46	0.71	0.71	0.81	0.17
Arithmetic avg.		0.44	0.60	0.61	0.27	0.67	0.62	0.72	0.24
Weighted avg.		0.45	0.59	0.60	0.30	0.65	0.61	0.72	0.22

Source: Own calculations based on data provided by the G20 Research Group
Note: Negative scores indicate that non-compliance with commitments dominates. Weights used for calculating weighted average were given by shares of priority commitments per summit

and emerging economies. The members of the EU, on average, perform better than the G20 advanced economies as a whole. Yet somewhat lower scores for the EU-3 make it evident that exceptionally high compliance was observed for the UK. The highest standard deviation, which captures the variation in compliance scores between the members of the G20, is observed in the case of the first three summits (Washington, London, and Pittsburgh). This suggests that during the global financial crisis compliance with commitments was largely unbalanced or incoherent among G20 countries. Since the global financial crisis of 2008 erupted in the advanced economies and it was their financial systems which were in need of reform, emerging economies felt less ownership over these reforms, resulting in lower compliance.

Compliance scores, and therefore effectiveness, by policy areas are demonstrated in Table 17.5. Without taking into consideration the category 'others', the highest compliance scores are found for 'labour and employment' and 'macroeconomic policy'. For these categories, more than half of priority commitments are complied with. High compliance scores are also observed in the cases of 'financial regulations' and 'food and agriculture' categories. The lowest scores, in turn, are observed for commitments related to 'corruption', 'trade', and 'climate change'. The G20 advanced economies are the most effective (compliant) in areas such as 'labour and employment', 'financial regulation', and 'macroeconomic policy', and the least effective in the areas of 'energy' and 'corruption'. The G20 emerging economies are effective (compliant) in 'labour and employment', 'macroeconomic policy', and 'food and agriculture' policy areas, while rather ineffective in the areas of 'trade' and 'climate change'. Thus, financial regulation reforms, for which the G20 was initially employed, have emerged as a domain of advanced economies. This is in line with the fact that global financial reforms were largely driven by EU member states, the European Commission, and the US, and hence the regulations were set in accordance with their own preferences (Kern 2011, p. 6). This undoubtedly distanced the G20 emerging economies from these reforms and led to less systematic compliance in this area.

One should further note that by enlisting various international bodies with universal membership, the G20 affects states beyond its own membership (Viola 2015).

Table 17.5 Compliance with main G20 commitments by policy area

	G20	G20 Advanced	G20 Emerging	N = 164
Macroeconomic policy	0.56	0.67	0.47	23
Financial regulations	0.49	0.73	0.30	18
Trade	0.23	0.57	−0.05	11
Development	0.35	0.59	0.16	45
Climate change	0.25	0.50	0.04	11
Energy	0.41	0.46	0.37	15
Corruption	0.13	0.13	0.13	5
Food and agriculture	0.49	0.58	0.42	5
Labour & Employment	0.73	0.84	0.63	10
Others	0.56	0.65	0.49	21

Source: Own calculations based on data provided by the G20 Research Group

Since the assessment exclusively considered G20 members' compliance with priority commitments, the approach taken here has been rather conservative as these 'spillover' or 'network' effects were not taken into account. Overall, based on this exercise, the G20 seems to have a fairly good record of compliance and delivery of outcomes. For some, this signifies output (result) legitimacy of the G20, covering up a possible lack of input (process) legitimacy.

It should also be stressed that these results are rather tentative. This analysis could be extended to include compliance with all commitments and not only the key ones selected by the G20 Research Group. It also remains to be verified how the G20 performs in the longer term. Some critiques point out that the G20 is only effective under crisis conditions, when a special political will exists and encourages them to pursue bold reforms. This political will may vanish in calm times when 'politics as normal' prevails (Angeloni and Pisani-Ferry 2012, p. 41). The global financial crisis did much to boost consensus building among the G20 members and international bodies; the question remains whether this impetus will last as the crisis recedes.

17.5 Concluding Remarks

This chapter was written with the purpose of providing answers to two questions: 'Why did the G20 become a leader in global economic governance?' and 'Is the G20 effective?' In what follows, this section will try to give a concise response to these questions, and touch upon some further issues regarding G20 institutionalisation.

As mentioned previously, the G20 is a collective body that comprises 20 'systematically important' economies, which together represent approx. 2/3 of the world's population, roughly 90% of global GDP and some 80% of global trade. Thus, the G20 has remarkably more 'input' legitimacy as compared to the G7/G8, for instance. Moreover, the fact that the G20 comprises countries with various economic and institutional backgrounds arguably leads it to have a more balanced decision-making process. Owing to this process, more countries may feel 'ownership' over the decisions made at the G20.

Besides the large economic weight of the G20, one should also stress its heavy political load, which is absent in cases of decisions made by international bodies, such as the IMF or WB, not to mention the SSBs. The decisions and commitments made by the G20 are unanimously backed by the leaders of executives or heads of states. This is crucial in that the leaders' support may facilitate the transposition and execution of commitments within the national legal frameworks of G20 economies.

What is arguably very important and what further makes the G20 a very attractive forum is its institutional informality and soft governance. The informal setting of the G20 enables consensus building on global issues 'quickly, flexibly, and effectively' (Cameron 2011, p. 14). The absence of a binding character of decisions seems to be suitable for those G20 members who need to reach decisions quickly despite diverse preferences and heterogeneous interests. Secret deliberation and unscripted discussions at the G20 furthermore allow for avoiding intransigent bargaining and reaching agreements rapidly (Viola 2015, p. 104). Overall, these features combined with a moderately positive record of G20 effectiveness, measured via compliance of G20 members with their commitments, demonstrate that the G20 is a useful platform for global cooperation. Nonetheless, one should be able to perceive negative aspects of the current institutional setting with an outlook on future reforms.

The limited and exclusive membership of the G20 means that around 170 countries of the world have no (direct) say in the negotiation processes at the G20 level. Yet, it is important to note that these 170 countries are likely to be targets of G20 governance without having any stake in it. For that reason, some academic and public commentators define this exclusion as 'input' illegitimacy of the G20 (Vestergaard 2011, p. 26), or 'elite multilateralism' (Richard Haass quoted by Moret 2016, p. 2). One should likewise be aware of the overrepresentation of some regions in the G20 (such as the EU) and the underrepresentation of others (in particular Africa). This regional bias may result in a situation where countries from underrepresented regions do not feel 'ownership' over the commitments made, and are left with the perception that commitments were imposed on them (Amtenbrink et al. 2015, p. 67). Logically, this may have some adverse implications for fulfillment of commitments by underrepresented regions. Given the fact that the G20 emerging economies record weaker compliance with G20 commitments, the above hypothesis regarding underrepresentation seems to be tentatively confirmed.

Furthermore, the much applauded 'power of informality' of the G20 may have some adverse effects. For instance, due to the prevailing informality, deliberations and their outcomes are generally non-transparent (negotiation behind closed doors and poor availability of documents), and formalized enforcement mechanisms do not exist (for more information on mechanisms of enforcement in the international law context see Chap. 18). As official sanctions for non-compliance are entirely missing, enforcement mechanisms rely upon peer pressure and 'naming and shaming' methods. However, these kinds of enforcement mechanisms arguably are of limited usefulness in an international context (Amtenbrink et al. 2015, p. 68).

By combining states with various economic backgrounds and institutional settings, the G20 risks negotiation deadlocks or agreements over very broad and largely meaningless commitments (see, for example, Angeloni and Pisani-Ferry (2012, pp. 14–15, 20), for a contentious discussion on global imbalances). The heterogeneity of countries can have further implications on the expansion of the G20 agenda. Prima facie, a broader agenda could be assessed as an advantage, as it allows the G20 to affect global policies in an increasing number of areas. However, the expansion of agenda and its large fluctuation can also be perceived negatively as it might mean the absence of clear-cut focus or specialisation, as well as the risk of impeding the G20 decision-making process (Amtenbrink et al. 2015, p. 67).

What could be done to remedy some of these problems related to the functioning of the G20? Some argue that the G20 could consider pursuing reforms aimed at its own institutionalisation, reducing the level of informality. Arguably, a higher degree of institutionalisation could improve the effectiveness and legitimacy of the G20. For instance, the establishment of a permanent secretariat would improve 'institutional memory', and the formalisation of G20 objectives and decision-making procedures would make the operations of the G20 much more transparent. The G20 could also examine the possibility of reforming its static membership system, so that membership could be opened up for other countries. To this end, the G20 would need to design clear admission criteria. Binding and unambiguous rules of the game would arguably lead to a situation where more countries and citizens at large accept the G20 leadership at the international level and are willing to comply with the G20 commitments. Of course, one must realise that, at least from a theoretical point of view, there is a clear trade-off between legitimisation via institutionalisation and overall effectiveness, as institutionalisation will most likely impair the quick and flexible process of consensus building.

However, the lack of institutionalisation and formalisation of membership criteria might have negative long-term effects for the G20, and global governance more broadly conceived. Growing frustration of countries which are affected by the G20 but remain outside this exclusive club may lead to the emergence of competitive fora for global economic cooperation. Without a doubt, this situation would undermine the role of the G20 as a key player in global economic governance.

Appendix

Table A1   Top 20 economies in terms of GDP (current prices, expressed in billions of US dollars) in 1999 (G20 establishment), 2008 (G20 upgrade), 2016 (current data)

	Ranking 1999	US Dollars Billion	Ranking 2008	US Dollars Billion	Ranking 2016	US Dollars Billion
1	US	9660.6	US	14,718.6	US	18,697.9
2	Japan	4417.0	Japan	4849.2	China	12,254.0
3	Germany	2202.8	China	4558.9	Japan	4170.6
4	UK	1558.4	Germany	3770.2	Germany	3472.5
5	France	1502.2	France	2937.3	UK	3054.8
6	Italy	1250.7	UK	2785.9	France	2488.4
7	China	1089.5	Italy	2403.2	India	2384.7
8	Canada	674.2	Brazil	1694.6	Italy	1867.6
9	**Spain**	634.4	Russia	1660.9	Brazil	1672.9
10	Brazil	602.0	**Spain**	1642.7	Canada	1592.4
11	Mexico	579.5	Canada	1542.6	Korea	1450.1
12	Korea	485.3	India	1224.1	**Spain**	1265.1
13	India	466.9	Mexico	1101.3	Australia	1253.0
14	**Netherlands**	442.6	Australia	1036.2	Mexico	1187.1
15	Australia	411.1	Korea	1002.2	Russia	1178.9
16	Argentina	339.8	**Netherlands**	940.7	Indonesia	875.8
17	**Taiwan**	304.2	Turkey	730.6	**Netherlands**	782.9
18	**Switzerland**	289.5	Indonesia	558.6	Turkey	721.2
19	**Sweden**	270.7	**Switzerland**	552.4	**Switzerland**	687.6
20	**Iran**	270.6	**Poland**	530.0	Saudi Arabia	643.2

Note: Bold figures refer to the G20 non-member states
Sources: own table based on the World Economic Outlook Database (IMF), retrieved in March 2016

Table A2 Commitments distributed by various policy areas and summits

	Washington 2008 (%)	London 2009 (%)	Pittsburgh 2009 (%)	Toronto 2010 (%)	Seoul 2010 (%)	Cannes 2011 (%)	Los Cabos 2012 (%)	St Petersburg 2013 (%)	Brisbane 2014 (%)	Antalya 2015 (%)
Macroeconomic Policy	6.3	11.6	21.9	23.0	19.0	32.3	39.4	23.5	16.6	18.6
Financial regulation	62.1	34.9	18.0	19.7	15.7	13.5	10.0	7.1	3.4	7.1
Development	4.2	11.6	7.0	13.1	14.4	6.0	5.6	17.8	9.8	21.2
Financial institutions	14.7	22.5	8.6	6.6	10.5	7.8	4.4	1.8	2.0	1.8
Trade	5.3	10.9	4.7	14.8	11.1	5.3	5.6	4.3	4.4	12.4
Energy	0.0	0.0	13.3	1.6	9.2	6.4	5.6	6.8	7.8	2.7
Employment and labour	0.0	3.1	2.3	0.0	2.6	2.8	10.0	10.3	7.8	8.8
Accountability	4.2	2.3	11.7	4.9	2.6	1.8	7.2	3.2	8.3	1.8
Crime and corruption	3.2	0.0	2.3	4.9	5.9	1.8	3.9	11.7	2.0	3.5
Food, agriculture, nutrition	0.0	0.0	2.3	3.3	1.3	12.8	2.2	3.9	0.0	2.7
Climate change	0.0	2.3	2.3	4.9	5.2	2.8	2.8	3.9	3.4	2.7
Health	0.0	0.0	0.0	0.0	0.0	0.0	0.0	0.0	16.1	1.8
G8/G20 governance	0.0	0.0	2.3	0.0	1.3	4.3	1.7	4.3	0.0	0.0
Infrastructure	0.0	0.0	0.0	0.0	0.0	0.0	0.0	0.0	13.7	0.0
Terrorism	0.0	0.0	0.0	0.0	0.0	0.0	0.0	0.4	0.0	10.6
Social policy	0.0	0.8	0.8	3.3	0.7	1.1	0.6	0.0	0.0	2.7
Others	0.0	0.0	2.3	0.0	0.7	1.4	1.1	1.1	4.9	1.8

Source: Own calculations based on data provided by the G20 Research Group

Further Readings

Amtenbrink, F., Blokker N., van den Bogaert, S., Cuyvers A., Heine K., Hillion C., Kantorowicz J., Lenk H., & Repasi R. (2015). *The European Union's role in international economic fora paper 1: The G20*. Study for the ECON Committee. IP/A/ECON/2014-15.

Hajnal, P. I. (2014). *The G20. Evolution, interrelationships, documentation*. New York: Routledge. G20 Information center provided by the G20 Research Group available at http://www.g20.utoronto.ca/

Luckhurst, J. (2016). *G20 since the global crisis*. New York: Palgrave Macmillan.

References

Amtenbrink, F., Blokker N., van den Bogaert S., Cuyvers A., Heine K., Christophe, H., Kantorowicz J., Lenk H., & Repasi R. (2015). *The European Union's role in international economic fora paper 1: The G20*. Study for the ECON Committee. IP/A/ECON/2014-15.

Angeloni, I., & Pisani-Ferry, J. (2012). *The G20: Characters in search of an author* (Bruegel Working Paper 2012/04).

Åslund, A. (2009). The Group of 20 must be stopped. *Financial Times*, 26 November 2009, available at https://www.ft.com/content/37deaeb4-dad0-11de-933d-00144feabdc0. Accessed on 9 Apr 2017.

Beeson, M., & Bell, S. (2009). The G20 and International Economic Governance: Hegemony, Collectivism, or Both? *Global Governance, 15*, 67–86.

Bertoldi, M., Scherrer, H., & Stanoeva, G. (2013). *The G20@5: Is it still delivering?* ECFIN Economic Brief 2013.

Callaghan, M. (2013a). *Relaunching the G20*. Sydney: Analysis, Lowy Institute for International Policy.

Callaghan, M. (2013b). *Strengthening the core of the G20: Clearer, objectives, better communication, greater transparency and accountability*. Sydney: Analysis, Lowy Institute for International Policy.

Cameron, D. (2011). *Governance for growth: Building consensus for the future. A report by David Cameron*, Prime Minister of the United Kingdom.

Çanacki, I. (2013). G-20 & Turkey's Presidency in 2015. Turkey in the Troika of G-20, Preparing to Assume the Chair. In *2015 AVİM – Center for Eurasian Studies*, 14 November 2013, Ankara, available https://www.hazine.gov.tr/File/?path=ROOT%2F1%2FDocuments%2FDi%C4%9Fer+Bas%C4%B1n+Duyurusu%2FSN_IHC_20131114_G20_AVIM_sunum.pptx. Accessed on 9 Apr 2017.

Cooper, A. (2010). The G20 as an improvised crisis committee and/or a contested 'steering committee' for the world. *International Affairs, 86*(3), 741–757.

Debaere, P., & Orbie, J. (2013). The European Union in the Gx system. In K. E. Jørgensen & K. V. Laatikainen (Eds.), *Routledge handbook on the European Union and international institutions: Performance, policy, power*. Abingdon: Routledge.

Der Spiegel. (2010). *Norway takes aim at G-20: 'One of the Greatest Setbacks Since World War II'*. Interview conducted by Manfred Ertel, 22 June 2010, available at http://www.spiegel.de/international/europe/norway-takes-aim-at-g-20-one-of-thegreatest-setbacks-since-world-war-ii-a-702104.html. Accessed on 9 Apr 2017.

Eccleston, R., Kellow, A., & Carroll, P. (2015). G20 endorsement in post crisis global governance: More than a toothless talking shop? *The British Journal of Politics & International Relations, 17*, 298–317.

G20. (2008). *The group of twenty: A history*. Available at www.g20.utoronto.ca/docs/g20history.pdf. Accessed on 9 Apr 2017.

G20. (2009a). *G20 action plan for recovery and reform.* Statement Issued by the G20 Leaders, 2 Apr 2009. Available at http://www.g20.utoronto.ca/2009/2009communique0402.html. Accessed on 9 Apr 2017.

G20. (2009b). *The leaders statement: The Pittsburgh Summit, including the Annex: Core values for sustainable economic activity and the framework for strong, sustainable and balanced growth,* 25 September 2009. Available at http://www.g20.utoronto.ca/2009/2009communique0925.html. Accessed on 9 Apr 2017.

G20. (2011a). *Final declaration: Building our common future: Renewed collective action for the benefit of all,* 4 November 2011. Available at http://www.g20.utoronto.ca/2011/2011-cannes-declaration-111104-en.html. Accessed on 9 Apr 2017.

G20. (2011b). *Final Communiqué,* 4 November 2011. Available at http://www.g20.utoronto.ca/2011/2011-cannes-communique-111104-en.html. Accessed on 9 Apr 2017.

G20. (2015a). *Process of working.* Available at http://www.g20india.gov.in/aboutg20-process-working.asp?lk=aboutg207. Accessed on 9 Apr 2017.

G20. (2015b). *Leadership and structure.* Available at http://www.g20india.gov.in/aboutg20-leadership.asp?lk=aboutg206. Accessed on 9 Apr 2017.

G20. (2015c). *Sherpas track.* Available at http://www.g20india.gov.in/sheraps-track.asp. Accessed on 9 Apr 2017.

Giovannini, A., Gros, D., Ivan, P., Kaczyński, P. M., & Valiante, D. (2012). External representation of the Euro area. European Parliament, Directorate General for Internal Policies. *Policy Department A: Economic and Scientific Policy, 2012.* https://doi.org/10.2139/ssrn.2149431.

Gradinis, S. (2013). The financial stability board: The new politics of International Financial Regulation. *Texas International Law Journal, 48,* 157–176.

Henley, P. H., & Blokker, N. M. (2013). The Group of 20: A Short Legal Anatomy from the Perspective of International Institutional Law. *Melbourne Journal of International Law, 14*(2), 550–607.

International Law Association. (2004). *Accountability of international organisations.* Final Report. Berlin 2004.

Jin-seo, C. (2010). Five non-G20 nations invited to Seoul Summit. *The Korea Times,* 9 September 2010. Available at http://www.koreatimes.co.kr/www/news/biz/2010/09/301_73469.html. Accessed on 9 Apr 2017.

Jokela, J. (2011). *Europe's declining role in the G20: What role for the EU in the club of the most important powers?* (FIIA Briefing Paper 96).

Kern, Steffen (2011). *The real G2: Americans, Europeans, and their role in the G20.* Transatlantic Academy Paper Series, 2011.

Kirton, J. (2000). The G20: Representativeness, effectiveness, and leadership in global governance. In J. Kirton, J. Daniels, & A. Freytag (Eds.), *Guiding global order. G8 governance in the twenty-first century* (pp. 143–172). Aldershot: Ashgate.

Kirton, J. (2008). Prospects for the G20 leaders summit on financial markets and the world economy. In: J. Kirton (Ed.), *The G20 leaders summit on financial markets and the world economy.* Available at: http://www.g8.utoronto.ca/g20/g20leadersbook/kirton.html. Accessed on 9 Apr 2017.

Kirton, John, Kokotsis, Ella, Guebert, Jenilee, Bracht, Caroline, G8 Research Group, G20 Research Group, BRICS Research Group, Munk School of Global Affairs at Trinity College University of Toronto. (2014). *Reference Manual for Summit Commitment and Compliance Coding.* Available at:. http://www.g8.utoronto.ca/evaluations/compliancemanual-140722.pdf. Accessed on 9 June 2019.

Lyngen, N., & Simmons, C. (2013). The financial stability board: The new face of international financial regulation. *Harvard International Law Journal.* Special Report, 54, i–x.

Moret, E. (2016). *Effective minilateralism for the EU. What, when and how.* EUISS Brief. 17/2006. June.

Nasra, S., & Debaere, P. (2016). The European Union in the G20: What role for small states? *Cambridge Review of International Affairs 2012, 29,* 209–230.

Nolle, D. (2015). Who's in charge of fixing the world's financial system? The un[?]der-appreciated lead role of the G20 and the FSB. *Financial Markets, Institutions & Instruments, 24*(1), 1–82.

Se-Jeong, K. (2010). Meeting shows hassle in G-20 agenda setting. *The Korea Times.* Available at: http://www.koreatimes.co.kr/www/news/special/2010/08/176_66750.html. Accessed on 13 June 2019.

Urban, M. (2017). *The quest for economic resilience in uncertain times* (showCASE, No 21).

Van Ham, P. (2012). *Upgrading the global financial system. The why and how* (Clingendael Policy Brief No. 12).

Vestergaard, J. (2011). *The G20 and Beyond: Towards Effective Global Economic Governance* (DISS Report 2011:04).

Vestergaard, J., & Wade, R. (2012). Establishing a new global economic council: Governance reform at the G20, the IMF and the World Bank. *Global Policy, 3*(3), 257–269.

Viola, L. A. (2015). Orchestration by design: The G20 in international financial regulation. In P. Genschel, D. Snidal, & B. Zangl (Eds.), *International Organizations as orchestrators* (pp. 88–113). Cambridge: Cambridge University Press.

Wouters, J., & Geraets, D. (2012). *The G20 and informal international lawmaking* (Leuven Centre for Global Governance Studies, Working Paper No. 86).

Wouters, J., & Ramopoulos, T. (2012). The G20 and Global Economic Governance: Lessons from Multilevel European Governance? *Journal of International Economic Law, 15*(3), 751–775.

Part V
Conflict, Conflict Resolution and International Security

Chapter 18
The Enforcement of International Law

Elena Kantorowicz-Reznichenko

> *That part of the law which provides the means by which it shall
> be enforced is of as much importance as the law itself.*
> Andrews (1909: 85)

18.1 Introduction

On-going conflicts and potential risks for emerging conflicts can be found all around the globe. Just to name a few: the escalating civil war in Syria, the humanitarian crisis caused by Islamic State (IS) terrorist groups, and the potential nuclear threats from North Korea and Iran.[1] Therefore, it is important to understand which instruments are available for the international community to enforce global order.

On the national level, the state has a monopoly over the enforcement of the laws. The procedure of law making and enforcement is clear. Legislators (or courts) enact laws and specify the expected consequences of failure to comply; police or other official authorities monitor compliance; prosecutors and courts impose punishment on violators who were apprehended; and finally, authorities such as prison service, probation service, fine collection agencies, execute the sanctions. On the contrary, there is no world governor and creation of international rules depends on the consent of States for whom those rules are binding. States enjoy sovereignty and have exclusive decision-making power over their territories. A question then arises – can international law be enforced?

The opinions on this question vary. The most optimistic view is captured by the famous quote by Louis Henkin: "*almost all nations observe almost all principles of*

---

[1] There are many more security threats in different parts of the world. For a recent overview see, Watch List 2017, Special Report No. 3 by the International Crisis Group (24 February 2017).

E. Kantorowicz-Reznichenko (✉)
Rotterdam Institute for Law and Economics (RILE), Erasmus School of Law,
Erasmus University Rotterdam, Rotterdam, The Netherlands
e-mail: Reznichenko@law.eur.nl

© Springer Nature Switzerland AG 2020
M. O. Hosli, J. Selleslaghs (eds.), *The Changing Global Order*, United Nations
University Series on Regionalism 17,
https://doi.org/10.1007/978-3-030-21603-0_18

international law and almost all of their obligations almost all of the time" (1979: 47). Realists, on the other hand, assume international law does not matter and has no effect on States' behaviour (e.g. Morgenthau 1985: 312–313). It seems that nowadays, the more prominent views lie in between those two extremes. Many scholars believe that States design international institutions with the purpose of promoting their interests, whether based on calculations of costs and benefits, or as a reflection of internalised international norms (Chayes and Chayes 1993: 179–182; Wendt 2001: 1025). States are considered to enter international agreements with an intention to comply with them. Lack of compliance stems either from the enforcement problem – a conflict between individual and collective incentives – (Koremenos et al. 2001: 7) or unintentional breaches (Chayes and Chayes 1993: 190–195). Therefore, States delegate limited powers to international institutions in order to overcome the enforcement problem and increase compliance.

The purpose of this chapter is to discuss the enforcement problem of international law, with a focus on security[2]; to analyse three of the enforcement institutions and the theoretical perspective on their design and significance; and finally to reflect on the changing global order and its implications for the enforcement of international law. Currently, the Security Council (SC) is the most important international organisation for the enforcement of global peace and security. It is an intergovernmental organisation to which states delegated authority to oversee compliance with international law. It constitutes an act of delegation from all United Nations (UN) Member States to a small number of States. The International Court of Justice (ICJ) is the judicial organ of the UN. Even though it has no enforcement capacity, and enforcement is under the authority of SC (Article 94 of the UN Charter) it facilitates coordination between States through allocation of rights and responsibilities to the disputing States (Llamzon 2007: 822). Such a body enables peaceful resolution of violations of international obligations and thus, plays a role in the enforcement of international law. Finally, States also delegated judicial powers to the International Criminal Court (ICC) as an independent body to adjudicate (specific) gross violations of human rights. Those three international institutions are the focus of this chapter.

This chapter is divided as follows. Part 2 presents the main concepts of public international law[3] and introduces the enforcement problem. It is followed by part 3, which addresses theoretical perspectives with a view on the enforcement problem. Part 4 introduces the three international institutions (SC, ICJ and the ICC) and explains their role in the enforcement of international law. In addition, this part briefly analyses those institutions from the perspective of the mainstream international relations (IR) theories. Part 5 concludes with the view on the implications the emerging powers have on the changing global order.

---

[2] International law includes many areas such as trade, environment, health, security, etc. The enforcement problem and States' solutions for it differs (see the extensive work of Koremenos 2016 on institutional design). This chapter deals only with the part of international law that concerns security, therefore, any reference to 'international law' is limited to this area.

[3] In this chapter, the concepts 'international law' and 'public international law' are used interchangeably.

18.2   Public International Law

Prior to discussing the different methods to enforce international law, it is important to understand what international law is. International law is a set of binding rules that were created by different States to govern their interactions. Its main goal is to preserve international order. There are multiple sources of international law and they are enumerated in Article 38 of the Statute of the ICJ (the Statute). Those sources include conventions and treaties agreed upon by States; international custom; and general principles of law recognised by civilised nations. Unlike a domestic legal system, which is reasonably certain and coherent, international law is not very accessible. It is difficult to identify a rule on each specific matter and there is no clear hierarchy between the different sources of law, no central legislator nor a hierarchical judicial system to enforce the rules (Anthony Aust 2005: 5).

International custom is a set of rules that emerged from the practice of States. It is binding on all States, but in order to qualify as a custom there must be evidence for a uniform practice of States over a certain period of time, and an indication that the rule is generally recognised by States. Such evidence can come in the form of State's observed actions, domestic legislation, UN resolutions, etc. For example, the prohibition on the use of force under the UN charter is an established customary rule (*Nicaragua v. U.S.*, 1986, para. 184). However, there is no single written source that contains the entire customary international law (Anthony Aust 2005: 7). Due to the imprecision of international custom, in the eighteenth century a movement emerged to codify international customary law. The meaning of codification is transformation of practices into 'statutes' or conventions. Until the nineteenth century there were mainly private attempts to codify international custom. Even though those attempts failed, they contributed to the development of the process of codifying international law. The first time States successfully codified international rules was in 1899 during the Peace Conference in The Hague. The two most important 'codes' that were produces in that event were the Convention for the Pacific Settlement of International Disputes and the Convention with Respect to Laws and Customs of War and Land. Over the years, many areas of international relationships were codified through an agreement of multiple states (Oppenheim 1992: 97–99).

Decisions of international courts are also part of international law, however, they are binding only on the involved parties (see section 4.1 on the ICJ). Furthermore, courts are allowed to apply recognised general principles, such as the obligation to act in good faith (Article 38(1) of the Statute).

The nature of international law is different from domestic law. In democratic societies people need to consent *ex ante* on their legislators through a voting system. However, once legislators are in office, they are not required to seek consent of the people for each new legal rule. Furthermore, enforcement of these rules are centralised and is not in the hands of individuals. In contrast, the legal basis of international law is the consent of States. Therefore, generally speaking, in order to bind States by certain rules, it must be clear that the State has consented to the application of such rules, either explicitly, or through evidence of a long-term practice. Hence, in domestic law, individuals are the main subjects of the law and in international law States are simultaneously the subjects of the law and also those who create the rules and are in charge of their enforcement (often through delegation).

Over the years States created various treaties with the purpose of increasing international security and minimising threats to peace. One example is the Treaty on the Non-Proliferation of Nuclear Weapons, which entered into force in 1970 (NTP). Nuclear weapons are extremely distractive and have the potential to cause enormous life loss if used for violent purposes. On the other hand, nuclear energy can also be used for peaceful objectives. Therefore the stated purpose of the treaty is to prevent the proliferation of nuclear weapon, and to enhance cooperative peaceful development and use of nuclear power.

However, the special structure of the international 'legal system', which is largely decentralised, creates enforcement problems. Global security is often viewed as a public good. It is costly to maintain, and its benefits are spread across all states. Therefore, states have incentives to free ride on the efforts of other States to maintain global order. If all States think in these lines, there is a 'collective action problem' and global security would be undersupplied (Kindleberger 1986: 2, 7–8; Thompson 2009a: 311). This situation might arise for instance, when enforcement requires sanctions which are imposed by all states. But sanctions are costly, and some States might prefer to avoid them and enjoy global security which is achieved by the efforts of others. On the other hand, the situation of global security is treated as a prisoner's dilemma where cooperation of all states is collectively efficient but defection is individually beneficial (Downs 1998: 322). For example, global order can be maintained if all states comply with the prohibition on the use of force. However, states might have incentives to deviate from this cooperation and unilaterally use force for strategic reasons.

18.3   The Problem of Enforcement from the Perspective of IR Theories

Currently, there is no world centralised governance that can enforce international law. Enforcement of international law is characterised by decentralised cooperation and delegation of powers by States to international institutions. The probability of delegation increases as the benefits from cooperation rise. However, the effectiveness of those institutions in enforcing international law depends on the extent to which they reflect the balance of powers, thus preserving the central role of sovereign states (Hawkins et al. 2006: 6).

International institutions, such as the ones discussed in this chapter (see section 3), can assist in mitigating the cooperation and enforcement problems. They are rationally designed by States to promote their interests and to facilitate cooperation. In particular, international institutions enable States to reduce uncertainty through diffusion of information (Koremenos et al. 2001: 764–768). The institutions that are the subject of this chapter assist in centralising enforcement of international law in the context of safety and security. Centralisation of enforcement can overcome the free riding problem since all States are obliged to contribute to the collective effort. In addition, it can place pressure on States not to deviate (or deviate less) from the collectively efficient behaviour (Stein 2010: 209). However, the extent of confidence in those institutions in the enforcement of international law varies across different IR theories.

According to realism theory, international law and international enforcement institutions merely reflect the distribution of power in the world rather than constraining States' behaviour. As strongly put by Anne-Marie Slaughter (2011: 2) – "*international law is thus a symptom of State behaviour, not a cause*". Therefore, realists view international law as irrelevant and assume States comply with international law only if it is costless (and beneficial) or when stronger States induce compliance (Morgenthau 1985: 312–313). However, this view fails to explain why States invest great resources in negotiating international agreements and designing international institutions (Koremenos et al. 2001: 762; Koremenos 2016: 199).

Similarly to realists, institutionalists follow the rational choice theory to explain international law and its enforcement. They as well believe States create international institutions to promote their own interests. However, they hold a more optimistic view on the significance of such institutions and emphasize cooperation between States. Institutions do matter and have an effect on the behaviour of States. They assist in overcoming the coordination and enforcement problems which is an important objective in increasingly interdependent world (Keohane 1984: 8; Keohane 1988: 386–387). Liberalists emphasize in addition the importance of domestic preferences in shaping international law. Interest groups and national political interests play a major role in State's foreign policy (Moravcsik 2010, p. 234). However, these theories have overly functional logic and disregard social context in which international institutions are created. Preferences are taken as exogenous without a deeper analysis of their origins. For example, in the context of international criminal law, how did 'international justice' become a public good? Atrocities were committed through history, why did States delegate enforcement powers to a centralised judicial authority in a specific point of time? (Fehl 2004: 370).

Finally, constructivists hold the most optimistic view on States' compliance with international law. They believe that international institutions are not merely reflections of state's interests, but are themselves shaping preferences and identities of States. Compliance with international rules is perceived as the default action, which is attributed to internalisation of norms (Wendt 1999: 360–362; Wendt 2001: 1025). Another 'channel' of compliance is naming and shaming. The more States care about their social reputation in the international community, the more they are pressured by external players to comply with international norms. For example, the increased emphasize on human rights enhances the vulnerability of States to external and internal pressure to comply with such norms (Risse and Ropp 2013: 20–21). However, if international norms are internalised, it is not clear why States violate them in important situations. For instance, the constructivist logic makes it difficult to understand U.S.'s invasion to Iraq in 2003 despite the dominant international norm against unilateral use of force.

18.4   Enforcement of International Law

As mentioned before, enforcement of international law in the context of global peace and security is done through delegation of this authority to international institutions. Since delegation is costly[4] it will take place only if the benefits of cooperation outweigh the costs. Powerful States are interested in delegation since it has a potential to advance common interests while reflecting their relative power in world politics. Weaker States have also interest in delegating enforcement authority to centralised international institutions since they can exert more influence through such institutions. For example, all Member States of the UN receive one vote in the UN General Assembly. This provides disproportional influence power to weak States (Hawkins et al. 2006: 9, 22).

Until the twentieth century, the international enforcement mechanism was decentralised. The decision power to impose measures in response to violations of international obligations was in the hands of each sovereign State. Even though wars were considered as a last resort, there was no international prohibition on the use of force. However, the twentieth century was characterised by the development of mass destruction weapons, large-scale conscription to national armies, and the emergence of multinational armed conflicts. Consequently, wars became too destructive and were no longer acceptable for the international community. This environment set the proper ground for the centralisation of enforcement power of international law and the general prohibition on the use of force by States. The latter ban allowed for the development of peaceful mechanisms for dispute resolution between States since it became truly essential (Kolb 2013: 5–6).

In mid-twentieth century, states delegated the authority to provide the public good of peace and security to the SC. The SC received a mandate to make centralised decisions about the enforcement of international norm violations on behalf of all UN Member States. Starting from that point, the primary legal source on the enforcement mechanisms of international law is the Charter of the United Nations. For the purpose of maintaining global peace and security, the Charter provides different means of (international) dispute resolution. Those means can be placed on a scale of growing level of external intervention. Chapter VI provides pacific instruments available for parties themselves to resolve their disputes. For instance, Article 33 provides that States should seek a solution through "negotiation, enquiry, mediation, conciliation, arbitration, judicial settlement" etc. Aside from judicial settlement through the ICJ, those instruments are not discussed in this chapter. They

---

[4]The direct costs are for instance, the long negotiations to agree on the nature and details of the delegation. The indirect costs of delegation is the partial forgone powers of the States to enable centralization of enforcement.

are however, addressed in the following chapter. Chapter VII of the Charter provides with more extreme measures to address threats to international peace and security that involve external intervention. Those measures are the focus of this part.

Another international body to which states delegated enforcement authority and that is discussed in the current part is the ICC. This is the only permanent judicial body that enforces international criminal law. Unlike the ICJ that is reserved for disputes between States, the ICC combats impunity and punishes individuals involved in grave violations of human rights. This is a complementary international institution to the UN organs in the perseverance of global order. Delegation to international courts differs from delegation to intergovernmental institutions. Courts are (in theory) independent third parties that act as trustees. They are empowered by states to make decisions on their behalf regarding norm violations based on professional criteria. This in turn, enhances the political legitimacy of states' actions (Alter 2008: 35).

The following sub-sections describe the three international enforcement institutions. In addition, they provide the perspective of the IR theories on the motivation and significance of these institutions. The order of analysing those institutions adheres to the following logic (which is partially reflected in the UN Charter). First the UN organs are discussed. The ICJ is described first forasmuch as it serves as a peaceful dispute resolution institution, which requires States' consent. It is followed by SC sanctions, which constitute an external intervention. The use of force is described at the end of the SC sub-section as it is the most invasive measure to enforce international law. The ICC is not a UN organ thus, it is analysed at the end.

18.5   International Court of Justice

The ICJ is the principal judicial organ of the UN and as such, the organ of the international legal order. Its legal mandate and powers are derived from the Statute of the International Court of Justice that is annexed to the UN Charter. Therefore, all States that are parties to the UN Charter are also parties to the ICJ Statute.

The establishment of the ICJ was not the first step in creating international centralised judicial body. It preceded by the Permanent Court of International Justice (PCIJ) that began its functioning under the League of Nations in 1922. This was the first permanent judicial body that offered States the possibility to bring their disputes before an international court that would rule according to existing sources of international law (Brownlie 2008: 708–710).

The ICJ's role in the enforcement of international law derives from its adjudication in contentious cases and its advisory opinions to UN organs upon request. Even though the ICJ has very broad jurisdiction – any dispute arising from international treaties, conventions or related to the UN Charter (Article 36 of the Statute) – there are important restrictions on its powers. Only States can bring their disputes before the ICJ (Article 34 of the Statute). Therefore, individuals or non-State organisations have no stand in the Court. The main purpose of contentious cases is to provide

States with peaceful mechanism to enforce the obligations of other States under different international treaties or conventions. Furthermore, the Court's decisions are only binding on the parties and not on the entire international community. However, the most important limitation of the ICJ that restricts its enforcement capacity is the lack of compulsory jurisdiction. In other words, if one State files a case against another State in the ICJ, the Court has no jurisdiction unless the other State consents for the adjudication of the matter before the ICJ (Article 36 the Statute of the ICJ). Therefore, the enforcement power of the ICJ entirely depends on the willingness of States to choose this method of settlement.

Nevertheless, States employed different methods to strengthen their commitment to the adjudicative authority of the ICJ. First, the majority of States in the world establish the Court's jurisdiction *ex ante* by including compromissory clauses in bilateral or multilateral treaties. Namely, the parties to the treaty agree in advance that in case of a dispute it will be resolved by the ICJ (Mitchell and Powell 2011: 166). Second, according to Article 36(2) of the ICJ Statute, States can accept compulsory jurisdiction of the ICJ (often with reservations). At the time of writing, a total of 72 States accepted such jurisdiction.[5]

The acceptance of the Court and its utilization changed over time. At the early stage of its existence, following the end of WWII, it enjoyed wide acceptance due to the sense of internationalisation and the need to learn from past mistakes. Its strength was in the idea of providing equal 'power' to all States regardless of their size. Furthermore, it was destined to help building the body of international law. However, following several cases where the Court limited its jurisdiction, the ICJ faced serious crisis when many countries turned its back on the Court. All this changed with the ICJ's ruling in the *Nicaragua* case in 1986. In this case, the ICJ ruled against the U.S. for the military and financial support they provided the *contra* rebels in their fight against the Nicaragua government. The Court ruled that the U.S. violated international law and ordered reparations to be paid by the U.S. to the Republic of Nicaragua (*Nicaragua v. United States of America*, 27 June 1986). The turning point can be attributed to the fact that the court 'dared' to rule against one of the most powerful States in the world. This move gained the Court respect from majority of the UN member States, and helped building trust in Court's impartiality, especially from developing countries (Kolb 2013: 1149–1155). Nevertheless, in recent decades the Court is largely under-utilised by the international community (Posner and de Figueiredo 2005: 607).

When considering the role of the ICJ in global order, an important question is compliance by States with the Court's judgments. An effective enforcement requires mechanisms to execute courts' rulings. Yet, the ICJ mainly relies on self-enforcement. Compliance by States is crucial for the prestige of the Court. In order to regard the ICJ as a true instrument to settle disputes in a peaceful manner, States must be committed to follow its rulings. High level of compliance is a reasonable expectation in light of the voluntary nature of the Court's jurisdiction. In practice, empirical evidence on this question demonstrates mixed results. Overall the compliance rate

---

[5] See http://www.icj-cij.org/en/declarations (accessed August 1, 2017).

with ICJ judgments is adequate. However, there is variation in the level of compliance between different cases, even though complete defiance is rare. Paulson (2004) identified several factors that are correlated with lower extent of compliance. First, States that are 'compelled' to accept jurisdiction (through compromissory clauses or *ex ante* adopted compulsory jurisdiction) and then lose the case, comply to a lesser extent with the Court's judgment. Second, the nature of a dispute is relevant to the level of compliance. Thus for instance, disputes over boundaries and existence of related armed conflicts tend to be associated with less compliance. Third, economic disputes have higher rates of compliance than political disputes. Other factors such as international pressure to comply and internal political drive to end a conflict also play a role in the level of compliance (Paulson 2004: 434, 456–457).

Nevertheless, to strengthen the significance of ICJ's decisions, Article 94 of the UN Charter offers parties an enforcement mechanism. This Article first states a general obligation of States that are parties to a case before the ICJ to comply with the judgment. If one State fails to fulfil its obligations, the aggrieved State can refer the matter to the SC. The SC is authorized to use recommendations or other measures to induce compliance with the judgment. Despite the existence of such mechanism States rarely use it and the SC has never implemented measures under this Article, even in cases of continuous non-compliance. One possible reason for this inaction might be the ambiguous nature of this mechanism. This refers to a situation of non-compliance that does not reach the threshold of threat or breach of peace. In such cases, the mandate of SC to use any measures is questionable. On the other hand, the SC might have decided not to take action under Article 94(2) because the recourse to the SC under this Article was sufficient to induce compliance (Llamzon 2007: 846–848).

From a realist's perspective, ICJ might be viewed as insignificant in the enforcement of international law. ICJ's jurisdiction depends on the consent of States, and only the SC can enforce its judgments. Therefore, if one of the permanent members (P5) rejects the judgment, it can never be enforced against them. The withdrawal of consent of the U.S. to the ICJ's compulsory jurisdiction following the unfavourable *Nicaragua* judgment (Delahunty and Yoo 2006: 110) is a case in point. Another problem with the ICJ is its potential bias. A study by Posner and de Figueiredo (2005) presented strong evidence that ICJ's judges are biased in their decisions, thus for instance, favouring States that appoint them, and States with wealth levels closer to their own States. Furthermore, by custom the composition of judges in the ICJ always includes judges from the P5, even though other States rotate (Posner and de Figueiredo 2005: 603).

The creation of the ICJ and the delegation of judicial authority to this institution can be explained from the institutionalist perspective as well. Such delegation increases commitment and reduces uncertainty, thus facilitating coordination between States. Legal preferences of States play a role in the rational design of the judicial institution. A court that mimics the domestic legal system of a state reduces uncertainty with respect to the interpretation of international law. Therefore, there is a higher probability for civil law States to accept ICJ's compulsory jurisdiction, a judicial institution that is designed as civil law courts, as compared to common law or Islamic legal traditions.[6] One implication of such trend is that the ICJ is more effective in facilitating coordination between civil law countries (Mitchell and Powell 2011: 10–14, 177).

18.6   United Nations Security Council

The SC is currently the primary body for the enforcement of international order. Chapter VII of the UN Charter enumerates the instruments available to the SC to enforce international law (Arts. 41 and 42 of the Charter). The Charter provides the SC broad discretional power with respect to the decision which measures should be applied and when. These measures can be divided into two groups: (1) measures that do not include use of force, in this chapter they are referred to as 'sanctions' and (2) use of force. The measures under Chapter VII are mandatory for States and can only be authorised to address situations of threat to peace, breaches of peace and acts of aggression. Therefore, prior to adopting any of the available measures, the SC needs to determine that one of the abovementioned situations exists, or that the measures are necessary to restore peace and security (Article 39 of the Charter).

The use of sanctions on the international level is not a new concept. The novelty of the twentieth century is the delegation of the power to impose sanctions from sovereign States to an international organisation. This power was already given to the League of Nations in 1920 (Article 16 to the Covenant of the League of Nations). With the entry to force of the UN Charter in 1945, the SC is the body that determines whether there is a violation of the Charter and which measures should be adopted. However, the SC has no centralised police force that can execute its sanctions. Therefore, it heavily depends on the cooperation of States. To strengthen the enforcement power of the SC and to mitigate the free riding problem, Article 25 of the Charter creates an obligation for the enforcing States to comply with the prescribed sanctions. This special structure of sanctioning apparatus requires a monitoring system and an 'enforcement mechanism within an enforcement mechanism'. For this reason, the SC established subsidiary bodies to oversee the implementation of its sanctions by States. Nevertheless, non-cooperative States with the sanctions regime are not automatically disciplined (Doxey 1980: 92), thus, potentially undermining the effectiveness of the sanctions.

Another challenge to international enforcement by the SC is the veto power. The voting structure increases the potential for inaction due to ideological conflicts within the SC. This point can be illustrated by the different levels of intervention of the SC through the years after its establishment. Shortly after the entry to force of the UN Charter, the Cold War commenced. This development had an effect on the

---

[6]Civil law originates from the Roman Empire and puts a great emphasize on the written law (codes). This is the most widespread legal system in the world. Common law is rooted in the British Isles and largely relies on courts' judgment (judge made law). Finally, the Islamic law is mostly based on religious principles (Mitchell and Powell 2011: 11–12).

exercise of the SC's sanctioning power. Until 1990, the activation of Chapter VII was very rare. Since its formation, the SC established 26 sanctions regimes (that do not include use of force). Only two of those (against Southern Rhodesia and South Africa) were impose between the years 1946–1990.[7]

The following sub-sections explain the different instruments available to the SC under Chapter VII of the Charter. Furthermore, it discusses the effectiveness of such measures.

18.6.1   Short-of-War Sanctions

The sanctions under Article 41 of the Charter are more frequently implemented than military interventions. This is not surprising in light of the destructive nature and the cost of wars.

The most frequently imposed sanctions are arms embargo. Arms sanctions specifically restrict import and export of arms and materials related to mass destruction weapons (Farrall 2007: 110). The second most used type of sanctions are the targeted sanctions. Those sanctions came to replace the comprehensive economic sanctions, which generally prohibited the import and export of all commodities. The latter type of intervention was enormously devastating for the civilian population of the target country. Targeted sanctions are imposed against specific individuals and sectors and come in the form of asset freeze, travel ban or restrictions, and financial restrictions. They mostly aim at placing restrictions on state leaders, decisions-makers, particular economic or regional sectors, non-state actors (e.g. Taliban in Afghanistan), etc., thus limiting the negative effects on innocent civilians (Biersteker et al. 2016a: 1–2). Commodity sanctions, which restrict the flow of certain goods in and out of the target State (e.g. timber, diamonds, oil), are used less frequently. Finally, diplomatic sanctions, which include restrictions on the activities or travel of the diplomatic personnel, suspension from intergovernmental institutions, etc., are less relevant nowadays and are rarely used (one example is the recent SC resolution, which imposes diplomatic sanctions against North Korea – DPRK –S/RES/2321, 30 November 2016).[8]

Starting from mid-1990, SC imposes only targeted sanctions. They are used to address various threats and to achieve different goals such as prevention of conflict and enforcement of peace agreements, counter terrorism instruments, protection of civilian population, restriction on the proliferation of nuclear weapon, etc. By its nature, targeted sanctions are more flexible than indiscriminate comprehensive sanctions, thus can be adjusted to the behaviour of the target State (or individuals).

---

[7] Information about the sanctions regimes can be found on the UN official website. *See*, https://www.un.org/sc/suborg/en/sanctions/information (accessed March 28, 2017).

[8] For the type of SC sanctions and the frequency of their application in the years 1990–2017, see Security Council Practices and Charter Research Branch, Graphs on currently active sanctions regimes and restrictions (31 March 2017).

Despite its advantage in terms of minimising humanitarian consequences, targeted sanctions are significantly more complex and difficult in implementation than comprehensive sanctions. The former requires thorough understanding of the economic and political structure of the target country and close monitoring of its appropriate execution by States (Biersteker et al. 2016a: 11–21).

The list of possible measures is not exhaustive, hence, leaving a wide range of discretion to the SC. For instance, while acting under Chapter VII of the Charter, the SC established the International Criminal Tribunal for the former Yugoslavia (ICTY) and The International Criminal Tribunal for Rwanda (ICTR) (SC Res. 827, 25 May 1993, and SC Res. 955, 8 November 1994, respectively) to address the armed conflicts in those countries.

Following the end of the Cold War, the SC increased rapidly its involvement in international situations that constituted threat to international peace and security. It authorised sanctions, *inter alia*, in Somalia: SC Res. 733 (23 January 1992); Liberia: SC Res. 788 (19 November 1992); Sudan (SC Res. 1054, 26 April 1996); Kosovo (SC Res. 1199, 23 September 1998); Ivory Coast (SC Res. 1478, 6 May 2003); Iran (SC Res. 1696, 31 July 2006); North Korea (SC Res. 1718, 14 October 2006); Central African Republic (SC Res 2127, 5 December 2013); Yemen (S/RES/2342, 3 February 2017, extending previously imposed sanctions), etc. The sanctions regimes include different measures, and have different levels of effectiveness.

In 2000, the SC formed an Informal Working Group to provide recommendations for the improvement of SC sanctions (UN Doc. S/2000/319, 17 April 2000). The Working Group concluded that in order to increase the effectiveness of sanctions several aspects of the enforcement mechanism ought to be improved. First, sanctions should be feasible and clearly communicated regarding its purpose, targets and instruments. Second, States should be encouraged to establish national coordination mechanisms to improve the implementation of the sanctions. Third, SC should perform periodic evaluation of the sanctions regime to identify its impact and unintended consequences. Fourth, SC should create independent monitoring groups for the sanctions regimes. The monitoring groups should visit States to verify compliance and report to the SC serious cases of non-compliance (UN Doc. S/2006/997, 22 December 2006). Due to their importance for the effectiveness of enforcement, monitoring groups became an integral part of SC sanctions regimes.[9]

An important question with respect to SC sanctions is the level of their effectiveness. The widespread belief among scholars, practitioners and the public is that sanctions generally do not 'work', especially as compared to the use of force. Biersteker et al. (2016b) point out that the driving force of this perception is the treatment of sanctions as an instrument to coerce behavioural change of the target. However, in their extensive study of SC targeted sanctions, the authors suggested that coercion of specific policy is not the sole goal of targeted sanctions. Some sanctions regimes are intended to constrain the target's ability to engage in certain activities (e.g. the financial sanctions against Al-Qaida to restrict their access to

---

[9] For information on the monitoring groups please visit SC official website https://www.un.org/sc/suborg/en/sanctions/information (accessed April 2, 2017).

resources), or to serve as a signal of the international community's discontent with the State's violation of an international norm (e.g. the prohibition of export of luxury goods to DPRK as a condemnation of their violation of the non-proliferation norm). Furthermore, to truly assess the effectiveness of the sanctions, the authors analysed each set of sanctions over a period of time. Their motivation for a deep examination was that the UN's goals and instruments, and the target's reaction change over time and cannot be evaluated in a single moment in time. Focusing on the entire sanctions regime and in a particular moment in time risks underestimating (or overestimating) its effectiveness (Biersteker et al. 2016b: 220–227).

The results of the comprehensive analysis by Biersteker et al. (2016b) demonstrated the following: (1) SC sanctions were effective only in 10% of the time when imposed as an instrument to change behaviour. For example, the halting of violence between the parties for the purpose of elections in 2005 and 2006 in Democratic Republic of Congo can be attributed to some extent to SC sanctions. (2) SC sanctions were more effective in constraining target's ability to engage in undesirable activities (in around 27% of cases). For instance, the SC managed to stabilise the situation in Sierra Leona following the departure of Charles Taylor partially by imposing financial sanctions on Taylor and other individuals who posed threat on the stability of the transitional government. (3) Finally, SC sanctions for the purpose of signalling were also found effective in about 27% of cases. In conclusion, SC sanctions were found to be effective in 22% of cases when combining the different goals together. An important finding of this study is that the level of effectiveness depends also on the area of intervention. Whereas SC sanctions were not effective in no-proliferation cases, they were very effective in terrorism cases (in about two third of the cases). Therefore, in order to truly understand effectiveness of sanctions, it is important to break down the analysis to different features of the targeted situations and the sanctions regimes (Biersteker et al. 2016b: 233–235).

It should be kept in mind that at times enforcement might fail due to states' lack of capacity to execute the prescribed sanctions (Chayes and Chayes 1993: 193), by e.g., not being able to enforce a travel ban against the target individuals. Moreover, inadequate design of the sanctions can occasionally explain their ineffectiveness. For example, the level of effectiveness of SC financial sanctions imposed on IS was limited inasmuch as this terrorist group was financially self-sustainable through control of oil reserves and criminal activities (e.g. Ryder 2016: 6–7).

18.6.2 Use of Force

The use of force is generally prohibited (Article 2(4) of the Charter). Two exceptions are provided in the UN Charter; collective use of force authorised by the SC under Chapter VII, and use of force for self-defence (Article 51 of the Charter).

Force ought to be used only as a last resort, in case other measures are inadequate to secure peace. Since the UN does not have its own military, States are required to make their forces available for the implementation of the enforcement actions (Arts.

43 and 45 of the Charter). Nevertheless, the agreements envisaged in Article 43 of the Charter to regulate such assistance were never concluded. This signalled the unwillingness of UN Member States to make the dispatchment of their military mandatory. Consequently, the UN does not have permanent military force that can enable urgent operations (Strydom and Juma 2016: 197–199).

Other aspects undermine the enforcement mechanism of the SC. First, the veto power might paralyze the SC and lead to inaction in cases where intervention is needed. For instance, this might be the case with the on-going civil war and violations of human rights and international humanitarian law in Syria. Repeated attempts to impose sanctions on Syria by the SC were blocked by the exercise of veto power by Russia and China.[10] However, the veto power was a necessary concession in the design of the SC in order to have the powerful countries, which are indispensable for an effective enforcement of international law, on board (Koremenos et al. 2001: 792).

Another problem that arises from the SC's exercise of its authority under Article 42 is the consequence of lack of precision. The SC often uses vague language when authorising the use of force. This creates grounds for States to abuse the authorisation and extend it beyond the original intention of the SC. For instance, in the case of Libya the purpose of SC Resolution 1973 (17 March 2011) was to solve the humanitarian crisis and to protect the civilian population. However, the vague authorisation "*to take all necessary measures*" led to 'mission creep'; namely, States used this authorisation to support rebel groups in removing Muammar Gaddafi and changing the Libyan regime (Breau 2016: 276).

Despite the limitations, the SC plays an important role in the enforcement of international peace through peacekeeping operations, often mandated under Chapter VII. Those operations are mainly aimed at controlling and resolving armed conflicts and are executed by the peacekeeping personnel. There are currently more than 80,000 troops and military personnel recruited from more than 124 countries. The core principles of the UN peacekeeping institution are the consent of the parties to intervene, impartiality, and no use of force except in self-defence or as specifically mandated. At present, there are 15 peacekeeping operations around the world led by the Department of Peacekeeping Operations. Those operations mainly concentrate in Africa and the Middle East.[11] From theoretical perspective, peacekeeping personnel are a good example of neutrality in the enforcement of international law. This institution enables States to support operations mitigating conflict without choosing sides. The neutrality derives from the fact that the troops are from countries

---

[10] See for instance, Russia and China veto UN resolution to impose sanctions on Syria (1 March 2017, The Guardian), available at https://www.theguardian.com/world/2017/mar/01/russia-and-china-veto-un-resolution-to-impose-sanctions-on-syria (accessed April 10, 2017). The mentioned draft resolution included sanctions short of force. However, it is clear that if economic and financial sanctions are vetoed, any suggestion to use force will be vetoed as well.

[11] For general information on the UN peacekeeping see, http://www.un.org/en/peacekeeping/ (accessed July 29, 2017). For the different SC resolutions authorizing peacekeeping operations see http://www.un.org/en/sc/repertoire/subsidiary_organs/peacekeeping_missions.shtml (accessed July 29, 2017).

that do not have stakes in the conflict, and their presence must be consensual. In addition, the operation is financed by the UN and not by particular States (Abbott and Snidal 1998: 21).

18.6.3   Theoretical Perspective on Enforcement of International Law by the SC

From the perspective of realist theory, the structure of the SC supports the claim that States merely promote their interests through those institutions and that international institutions do not play a role in changing behaviour. The veto power in the SC assures that sanctions under the UN Charter will never be imposed on the P5. Furthermore, those States can protect their interests by vetoing measures against their allies. Inconsistency in the SC's decisions suggests that the SC is promoting national interests rather than enforcing international legal norms (Hehir 2013: 137–138). For example, States' interests could potentially explain the difference of Russia's voting practice in the SC in response to the humanitarian crisis in Libya (2011) as compared to the gross violations of human rights in Syria. Russia is the main exporter of arms to Syria, constituting 10% of its total arms export. This is an especially important factor in light of the financial hardship caused to Russia by the sanctions against them in recent years (Gifkins 2012: 391). In the case of Libya, the strong support expressed by the African Union and the League of Arab States for SC sanctions (Hehir 2013: 153) could increase Russia's political costs of vetoing the SC resolution 1973 (which approved the use of force in Libya).

Moreover, the SC heavily depends on States to execute their measures, thus subjecting the enforcement of international law entirely to States' will. This structural design of the SC provides support for the realists' claim that the success of international organisations depends on the question whether they serve the interests of the States. The examples of unilateral use of force without the approval of the SC, the 2003 Iraq war, the 1999 NATO air campaign in Kosovo (Mcglinchey 2015: 53–54), and the recent U.S. missile attack on the Syrian military base as a response to chemical attack on civilians,[12] illustrate this point.[13]

From the perspective of liberalism, international institutions are not perfect but they are preferable to the anarchy state before their creation. International institutions balance the power differences between States through information exchange, and in turn, reduce uncertainty (Keohane 1992). Furthermore, the large resources that were invested in negotiating and designing the SC as a representative international institution to solve cooperation problems and enforce peace and security cannot be

---

[12] "Syria war: US launches missile strikes in response to 'chemical attack'" (BBC News, April 7, 2017), http://www.bbc.com/news/world-us-canada-39523654 (accessed April 16, 2017).

[13] The three mentioned events have different levels of justification, which are not discussed in this chapter. Those examples are only presented as situations where the formal procedure of the UN Charter for the use of force was not followed.

explained if states had no intention for it to affect international outcomes (Koremenos et al. 2001: 762). Institutionalists also view the SC as a 'strategic information transmission' device to reduce political costs of military actions. The SC constrains States' use of force by signalling to others whether those States' coercive actions are desirable or not. SC is viewed as a neutral body partially due to its voting structure. To approve any use of sanctions or force, a majority of the SC must favour it (nine out of 15 members) and no permanent member should veto it. The heterogeneity of States in the SC increases its credibility as an information provider. Therefore, actions that are approved by the SC are viewed as legitimate, and in turn reduce uncertainty and the sense of threat caused by the 'aggressor'. The fact nowadays there are almost no military interventions without first seeking the approval of the SC,[14] indicates its institutional significance (Thompson 2006: 1–4, 8–10, 2009a: 317–318). For example, if the SC as an international enforcement institution did not matter, it is not clear why so many attempts were made by some States to draft resolutions and seek the approval of the SC for imposing sanctions on Syria in the past few years, instead of pursuing a unilateral intervention.[15]

Constructivists emphasize shared international norms and their importance in shaping behaviour. The SC might be reflecting internalised norms by legitimising or delegitimising some actions of enforcement. For instance, the unilateral invasion of the U.S. to Iraq in 2003 without the approval of the SC was against the 'norm' of international relations at the time. Even though there were no formal sanctions imposed, it did not go without consequences as can be seen from the hurdles the U.S. faced in its international relations and the political costs incurred following the invasion (Thompson 2009b: 195–203). Nevertheless, unilateral actions can also express emerging norms. For example, the NATO operation in Kosovo in 1999 might have signified an emerging norm of humanitarian intervention. Despite the heavy criticism it faced, it triggered the development of States' Responsibility to Protect[16] (Breau 2016: 15–29).

18.7   International Criminal Court

The ICC, which was established in 1998 and entered into force in 2002, is the first permanent court for judging the most serious international crimes – genocide, crimes against humanity, war crimes, and crimes of aggression (preamble and

---

[14] This is not to say that States do not act unilaterally. The argument only stresses the fact that in most cases, prior to taking actions unilaterally, States seek SC's approval to reduce political costs. Political costs refer to condemnation (and other active negative responses) by other States.

[15] For all resolutions on Syria see http://www.securitycouncilreport.org/un-documents/search.php? IncludeBlogs=10&limit=15&tag=%22Security%20Council%20Resolutions%22+AND+%22Syria%22&ctype=Syria&rtype=Security%20Council%20Resolutions&cbtype=syria, and for the drafts that were vetoed see, http://research.un.org/en/docs/sc/quick (accessed July 30, 2017).

[16] This concept and its development are discussed in Chap. 18.

Article 5 of the Rome Statute). It is a product of a long development of international criminal law. Traditionally, international law concerns obligations and rights of States, and criminal law imposes restrictions on individuals who can be punished by a State. The Nuremberg and Tokyo trials constituted therefore, an important turning point for international criminal law. In 1945, the four victorious Allies (United Kingdom, France, United States and the Soviet Union) created the International Military Tribunal to try Nazis for crimes against peace, war crimes and crimes against humanity. In the same period, the Allies also established the International Military Tribunal for the Far East that prosecuted Japanese war criminals for similar crimes (Schabas 2011: 3–9).

In the aftermath of the trials, the UN created the International Law Commission (ILC) to prepare for the establishment of a permanent and impartial judicial body for prosecuting international crimes. However, due to the Cold War there was stagnation in the process of forming international criminal court. Thus, the ILC resumed its work only during the 1990s. In addition, during this period the two ad hoc tribunals – ICTY and ICTR – were created by the SC to address the atrocities committed in Former Yugoslavia and in Rwanda. Those events set the ground for the establishment of the ICC (Cassese 2002: 9–16).

The Rome Statute of the International Criminal Court was negotiated and eventually adopted in the Diplomatic Conference in Rome in July 1998. It is not a UN organ but a newly established international institution to which the States delegated judicial authority. Currently there are 124 States parties to the Rome Statute.[17] However, the definition of the crime of aggression was adopted only during the Review Conference of the Rome Statute of the International Criminal Court in Kampala in 2010. This crime, contrary to the other international crimes under the jurisdiction of the ICC, was not criminalised before (against individuals). Furthermore, it touches upon a question that is under the authority of the SC – determination of the occurrence of act of aggression. Therefore, it was dealt with separately and places special restrictions on the Court's jurisdiction (Ambos 2013: 184–190). At the time of writing, 32 States had ratified the crime of aggression.[18]

The ICC has a limited jurisdiction. The Court may try a case only if the State where the crime was committed or the State of the accused (by nationality) is a State Party to the Rome Statute. In addition, any non-party State can accept the Court's jurisdiction with respect to the crime in question (Article 12 of the Rome Statue). As a general matter, the ICC has a complementary jurisdiction. Namely, prosecution of international crimes is a domestic matter. Only if a State is not willing or unable to investigate such crimes, will the ICC intervene. In addition, due to scarce resources of the ICC, situations need to meet a certain threshold of gravity in order to be adjudicated by the ICC (Article 17 of the Rome Statue).

---

[17] See the official website of the ICC: https://asp.icc-cpi.int/en_menus/asp/states%20parties/Pages/the%20states%20parties%20to%20the%20rome%20statute.aspx (accessed April 11, 2017).

[18] See the official website of the ICC https://asp.icc-cpi.int/en_menus/asp/RomeStatute/Pages/default.aspx (accessed April 11, 2017).

There are several ways to trigger jurisdiction of the ICC (Article 13 of the Rome Statute). The first is referral by a State Party. Even though having a broader meaning, in practice this became a self-referral mechanism. The first case that was referred to the ICC was by the Government of Uganda in 2003 following an on-going internal armed conflict. Other referrals followed. The second possibility to trigger jurisdiction is through SC referral when acting under Chapter VII of the Charter (also non-States Parties). In 2005, the SC exercised its right and referred the case of Darfur to the ICC. Following the referral, the acting president of Sudan, Omar Al Bashir, was charged with multiple counts of genocide, crimes against humanity and war crimes (ICC-02/05–01/09). However, an arrest warrant that was issued against him is still pending.[19] The SC has also an authority to request the ICC to temporary defer a case (Article 16 of the Rome Statue). Finally, jurisdiction of the Court may be triggered by the prosecutor (*proprio moto* authority). This power was exercised for the first time in 2009 following the on-going violence in Kenya (Schabas 2011: 159–186).

An important question in the context of ICC's work is the enforcement mechanism of the Court's rulings. As have been stressed before, the international community does not have a centralised body to execute enforcement decisions. Therefore, the ICC depends on the cooperation of States, especially for arresting individuals that were indicted and are staying on their territories (Article 89 of the Rome Statute), and for executing the imprisonment sentences (Article 103 of the Rome Statute). With respect to the former, which is mandatory for States Parties, experience demonstrates that not all States Parties perform their obligations under the Rome Statute, and SC does not always exercise its authority to impose cooperation obligations on non-States Parties. For instance, the president of Sudan, Al-Bashir, was traveling freely in different countries around the world, as an ICC arrest warrant against him is pending (Kreß and Prost 2016: 2037). Regarding the latter – execution of imprisonment sentences – cooperation is voluntary for States. Only States that agree to place a convicted international criminal under their custody are obliged to do so (Strijards and Harmsen 2016: 2176).

Given the structure of the ICC, a question arises to which extent it contributes to the enforcement of international law. A recent study attempted to answer this question and concluded that effectiveness of the ICC is conditional. On the one hand, the broad jurisdiction of the ICC increases the risk of prosecution as compared to a world of immunities. On the other hand, the actual probability of being prosecuted and punished is low (partially due to lack of cooperation from States), thus reducing the general deterrence effect. Therefore, the authors assert that the ICC can mainly deter actors who are concerned with the national and international opinions about their legitimacy (Jo and Simmons 2016: 460–470).

From a theoretical perspective, the significance of the ICC depends on the given IR theory. Realists would suggest that the ICC, similarly to other international institutions, has limited (or no) effect on States' and individuals' behaviour. One indication might be the relationship between the powerful States and the ICC. As

---

[19] https://www.icc-cpi.int/darfur/albashir/Documents/albashirEng.pdf (accessed April 11, 2017).

explained before, from realist's perspective States will delegate authority to an international institution only if it reflects the balance of powers. The ICC by design is meant to be independent from the UN and gives only limited powers to the SC to constrain its jurisdiction. Furthermore, none of the States have a special stand in its decisions, unlike the voting structure in the SC. In light of this institutional design, and congruent with the realist approach, none of the three world's major powers (U.S., Russia and China) ratified the Rome Statue.[20] This implies that the ICC has only a limited jurisdiction over their nationals. The U.S. took further steps to limit the Court's jurisdiction with respect to American nationals by enacting the American Service Members Protection Act 2002, which restricted the cooperation with ICC (e.g. authorising use of force to 'liberate' American nationals held by the ICC). Additionally, the U.S. pursued bilateral agreements in which countries pledge not to surrender each other's nationals to the ICC (Van Schaack and Slye 2015: 171–173). Russia on the other hand, recently withdrew its signature from the Rome Statute following the Court's report that the Russian annexation of Crema is an occupation.[21] Finally, in recent years, the ICC is under heavy criticism of targeting African countries, while leaving the powerful States and their allies untouched. This move led some countries to pronounce their intention to withdraw from the Court's jurisdiction.[22]

Institutionalist approach on the other hand, would suggest that the ICC is a product of a careful and rational design by States. According to the conjectures of rational design paradigm, States will centralise enforcement through international institutions when the enforcement problem is more acute (strong individual incentives to deviate from a collectively efficient cooperation). However, even then the decision to delegate the enforcement authority is restricted by 'sovereignty costs' (Abbott and Snidal 2000: 437–440). Therefore, from a rational choice perspective the ICC might have been designed to solve the cooperation problem of prosecuting international criminals in national courts. Prosecution of international crimes contributes to international security and stability. On the other hand, without a centralised authority, only the prosecuting States bear the costs (which are significant). Given States' scarce resources, States will prefer to free-ride on the efforts of others to eradicate atrocities. Therefore, the public good of prosecuting and deterring international crimes is undersupplied. Creation of an international permanent court can overcome this problem (Abbott 1999: 373–374). The sovereignty costs, on the other hand, can explain the ratification record and the

---

[20] There is a difference between signature and ratification of an international agreement in general and the Rome Statute in particular. Representatives of States signed the Rome Statute at the Diplomatic Conference. However, ratification was required to make the Statute binding on the State.

[21] Russia Withdraws Signature from International Criminal Court Statute (November 16, 2016, The Guardian), https://www.theguardian.com/world/2016/nov/16/russia-withdraws-signature-from-international-criminal-court-statute (accessed August 1, 2017).

[22] South Africa to quit international criminal court (October 21, 2016, The Guardian), https://www.theguardian.com/world/2016/oct/21/south-africa-to-quit-international-criminal-court-document-shows (accessed August 1, 2017).

restrictions placed on ICC's jurisdiction. Sovereignty costs are especially high in the context of the ICC forasmuch as its jurisdiction often intervenes in the relationship of States with its citizens. The high sovereignty costs can potentially explain why the most powerful States did not ratify the Rome Statute. In fact, the extent of control of the SC over the ICC was a major issue in the Rome Statute negotiations, with the P5 insisting on more control (Fehl 2004: 375–376).

From the perspective of constructivism, the interesting question is how did the norm that shaped State's preferences to establish an international criminal court develop? One argument is that the proliferation of human rights norms in the years preceding the ICC's establishment led to this choice. In this period, a large number of countries ratified the different Conventions on human rights (e.g. UN Covenant on Civil and Political rights). Those conventions are not merely formal rules but they shaped the identity of the States, which in turn internalised the human rights norms. The universality of acceptance of human rights made gross violations of it a collective problem (Risse and Ropp 2013: 8–10; Fehl 2004: 371–372). An additional argument can be that states established a permanent international criminal court because it is more appropriate and legitimate than UN-established *ad hoc* tribunals, which are perceived by some as the 'victor's justice' (Fehl 2004: 374–375).

18.8   Conclusion

In recent decades there is a move to a stronger international community with more delegation to international institutions and tribunals and an increased demand for international enforcement through collective actions (Hurrell 2006: 4). The international enforcement institutions discussed in this chapter are complementary in the task of securing global peace and order and mitigating the enforcement problems discussed through the chapter. The ICJ provides States with a forum to resolve their disputes in a peaceful manner without resorting to coercive mechanisms. Even though it is voluntary by nature, the ICJ allows addressing belligerent situations prior to their escalation. When such methods are not chosen, and a situation emerges that threatens international peace and security, the SC is endowed with the authority to impose measures. SC sanctions can take different forms, thus enabling it to remain flexible in addressing various problems. The use of force constitutes another enforcement measure in the arsenal of the SC to restore global peace. Finally, the ICC complements those institutions by criminalising grave actions of violence on the international level and placing individuals under the jurisdiction of a centralised justice system.

In the last two decades there are also new emerging powers. For example, the BRICS (Brazil, Russia, India, China and South Africa). Some commentators claim that the main common dominator of this group is their anti-Western approach. For example, whereas the Western countries sanctioned Russia for annexing Crimea, none of the BRICS countries condemned Russia's behaviour. In fact, China and

South Africa condemned the West for imposing sanctions on Russia in violation of international law (Stuenkel 2015: ix–x, 148–154). The increasing significance of these States is important when thinking about changing global order. From a theoretical perspective changes often come from States that have the capacity and political power to demand revisions of the established international order in a way that will reflect their own norms and interests (Hurrell 2006: 2–4).

In terms of enforcement of international law, the emerging powers are less supportive of the use of force and interventions in States' sovereignty as compared to the Western-led global order. In addition, the BRICS are discontent with the fact that the international institutions are not reflecting the distribution of powers. Brazil and India for instance, wish to become permanent members in the SC. BRICS' increasing power and the role they play in the main international enforcement institution (China and Russia as current members of the P5) might weaken the enforcement of international law (Stuenkel 2015: 125–127, 154–156).

The on-going civil war in Syria and the international reaction to it is a case in point. Since the start of the civil war, the Western countries are strongly promoting international interventions through SC drafts to condemn and impose sanctions on the Syrian government. Russia and China on the other hand, largely oppose such interventions in spite of the deteriorating humanitarian situation in Syria. In the early stage of the conflict, all BRICS States were in the SC and have voted on the first draft resolution related to the human rights violations in Syria (S/2011/612, October 4, 2011). This resolution was rejected due to the veto by Russia and China. Brazil, India and South Africa abstained (6627th SC meeting, S/PV.6627, October 4, 2011). Since then the SC is in a continuous deadlock as the last eight attempts to impose measures on Syria were vetoed by Russia and China (or Russia alone).[23] In addition, the ICC does not have jurisdiction unless the SC uses its power to refer the situation to the Court. An attempt to do so was blocked in the SC by Russia and China who invoked their veto power.[24] Following this deadlock, the U.S. recently launched a unilateral missile attack against the Syrian regime destroying its air base as a reaction to the use of chemical weapons against civilians.[25] In light of such events, it remains to be seen whether the international enforcement institutions as we know them today will be weakened.

---

[23] See, https://www.un.org/press/en/2017/sc12791.doc.htm; http://research.un.org/en/docs/sc/quick (accessed April 16, 2017).

[24] See http://www.un.org/apps/news/story.asp?NewsID=47860#.WPNunxSZzjA (accessed April 16, 2017).

[25] See, "Syria war: US launches missile strikes in response to 'chemical attack'" (April 7, 2017, BBC News), http://www.bbc.com/news/world-us-canada-39523654 (accessed April 16, 2017).

Further Readings

Bull, H. (1971, September). Order vs. justice in international society. *Political Studies, 19*(3), 269–283.

Gaddis, J. L. (1986, Spring). The long peace: Elements of stability in the postwar international system. *International Security, 10*(4), 99–142, MIT Press.

Ratner, S. (1998). International law: The trials of global norms. *Foreign Policy, 110*, 65–80.

Schweller, R. (1993, March). Tripolarity and the Second World War, *International Studies Quarterly, 37*(1), 73–103.

Schweller, R. (1994, Summer). Revisionist state. *International Security, 19*(1), 72–107, MIT Press.

Waltz, K. (1959). Man, the state, and war: A theoretical analysis. *Political Science Quarterly, 75*(3), 75–90.

Waltz, K. (1979). The consequences of anarchy: The anarchic Structure of World Politics. In *Theory of international politics*. New York: Free Press.

Waltz, K. (2000). Structural realism after the Cold War. *International Security, 25*, 5–41.

Wendt, A. (1992, Spring). Anarchy is what states make of it. *International Organization, 46*(2), 391–425.

References

Abbott, K. W. (1999). International relations theory, international law, and the regime governing atrocities in internal conflicts. *American Journal of International Law, 93*(2), 361–379.

Abbott, K. W., & Snidal, D. (1998). Why states act through formal international organizations. *Journal of Conflict Resolution, 42*(1), 3–32.

Abbott, K. W., & Snidal, D. (2000). Hard and soft law in international governance. International Organization, 54(3), 421–156.

Alter, K. J. (2008). Agents or trustees? International courts in their political context. *European Journal of International Relations, 14*(1), 33–63.

Ambos, K. (2013). *Treatise on international criminal law. Volume 1: Foundations and general part*. Oxford: Oxford University Press.

Anthony Aust, A. (2005). *Handbook of international law*. Cambridge: Cambridge University Press.

Biersteker, T. J., Marcos, T., & Eckert, S. E. (2016a). Thinking about United Nations Targeted Sanctions. In T. J. Biersteker, S. E. Eckert, & M. Tourinho (Eds.), *Targeted sanctions: The impacts and effectiveness of United Nations Action* (pp. 11–37). Cambridge: Cambridge University Press.

Biersteker, T. J., Marcos, T., & Eckert, S. E. (2016b). The effectiveness of United Nations Targeted Sanctions. In T. J. Biersteker, S. E. Eckert, & M. Tourinho (Eds.), *Targeted sanctions: The impacts and effectiveness of United Nations Action* (pp. 220–247). Cambridge: Cambridge University Press.

Breau, S. (2016). *The responsibility to protect in international law: An emerging paradigm shift*. London and New York: Routledge.

Brownlie, I. (2008). *Principle of public international law*. Oxford: Oxford University Press.

Cassese, A. (2002). From Nuremberg to Rome: International military tribunals to the international criminal court. In A. Cassesse (Ed.), *The Rome statute of the international criminal court* (Vol. 1, pp. 3–19). Oxford: Oxford University Press.

Chayes, A., & Chayes, A. H. (1993). On compliance. *International Organization, 47*(2), 175–205.

Delahunty, R. J., & Yoo, J. (2006). Executive power vs. international law. *Harvard Journal of Law & Public Policy, 30*(1), 73–113.

Downs, G. W. (1998). Enforcement and the evolution of cooperation. *Michigan Journal of International Law, 19*(2), 319–244.

Doxey, M. P. (1980). *Economic sanctions and international enforcement*. London: Palgrave Macmillan UK.

Farrall, J. M. (2007). *United Nations Sanctions and the rule of law*. Cambridge: Cambridge University Press.

Fehl, C. (2004). Explaining the international criminal court: A 'practice test' for rationalist and constructivist approaches. *European Journal of International Relations, 10*(3), 357–394.

Gifkins, J. (2012). The UN security council divided: Syria in crisis. *Global Responsibility to Protect, 4*(3), 377–393.

Hawkins, D. G., Lake David, A., Nielson Daniel, L., & Eds, T. M. J. (2006). *Delegation under anarchy: States, international organizations, and principal-agent theory*. Cambridge: Cambridge University Press.

Henkin, L. (1979). *How nations behave* (2nd ed.). New York: Columbia University Press.

Hurrell, A. (2006). Hegemony, liberalism and global order: What space for would-be great powers. *International Affairs, 82*(1), 1–19.

Hehir, A. (2013). The permanence of inconsistency: Libya, the security council, and the responsibility to protect. International Security, 38(1), 137–159.

Jo, H., & Simmons, B. A. (2016). Can the international criminal court deter atrocity? *International Organization, 70*, 443–475.

Keohane, R. O. (1984). *After hegemony: Cooperation and discord in the world political economy*. Princeton: Princeton University Press.

Keohane, R. O. (1988). International institutions: Two approaches. *International Studies Quarterly, 32*(4), 379–396.

Keohane, R. O. (1992). *Institutional theory and the realist challenge after the Cold War*. Cambridge, MA: Center for International Affairs, Harvard University.

Kindleberger, C. P. (1986). International public goods without international government. *American Economic Review, 76*(1), 1–13.

Koremenos, B. (2016). *The continent of international law: Explaining agreement design*. Cambridge: Cambridge University Press.

Koremenos, B., Lipson, C., & Snidal, D. (2001). The rational design of international institutions. *International Organization, 55*(4), 761–799.

Kolb, R. (2013). *The international court of justice*. Oxford: Hart Publishing.

Kreß, C., & Prost, K. (2016). International cooperation and judicial assistance. In O. Triffterer & K. Ambos (Eds.), *The Rome Statute of the International Criminal Court: A commentary* (3rd ed., pp. 2003–2013). Oxford: Beck/Hart.

Llamzon, A. P. (2007). Jurisdiction and compliance in recent decisions of the international court of justice. *European Journal of International Law, 18*(5), 815–852.

Mitchell McLaughlin, S., & Powell, E. J. (2011). *Domestic law goes global: Legal traditions and international courts*. Cambridge: Cambridge University Press.

Moravcsik, A. (2010). The new liberalism. In C. Reus-Smit & D. Snidal (Eds.), *The Oxford handbook of international relations* (pp. 234–254). Oxford: Oxford University Press.

Morgenthau, H. J. (1985). *Politics among nations: The struggle for power and peace* (6th ed.). Beijing: Perkin University Press (Revised by K. W. Thompson).

Mcglinchey, S. (2015). International relations. In S. Mcglinchey (Ed.), *International relations* (pp. 46–70). Bristol: E-International Relations Publishing.

Oppenheim, L. (1992). In S. R. Jennings & S. A. Watts (Eds.), *Oppenheim's international law. Volume 1* (9th ed.). Harlow: Longman.

Paulson, C. (2004). Compliance with final judgments of the international court of justice since 1987. *American Journal of International Law, 98*(3), 434–461.

Posner, E. A., & de Figueiredo, M. F. P. (2005). Is the international court of justice biased? *The Journal of Legal Studies, 34*(2), 599–630.

Risse, T., & Ropp, S. C. (2013). Introduction and overview. In T. Risse, S. C. Ropp, & K. Sikkink (Eds.), *The persistent power of human rights: From commitment to compliance* (pp. 3–25). Cambridge: Cambridge University Press.

Ryder, N. (2016). Out with the old and…in with the old? A critical review of the financial war on terrorism on the Islamic state of Iraq and Levant. *Studies in Conflict & Terrorism*, 1–17.

Schabas, W. A. (2011). *An introduction to the International Criminal Court* (4th ed.). Cambridge: Cambridge University Press.

Slaughter, A.-M. (2011). International relations, principal theories. In R. Wolfrum (Ed.), *Max Planck encyclopedia of public international law*. Oxford University Press. Published at www. mpepil.com

Stein, A. A. (2010). Neoliberal institutionalism. In C. Reus-Smit & D. Snidal (Eds.), *The Oxford handbook of international relations* (pp. 201–221). Oxford: Oxford University Press.

Strijards, G. A. M., & Harmsen, R. O. (2016). Enforcement. In O. Triffterer & K. Ambos (Eds.), *The Rome Statute of the International Criminal Court: A commentary* (3rd ed., pp. 2173–2186). Oxford: Beck/Hart.

Strydom, H., & Juma, L. (2016). Maintaining international peace and security: The enforcement of international law. In H. Strydom (Ed.), *International law*. Oxford: Oxford University Press.

Stuenkel, O. (2015). *The BRICS and the future of global order*. London: Lexington Books.

Thompson, A. (2006). Coercion through IOs: The security council and the logic of information transmission. *International Organization, 60*, 1–34.

Thompson, A. (2009a). The rational enforcement of international law: Solving the Sanctioners' dilemma. *International Theory, 1*(2), 307–321.

Thompson, A. (2009b). *Channels of power: The UN Security Council and U.S. Statecraft in Iraq*. Ithaca: Cornell University Press.

Van Schaack, B., & Slye, R. C. (2015). *International criminal law and its enforcement: Cases and materials* (3rd ed.). Saint Paul: Foundation Press.

Wendt, A. (1999). *Social theory of international politics*. Cambridge: Cambridge University Press.

Wendt, A. (2001). Driving with the rearview Mirror: On the rational science of institutional design. *International Organization, 55*(4), 1019–1049.

Chapter 19
The International Norm Dynamics of Responsibility to Protect

Jérémie Speiser

19.1 Introduction

The responsibility to protect (R2P) is a United Nations principle enshrined in the 2005 World Summit Outcome Document. According to paragraph 138 of the latter text, 'each individual state has the responsibility to protect its population from genocide, war crimes, ethnic cleansing and crimes against humanity'. Paragraph 139 further adds that 'the international community, through the United Nations, also has the responsibility to use appropriate diplomatic, humanitarian and other peaceful means' to protect civilian populations from the aforementioned crimes. Paragraph 139 continues by stating that the international community is 'prepared to take collective action, in a timely and decisive manner, through the Security Council, in accordance with the Charter, including Chapter VII, on a case-by-case basis and in cooperation with relevant regional organizations as appropriate, should peaceful means be inadequate and national authorities manifestly fail to protect their populations from genocide, war crimes, ethnic cleansing and crimes against humanity'. After engaging in theoretical considerations, this chapter contributes to assessing the extent to which R2P has become a norm in global politics by firstly delving itself into the narrative accompanying the emergence of R2P before analyzing the discourse held by the permanent members of the Security Council in General Assembly debates concerning R2P since 2009.

This chapter assesses R2P's stage of normative progress through the constructivist theoretical framework of the norm 'life-cycle'. Developed by Finnemore and Sikkink (1998), this framework comprehensively integrates inter-subjective features in a manner distinguishing three particular stages of norm dynamics in international relations, which are norm emergence, norm cascade, and internalization.

J. Speiser (✉)
Independent researcher, Strasbourg, France
e-mail: jeremiespeiser@hotmail.com

© Springer Nature Switzerland AG 2020   385
M. O. Hosli, J. Selleslaghs (eds.), *The Changing Global Order*, United Nations
University Series on Regionalism 17,
https://doi.org/10.1007/978-3-030-21603-0_19

Accordingly, this theoretical framework offers the tools to measure to what extent R2P is a norm 'that set standard for the appropriate behavior of states' (Finnemore and Sikkink 1998: 891). This leads us to the following research questions. What is the current stage reached by R2P on Finnemore and Sikkink's scale of international norm dynamics? Why has it reached this particular stage?

For the sake of consistency, Finnemore and Sikkink's (1998: 891) definition of norms as 'a standard of appropriate behavior for actors with a given identity' is used throughout this chapter. According to the authors of 'International Norm Dynamics and Political Change', norms are particularly relevant in world politics because they have a systematic impact on behavior. For this reason, Finnemore and Sikkink (1998: 894) argue that 'idea shifts and norm shifts are the main vehicle for system transformation'. To go further in their analysis of how norms influence behavior and may find themselves in the position of being a driver of political change, the authors coined the concept of the norm 'life cycle' (Finnemore and Sikkink 1998: 895). Accordingly, the three successive stages of a norm's potential life cycle are firstly 'norm emergence', then 'norm cascade' and finally, 'internalization' (Finnemore and Sikkink 1998: 898). Acharya (2014: 405) concurs by arguing that the creation of a particular norm does involve multitudes of actors and is impacted by the issues and context around which it arises.

According to Finnemore and Sikkink (1998: 896), norms are promoted by so called 'norm entrepreneurs' who develop strong notions of what constitutes appropriate behavior in international politics. Norm entrepreneurs are essential in the stage of norm emergence because they raise awareness around issues and frame an international debate around them. The goal of norm entrepreneurs is 'to secure the support of state actors to endorse their norms and make norm socialization a part of their agenda (Finnemore and Sikkink 1998: 900). Framing has been defined by Keck and Sikkink (1999: 90) as to 'mobilize information strategically to help create new issues and categories, and to persuade, pressurize, and gain leverage over much more powerful organizations and governments'. Norm entrepreneurs are usually associated with individuals but they can also take the shape of non-governmental organizations (NGOs) or transnational advocacy networks. Keck and Sikkink (1999: 91) argue that transnational advocacy networks frame to raise awareness among selected publics, urge governments and other stakeholders to act, and press for institutionalization.

The fluctuating nature of norm diffusion implies that following their emergence, norms can break through in order to obtain the adherence of a wider amount of states. The tipping point between the stages of norm emergence and norm cascade happens when norm entrepreneurs have convinced a sufficient amount of states to support and adopt their norm. The theoretical framework suggests that a tipping point is reached when approximately one third of states in the international system adopt the norm (Finnemore and Sikkink 1998: 901). After the tipping point has been attained and the stage of norm cascade begun, Finnemore and Sikkink (1998: 902) argue that more states start adopting the norm at a higher pace due to an 'active process of international socialization intended to induce norm breakers into norm followers'. At the second stage of the norm life cycle, this socialization mechanism is comparable to a system of peer-pressure where norm entrepreneurs use appropriate organizational platforms in order to pressure targeted states to adopt the norm through the application of new laws and policies or treaty ratification. Finnemore and Sikkink (1998: 902) also recognize that during the stage of norm cascade, norm adoption becomes part of an identification process that states use to be perceived as part of an international society. The last stage of the norm life cycle is when actors have internalized the norm until the point where they consider the norm as taken for granted and conform to it in automatic fashion (Finnemore and Sikkink 1998: 904).

19.1.1 The Emergence of the Responsibility to Protect

The substance of the R2P principle can be declined in three main pillars. First, there is recognition of the responsibility of the state to protect its own civilian population from mass atrocities. Second, the international community indicates its formal commitment to help states in meeting these obligations. Third, the declaration endorses the international community to provide a timely and decisive reaction when a state fails to protect its citizens. The adoption of the R2P principle is the result of a succession of debates that took place in the wake of humanitarian catastrophes in the 1990s such as Somalia, Rwanda, Bosnia-Herzegovina and Kosovo. Several new concepts were brought to the table by high-profile politicians in order to propose to the international community new policies to protect civilians from mass atrocities. Notably, United Nations Secretary General Kofi Annan suggested the idea that individual sovereignty – a form of individual right to self-determination – existed alongside the conventional concept of state sovereignty stemming from the 1648 Peace of Westphalia (Evans 2008: 37). Francis Deng, former United Nations Secretary General representative on Internally Displaced Persons, attempted to pioneer a new model of humanitarian intervention which would not place state sovereignty at odds with the responsibility of states to guarantee their population a primary set of human rights. Francis Deng proposed to merge the principles of state sovereignty and the responsibility of states towards their population into the wider concept of R2P. As the title of his book, *Sovereignty as Responsibility* (Deng et al. 1996: 32–3) aptly suggests, state sovereignty and R2P are two sides of the same coin. Francis Deng's idea was further examined, debated, and elaborated with the contribution brought by the International Commission on Intervention and State Sovereignty (ICISS) and Kofi Annan's establishment of the High-Level Panel on Threats, Challenges and Change.

Subsequently, R2P's endorsement by the High-Level Panel on Threats, Challenges, and Change and the publication of the Panel's report *A More Secure World: Our Shared Responsibility* in late 2004 created an important momentum for the norm's progress towards norm emergence. In March 2005, Kofi Annan released an additional report titled *In Larger Freedom: Towards Development, Security and Human Rights for All*. In this way the report encouraged heads of states to 'embrace the responsibility to protect' (Annan 2005: 59). Kofi Annan's call for states to endorse R2P was heard and they would adopt R2P as an official

UN principle following the negotiations leading up to the 2005 UN World Summit. Therefore, the reasons why it can be considered that R2P has reached the stage of norm emergence are threefold. Firstly, norm entrepreneurs such as Francis Deng and Kofi Annan used their work and notoriety to mobilize the international community around the issue and persuade states that further discussion was needed around the topic of state sovereignty and humanitarian intervention. Secondly, these norm entrepreneurs have promoted R2P with altruistic motives, as they called states for action to prevent civilians from atrocities similar to the ones encountered in Somalia, Rwanda, and Bosnia during the 1990s. Last but not least, the 2001 ICISS and the 2004 High-Level Panel provided the organizational platform for R2P to emerge as a norm in international politics as it encouraged states to frame the issue around the concept of 'sovereignty as responsibility' and refer to the abovementioned reports as references for further negotiation with other state counterparts on the issue.

The critical observation to make in the event of R2P's adoption as a UN principle is that states unanimously agreed on its inclusion within the final document of the World Summit. Using the terminology of Finnemore and Sikkink (1998), one can consider that this uncontested rate of approval convincingly fulfils the threshold for it to be considered that a critical mass of states supported R2P's institutionalization, hence representing a tipping point leading R2P from the stage of norm emergence to the stage of norm cascade. In the aftermath of the 2005 World Summit, R2P encountered further favorable events that legitimated the norm's rise within the United Nations system. In this way, the Security Council reaffirmed its commitment towards R2P in resolutions 1674 and 1894, voted respectively in 2006 and 2009. Finally, the appointment of Ban Ki-Moon as Secretary General confirmed the trend of widespread support for R2P that was found within the United Nations secretariat and did not decrease as Kofi Annan's mandate expired. In this way, the publication of a report titled *Implementing the Responsibility to Protect* by Ban Ki-Moon clarified some aspects related to the manner in which R2P is to be put into practice by dividing it into three distinct pillars. Pillar one's focus is on the primary responsibility of the state to protect its civilian population (Ban 2009: 10). Pillar two emphasized the necessity to develop preventive efforts along with regional organizations, as well as improve international assistance and capacity-building mechanisms along the lines of early-warning systems (Ban 2009: 15). Pillar three focuses on the international community's timely and decisive response to R2P crimes (Ban 2009: 22). Ban Ki-Moon's report confirmed R2P's institutionalization was by then deeply rooted within the United Nations system. Finally, this report urged the General Assembly to further discuss the conditions that would surround R2P's implementation within the General Assembly (Ban 2009: 29). The Secretary General's recommendation that discussions about R2P's implementation should be reopened at the highest level represented a particularly decisive test for R2P, determining whether its normative rise was supported by UN member states.

19.1.2   Libya and the Contestation of R2P Amongst the Permanent Members of the Security Council

Since the emergence of R2P in global politics, humanitarian intervention on the grounds of this principle has been only authorized in the case of NATO's Operation Unified Protector in Libya in 2011. Importantly, this event constitutes the first time the use of force has been authorized by the Security Council by invoking R2P. In this regard, it is interesting to observe whether the demonstration of R2P implementation in Libya altered the norm's internalization prospects. The respective positions of the five permanent members of the Security Council, being the United Kingdom, France, the United States, Russia, and China, concerning R2P from 2009 until 2014 are examined below. Examining the position of the latter states is crucial in assessing the advancement of R2P as a norm not only because these are leading countries in world politics with considerable influence on the global normative debate, but also because of the role of permanent members of the Security Council in authorizing the use of force. Since only permanent members of this institution have the right to veto resolutions authorizing the use of force against other states, including in operations conducted within the framework of R2P, the Security Council's position on the R2P concept is determinant for R2P's normative advancement. The timeframe of the subsequent analysis takes place between 2009 and the start of the General Assembly Dialogue on R2P and 2014, when the last Security Council Resolution mentioning R2P in relation to the Syrian conflict was vetoed.

19.1.3   The United Kingdom

In the framework of the 2009 General Assembly Dialogue on R2P, the United Kingdom demonstrated support for making R2P an operational principle. After having welcomed Ban Ki-Moon's report *Implementing the responsibility to protect* published earlier in 2009, the United Kingdom's final remarks at the Dialogue were unequivocally supportive of the concept:

> I will conclude by saying a little about what I think we should be trying to achieve here, that is an R2P-culture, a culture of prevention that is as much about responsible sovereignty as it is international assistance. A culture that in the long-term will help us to prevent mass atrocities and reduce conflict and the cost of conflict. A culture that will help us to build an international system which is better equipped and more effective at preventing and responding to conflict. A culture which fosters our ability to reach consensus on timely and decisive action. I don't think anyone here would disagree with those goals. And I very much hope that none would seek to delay implementation through procedural or administrative means. This is too important to us all – we made a commitment in 2005, a commitment to practical action. We must now live up to that (United Kingdom* 2009).

The United Kingdom is doing more than simply conveying its approval of R2P as a concept in this statement. By calling for the establishment of a 'R2P-culture', London is encouraging other states to make the protection of civilians from mass crimes an every-day priority. The use of the term 'R2P-culture' is significant as it implies that the concept should become usual practice among UN member states. Additionally, Britain is warning other member states that they should not try to obstruct the process of R2P implementation in the light of the engagement they took at the World Summit. Two years later in 2011, the United Kingdom issued a position endorsing 'the continued efforts to refine and to implement the principle of responsible sovereignty, which is the corollary of the principle of responsible sovereignty' (United Kingdom∗ 2011). By calling on states to respect what they agreed upon in 2005 and urging them not to obstruct R2P implementation, the United Kingdom is pressuring other states to follow its example by fully adhering to R2P and considering it as a concept they ought to put into practice as soon as possible in exchange for tangible benefits in terms of worldwide civilian protection.

In February and March 2011, the United Kingdom led the efforts alongside France and the United States to submit draft resolutions to the Security Council advocating an intervention to protect civilians in Libya. The results of these efforts were resolutions 1970 and 1973 providing NATO with a mandate to establish a no-fly zone over Libya's aerial territory. London's stance remained supportive of an active implementation of the R2P principle and diplomats in the Foreign Office were convinced that NATO's intervention in Libya was an example of its successful demonstration. In a General Assembly statement on 5th September 2012, almost a year after the end of the operation, a British representative at the UN defended NATO's intervention in Libya in the following terms:

> On Libya, we believe the UN Security Council-mandated action taken by NATO was necessary, legal and morally right. By taking prompt action, the UN Security Council and NATO saved tens of thousands of people from becoming victims of crimes against humanity and war crimes (United Kingdom∗ 2012).

An illustration that the implementation of R2P in Libya has not modified the United Kingdom's position on the concept is London's stance on the ongoing conflict in Syria. The United Kingdom has pushed for coercive intervention alongside France and the United States in the case of Syria by submitting four draft resolutions on the situation to the Security Council between 2011 and 2014. The United Kingdom's support for coercive intervention in Syria conducted on the grounds of R2P is apparent in the following statement:

> The overwhelming majority vote in favor of the UN General Assembly Resolution on Syria on 3rd August 2012 sent a clear statement that the world condemns escalating violence and human rights violations by the Syrian regime. But the collective response by the international community to the situation in Syria has been thwarted by a lack of consensus in the United Nations Security Council. We reiterate the call for all members of the Security Council to shoulder their responsibility in taking the decisive action required to compel the Assad regime to cease the violence and engage in a political process (United Kingdom∗ 2012).

In the years that followed, statements issued by the representatives of the United Kingdom to the General Assembly conveyed a similar message, highlighting that the controversy that surrounded Qaddafi's death in the final stage of NATO's intervention in Libya did nothing to change London's position on R2P. In 2013, the United Kingdom declared that 'the situation in Syria [...] is a clear example of where the state has failed to protect its citizens' (United Kingdom* 2013). One year later, the British representative to the General Assembly stated that 'the situations in Syria and Iraq, where hundreds and thousands have been killed and minority groups persecuted, highlight the need for the international community to stand firm and take decisive action' (United Kingdom* 2014). Through the abovementioned statements, it is clear that the United Kingdom strongly supports R2P's implementation in principle and in practice, which signifies that its government has internalized the concept.

19.1.4 France

France has continued its efforts to make R2P ready for practice and advocated the principle's legitimacy in the years following the World Summit. Paris has taken initiative alongside London to promote resolution 1674, reaffirming the Security Council's commitment to R2P (Brockmeier et al. 2016: 440). In a statement to the General Assembly in 2009, France encouraged other states to further their efforts to make R2P an operational concept. As such, French representative to the UN Jean-Pierre Lacroix declared:

> The responsibility to protect already largely exists; our heads of state and government recognized it as a universal principle nearly four years ago. We are therefore meeting not to discuss the definition of the concept, but rather to debate the means to strengthen its implementation and its respect (France* 2009).

As France considers R2P to be institutionally embedded within the United Nations system, its stated objective for the further discussion of the norm within the General Assembly is to improve the procedure of R2P implementation along its three pillars. In 2009, the French representative to the UN spoke out to the General Assembly in the following terms:

> The responsibility to protect is certainly not only the response to a crisis situation, its success depends on the ability of all of us to strengthen the prevention of mass crimes. But the responsibility to protect would not be complete without the third pillar that gives it its meaning – that is the international community's reaction when one of the four crimes is about to be or is being committed (France* 2009).

The latter quote particularly shows that France fully adhered to R2P in both principle and practice as it underlines the importance of both prevention and action to protect civilians from crimes against humanity. France also gives a prime importance to international law as an institutional barrier preventing R2P-related crimes to take place. France particularly promotes the respect for 'human rights law, international humanitarian law and refugee law' (France* 2009). In this manner, France considers that international legal institutions such as the International Criminal Court are essential to guarantee that mass crimes do not go unpunished and has pushed UN member to complete the ratification process of the Rome Statute, the founding document of the International Criminal Court (France* 2011). France attempts in this way to locate R2P within a network of international institutions fighting impunity against genocide, war crimes, crimes against humanity, and ethnic cleansing. France conveys the message that R2P is an integral piece within the wider puzzle of international law. France's strategy of framing R2P further legitimizes the concept and brings a sense that all UN member states ought to become norm followers in the spirit of international law, while norm breakers isolate themselves from the rest of the international community.

Concerning the situation in Libya during the Arab Spring, the French government was an unmitigated supporter of humanitarian intervention on the grounds of R2P. France, as mentioned above, submitted alongside the United Kingdom the drafts that led to Security Council resolution 1970 and 1973 calling for and authorizing the international community to protect civilians in Libya. In a joint effort with the United Kingdom, France took a leading role within the NATO coalition performing Operation Unified Protector by providing troops, logistics, and materiel to the mission. For France, R2P effectively stood the test of demonstration in the case of Libya. Paris considers Operation Unified Protector as much of a success as the other peacekeeping operations it had recently been involved in on the African continent. French representative to the UN Gérard Araud declared to the General Assembly that 'in Libya, Cote d'Ivoire, Mali, and Kenya, the international community stood up to its responsibilities and effectively prevented atrocities' (France* 2013).

As it remained an advocate of R2P in both principle and practice after NATO's intervention has ended, France also supported coercive intervention against the Assad regime and the perpetration of mass crimes in Syria. In the context of the use of chemical weapons in Syria in late August 2013, France attempted to apply diplomatic pressure on the international community in order to react to this atrocity. French representative Gérard Araud declared in front of the General Assembly:

> The Syrian government is in the process of murdering its own people. More than 100,000 people have died. The Syrian government, while showing complete indifference, used its air assets and then artillery against civilian neighborhoods, in violation of international humanitarian law, and is now using chemical weapons. It first of all tested the waters by using them in a limited way. It's now using them on a massive scale, meetings focusing on "never again" will do absolutely nothing to respond to the brutality of a regime that wants to murder its own people (O'Donnell 2014: 575).

France has also been at the forefront of combating gridlock within the Security Council (O'Donnell 2014: 576). It acted accordingly by proposing its permanent members to collective restraint in their use of veto in cases of mass crimes, a suggestion originally included in the ICISS report on R2P. On this topic, French representative François Delattre stated:

When mass atrocities are committed, the Council must not add to the failure of prevention by failing to act. In Syria, four double vetoes did not allow us to take the necessary preventive measures and to put an end to impunity for the perpetrators of these crimes. This is why France is working with its partners in order to regulate the use of the veto in cases of mass crimes, in the framework of a voluntary and collective commitment of the Permanent Members (France∗ 2014).

In sum, France supports R2P in both principle and practice. Throughout its speeches to the General Assembly, France has shown its adherence to values of human rights, good governance, and responsible sovereignty in pressuring states to live up to their responsibility to protect their own citizens from R2P crimes. Furthermore, France has called for states to improve R2P prevention by empowering international justice and regional organizations as well as creating local mechanisms of conflict prevention on their domestic territory. France has been a supporter of coercive intervention by the international community in cases of R2P crimes so as to implement the concept's third pillar. Last but not least, France urged other permanent Security Council to be more responsible in their veto uses in such situations. In view of the above, France's position on R2P can be qualified as being one of strong support. Therefore, it can be concluded that France has internalized R2P.

19.1.5   The United States

With the arrival of Barack Obama in the White House in 2009, the US president's foreign policy preferences resulted in the United States increasing its support for R2P. Washington's speeches on R2P in the framework of the 2009 General Assembly debates have greatly emphasized the importance of prevention and early warning mechanisms in order to avoid mass crimes on a large scale. In this aspect, the United States has called for the increase in means provided to the United Nation's mediation teams (United States∗ 2009). Furthermore, the Obama administration has proved to be particularly proactive on this front by creating the U.S. Atrocities Prevention Board and the Genocide Prevention Task Force in 2009. Importantly, the latter issued a recommendation that the permanent members of the Security Council should commonly consider to renouncing their use of veto in R2P situations (Reinold 2011: 81). The institutionalization of the Atrocity Prevention Agenda shows the extent to which US policymakers have made the prevention of crimes against humanity a priority in US national security and foreign policy (Junk 2014: 551). The United States remain cautious concerning coercive interventions on the grounds of R2P as it does not want it to create a legally binding obligation for the international community to intervene in situations of grave humanitarian distress. US ambassador to the UN Rosemary DiCarlo's statement to the General Assembly adequately illustrates Washington's position on R2P:

Where prevention fails, and a state is manifestly failing to meet its obligations, we also need to be prepared to consider a wider range of collective measures. Only rarely, and in extremis, would these include the use of force (United States∗ 2009).

This declaration mirrors that in 2009, although the United States supported R2P in principle, it wished to maintain decision-making over coercive intervention on a case-by-case basis. In view of preserving full-control over its use of force, Washington wanted to avoid R2P resulting in a legal obligation for the United States to mobilize troops in cases of crimes against humanity (Rotmann et al. 2014: 365). The context around which this statement was issued explains the caution displayed by the United States concerning the use of force. Rosemary DiCarlo's declaration was pronounced during the first General Assembly debate on R2P. Consequently, the United States' position should not be interpreted as restrictive towards the use of force but rather as a reminder to other delegations that the 2005 World Summit Outcome Document did not include a clause legally binding the international community to conduct coercive intervention in R2P situations. In light of the support brought to R2P's three pillars and the efforts made by the Obama administration to strengthen preventive measures, the latter can be considered to have been a strong supporter of the concept.

The humanitarian crisis in Libya is a compelling case to determine whether the first demonstration of the use of force on R2P grounds would change Washington's position on R2P. In this case, the United States voted in favor of Security Council resolutions 1970 and 1973, respectively placing sanctions on the Qaddafi regime, and authorizing a no-fly zone over Libya in order to protect civilians. Furthermore, the United States' support for coercive intervention for R2P reasons was illustrated by the US army providing the NATO coalition with logistical and intelligence resources. It was the explicit nature of Qaddafi's threats towards his own civilian population that convinced the Obama administration to support R2P implementation in Libya (Chesterman 2011: 282). Significantly, the United States has used R2P language to justify the necessity to intervene. For example, a legal advisor of the State Department is quoted as saying that 'Qaddafi has forfeited his responsibility to protect his own citizens and created a serious need for immediate humanitarian assistance and protection' (O'Donnell 2014: 566). The United States' stance on R2P therefore remained one of strong support, as US Ambassador to the UN Rick Barton was adamant about the way the international community had implemented R2P in Libya:

> The Security Council's decisive action in Libya shows the progress we have made in learning from our past failures to prevent mass atrocity crimes and in living up to the aspirations we set for ourselves under Responsibility to Protect (United States∗ 2012).

The United States' position on the humanitarian crisis in Syria further illustrates that Washington's present stance on R2P remains one of strong support. Shortly after the use of chemical weapons was observed in Syria in late August 2013, US Ambassador Samantha Power declared at the General Assembly on R2P:

> All attacks on civilians are an outrage that should shock the conscience. We must also recognize that the use of chemical weapons crosses a line. These weapons are particularly grotesque, efficient, and indiscriminate. Their use cannot be reconciled with basic principles of humanity that apply, even in wartime (United States∗ 2013).

The United States' position on R2P between 2005 and the present has not been as consistent as the stances displayed by France and the United Kingdom. During the run up to the 2005 World Summit, the Bush administration received R2P with considerable reluctance. This was notably the case concerning the question of establishing criteria on the use of force (Bellamy 2009: 86). After having decided to support the concept in principle, the United States took a posture of active support for R2P under the Obama administration. The discrepancy between the rhetoric used by the Bush and Obama administrations concerning R2P demonstrates that the support given by the United States to the principle is reliant on the foreign policy strategy of the government in power and may evolve more or less abruptly depending on the personality, and first and foremost, the party taking over the presidency. The efforts made by the United States to create institutions supporting the prevention of crimes against humanity such as the Genocide Prevention Task Force and the Atrocity Prevention Agenda demonstrate Washington's willingness to make R2P a working principle. The United States' calls to intervene in Libya and Syria for R2P reasons confirm that the United States consider R2P as a principle that should govern states' behavior in the international system. For instance, US ambassador to the UN spoke about R2P as a 'normative concept' in front of the General Assembly (United States∗ 2014). In view of its position on R2P during the second and third timeframes, the United States can be considered as a strong supporter of R2P. As a result, the United States has demonstrated its internalization of R2P as a norm in international relations under the Obama administration.

19.1.6 Russia

Prior to the 2009 General Assembly debate, Russia's intervention in Georgia in 2008 constitutes an illustration of the extent of Moscow's recognition of the R2P principle in the years following the World Summit. In this event, Russian Minister of Foreign Affairs Sergei Lavrov invoked the necessity for Russian intervention to protect its citizens and to justify the Kremlin's use of force in Georgian territory, with President Medvedev referring several times to the term 'genocide' (Kurowska 2014: 500). Although this intervention had been widely condemned by the international community, one of Russia's statements to the General Assembly debate on R2P referred to its 'legitimate right to self-defense' in this particular situation (Russian Federation∗ 2011). The fact that Moscow attempted to legitimize its action on the grounds of protecting its citizens is a sign of the Kremlin's implicit acknowledgement of coercive intervention for R2P reasons as being acceptable practice, yet only when its own geopolitical interests are not compromised. In this way, Moscow justified its decision to annex Crimea in 2014 by invoking the necessity to protect Russian speaking minorities as well as reminding the international community of its long-standing cultural ties with the region (Kurowska 2014: 502; Ziegler 2016).

Russia's invocation of R2P to use force in Georgia can be considered as selective because of the fact that Russian policymakers did not modify their cautious discourse on the international stage. The stance of Russian ambassador to the UN Margelov to the first General Assembly debate on R2P in 2009 mirrors the Kremlin official position:

> The concept of the responsibility to protect has enormous potential for change. Its development and implementation could significantly shape key trends that will determine the future of the entire system of international relations and the international rule of law. That is precisely why we are convinced that we should be measured and cautious in addressing any idea regarding implementation of the authoritative and relevant ideas of the 2005 World Summit Outcome document on the responsibility to protect (Russian Federation* 2009).

The Russian Federation adheres to a restrictive interpretation of Paragraphs 138 and 139 of the World Summit outcome document. Russia's perspective on R2P is strongly driven by the primacy it places on international law and the Charter-based system (O'Donnell 2014: 577). Accordingly, Russia adopts a literal reading of international law because it considers it as the main barrier protecting less politically influential and militarily strong states from external interference (Rotmann et al. 2014: 371). Furthermore, Russia's perspective on R2P is rooted in the Kremlin's adherence to pluralist values and the perception that the international community should favour the coexistence of different political regimes in order to obtain a stable world order (O'Donnell 2014: 577). Russia's stance on R2P is described as a 'nuanced position' (Kurowska 2014: 490). Indeed, the first two R2P pillars on the responsibility of states to protect their population and preventive measures do not represent a cause for concern for Russia (Ziegler 2015: 8). In fact since March 2011, out of 25 Security Council resolutions mentioning R2P, Russia voted in favour of 23 of them (Ziegler 2016: 348). Crucially, all of these resolutions concerned the first two R2P pillars. Nevertheless, Russia remains extremely cautious concerning R2P's third pillar referring to the use of force by the international community after all peaceful means have been exhausted.

Russia's position on R2P encountered an important test in the case of the 2011 Libyan crisis. Moscow's stance, which was to recognize the necessity of preventing crimes against humanity while expressing caution towards conducting coercive intervention in R2P situations was to be stretched during the early stages of the crisis. Although it did not participate in the operation itself, the Kremlin initially tolerated NATO's intervention in Libya by abstaining during the vote of Security Council Resolution 1973. Russia did not oppose coercive intervention in the first place because the situation of humanitarian distress in Libya was exceptionally clear-cut as Qaddafi issued extermination threats towards civilians early on in the civil war, and regional organizations such as the Arab League had given approval for an intervention to take place (Garwood-Gowers 2013: 608). This decision was subject to a heated debate within the Kremlin, with Putin, the Prime Minister at the time, openly criticizing President Medvedev's decision to contribute to the West's 'medieval call for a crusade' (Kurowska 2014: 501). The manner in which NATO implemented R2P in Libya was subject to Moscow's condemnations already in the early stages of Operation Unified Protector. Denouncing the occurrence of civilian casualties in the framework of the intervention, Russia stated:

any use of force by the coalition in Libya should be carried out in strict compliance with Resolution 1973. Any act going beyond the mandate established by that resolution in any way or any disproportionate use of force is unacceptable (Bellamy and Williams 2011: 845).

In the eyes of Putin, Qaddafi's death shortly before the end of NATO's intervention in Libya definitely sealed Medvedev's decision of abstaining on resolution 1973 as a mistake not to be repeated. The perception that NATO contravened its mandate to use force by fostering regime change in Libya hardened Russia's stance on R2P. For example, the 2013 Russian Foreign Policy Concept considers the following:

> It is unacceptable that military intervention and other forms of interference from without which undermine the foundations of international law based on the principle of sovereign equality of states, be carried out on the pretext of implementing the concept of "R2P" (Ziegler 2015: 9).

The Kremlin's toughened position on R2P was to be further illustrated by Russia joining China in vetoing four successive draft Security Council resolutions on the situation in Syria since 2011. Shortly before his election as President in 2012, Putin went on to declare 'No one should be allowed to employ the Libyan scenario in Syria' (Ziegler 2015: 14). The events of Libya did not lead Russia to reject R2P as a whole however. Instead, Moscow opted for a strategy of norm subsidiarity. This strategy was characterized by Russian support for the norm of 'Responsibility while Protecting' coined by Brazil, which advocates the establishment of mechanisms verifying that the conduct of interventions on R2P grounds conform to their relevant Security Council mandate (Russian Federation* 2012).

In sum, Russia's position on R2P is nuanced in the light of its attachments to the principles of state sovereignty, territorial integrity, and non-interference. On one hand, Russia supports R2P's first two pillars, as they are compatible with the stipulations of the UN Charter concerning the prohibition on the use of force. On the other hand, Russia has largely sought to avoid the practice of coercive intervention under R2P's third pillar, as it remains concerned that the latter is affected by politicized abuses and the lack of criteria on the use of force. The Kremlin's fears in this regard culminated in the aftermath of Qaddafi's death during NATO's intervention in Libya, an event that toughened Russia's stance on the use of force on R2P grounds. Yet, the fact that Russia invoked R2P during the 2008 Georgian crisis, however selectively, illustrates that it recognizes R2P's legitimacy in the international order. These reasons lead to the conclusion that Russia is a cautious supporter of R2P. Moscow's interaction with the norm suggests that R2P internalization within policy-making ranks in the Kremlin is reliant on the future development of the norm, notably through its continued discussion within the General Assembly. In this light, the assessment is that although Russia recognizes R2P in principle, it has so far not internalized R2P as a norm to be practiced in the realm of international relations under the circumstances stipulated in the 2005 World Summit declaration. The specificity of Russia in this case is that instead of recognizing R2P as a universal norm, it selectively advances the concept when it suits its domestic geopolitical interests, like it did in the case of the 2008 Georgian crisis. Following a similar logic, Moscow vetoes military interventions framed around R2P when it views such operations as contrary to their domestic geopolitical interests, as has been the case in discussions revolving around the Syrian conflict. Russia's position illustrates the lack of consensus within the Security Council in considering R2P as a universal principle to be applied in both principle and practice. It can therefore be concluded that in light of Russia's position on the principle, R2P remains at the stage of norm cascade.

19.1.7   China

When the first General Assembly debate on R2P took place in 2009, China's stance on R2P remained consistent with the cautious position it held on the concept in the previous years. During the debate, Beijing emphasized that R2P had to be considered within the wider framework governed by the UN Charter. China's representative to the General Assembly declared:

> When a crisis involving one of the four crimes emerges, to ease and curtail the crisis will be the common aspiration and legitimate demand on the part of the international community. But the relevant actions must strictly abide by the provisions of the UN Charter, and respect the views of the government and regional organizations concerned. The crisis must be addressed in the framework of the UN, and all peaceful means must be exhausted. It is necessary to prevent any state from unilaterally implementing R2P. [...] The prerequisite for [the Security Council] taking action is the existence of "any threat to the peace, breach of the peace, or act of aggression". The Council must consider R2P in the broader context of maintaining international peace and security, and must guard against abusing the concept (People's Republic of China∗ 2009).

China is not questioning whether the international community should intervene in protecting civilians confronting these core crimes, but rather the way in which R2P should be implemented. More particularly, China has been an advocate of the first two pillars of R2P rather than being a proponent of coercive military interventions (Teitt 2011: 308). Aside from recalling Beijing's cautious reading of the concept along the lines of the UN Charter, the statement reveals the importance China places on the agreement of the host state and of regional organizations in the use of force for R2P reasons. China advocates that states, as primary bearers of the responsibility to protect civilians on their territory, should be able to authorize or discard interventions within their borders because of the principle of non-interference in the internal affairs of a sovereign country. China emphasizes the importance of regional organizations as gatekeepers against the misuse of the R2P concept such as unilateral interventions. This position has been particularly influenced by past experience, as China did not approve of NATO's intervention in Kosovo in 1999, which was devoid of Security Council authorization (Wheeler 2000: 272). Finally, the fact that China's representative considers that 'R2P so far remains a concept' that 'does not constitute a rule of international law' illustrates Beijing's will to contain R2P as a principle located on the fringes of the wider Charter-based system (People's Republic of China 2009).

China's position on R2P did not change in the case of a humanitarian crisis in Libya in 2011. Although China abstained on resolution 1973, it nevertheless expressed deep reservations concerning the mandate given by the Security Council for NATO's intervention. Chinese representative Li Baodong clarified his country's position on the resolution in a statement to the Security Council:

> China has serious difficulty with parts of the resolution. Meanwhile, China attaches great importance to the relevant position by the 22-member Arab League on the establishment of a no-fly zone over Libya. We also attach great importance to the position of African countries and the African Union. In view of this, and considering the special circumstances surrounding the situation in Libya, China abstained from the voting on resolution 1973.

This declaration illustrates that rather than departing from its initial position on R2P, China's abstention adheres to the stance it had held so far. In conformity with the importance Beijing placed on regional organizations as gatekeepers against R2P misuse, the Arab League's approval of resolution 1973 was essential in China's decision to refrain from using its veto in the case of Libya. In addition, the immediacy of the threat issued by Qaddafi on his civilian population pressured China not to form an obstacle from intervening in a situation with potentially sordid consequences. These 'special circumstances' referred to by Li Baodong underlined the exceptional nature of the situation, which meant that China did not want to consider resolution 1973 as a template for future cases of R2P implementation (Garwood-Gowers 2012: 387). Alongside Moscow, Beijing perceived Qaddafi's death in the streets of Sirte as a case of regime change, with NATO abusing the mandate it had been conferred by the Security Council to protect civilians in Libya. This event noticeably toughened China's stance on the use of force in R2P situations. In the aftermath of Operation Unified Protector, Chinese Foreign Minister Le Yusheng said:

> We should not forget the lessons we have learnt from Libya. On the first "protection" day led by NATO in Libya, there were 64 civilians killed and 150 injured. And the final result of the "protection" is that over 20,000 civilians killed and 900,000 displaced. [...] The courage to say "no" to it absolutely demonstrates our determination to be responsible. We respect "Responsibility to Protect" and at the same time we value "Responsibility while Protecting" even more (Liu and Zhang 2014: 418–419).

During the General Assembly debate on R2P in 2012, China refers to 'Responsibility while Protecting' in the attempt to promote the norm created by Brazil that addresses the lack of monitoring and accountability of R2P interventions as experienced in the case of NATO's intervention in Libya (People's Republic of China* 2012). The latter demonstrates that China, along with other BRIC states, engages in a strategy of norm subsidiarity in order to contain and shape R2P's development along its own perspective. In this fashion, Beijing aims to spread a worldview emphasizing territorial integrity as well as non-interference in order to limit Western influence in developing countries (Van der Putten 2013). China's hardened stance on R2P has resulted in the deadlock of the Security Council on the humanitarian crisis in Syria. Alongside the Kremlin, Beijing vetoed four resolutions on this situation between 2011 and 2014. China's objection to pass these resolutions is linked to its aversion of a repetition of the Libyan scenario in Syria. A quote of Chinese Ambassador Chen Shiqiu is unequivocal in this regard:

> If the Syrian tragedy was taken as a humanitarian disaster, how should we understand the fact that the opposing faction was provided with weapons? Therefore, it seems that it was not meant to terminate the conflict, but to topple the Bashar al-Assad administration and turn Syria into a second Libya (Liu and Zhang 2014: 419).

In sum, China has demonstrated support for the first two pillars of R2P and has encouraged the continuation of the debate on the norm within the framework of the General Assembly. However, Beijing remains cautious in its interpretation of R2P and advocates that its implementation strictly abides to the limits imposed by the UN Charter. China's abstention in the situation of Libya demonstrated that it did not reject the use of force in R2P situations outright. The latter case increased China's wariness towards the abuse of R2P, hardening its stance on the use of coercive intervention in R2P situations such as Syria. China's position is similar to Russia in the sense that it recognizes R2P in principle but is reluctant towards its universal implementation in practice. However, China's position on R2P differs with the Russian one in the sense that it has not attempted to use R2P to justify military interventions without Security Council approval, as Moscow has done in the event of the 2008 Georgian crisis. Adopting a more conservative approach than Russia in contesting R2P's universal implementation, China invokes international legal provisions such as Article 2(4) of the United Nations Charter prohibiting the use of force in international relations. Finally, the fact that China stands strong along Russia in using R2P on a highly selective basis is revealing about R2P's stage of normative advancement. In this way, it highlights a split within the Security Council between two groups of states. On one side, the United Kingdom, France, and the United States argue in favor of implementing a universal duty to protect civilians against war crimes. On the other hand, Russia and China resist the latter, advancing concerns towards the integrity of the territorial sovereignty of states. The lack of consensus within the Security Council, which is the sole institution that is entitled to authorize the use of force on R2P grounds, leads to the final assessment that the international community as a whole has not yet internalized the concept.

19.2 Conclusion

In sum, R2P remains at a stage of 'norm cascade' on Finnemore and Sikkink's scale of international norm dynamics. Less than a decade following its inception by Francis Deng, the idea that state sovereignty conferred heads of state with the responsibility to protect their citizens from genocide, war crimes, crimes against humanity, and ethnic cleansing has taken the form of an institutionalized principle at the 2005 World Summit. Nevertheless, R2P's institutionalization does not represent an end in itself as the principle is entirely based on practice. Due to the protracted nature that surrounded its negotiation, the summit's outcome document does not provide specific guidelines concerning the use of military force in order to implement R2P. Consequently, this means that R2P's further progression towards internalization will be subject to an international consensus on coercive intervention and R2P. More specifically, this means that states will have to agree on which thresholds and modes of operations apply to the use of R2P's third pillar. As recently witnessed in the case of Syria, the importance of Security Council permanent member states remain crucial as any dissent concerning R2P and coercive intervention within this institution is likely to lead towards institutional deadlock and protracted reactions from the international community to R2P crimes.

What Future for R2P?

The Russian and Chinese allegations that R2P was used by NATO for ends of regime-change as opposed to fulfilling humanitarian objectives in Libya as well as the firm stance displayed by Beijing and Moscow through successive vetoes of United Nations Security Council resolutions referring to the use of R2P in Syria show that R2P has not yet matured into a norm gathering swift consensus amongst the international community in favor of protecting civilians from war crimes. However, the story behind the conceptualization and early implementation attempts of R2P illustrates how the diffusion of norms in international relations, as opposed to being a linear process, is subject to breakthroughs and setbacks. Concepts built around the notion of humanitarian intervention such as R2P are to be judged on whether they succeed in protecting the civilian lives in times of crises. R2P's first-ever use in Libya represents a controversial start for what had been a theoretically promising rekindling of the concept of state sovereignty. Furthermore, the stocktaking on R2P's potential for successful implementation in the future is prone to pessimism in light of the ensuing Security Council deadlock on the issue of R2P-use in Syria. Nevertheless, definitive conclusions about the disappearance of R2P from the normative debate regarding humanitarian intervention are premature at this stage. In times dominated by global news outlets, live-coverage channels and social media, humanitarian crises catch a considerable level of attention amongst policymakers, scholars, and civil society. The intense violence and complexity of contemporary humanitarian crises and the international community's current inability to gather consensus around effective solutions to relieve emergency situations on the ground is alarming. However, focusing on the fast-paced developments of conflicts occupying the forefront of international affairs should not eclipse the diplomatic marathon operating in the backstage of global politics. Institutional bodies of the United Nations, namely the Security Council, the General Assembly and the Secretary General hold the key towards R2P's future in the fact that they are the pillars of the normative debate on the concept. By the time the dialogue on R2P amongst United Nations member States is maintained in institutional forums such as the Security Council and the General Assembly and that this conversation is fed by the input of the Secretary-General, R2P will stay alive as a norm guiding international civilian protection. Rather than the mere failure of its implementation on the ground, it is the very prospect of its progressive disappearance from the international debate on humanitarian intervention that could spell the end of R2P.

*Please note that the respective statements issued by the United Kingdom, France, the United States, the Russian Federation, and the People's Republic of China cited in this chapter are accessible at: http://www.responsibilitytoprotect.org/index.php/about-rtop/government-statements-on-rtop.

Further Readings

Acharya, A. (2013). The R2P and norm diffusion: Towards a framework of norm circulation. *Global Responsibility to Protect, 5*(1), 466–479.

Brockmeier, S., Stuenkel, O., & Tourinho, M. (2016). The impact of the Libya intervention debates on norms of protection. *Global Society, 30*(1), 113–133.

Kurz, G., & Rotmann, P. (2016). The evolution of norms of protection: Major powers debate the responsibility to protect. *Global Society, 30*(1), 3–20.

References

Acharya, A. (2014). Who are the norm makers? The Asian-African conference in Bandung and the evolution of norms. *Global Governance, 20*(1), 405–417.

Annan, K. (2005). *In larger freedom: Towards development, security and human rights for all.* New York: United Nations Publications.

Ban, Ki-Moon. (2009). *Implementing the responsibility to protect.* Rep. United Nations Publications.

Bellamy, A. J. (2009). *Responsibility to protect: The global effort to end mass atrocities.* Cambridge: Polity.

Bellamy, A. J., & Williams, P. D. (2011). The new politics of protection? Côte d'Ivoire, Libya and the responsibility to protect. *International Affairs, 87*(4), 825–850.

Chesterman, S. (2011). Leading from behind: The responsibility to protect, the Obama doctrine, and humanitarian intervention after Libya. *Ethics and International Affairs, 25*(3), 279–285.

Deng, F. M., Kimaro, S., Lyons, T., Rothchild, D., & Zartman William, I. (1996). *Sovereignty as responsibility: Conflict management in Africa.* Washington, DC: Brookings Institution.

Evans, G. J. (2008). *The responsibility to protect: Ending mass atrocity crimes once and for all.* Washington, DC: Brookings Institution.

Finnemore, M., & Sikkink, K. (1998). International norm dynamics and political change. *International Organization, 52*(4), 887–917.

Garwood-Gowers, A. (2012). China and the "Responsibility to protect": The implications of the Libyan intervention. *Asian Journal of International Law, 2*(2), 375–393.

Garwood-Gowers, A. (2013). The responsibility to protect and the Arab spring: Libya as the exception, Syria as the norm? *UNSW Law Journal, 36*(2), 594–618.

Junk, J. (2014). The two-level politics of support—US foreign policy and the responsibility to protect. *Conflict, Security and Development, 14*(4), 535–564.

Keck, M. E., & Sikkink, K. (1999). Transnational advocacy networks in international and regional politics. *International Social Science Journal, 51*(159), 89–101.

Kurowska, X. (2014). Multipolarity as resistance to Liberal norms: Russia's position on responsibility to protect. *Conflict, Security and Development, 14*(4), 489–508.

Liu, T., & Zhang, H. (2014). Debates in China about the responsibility to protect as a developing international norm: A general assessment. *Conflict, Security and Development, 14*(4), 403–427.

O'Donnell, C. (2014). The development of the responsibility to protect: An examination of the debate over the legality of humanitarian intervention. *Duke Journal of Comparative and International Law, 24*(1), 557–588.

Reinold, T. (2011). The United States and the responsibility to protect: Impediment, bystander, or norm leader? *Global Responsibility to Protect, 3*(1), 61–87.

Rotmann, P., Kurtz, G., & Brockmeier, S. (2014). Major powers and the contested evolution of a responsibility to protect. *Conflict, Security and Development, 14*(4), 355–377.

Teitt, S. (2011). The responsibility to protect and China's peacekeeping policy. *International Peacekeeping, 18*(3), 298–312.

United Nations, Security Council. (2011, March 17). *Verbatim records: 6498th meeting*, S/PV.6498. Available from http://daccess-ddsny.un.org/doc/UNDOC/PRO/N11/267/18/PDF/N1126718.pdf?OpenElement

Van der Putten, F.-P. (2013). Harmony with diversity: China's preferred world order and weakening Western influence in the developing world. *Global Policy, 4*(1), 53–62.

Wheeler, N. J. (2000). *Saving strangers: Humanitarian intervention in international society*. Oxford: Oxford University Press.

Ziegler, C. E. (2015). Contesting the responsibility to protect. *International Studies Perspectives, 17*(1), 1–23.

Ziegler, C. E. (2016). Russia on the rebound: Using and misusing the responsibility to protect. *International Relations, 30*(3), 346–361.

Chapter 20
Methods of Conflict Resolution: Negotiation

Paul Meerts

This chapter will analyse international negotiation from the perspective of procedure and process, party and people, perception and power, preference and product. It will ask the question of the nature and of the conduct of international negotiation, its past and prospects. Negotiation is one of the main instruments of conflict resolution. Chapter VI article 33.1 of the Charter of the United Nations, concerning the 'Peaceful Settlement of Conflicts' sees negotiation as the first instrument of seven methods in resolving conflicts: 'The parties to any dispute, the continuance of which is likely to endanger the maintenance of international peace and security, shall, first of all, seek a resolution by negotiation, enquiry, mediation, conciliation, arbitration, judicial settlement, resort to regional agencies or arrangements, or other peaceful means of their own choice' (https://treaties.un.org/doc/publication). Furthermore the United Nations General Assembly adopted Resolution 53/101 on 'Principles and Guidelines for International Negotiations' (www.refworld.org/docid/3b00f5254a.html). In the preamble, it stresses 'the important role constructive and effective negotiations can play in attaining the purposes of the Charter by contributing to the management of international relations.'

International negotiation processes have been studied for centuries, but especially since the last quarter of the twentieth century. The majority of negotiation scholars and practitioners are analyzing baskets of different inroads to the negotiation processes and all these inroads look alike. The difference is their emphasis: many authors take the process and its phases as a starting point; others focus first on different factors influencing these processes; while some will take the actors in the process as their point of departure. Whatever their main focus is, however, the vast majority of the 'negotiationists' will deal with the same elements in the end. For the processes, these will be diagnosing, exploring, selecting, deciding and implement-

P. Meerts (✉)
Netherlands Institute of International Relations 'Clingendael', The Hague, The Netherlands
e-mail: pwmeerts@gmail.com

© Springer Nature Switzerland AG 2020
M. O. Hosli, J. Selleslaghs (eds.), *The Changing Global Order*, United Nations
University Series on Regionalism 17,
https://doi.org/10.1007/978-3-030-21603-0_20

ing. The main factors analyzed are the political and diplomatic context of the negotiation, the nature of and the distance between positions and interests, the strategies and tactics employed, the impact of power and influence, as well as the shadow of the past and the future. For actors, the authors deal with parties such as states and international organizations and their structure, the people representing them and the delegations they are managing, their character, experience and skill, their societal and professional background, and the question of what extent they are included in or excluded from the negotiation process.

This triangle of 'Actors–Factors–Processes' is of course incomplete and much more complicated in reality. It is but one way to look at all the issues at hand. Another approach would structure by asking questions like why, who, how, when and where? This approach cuts through the construction of actors, factors and processes. The question here is: what are the independent and dependent variables? There is no answer to this, as all elements are dependent on each other and it is up to the authors to choose the starting points. The problem is that different authors take different starting points and there are only subjective ways to separate the independent variables from the dependent. The choice is for pragmatic reasons; there is unfortunately no objective scientific choice. As negotiation is situational, so is the study of it. A one-dimensional approach can be helpful, as long as it is understood as such. We go off-track if we pretend that our approach to negotiation is the one and only truth.

The definition of international *negotiation* depends on the question of *which definition is most suitable to describe and analyze the process as an explanation of its outcome.* Maxim Kaplan (2010: 13) found 161 different definitions of negotiation. In 115 of these, *agreement* is the issue that these definitions want to clarify, 71 definitions stress *communication* as the main factor to be analyzed, 64 focus on *conflicting interests*, and another 64 perceive negotiation from the point of view of elements such as *process* and *behaviour* (Kaplan 2010: 14–15). He sums them up in an annexe (Kaplan 2010: 351–375). It is neither possible nor useful, however, to refer to a long list of definitions in this treatise. Christer Jönsson and Martin Hall attempt to define the international dimension of negotiation by its diplomatic actors: 'While negotiating to further the interests of their particular polities, diplomats typically identify the peaceful resolution of conflicts and the avoidance of war as common interests' (Jönsson and Hall 2005: 82). They stress the fact that diplomats are negotiating as 'agents of a principal with ultimate authority' (Jönsson and Hall 2005: 84). The same is true for Machiavelli, who limits himself to the observation that the diplomat must, 'if his instructions require it, engage in formal negotiations, and be especially industrious in obtaining information and reporting it home' (Berridge 1999: 13).

Henry Kissinger views negotiation thus: 'In simple terms, negotiation is a process of combining conflicting positions into a common position, a phenomenon in which the outcome is determined by the process' (Kissinger 1969: 212). In serious conflictual situations, it might be seen as *war by peaceful means*; in continuous decision-making as *the policy of give and take*. Between these two extremes there is a grey area of mixture, where either the one or the other is the predominant mode of processing.

'Negotiation and conflict management research is thriving, as shown by the success of international conferences, the vast number of research and teaching programs held in an expanding list of countries, and the quantity and quality of articles, books, dissertations, and working papers' (Colson et al. 2013: xi). New scholarly interest in international negotiation processes started after the Second World War (Lewicki et al. 1994: 15–19). Before then, one can point to the work of diplomats like Francesco Guicciardini (1483–1540) (Berridge 1998), the Archbishop Fénelon (1651–1715) (Koskenniemi 2011), the Abbé de Saint-Pierre (1658–1743) (Koskenniemi 2011), the diplomatic negotiator Francois de Callières (1983), and at a much later stage Harold Nicolson (1963), who have said many things worthy of consideration about the phenomenon of negotiations between states. Scientific interest was raised more seriously in the 1960s. Academics like Fred Iklé (1964) and Howard Raiffa (1982) tried to find patterns in something as intangible as a process. For this purpose various methods were used, from the description of real negotiations to mathematical models in which the factors of the negotiation process were objectified. In that way there was common ground between the authors for whom negotiation did not take a central role, but who had carried out research into facts and factors that played a major role in the negotiation process. It relates, for instance, to the power factor (Zartman and Rubin 2000), the psychological factor (Rubin 1991), and the game theoretical aspects (Axelrod 1984).

Negotiation is 'just' one way – although if it can be applied, it is very cost-effective – to create and enhance peace, security and justice. This is especially true if the circumstances help to foster sustainability. 'Negotiators who respect Procedural Justice principles are more likely to produce agreements based on equality, and such agreements are more durable' (Albin and Druckman 2012: 23). Other tools can be facilitation, mediation, arbitration, adjudication and warfare, etc. This study limits itself to inter-state negotiation, asking questions about negotiation's nature and utility, and relating it on its fringes to warfare and adjudication. Negotiation can be used to avoid wars, and it is nearly always used after wars are over. Negotiation can be used to avoid adjudication, but it is always used to give rise to adjudication. This means that so-called 'black letter laws' are products of negotiation processes, especially on the international level. Negotiation is a cost-effective mechanism aspiring to create peace, creating a secure environment for that peace to flourish, and establishing sustainability through the implementation of justice. It is, of course, a question of interrelationships. Peace creates favourable conditions for negotiation processes, because security is needed to protect the negotiators – there have been times when killing the enemy's ambassador was seen as a way to show strength – and justice secures the implementation of the fruits of the negotiation process.

20.1   Practitioners, Researches, Trainers

From an academic point of view, the thinking about – and research in – international negotiation processes cannot be described as a separate discipline (Faure 2003: 11, 203). However, multidisciplinary research programmes can be found within the social sciences in which an increasing number of political scientists, sociologists, psychologists and also mathematicians are already involved. This upward trend is shown in the increasing number of books and articles in journals, and the founding of periodicals such as *Negotiation Journal* (Plenum Press) and *International Negotiation* (Martinus Nijhoff Publishers).

We might expect these academics to use their findings to train practitioners, and we could expect practitioners to help academics with their research, but strangely this is not the case. Practitioners, researchers and trainers do not communicate at the same level. Leaving aside the fact that many of the researchers are also lecturers on international negotiation at universities, and that they use their discoveries of the 'secrets' of negotiation to enhance their students' insight, they are not by definition skilled trainers. Teaching is mostly about literature, and although simulation games are used to illustrate theory, teaching is still a far cry from real training. Trainers are – if everything is up to standard – capable of providing participants with experience in negotiation processes. However, contrary to teachers and researchers, trainers are often not aware of the bulk of modern literature. They often copy what others copied from someone who once upon a time developed a practicum on the basis of academic insights. Yet these trainers can be charismatic people, who may not know as much about negotiation as they do about private-sector management, but who have the empathy to influence the thinking and frame of mind of their course participants. They may radiate strength. Participants will often remember their personality many years thereafter, but they will forget what they learned about negotiation.

One would expect a 'natural life cycle' – that is, practitioners help researchers to understand the soul of the negotiation process, while trainers would use the insights from research to train effective (future) practitioners. One could expect common understanding to grow as the sub-discipline of negotiation processes developed over the past 20 years, bringing the three groups together in joint forums. There is indeed some more communality, but on average the cleavages between practitioners, academics and trainers have not been bridged.

We must first look at the reasons behind the persons. Many practitioners, especially those in the Inter-state Negotiations Arena – first and foremost diplomats – do not really believe that negotiation is a science; they perceive it as art. They are not alone on this. To many diplomats and other practitioners, it is an art that is inborn and cannot be learned, a feeling that is especially true for the old-fashioned diplomats. One might hope for change as time goes by, but for the moment these senior diplomats dominate the scene, as they hold the most important diplomatic posts. Apart from their perception – and perception determines reality – they are often handicapped by not fully understanding their own behaviour. They may be effective diplomatic negotiators, but they tend not to be fully aware of the 'why' questions.

What does one do in order to be effective? How do we negotiate? They are so deep in their routine that they do not have the insight of efficacy traits in their own dealings with other states. It is a little like an excellent car driver, who is so good because he does not need to bother about the technicalities of driving; he has his routine, and can therefore develop a helicopter view. The mind and eyes concentrate on the environment and not so much on the mechanics. In itself this is good, and the most effective negotiators have a grip on both process and context, but this does not mean that they really understand what they are doing in order to be effective. They often negotiate on automatic pilot.

Practitioners – in particular ambassadors of the older generation – often have a certain disdain for academic negotiation research and education. They do not really believe in training as a tool to become a better negotiator. Many practitioners do not want to lose time by conferring with academics on the issue of international negotiation processes. Moreover, they do not want negotiation 'experts' to have a look in their kitchen, first because this might harm their country's national interests (the secrecy of the negotiation in order to keep some room for manoeuvre), and second, because they might lose face if consultants observe that mistakes are made and opportunities are lost. Negotiators often show their emotions, they have non-verbal leaks (such as unconscious body language), and they do not want this to be revealed to the outside world.

More serious is the second 'reality dilemma' (Klabbers 1988), in that practitioners do not allow researchers (and trainers) to observe real-time negotiations. Negotiation 'experts' are sometimes invited to witness bilateral negotiations, but closed sessions are the rule, especially in multilateral inter-state bargaining. The consequence of this is twofold. First, practitioners do not profit from the insights of negotiation research, and indeed serious mistakes are made on matters like timing and trust, strategy and tactics, skills and styles. Indeed, obvious mistakes have been made at many conferences, and process experts would probably have noticed these and might have helped the process to avoid going off-track. Second, this attitude of the practitioners hampers academics and trainers in a serious way: unable to observe real negotiation processes has the consequence that alternative means, such as the observation of mock communication, and the study of 'memoirs' and other written accounts, have to be used in order to come as close as possible to the real processes. Interviews and surveys might help somewhat, but interviewees have a tendency to omit the things they did wrong and to stress their glorious moments.

As negotiation is not only art but also science (Raiffa 1982), training of negotiators will be very helpful, notwithstanding the problem of having a shortage of insights delivered by practitioners and researchers (Meerts 2012; Westerman 2016). The 'ideal' training seminar would look roughly like this:

1. Day I: Introduction, Distributive and Integrative Bilateral Bargaining
2. Day II: Trilateral Negotiation, Strategy and Tactics, Culture and Emotion
3. Day III: Multiparty Negotiation, Chairing, Mediating, Skills and Styles
4. Day IV: Multilateral Negotiation: Drafting, Debriefing, Non-verbal Behaviour

The first day helps to get a better understanding of process, procedure, parties, people, preferences and products. Day II and III elaborate this and prepare for the last day's exercise. The simulation of day IV should be based on reality by using real agreements and films showing how negotiations have been navigated by real international.

Negotiators (Meerts 2009). The aim of the seminar is to give participants more grip on the negotiation process by raising awareness of their own behaviour. As people have different experiences, skills, styles, characters, chemistry and cultural background, a 'one-size fits all' will not be helpful.

20.2   Parties, People, Preferences

Who conducts the negotiations? This section will limit analysis of the phenomenon of international negotiation to negotiations between representatives of governments. These state representatives can be divided into two categories: politicians; and diplomats/civil servants. Consequently, negotiations between states can be held either on a political or on a diplomatic/official level. The political level is the highest level and mostly preceded and followed by diplomatic/official consultations. The category of diplomats and civil servants can also be subdivided, depending on the question of whether an ambassador/director-general, a young diplomat/policy adviser, or someone in between these ranks, is conducting the negotiations.

The actors appear at the negotiation table from different positions. Apart from the interests that they have to consider, one can assume that one negotiator will be more skilled than the other, will have a better knowledge of his dossier, is more motivated, better trained and could have more credit within his delegation, ministry or government than the other. Human differences will influence the course of the negotiations, not in the sense that they would be the most influencing factor on their own, but at decisive moments they can tip the balance. In other words, the more the other factors (that influence the negotiation process) are balanced against each other, the greater the margins in which the negotiator's personal characteristics will play a role. Personal influence might be relatively marginal in most inter- and intra-state negotiations, margins can determine outcomes in the same way as profit margins determine a company's success.

The readiness of actors to be involved in the process depends on their interests. Negotiations will only take place when the parties, in one way or another, actually need each other. A relationship should exist between (parts of) the parties' interests. It is very important for the negotiator to know to what extent the interests of both parties run parallel, or whether they largely exclude each other. For parallel interests, a strategy of cooperation will be chosen (integrative negotiating); the second case will see a more competing approach (competitive negotiation). The negotiations take place in a situation where interests practically converge with reasons to cooperate (the lower limit), or when the interests do not converge but enough reasons exist for consultation (the upper limit). Outside these limits, there is no question of negotiating but instead of conflict or staying aloof.

In most cases, the mutual (overlapping) and competing (conflicting) interests will play a mixed role. In addition, there is often a third category of interest, in which matters are important for one's own party, but do not touch the other (neutral interests). However, one always needs to keep an eye on the latter category. To be neutral concerning interests can be of importance for those parties who are not participating in the consultations, but who will (or can) speed up the ongoing negotiations. Thus, for example, in a case when the Dutch and the Belgians will not reach an agreement, but the Dutch can offer the Germans something, in exchange for which the Germans will give something to the Dutch that is useful for the Belgians, this can lead towards a positive rounding-up of the Dutch–Belgian negotiations ('expanding the cake').

In other situations, interests can be arranged in such a way that even with the lack of parallel interests, reasons may occur for negotiating. No agreement will be reached regarding the subject in those cases, but that is not in fact what the parties involved have in mind. For example, two countries have the intention to enlarge their armaments but public opinion opposes their plans and demands negotiations on arms control before upgrading any defence. Through negotiating, both states meet the conditions that will make enforcement of their defence possible. Not only are the stated conditions met, but there is also the opportunity to point out that the other party is unwilling, and obviously has aggressive intentions in mind. Moreover, it is advantageous that both states are in consultation with each other and can exchange information. In some cases the desire to negotiate has only been prompted by the necessity to open up a flow of information. In that way, the mutual desire to negotiate has only been prompted by each party's wish to prevent an agreement from being reached. In such a situation there is an agreement of intentions *not to* come to an agreement. Much more difficult is the situation where one of the parties does want an agreement, and the other does not (as with Chamberlain versus Hitler before the Second World War). The latter party abuses the former for totally different goals. As previously mentioned, the negotiation disguises the idea to use means other than negotiations. The question is whether, in this case, one can speak of genuine negotiations, when not all parties were striving for a negotiated agreement that had to be successfully implemented in the future.

This issue leads to the question of Forward and Backward-Looking Outcomes (Zartman and Kremenyuk 2005). On the question of Forward and Backward-Looking Outcomes, it should be noted that a lasting peace is in need of justice to be done, plus the instalment of institutions guiding future cooperation between the contending parties – in other words, the institutionalization of the process of cooperation. The European Union is a typical example of such an institutionalized process, while the Peace of Westphalia created the very system of sovereign states in which we are living today. The Dayton Agreement of 1995, however, which settled the Bosnian question, might be viewed as a Backward-Looking Outcome. It put an end to the war, but it did not create a truly stable framework for the future. International governance and troops therefore had to be called in to stabilize the situation until Forward-Looking rules and regulations could create a platform for successful home rule.

Parties might also have reasons for concluding peace, in other words their interests might converge, while they have opposing positions concerning justice being done. Ruling elites might very well be ready to implement a cease-fire, and to quit their posts, but they would not be happy to be prosecuted before the International Criminal Court, or any other tribunal. They will therefore refuse to conclude a peace, because they want to be protected against prosecution. We are confronted here with the dilemma of 'peace versus justice'. In some cases peace can therefore not be attained, or, when it can be attained, doing justice will be difficult, if not impossible. Institutions might not be created as the parties cannot agree on them. And if they did agree, the institutions might be so weak that peace and justice would be under a constant threat of collapse.

We need to analyze the countries' positions in order to know whether an outcome can be expected. If positions and underlying needs are completely in opposition, then we cannot expect a successful negotiation process. As soon as there is an overlap of interest, however, an outcome can be expected. Even without the contending parties having overlapping minimum and maximum reservation points, an outcome could still be constructed, provided that the parties have included more than one issue in their negotiation process, and that by combining these issues, zones of overlap come into reach ('package deals'). Depending on the interrelationship between the interests of the participating parties, we can expect more or less peace and/or justice, and thereby more or less security and/or stability.

There is one more element at stake here: the question of context. What situation are we in? Negotiation is highly situational; what is effective in one context can be disastrous in another. The question of whether negotiation and bargaining will be effective as a tool in conflict resolution is also very much connected to its context. William Zartman (2005) postulates that we need a push and a pull in order to start any negotiation process and to create an outcome. The push is the 'mutual hurting stalemate' (MHS): a status quo that is painful for all the involved parties, to the extent that they prefer a change (through negotiation) over the situation into which they are locked. At the same time there should be a perceived way out of the deadlock: the pull in the form of a 'mutual enticing opportunity' (MEO). We should note here that not everything is negotiable, but in cases where there are structural problems instead of situational problems to be solved, we might at least hope for mutual respect, such as the (in)famous 'Peaceful Coexistence' at the time of the Cold War, which might be called a 'mutual beneficial stalemate' (MBS) – beneficial and satisfactory as it ensures a peaceful situation in such a way that the major powers can use the stand-off to control their own 'allies'. The MBS is stable compared to the MHS, but it thereby paradoxically precludes negotiation from being used as a tool in dealing with the underlying conflicts, because the dominant powers have no interest in solving them. Their allies may have such an interest, however, and they will do everything to undermine the MBS in order to open the situation to change. They will only be successful, however, if there is a regime change in the capitals of the hegemonic powers. In other words, negotiation can only be a successful tool if the context can be changed first. Additionally, while context determines perception, perception determines reality (Goodfield 1999).

20.3   Procedure, Process, Power

The way in which parties reach a settlement can also be divided into three categories. In the first place, there is the procedure whereby parties would like to see what are, for them, the all-important points included in the settlement: the synthesis of interests. A synthesis is often difficult to reach and even more difficult to implement. Second, there is the synergy of interests, when one tries to work not from a partial interest, but from a mutual interest. These kinds of results can be very satisfying, and can be well implemented. However, requirements include a very good atmosphere during the negotiations, and lots of time. Third, there are compromise and compensation. Compromise comes in the form of mutual concessions, in which each party loses some points and wins some, or in which parties compensate each other for their losses by trading concessions ('package deals'). Especially in unequal power situations where one party has to deal with fewer concessions than the other, this formula can lead to 'operation accomplished, patient deceased'. Agreement may be reached, but the loser might end up wanting to sabotage its implementation.

In connection with the aforementioned problems with implementation, experienced negotiators will arrange the agreement in such a way that it can be implemented step by step in order to reduce uncertainty (Jönsson 2001).

If the implementation does not proceed according to plan, the damage will be limited. The implementation is, as it were, ingrained in the agreement and still leaves room for negotiations during the implementation process. One disadvantage of such a course of action is that trust between the parties – especially at the beginning – will remain slight, and trust is the basis of every negotiation when an agreement is required.

A negotiation process means going through various phases: preparation and diagnosis, information, searching for formulations, bargaining, and the drafting of all the details (Dupont and Faure 1991). The factors influencing this process are so numerous that a thorough understanding of the actual proceedings is almost impossible. Previously it was pointed out that the negotiators, with their own characteristics and circumstances, have a certain influence, but that the real determining factor does not rest with them but is ingrained in the power of the countries that they represent, or, in other words, in the power structure, the measure of asymmetry. How 'distorted' is that power structure and which factors determine this 'distortion'?

The question of the direction in which the negotiation process is moving is therefore predominantly a question of power, at least in inter-state negotiation processes. It is interesting to note here that negotiation processes between equal powers are as a rule not very effective. Some power difference is needed in order to get the negotiation process to flow. Power can be distinguished in three components: power that is marginal and originates from the negotiator (power of conduct); power of the state being represented (structural power); and power that belongs to the state regarding the issues being negotiated (comparative power). In that context, Habeeb speaks of 'behavioural power', 'structural power' and 'issue-specific power' (Habeeb 1988).

Structural power involves the total of power factors that are available to a country in relation to that of other nations. This power is determined by issues such as the size and location (for example, a strategic position) of the territory or state, the nature of its borders, its inhabitants, the presence of natural resources, its economic structure, the level of technological development, its financial power, ethnic diversity of its population, social homogeneity, the stability of its political system (that is, how legitimate is the government?) and the nature of its people (whatever that may be, and whether it exists at all). The question that then follows is: in which way does a country handle its power? What is its 'national strategy'? Is the country reticent about using its power (as was Germany before reunification), or does it use its power in a more self-conscious manner (Germany after 1990)?

Structural power is of importance when answering the question of which countries involved in negotiations will reach the best negotiation results in the end. It is a necessary, but not a sufficient, condition for explaining negotiation results (Habeeb 1988). In other words, it is not correct to more or less assume that in negotiations between a large and a small state the 'stronger' state will acquire the best negotiation results. History provides too many examples to the contrary, about the power of the weak and the impotence of the strong (such as the United States and Vietnam, the Soviet Union and Afghanistan, the United Kingdom and Iceland) to be able to come to a simple comparison by predicting the total weight of power of one country or the other. To obtain a better understanding, their comparative power should be drawn into the analysis. By comparative power, we mean the power structures around the issues being negotiated, or the power that is relevant in a particular situation. In practice it is impossible for a country to put forward every power potential in every field. For example, does the Russian Federation, or the Republic of Turkey for that matter, because of its enormous army, have increased power over, for example, Italy when negotiations are taking place in the field of economic cooperation? That is very doubtful. The existence of such an army certainly plays a role, but the danger is neutralized by the politico–military coalitions in which Italy finds itself. From an economic point of view, one could argue that the gigantic potential of the Russian Federation – because of its energy resources – could result in it having a strong position in the negotiations, but the time when this potential will be converted into a strong economic position is still a long way off. Italy's comparative power is bigger than the Russian Federation when, for example, the modernization of Russia's car industry is the issue.

Comparative power is built of three components: the internal sources of power; (im)balance with the sources of power of the other states involved; and the relevance for the issues being negotiated (Habeeb 1988). There are, however, famous examples of countries with minimal internal sources of power that, through special circumstances (such as playing powerful states, or factions within those powerful states, against each other), can build up a great relevant 'blackmail power'. Take, for example, the case of the Netherlands and Surinam during the negotiations about development aid since Surinam became independent in 1975. Comparative power is decisive, and structural power plus the power of conduct will enforce or weaken the relevant factors of power. Surinam has been capable of building up process power, or relational power, because it has been dependent on Dutch resources. Add to this the historical dimension (the Netherlands as the colonial power felt guilty about what it had done to its colonies in the past) and we can expect quite a favourable negotiation process as far as Surinam is concerned, notwithstanding – or better, because of – its weaker position.

Comparative power is influenced by three factors. The first factor is the alternatives that might be available for the relevant issue: the fewer alternatives a country has, the weaker its cause. Second, to what extent has the country committed itself: how far will willingness go to make use of its power factors? Is there, for example, a willingness to weaken a country's economic power in favour of its military power? Third, to what extent does the country have control over the issues under negotiation? A small nation can have a lead position over a bigger country when it controls the dispute in question, as was the case for Iran in connection with the American diplomats who were taken hostage during the so-called 'Iranian Hostage Crisis'. The hostages were at first in the hands of fanatics who were outside the control of the Iranian government, but once the hostages were being held by the Iranian government, it was possible to negotiate their freedom.

20.4 Competing, Conceding, Coordinating

A distinction should be made about negotiating in relation to other interactions between states, such as armed conflict, the use of international courts of law or arbitration, the use of services from third states as honest brokers, and diplomatic consultations in which certain issues are being clarified and points of view exchanged, as opposed to the phenomenon of imposed settlements or '*diktat*' such as 'Versailles', in which interaction was hardly the case. The following question presents itself here: in which cases will states prefer the instrument of negotiation, and when will they choose alternatives in international relations? If war is the continuation of politics with the admixture of other means (Clausewitz 1984), could we then postulate that negotiation is war by other means? In other words, while the use of force is one way to manage a conflict, negotiation is another, and adjudication is a third road to be followed.

The choice has everything to do with the question of whether negotiation in a given situation is preferable to the use of other international interactions. Negotiating will be 'more advantageous' in cases where the state would be able to acquire what it has in mind in a 'cheaper' way through negotiations than in any other way. In short, the question about the limitations of the negotiation process is a matter of cost-benefit analysis. Depending on the situation at that moment, the balance will be different each time. When the expected benefit is considerably higher than the cost, the desire for a stable negotiation process is obviously justified.

The problem remains that cost-benefit analysis can, relatively speaking, rarely be determined, keeping in mind the influence of other states with their own cost-benefit situations, and given the impossibility, up to the present day, to verify costs. That is the first and biggest obstacle to providing at any one time an instrument for totally getting to the bottom of 'the science of negotiation'. The second obstacle, as mentioned before, is that the researcher is not allowed to attend really important negotiations, or to carry out research in a systematic manner. Reports by the negotiators themselves are usually too biased, and not systematic enough, to enable a real scientific analysis. Third, in cases where good analysis should be possible, the results will nonetheless be so abstract because of the many factors playing a role that a more or less practical application, such as through training courses, will be difficult.

Nevertheless, the number of useful explanations about the role and direction of international negotiation processes is increasing. Slowly, but surely, there is a growing convergence of views. However, one has to be wary of those who think that they have found the stone of wisdom. They may have carried the building stones, perhaps even a keystone, but certainly not a cornerstone. Perhaps that cornerstone will present itself in the form of sound research, analysing in which cases negotiating can, and in which circumstances negotiating cannot, be an instrument of international relations.

It is interesting to observe that the notions of international negotiation processes as a method of bridging opposing interests, views and perceptions have evolved over time. In the seventeenth and eighteenth centuries, negotiations were often used as a tool in warfare. Notably King Louis XIV of France used this constellation in order to break up coalitions formed against him, resulting in a series of short-lived peace treaties and ongoing warfare on the European continent. Moving into the nineteenth century, the role of negotiation in inter-state relations became more and more substantial, as the costs of war soared with the development of modern weapons technology, which resulted in an enormous toll of human lives. In the twentieth century, states tried to strengthen the value, and enhance the stability, of international negotiation processes through institutionalization – that is, the building of institutions in order to channel and stabilize negotiation processes and thereby to secure assured outcomes. Thus we witnessed the creation of the League of Nations, the United Nations, the Organization for Security and Cooperation in Europe, the North Atlantic Treaty Organization, and the European Union, etc. With the Second World War as a turning point, we might postulate that warfare nowadays can be a tool in negotiation, whereby negotiation is seen as the main tool in managing inter-state and other conflicts. We have come a long way since the seventeenth century. The institutionalization of the processes and the relative ineffectiveness of war (by using military means we can win the war, but not the peace) greatly enhanced the effectiveness, and therefore the role, of negotiation as a tool in conflict resolution.

20.5 Changes Over the Centuries

An important difference between international negotiation processes of the past and present is the question of the *relevance* of the bargaining process in conflict management. If warfare and negotiation are seen as alternatives – if both are politics by other means – warfare was the priority tool in inter-state conflict until the twentieth century. This is an interesting paradox, as no other era has seen such massive warfare as the last century. On the other hand, no other period in European history has witnessed such substantial periods of stable peace as the nineteenth century. Throughout the centuries, negotiation became a more relevant tool, although warfare for a long time remained the preferred means to settle problems. In Europe, negotiation gained strength because of four developments.

The first development was *technology*. If anything characterizes human history, it is the change in technological devices. One can question the development of culture, for are we at a higher level than in the past? Perhaps not. One can state that art did not develop into a higher stage, but who is to judge the quality of Rembrandt's work compared to modern and ancient art? One can question the development of the human psyche, of human health, yet are we better off than in the past? Perhaps we can acknowledge that our political systems reached some sort of ripeness. We can definitely prove, however, that technology evolved in a positive way, that it reached a higher standard than in classical times, medieval times, or the Renaissance. Technology influenced warfare in the sense that it created more destructive weaponry than ever. At the same time, technology gave diplomacy the sophisticated tools needed to forge organizations channelling negotiation processes. It contributed to the availability and speed of information facilitating effective negotiation. While technology made warfare an often too dangerous sword to wield, it made negotiation a more effective tool to bridge the gap.

The second development was that of *regime-building*. Regimes, in the form of international agreements stipulating rules and regulations of conduct and – at best – allowing for sanctions against those parties that do not comply with the understandings that have been made, can compensate for lack of trust by imposing control. They provide information about the parties' behaviour and monitor their activities. Regimes can go a step further by establishing international organizations in order to have a more durable and ongoing surveillance of the (mis)behaviour of states. Surely, leaders might trust each other, but why should states set their *raison d'état* aside for something as feeble as trust, which can be turned over from 1 day to another? Not having any regimes to stabilize negotiation processes and secure the outcome contributed to the idea that bargaining could be – at most – a sideshow in warfare. Trust has always been *the* pre-eminent problem in negotiation. As long as one cannot be sure about the intentions of the other side and its willingness to stick to an agreement, governments have proven to be reluctant to put all their eggs in the basket of negotiation as an alternative to warfare.

Negotiators tried to deal with this problem in different ways. They swore pious oaths and asked all the available gods to bless the treaties that they forged, but as this clearly did not guarantee any solid implementation of any holy pact, negotiators had to think of other ways, such as strengthening relationships, for example, or exchanging hostages, or, as in the seventeenth century, asking guarantors (like France and Sweden in the Peace of Westphalia in 1648) to help implement the treaty. In the eighteenth century, after the (in essence) multi-bilateral Peace of Utrecht (1713), the number of conferences multiplied in an attempt to stop wars ravaging the European continent and to make bargaining the dominant mode in conflict management. In the nineteenth century, starting with the multilateral Vienna Conference (1814–1815), the meetings between heads of states and diplomats became a systemic feature, but ongoing organizational structures were still lacking. This changed in the twentieth century after the devastating First World War (with the Paris Conference and the Peace of Versailles in 1919) and then the Second World War (Conference of San Francisco in 1945), by creating regimes of ever-better quality and strength, not only on a regional, but also on a global level.

Regimes, in transforming negotiations into increasingly rationalized tools, dealt with the problem of *trust* in an effective way. The development of trust is the third remarkable trend in the evolution of inter-state negotiation. Secrecy was a major issue in early European diplomacy, much more than today. Ambassadors had to be versed in publicly representing their monarchs as well as dealing with issues under conditions of complete secrecy. Being able to keep secrets, to be specialized in treason, maintaining a poker-face and the like were the qualities of the effective ambassador-negotiator (Colson 2008; Berridge 1999). Distances, time-lags, transportation problems and communication distortions all helped secrecy. There are of course still secrets nowadays in diplomatic negotiation and the WikiLeaks revelations pushed them to the forefront of the public debate (Rosoux 2013; Meerts 2013). Modern authors on negotiation even plea for openness as a means to further the effectiveness and speed of negotiation processes, although it remains unwise to show your trump-cards 'in public'. So-called 'corridor work' (outside the conference room) and 'huddling' (small groups of negotiators talking informally in the conference room during a break in the formal session) are still an essential part of bargaining, also for cultural reasons. Open concession-making can lead to losing face, as negotiators might refuse to give in openly, only in informal sessions.

The fourth evolving element is *power*. The political context is changing. Power is more equally distributed today than in the past, even internationally (Cohen and Meerts 2008: 155), although it is still more bluntly used in international relations than in national politics, at least in and between democracies. This clearly has to do with the evolution of human history, the development of democracy, creating more diffusion of power, and the protection of minorities and human rights. At the same time, the distribution of power among states has become less volatile, while intergovernmental and non-governmental organizations are on the rise (Van Staden 1987: 14), helping to stabilize power or to diffuse it.

Non-state groups, including regional and terrorist organizations, are able to undermine the hegemony of the state, because weapons technology has been globalized so much that the state's monopoly of structural advantage is washing away. Nuclear states still hold this prerogative, but even they might be under attack in the future, as nuclear weapons are of no avail against regional or global insurgencies. Furthermore, the idea that states should not be wiped out just like that, even with the rationale that the stronger state might use nuclear weapons in the future against other major powers, gave minor powers a rightful and legitimate niche in international politics, and therefore in international bargaining. Negotiation is situational and contextual. Major changes in the political context will influence the character and the effectiveness of international negotiation processes.

Can one therefore conclude that negotiation evolved into a more valuable and legitimate instrument in international conflict and international relations than other methodologies, such as, first and foremost, warfare? Indeed, 'Negotiation becomes the prevailing method in conflict resolution and the prevention of further violent conflicts'. However, this does not mean – at all – that warfare has lost its significance. And in many cases it is still easier to go to war than to open negotiations. Given the present levels of technology, regime strength, the instruments to compensate for lack of trust and the attempts to respect minor powers, it can indeed be hypothesized that negotiation evolved into one – if not the main – tool in international conflict management and resolution. With disasters and scarcity ahead, the world might well want to learn from the experiences of the past, to be better equipped in dealing with the future.

20.6 Regimes and Negotiations

Depledge observes that '[g]lobal negotiations are often closely associated with the formation and development of regimes, defined as sets of both formal and informal rules, institutions and procedures aimed at governing action in a particular issue area, usually based on a founding treaty', while 'an important function performed by regimes is precisely to provide an efficient framework for negotiations' (Depledge 2005: 13). On the nature of negotiations within regimes, he notes that they:

> [...] have a special character. Like all intergovernmental negotiations, they are repetitive, but more intensively so, often involving not only the same governments, but also the same individuals. [...] The negotiation process within the regime typically gives rise to its own set of informal practices and procedures, even its own culture. While such intensively repeated games can provide important opportunities for learning and therefore improving ways of negotiating, the flipside is the danger of ossification: the negotiation process gets stuck in old ways of thinking and doing that drag down substantive progress (Depledge 2005: 13–14).

Similarly, William Zartman points to the connectedness between negotiation processes and international regimes by arguing that 'international regimes are continuous two-dimensional negotiations among sovereign states for the purpose of resolving a problem of coordination under conditions of uncertainty' (Zartman 2003: 14). Zartman sees regime-building as an ongoing negotiation.

Like Depledge and Keohane, Zartman believes that 'the concept of "regime" was devised to meet the need for something looser and less rigid than "international law" or "international organization'" (Zartman 2003: 17), although nowadays an international organization is regarded as a highly structured regime mode. Spector and Zartman point out that regime building is a painful negotiation process: 'Fear of relinquishing sovereign legal authority is obviously a very serious issue that constrains the evolution of any regime. International regimes constitute governing in the absence of government through the processes of negotiation' (Spector and Zartman 2003: 282).

There is a rich variety of regimes. Spector distinguishes three kinds of national, and three kinds of international regime negotiations. On the national level, he identifies: (1) acceptance/ratification negotiations; (2) rule-making negotiations and enforcement; and (3) monitoring and reporting negotiations. As for international regime negotiations, he classifies: (1) regime formation negotiations; (2) regime governance negotiations; and (3) regime adjustment negotiations (Spector 2003: 65–66). Together with Zartman, Spector concludes that the following categories of regimes can be observed: those that remain more or less in force as originally negotiated; regimes that grow and evolve; and regimes that follow a jagged course (Spector and Zartman 2003: 372). The second kind of regime, those that grow and evolve, is seen most frequently in the world.

It is important to recognize that regime and negotiation are symbiotic: while regimes are created through national and international negotiation processes, they then protect these processes and thereby enhance their effectiveness in reaching outcomes. Moreover, *'for the most part, exogenous shocks or crises increase the probability of success in efforts to negotiate the terms of international regimes'* (Young 1989: 371). These outcomes 'are not monocausal events, but rather the product of a multitude of strategic, political and [...] psychological factors' (Terris and Tykocinski 2014: 14). 'As in any negotiation, personal skills are an important factor in the process, but in the multilateral setting, the context, the jargon and the procedures rule the day' (Perlot 2014: 27). Nevertheless: *'Institutional bargaining is likely to succeed when effective leadership emerges; it will fail in the absence of such leadership'* (Young 1989: 373).

How structured or how fluid are regimes nowadays? According to Spector and Zartman, regimes tend to be more fluid than before: 'In the early twenty-first century, reality tends to lie on the softer end of the spectrum' (Spector and Zartman 2003: 292). Taking the number of regimes in the world, this statement is true for sure, especially after the present-day erosion of the multilateral system through unilateral action. Yet if one divides regimes into 'strong' and 'weak', 'important' and 'less important', or looks at strength and effectiveness, the world might look very different. Regimes with most added value are normally more structured than those of a more fluid nature. In other words, more *'regimist'* regimes seem to be more structured. As they matter more to the international system, one could make the statement that *effective regimes in the twenty-first century tend to lie on the institutional side of the spectrum.*

However, as regimes' effectiveness seems to be dependent on their flexibility, one should add that *effective regimes are highly structured institutions that are managed through fluid processes.* If the processes become less fluid and more bureaucratic, as tends to be the case with successful regimes (which therefore have a long life-span in general), '*regimist*' regimes might hamper their own success in the long run, just as diseases tend to affect a body more as it grows older and older. The fluidity of the process is even more important if one looks at the political dimensions of the regime. According to high-ranking German diplomat Michael Schäfer: 'Negotiations are the art of consensus-building, and the more political the subject matter is, the less formal the formats of the negotiation process will be to prepare for the best possible outcome. Why? Because of the heterogeneity of the various interests involved in that process (Hanschel 2005).

20.7   Coping with Challenges

New international orders often come into being after man-made disasters. The world apparently needed a first and a second world war in order to finally create global political organizations: the League of Nations and the United Nations, respectively. The Cold War gave rise to the North-Atlantic Treaty Organization (NATO) and Warsaw Pact. Meanwhile, German–French animosity needed three wars before it was understood that a problem cannot be solved on the level that it arises, so the European Union was created.

As soon as a major threat arises, regimes are put in place. The more serious the challenge, the more willingness there is to invest in dealing with it, but if and only if the threatened party cannot deal with it on its own and needs allies, and moreover if an ad-hoc alliance cannot be the answer and an institutionalized structure is needed. If the party under threat is strong enough to deal with the issue, regime formation is not needed and will actually hamper the room for manoeuvre of the state involved so that an effective negotiation process cannot be expected to take place.

New challenges might put life into existing organizations that never really got off the ground or that lost their significance. The need for peacekeeping operations led by countries in the region itself thus vitalized the Organization of African Unity, now the African Union (AU). The need for security, stability, protection of human rights and the emergence of new democratic systems gave new meaning to the Conference for Security and Organization in Europe (CSCE), now the Organization for Security and Organization in Europe (OSCE). But how effective are these regimes in comparison to the needs of the international community? How effective are new institutions such as the Yugoslav Tribunal and the International Criminal Court? They want to move from peace to justice, but peace versus justice is often the problem (Zartman and Kremenyuk 2005) and there is not enough external and/or internal pressure to start a 'common project', to establish a regime that is strong enough to cope with the challenge.

Although many techniques have been developed in order to get regimes to deal with problems effectively, for example in the European Union, they can hardly be successful if the major powers within and outside the regime want to handle regime change unilaterally, bilaterally, or trilaterally, or indeed outside the existing regime(s), as the restraints of the regime might block an effective '*Alleingang*' (going it alone). Here we have the paradox that rules and regulations, and institutions and vested interests, strengthen the capability of a regime to cope with problems. This creates a bargaining platform, but at the same time it restricts the bargaining range and freedom of the more powerful states. They will therefore work in the spirit of negotiation, being a context-dependent process, by acting in a situational way. This might then be favourable for some parties involved, but it can be disastrous for the common good. In the European Union, this is the classical dilemma of full or partial integration of new member states; in the United Nations Framework Treaty on Climate Change and the World Trade Organization, it is about short-term over long-term interests.

In other words, the constraints to having adaptable and effective regimes are of both an internal and an external nature. Internal delimitations are often difficult to handle if outside pressure is lacking. This is not so much an issue of a 'mutual hurting stalemate', but of lack of 'painful pressure from outside' (PPO). Perhaps this was comfortable hurting pressure from outside, which is what kept the Socialist Federal Republic of Yugoslavia together. When the Cold War was over, this pressure fell and so did Yugoslavia. PPO can, of course, be created by the regime itself, as with Indonesia's regime, which sought to strengthen its internal position by seeking the '*konfrontasi*' (confrontation) with Malaysia from 1963–1966, and like the Soviet Union and United States, which gained more control over their allies in the Warsaw Pact and NATO, respectively, by overplaying the external threat. Both regimes flourished in this way, as a regime at least, but somebody of course had to pay for this – the civilians of the particular regime's member states. NATO hardly survived the end of the East–West confrontation and the Warsaw Pact died on the spot, yet with the regimes gone or destroyed, instability entered the European theatre (Davies 1996).

Negotiation processes within the regimes – a regime's lifeblood, it has been said – are quite defenceless without their cover. Like a turtle, the process of international negotiation is a peaceful, but slow animal. It needs the shell of the regime to survive, or at least to be effective and sustainable. At the same time, the shell is a heavy burden that slows down the turtle even further, with the turtle thereby losing its relevance and perhaps being trod upon. If the shell is hard enough, however, the animal will survive and can wait for a better future.

20.8   Prospects

So what about that future, let us say the first half of the twenty-first century? From a political point of view, it will be impossible to calculate the evolution of international regimes as international organizations if national regimes in the form of the sovereign states are overlooked. The central question seems to revolve around the extent to which (member) states need each other in order to expect further regime growth.

As centuries pass by and violence becomes a more costly affair, one can observe an evolution in regimes in the sense of their international organization and cooperation. In general, regimes become more complex and more effective, although the one does not always favour the other. Interdependency fosters regime-building, but because it removes stimuli (threats), it also puts the brakes on.

At the beginning of the twenty-first century, there does not seem to be much room for optimism as far as the further growth of international regimes is concerned. The present distribution of power among states, which still continue to prioritize sovereignty over international cooperation and international organization, works against further regime-building. Some kind of equilibrium – whether mutual assured destruction or risk management, a Concert of Europe approach or a well-understood balance of interests (Dupont 2003) – seems to be needed to create the cradle in which the international regime can grow old and flourish. So we cannot expect too much from regimes as long as a new balance between major regimes has not been established, and this might take the whole first half of the twenty-first century.

Strengthening regimes in the coming 50 years will only be possible if states not only focus on structured international cooperation and multilateral bargaining, but also prioritize ad-hoc negotiation processes and bilateral bargaining. Multilateralism, i.e. 'Conference Diplomacy' (Meerts 2014), does not work without bilateralism. As negotiations are the life-blood of regimes, so bilateral negotiation is the gist and juice in creating a new balance of power among the major regimes, whether they are states or international organizations. In other words, we have to look at both structured and less-structured modes of cooperation. Negotiation processes are fit for both.

Another important point is the level of negotiation. National problems will have to be negotiated at the national level. This seems self-evident, but in the European Union in particular, problems are shifted to inappropriate levels. Governments tend to get rid of difficult issues by pushing them to higher levels, then blaming 'Brussels' for not being effective.

Inclusiveness is also important. Inclusiveness might give rise to opportunities (such as trade-offs and multiple outcomes) and to problems (such as complexity). William Bottom gives an example of the disastrous consequences of exclusion at Versailles, while Dupont shows both the importance of including the major players and excluding the minor ones in Vienna in 1814–1815 (Dupont 2003). Regimes may assume a life of their own, a life independent of the basic causal factors that led to their creation in the first place. There is not always congruity between underlying power capabilities, regimes, and related behaviour and outcomes. Principles, norms, and procedures may not conform with the preferences of the most powerful states. Ultimate state power and interests condition both regime structures and related behaviour, but there may be a wide area of leeway (Krasner 1983: 357).

Polarization is the phenomenon of the new millennium. The growth of international regimes, and in particular the European Union, raised hopes for enhancing the role of international negotiation processes as an antidote for violence. However, the attacks on the World Trade Centre, the international wars in Afghanistan and Iraq, followed by the 'Arabic Spring' and the civil wars in Syria and Yemen, as well as the return of Russian – American and American – Chinese antitheses re-polarized the world after the thaw in international politics in the last decade of the twentieth century. These tensions threaten to unravel and paralyze the multilateral framework facilitating effective negotiation processes while some treaties, that were success-fully negotiated, will remain in a non-ratified limo. On top of this the European – American alliance seems to crumble both in the political, economic and security realm.

The European Union itself is moaning under external pressures like the refugee crisis and the export of terrorism to continent, while its relationship with its direct neighbourhood in the East and in the South is deteriorating. At the same time inter-nal centrifugal tendencies are seriously undermining the cohesiveness and therefore the strength of the EU. Not only because of the pressure on the euro and Brexit, but also as a consequence of the rise of nationalism and populism inside and outside the Union. The election of Donald Trump will have a negative effect on the strength of the fabric of international negotiation processes as a means to wage war by peace-ful means.

20.9 Conclusions

International negotiations are being nationalized and national negotiations are being internationalized. The domain of international relations and a country's carefully separated area of internal affairs are beginning to merge with each other. If it is no longer clear where the demarcation lies for the international dimension, how can the diplomat's position as the monopolist in international relations be maintained? In this way, the diplomat loses his prerogative as an international negotiator. He or she is in competition with colleagues (departmental civil servants) who often know more about the specialized subject than the diplomat. The increasing complexity of inter-national affairs increases the influence of the non-diplomat expert. The diplomat maintains her or his function as a generalist who is necessary for coordination. Improved means of communication make it easier for the civil servant to negotiate directly with his or her counterpart in another country. The same is true for ministers and heads of state who do business directly at summit conferences, sometimes osten-tatiously closing out their assistants. It is extremely difficult to keep them on track, especially if they feel that the defence of their reputation might be more important than the interest of their country, the phenomenon of *egotiation*. In summary, the role of the diplomat as negotiator is being undermined. Inter-state negotiation is increas-ingly 'inter-civil-servant' and 'inter-politician' negotiation and less often diplomatic negotiation in the sense of an international negotiation process between diplomats.

Above all, within the European Union, there are visible processes that threaten to marginalize the diplomat's role in relation to the negotiator of the specialized departments. Also outside of the Union, there are developments that threaten to diminish the role of the diplomatic negotiator. In addition to the civil servant, there are other competitors. The democratization of society leads to increasing interventions by politicians and non-governmental groups and organizations. This leads to greater openness and increases the role of the media and journalists as players in the international arena. Companies also play an increasing role in international affairs, certainly now that there is a higher priority placed on economic developments. The businessman and his interests can no longer be ignored by diplomacy. For example, the effort to increase exports has become a larger part of the diplomatic task. Saner describes and analyzes the divergent post-modern diplomatic roles in the economic sphere of representatives of states and of non-state actors. Commercialization, privatization, democratization, politicizing, professionalizing, increasing interdependence, improved communication, improved transport, greater security risks and the increasing number of international issues: in short, the quality and quantity of the international questions to be negotiated is on the rise.

International negotiations are thus less often synonymous with inter-state negotiations. The state has lost influence, and within the state, the diplomat. Paradoxically, because of the increase in importance of diplomatic negotiations, a more modest role is set aside for the diplomat. It would perhaps be better to speak nowadays about 'inter-state negotiations' – that is, negotiations in which diplomacy is only one of the players. In addition, it can be concluded that inter-state negotiations will have competition from an increasing number of other forms of negotiation, while the state-like character of negotiations between countries will lessen.

Does this mean that the roles of diplomacy and of the state are becoming so marginalized that international negotiations will lose their meaning as a theme for study and training? The answer is just the opposite (Flemish Foreign Affairs Council 2013: 1). The study of, and training in, international negotiations are increasing, just as the world is becoming more internationally oriented, just as international developments have an increasing influence on the internal development of states, and just as the increasing complexity of international developments bring greater pressure on the ability of states and their representatives to create order, without which further peaceful development is not possible. It is precisely in these circumstances that the role of the diplomat as coordinator, shaper and negotiator – in short, communicator – will gain in significance. The tasks of the modern diplomat of the twenty-first century will be difficult to compare to that of the twentieth century, not to mention of the nineteenth or eighteenth centuries.

The unpredictability of international negotiations and their outcomes is problematic. Unpredictability is bad for stable relations between states and is bad for effective negotiations. It is up to the diplomat to demonstrate his abilities and to improve predictability. In order to do this, the diplomat must be formal and flexible at the same time. He or she must maintain relations and continue to work precisely in those instances in which the conflicts threaten to become the most serious. Power must be used in situations in which states consider themselves inviolable, which calls for great knowledge of the dossiers. Diplomats work in extremely complex situations, making it necessary for them to have a lot of professionalism and general skills and knowledge. In negotiating, which by definition is a paradoxical method because of competitive and cooperative elements at the same time, the diplomat is confronted with difficult situations for which an acceptable solution must be found.

Diplomats will be inclined to take into account the consequences of their decision making in the future: 'diplomats involved in international bargaining are almost always less concerned about the issue immediately at hand than about the impact of the settlement on resolving future issues' (Ray 1998: 143). Furthermore they 'are anxious to avoid giving the impression that they make concessions easily' (Ray 1998: 145). Daniel Druckman highlights this problem by making a distinction between settlement and resolution: 'the former emphasizes getting deals; the latter promotes longer term relationships' (Druckman 2013: 201). Seen from this perspective, international negotiation is still a useful tool in conflict management, but it might be an obstacle to conflict transformation.

While globalization and polarization are going hand-in-hand, national and international negotiation are more than ever needed as an instrument in peaceful conflict resolution. At the same time its underpinnings are undermined by the way states and their unruly citizens deal with each other in the second millennium of the twenty-first century (Janush 2016).

Further Readings

Gaddis, J. L. (1986, Spring). The long peace: Elements of stability in the postwar international system. *International Security, 10*(4), 99–142, MIT press.

Gross-Stein, J. (2013). Building politics into psychology: The misperception of threat. In L. Huddy, D. O. Sears, & J. S. Levy (Eds.), *The Oxford handbook of political psychology* (2nd ed.). Oxford: Oxford University Press.

Jervis, R. (1976). *Perception and misperception in international politics.* Princeton: Princeton University Press.

Jervis, R. (1978). Cooperation under security dilemma. *World Politics, 30*(2, January), 167–214, Cambridge University Press.

Jervis, R. (1988, Spring). War and misperception. *The Journal of Interdisciplinary History, 18*(4), The origin and prevention of major wars, pp. 675–700, MIT Press.

Keohane, R. O., & Nye, J. S. (1997). Interdependence in world politics. In G. T. Crane & A. Amawi (Eds.), *The theoretical evolution of international political economy.* New York: Oxford University Press.

Kissinger, H. (1994). *Diplomacy.* New York: Simon & Schuster.

Mearsheimer, J. (2010). The gathering storm: China's challenge to US power in Asia. *The Chinese Journal of International Politics, 3*, 381–396.

Morgenthau, H. (1978). *Six principles of political realism.* New York: Alfred A. Knopf.

Ratner, S. (1988, Spring). *International law: The trials of global norms.* Foreign policy no. 110, Special edition: Frontiers of knowledge, pp. 65–80.

Schweller, R. (1993). Tripolarity and the Second World War. *International Studies Quarterly, 37*(1, March), 73–103.

Snyder, J., & Christensen, T. J. (1990, Spring). Chain gangs and passed bucks. *International Organization, 44*(2), 137–168.

Van Evera, S. (1985). Why cooperation failed in 1914. *World Politics, 38*(1, October), 80–117.

References

Albin, C., & Druckman, D. (2012). Equality matters: Negotiating an end to civil wars. *Journal of Conflict Resolution, 00*(0), 1–28.

Axelrod, R. (1984). *The evolution of cooperation.* New York: Basic Books.

Berridge, G. R. (1998). *Harold Nicolson and diplomatic theory: Between old diplomacy and new.* Leicester: Diplomatic Studies Programme, Discussion papers, 44.

Berridge, G. R. (1999). *Machiavelli on diplomacy.* Leicester: Diplomatic Studies Programme, Discussion papers, 50.

Cohen, R., & Meerts, P. W. (2008). The evolution of international negotiation processes. *International Negotiation, 13*(2), 149–156.

Colson, A. (2008). The ambassador, between light and shade: The emergence of secrecy as a norm in international negotiation. *International Negotiation, 13*(2), 179–195.

Colson, A., Druckman, D., & Donohue, W. (2013). Foreword. In A. Colson, D. Druckman, & W. Donohue (Eds.), *International negotiation: Foundations, models, and philosophies. Christophe Dupont* (pp. 225–232). Dordrecht: Republic of Letters.

Davies, N. (1996). *Europe, a history.* Oxford/New York: Oxford University Press.

de Callières, F. (1983). *The art of diplomacy* (English translation). New York: Addison Wesley Longman.

Depledge, J. (2005). *The organization of global negotiations: Constructing the climate change regime.* London: Earthscan.

Druckman, D. (2013). Frameworks, cases, and risks: Dupont's legacy. In A. Colson, D. Druckman, & W. Donehue (Eds.), *International negotiation: Foundations, models and philosophies.* Dordrecht: Republic of Letters.

Dupont, C. (2003). History and coalitions: The Vienna congress (1814–1815). *International Negotiation, 8*(1), 169–178.

Dupont, C., & Faure, G. O. (1991). The negotiation process. In V. A. Kremenyuk (Ed.), *International negotiation* (pp. 40–57). San Francisco/Oxford: Jossey-Bass.

Faure, G. O. (2003). *How people negotiate.* Dordrecht/London/Boston: Kluwer Academi Publishers.

Flemish Foreign Affairs Council. (2013). *Een Nieuwe Vlaamse Diplomatie in een Veranderende Wereld: naar een Efficiënt Buitenlands Netwerk.* Brussels: Jan Wouters.

Goodfield, B. A. (1999). *Insight and action: The role of the unconscious in crisis from the personal to international levels.* London: University of Westminster Press.

Habeeb, W. M. (1988). *Power and tactics in international negotiation.* Baltimore/London: Johns Hopkins University Press.

Hanschel, D. (2005). Assessing institutional effectiveness: Lessons drawn from the regimes on ozone depletion and climate change. In E. Riedel & D. Hanschel (Eds.), *Institutionalization of international negotiation systems: Theoretical concepts and practical insights.* Mannheim: Universität Mannheim, 24.

Iklé, F. (1964). *How nations negotiate.* New York: Harper & Row.

Janush, H. (2016). The breakdown of international negotiations: Social conflicts, audience costs, and reputation in two-level games. *International Negotiation, 21*(3), 495–520.

Jönsson, C. (2001). *Conceptualizations of the negotiation process.* Canterbury: Paper prepared for the 4th Pan-European International Relations Conference, section 33.

Jönsson, C., & Hall, M. (2005). *Essence of diplomacy.* Houndmills: Palgrave Macmillan.

Kaplan, M. (2010). *Commercieel onderhandelen: een transdisciplinaire aanpak.* Universiteit van Leiden, dissertatie.

Kissinger, H. A. (1969). The Vietnam negotiations. *Foreign Affairs, 47*(1), 211–234.

Klabbers, H. G. (Ed.). (1988). *Simulation-gaming.* Oxford: Pergamon Press.

Koskenniemi, M. (2011). *Histories of international law: Dealing with eurocentrism.* Inaugural Address, University of Utrecht, Faculty of Humanities.

Krasner, S. D. (1983). Structural causes and regime consequences: Regimes as intervening variables' and 'regimes and the limits of realism. In S. D. Krasner (Ed.), *International regimes.* Ithaca/London: Cornell University Press.

Lewicki, R. J., Litterer, J. A., Minton, J. W., & Saunders, D. M. (1994). *Negotiation* (2nd ed.). Homewood/Boston/Sydney: Irwin.

Meerts, P. W. (2009). Training and education. In J. Bercovitch, V. A. Kremenyuk, & I. W. Zartman (Eds.), *The sage handbook of conflict resolution* (pp. 645–668). Thousand Oaks: Sage.

Meerts, P. W. (2012). Simulare Necesse Est. *Simulation & Gaming, XX*(X), 1–6.

Meerts, P. W. (2013). Public opinion and negotiation: The dilemma of openness and secretiveness. *PINpoints Network Perspectives, 39,* 22–24.

Meerts, P. W. (2014). Conference diplomacy. In C. M. Constantinou, P. Kerr, & P. Sharp (Eds.), *The sage handbook of diplomacy* (pp. 499–509). Thousand Oaks: Sage.

Nicolson, H. (1963). *Diplomacy.* London: Oxford University Press.

Perlot, W. (2014). Visit to the 26th session of the human rights council. *PINpoints Network Newsletter, 40,* 46–47.

Raiffa, H. (1982). *The art and science of negotiation.* Cambridge, MA/London: Belknap Press of Harvard University Press.

Ray, J. L. (1998). *Global politics.* Boston/New York: Houghton Mifflin.

Rosoux, V. (2013). Secrecy and international negotiation. *PINpoints Network Perspectives, 39,* 18–20.

Rubin, J. (1991). Psychological approach. In V. A. Kremenyuk (Ed.), *International negotiation* (pp. 216–288). San Francisco/Oxford: Jossey-Bass.

Spector, B. I. (2003). Deconstructing the negotiations of regime dynamics. In B. I. Spector & I. W. Zartman (Eds.), *Getting it done: Post-agreement negotiation and international regimes* (pp. 51–87). Washington, DC: United States Institute of Peace Press.

Spector, B. I., & Zartman, I. W. (2003). Regimes in motion: Analysis and lessons learned. In I. B. Spector & I. W. Zartman (Eds.), *Getting it done: Post-agreement negotiation and international regimes* (pp. 271–292). Washington, DC: United Nations Institute of Peace Press.

Terris, L. G., & Tykocinski, O. E. (2014). Inaction inertia in international negotiations: The consequences of missed opportunities. *British Journal of Political Science, 46*(3, July), 1–17.

van Staden, A. (1987). De heerschappij van staten: het perspectief van het realisme. In R. B. Soetendorp & A. van Staden (Eds.), *Internationale betrekkingen in perspectief.* Utrecht: Uitgeverij Het Spectrum.

von Clausewitz, C. (1984). *On war* (M. Howard & P. Paret, Ed. & Trans.). Princeton: Princeton University Press.

Westerman, F. (2016). *Een Woord Een Woord.* Amsterdam/Antwerpen, De Bezige Bij, 121.

Young, O. R. (1989). The politics of international regime formation: Managing natural resources and the environment. *International Organization, 43*(3), 349–375.

Zartman, I. W. (2003). Negotiating the rapids: The dynamics of regime formation. In B. I. Spector & I. W. Zartman (Eds.), *Getting it done: Post-agreement negotiation and international regimes* (pp. 13–50). Washington, DC: United States Institute of Peace Press.

Zartman, I. W. (2005). Concepts: Mutual Enticing Opportunity (MEO). *PINpoints Network Newsletter.* Laxenburg: IIASA, 24, 1–4.

Zartman, I. W., & Kremenyuk, V. A. (Eds.). (2005). *Peace versus justice: Negotiating forward- and backward-looking outcomes* (pp. 35–71). Oxford: Rowman & Littlefield.

Zartman, I. W., & Rubin, J. Z. (Eds.). (2000). *Power and negotiation.* Ann Arbor: University of Michigan Press.

Chapter 21
Debunking the Myths of International Mediation: Conceptualizing Bias, Power and Success

Siniša Vuković

21.1 Introduction

Despite their widely acknowledged success, some of the most significant peace-making processes in the twentieth century – such as the *1978 Camp David Accords* that sanctioned a first of its kind political rapprochement between an Arab country and Israel, the *1993 Oslo Accords* that saw the PLO and Israel exchange letters of mutual recognition, the *1995 Dayton Agreement* that ended a violent conflict in war-torn Bosnia, and *1988 Tripartite Accord* between Angola, Cuba and South Africa which granted independence for Namibia – failed to address all of the driving mechanisms that fuelled the respective conflicts. In fact, during the Camp David talks between Israel and Egypt, the matter of Palestinian autonomy was treated only marginally, while main issues – such as the final status of Jerusalem and the Palestinian right to return – were intentionally ignored. Similarly, during the Oslo talks in 1993 between Israel and PLO the issue of Jerusalem was once again deliberately left out as a way to reach an accord that will strongly condition any future negotiation attempts. The 1995 peacemaking process in Dayton that ended the conflict in Bosnia never discussed the situation and the future of Kosovo. Lastly, the peacemaking process that resulted in Namibia's independence in 1988 intentionally avoided discussing the internal issues both in Namibia – between SWAPO and DTA – and in Angola – between MPLA and UNITA – and rather focused on the regional dynamics of the ongoing conflicts in Angola and Namibia, by primarily addressing the presence of foreign troops in those areas and the urgent need to tie in their withdrawal into a peace deal. As experience shows, the peacemaking processes are often

S. Vuković (✉)
Johns Hopkins University, SAIS, Washington, DC, USA

Leiden University, FGGA, The Hague, The Netherlands
e-mail: sumosika@yahoo.com

© Springer Nature Switzerland AG 2020
M. O. Hosli, J. Selleslaghs (eds.), *The Changing Global Order*, United Nations University Series on Regionalism 17,
https://doi.org/10.1007/978-3-030-21603-0_21

characterized by a decision to leave out from discussion a major item of contention. While the decision might have been out of fear that discussing these issues might derail the other items on which agreement was in sight, it is still not clear *how* this decision is actually made. Reflecting back at these examples, a common puzzle comes to light: was the exclusion of a major issue the price of eventual success in reaching an agreement?

All four mentioned peacemaking processes dealt with highly intractable conflicts (Kriesberg 1993; Coleman 2000; Zartman 2005). Each conflict displayed heightened instability, wariness, and uncertainty between the parties, who resorted to hostile and harmful practices in pursuit of their unilateral solutions. Such an overly-incendiary environment, incited by accusatory and dehumanising rhetoric, is effectively void of any type of constructive communication between the parties. As a result, parties are increasingly unaware of each other's true interests, capabilities and levels of resolve. In situations where parties lack disposition or demonstrate inability to reach a mutually acceptable solution on their own, they may request or consent to external assistance in the form of mediation (Crocker et al. 2004; Bercovitch 2005). Mediation is an ad hoc, voluntary and legally non-binding form of assisted negotiation through which an external actor helps the parties in reaching a solution that they are unable or unwilling to find themselves (see also Touval and Zartman 1985; Bercovitch et al. 1991; Beardsley 2011; Grieg and Diehl 2012; Vuković 2015: Wilkenfeld et al. 2019). Since the presence of mediators was crucial in shaping outcomes in all four cases, in order to answer what prompted the decision to leave some of the major issues out and move to agreement on other points, the present study will focus on the role of third parties on three tactical dimensions: strategic issue sequencing (i.e. decision which issue should be addressed first), party arithmetic (i.e. who should they engage with in the peace talks and which spoilers should be excluded), and the feasibility assessment of a potential solution (i.e. what kind of a deal is sustainable and achievable at the same time). All three dimensions will be further scrutinized as the building blocks of a specific type of bias that third-parties bring to the peacemaking process: bias of outcome.

21.2 Mediator's Power and Strategies

In order to see a particular outcome materialize, mediators resort to different strategies. The most common taxonomy classifies mediators' behaviour and corresponding strategies on an intervention scale ranging from low to high, from facilitation (both communication and formulator) to directive-manipulator strategies (Touval and Zartman 1985, 2006; Zartman and Touval 1996). Facilitation strategies are most successful in low intensity conflicts in which parties are willing to settle, but are unable to communicate this willingness. However, in cases where disputants lack the motivation to settle and show unwillingness to compromise, a more powerful intervention from a third party is needed (Carnevale 2002; Sisk 2009; Bercovitch 2009).

The least assertive role taken on by mediators in the process of peacemaking is characterized by the reliance on facilitative strategies. In these cases, mediators focus in large part on improving ineffective communication (or establishing lines of communication where they did not previously exist) between the parties to a conflict and facilitating cooperative behavior, while maintaining very limited control of the substantive aspects of negotiations. This type of strategy is directly related to integrative bargaining behavior (Carnevale 1986; Hopmann 1996; Beardsley et al. 2006), the goal of which is to assist disputants in identifying existing mutual interests, in an effort to encourage non-violent conflict resolution. However, since mediation tends to be applied in the most intransigent cases, those in which conflict dynamics have bred high levels of suspicion and distrust, disputing sides are often unable to come up with and agree upon a specific formula for resolution, even when a well-defined zone of possible agreements (ZOPA) has been established. This situation is produced by parties not enjoying complete information about their opponent's goals, level of resolve, and resources. This, in turn, limits the parties' ability both to recognize a zone of mutually acceptable alternatives to ongoing conflict and to formulate a solution, even in the awareness that one exists. As such, a facilitating mediator may provide the conflicting parties with information that is essential to minimizing their differences and convince them of the existence of a ZOPA. This type of mediator may also assume responsibility for formulating specific solutions within that ZOPA. This type of strategy, usually referred to as formulation, is far more assertive in nature and requires mediators to exert a greater degree of control over the actual process and delve into the substance of a negotiated solution. Formulation requires mediators to identify and sell attractive trade-offs and creative solutions with the aim of assuaging security concerns and mitigating commitment problems as perceived by the parties. As noted by Zartman and Touval "formulas are the key to a negotiated solution to a conflict; they provide a common understanding of the problem and its solution or a shared notion of justice to govern an outcome" (Zartman and Touval 1996, 454). The formulas that mediators propose are attractive insomuch as they offer a useful political cover for the parties to accept solutions that they can easily justify to their constituencies. Thanks to this transfer of political legitimacy, conflicting parties may agree on solutions which while formally within their ZOPA would still be very difficult to sell.

Political cover is one of many incentives that mediators rely on to manipulate payoff structures and change perceptions of the utility of a proposed agreement. In cases in which facilitation alone fails to convince the parties of the existence a ZOPA, mediators may resort to manipulative strategies that actually create new (and artificial) ZOPA. These manipulative strategies may involve coercion and the threat of the use of force in an effort to make non-compliance and continued confrontation seem less attractive. Mediators may also make promises, offering inducements that might make a negotiated solution more appealing. With this in mind, the difference between facilitation and formulation on the one side, and mediating with muscle or manipulation on the other becomes obvious. While the strategies of facilitating communication, disseminating useful information, and formulating viable solutions are used to assist the disputants in identifying a mutually acceptable solution within a range of available alternatives, the main purpose of manipulative strategies is to enlarge the spectrum of potential solutions that are preferable (from the standpoint of both parties) to continued conflict (Hopmann 1996; Beardsley et al. 2006; Terris 2016).

Traditionally, manipulative strategies have been associated with coercive forms of power that are tangible in nature (Svensson 2007). While this type of power is easy to observe in the context of a mediator's use of carrots and sticks, power in mediation can be defined much more broadly. In fact, power, or leverage, represents "the ability to move a party in an intended direction" (Touval and Zartman 2006, 436). Leverage is a direct consequence of the fact that parties in conflict still need a mediator's help to reach a compromise (Touval and Zartman 1985; Touval 1992). Carnevale (2002) classifies sources of power into two groups based on mediator's "will and skill". On one hand there is the resource-based aspect of social power (strategic strength) and on the other there is the behavioral aspect of mediation (tactical strength). According to this categorization, "strategic strength in mediation refers to what the mediator has, to what the mediator brings to the negotiation table; the tactical strength refers to what the mediator does at the negotiation table" (Carnevale 2002, 27–28).

Tactical strength is exemplified through a mediator's premeditated choice of specific techniques and the ability to follow a particular procedure; for instance the ability to create a framework which will enhance trust between the parties and alter negative images that they have of each other. On the other side, strategic strength includes different types of social power. Social power is most commonly observed as a mediator's ability to employ 'carrots and sticks', which in Carnevale's typology are referred to as coercive power and reward power (Carnevale 2002, 28). While reward power involves forms of 'compensation' for disputants' cooperative behavior, coercive measures are generally exercised through various forms of threat or punishment, such as diplomatic pressure, the imposition of sanctions regimes, and the use of military power. These forms of power are used to manipulate the mediation process, by creating necessary inducements for the parties to move toward a commonly acceptable solution.

However, mediators might also be perceived as actors with legitimate power to prescribe behavior for the disputants. According to Carnevale, this power "derives from a norm that has been accepted by the disputants… and influence rests on a judgment of how one *should* act, and the authority determines the standard" (Carnevale 2002, 28). Legitimacy as such, could be seen as the other extreme form of power from coercive and reward powers. So while the latter are commonly observed as instrumental in manipulative strategies, the former usually complements communication and formulation efforts. Studies have shown that legitimate power is more commonly attributed to international organizations than to individual states (Touval 1992). This hints at the idea that a mediator's legitimacy (or lack thereof) is directly related to the disputants' perception of his or her agenda and motivation to engage in the process at all.

Mediating states often "seek terms that will increase the prospectus of stability, deny their rivals opportunities for intervention, earn them gratitude of one or both parties, or enable them to continue to have a role in future relations in the region" (Zartman 2008, 156). This type of agenda or motivation on the part of an individual state might be perceived by disputants as being overly intrusive or, perhaps, biased toward a particular outcome. International organizations, on the other hand, tend to be motivated to intervene by a more complex set factors. As Touval and Zartman point out, "peacemaking is the raison d'être of several international organizations and thus enshrined in their charters" (Touval and Zartman 2006, 431). At the same time it should be noted that international organizations are also subject to specific policies and interests of their member states (Fretter 2002; Iji 2017). Nonetheless, international organizations are often seen as bodies that channel conflicting interests of member states in order to produce a specific set of interests that are still in line with the spirit of an organization's establishing charters (which tend to focus on the preservation of peace and encouragement of cooperation). A mediator with a balanced set of interests and an underlying commitment to the spirit of peacemaking could thus be seen as less intrusive and more acceptable from the standpoint of the disputants. As a consequence, disputants might be more inclined to perceive an international (or regional) organization as being legitimate a state.

21.3   Mediator's Bias of Outcome

The role of a mediator is quite diverse. A mediator facilitates impaired communication between the parties, assists them in formulating viable alternatives to settle their dispute, and finally, guides them toward a mutually acceptable solution. At the same time, a mediator also assumes the responsibility to present the proposed agreements as mutually enticing opportunities, by offering various incentives such as political cover, international legitimacy and guarantees of implementation assistance. Evidently, in order to help parties in conflict reframe their relationships and promote cooperative behaviour, mediators are often called upon to make considerable investments of both material and non-material resources. For this reason, mediators are rarely indifferent to the terms that are being negotiated. While their intervention is usually justified as a method of conflict reduction, humanitarian concerns are almost always also intertwined with particular interests that drive a mediator to get involved in the first place. As matter of fact, for many actors, international mediation is a useful (foreign) policy instrument through which they can pursue some of their strategic interests without causing significant international resistance (Touval 2003; Kamrava 2011, 2013; Akpınar 2015; Rieger 2016; Sun and Zoubir 2018). As Touval and Zartman point out, "mediators are no less motivated by self-interest than by humanitarian impulses… [T]he mediator is a player in the plot of relations surrounding a conflict, and has some interest in the outcome (else it would not mediate)" (Touval and Zartman 1985, 8). Although, mediators aim to promote an outcome that is in line with their self-interest, their interests are not as restrictive in terms of potential outcomes as those of the conflicting parties are.

Not all conflicts attract the same level of international scrutiny. Depending on the situation at hand, as Young notes, "it is perfectly possible for situations to arise in which there is a distinct role for an intermediary, but in which no third party finds it worth his while to assume this role" (Young 1972, 55). As an ad-hoc dynamic, each iteration of international mediation draws a distinct type of international actors to the peacemaking process. Participating mediators are commonly as diverse in their interests, capabilities and levels of resolve as the conflicting parties themselves. As no political process happens in a vacuum, mediators' interests to get involved may encompass both endogenous motives – stemming from specific issues that are central to the conflict itself – as well as exogenous drivers grounded in broader geopolitical considerations that mediators may have (Carnevale and Arad 1996). As a consequence, each mediation process is affected by a wide variety of preconceived notions about the conflict and conflicting parties, as well as preferences regarding specific outcomes that mediators bring with them to the process. Current studies of mediation have generally operationalized a specific type of preferences or mediator's bias as the manifestation of preferential treatment of one of the parties in conflict (Kydd 2003; Beber 2012; Svensson 2009; Savun 2008; Favretto 2009; Gent and Shannon 2011; Vuković 2011). To this end, Carnevale and Arad provide a useful taxonomy of such mediator biases. On the one hand, they refer to closer ties with one of the disputing parties as 'bias of source characteristic', while on the other, they label a mediator's settlement proposal(s) that favours one conflicting side as 'bias of content' (Carnevale and Arad 1996, 45).

Although bias has often been seen as a liability in the mediation process, mediator impartiality appears to be quite an elusive concept in international mediation. Even if we try to differentiate between biased and impartial mediators – the former being one that has something at stake, and/or is potentially more partial to one of the disputing sides, and the latter being allegedly more even-handed and having no opinion regarding the disputed issue – both terms appear to lose their original meanings if we look at the way mediators influence the overall process. Numerous studies have shown that presence of a mediator that has a bias toward one of the disputants is not automatically a liability. It can entice the partner party to accept a solution that would not have been accepted otherwise (Touval and Zartman 1985). Furthermore, information delivered by a biased mediator is argued to be more credible (Kydd 2003). Finally, biased mediation processes are more predisposed to ending with robust institutional arrangements, which, in turn, have the propensity to promote a more durable peace between the disputants (Svensson 2009).

As mentioned earlier, mediators are seldom indifferent to the terms that are being negotiated. Mediators will never endorse an outcome that is not in line with their interests, even if conflicting parties agree to such terms. For instance, it is implausible to imagine a scenario in which the United Nations or the European Union would ever mediate a treaty that would explicitly prescribe forced expulsion and exchange of populations between two countries. In other words, a solution similar to the one signed by the Greek and Turkish delegations in Lausanne, Switzerland on January 30, 1923, entitled "Convention Concerning the Exchange of Greek and Turkish Populations" as part of the peace negotiations which put an end to the Greco-Turkish War (1919–1922), would never be endorsed by an international actor that has the respect and promotion of human rights as one of its core values and principles. It is important to remember that mediators are invited and accepted by conflicting parties because they can grant political cover and international legitimacy to very delicate and often unpopular decisions. Nevertheless, they would never grant political cover or international legitimacy to a solution that damages their core interests or reputation.

Conflict resolution efforts on the domestic level (i.e. labour-management disputes, domestic litigations, etc.) commonly find useful and practical focal points within the existing legal frameworks. At the same time they can rely on enforcement mechanisms which are inexistent on the international level. Since internationalised disputes lack similar structures, mediators are called upon to provide the necessary guidance and clarity about the possible solutions, which can enjoy the needed degree of international legitimacy. With this in mind it is essential to sophisticate the existing notions of mediator bias, in order to accommodate third parties' preferences and support for specific outcomes. Bias of outcome can be seen as an intrinsic characteristic of any mediator (Vuković and Hopmann 2019). While it certainly reduces the bargaining range for the conflicting parties, it also provides them with clarity and direction so they can focus their efforts on a specific set of outcomes that the mediators are ready to support and legitimize. Therefore, the bias of outcome offers a solid frame of reference for the parties, who can get a better idea of what might be the endgame for their peacemaking efforts (Vuković 2019).

21.4 Operationalization of Mediator's Bias Outcome

Bercovitch and Jackson noted that "mediators bring with them consciously or otherwise, ideas, knowledge, resources and interests, of their own or of the group they represent. Mediators often have their own assumptions and agendas about the conflict in question" (Bercovitch and Jackson 2009, 35). These partialities inevitably affect a wide range of mediators' choices pertinent to the structure and the process of the peacemaking efforts. Who should be invited to the talks, where to conduct them, how to use back-channel communications, should the process be more formal or informal, public or secret, and many other similar choices are contingent upon mediators' bias of outcome.

Although mediation is an iterative process, where newly acquired information and potential changes in context may induce mediators to reconsider their choices, most of the choices are still made very early in the process as mediators start to prepare for peacemaking. This preparatory stage, during which the parties get encouraged to abandon their unilateral strategies and consider exploring cooperative methods to resolve their differences, represents the prenegotiation phase (Zartman 1989a; Saunders 1996). According to Saunders, prenegotiation starts as soon as the third parties decide to pursue negotiation, and accordingly covers two functional needs: "defining the problem" and "developing a commitment to negotiation on the part of the parties", which are followed by a third phase, "arranging the negotiations" (Saunders 1985).

In the earliest stages of the process, mediators face a significant challenge to alter the parties' perceptions, preferences and priorities which are shaped by conflict dynamics. As parties are seldom capable and willing to foster a sense of awareness that their confrontational approaches may not yield expected results, mediators are frequently tasked with the responsibility to ripen the conflict and drive the parties out of their predicament. Using a broad range of resources and tactical moves, mediators may generate a sense of urgency among the parties, who start perceiving the ongoing conflict as unbearable and their escalatory strategies as counterproductive. In turn, mediators start projecting creative solutions as enticing opportunities which may not only lead them out of the conflict, but also allow them to achieve essential underlining interests that they wanted to preserve and promote throughout the conflict (Zartman 1989a, 2001; Pruitt and Olczak 1995; Ohlson 2008; Zartman and de Soto 2010). Thus, from the onset of the peacemaking process, already in the prenegotiation phase, mediators may assume a dual role: on the one hand to incite awareness of increasing costs, which may result in a very destructive stalemate, and on the other to increase the attractiveness of a negotiated solution as a suitable alternative to their destructive methods (Vuković 2019). These creative formulas represent a clear indication of a mediator's prerogatives and preferences in the peacemaking process.

21.4.1 Bosnia

The most assertive mediating role in the prenegotiation phase was assumed by the United States and its special envoy Richard Holbrooke in order to ripen the conflict in Bosnia for resolution. Prior to the US involvement in the summer of 1995, the situation on the ground clearly favoured the Bosnian Serbs, who controlled more than 60% of the territory and had an undisputed military upper hand over their counterparts. Approximately 1/3 of the Republic of Croatia. Faced with European inability to successfully manage the conflict, the US decided to 'level the playfield' by changing the power balance on the ground. Using the unprecedented acts of genocidal atrocities in Srebrenica and Sarajevo market place 'Markale' as a justification for humanitarian intervention, the US started a full scale air offensive against Bosnian Serb military infrastructure. The rapid weakening of Bosnian Serb military superiority prompted its counterparts – Bosnian Muslims and Bosnian Croats, assisted by Croatian forces – to commence an offensive and tilt the power balance in their favour. The military intervention was a signal for the Bosnian Serbs – and their patrons in FR Yugoslavia – that the ongoing conflict is increasingly becoming unbearable. Knowing that this sense of a 'hurting stalemate' was developing among Bosnian Serbs, Holbrooke begun his shuttle diplomacy trying to sell the prospects of a negotiated solution, in return for a cessation of the US led air strikes (Touval 1996; Holbrooke 1999). The formula he was proposing entailed an administrative division of Bosnia along ethnic lines, where Serbs would control 49% of the territory and the Croat-Muslim federation would assert their authority over the remaining 51% of Bosnia (Silber and Little 1996). The proposed solution was largely based on previous formulas that the conflicting parties continuously rejected as they still believed that they can gain more by fighting (Daalder 2000).

The uniqueness of the US initiative was in the fact that they were able to directly alter the power balances on the ground, making the ongoing conflict costlier then ever. However, while this was certainly the case for Bosnian Serbs, their counterparts were using the new circumstances to increase their gains through a military offensive. Viewing potential Croat-Muslim military gains as detrimental for the creation of a mutually hurting stalemate, Holbrooke resorted to the US' bias relations to manipulate their perceptions over an impeding catastrophe in the form of a Bosnian Serb counteroffensive while simultaneously selling them the prospects of a 49–51 negotiated solution. Although both the Croats and Muslims were apprehensive of Holbrooke's trustworthiness – fearing that he was deceiving them over the Serb counteroffensive for which neither side had any valid confirmation from their intelligence communities – they both accepted his offer to negotiate a solution that would fit the proposed 49–51 formula. They knew that only the US could provide the much needed political cover, security guarantees and implementation assistance that would help the conflicting sides sell the proposed framework to their respective constituencies as an enticing opportunity (Silber and Little 1996; Touval 2002). More importantly, they also knew that by accepting the US initiative, all other solutions which would involve any form of formal partition or deeper centralization of Bosnia would no longer be possible. In other words, by narrowing down the framework for a negotiated solution Holbrooke clearly provided an indication of the possible endgames.

21.4.2 Namibia

Although not as assertive as Holbrooke in Bosnia, the US Assistant Secretary of State for African Affairs Chester Crocker also made sure to provide a clear set of indicators and guidelines for a negotiated solution on Namibian independence. His 'linkage strategy' prescribed a tripartite negotiation process between Cuba, Angola and South Africa, which would sanction internationally recognized Namibian independence with a simultaneous withdrawal of South-African and Cuban troops from South-western Africa. Although this initiative could not find immediate support among the conflicting parties and other external actors, given the futility of all other peacemaking initiatives, Crocker gradually asserted his approach as 'the only game in town' (Zartman 1989b). In fact, the 'linkage strategy' was a response to the fruitless insistence on the respect of the UN Security Council Resolution 435 from 1978, which heavily criticized South African apartheid policies and occupation of Namibia, and in its own way 'linked' South African withdrawal from the occupied territories with a cease-fire and UN supervised elections in independent Namibia.

Looking at the developments on the ground, Crocker was aware that Namibian independence could not be achieved unless the presence of foreign troops (i.e. South African and Cuban) in the neighbouring conflict affected Angola is addressed. Against the backdrop of Cold War politics, where the Cuban presence in Angola was seen as an assertion of the communist block in the region, Crocker formulated a policy of 'constructive engagement' with South Africa, which instead of outright international isolation of the apartheid regime in Pretoria, prescribed a practical cooperation between the US and South Africa over the issue of Namibian independence (Crocker 1980). Tying in the potential improvement of US-South African relations with a departure of Cuban and South African troops from Angola, Crocker's linkage strategy induced a change of perception in South Africa on the utility of relinquishing control over Namibia. This ripening through the projection of mutually enticing opportunities was coupled with the realization of a painful stalemate on the ground and decreasing ability of the communist countries to assert their presence in the region (Zartman 1989a; Crocker 1992; Vukovic 2015). Therefore, even prior to the formal commencement of the negotiations, the parties in conflict were fully aware what will be the focus of the talks. The linkage strategy excluded any prospects of talking about internal political issues in either Namibia and/or Angola, as it rather primarily focused on the disengagement of foreign troops from the region. Just as was the case of Holbrooke's approach in Bosnia, Crocker provided a very clear framework of potential solutions for the conflicts in South-western Africa.

21.4.3 Oslo Accords

One of the main advantages of the prenegotiation rests in its informality (Touval 1989; Druckman 1997). In fact, informal issue-oriented discussions prove to be much more efficient than any form of 'tactical preparation' and 'no pre-negotiation communication' between the parties involved, since it may contribute in developing psychological effects conducive for the creation of a constructive negotiation atmosphere. Moreover, informal secret talks in the prenegotiation phase provide everyone with a mechanism of deniability: as these talks are non-binding parties can always deny that any politically sensitive issue was discussed at all. Such informal issue-oriented talks were pivotal in creating the necessary breakthroughs between Israel and PLO during the Norwegian mediation in Oslo (John 2011). The talks were held under the guise of a Norwegian think-thank FAFO, used as a smokescreen for secret talks that were known to only a handful of high ranking officials in Israel, Norway and PLO. It is worth noting that the talks were formally detached from the official governmental structures, such as the Norwegian Ministry of Foreign Affairs. This in turn meant that no official (governmental) record of the talks has been preserved.

Deprived of traditional carrots and sticks, Norway was a very unlikely mediator for the highly intractable conflict in the Middle East. Although, its relatively small size and lack of coercive means may be conflated into an assumption that Norway lacks any agenda or bias in this conflict, a closer look at Norway's involvement depicts a more complex picture. In fact, throughout the 1970s and 1980s Norway had extremely close ties with Israel. Especially close were relations between the ruling Norwegian Labour Party and their namesake in Israel (Egeland 1999, 532). Moreover, Norway was very sympathetic to the Israeli stand in the conflict: 1974 it was one of only eight countries that voted against the UN General Assembly Resolutions 3236 and 3236 on the Palestinian people's right for self-determination and PLO's observer entity status within the UNGA. The first contact between Norwegian authorities and PLO was established in 1978 when Norway took part in the UNIFIL Mission in South Lebanon. This contact proved to be essential in 1979, when Norway was asked to provide crucial energy supply guarantees to Israel which until that moment were provided by the deposed Shah regime in Iran. Fearful for the security of their troops in South Lebanon, Norwegians reached out to Yasser Arafat, who had no objections to Norwegian oil shipments to Israel as long as Norway accepts to provide a secret back channel with Israel when needed (Al Jazeera 2013). For over a decade, Norwegian initiatives were falling short of any significant breakthrough, due to the fact that Israel had an unequivocal upper had in this conflict and saw no utility in negotiating directly with PLO. However, the situation dramatically changed with the escalation of the first Intifada in 1988 which put Israel under considerable economic and moral pressure for using disproportionate force. In a secret message, the Norwegian Minister of Foreign Affairs provided his counterpart in Israel Shimon Peres with the Norwegian diagnosis of the situation, claiming that "only by relieving itself of the burden of the occupied territories, can Israel succeed and prosper" (Al Jazeera 2013). While the situation on the ground and Norwegian willingness to facilitate the talks provided sufficient impetus for Israel to accept the talks, Israeli officials were still reluctant to accept any explicit framework or negotiation agendas that came from either Norway and PLO. In fact, Israeli delegation set the tone of the secret talks by immediately drafting a 'Declaration of Principles' which excluded the core issues related to security, borders, status of Jerusalem, and refugees' rights to return (Al Jazeera 2013). Evidently, Norwegian lack of coercive power which could increase the costs of an ongoing conflict for *all* parties involved, coupled with the nature of its relations with the conflicting parties and the vail of secrecy surrounding the talks, provided an opportunity for a stronger party to assert its list of negotiable items.

21.4.4   Camp David Accords

Norwegian experience in Oslo is by no means an exception. In fact, during the 1978 Camp David talks between Israel and Egypt, the US was also faced with the dilemma of balancing between its initial ambition and the reality on the ground (Quandt 2010). The Carter administration initial assessment of the situation in the Middle East pointed out that sufficient momentum was created for a significant and robust appeasement between Arab states and Israel. Already in March 1977 Jimmy Carter laid down five basic principles for the peace in the Middle East: (1) comprehensive peace, (2) reaffirmation of UN Resolutions 242 and 338 as the bases for negotiations, (3) peace not just as an end of belligerent activities, but as an establishment of normalized relations between the parties, (4) question of borders and a phased withdrawal, and (5) the issue of Palestinian rights, including measures to "permit self-determination by the Palestinians in deciding their own future" (Quandt 2010, 184). The US ambition to foster a comprehensive peace in the Middle East immediately ran into trouble. First of all, Israel made it quite clear that it refused to engage in any discussions over "Palestinian rights", it was unwilling to link the withdrawal from the West Bank and Gaza with the Resolution 242, and was very apprehensive of talking with PLO in any capacity. Secondly, Carter administration was remarkably unaware of the intra-Arab split, exemplified by the rivalry between Syria and Egypt, which strongly conditioned the chances of assembling a unified Arab delegation. To this end, each Arab country had its own concern with Israel and a diagnosis of the Palestinian issue, which in turn made it quite difficult for the Carter administration to accommodate all of them in a comprehensive peace agreement. Finally, not every Arab state was equally enthusiastic with the Carter's platform.

As time went by, Carter administration was becoming increasingly aware that the only regional leader truly interested to engage in talks with Israel was the Egyptian president Anwar el Sadat. Hoping to build upon Sadat's unexpected and unprecedented visit to Jerusalem, and increasingly frequent secret consultations between high ranking Egyptian and Israeli envoys, the US decided to abandon its goal of a robust peace conference and opt to support direct negotiations between Israel and Egypt instead. In preparing for the direct talks, the Carter administration diagnosed 'pivotal issues' and most likely obstacles to negotiations. According to their assessment, the talks should primarily focus on issues which can be 'linked' and used as building blocks for the future more robust peace talks in the Middle East. Compared to the initial proposal, now the list of issues that the two parties would negotiate on was considerably narrowed down to two main points: the issue of Sinai (i.e. Egyptian-Israeli relations) and the issues of an interim period of self-government for Palestinians living in the West Bank and Gaza (Quandt 2010, 198). Carter administration hoped to use a potential peace deal between Egypt and Israel as an incentive for Israelis to soften up on the Palestinian issue, without making the improved Egyptian-Israeli relations subject to the prospects of finding an actual solution to the most intractable issue in the Middle East. As noted by Quandt, "the Americans felt that the questions of sovereignty over the West Bank and Gaza, as well as the status of Jerusalem, should be differed. Instead they thought that Egypt and Israel could make some headway on outlining a transitional regime for the West Bank" (Quandt 2010, 198). Clearly, the prenegotiations that led to the Camp David talks already narrowed down the list of items that could be discussed and as such the nature of the endgame that the parties may expect from these negotiations.

21.5   Party Arithmetic

One of the most fundamental choices that are made already in the prenegotiation phase is the list of participates that mediators are willing to engage with in the process (Touval 1989). In order to achieve their self-defined goals, mediators need to develop a nuanced understanding who may be the most constructive actors that demonstrate propensity to compromise and ability to implement an eventual agreement. At the same time, mediators need to deter spoiling activities of those actors that see no utility in what may be achieved at the negotiating table (Stedman 1997). The selection process is grounded in a genuine cost-benefit analysis, which assesses if granting international legitimacy, political cover and implementation assistance to specific parties will yield adequate returns in line with mediators' motives to get involved as peacemakers. In order to simplify the selection process, and streamline the incentives in an adequate manner, mediators may opt to facilitate the creation of coalitions, composed of parties that share specific goals in the peacemaking (Lax and Sebenius 1991). While this may simplify the distribution of resources for mediators, it also permits the parties to pool in their leverages and consequently improve their bargaining power with the other side.

21.5.1 Bosnia

In the case of Bosnia, Holbrooke made it explicitly clear that his team will not engage directly with the Bosnian Serb leadership, which was already indicted for war crimes and crimes against humanity. The choice to isolate them from proposed talks was a signal that a potential solution should not and could not be used to legitimize their role in the post-conflict peacebuilding phase. For this reason, he chose to empower the President of Serbia Slobodan Milosevic to negotiate on behalf of the Serbian side. Although formally unable to represent Bosnian Serbs, Milosevic and his regime in Belgrade were granted a blessing from the Patriarch of the Serbian Orthodox Church to represent a unified Serb cause in the talks. The presence of Milosevic greatly influenced the bargaining dynamics, as he was far more flexible in granting concessions which were unthinkable for Bosnian Serbs. He accepted a corridor from the last remaining enclave (Gorazde) to the Bosnian capital Sarajevo, gave away control of Sarajevo to the Muslim-Croat coalition, and even decided to accept that the future control of the city of Brcko gets decided through international arbitration (Silber and Little 1996). While Holbrooke chose to grant a leading role to Milosevic, he also decided to narrow down the list of participants to only three conflicting sides in Bosnia. This meant that the delegation of Kosovo Albanians was automatically excluded from the talks. Holbrooke was aware that the issue of Kosovo is too important to ignore, yet for the purposes of ending hostilities in Bosnia, adding another delegation to the table would only complicate an already very fragile balance between the parties (Holbrooke 1999). This party arithmetic was an implicit signal that a major issue will be ignored, in order to sort out issues that were deemed by mediators as more salient and urgent at that time.

21.5.2   Namibia

A similar decision was made by Crocker during the tripartite talks over Namibia. The choice of inviting only representatives of Cuba, South Africa, and Angola was not only an indication that the main scope of the talks will be to address the presence of foreign troops in Angola, but also that a major player in the conflict will inevitably be ignored. In fact, as Crocker's initiative focused on reaching a deal between states, two main guerrilla movements in the region did not participate in the final talks. This meant that the National Union for the Total Independence of Angola (UNITA), which contested the authority of the Popular Movement for the Liberation of Angola (MPLA) in Luanda, despite getting logistical support from the US was excluded from the talks. More importantly, the main force fighting for Namibian independence, South West Africa People's Organization (SWAPO), was also excluded from the process. The decision to link Namibian independence with a parallel and simultaneous withdrawal of South African and Cuban troops from Angola meant that once foreign armies leave the region the issue of Namibian independence cannot and would not be challenged by anyone. In other words, the US believed that the acceptance of the tripartite talks was an implicit message that SWAPO's demands for an independent Namibia will be fully endorsed. While this might have been the case, SWAPO's and UNITA's absences were also an indication that the domestic dynamics in Namibia – which saw SWAPO challenging the authorities in Windhoek – and in Angola – embroiled by a devastating civil war between MPLA and UNITA – were not on the agenda, and as such will not be part of the negotiation endgame.

21.5.3   Oslo Accords

While SWAPO's absence was (maybe counterintuitively) a message that their interests were fully protected by the format of the talks, the breakthrough of Oslo is mirrored in the ability of the Norwegians to encourage Israel to negotiate directly with PLO. As was mentioned previously, secrecy and informality of the talks, provided the parties with the necessary degree of 'deniability'. Only a handful of people on all three sides were aware that the talks were held. Until Oslo, Israel was continuously rejecting any idea of negotiating directly with PLO. They were apprehensive that negotiating with PLO would implicitly legitimize their terrorist tactics and calls for Israel's demise. Norway's ability to provide a secret channel for negotiations, absolved Israel from any culpability of negotiating with terrorists and enemies of the state. However, in case of success this type of rapprochement meant it was inevitable that some form of mutual recognition between Israel and PLO would have to take place. Not surprisingly, the biggest breakthrough of Oslo was indeed the mutual recognition of PLO as authentic and sole representative of Palestinian people and Israel's right to exist as an independent state. In other words, Norwegian insistence that Israel should engage directly (albeit in secret) with PLO, identified possible endgames in their first of its kind negotiations.

21.5.4 Camp David Accords

Evidently, prior to Oslo, direct negotiations between Israel and PLO were impossible to expect. Given the sheer complexity of the issues and interests that all Middle Eastern parties would have brought with them to the initially envisioned comprehensive peace conference, the US decided to focus their efforts in supporting the two parties that were at that time most likely to succeed in finding a sense of compromise. Thus, when it became clear that Egypt and Israel would be the only ones negotiating at Camp David, the US decided to exclude issues that could not be endorsed or guaranteed by either one of the parties. For instance, on the issue of borders, the US realized that Israeli-Jordanian border could not be discussed, even though this aspect was crucial for the achievement of a robust settlement on the issue of Palestine. The final text deferred this issue to future negotiations, hoping that the Egypt-Israel rapprochement would trickle down to other Arab countries in the region. Similarly, knowing that Egypt-Israeli peace deal was too valuable to be conditioned by an elusive solution of the Palestinian question, the US decided to avoid any talks about Palestinian sovereignty in the West Bank, Gaza and Jerusalem, and instead focus on a less controversial transitional plan for the West Bank, "building on Dayan's idea of dismantling the military occupation and replacing it with an elected Palestinian body with broad responsibility for day-to-day affairs" (Quandt 2010, 198–199).

21.6 Issue Sequencing

Another crucial decision that mediators make already in the prenegotiation phase relates to the formulation of appropriate peacemaking agenda. A well-structured agenda reduces uncertainties and provides clarity about the intentions mediators have with the process (Druckman 1997). In a highly informal manner, characterized with a strong degree of plausible deniability, mediators may explore parties' actual interests and needs, in an effort to subsequently formulate adequate solutions to settle their conflict. These solutions are imbedded in the agenda around which mediators structure their peacemaking efforts. The purpose of the agenda is to project a sense that parties have overlapping interests, and that compromise is real possibility. The compromise is found within the zone of possible agreement (ZOPA), which consists of all solutions that are not only in line with parties' interest but also better than their no-deal alternatives (Fisher and Ury 1981; Raiffa 1982; Hopmann 2001; Lax and Sebenius 2006).

The choice of specific items to be included in the agenda, and the order in which these issues should be addressed, are subject to mediators' reading of the situation and ability to generate momentum which may foster a sense of compromise between the parties (Lim and Carnevale 1990; Carnevale 2002). Moreover, inclusion or exclusion of specific items from the agenda is primarily based in the expectation that certain issues may be best addressed through specific package deals, i.e. creative trade-offs. Therefore, the decision on how to structure the agenda is subject to mediators' estimates of the costs particular incentives may generate vis-à-vis the likelihood they may produce a compromise on specific issues.

21.6.1 Bosnia

Holbrooke initial assessment of the main issues was quite elaborate. Accordingly, the final agreement should include:

> eastern Slavonia, the Federation, a constitutional framework, elections, a three-person presidency, a national assembly, freedom of movement and the right of refugees to return to their homes, compliance with the international War Crimes Tribunal, and an international police force. Finally, we would face our most contentious task: determining the internal boundaries of Bosnia, those between the Serb portion of Bosnia and the Croat-Muslim Federation (Holbrooke 1999, 233).

Indeed, Holbrooke's team feared the most an outcome that would endorse an eventual partition of Bosnia, where Serbian and Croatian parts would drift away to their respective "motherlands". According to Holbrooke, any agreement produced under American leadership should promote a multi-ethnic Bosnian state, as a way of preventing further ethnic and border conflicts in Central and Eastern Europe (Holbrooke 1999, 233). Holbrooke's team approached the negotiations with the spirit 'nothing is agreed until everything is agreed'. Given the fact that the saliency of issues was not identical among the parties, Holbrooke encouraged package-deals in order to create attractive trade-offs between the parties. Nevertheless, everything was contingent upon the realisation of Holbrooke's 49–51 formula. Since this was the premise that made the talks enticing for all parties, everyone was focused to retain the maximum benefits from that type of divide. Thus, when the corridor between Gorazde and Sarajevo was created, followed by a handshake between Milosevic and Haris Silajdzic (who was the Bosnian Prime Minister at that time), it all fell apart when Milosevic realized that this corridor gave away more than 51% of the Bosnian territory to the Croat-Muslim Federation. Subsequently, even when other territories were exchanged between Serbs and Muslims in order to reach the 49–51 balance, the 'thirty seven minute peace' collapsed because the parties actually exchanged territories that Croat forces conquered in their recent counteroffensive against Serbs, making the agreement 'zero point zero zero' chance acceptable for the Croats (Silber and Little 1996; Holbrooke 1999, 299). Therefore, even with a very clear formula proposed by the US delegation, regarding the issues that will be included in the final agreement, the actual 'division of the pie' was far more difficult than anyone expected. This is clearly in line with the theoretical expectation that 'expanding the pie' (i.e. integrative bargaining or problem solving) that mediators are regularly called upon to promote, eventually has to end with distributive bargaining or the 'division of the pie' (Wetlaufer 1996). In the case of Bosnia, this division was unequivocally conditioned and guided by a principle that was predefined by the mediator.

21.6.2 Namibia

Crocker's mediating platform clearly prioritized on the achievement of a settlement that would primarily focus on the departure of foreign troops from Angola, which was seen as a fundamental step in brining peace to the region and sustainable independence for Namibia. Therefore, just as was the case of Bosnia, the three sides in the tripartite talks tried to outmanoeuvre each other within the pre-established framework of troop withdrawal. During the exploratory meeting in London in 1988, Angolans proposed that the Cuban troops withdrew within 4 years, while grating only 1 year for the withdrawal of the South African Defense Forces (SADF) from Namibia. At the same time, Angolans requested that prior to any withdrawal, the US and South Africa cease any support for UNITA. The South African counterproposal requested a Cuban withdrawal before Namibian independence can be achieved and at the same time reconciliation between MPLA and UNITA (Zartman 1989b, 230). The US was becoming aware that the issue of timetables for withdrawal was reaching a deadlock, and in order to 'increase the pie' pushed for a set of 'indispensable principles' that all parties should adhere. These included:

> aspects of cooperation (aid) for development, right to peace, right to self-determination, non-aggression, non-interference, non-use of force, and respect for territorial integrity and inviolability of frontiers, as well as recognition of roles – the United States as mediator and permanent members of the Security Council as guarantors (Zartman 1989b, 231).

These principles provided sufficient tradeoffs for the parties to accept a final formula for withdrawal, which saw Cuban troops departing Angola in stages over a period of 27 months, while South Africa agreed to relinquish its control over Namibia and grant it independence as prescribed by the UN plan adopted in 1978.

21.6.3 Oslo Accords

According to Terje Rod-Larsen, chief architects of the Oslo accords and director of FAFO, "the logic of Oslo is that you start with the easiest and then you postpone the most difficult, hoping that the parties would find a way as they walked that road to resolve the most difficult issues" (Rod-Larsen interview in Al Jazeera 2013). However, as mentioned earlier, all of the most difficult questions – such as the issue of Jerusalem, refugees, borders, security – were taken out from the agenda from the start, on the suggestion of Israel that saw them as an impediment to a possible agreement. Thus the only issues left for discussion were the self-rule of Palestinians in Gaza and in the city of Jericho, and matters of Palestinian self-governance in the domains such as education, tourism and health (Al Jazeera 2013).

21.6.4   Camp David Accords

The Camp David peace talks have been long recognised not only by what has been achieved, but also by what has been eventually omitted from the talks. Despite the initial expectations that these talks may resolve a broad range of issues that have been central to the disputes in the Middle East – from the future status of Jerusalem to the question of Palestinian refugees – the U.S. realised that an extended framework may be counterproductive to the scope of the talks. In preparation for the talks, Carter realised that the differences between the parties were quite substantial, that a fixed agenda would hamper the creation of the necessary momentum in the peace process. As a solution he decided to foster incremental search for compromise, by drafting single drafts papers, which parties may comment on and use those comments for subsequent drafts. As noted by Bercovitch, "single negotiating draft permitted negotiation to go until the right blend of agreement and ambiguity was found… Fewer decisions were needed, fewer complex issues were faced and fewer trade-offs were require. The parties were merely asked to listen, criticize and suggest improvements to a single document. The advantages of working with a single, comprehensive text were evident at Camp David" (Bercovitch 1986, 58).

21.7   Outcome Feasibility Assessment

From the onset of the peacemaking process, mediators continuously explore if and how constructive may be specific issues for the achievement of intendent goals that motivated mediators to get involved. While they have the previously described procedural importance, issues are also carefully chosen based on their implementability. In selecting issues to be included in the agenda, mediators are also attentive to opt for those that may not create unrealistic expectations in the implementation phase (Vuković and Hopmann 2019). As mediators provide the necessary incentives, which drive the parties toward mutually acceptable agreement, the uninterrupted delivery of these incentives becomes essential for the long term stability of the mediated solution. Not surprisingly, mediators may be hesitant to include those issues which would require an enduring involvement in managing the dispute. Mediators may face pressures from the unenthused domestic constituencies, which may object to a costly and long-lasting commitment.

Previous discussions of all four cases indicate that mediators were fully aware that there are certain realities on the ground that they need to acknowledge and accommodate in the final solution. Nevertheless, no mediator was willing to endorse a final solution that would go against its essential interests in the conflict. For Holbrooke this was a multi-ethnic Bosnia, for Crocker this was the withdrawal of foreign troops, for Norwegians this was the mutual recognition of PLO and Israel, and for Carter this was a rapprochement between Egypt and Israel as a building block for a more robust peace in the Middle East. These outcomes were a product of mediators' conflict assessments and policy preferences that could be easily justified not only domestically, but also globally as no foreign policy decision occurs in a vacuum.

21.8   Discussion and Implications for Theory and Practice

Evidently, all four cases unanimously indicate that the "Big Ones" were excluded already during the mediated prenegotiation phase. Although the mediators realized the relevance and utility of discussing (and potentially solving) such issues, they were also aware that including the most difficult issues would jeopardize the ability to find a minimum level of compromise. Based on their assessments and policy preferences mediators formulated their own set of goals and outcomes that they believed were most likely to be achieved. These initial formulas did not preclude a possibility that during the process certain newly developed or realized contentious issues get eliminated. Nevertheless, the 'Big Ones' were by large left out already in the exploration phase of prenegotiation. Most importantly, in all four processes mediators controlled the agenda, and as such controlled the focus of the talks. Thus, their interests and preferences were the cornerstone of the final outcome. Therefore there are several conclusions that have wider implications for theory and practice.

First, the choices made in the prenegotiation directly affect the actual scope of the talks. As such, even when mediators' general ambition might be to fully resolve the conflict, the sheer complexity of the conflict and contentious nature of the Big issues will allow the mediators to conduct primarily conflict management activities. The ability to make initial agreements (conflict management) might be used to create momentum and confidence in future management activities in order to fully resolve the conflict. Therefore, leaving the big one out is a calculated decision made by third parties when all they can achieve is conflict management, hoping that it will serve as a building block for future conflict resolution.

Second, mediators enter the conflict management with a limited set of information. In their initial calculations they might hope for full resolution. However, after obtaining new information directly from the conflicting parties, they might realize that they need to reduce their hopes from full settlement to a more limited one. This new information is tactically used and employed by conflicting parties, as they might already be apprehensive of mediators' plans and preferences. So, looking at what Kydd is saying about information, such information is systematically used through out the process, starting from the prenegotiation.

Third, mediators might be using the same tactics as conflicting parties in the last moments of the talks. Insights from these four cases show that they do not mediate aimlessly, nor are they just passive bystanders in the process. They are rather driven by their own preferences about the most feasible outcomes (i.e. bias of outcome) and consequently drive the parties toward it using various tactical tools: agenda setting, image control, information manipulation, threats and promised, imposition of deadlines, walk-away tactics, etc.

Lastly, these four cases provide sufficient evidence in support of an argument that endgames are not just a matter of last moments. Rather they represent a culmination of a wider set of preferences that are formulated throughout the process: who to talk to, about what, and how. Thus, when it comes to the role of mediators, these types of preferences give guidance to the conflicting parties about what kind of outcomes they can expect.

Further Readings

Beardsley, K. (2011). *The mediation dilemma.* Ithaca: Cornell University Press.
Bercovitch, J. (1996). *Resolving international conflicts: The theory and practice of mediation.* Boulder: Lynne Rienner Publishers.
Butler, M. J. (2009). *International conflict management.* London: Routledge.
Collier, J. G., & Lowe, V. (1999). *The settlement of disputes in international law: Institutions and procedures.* Oxford: Oxford University Press.
Greig, J. M., & Diehl, P. F. (2012). *International mediation.* Cambridge: Polity Press.
Kleiboer, M. (1998). *The multiple realities of international mediation.* Boulder: Lynne Rienner Publishers.

References

Akpınar, P. (2015). Mediation as a foreign policy tool in the Arab Spring: Turkey, Qatar and Iran. *Journal of Balkan and Near Eastern Studies, 17*(3), 252–268.
Aljazeera. (2013). *The price of Oslo.* Documentary.
Beardsley, K. (2011). *The mediation dilemma.* Ithaca: Cornell University Press.
Beardsley, K. C., Quinn, D. M., Biswas, B., & Wilkenfeld, J. (2006). Mediation style and crisis outcomes. *Journal of Conflict Resolution, 50*(1), 58–86.
Beber, B. (2012). International mediation, selection effects, and the question of bias. *Conflict Management and Peace Science, 29*(4), 397–424.
Bercovitch, J. (1986). A case study of mediation as a method of international conflict resolution: The Camp David experience. *Review of International Studies, 12*(1), 43–65.
Bercovitch, J. (2005). Mediation in the most resistant cases. In C. Chester, H. Fen, & A. Pamela (Eds.), *Grasping the nettle: Analyzing cases of intractable conflict* (pp. 99–122). Washington, DC: United States Institute of Peace.
Bercovitch, J. (2009). Mediation and conflict resolution. In J. Bercovitch, V. Kremenyuk, & I. W. Zartman (Eds.), *The Sage handbook of conflict resolution* (pp. 340–357). London: SAGE.

Bercovitch, J., & Jackson, R. (2009). *Conflict resolution in the twenty first century: Principles, methods and approaches.* Ann Arbor: Michigan University Press.

Bercovitch, J., Anagnoson, J. T., & Wille, D. L. (1991). Some conceptual issues and empirical trends in the study of successful mediation in international relations. *Journal of Peace Research, 28*, 7–17.

Carnevale, P. J. (1986). Strategic choice in mediation. *Negotiation Journal, 2*(1), 41–56.

Carnevale, P. J. (2002). Mediating from strength. In J. Bercovitch (Ed.), *Studies in international mediation* (pp. 25–40). New York: Palgrave Macmillan.

Carnevale, P. J., & Arad, S. (1996). Bias and impartiality in international mediation. In J. Bercovitch (Ed.), *Resolving international conflicts: The theory and practice of mediation* (pp. 39–53). London: Lynne Rienner.

Coleman, P. T. (2000). Intractable conflict. In M. Deutsch & P. T. S. F. Coleman (Eds.), *The handbook of conflict resolution: Theory and practice* (pp. 428–450). San Francisco: Jossey-Bass.

Crocker, C. A. (1980). South Africa: Strategy for change. *Foreign Affairs, 59*(2), 323–351.

Crocker, C. A. (1992). *High noon in Southern Africa: Making peace in a rough neighborhood.* London: WW Norton.

Crocker, C. A., Hampson, F. O., & Aall, P. R. (2004). *Taming intractable conflicts: Mediation in the hardest cases.* Washington, DC: US Institute of Peace Press.

Daalder, I. H. (2000). *Getting to Dayton: The making of America's Bosnia policy.* Washington, DC: Brookings Institution Press.

Druckman, D. (1997). Negotiating in the international context. In I. W. Zartman & J. L. Rasmussen (Eds.), *Peacemaking in international conflict: Methods and techniques* (pp. 81–124). Washington, DC: United States Institute of Peace Press.

Egeland. (1999, January). The Oslo accord: Multiparty facilitation through the Norwegian channel. In C. A. Crocker, F. O. Hampson, & P. Aall (Eds.), *Herding cats: Multiparty mediation in a complex world* (pp. 527–546). Washington, DC: U.S. Institute of Peace Press.

Favretto, K. (2009). Should peacemakers take sides? Major power mediation, coercion, and Bias. *American Political Science Review, 103*(2), 248–263.

Fisher, R., & Ury, W. (1981). *Getting to yes: Negotiating agreement without giving in.* Boston: Houghton Mifflin.

Fretter, J. (2002). International organizations and conflict management: The United Nations and the mediation of international conflicts. In J. Bercovitch (Ed.), *Studies in international mediation.* New York: Macmillan.

Gent, S. M., & Shannon, M. (2011). Bias and the effectiveness of third-party conflict management mechanisms. *Conflict Management and Peace Science, 28*(2), 124–144.

Greig, J. M., & Diehl, P. F. (2012). *International mediation.* Cambridge: Polity.

Holbrooke, R. (1999). *To end a war.* New York: Modern Library.

Hopmann, P. T. (1996). *The negotiation process and the resolution of international conflicts.* Columbia: University of South Carolina Press.

Hopmann, P. T. (2001). Bargaining and problem solving: Two perspectives on international negotiation. In C. A. Crocker, F. O. Hampson, & P. Aall (Eds.), *Turbulent peace: The challenge of managing international conflict* (pp. 445–468). Washington, DC: U.S. Institute of Peace Press.

Iji, T. (2017). The UN as an international mediator: From the post–cold war era to the twenty-first century. *Global Governance: A Review of Multilateralism and International Organizations, 23*(1), 83–100.

John, A. W. S. (2011). *Back channel negotiation: Secrecy in the Middle East peace process.* Syracuse: Syracuse University Press.

Kamrava, M. (2011). Mediation and Qatari foreign policy. *The Middle East Journal, 65*(4), 539–556.

Kamrava, M. (2013). Mediation and Saudi foreign policy. *Orbis, 57*(1), 152–170.

Kriesberg, L. (1993). Intractable conflicts. *Peace Review, 5*(4), 417–421.

Kydd, A. (2003). Which side are you on? Bias, credibility and mediation. *American Journal of Political Science, 47*(4), 579–611.

Lax, D. A., & Sebenius, J. K. (1991). Thinking Coalitionally: Party arithmetic, process opportunism, and strategic sequencing. In H. P. Young (Ed.), *Negotiation analysis* (pp. 153–193). Ann Arbor: University of Michigan Press.

Lax, A. D., & Sebenius, J. K. (2006). *3-D negotiation*. Boston: Harvard Business School Press.

Lim, R., & Carnevale, P. J. (1990). Contingencies in the mediation of disputes. *Journal of Personality and Social Psychology, 58*, 259–272.

Ohlson, T. (2008). Understanding causes of war and peace. *European Journal of International Relations, 14*(1), 133–160.

Pruitt, D. G., & Olczak, P. V. (1995). Beyond hope: Approaches to resolving seemingly intractable conflict. In B. B. Bunker & J. Z. S. F. Rubin (Eds.), *Conflict, cooperation, and justice: Essays inspired by the work of Morton Deutsch* (pp. 59–92). San Francisco: Jossey-Bass.

Rieger, R. (2016). *Saudi Arabian foreign relations: Diplomacy and mediation in conflict resolution*. Milton Park: Routledge.

Quandt, W. B. (2010). *Peace process: American diplomacy and the Arab-Israeli conflict since 1967*. Washington, DC: Brookings Institution Press.

Raiffa, H. (1982). *The art and science of negotiation*. Cambridge, MA: Belknap.

Saunders, H. (1985). We need a larger theory of negotiation: The importance of pre-negotiation phases. *Negotiation Journal, 1*(3), 249–262.

Saunders, H. (1996). Prenegotiation and Circum-negotiation: Arenas of the peace process. In C. A. Crocker, F. O. Hampson, & P. R. Aall (Eds.), *Managing global Chaos: Sources of and responses to international conflict* (pp. 419–432). Washington, DC: United States Institute of Peace Press.

Savun, B. (2008). Information, Bias, and mediation success. *International Studies Quarterly, 52*(1), 25–47.

Silber, L., & Little, A. (1996). *The death of Yugoslavia*. New York: Penguin.

Sisk, T. (2009). *International mediation in civil wars: Bargaining with bullets*. London: Routledge.

Stedman, S. J. (1997). Spoiler problems in peace processes. *International Security, 22*(2), 5–53.

Sun, D., & Zoubir, Y. (2018). China's participation in conflict resolution in the Middle East and North Africa: A case of quasi-mediation diplomacy? *Journal of Contemporary China, 27*(110), 224–243.

Svensson, I. (2007). Mediation with muscles or minds? Exploring power mediators and pure mediators in civil wars. *International Negotiation, 12*(2), 229–248.

Svensson, I. (2009). Who brings which peace? Neutral versus biased mediation and institutional peace arrangements in civil wars. *Journal of Conflict Resolution., 53*(3), 446–469.

Terris, L. G. (2016). *Mediation of international conflicts: A rational model*. New York: Routledge.

Touval, S. (1989). Multilateral negotiation: An analytic approach. *Negotiation Journal, 5*(2), 159–173.

Touval, S. (1992). The superpowers as mediators. In J. Bercovitch & J. Z. Rubin (Eds.), *Mediation in international relations*. New York: St Martin's Press.

Touval, S. (1996). Coercive mediation on the road to Dayton. *International Negotiation, 1*(3), 547–570.

Touval, S. (2002). *Mediation in the Yugoslav wars: The critical years, 1990–95*. New York: Palgrave.

Touval, S. (2003). Mediation and foreign policy. *International Studies Review, 5*(4), 91–95.

Touval, S., & Zartman, I. W. (1985). *International mediation in theory and practice*. Boulder: Westview.

Touval, S., & Zartman, I. W. (2006). International mediation in the post-cold war era. In C. A. Crocker, F. O. Hampson, & P. R. Aall (Eds.), *Turbulent peace: The challenges of managing international conflicts* (pp. 427–443). Washington, DC: United States Institute of Peace Press.

Vuković, S. (2011). Strategies and Bias in international mediation. *Cooperation and Conflict, 46*(1), 113–119.

Vuković, S. (2015). *International multiparty mediation and conflict management: Challenges of cooperation and coordination*. London: Routledge.

Vuković, S. (2019). Mediating closure: Mediator as a driver. In I. W. Zartman (Ed.), *How negotiations end: Negotiating behavior in the endgame*. Cambridge: Cambridge University Press.

Vuković, S., & Hopmann, P. T. (2019). Satisficing in international mediation: Framing, justifying and creating outcomes in peacemaking. In J. Wilkenfeld, K. Beardsley, & D. Quinn (Eds.), *Research handbook on mediating international crises*. London: Edward Elgar Publishing.

Wetlaufer, G. B. (1996). Limits of integrative bargaining. *Georgetown Law Journal, 85*, 369.

Wilkenfeld, J., Beardsley, K., & Quinn, D. (2019). *Research handbook on mediating international crises*. London: Edward Elgar Publishing.

Young, O. R. (1972). Intermediaries: Additional thoughts on third parties. *Journal of Conflict Resolution, 16*, 51–65.

Zartman, I. W. (1989a). Prenegotiation: Phases and function. *International Journal, 44*, 237–253.

Zartman, I. W. (1989b). *Ripe for resolution: Conflict and intervention in Africa*. New York: Oxford University Press on Demand.

Zartman, I. W. (2001). The timing of peace initiatives: Hurting stalemates and ripe moments. *The Global Review of Ethnopolitics, 1*(1), 8–18.

Zartman, I. W. (2005). *Analyzing intractability. Grasping the nettle: Analyzing cases of intractable conflict* (p. 47).

Zartman, I. W. (2008). Introduction: Bias, Prenegotiation and leverage in mediation. *International Negotiation, 13*(3), 305–310.

Zartman, I. W., & De Soto, Á. (2010). *Timing mediation initiatives*. Washington, DC: United States Institute of Peace.

Zartman, I. W., & Touval, S. (1996). International mediation in the post-cold war era. In C. A. Crocker, F. O. Hampson, & P. Aall (Eds.), *Managing global Chaos: Sources of and responses to international conflict* (pp. 445–461). Washington, DC: United States Institute of Peace Press.

Closing Remarks

Madeleine O. Hosli, Joren Selleslaghs, Rory Johnson, and Ewout Ramon

This edited volume, largely created as a result of the Massive Open Online Course (MOOC) 'The Changing Global Order', was written in order to present to its readers an understanding of the complexities and dynamics of the contemporary global system. It demonstrates how regions develop within this system and how the global and regional levels interact. In terms of academic disciplines, the volume falls within the discipline of IR and political science, but is also multifaceted in nature with a number of chapters having been written using legal as well as economic aspects of IR, such as international law and international political economy. The end result is that the reader is presented with an opportunity to understand related topics such as political economy, international law and institutions of global governance, in conjunction with the academic field of IR. The volume highlighted some of the tremendous changes that have occurred over the past few decades including the significant global power shifts and changes in the dynamics of international and

M. O. Hosli
Institute of Security and Global Affairs, Leiden University, The Hague, The Netherlands
e-mail: m.o.hosli@fgga.leidenuniv.nl

J. Selleslaghs
Faculty of Governance and Global Affairs, Leiden University, The Hague, The Netherlands
e-mail: selleslaghs.joren@gmail.com

R. Johnson
United Nations University Institute on Comparative Regional Integration Studies (UNU-CRIS), Bruges, Belgium
e-mail: rjohnson@cris.unu.edu

E. Ramon
Chamber of Commerce and Industry (Voka), Flanders, Belgium
e-mail: ewout.ramon@voka.be

© Springer Nature Switzerland AG 2020
M. O. Hosli, J. Selleslaghs (eds.), *The Changing Global Order*, United Nations University Series on Regionalism 17,
https://doi.org/10.1007/978-3-030-21603-0

regional institutions. It focuses on both state and non-state actors in these developments.

The edited volume is divided into five separate parts to logically combine different but related topics. The first part of the volume addresses the various theoretical approaches to IR and provides the readers insights into both more traditional and modern approaches in this area. More traditional approaches in political science and international relations use methods and theories similar to those used to study the natural world. In IR and political science, such an approach is known as positivism. Accordingly, the mainstream schools of thought, or theories of IR are characterised as positivist in nature. These are (neo-) Realism and Liberalism. These theoretical approaches are grounded on positivist methodology, which is the foundational epistemology of the mainstream schools of IR theory. The first two chapters address these mainstream schools of IR theory, known as positives approaches, as well as alternative theoretical angles, known as post-positivist approaches. The debate between the two camps, i.e. positivism and post-positivism is addressed in detail, and the advantages and importance of either camp in light of the wider international and social context. Both camps of thought are important to the study of international relations.

Part II of the volume addresses the changing nature of the global order, beginning with Chap. 3 on power politics. It discusses in detail the fundamental elements of power and its practice, utility, and role in the changing global order. The remaining chapters of part II address the rise and role of new powers in the global order. Chapter 4 focuses on the rise of China and examines in detail a range of aspects related to China's rise, such as: relations with the United States, Beijing's relations and influence in the East Asian region, the Chinese worldview and practice of IR. Chapter 5 addresses the role of Russia on the global stage, and succinctly analyses different domains of Russian statecraft, for example: the historic role of Russia as a power and its permanent seat on the UNSC, the notion of multipolarity and multilateralism and its place in Russian politics, the importance of the Eurasian region which is composed of post-Soviet countries, and Russia's relations with the United States. Both Chaps. 4 and 5 also address the increasingly close relations between China and Russia and both countries' aspirations for regional hegemony and control.

Part III is dedicated to the incremental role of regions in global politics, regional integration, regional organisations, regional cooperation, and other crucial theoretical and conceptual aspects pertaining to the study and role of regions in global politics. Individual chapters are designated to different regions and regional contexts. The relevance and importance of these various regions is investigated in detail. The first chapter of part III, Chap. 8, outlines the rise of regions in the theory and practice of IR and serves as a starting point in order to examine regions and their role in the global order. Chapter 9 addresses the most advanced manifestation of regional integration in the world and discusses various aspects of the European Union such as its history, institutional framework and external relations. Chapter 10 examines the Shanghai Cooperation Organisation, and outlines its increasing relevance on the global stage. It describes in detail important elements related to this organisation,

such as rising popularity and increase in states seeking membership, the cooperation between Russia and China and its effect on IR. Chapter 11 then addresses
another aspect, or rather function of regional integration, and organization: conflict
management. This chapter specifically looks at the case study of ASEAN's role as a
conflict manager, and analyses three different cases; the Cambodia conflict, the
Aceh conflict, and the East Timor conflict. Chapter 12 examines regionalism and
regional trends in Latin America. It outlines regional international relations in this
area, the numerous (and often overlapping) regional institutions and the relations
between regional members. The succeeding chapter investigates regional integration in South Asia and discusses the regional organisation SAARC. It highlights the
vital dynamics concerning the region, including the nuclear rivalry between India
and Pakistan, and the intractable conflict in Kashmir. Chapter 13 presents a critical
outlook on regional integration and argues that the cooperation and partnership
between key regional players is fundamental for the manifestation and maintenance
of regional integration.

The fourth part of this edited volume is directed towards international organisations and global governance, and their relevance to the changing global order. The
first chapter (14) of part IV addresses trends in global governance. This chapter also
examines additional related aspects such as the notion of sovereignty, and critically
compares democratic and authoritarian governments. Chapter 15 addresses in detail
the most important international institution related to the maintenance of global
peace and security, the United Nations Security Council. It focuses on crucial
debates within the UN related to reform of the institution, partially as a direct
response to the changing global order. The chapter also addresses additional aspects
related to the UNSC, such as its history and composition. Chapter 16 examines an
important security organization; the North Atlantic Treaty Organisation (NATO).
The fluctuating relevance of NATO through changing global contexts is evaluated,
as is the organisation's involvement in global crises. Chapter 17 looks at the case
study of the G20 as a crucial aspect of current global governance, presenting an
analysis of the main features of this leading global economic organisation.

The fifth and final part of this volume focuses on conflicts, methods for conflict
resolution, and related aspects of international security. Chapter 18 addresses the
enforcement of international law. This chapter considers the history, composition,
as well as the function of key international legal organisations, such as the
International Criminal Court, and the International Court of Justice. Chapter 19 follows on from this legal theme by addressing a topic related to international law and
international relations; the responsibility to protect (R2P) norm. The chapter focuses
on an important debate in IR, demonstrating the evolution of role perceptions in the
international community in general, and the UNSC in particular, when considering
mass atrocities in an international context, where domestic governments are often
either unable or unwilling to stop massive violence. R2P involves legal complexities, related to sovereignty and territorial integrity, in light of (forced) humanitarian
intervention in cases of mass atrocities. Chapter 19 studies cases where R2P was
invoked and examines the norm in detail. The final two chapters focus on the most
important methods to conflict resolution; negotiation and mediation. Chapter 20

addresses international negotiation, presenting a candid account from the perspective of procedure and process, party and people, perception and power, preference and product. It also examines the nature and conduct of international negotiation, as well as its past and prospects. The author is an expert in the theory and practice of negotiation, and presents important insights for scholars and practitioners alike. The volume concludes with a chapter (21) addressing mediation as alternative method of conflict resolution.

Concerted efforts were made to ensure that this volume is both thorough in its approach, and wide-reaching in its scope. Acknowledging that Plato's maxim 'everything changes and nothing stands still' is as applicable to the field of IR as it is to any other topic, the editors of this volume recognise that global events are constantly shaping and moulding the international system. Although certainly not insignificant, there is often a tendency to overemphasise the impact that individual people, or events, can have on the broader trajectory of global affairs. This volume has tried to demonstrate this by striking a balance between the use of specific case studies and the presentation of broader trends and theoretical developments. One overarching conclusion that should have become clear is that developments within IR do not necessarily occur in a straightforward, chronologically linear fashion. Rather, the global system tends to fluctuate between periods of increased order and disorder. A second fundamental message that should be taken away from this work is that regional organisations and integration processes continue to have much relevance within the current global system. There seems to be a current perception that apathy levels towards regional organisations have been steadily growing, but this should not distract us from realising the ongoing need for regionalism in the current world order. Alongside and through international organisations, regional enterprises have the ability to tackle a broad range of pertinent issues including, specifically, those relating to international security where they often take the lead in trying to prevent and solve episodes of conflict. Collaboration between international institutions – among them the United Nations – and regional integration schemes to tackle challenges to peace and security are crucial in this context.

This volume was written with students, scholars, practitioners, specialists, and non-specialists in mind; the primary objective was to help readers understand the theoretical and practical foundations that seek to explain the changing nature of global affairs. Readers should have obtained a nuanced perspective on various aspects of international relations, of cataclysms, wars and peace, conflicts, conflict resolution and security. Fundamentally, this volume represents an overview of many different ideas, concepts and approaches. It is hoped that it will also act as a foundation and tool from which to begin exploring more in-depth some of the subjects covered, as it has sought to highlight recommended further reading in each topic area. The volume, with this, aims to make a contribution to the continued search for stability and peace, on the global and regional level, in view of the current changing global order.

Printed by Printforce, the Netherlands